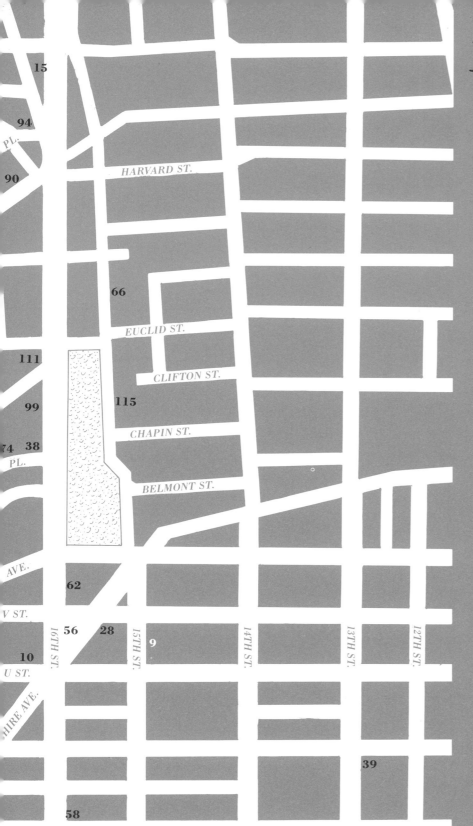

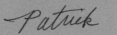 
9. PORTNER FLATS
10. BALFOUR
12. MENDOTA
13. HIGHLANDS
15. KENESAW
16. ONTARIO
18. CORDOVA
20. FLORENCE COURT
21. WESTMORELAND
22. WYOMING
25. DRESDEN
28. NORTHUMBERLAND
29. 2852 ONTARIO ROAD, N.W.
30. WOODWARD
31. WINDSOR LODGE
32. ST. REGIS
34. ALTAMONT
36. 2029 CONNECTICUT AVENUE, N.W.
37. 1870 WYOMING AVENUE, N.W.
38. MERIDIAN MANSIONS
39. WHITELAW
40. ALBEMARLE
48. WOODLEY
52. NETHERLANDS
53. STAFFORD
54. COVINGTON
55. BILTMORE
56. 2001 16TH STREET, N.W.
57. 1868 COLUMBIA ROAD, N.W.
58. SOMERSET HOUSE
62. ROOSEVELT HOTEL
63. CATHEDRAL MANSIONS
66. MERIDIAN HILL STUDIO
68. 2500 MASSACHUSETTS AVENUE, N.W.
72. ARMY AND NAVY
73. CHALFONTE
74. 1661 CRESCENT PLACE, N.W.
75. 2120 KALORAMA ROAD, N.W.
79. 2101 CONNECTICUT AVENUE, N.W.
82. HARVARD HALL
83. WARDMAN TOWER
86. SHOREHAM HOTEL
90. ARGONNE
93. 1705 LANIER PLACE, N.W.
94. EMBASSY
99. PARK TOWER
102. 2929 CONNECTICUT AVENUE, N.W.
107. CRYSTAL HEIGHTS (never built)
110. DELANO
111. DORCHESTER HOUSE
115. 2407 15TH STREET, N.W.
126. SHOREHAM WEST

BEST ADDRESSES

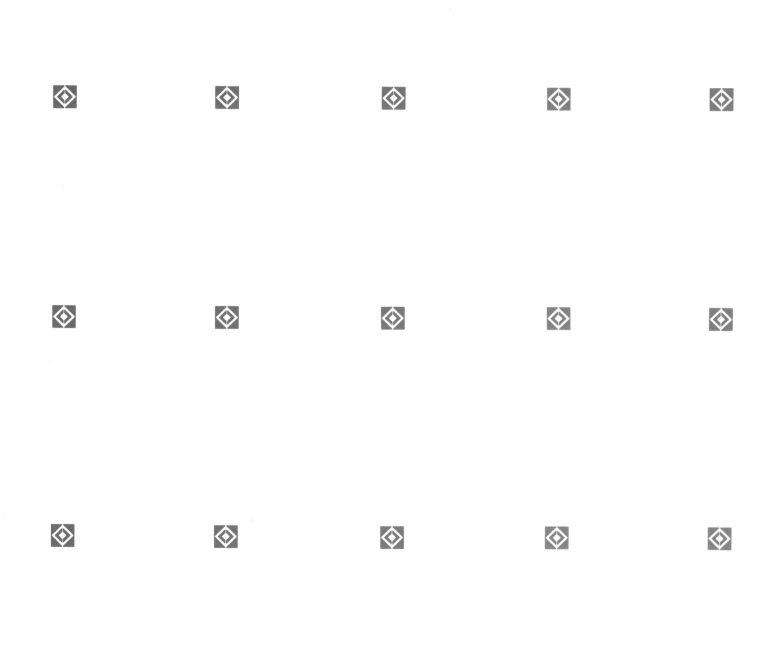

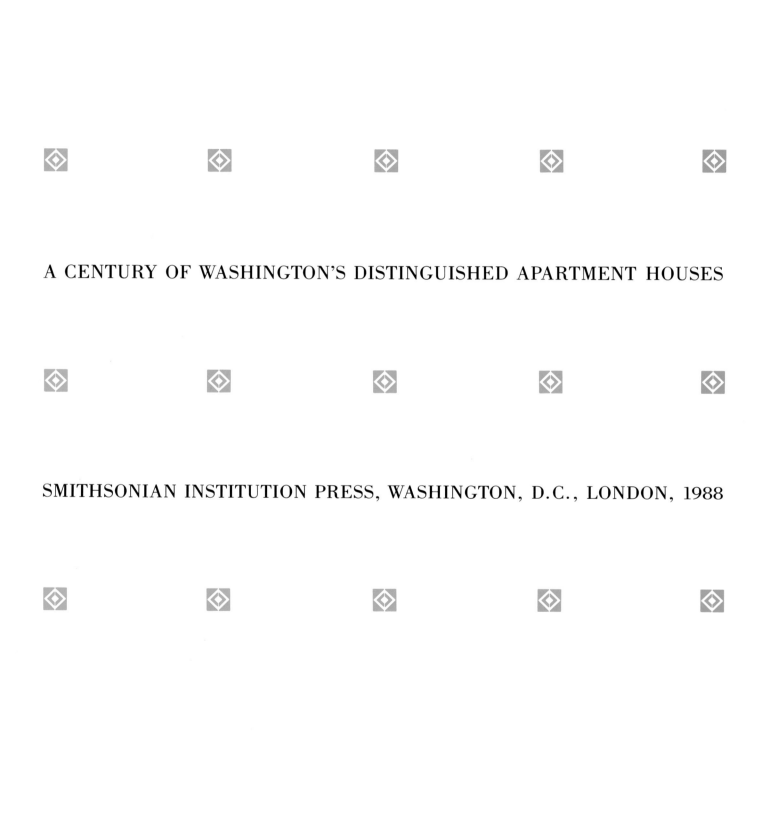

A CENTURY OF WASHINGTON'S DISTINGUISHED APARTMENT HOUSES

SMITHSONIAN INSTITUTION PRESS, WASHINGTON, D.C., LONDON, 1988

JAMES M. GOODE

BEST ADDRESSES

PHOTOGRAPHERS: JAMES STAFFORD PHILLIPS and JAMES F. TETRO

Senior Editor   Caroline Newman
Copy Editor   Joan Holleman
Designer   Janice Wheeler

Endpapers: Cartography by Stephen Kraft.

Frontispiece: Each of the well-designed apartments at Wendell Mansions has an elegant elliptical foyer, from which radiate the principal drawing room, right, a small reception room, center, and the dining room, left.

Page 602: Lobby staircase, Northbrook Courts.

Library of Congress Cataloging-in-Publication Data
Goode, James M.
  Best addresses.
  Bibliography: p.
  Includes index.
  1. Apartment houses—Washington (D.C.) 2. Architecture, Modern—19th century—Washington (D.C.) 3. Architecture, Modern—20th century—Washington (D.C.) 4. Washington (D.C.)—Buildings, structures, etc. 5. Washington (D.C.)—Social life and customs. I. Title.
NA7860.G66   1988   728.3'14   88-600058
ISBN 0-87474-476-8 (cloth edition)
ISBN 0-87474-478-4 (deluxe edition)
British Cataloging-in-Publication data is available.

⊗ The paper used in this publication meets the minimum requirements of the American National Standard for Permanence of Paper for Printed Library Materials Z39.48-1984.

DEDICATED TO WASHINGTONIANS WORKING TO PRESERVE
THE DISTINGUISHED APARTMENT HOUSES THAT FORM A SIGNIFICANT PART OF THE
ARCHITECTURAL HERITAGE OF THE NATION'S CAPITAL

James M. Goode
Washington, 15 Dec. 1988

CONTENTS

FOREWORD

Most Americans can quickly call to mind Washington's distinct and memorable public image, composed as it is of an orderly disposition of structures and open spaces—the seats of the three principal branches of our government, monuments to indubitable national heroes, a string of museums planted in prominent places on the city's great common space, the Mall.

Lying beyond and between these massive edifices and giving them prominence is a wide range of other buildings we tend to ignore. They provide places for Washingtonians to work, play, and live. Not until they are gone, however, do we pay them much heed, as illustrated in James Goode's *Capital Losses*, issued by the Smithsonian Press in 1979.

In the present volume, Mr. Goode turns his attention to some of the best of Washington's overlooked buildings. *Best Addresses* provides a detailed history of more than a hundred of the capital's distinguished surviving apartment houses, as well as many landmarks that have been demolished. The result is a carefully researched book with social history and architectural history uniquely combined in

Opposite: The richly eclectic facade of 2101 Connecticut Avenue.

the author's personal style. Mr. Goode offers splendid insight into how people have lived in Washington's best-designed apartment houses over the past century. Hundreds of handsome photographs and carefully drawn floor plans of these residences provide a vivid and detailed record never before available. The book is filled with information about who built what when, and it is laced with delightful anecdotes that assure the reader that buildings are to be lived in and not simply put up for the convenience of the architect or the profit of the builder.

Best Addresses is surprisingly the first serious attempt to document the development of this important kind of building not only in Washington but anywhere in the country. It sets a standard for other cities to follow, both in this country and abroad, in dealing with a kind of structure that is ignored in studies of buildings and cities. Historians dealing with urban development would have us believe that our cities have a dense core of tall commercial towers devoted to commerce, are sprinkled with monuments such as churches, libraries, and museums, and are ringed with suburbs and small towns with the exquisite freestanding residences that ever since Europeans settled in North America have meant home to Americans. We all know that this is a deceptively restrictive coverage of our cities' architectural landscapes.

In thinking we have been erecting a nation of single-family houses, we have been neglecting and misunderstanding our cities. Since the turn of the century, a majority of all residential structures built in our cities, both in Washington and elsewhere, have been some form of apartment building. Nevertheless, we know less about America's apartment buildings than about any of the other important structures in our cities.

In ignoring our cities, we have ignored the diversity of our architecture. We know less about how the buildings in our various cities differ from one another than we do about what they have in common. We have apparently wanted to assure ourselves that every corner of the country has something American while remaining indifferent to seeing that the diversity and variety guaranteed under the American system of government take architectural form.

Best Addresses shows how an apartment building can represent a successful response to local circumstances. Because each city presents unique circumstances, it follows that successful buildings in one city are different from those in another city. This simple syllogism holds anywhere, but our understanding of our cities suffers because it is seldom invoked.

Best Addresses also celebrates local achievement. Concentration on the general rather than the specific has led us to applaud those who have achieved national or international reputations even though they usually have done so by swamping local sensibilities with the fashions of the larger world. As a result, we have remained largely indifferent to those who have won local fame by excelling even while, or especially by, respecting local properties. In this book, however, James Goode pays proper attention to local architects, that is, to those who knew how to respond properly to local circumstances.

We have also tended to make the history of architecture synonymous with the history of what architects did on their own. As *Best Addresses* shows, however, this is a much more interesting topic than a simple list of individual achievements. Here is the story of the complex interplay between the professional skills of the developer and those of the architect, the constraints of local laws, the rigid logic of economics, the fickle tastes of the marketplace, the momentum of urban development, the whims that determine the names buildings are given, and much more.

Those who love Washington and those who are only coming to know it are both well served by this book. One can now hope that other cities will soon receive similar penetrating scrutiny and pleasant presentation of their important and overlooked buildings. These structures have earned their place in history by providing places for people to live and by filling in the spaces along the streets and between the monuments of our cities.

Carroll William Westfall
Division of Architectural History
School of Architecture
University of Virginia

PREFACE

This study of apartment houses in Washington, D.C., originated with a tour I conducted for the Smithsonian Resident Associates in the spring of 1978. In my research for this tour I was surprised by the dearth of published information not only on Washington apartment houses but on American apartment houses in general. In fact, I soon learned that the last comprehensive work, Sydney Perks's *Residential Flats of All Classes*, which is concerned primarily with the development of European apartment houses, was published in London in 1905. This conspicuous neglect of an important part of architectural history inspired me to begin intensive study of Washington apartment houses. Little did I know then that I had embarked on a project that would occupy me for ten years.

At the same time that I began my research, two other historians, Carroll William Westfall, then a professor of architectural history at the University of Chicago, and Elizabeth Cromley, then a graduate student at New York University, began similar studies on Chicago and New York apartment houses. After meeting these two scholars and several graduate students involved in related studies, I organized a symposium at the annual meeting of the Society of Architectural Historians in Minneapolis in 1984 on the development of the American building type before World War I. The lectures demonstrated the significance of the social and architectural history of the American apartment house as a uniquely urban structure.

Intrigued by the evolution of apartment design, I visited architecturally prominent examples outside of Washington in New York, Boston, Philadelphia, Baltimore, Richmond, Los Angeles, and San Francisco, and also their European precursors in Vienna, Paris, London, Edinburgh, and Glasgow. It was interesting to discover firsthand how the building type evolved in significantly different ways in each city. To help place the development of the Washington apartment house in the context of other urban centers, a brief comparative history is offered in appendix 1.

The buildings included here have been selected primarily for their excellence in architectural design. Other criteria are innovative technological features, a building's importance to social history, or the representation of a style or plan in vogue at a particular time. Although a majority of these buildings are luxury apartment houses, some modest but well-designed examples, such as garden apartments, are included because they are the best of their class.

Certainly the most difficult moment in the history of this project was the decision to eliminate some buildings originally treated in a first draft of this book. Although

200 Washington-area apartment houses were studied, only 162 could ultimately be included in an already oversized volume. Space restrictions further limited full coverage of one-third of these buildings; they appear here as "notable additions" in pictorial "essays" at the end of each chapter that suggest the full range of styles available in a particular time period. Fortunately, most of the apartment houses that were eliminated are similar in general design and plan to others retained. The Promenade in Rockville, for example, is basically similar to the Towers at Cathedral and New Mexico avenues, N.W., since both consist of two separate rectangular blocks connected in the center by a common lobby. Likewise the Westmoreland of 1905 shares the plan (double-E) and the facade treatment of the Plymouth at 1236 11th Street, N.W., built in 1903. Thus most types and styles typical of the approximately seven thousand apartment buildings in the Washington metropolitan area are fully represented. The floor plans reflect the original designs of the buildings and do not, as a rule, show subsequent alterations. A site plan for large apartment houses, usually consisting of two or more buildings, is often included as well.

This study has been a long but fascinating project, involving a cross section of urban architectural history and social history. It is hoped that the findings presented here will not only acquaint Washingtonians, and others, with the rich architectural heritage inherent in the design of local apartment houses but also encourage their preservation. Although some have fallen on hard times and deteriorated, and others have been razed, they all were, at one time, best addresses in the nation's capital.

ACKNOWLEDGMENTS

More than a thousand people, mostly Washingtonians, have helped with the preparation of this volume over the past decade. The largest group involved the residents of the two hundred apartment houses that my two photographers and I visited on weekends between January 1980 and January 1987. I am extremely grateful to these apartment residents; without their hospitality in opening their doors for study and for photography, this book would not have been possible. Only a small number of the photographs could be included here, but all of the negatives have been preserved in the Photographic Archives of the National Gallery of Art and form a permanent record of how Washingtonians lived in a given period of time. The second part of my collection, including extensive notes and files on apartment houses that do not appear in this volume as well as many photographic prints, has been deposited at the Columbia Historical Society in Washington. These two holdings form an important and unique record of American architectural, decorative art, and social history.

The staffs of the apartment buildings selected for study were invariably helpful. Resident managers generously took time from busy schedules to discuss the history of their buildings, explain peculiarities in design, and escort my photographers and me through both public and private areas. The boards of directors of both cooperatives and condominiums as well as the owners of rental buildings were equally cordial in opening their files to my study and in answering numerous questions.

At the Smithsonian, I am indebted to Moya King for her support of the initial tour, conducted for the Smithsonian Resident Associates in May 1978, that led me to embark on a comprehensive study of Washington apartment houses. My request for research time to work on the book was approved and encouraged by Secretary S. Dillon Ripley in 1979 and by Secretary Robert McC. Adams in 1984. Assistant Secretary David Challinor approved a Smithsonian research grant that in 1985 enabled me to study the development of apartment houses in five European cities.

Other members of the Smithsonian staff who helped in various ways include James McKim Symington, Jeff Stann, and Arthur Gardner of the Office of Development, who assisted me in applying for both research and publication grants from local foundations. In the Smithsonian photo lab help came from Jim Wallace, Mary Ellen McCaffrey, Wilnette Harrington, Louie Thomas, and Lorie Aceto. My immediate colleagues in the Castle, Amy Ballard and Colin Varga, were supportive in many ways over a number of years.

A large number of Smithsonian volunteers, all interested in Washington's social and architectural history, assisted on this project for various lengths of time. Several helped locate hundreds of articles on apartment houses in American architectural magazines published between 1873 and 1980. Others carefully scanned the microfilm reader at the D.C. Public Library, searching a century of issues of the [Washington] *Evening Star* newspaper for local apartment house articles. A number arranged appointments for my photographers and me to visit apartment houses over the weekends. Those who offered suggestions for the elimination of photographs in the final selection were especially helpful. The volunteers included Pat Eames, Constance Minkin, Scott Wayne Hall, Marie T. Norris, Melanie Richardson, Marian Israel, William A. Savin, Robert M. Pajer, Adam Sher, James Matthew Evans, Margaret Martin, Clark Hollis Blouir, and Sam J. Profeta. Others who gave assistance included Jan Evans, Mrs. T. C. Alford, Michael Sullivan, Keith Scripps, Richard Stoltz, Virginia L. Blodgett, Lorijon Bacchi, Julie Rose, and Amy Loveless.

Washington architects Arthur Keyes, Richard Ridley, and Tom Ahmann read the post–World War II chapters on modern architecture and suggested ways of improving the stylistic descriptions. Parts of the manuscript were edited by Arthur Warren, Robert W. Kilpatrick, Betty Bird, Thomas Pursley, Knight Kiplinger, and H. Bartholomew Cox. Those who read the entire manuscript and offered suggestions include Richard Longstreth, Judy Frank, Robert Cullinane, Richard Cote, Emily Eig, Russell Adams, Catherine Ray, Roxanna Deane, Mark Andrich, Sue Kohler, Jeff Carson, and Larry Baume. In the last two months Constance Minkin, a retired editor at the Smithsonian Institution, helped me considerably to polish the grammar and style. Professor C. William Westfall of the University of Virginia interrupted a busy schedule both to serve as a principal reader and to write the foreword.

I am particularly appreciative of the research completed by Imogene Baumgardner. Over a period of six years, she located the building and demolition permits for all of the apartment houses included here. Pat Eames researched a number of buildings and set up dozens of appointments over the same length of time. In the final weeks of work on the manuscript, four neighbors in my former apartment house, the Northumberland, worked with me at night to renumber pages, renumber photographs, and help with corrections—Elsie Anderson, Woodrow W. Reagan, Jr., Henry A. Willard III, and Russell Adams.

The site and floor plans were prepared by local draftsmen, most of whom were enrolled in the School of Architecture of the University of Maryland in College Park. The chief draftsman was Thomas Ahmann, who not only redrew dozens of floor plans and site plans but organized most of the work produced by the draftsmen whose names are listed in the credits for drawings in the back of the book.

On the recommendation of a member of the staff of the Commission of Fine Arts, Jeff Carson, I enlisted the aid of a local photographer, James Stafford Phillips, in photographing the fifty Washington apartment houses that I had initially selected for inclusion in early 1980. Mr. Phillips and I worked closely together to photograph Washington apartment houses from 1980 to 1982. After he moved to New York, his assistant, James F. Tetro, assumed the position of principal photographer for the project and worked until early 1987 on many additional apartment houses. The resulting collection of more than five thousand exceptionally fine photographic negatives, known as the Goode-Phillips Collection, was generously donated by these two photographers to the Photographic Archives of the National Gallery of Art.

A great deal of information came from the extensive archives of the Edmund J. Flynn Company, the earliest surviving realty firm in Washington to specialize in cooperative apartment house sales. Russell Adams opened the files there for my use and was particularly helpful in keeping me posted on changes in the status of many apartment houses while research was in progress. His extensive knowledge of Washington cooperative and condominium apartment houses was very helpful.

Several individuals working on specialized studies of Washington apartment houses contributed in many ways to my own research. We shared information and frequently worked together on research problems. These include Paul Alley, who studied the early Beaux Arts facade treatment of Washington apartment houses from 1900 to 1905 for his M.A. thesis in architectural history at the University of Virginia, and Clark Hollis Blouir, who studied the development of mixed-use buildings in Washington from 1970 to 1986 for his M.S. thesis in architecture at the Virginia Polytechnic Institute. Mark Andrich produced several important papers on the influence of Washington zoning on apartment house development and the development of Connecticut Avenue as a major apartment house corridor while working on his M.A. in urban and regional planning at George Washington University. Emily Eig of Traceries, Inc., and her staff worked with me for more than a year, beginning in 1985, when she began her study for the D.C. Preservation League and the D.C. government on all types of Washington apartment buildings built between 1880 and 1945. Glen B. Leiner was helpful in providing additional information on Langston Terrace.

As much as time would allow, I visited the best-designed apartment houses in other cities to study the differences in regional design and development from those of Washington. In the United States I was shown apartment houses in Boston by Alexander Cassie; in New York City by Richard Wrobelenski and Andrew Alpern, and by Wilbur L. Ross, Jr., who gave me a three-hour tour of the Dakota from attic to basement; in Baltimore by Debora Fulton; in Richmond by Richard Cote; in Los Angeles by G. Peyton Hall and Robert Sweeney; and in San Francisco by Christopher H. Nelson. My tour guides in Europe included Frau Olga Prehsfreund and Frau Eberhart Winkelbauer in Vienna; Paul A. Elby, Sir Valentine Abdy, Harry H. Lunn, Jr., Robert Carlhian, and Frazier Draper of the U.S. Embassy in Paris; Robert Thorne in London; and Peter Robinson and Charles Prosser and the staff of the Royal Scottish Commission of Fine Arts in Edinburgh.

Within the Photographic Archives of the National Gallery of Art, Ruth Philbrick, Jerry Mallick, and Kathy Buchalew were especially helpful in organizing and cataloging the negatives produced for this book, which were donated by my photographers. They also produced numerous improved prints at the last minute. Both Larry Baume, curator of the Columbia Historical Society, and his two volunteers, Jack Brewer and Selena Hoyle, skillfully assisted with organizing my files there. The reference staff at the Washingtoniana Collection of the Martin Luther King, Jr., Public Library, including Roxanna Deane, Katherine Ray, G. R. F. Key, and Mary Ternes, were helpful for eight years in locating important clippings and rare photographs. The staff of the American Institute of Architects, including librarian Stephanie Burnes and archivist Tony Wrenn, were also of constant assistance in locating rare magazine articles. Many of the rare photographs taken by Theodore Horydczak in the collections of the Prints and Photographs Division of the Library of Congress were provided by C. Ford Peatross, Beverly Brannan, and Jerry Kerns.

At the Smithsonian Institution Press Maureen Jacoby, assistant director, Caroline Newman, editor, and Janice Wheeler, designer, offered expert counsel and guidance. I am also grateful to Joan Holleman for copy editing the final manuscript. Fourteen friends helped with the arduous task of proofreading galleys: Russell Adams, Mark Andrich, Amy Ballard, John Brewer, John Hazzard, Michael Kopp, Kenneth Love, Connie Minkin, Joy Pierce, Thomas Pursley, Woodrow Reagan, Keith Scripps, Florence Stanley, and Hank Willard. The endpaper maps were skillfully produced by Stephen Kraft, and the map of apartment houses in Southwest Washington by Mame Cohalan.

The production of this volume would have been impossible without the financial backing of several individuals and organizations. The research cost of photography and plans was far above what was projected in the beginning. These costs were covered by several generous local grants, extending over a period of seven years, endorsed by Robert Alvord of the Alvord Foundation and Knight Kiplinger of the Kiplinger Foundation. The cost of publication of the clothbound edition was generously provided for by a major grant from the Gwendolyn and Morris Cafritz Foundation. In addition, Mark G. Griffin made a contribution to the Smithsonian to allow publication of a limited deluxe edition. B. Francis Saul II has taken a personal interest in this project for the past five years and has contributed funds for both research and publication costs. Finally, without the gift of a computer by my father, George Browne Goode of High Point, North Carolina, in 1985, I would not have been able to complete the manuscript on time. My appreciation is extended as well to the hundreds of individuals who remain unlisted for lack of space.

INTRODUCTION

Millions of visitors and even many residents of Washington are unaware of the capital's great tradition of apartment living. Presenting a veritable tapestry of architectural styles and compositions, the area's seven thousand apartment buildings make up one of the richest ensembles in the country. Washington's percentage of apartment dwellers is surpassed only by those of New York and Chicago.

As in most urban centers, Washingtonians take their built environment for granted; in a city of world-famous monuments, the everyday is all the more obscure. This book is the first published effort to recognize the importance of Washington's apartment houses and to delve even into their interiors, to date a mystery to all but their inhabitants. *Best Addresses* has been written to acquaint Washingtonians with the outstanding—and hidden—wealth of apartment residences. What a revelation it is to see the insides—beyond the lobbies and private paneled doors! Apartment living in Washington is a very special world. The casual reader as well as the historian will find much to use and enjoy in the major elements that are included: history, architectural drawings, rich documentary, and original photographs, made specifically for this book.

The apartment house was introduced to Washington in the 1880s and has increased in popularity ever since.

Just fifty years after its appearance, half the city's population was residing in apartment houses. By 1987 approximately 70 percent of the residents of the city and 50 percent of those in the suburbs lived the apartment life.

UNIQUENESS OF WASHINGTON APARTMENTS

The presence of the federal government, with its large number of transient workers, has given the apartment house a place in Washington surpassing that in most American cities. The rowhouse, for example, has remained the traditional residential mode in the nearby cities of Baltimore and Philadelphia. This study shows that the Washington apartment house also differs in other significant ways from those elsewhere. In the early decades, Washington apartment houses, more than those in other American cities, were built to look like large houses. They had domestic-looking facades awkwardly designed with rows of quaintly projecting bays and inside revealed rooms arranged house-like along a long hall.

It was only after the turn of the century that local architects began to do something interesting with apartment houses. A number of awkward Victorian elements began to disappear, and plans gained an orderly, self-contained, and logical arrangement. Indeed, local architects in the decade before World War I produced a number of apartment houses of the Beaux Arts mode, some equal to the best then being built in New York. Those prewar years have never been equaled in Washington for elegant detailing and original planning. If Washington's apartment houses had a golden age, that was it.

Differences between Washington apartment houses and those of other cities can also be attributed to the 1894 height limitation law, under which apartment houses could rise to only 90 feet—then seven stories. The first height limitation law, which limited all buildings to a maximum of 40 feet and required those built on wide avenues to rise to a minimum of 35 feet, had been instituted by President George Washington when the city was laid out in 1791 but was soon abolished to encourage more rapid development of the infant city. Under the next height limitation law, established in 1894, local developers secured the prestige of their first-class apartment houses not by height, as in New York or Chicago, but by the splendor of their facades and the luxury of their lobbies. Today both the 1894 law and the trend continue. Another local peculiarity resulting from the height law was the development in the 1920s of step-down lobbies, which allowed an additional floor of apartments above. This device is still seen in many new intown apartment houses.

The resort hotel also influenced the development of the Washington apartment house. Beginning in the early 1920s, dozens of large multibuilding apartment houses with spacious lawns were built in all parts of the city and suburbs. The happy availability of vacant sites within easy commuting distance of the downtown business core made this possible economically.

Apartment house corridors began to appear locally at the turn of the century. The first two such corridors—14th Street, N.W., and lower Connecticut Avenue, N.W.—originated because of the existence of streetcar lines. By World War I Columbia Road had developed as the third apartment house corridor after the streetcar line between Connecticut Avenue and 16th Street was completed in 1901. Even though the streetcar line had been

extended out Connecticut Avenue from Calvert Street to Chevy Chase Circle as early as 1892, it was not until the 1920s that upper Connecticut Avenue developed as the city's most fashionable apartment house corridor.

General prosperity and the continued growth of the federal government during the 1920s caused a building boom of apartments that has never been equaled. The popularity of the automobile, moreover, made it possible for developers to build apartment houses in parts of the city far removed from downtown, such as Hampshire Gardens in Petworth and Alban Towers near the Washington Cathedral. During the twenties the cooperative apartment house—the "co-op"—became popular. Architects devised innovative site plans, featuring abundance of light and air. The traditional corner apartment house with its rear U-shaped courtyard and long halls disappeared.

The 1930s saw the construction of more than three hundred garden apartment complexes in the city and the suburbs. Designed with both Georgian and modernist imagery, these complexes constitute as a building type the most important collection of garden apartments of any American city. At the time they were built, the construction industry was stifled elsewhere; because of the government's efforts to deal with the Great Depression as well as strengthen national defense, however, Washington experienced a building boom. Nor did this boom end when the United States entered World War II at the close of 1941. The nationwide restrictions on construction materials did not apply to many new apartment buildings in the capital. In Washington large-scale garden apartment complexes continued to be built during the war years to help alleviate the critical shortage of housing for defense workers. Most of these large complexes, such as Parkfairfax and Fairlington, were financed by private insurance companies through the encouragement of the federal government, while others, such as Naylor Gardens and McLean Gardens, were built by the government itself. The housing shortage continued, even with construction of these many garden apartments, causing the division of hundreds of houses into small apartments.

When full-scale private construction resumed in the late 1940s, most apartment houses in Washington were designed in the International Style, a tendency that would last for twenty-five years. Their relatively plain facades signaled a theme of spareness throughout. Almost none of the interior ornament found in prewar apartment buildings—such as crown moldings, paneled and French doors, and finely detailed wooden window jambs—appeared here. Both their design and their resulting popularity represented a reaction against the ornamentation found in the more "architectural" Beaux Arts and Art Deco apartment houses. They had their day, however, like previous episodes in design.

By the 1970s the next generation of Washingtonians increasingly found many features of the International Style boring. Ribbon windows and blond-brick facades, relieved—indeed often rescued—by the site planning of trees and slopes, came to seem bland and too often repeated. A number of these same concepts, the clusters of buildings, the inner plazas, the buildings raised above the ground with garages below, are found in the apartment house complexes built under urban renewal in Southwest Washington during this period.

Postmodern architecture became popular in the mid-1970s, relieving the often repetitive similarity of Washington's International Style apartment houses. With renewed interest in—but painfully little knowledge of—historical styles, Postmodern architects explored the adaptation of Georgian, Victorian, classical, and even Art Deco detailing. These Postmodern residences are, in a traditional sense, more sensitive to their immediate neighbors and to the overall streetscape. During the 1970s major changes in the Washington building and zoning codes allowed "planned unit development," in which a single building could contain both residential and commercial space. By the late 1980s more than forty of these mixed-use structures had been built in the Washington metropolitan area—from the Watergate, the earliest example from the 1960s, to the most recent controversial undertaking, Washington Harbour, completed in 1987.

A major influence on the development of the apartment house in Washington was the reestablishment of rent control in 1974. It resulted in the halt of construction of all rental apartment houses except for the very few built as public housing. Apartments built in the city since that time have almost universally been designed as condominiums. Because of this development, the city government passed a 1983 law exempting new apartment

houses from rent control, to encourage their contruction. Rent control also spurred the conversion of hundreds of apartment houses, both large and small, into condominium apartments. Today the city has more than 4,000 apartment buildings—approximately 110 cooperatives, 400 condominiums, and 3,500 rental structures. The Virginia and Maryland suburbs add to this housing supply with approximately 3,000 apartment buildings.

IN THE NAME OF "PROGRESS"

In looking back over the first century of Washington's apartment house development, one learns that almost all of the city's important nineteenth-century examples, such as the Portland Flats, have been demolished. Dozens of other grand Beaux Arts apartment houses built in the first decade of the twentieth century, such as Stoneleigh Court, the Warder, the Farragut, the Rochambeau, the Sherman, and the Cecil, have also been lost. Most of these were razed as the city's downtown commercial center shifted northwest from F and 12th streets, N.W., toward K and 17th streets, N.W., following World War II.

The destruction of these apartment houses and hundreds of other important landmark Washington buildings during the boom period of development in the 1950s and 1960s caused a terrible wound in the harmony of the cityscape. Beginning in the 1950s elegant lobbies and apartment units themselves were often gutted and crudely adapted for office or hotel use. Notable examples of these insensitive changes include the Toronto and the Highlands. Even the 1980s saw landmark apartment houses such as the Story Flats, the Burlington, the Marlborough, the Gwenwood, and the Governor Shepherd razed for the construction of innocuous new commercial buildings. Many more were insensitively converted to condominiums during the 1970s and 1980s. It was only with the threat of razing the Falkland and the Governor Shepherd in the early 1980s that preservationists began to try to save historically significant local apartment houses.

Although a number of historic apartment house facades have recently been saved, many developers elected to strip the interiors, since the restoration of elaborate and ornate lobbies is expensive and architects are un-

Preservation of historic apartment houses has been a neglected subject. Here in the lobby of Tudor Hall are stacked many of the columns and other architectural detailing removed when the World War I apartment house was gutted in 1981 for conversion to the Henley Park Hotel.

accustomed to that sort of work. In early 1980, for instance, the classical lobby of 2001 16th Street, N.W., now called the Brittany, was gutted and three apartments built in that space, permitting the developer to make a far greater profit on his initial investment, while ruining a great interior. No vestige of the original detailing survives, and the once-spacious apartments above were replaced with mean little units with tiny rooms. The Balfour, located across 16th Street from the Brittany, built in 1900 and still in original condition in 1980, was likewise unhappily gutted the same year for condo conversion.

Not all of the renovations of historic apartment houses have been so thoughtlessly carried out. Fortunately a number of realtors, businessmen, and entrepreneurs have completed harmonious conversions, retaining the best features of historic interiors. Even though some of them have been converted to office buildings or hotels, their interior details and character have been retained. Examples include the Bachelor Flats, the Jefferson, 1509 16th Street, N.W., the Chastleton, the Mayflower Hotel,

and the Wardman Tower, all covered in this book.

One of the most exciting recent restorations occurred at the Embassy, where four apartments that had been built in the spacious lobby in the 1950s were removed, revealing all of the original Gothic detailing. After careful study and at considerable cost, the gilt strapwork ceiling, the mahogany columns, and the intricately laid terrazzo floor with its quatrefoil design were restored to their brilliant original appearance. It is today once again one of the finest lobbies in the city. The original workmanship here is so superior that it would be prohibitively expensive to reproduce it today. The Embassy restoration was undertaken primarily because current tax laws make such a project economically practical for investors.

PRESERVATION AND DISCOVERY

Listing landmark apartment houses in the National Register of Historic Places of the United States Department of the Interior can help save these symbols of Washington history. While historic buildings placed in the National Register (established in 1966) are not guaranteed preservation, listing helps considerably. Such buildings cannot be razed for projects with federal funding, including the construction of highways, subways, or government office buildings, without adequate public hearings. More than a hundred Washington apartment houses are now included in the list, some as individual listings but most as part of historic districts.

Another aid to the preservation of architecturally significant apartment houses was the federal Tax Act of 1981, which allowed developers to deduct 25 percent of renovation costs from their federal taxes. A 1986 revision in the federal law reduced the deduction to 20 percent, but it still provides a sufficient business incentive for rehabilitation of historic buildings. Much remains to be accomplished in Washington, however, including the listing of apartment house interiors, primarily lobbies, in the National Register for their protection and preservation. This common practice in most European countries over the past thirty years is almost unknown in the United States.

Best Addresses, begun in 1978, has concentrated only on the most architecturally significant apartment buildings, extant and demolished, built over the past century. A different type of survey of Washington apartment buildings was initiated by the city government in 1985 when the D.C. Preservation League received a grant to survey apartment houses in Washington, D.C. Awarded by the District of Columbia's Division of Historic Preservation, it was supported by the National Park Service's Historic Preservation Fund and required matching cash and in-kind services. The D.C. Preservation League commissioned the survey to be completed by Traceries, Inc., one of several local consulting firms specializing in architectural and historic preservation. This survey will establish a context for evaluating the significance of individual apartment houses built throughout the city when they are nominated for landmark status.

The development of the Washington apartment house has a fascination all its own. We read histories of houses and of public buildings; apartments are less common subjects of study. The chapters of this book are arranged chronologically to trace the social and architectural development of the best-designed local examples. They fall into six distinct phases: (1) Victorian structures of the 1880s and 1890s; (2) Beaux Arts classicism from the turn of the century to World War I; (3) great expansion during the 1920s in which the classical uniformity of the prewar period gave way to a variety of architectural modes such as Gothic, Colonial Revival, Moorish, and Art Deco— and even mixtures of two of these in one building; (4) stylistic changes influenced by the Great Depression and the growth of the garden apartment, 1932–45; (5) the postwar years, 1946–73, the International Style; and (6) contemporary development of condominium apartment houses as well as mixed-use buildings, most of them Postmodern in design, based on the revival of historical styles. With the exception of the first or Victorian phase, Washington's best examples of apartment houses date from 1900 on. The apartment lifestyle is a unique and largely unknown heritage in a city famous for its grand government buildings and national memorials.

1

VICTORIAN BEGINNINGS,

1880–1896

INTRODUCTION

1.

PORTLAND FLATS, 1129 Vermont Avenue, N.W.

2.

RICHMOND FLATS, 801 17th Street, N.W.

3.

CAIRO, 1615 Que Street, N.W.

NOTABLE ADDITIONS

The appearance of the apartment house in Washington in 1880 was facilitated by earlier experiments with the building type in Boston, Chicago, and especially New York. Even though apartment living had been popular in ancient Rome and had been well known in most of Europe since the Renaissance, it was relatively new to the United States. The apartment was uniquely suited to Washington and other American cities because of rapid urban growth during the Victorian period. (A broad historical survey of how the apartment house developed elsewhere before its introduction to Washington can be found in appendix 1.)

The development of the apartment house in Washington over the past century makes a complex story. Architecturally, the apartment has been affected constantly by changes in style and social patterns, war, depression and inflation, building codes, zoning laws, rent control, public transportation systems, demographic shifts, and technological developments. Architecture always reflects the forces that surround its inception; this maxim is magnified with the apartment.

Most of the one hundred apartment buildings erected in Washington during the first two decades of development—the 1880s and 1890s—were small, with two to fifteen units. They were immediately popular with lower-income residents, especially clerks and mechanics. Only a dozen were "apartment houses," however, possessing a lobby, elevator, and staff. Although the apartment house was favored by the capital's rich during this period, it did not become popular with the city's middle-income population until the last of the 1890s. Conversely, with little industry and fewer factories, the city never realized a large blue-collar population, so no tenements were built. But then Washington has always shown marked differences in its social and architectural makeup from other American cities. It was created and is still strongly influenced by the presence of the federal government. And, unlike most capital cities of the world, it is not the nation's economic center.

Throughout most of the nineteenth century, Washington remained relatively small in both size and population when compared with Boston, New York, Philadelphia, and Chicago. The city had been laid out by French military engineer Pierre Charles L'Enfant in 1791, and the federal government moved to Washington from Philadelphia in 1800, after a few government buildings had been built to the point of being habitable. Washington failed to grow at the rapid rate of other Eastern cities because it lacked a significant industrial base. Its "industry" was government.

Housing for the government's salaried employees was limited to private rowhouses, boarding houses, and numerous hotels until after the Civil War when the city began to grow quickly. Alexander R. Shepherd, governor of the District in the early 1870s, made numerous civic improvements to keep pace with this growth. Streets were leveled, paved, and flanked by sidewalks, new gas streetlights were installed, and public landscaping projects were initiated. The improved city began to attract an affluent community of part-time residents who built second houses in Washington primarily either to extend their political influence or to enjoy the brilliant winter social season. Preferred neighborhoods for the new private mansions were all in the northwest sector of the city—on K Street, Massachusetts Avenue, New Hampshire Avenue, 16th Street, and Dupont Circle.

A building boom started in the 1870s to supply rowhouses for the growing population of middle-class residents. At that time developers began the earliest important residential area north of the old city limits at Boundary Street (now Florida Avenue)—Le Droit Park, the first suburb. The success of this venture caused other developers before World War I to build hundreds of entire blocks of speculative rowhouses in areas only recently considered to be remote—Georgetown, North Capitol Street, Logan Circle, Capitol Hill, and Mount Pleasant.

The federal government was at the same time rapidly building many large structures to house its expanding departments and agencies. These included the enormous State, War, and Navy Department Building (now the Old Executive Office Building), Government Printing Office, Pension Building, Agriculture Department, Bureau of Engraving and Printing, Naval Observatory, Navy Yard, and Washington Barracks (now Fort McNair)—all dating from the decades between the Civil War and World War I.

The growth of the federal government actually played the major role in a housing shortage beginning in the 1870s. Although most of the new clerks and secretaries and their families became permanent residents, a large percentage of the population was transitory. It was composed of congressmen, senators, justices, political appointees, and lobbyists whose number expanded each decade due to the admission of new states to the union. Many were employed during only one presidential administration; unwilling to invest in private houses, they usually lived in boarding houses and hotels. While many of the lesser clerks purchased or rented the hundreds of new two-story Victorian rowhouses being built in the outlying areas of the city, higher-paid government officials preferred to live in the old downtown residential section near Lafayette Square, which was far more convenient to government offices, businesses, and clubs. They were almost universally unhappy with their living conditions there, however. The rental of downtown houses was too expensive, and hotels and boarding houses offered little privacy. The arrival of the apartment house was a welcome answer to their needs.

Several buildings in Washington were subsequently converted to apartments to relieve this shortage. The earliest of these conversions involved the former Miss Lydia English's Georgetown Female Seminary building at 1305–1315 30th Street, N.W. Built in 1820 and today known as the Colonial Apartments, it was converted to a "flat building" in 1870. This example and many others adapted from large houses are known as *apartment buildings*—which were distinctly different from *apartment houses*, which were designed with lobbies, elevators, and provision for staffs.

The first attempt to build an apartment house in Washington occurred in 1873 when construction began on the 200 block of East Capitol Street, N.E., adjacent to the Capitol and across the street from the present Folger Shakespeare Library. Although the foundation was completed, the developer declared bankruptcy in the depression of 1873 and the structure was never finished.

NEW YORK INFLUENCE

The city's first realized apartment house, the Portland Flats on Thomas Circle, was built in 1880. It is not surprising that the developer was Edward Weston of New York, where apartment houses had been prevalent for the previous eleven years. Even while construction was underway on the Portland Flats, the city's second apartment house, the smaller Fernando Woods Flats, located at 1418 Eye Street, N.W., was begun in May 1880. This four-story structure, built by another New York developer, was named for the former mayor of New York City.

During the Victorian period Washington's apartment houses were mostly designed as six-story U-shaped elevator buildings, located downtown, each with an average of forty apartments. They were built at intersections to have two street exposures for maximum light and air circulation.

Unlike the designers of Washington's federal government buildings, the architects of these private residences were, for the most part, locally trained. They attempted in every way to design domestic facades for the apartment house in order to differentiate it from an office building, the only other type of high-rise. While office buildings had relatively flat facades and flat roofs, early apartment houses were designed with features found on typical rowhouses—projecting bays, cornices, turrets, porches, and gabled roofs.

Projecting bays became virtually standard on Washington rowhouses when architects took advantage of an 1871 law first allowing them to be built out onto public property. Because the 1791 L'Enfant Plan provided for streets much wider than necessary in residential areas, the Victorian law permitted rowhouse bays to extend 4 feet out from the actual lot line, with a front lawn extending even farther into the public right-of-way. This rowhouse feature is more pronounced in Washington than in any other Eastern city.

Facades of the Victorian Washington apartment house varied in design from the Châteauesque style, such as the Richmond Flats of 1883 by Gray and Page, and the Queen Anne style, exemplified by the Analostan of 1893 by George S. Cooper, to the Romanesque Revival 1889 Story Flats by T. Franklin Schneider. Others were eclectic, combining two or more different Victorian styles, such as the Portland Flats of 1880 by Adolph Cluss. The richness, the variety, and the texture of these "French flats" (as early American apartment houses were first termed, because of their so-called Parisian models), usually executed in finished red brick and trimmed in stone—

T. Franklin Schneider was Washington's
first architect to specialize in apartment
house design, beginning in the 1880s. This
photograph was taken in 1894, at the time
he designed the Cairo.

typical of the better rowhouse—allowed the early apartment house to fit successfully into the domestic Washington streetscape. Paradoxically, even though Paris was the center for nineteenth-century apartment house design, most American examples between 1870 and 1900 were influenced by those built in London—in both facade treatment and plan.

Washington apartment house floor plans were never really convenient in the late nineteenth century. A series of rooms was usually arranged along a narrow hall, and bedrooms were often adjacent to parlors. These features were not particularly upsetting to their upper-income residents at the time, since most of their entertaining and dining took place outside their apartment in the building's numerous public rooms. Washingtonians were also accustomed to the long hall, the worst feature of the plan, since such halls were common in the rowhouses after which the apartment's plans were patterned.

Despite their plans, these new apartments often afforded luxurious accommodations. The ground floor of the usual Victorian apartment house in Washington included many features of a hotel—large lobby, desk with receptionist, drugstore, barbershop, and public dining room. The people who resided in the better Washington apartment house in this period included both permanent and transient residents—high-level federal government offi-

cials and members of Congress, as well as the newly rich social elite from New York, Chicago, and Philadelphia who lived in Washington during the three-month winter social season. Conveniently located large rowhouses were expensive rental properties when used for only a short time. Downtown luxury apartments with permanent staff, providing full service and security from burglary, were economical as well as convenient. They provided much more privacy than either a boarding house or a hotel, the previous modes of living for many of the new apartment house residents.

During the 1880s and early 1890s few Washington apartment houses contained kitchens. Although the Portland Flats had kitchens in a few apartments when it opened in 1880, they were not in use a decade later. The Richmond Flats of 1883 included kitchens for all apartments, but they were located in such peculiar places as the basement or attic. Since servants were then plentiful and low-paid, all residents had their own cooks. Nevertheless, such odd arrangements constituted a serious drawback for a family with children. Parents found it undesirable to reside in an apartment without a kitchen. This problem was pointed out in a rare early glimpse of Washington apartment house life as reported in the [Washington] *Evening Star* in 1891:

> An apartment house is being erected in the extreme
> northwestern portion of the city [The Concord, at New
> Hampshire Avenue and Swann Street]. The projectors of
> this enterprise design to supply accommodations equal to
> those afforded by a small house at a rental which will not
> be more than such a house would command in a similar
> locality. To a certain extent the apartment house is still
> in an experimental stage in this city. The oldest and most
> successful building of this kind is more of a private or
> family hotel than an apartment house [The Portland Flats,
> at Thomas Circle]. The suites have no kitchens in use,
> and the occupants get their meals in the general dining
> room. There are practically only two buildings in this city
> which are apartment houses in the real meaning of that
> term. In these buildings each suite has a kitchen at-
> tached and is a separate and distinct house. The rentals
> range from $35 to $50 per month. The experiment will be
> made in this new building, as well as in several others
> which are now projected, of supplying the accommoda-
> tions of a complete house at a rental which will not ex-

Intricate Moorish designs on the 1894 twelve-story Cairo decorate the carved front stone entrance and the wide pressed metal cornice. Such elaborate architectural detailing was typical of Washington's better Victorian apartment houses; few still survive.

ceed for the best suite $75 per month. It is believed that such buildings will supply a need and will yield a good revenue upon the money invested, but so far this had been a mere theory. The results of the experiments to be made will be watched with considerable interest by men who have the money to invest in such undertakings.

At the time that this article was written, only five apartment *houses* existed in Washington—the Portland Flats, the Everett, the Richmond Flats, Maltby House, and the Albany. The two that included kitchens in every apartment were the Albany and the Everett—both located downtown at 17th and H streets, N.W. The apartment house mentioned as under construction, the Concord, opened in 1892 as the city's first cooperative apartment house. Here every apartment included its own kitchen. Because of this feature, the Concord enjoyed such popularity that a six-story addition, even larger than the original five-story building, was erected in 1893.

Developers followed the Concord's plan when the harsh economic effects of the depression of 1893 finally waned and allowed normal building to resume in 1897. The original Concord unfortunately was demolished in 1962 for the rather dull International Style apartment house of the same name that now occupies the site.

ROWHOUSE FEATURES

The interior details as well as the facade treatment of Washington's Victorian apartment houses reflected rowhouse features. An elaborate, decorative fireplace mantel, with mirror above, was always found in the parlor. All of these luxury buildings had central heating, but a decorative fireplace mantel was considered essential to a homelike atmosphere. Another rowhouse feature was the sliding door that separated the parlor from the dining room. About 1905 the sliding door (also known as an envelope or pocket door), as well as the built-in mirror over the mantel, disappeared, but the decorative mantel itself remained in place. The living room mantel in the better-class Washington apartment house did not finally disappear until the late 1930s.

Three apartment houses from these early years that greatly affected the future development of this building type in Washington were the Portland Flats (1880), the Concord (1891), and the Cairo (1894). The Portland Flats, Washington's first apartment house, with its hotel-like features, served as a model for others. The Concord, with its kitchen in every apartment, became extremely popular and was a model that developers followed a few years later. The Cairo was important because concerted public criticism of its great height resulted in passage of the city's 1894 height-restriction law, still in effect.

These landmark Washington buildings were designed with hotel-like features and were reserved for the affluent. The rent for a five-room apartment at the Portland Flats, for instance, was $150 a month, while a modest but new rowhouse in Mount Pleasant rented for $16 a month in 1880!

Few records and even fewer photographs have survived to give us detailed information on most of Washington's important Victorian apartment houses. Only the 1894 Cairo remains standing from this class, but at least five middle-class pre–1900 walk-up apartment buildings are still in place. Although altered on the interior, the oldest surviving example is the 1888 Canterbury (now the Harrison) at 704 3rd Street, N.W. Most of these, like the once-grand Cairo, have been gutted for total modernization or their plans have been drastically altered over the years.

Of particular interest is the design of the Cambridge, built in 1894 at 510 Eye Street, N.W., in the city's present Chinatown. Although not in the luxury category, it remains important as one of the oldest surviving apartment buildings in the city. It needs paint and a good cleaning, but it remains in original condition on both the exterior and the interior. Here are still found the brass speaking tubes at its front entrance, the sleeping porches at the rear, the pass-through kitchens, the pressed-tin facade simulating stone blocks and decorative shingles, the elaborate woodwork used for the apartment entrances and for the public staircase, and its original floor plan in all eight units. The four-story walk-up has two apartments per floor, each with four rooms. Its eclectic facade combines Romanesque, Shingle Style, and Queen Anne elements. The design of the Cambridge was typical of dozens of other modest Washington apartment buildings of the Victorian era—most of them now demolished for commercial development or gutted for condominium conversions.

The Story Flats at 715 13th Street, N.W., held the claim of being the second oldest surviving apartment building in the city until it was demolished in 1984 to allow construction of the new Hecht's department store. Built in 1889 in the Romanesque Revival style, it had been one of the first apartment houses designed by T. Franklin Schneider, the city's first apartment house specialist. Each of the four apartments occupied one entire level in the five-story building. The ground floor contained two entrances: the right door led to a shop and the left door to an elevator and staircase for the apartments. One servant's bedroom for each apartment was located in the basement.

Beginning in 1897, a major change in design began: the apartment house would undergo an awkward transition to adapt to modern planning. The eclectic Victorian facade began to change to a well-ordered Beaux Arts classicism, but the floor plan remained unimproved for a number of years. Before moving to this second phase, it is worthwhile to survey the history of three important early Victorian apartment houses—the Portland Flats, the Richmond Flats, and the Cairo.

1

PORTLAND FLATS

1129 Vermont Avenue, N.W.; south side of Thomas Circle at the intersection of Vermont Avenue and 14th Street

ARCHITECT: Cluss and Schulze, 1880; 1883 addition

ORIGINAL APARTMENTS: 39 (12 one-bedrooms; 7 two-bedrooms; 20 three-bedrooms)

STATUS: opened as rental in 1880; converted to hotel ca. 1926; converted to office building ca. 1940; razed in 1962

The Portland Flats, Washington's first apartment house, was designed by architect Adolph Cluss in 1880.

The Portland Flats, Washington's first luxury apartment house, served as a model for later Victorian apartment houses, most of which copied its hotel-like features— lobby, public dining room, drugstore, and full staff. It took a New York investor, Edward Weston, who was familiar with the rapid development of the apartment house in Manhattan during the 1870s, to realize its potential in the nation's capital. Even so, Weston cautiously built the Portland Flats in two sections, and the rear half of the building was only completed in 1883. Other local developers built their major Victorian apartment houses in two sections as well, since it was uncertain if the new building type would be a success.

When completed, the Portland Flats contained a total of thirty-nine apartments, half of which were large units comprising a parlor, dining room, three bedrooms, and bath. A significant number of units did not have kitchens as most residents took their meals in the first-floor public dining room. Steam heating was used throughout, but every apartment dining room and living room had a coal-burning fireplace that enhanced the homey feeling. A unique feature was the telephone in every apartment, connecting the public dining room, janitor's room, and elevator. The larger suites also had dumbwaiters to the basement and brick shafts for disposing of

The elegant Beaux Arts marquee at the Vermont Avenue entrance to the Portland Flats was added about 1905 to keep the building up to date. The marquee was fabricated and installed by Frederick Gichner, founder of the Gichner Iron Works, shown seated under it.

Ground and typical floor plans of the Portland Flats.

ashes. The two principal iron staircases and servant's stairs were lit by skylights, and the building boasted two hydraulic elevators—a technological development that had indeed made the luxury apartment house possible. The Portland Flats was an immediate success with its first occupants. Many were high-ranking government officials seeking the privacy they missed in Washington's hotels and boarding houses but without the problems involved in maintaining a second house.

The high cost of housing in Washington toward the end of the nineteenth century prevented the majority of politicians from purchasing houses appropriate to their status. Of the thirty-seven senators and representatives from the six New England states in 1900, twenty-five lived in hotels and boarding houses. With an annual salary of $5,000, few could even afford to rent a single-family dwelling with suitable space for entertaining. As Senator George F. Hoar of Massachusetts wrote in 1890:

> During all this time [as a representative and then a senator] I have never been able to hire a house in Washington. My wife and I have experienced the varying fortune of Washington boarding houses, sometimes very comfortable, and sometimes living in a fashion to which no Pittsburgh mechanic, earning two dollars a day, would subject his household.

The high rents at the Portland Flats offered no immediate solution to Senator Hoar's problems. By the end of the nineties, however, the apartment house had become common and units increasingly competitive.

The V shape of the six-story residence was dictated by the wedge-shaped lot on which it was situated—formed by the intersection of 14th Street and Vermont Avenue. The main entrance, approached by a circular drive, faced Vermont Avenue. The building had three other secondary entrances—one on 14th Street and two to the public drugstore located on its apex, facing Thomas Circle. The principal architectural feature was an imposing circular tower, embellished with balconies and crowned by a turret. Built at a total cost of $350,000, the structure combined Renaissance and [British] Indian influences.

The Portland Flats was designed by Adolph Cluss, a local architect unfamiliar with apartment house design. Although then the city's leading architect, he had made his reputation as a prominent designer of rowhouses, school buildings, and public markets. Indeed many features of the rowhouse were adopted in the design of the Portland Flats: the apartments had rooms arranged along a long hall, and the facades consisted of two long ranges of projecting bay windows on Vermont Avenue and 14th Street.

Only two exterior photographs of the Portland Flats survive, and no interior views have been located. The rare photograph of the main entrance facing Vermont Avenue is the only known close-up of the facade. The photograph was found in the archives of the Gichner Iron Works, the local firm that fabricated and installed the Portland's elaborate Beaux Arts marquee about 1905. The founder of the firm, Fred G. Gichner, is shown seated on the porch. Besides the handsome iron and glass marquee, another interesting architectural detail that appears in this photograph is the belt course. Actually, a series of polychrome glazed-brick belt courses circled the building, both at the base and in the center of each story. The 12-foot ceilings helped keep apartments cool during the summer months.

The construction of this fashionable residence on the south side of Thomas Circle influenced the location of more than fifteen other apartment houses on four adjacent blocks during the following twenty-five years. To the east of the Portland Flats, on square 247, were the Clifton, the Cumberland, the Valois, and the DeSoto; on the block to the west, square 214, were the Burlington, the Thomas, the Iroquois, the Manchester, and the Sherman; and to the north, on square 245, were the Laclede and the Blar. The proximity of several embassies on Massachusetts Avenue further enhanced the prestige of the Thomas Circle neighborhood. Unfortunately, all of these landmark apartment houses were demolished after World War II for office buildings as the downtown commercial area on F Street, N.W., expanded rapidly northward.

2

RICHMOND FLATS

801 17th Street, N.W.; northeast corner of 17th and H streets

ARCHITECT: Gray and Page, 1883; Henry T. E. Wendell, 1887 addition

ORIGINAL APARTMENTS: 10 (all five-bedrooms)

STATUS: opened as rental in 1883; converted to a hotel ca. 1900; razed in 1922

Once an imposing pile of masonry, the Richmond Flats offers a case study in how familiar historical styles were adapted to the monumental residences of Washington. In this instance, the châteaux of the Loire Valley (from which the American Victorian architectural style, the Château-esque, took its name) were dominant influences. From a rusticated base of stone, the predominantly brick building soared above the street, dwarfing the neighboring antebellum Greek Revival houses. The heavily fenestrated facade was articulated by window surrounds of smooth, lighter stone and by projecting bays. The steep roof was pierced and intersected by dormers, turrets, and chimneys with late Gothic lancet arches and delicate finials. The corner tower was an interesting translation of those found at Chambord, one of the greatest early sixteenth-century châteaux of Europe. At the top of the tower a delightful metal flag announced the Richmond Flats with a capital *R*.

Sensitively built in two sections, following the design of different architects, it is almost impossible to define the addition in the one surviving photograph of this landmark (the original structure was to the right). Until the early 1880s, the neighborhood around Lafayette Square remained much as it was before the Civil War, boasting the city's most prestigious collection of massive Greek Revival rowhouses. The construction of the Richmond Flats was one of the first major inroads into this neighborhood of houses, none of which survives today except for Blair House. Two mansions were torn down to provide the space; in the photograph, to the right of the Richmond Flats on H Street, can still be seen the Bancroft House. The transition of the old downtown area from residential to commercial use progressed in stages. After a number of Greek Revival houses were razed for luxury apartment houses in the 1880s, they in turn were razed for even more valuable large office buildings during the 1920s.

Contemporary newspaper accounts of new buildings "going up" provide us with some of the most reliable records of an architect's design. In the case of the Richmond Flats, the real estate editor for the *Evening Star* reported in 1883:

> Calling upon Messrs. Langley & Gettinger [builders], at their shop, No. 20 12th Street, a *Star* reporter found both of these gentlemen, with a full corps of carpenters, busy at work, as was soon ascertained, on material which is to enter into the internal construction of the new apartment building now in the course of erection at the corner of 17th and H streets. . . . The walls are now up to the third story. This building is to be seven stories in height, with a fine round tower at the corner of 17th and H

The Richmond Flats of 1883 was Washington's only example of the châteauesque style apartment house.

streets, 112 feet high above the basement floor, with spiral top and galvanized iron and Hummelstown brown stone trimmings all the way up. The same stone is used for the front up to the second-story windows, with all the rest of pressed and moulded brick and galvanized iron cornices. The stone is brought from New York in rough ashlers [sic], and cut here to suit.

The plan of the building shows it to be 109 feet on 17th street by 130 feet on H street. It will contain ten apartments, with seven rooms in each apartment, all complete, making a distinct and separate dwelling of each. There are to be four bay window projections, each fourteen feet wide, and three feet projections running to the topmost story. These start in a square form from basement and first story, changing with corbels to an octagon form on the second and third stories, then a change with other corbels to a circular form, which continues all the way up to a mansard roof, covered with tiling. One iron winding stairway is to run all the way up, with also a Murtaugh's patent dumbwaiter, running all the way up, to serve each dining room. An Otis [hydraulic] passenger elevator will occupy the well-hole space of the immense iron stairway, and will be run by steam and always ready at a moment's notice. The internal finish throughout is in natural poplar with hand oil dress. No paint will be used

at all. Each bathroom and water closet will be finished up in cherry wood.

The dining room [of each apartment] will be filled up with panel wainscotting and panel ceilings. Stationary buffets will be made in each corner, with leaded glass panels in each one. The kitchen for the first story [apartments] will be in the basement, and for the fifth story [apartments] in the attic, those for the second, third, and fourth floors will be constructed on the same floors. Each apartment will have the advantage of the dumbwaiter from the basement. The walls are very substantially made throughout—of the best arch brick, eighteen inches thick for basement and first story, the balance, including partition walls, etc., thirteen inches thick. The whole building will be heated by steam. The architects are Messrs. Gray & Page. The entire cost, including the ground, will be $100,000. It is thought that the building will be ready to occupy by October 1st, next.

This account provides some important clues to what people wanted and expected in luxury apartment houses in the 1880s. The building is clearly more sophisticated than the slightly earlier Portland Flats, and despite the addition by another architect five years later, its parts are well proportioned. Designed with red-brick eclectic facades, the structure resembled many of the luxury apartment houses then being built in New York (which were similar to those in London rather than Paris). The author carefully describes the large apartments as "distinct and separate dwelling[s]" to distinguish them from hotel rooms. The most modern and expensive conveniences were installed in the Richmond Flats—dumbwaiters for delivery of groceries by the servants directly from the basement to each of the apartments' pantries, and a passenger elevator that was manned around the clock. Each parlor featured a decorative fireplace mantel—a pattern that would be followed in Washington apartment houses for the next four decades. The elaborate dining room of each suite, with built-in corner china cabinets and paneled wainscoting, indicates the attention to detail common in all of the city's early luxury apartment houses. (See the photograph of a typical dining room in the Balfour— included in the next chapter—before it was unfortunately gutted in 1980.)

A peculiarity in the design was the location of communal kitchens for apartments in the basement, middle floors, and attic. While the scheme saved valuable space for the principal rooms in the apartments, the awkwardly located kitchens meant additional servants and expense, and the experiment was never repeated. Washington's first-class apartment houses were new and developers and architects were feeling their way. Despite the unsuc-cessful kitchen arrangement, however, the Richmond Flats was completely rented before construction was completed in late 1883.

ARCHITECTS GRAY AND PAGE

One of the leading Washington architectural firms at the end of the nineteenth century was Gray and Page. The firm was formed in 1879 by Harvey L. Page (1859–1934), a native of Washington, and William Bruce Gray, a New Yorker. (Page acquired sole control of the firm in 1885.) The firm designed Albaugh's Opera House, the annex to the Arlington Hotel, the old Army and Navy Club, the first Metropolitan Club, and the original First Baptist Church at 16th and O streets, N.W. Gray and Page were most noted for the dozens of prominent large houses they designed in the Dupont Circle area of Northwest Washington. These included the Noble House at Massachusetts Avenue and 18th Street (demolished for the McCormick apartment house); the Bryan House at 2025 Massachusetts Avenue; the Needham House at 1730 16th Street; the Bonaparte House at 1627 K Street; and the Cox House on the south side of Dupont Circle at New Hampshire Avenue. They worked in the Gothic Revival, Romanesque Revival, Colonial Revival, and Queen Anne styles. After 1897, Page worked as an architect in Chicago and ended his prolific career as a prominent architect in San Antonio.

CAIRO

1615 Que Street, N.W.
ARCHITECT: T. Franklin Schneider, 1894; 1904 addition
ORIGINAL APARTMENTS: approximately 110 (mostly one-bedrooms) and approximately 100 hotel rooms
STATUS: opened as rental in 1894; interior gutted and rebuilt, reopened as rental in 1976; converted to condo in 1979

Soaring twelve stories above Que Street, the Cairo led—in 1894—to Washington's present height limitation law.

While most luxury Washington apartment houses of the Victorian period were basically the same size and scale, with an average of six stories and forty units, one literally stands out as unique: the Cairo. No apartment house has left a more lasting impact on the development of the nation's capital than the twelve-story steel-framed Cairo, built at the then-record cost of $425,000 in 1894.

The Cairo was the most significant although not the best-designed building in the long career of Washington architect T. Franklin Schneider (1858–1938). The son of German immigrants, Schneider became the city's first large-scale architect-developer. He produced more than a thousand Romanesque Revival rowhouses (many designed as streetscapes covering whole blocks) and more than twenty Romanesque Revival and Beaux Arts apartment houses between 1883 and 1906. Trained in the office of Washington architect Adolph Cluss from 1875 to 1883, Schneider developed a keen sense of when and where to build. He was enormously successful both as an apartment house architect who made the Beaux Arts

Opposite: The impressive stone Romanesque Revival arch and Moorish Revival carved frieze at the entrance of the 1894 Cairo were based on the design of the Transportation Building at the Chicago World's Fair of 1893.

CAIRO
15

style popular in Washington as early as 1900, and as a businessman who built and owned many of the apartment houses that he designed, including the Cairo. Because of failing eyesight, he reduced his architectural practice in 1906 and gave it up entirely in 1909 to manage his extensive real estate holdings. The last building he designed was his own imposing Art Deco house of 1926 at Military Road and 31st Street, N.W. He developed this large tract of land as a family compound, designing two adjacent houses in the mid-1920s as wedding presents to his daughters, Florence and Ethel. His own house was razed in the late 1950s for the site of the present Presbyterian Retirement Home.

Almost square in plan, 120 by 100 feet, the Cairo soars 156 feet above its front step and 160 feet above the sidewalk. A large rear court eliminates any inside rooms, so that all of the 350 rooms have natural light. The front facade includes small projecting corner pavilions and a projecting three-bay-wide central entrance pavilion. The latter includes small columned balconies for selected apartments on the fifth, sixth, and twelfth stories. The principal decoration is the Romanesque Revival entrance, a massive stone arch framed by an elaborate carved frieze of flat ornament. Another major decorative feature is the massive 6-foot-high ornamental flat metal cornice that embellishes the building at the roof line on the front and side facades.

Schneider's visit to the Chicago World's Fair in 1893 was a major influence on his design of the Cairo a few months later. There is no question that he based the elaborate entrance, cornice, and balconies on Louis Sullivan's two-story Transportation Building at the fair. Even the Cairo's name was taken from the Midway or entertainment section of the fairgrounds, where the buildings were designed in Egyptian Revival and Moorish styles. The main street that ran through this complex of dance halls, Near Eastern exhibitions, bazaars, and cafes was called Cairo Street.

The Cairo is one of the few buildings in Washington with elements of the so-called Sullivanesque style, based in part on Islamic design elements. While the highly personal style of Louis Sullivan was popular in Chicago, it was rarely used in Washington for total facade treatments. Elements did occasionally appear on some Ro-

Architect Louis Sullivan's 1893 Transportation Building at the Chicago World's Fair.

manesque Revival houses of the period, however. The porch and balconies of two Victorian houses in Washington (both now demolished) contained Moorish details—architect Harvey L. Page's remodeled Hearst House of 1889 at 1400 New Hampshire Avenue, and Schneider's own 1890 house on the southeast corner of 18th and Que streets. More often, Washington architects of the late Victorian period used this style in the interior of their houses. One could find a Moorish room, a Japanese room, or a Colonial Revival room in the same house—it was all part of the then-fashionable eclecticism. Perhaps the most significant example of Moorish architecture ever erected in Washington was the Almas Temple, a 1926 Masonic hall built on K Street, opposite Franklin Park.

In addition to the influence of the Chicago World's Fair, Schneider based the massing and general shape of the Cairo on a New York apartment house, the Osborne, which had been built in the previous decade. Schneider must have visited the Osborne on his many trips to New York or seen photographs of it in architectural journals, for its design is too similar to the Cairo not to have been known by him. Both structures had iron and steel frames, but the Osborne was faced entirely in stone, a more expensive building material than brick. Now on New York's landmarks list, the Osborne still stands at 205 West 57th Street.

Seen from a distance, the elaborate buff-brick and

The classical lobby of the Cairo was still in original condition when photographed in 1925.

stone trim on the front facade of the Cairo created a jarring contrast to the austere red-brick walls on the sides and rear of the building. An editor of the *Architectural Record*, Montgomery Schuyler, reviewed the Cairo's design in a scathing critique published months after the apartment house was completed:

> It is a box full of holes. True, the bottom is stone, which is presumably stronger than brickwork, and therefore is properly used as a substructure when the substructure supports the superstructure, but meaningless when both substructure and superstructure are hung on steel frames. Of course this is the case with the best architectural renderings of the Chicago construction, as well as the worst. The architects play [pretend] that these envelopes of masonry are real buildings, and they ask the spectators to pretend the same thing. It is, from this point of view, proper that the basement should be massive enough, apparently, to carry what is over it, that the bottom should be the strongest and simplest, and the top the lightest and richest part of the assumed structure, and that the same canons of criticism should be applied as if the assumed structure were the real one. This structure goes to pieces at once under such a scrutiny. True the basement is of masonry, but it is not massive or strong of aspect, being painfully weak and thin. Moreover, it is not set off by any architectural devices as an essential division of the building. It is not even clear where it stops, for in the

middle it goes a story higher than in the flanks, and in both places stops without any architectural punctuation, as if the builder had merely run out of stone and had to take to brick at this point.

> As to the relation of voids and solids there is properly no such relation. The ends and the centre are projected a little, and the windows are varied in form, some being square-headed and some round-headed. But it is plain that these dispositions have had no more artistic origin than the desire to "obtain variety," and variety without purpose is mere confusion. The terminal pavilions are lean and hard, the central projection confused in mass and crude in detail, the fenestration architecturally nothing at all. Making this front various has only accentuated the fact that it is monotonous. "The more it changes, the more it is the same thing," as the lively Gaul observes. It is curious how the effect of boxiness, inherent in the original parallelepiped, is enhanced by all the things the architect has put on it ostensibly to relieve it of that appearance. The balconies at the angles, at the centre, and between the two, are merely box-like troughs, and so is the cornice a mere projecting box. It almost seems as if the designer must have projected these boxes in a cynical spirit, as if instead of trying to mitigate the boxiness of the building he were intent upon aggravating it and "rubbing it in."

The local criticism of the Cairo's height caused the three-member Board of Commissioners of the District of Co-

Adjacent to the Cairo's lobby was this Moorish Revival public parlor.

The floor plan of the Cairo was typical of many early Washington apartment houses: it included suites of rooms that could be used with or without kitchens.

lumbia, which then governed the city, to pass the [still-current] 1894 height-limitation regulation. The Cairo was by far the city's tallest privately owned building. Until it was erected, the [Baltimore] *Sun* newspaper building at 1317 F Street, N.W., was the city's tallest office building, with nine stories, crowned by a steep spire. Only three

Washington churches with tall steeples could come close to the Cairo's height. The new rule limited future privately owned residential buildings to 90 feet and commercial buildings to 110 feet. The commissioners explained their action in this press release:

> It was the erection of the Cairo Flats that directed the attention of the Commissioners to this matter. When the permit was granted several protests were filed with the Commissioners by the neighbors in the vicinity who claimed that the building would not only be a menace to the surrounding dwellings in case of fire or other catastrophe, but would depreciate their property by shutting off light and air. When the Board of Commissioners met several days after receipt of the protests, Commissioner Truesdell called the matter up for consideration. He agreed with the protestors and argued at length against such a building. Should a fire break out in any of the upper stories, there was not an engine in the city that could throw a stream high enough to extinguish it, and there was no ladder or series of ladders in the fire department long enough to reach a roof 160 feet above the sidewalk. Then, again, there was the argument advanced by the surrounding property owners that such a high building was a constant menace and depreciated adjacent property.
>
> He [Commissioner Truesdell] believed it did, and while nothing could be done to stop the erection of the present building, he thought the Commissioners should pass an amendment to the building regulations forbidding such high buildings in the future. Further, there was necessity for such high buildings in the commercial cities where there was little room, but here in Washington, where there was ample space, he did not see the necessity for such high structures.

Acts of Congress in 1898 and 1910 buttressed the board's ruling of 1894—reinforcing Washington height limits of 90 and 110 feet, respectively, for residential and commercial buildings. Since these laws are still in effect—although there are several recent exceptions—Washington has become the only major city in the United States to maintain a low skyline.

Upon entering the original Cairo, the visitor found a large lobby, with an ornate public desk to the left and classical pillars surrounding a marble fountain in the

The dining room of the Cairo originally occupied half of the top floor.

center. The lobby extended into the rear courtyard, where it was lighted by an arched skylight. Adjacent to the lobby was a public parlor, called the Oriental Room, with Moorish and [British] Indian furnishings and detail. Other public spaces on the first floor included the office, reading room, ballroom, and drugstore. In the basement an artesian well supplied the Cairo with fresh water. Although most of the apartments contained decorative fireplace mantels with gas logs, only electricity was used for lighting, a unique feature for an apartment house of this period.

Most of the 110 apartments on the floors above contained two rooms with bath. Only a few units had kitchens, since most residents took meals in the spacious public dining room that originally occupied more than half of the twelfth floor. Almost all of the rooms on each floor connected so that an apartment could be expanded to any size by unlocking adjacent doors. A bowling alley, billiard room, and numerous service rooms were located in the high English basement.

The roof garden, where refreshments were served in the summer months, was one of the first in the city and proved popular with Washingtonians. Many visitors, unaccustomed to such a height, tossed pebbles from the roof to time their fall. After a number of runaway carriage accidents on Que Street below, the police closed the roof.

As a result, in 1904 Schneider purchased and then demolished the rowhouse adjoining the Cairo to the east for the site of a new wing, 45 by 100 feet. The dining room was then moved from the top floor to the new first-floor addition.

Many inner-city Washington neighborhoods declined after World War II, causing Schneider's two daughters and heirs to sell their nine inherited apartment houses, including the Cairo, for a total of $3 million in 1955. The Cairo had deteriorated significantly by the time it was vacated in 1972. The following year it was purchased by the Inland Steel Development Corporation, which commissioned Washington architect Arthur Cotton Moore to redesign the interior. At that time the interior of the building, including the intricate wrought-iron elevator cage and most of the lobby detailing, was unfortunately gutted. The new design includes 192 apartments: 66 efficiencies, 44 one-bedroom units, 66 two-bedroom apartments, and a series of 8 new two-bedroom garden apartments and 8 duplex apartments created in the old rear courtyard. Although the view from the top floors is spectacular, the rooms in the new apartments—many with an exposed brick wall (a fad that has since passed)—are very small. The Cairo reopened as a rental building in 1976 and was converted to a condominium in 1979.

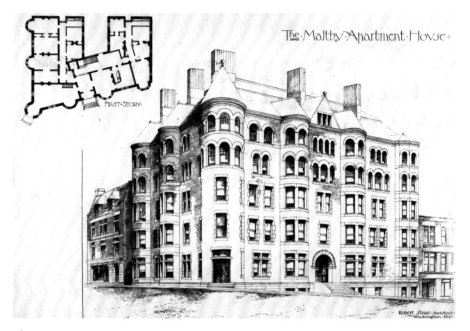

4. **MALTBY HOUSE**
200 New Jersey Avenue, N.W.
ARCHITECT: Robert Stead, 1887. (H. H. Richardson's Sever Hall of 1878 at Harvard University provided the inspiration for the principal facade.)
STATUS: opened as rental in 1887; converted to offices in 1891; razed in 1930

5. **STORY FLATS** (*above*)
715 13th Street, N.W.
ARCHITECT: T. Franklin Schneider, 1889
STATUS: opened as rental in 1889; converted to hotel in 1906; converted to retail and office use in 1922; razed in 1984

6. **ANALOSTON** (*left*)
1718 Corcoran Street, N.W.
ARCHITECT: George S. Cooper, 1893
STATUS: opened as rental in 1893; converted to condo in 1978

7. CAMBRIDGE

510 Eye Street, N.W.
ARCHITECT: Nicholas T. Haller, 1894
STATUS: opened as rental in 1894

8. MOUNT VERNON FLATS

904 New York Avenue, N.W.
ARCHITECT: unknown, 1896; B. Stanley Simmons, 1903 addition
STATUS: opened as rental in 1897; original building razed in
1950; addition razed in 1980

2

THE GOLDEN AGE, 1897–1918

INTRODUCTION

THE GOLDEN AGE

NOTABLE ADDITIONS

Washington underwent considerable civic improvement as a result of the McMillan Commission Plan of 1901. Established by the U.S. Senate to study ways to improve the physical aspect of the nation's capital, the McMillan Commission recommended that all future government buildings be in classical harmony with the Capitol and the White House. As a result, many new monumental federal government buildings were designed according to Beaux Arts classicism, including the Senate and House office buildings, Union Station, the U.S. Treasury Annex, the Veterans Administration Building on Lafayette Square, the Department of Agriculture Building, and the Smithsonian's National Museum of Natural History and Freer Gallery of Art on the Mall.

City government officials as well—including the three District Commissioners and the directors of the Board of Trade—ordered classical revival designs for all new city government buildings, such as the District of Columbia Building on Pennsylvania Avenue and the D.C. Public Library on Mount Vernon Square. They strongly encouraged private organizations, such as the Red Cross, the Daughters of the American Revolution, and the YMCA, as well as private developers who were building both office buildings and apartment houses to employ the new style.

Dozens of classical office buildings, clubs, museums, apartment houses, and outdoor sculptures were erected as a result. One of the most elegant additions to the cityscape was the Pan American Union building at the corner of Constitution Avenue and 17th Street, N.W. The McMillan plan, which called for a vast program of public improvements in Washington and endorsed classicism, gave real impetus to a national movement called the City Beautiful. Indeed, Washington became the model for the nation to follow. Certainly the introduction of the classical style in architecture in America had come much earlier—with pioneering examples in the Villard Houses in New York in 1882 and the Boston Public Library of 1887 (both by McKim, Mead, and White) and later in Washington, with the construction of the Leiter House at Dupont Circle in 1892. The movement gained national attention, however, from the influence of the Chicago World's Fair of 1893, which introduced Beaux Arts classicism to the American public and helped make it popular. Indeed, by World War I most of the major new public and private buildings in American cities were being built in the style of monumental white marble palaces.

Part of this City Beautiful movement involved the construction of dozens of major Beaux Arts luxury apartment houses. They were built at this time in much greater numbers than in the previous Victorian period, as the city's population continued to swell. Because of the Spanish-American War, the United States emerged as a world power with responsibility for the administration of the Philippines, Cuba, and Puerto Rico. New agencies were established in Washington, and thousands of new federal employees arrived to fill civil service positions. The apartment house was the answer to the housing needs of many of these new arrivals.

Washington apartment house design, dominated superficially by the French-inspired classicism, nevertheless saw other important changes during this period, including the introduction of apartment house districts or corridors, influenced by the expanding electric streetcar system and the perfection of a sophisticated apartment floor plan. It was a time when a discerning clientele demanded a quality of construction, facade treatment, floor plans, and fine interior detailing. Architects were immersed in the aesthetics and the models of the past—"time tested" models, they said—and not the dubious classical detailing inserted in Postmodern buildings in the 1980s. The Washington apartment house, reserved for the affluent during the Victorian era, became popular with the middle class at the turn of the century. The functions and reasons affecting Washington apartment house design at this time are complex.

BEAUX ARTS PRINCIPLES

A turning point in the development of the Washington apartment house was marked in the late Victorian period when Beaux Arts influence was first employed in its design. The various eclectic Victorian styles common to Washington apartment houses during the 1880s and most of the 1890s gave way to full-blown Beaux Arts in 1897. The new design called for the division of the facade into base, shaft, and capital, following the balance and symmetry advocated by the classical order. The base was usually defined by a first floor of rusticated limestone, the shaft by tan or "buff" brick as it was called at the time, and the capital by a wide cornice, usually made of pressed tin painted to resemble stone. Stringcourses of limestone typically further defined the tripartite division. Often the front entrance was embellished by an impressive one-story-high limestone portico. Buff brick was used to simulate stone. Few luxury apartment houses of the Beaux Arts period were entirely faced with limestone because of the high cost involved.

Many of the Beaux Arts apartment house facades designed during the first seven years of using the classical style were awkward. Local architects, with limited knowledge of the classical style's possibilities, mixed it with Victorian elements. Most of these transitional buildings were constructed near 14th Street and Florida Avenue, N.W., then a newly fashionable residential section. They included more than a dozen important apartment houses, such as the Savoy Flats, the Victoria Flats, the Portner Flats, and the Olympia Flats. In these, all designed in 1897–98, the architects superimposed projecting bays borrowed from Victorian rowhouses on the classical tripartite division. At the nearby Balfour of 1900, the architect included round-headed windows, left over from the Romanesque Revival, on the top floor. In the monumental Ontario of 1903, the architect included a Victorian-inspired octagonal tower above the original main entrance. Even though he embellished it with a handsome classical roof pavilion on the top and a classical entrance porch on its base, it remained oddly out of place. The same architect, James G. Hill, designed the 1901 Mendota in the Beaux Arts mode but included the same projecting Victorian bays as in the Olympia Flats.

Beaux Arts principles began to be applied with sophistication in 1900, when architect T. Franklin Schneider developed the first successful classical apartment house facades in the Iowa and the Albemarle. Many of the other apartment houses he designed over the next six years were also notable Beaux Arts successes, including the Farragut, the Cecil, the Burlington, the Woodley, and his most exuberant of all, the Rochambeau. Jules H. de Sibour designed the most refined Beaux Arts facades for

the Warder and the McCormick. These two landmarks, inspired by the classicism of Louis XV, fit into the streetscape much better than most apartment houses of the time because of their more domestic appearance, resulting in part from their mansard roofs. Even though the facade became sophisticated during these early years of the twentieth century, the floor plan remained traditional, with the long corridor and other interior features usual to the Victorian rowhouse.

The demand for apartments grew so rapidly after 1900 that a number of large houses were converted into apartments. The imposing group of Victorian rowhouses on the south side of East Capitol Street between 2nd and 3rd streets, S.E., known as Grant Row after their builder, were early examples. The owner converted three of the houses into apartments in July 1903; each house had three five-room apartments, one to a floor. Since they were rented immediately, he converted three more houses the same way several months later. In another case, the Italianate style Francis Dodge, Jr., House at the southeast corner of 30th and Que streets, N.W., in Georgetown was purchased by architect-developer C. B. Keferstein and converted to apartment use in early 1904. Two large wings were added to the original house to create a total of twenty large apartments. It too was an immediate success.

TWO-STORY FLAT BUILDINGS

The demand for apartments for both lower-middle- and middle-income residents grew enormously from the late 1890s to World War I. Developers built more than a thousand two-story flat buildings during this twenty-year period. Since their exteriors closely resemble single-family rowhouses, most of them can be recognized as flat buildings only by their two adjacent doors, one leading to the first-floor apartment and the second opening onto an interior stair leading to the second-floor apartment. Many have since been converted to single-family rowhouses.

In 1904 developer Alonzo O. Bliss built twelve two-story flat buildings on the northwest corner of 6th and K streets, N.E. He incorporated a novel heating system in which a central hot water plant in one of the buildings would provide heat for all twenty-four flats. In the same year another developer built eleven two-and-one-half-story-and-cellar flat buildings, each containing two flats of five and six rooms, respectively. In another instance, developer F. P. Dodge built four two-story flat buildings on the south side of North Carolina Avenue, N.E., just east of Lincoln Park, on Capitol Hill, in 1904. Nearby, at the same time, developer John F. Lynch was building thirteen two-story flat buildings on the northeast corner of 5th and E streets, N.E.

Today four surviving adjacent two-story flat buildings, still in use as originally planned, are located at 1621–27 V Street, N.W. They were designed in 1911 by architects Speiden and Speiden of Washington for investors Samuel Saks and Robert Plyum. In 1902 and 1903 Harry Wardman, who became the city's most prominent developer before the Great Depression, got his start building modest two-story flat buildings. During these two years he built more than a hundred such buildings, many in Georgetown. By 1909 Wardman had given up building these low-income dwellings for luxury apartment houses.

George W. Stone, Sr., in 1902, a year before he designed the Kenesaw.

Before World War I there were dozens of small developers of Washington apartment houses who built and owned an average of three or four buildings. Most of the owners were businessmen, such as Samuel W. Woodward, a department store magnate, Christian Heurich, a brewer, and Stilson Hutchins, a publisher, who built apartment houses along with office buildings as sound real estate investments. The most prominent apartment house developers during this early period were Robert Portner, William M. and Edgar S. Kennedy, Lester Barr, Charles McLaughlin, T. Franklin Schneider, and Harry Wardman. Schneider was the principal developer before 1910—designing and building more than twenty-five Washington apartment houses, half of which he owned. He later was exceeded by Wardman, who by 1929 had built more than four hundred Washington apartment houses—a record that has never been equalled in any other American city.

APARTMENT HOUSE CORRIDORS

The concentration of Washington apartment houses along certain streets or "corridors" coincided with the extension of the electric streetcar system. In 1896 the new 14th Street, N.W., streetcar line opened: this was the nucleus of the first apartment house corridor in Washington. Soon it extended for more than two miles along 14th Street between Thomas Circle on the south and Park Road on the north. By World War I more than 150 apartment houses were situated directly on 14th Street, N.W., or within one block on both the east and west sides, between 13th and 15th streets. This corridor, as well as those on Columbia Road and Connecticut Avenue, would develop in the early years of the twentieth century.

The 14th Street apartment house corridor was initiated by the construction in 1897 of four classical luxury apartment houses. Three were built adjacent to one another on Columbia Heights (the top of the hill above 14th Street and Florida Avenue, N.W.)—the Columbia Flats by Clement A. Didden, Jr., at 14th and Girard streets, N.W.; the Savoy Flats by A. B. Morgan, at 14th and Harvard streets, N.W.; and the Victoria Flats by Nicholas T. Haller, at 14th and Clifton streets, N.W. The fourth was located four blocks south at 15th and U streets, N.W.—the Portner Flats, also by Clement A. Didden, Jr. All were six stories and designed in a transitional vein, combining Romanesque and classical architectural elements. All have been unfortunately demolished. Only one from this early period, the 1898 Olympia Flats, remains standing at 14th and Euclid streets, N.W.

The second apartment house corridor began not long after, in 1900 with the construction of more than a dozen apartment houses, including the Rochambeau, Stoneleigh Court, and the Connecticut, on lower Connecticut Avenue south of Dupont Circle. This corridor was extended farther north to the Taft Bridge by World War I with the construction of the Highlands, the Woodward, the Dresden, and 2029 Connecticut Avenue, N.W. In the 1920s it spread five miles out to the Maryland line at Chevy Chase, making Connecticut Avenue the premier apartment house corridor in the city and one of the major ones in the country. Its development was greatly influenced by zoning, which was established in the city in 1920.

The third apartment house corridor was along Columbia Road, which became a major thoroughfare because of its early streetcar line. Apartment houses appeared there rapidly, between Connecticut Avenue and 16th Street, N.W., beginning in 1903 with the construction of the Kenesaw toward its eastern end. After the Wyoming was built at its western end in 1905, many other prominent Beaux Arts apartment houses were built between these two landmarks before World War I.

Developers had carefully watched the construction of the Concord, the first cooperative, at New Hampshire Avenue and Swann Street, in 1891. One of the first luxury apartment houses designed with large kitchens in every apartment, this building proved so popular that a large addition was built in 1893. Before local developers could build other apartment houses with a kitchen in each unit, the depression of 1893 began and almost all construction in the city stopped until economic conditions improved in 1897. All of the units in the apartment houses built that year on upper 14th Street, N.W., had kitchens. That feature and their location on the new streetcar line made them immediately popular with the middle classes. Before this time Washington apartment house living (as distinguished from that in cheaper flat buildings with no lobby,

An important architect of Washington classical apartment houses was B. Stanley Simmons, most noted for his Wyoming.

elevator, or staff) had been limited to the affluent who could afford to take most of their meals in the public dining room. The popularity of the new trend in housing accommodations on 14th Street, N.W., was reported in the *Evening Star* in September 1897 in an article entitled "Flocking to Live in Flats":

The apartment houses that are rapidly approaching completion on Columbia Heights will doubtless have a full complement of tenants before even the final touches are put to them. Over half of the apartments in the Victoria flats, at the corner of 14th and Welling [now Clifton] streets, have been taken, and several of the tenants have already moved in. Very animated inquiry is reported from those who desire to make their prospective residences in the Albert Carey [renamed the Columbia before it opened] flats at the corner of 14th and Binney [now Girard] streets, and the Savoy flats which are approaching completion immediately north of the latter.

Each succeeding apartment built in this area in the late 1890s was occupied as soon as it was completed. These 14th Street, N.W., apartment houses initiated a building boom that did not stop until World War I cut off the supply of construction materials. The real estate editor of the *Evening Star* evaluated the development of the Washington apartment house in an unusual article in late 1905:

The apartment house situation in this city still continues to be one of the most interesting phases of the [real estate] market. This is the case from almost any standpoint one chooses to look at it. Although during the past ten years, including the present year, nearly 500 of these structures, from the seven-story to the two-story, have been built, the large proportion of that number during the latter part of the decade, yet they continue to be profitable as investments, and there is no indication that they have ceased to be popular as places of residence.

In fact, while there is a constant shifting of apartment house population, and people are continually going from the old to the new, just as is done in the case of individual houses, still there are few vacancies. The places that are left in the older buildings are taken up, and so it goes. Even with buildings which are in course of construction, and which will not be finished until the end of December, there are lists of applicants, and the available space is about all taken up.

It is quite evident from the experience of the present season, following, as it does, the very prosperous season of last year, that the apartment house has come to stay, that it is one of the assured institutions of life in this city and that it is not merely a temporary vogue. It is no longer an experiment, and that being assured and everybody convinced that such buildings are meeting a real want, it is likely that second stage will soon be reached and apartment houses as an investment will find a place in the market.

Thus far this class of property has been looked upon with more or less suspicion, and the market for it has been rather limited. Those that have been built, as a rule, are owned by the men who put their money in them, and while it is not claimed that there has been any great pressure to sell, yet it has been recognized that they are not a very salable property. It is believed there will be a change, in this particular and that apartment houses will take their places in the investment list just as other classes of property.

FLOOR PLAN PERFECTION

Beginning in 1905, after twenty-five years of experimentation—but apparently ignoring examples elsewhere—Washington architects finally began to perfect the apartment floor plan. It was an age with a taste for elegance that produced Washington's five most outstanding pre–World War I landmark apartment houses—the Warder, Wendell Mansions, 2029 Connecticut Avenue, the Altamont, and the McCormick. Four of these five buildings were designed by architects trained at the Ecole des Beaux Arts in Paris, which accounted for much of their sophistication. The French requirement of the tripartite separation of interior space into the public, private, and service areas was carefully followed in all five. For the first time luxury apartment houses in the city began to lose their hotel-like characteristics—large lobby, public dining room, and drugstore. In these buildings the goal was to remove all aspects of commercialism and to maintain the greatest amount of domestic privacy.

The 1905 Warder offered one thirteen-room apartment per floor—the largest units in the city at the time. The principal rooms in each apartment—the parlor, dining room, and library—were all arranged along the front facing 16th Street, N.W., to provide the best view. These three public rooms were also conveniently connected to the foyer and adjacent to the elevator. The private spaces—the four large bedrooms—were arranged together on the next most desirable location—facing M Street, N.W. The service area included four servants' bedrooms and bath, as well as the laundry, servants' hall, and kitchen. This space was cleverly arranged along the east and south sides of the building, the least desirable locations because of the lack of a view. A large lightwell provided natural light to the two inside hallways connecting the public, private, and service areas. In addition to the public elevator, the kitchen of each apartment was connected to a service elevator and stairs so that movement of provisions and staff was isolated from the rest of the apartment. Bedrooms were connected to each other as well as to the two bathrooms to ensure privacy from the servants. This was a practice common in the better Parisian apartment houses of the time—but uncommon elsewhere in Washington and other American cities.

The following year another important floor plan was conceived for the five-story Wendell Mansions. Again the three divisions of the apartment were carefully segregated from one another. In each apartment an elegant elliptical foyer allowed guests to view three of the public rooms simultaneously—parlor, reception room, and dining room.

Each of the three master bedrooms had its own bathroom—the first such plan in Washington. To maintain its quiet domestic appearance, only one public room on the ground floor was allowed—the lobby: quiet, unostentatious, with decorative fireplace mantel, beamed ceiling, wainscoting, and fluted pilasters. The public entrance hall extended to the rear, where a square marble staircase encircled the French-inspired wrought-iron Otis elevator car. Privacy was ensured with only one twelve-room apartment on each floor.

Washington architects Hunter and Bell designed their best building, 2029 Connecticut Avenue, N.W., in 1915. It remains intact to this day. The Beaux Arts buff-brick facade includes two prominent entrance porches ornamented by terra cotta details. Of the three apartments on each floor, the most important, comprising 5,400 square feet of space, faces Connecticut Avenue. The design begins with an 18-foot-long private entrance hall, which connects perpendicularly to a spectacular 13-by-45-foot gallery. The 30-foot-long living room, as well as the library and dining room, connect to the gallery. The bedroom areas are approached from each end of this long gallery. (The master bathroom was the first in Washington to contain both a bathtub and a shower stall!) Attention to detail in the plan is shown by the unusual pair of reception rooms with bathrooms in the lobby for guests to freshen up upon arrival in the building.

Another outstanding floor plan, no longer extant because it was later subdivided, was found in the 1915 Altamont, one block to the rear of 2029 Connecticut Avenue, N.W., at the corner of Wyoming Avenue and Columbia Road. Designed by Arthur B. Heaton, the seven-story Altamont was unusual for an important luxury apartment house because it had two distinctly different "typical" floor plans. The lower (and less desirable) first three floors included only small units of one and two bedrooms. Two very large and one small apartment were found on each of the fourth, fifth, and sixth floors. On these upper levels a small one-bedroom apartment was located in the center of the irregular U-shaped building, while each of the two wings was reserved for one twelve-room apartment. By having the one-bedroom unit in the center, each of the two large apartments on each floor could have three exposures.

Architect Arthur B. Heaton's best apartment houses in the nation's capital were the Highlands and the Altamont.

Not only were these large, airy apartments carefully separated into public, private, and service areas, but they also included a new feature, sleeping porches. Praised by hygienists for fresh air and thus the prevention of tuberculosis, the best sleeping porches, as these, were located on corners to provide better circulation. The hallways in the large apartments at the Altamont were carefully laid out, with the private hall of the bedrooms closed off completely by a door from the public rooms. The servants' area was also completely separated from the residents' area by its own hall, which connected the kitchen, pantry, two maids' bedrooms, and bath. Servants could enter and leave their area from a private door in the rear, next to the servant staircase. Each of these large apartments included elegant spaces—circular reception halls and, in the case of units in tier No. 3, an unusual elliptical drawing room.

THE ULTIMATE IN LUXURY

The Beaux Arts Washington apartment house with the most luxurious floor plan was the McCormick, now the home of the National Trust for Historic Preservation. Located on the northeast corner of Massachusetts Avenue and 18th Street, N.W., the five-story McCormick housed six families with their forty servants when it opened in 1917. One enters beneath an iron and glass marquee into an elegant circular public foyer. The floor of the foyer, as well as its wainscoting and mantel, is of white marble, while the circular walls are executed in decorative plaster panels.

Although the ground floor contained two apartments, only one apartment of twenty rooms occupied each of the floors above. Special features in these 11,000-square-foot upper apartments included private elliptical foyers, which connected small salons, massive dining rooms, and 24-by-45-foot drawing rooms. Upon entering, a corridor on the right led from the foyer to six bedrooms, which were carefully separated from public spaces. There was even a separate set of hallways connecting the five servants' bedrooms and the servants' dining hall, pantry, and kitchen. Servants could circulate through the service area without being observed. This plan was unique in Wash-

One of Washington's first architects to receive Beaux Arts training in Paris was Jules H. de Sibour, who designed the McCormick, the finest apartment house ever built in the city.

ington. Although the building has been used for offices since 1940, many of its handsome original details were restored in 1977 by the National Trust.

In addition to perfecting the floor plan, local architects began to experiment with the duplex apartment, two stories per unit. Although common in New York since the 1890s, the duplex was not well received in Washington, being associated somehow with seedy old mansions made over into apartments. During this golden age of apartment house design in the decade before World War I, two apartment houses were built in Washington with a few duplex units in each—the 1905 Cordova and the 1909 Woodward. Washingtonians disliked the duplex because the traditional Washington apartment allowed them to escape the three-story rowhouse with its many stairs and offered them the convenience of housekeeping on one level.

It would not be until the 1970s, six decades later, that the duplex apartment would be accepted. Its popularity resulted in part from retired couples moving from detached houses to apartments. The second floor in the duplex apartment seemed a natural arrangement and provided the added amenity of increased privacy to the bedroom areas from the living room and dining room on the lower level.

Although the vast majority of first-class apartment houses built in Washington between 1897 and 1918 were based on classicism, two other modes in the Beaux Arts vein were employed for first-class buildings—Spanish Colonial and Georgian. The best examples of the Spanish Colonial are the Cordova (now the President Madison), the Woodward, and the Chevy Chase. These buildings have either partial or complete stucco facades, red-tile roofs, and elaborate baroque entries. Two also have summer pavilions on their roofs. In an attempt to reflect an Anglo-Saxon background, Georgian motifs also became popular, with such early examples as 1509 16th Street, N.W., the Dresden, and the Northumberland. For this mode red brick was used, while nearly all Beaux Arts–inspired apartment houses were buff brick.

Most apartment houses of this pre–World War I period continued to include public dining rooms. The first buildings appeared without them, however, offering residents greater privacy—Wendell Mansions, 2029 Connecticut Avenue, N.W., and the McCormick. The luxury apartment house began to shed hotel-like characteristics, and architects began to experiment with alternate uses of public spaces. At the Altamont, architect Arthur B. Heaton placed the individual storage rooms for each apartment on the seventh, or top, floor instead of in the basement. Not only did this location provide a drier and safer storage area for the residents' possessions, but it also insulated the apartments on the sixth floor from the excessive heat and cold that were common complaints of residents in top-floor apartments. The St. Regis of 1915 included a series of five separate garages for automobiles in the rear alley—the first apartment house to have this convenience. It was not until the mid-twenties that garages became popular for apartment houses.

TECHNOLOGICAL INNOVATIONS

Architects began to employ new technological improvements as they experimented with changing space arrangements. A number of buildings between 1905 and 1918 had central vacuum systems. The residents (or their servants) would connect the hose of their vacuum cleaner to one of the two or three outlets in their apartment that led to a suction air machine in the basement, which the janitor operated. In another new arrangement, speaking tubes were provided in a number of buildings, especially those without elevators, such as Dumbarton Court. Several of the better apartment houses were equipped with gas-fired clothes dryers in the basement, such as those still intact at the Chevy Chase and the Altamont. Wall safes were another innovative feature. These were almost always located in the outer wall of the building: if the building burned, the outer wall would hold up longest. The safes were usually located in bedrooms, the most private part of an apartment, and next to a window so that curtains could conceal them.

Revolving doors, usually mahogany, became common in many of the best apartment houses built between 1910 and 1917. They have survived in only two such buildings today because the city's fire code, revised in the early 1960s, required that revolving doors be removed

from apartment houses with only one lobby exit. The lobbies of the two surviving examples, at 2029 Connecticut Avenue, N.W., and the Altamont, have two exits, permitting one revolving door to remain in each.

Another important design feature in these Beaux Arts apartment houses was the manually operated elevator car. Many were elegant devices, enclosed by iron grilles with wrought-iron doors. The interiors had coved ceilings and often mirrored panels on three sides. Some had folding benches for passenger use. In several the marble staircase wrapped around the elevator shaft. Again, almost all of these cars have been removed. Most early apartment house elevators operated on DC current and were connected to the closest streetcar tracks. When the streetcar system was removed in 1962 and replaced with buses, almost all original elevator cars had to be replaced with AC current and consequently automatic push-button cabs. The best surviving elevator car is a 1908 Otis located in Wendell Mansions. At the Northumberland the elegant hand-operated 1910 freight elevator, with its wrought-iron grillwork and coved ceiling, also remains in use.

An important prestige factor in luxury apartment houses of other American cities, especially New York, was their height of twelve to eighteen stories. Washington's 1894 height-limitation law, however, restricts apartment houses to a height of 90 feet. In place of height, therefore, the local architect often devised either an elaborate facade or a spectacular lobby to provide prestige for a new luxury apartment house. This development in Washington is illustrated in two companion buildings, the Dresden at Connecticut Avenue and Kalorama Road, N.W., and the Northumberland at New Hampshire Avenue and V Street, N.W. Both designed in the Georgian mode by Washington architect Albert H. Beers in 1909 with a U-shaped plan and rear court, they were the first of the four hundred large Washington apartment houses built by Harry Wardman, the city's greatest real estate developer. The Dresden's handsome, curved, red-brick Georgian facade remains one of the most impressive in the city. Yet its lobby is small and simple. In contrast, the Northumberland's rather simple Georgian facade belies its large, richly appointed, muted yellow marbleized lobby with baronial detailing and handsome cast-iron grand staircase. The lobby, the first view of the interior, usually was treated in a formal manner to indicate the augustness of the residents.

In addition to the Northumberland, twenty other elaborate pre–World War I luxury apartment house lobbies remain intact today. These include the Wyoming with magnificent marble columns and richly plastered ceiling, the Altamont with its paneled ceiling and massive fireplace mantel, and the round domed lobby of the McCormick. Other surviving treasures include 1870 Wyoming Avenue, N.W., with its gray marbleized walls and strapwork plaster ceiling; the pair of curved stairs and elaborate tilework in the lobby floor of the Cordova (now the President Madison); the columns and series of blind arches in the lobby walls of the Westmoreland; the iron door grilles and classical detailing in both the Woodward and the Avondale; and the delicate Regency plasterwork in the Somerset House at 16th and S streets, N.W., and at Northbrook Court. Even in a small luxury apartment house like the Bachelor Flats of 1905, great attention was paid to such lobby details as the intricate hand-laid mosaic floor, the classical paneled ceiling, and the handsome wrought-iron staircase balustrade.

Washington apartment houses evolved through several phases from their awkward floor plans of the 1880s, and disjointed transitional facade designs in which Victorian and classical elements were mixed in the late 1890s to considerable design sophistication by World War I. Both the quality of workmanship and the spacious and well-ordered facade treatment and floor plan of the prewar apartment house would rarely be repeated after 1918. Wartime inflation and the new income tax were among many factors that turned developers from building such opulent places. Their likes will never be seen in Washington again.

9

PORTNER FLATS

2015 15th Street, N.W.; east side of 15th Street between U and V streets

ARCHITECT: Clement A. Didden, Jr., 1897; 1899 addition; 1902 addition

ORIGINAL APARTMENTS IN 1902: 123 (mostly three-bedrooms) and approximately 30 hotel suites

STATUS: opened as rental in 1897; converted to hotel in 1946; razed in 1974

Built by Washington brewer and investor Robert Portner (1837–1906), the Portner Flats was one of the city's most fashionable apartment houses when it opened in 1897. After second and third additions were completed in 1902, the Portner was briefly the city's largest apartment house until Stoneleigh Court opened on Connecticut Avenue the following year. The public referred to the original Portner Flats in 1897 as Portner's Folly because of its then-remote location from downtown. It was an immediate success, however, because of its location one block from the 14th Street streetcar line, which had been extended from Florida Avenue to Park Road in 1892.

Reading the real estate sections of local newspapers today, one might think that tennis courts and swimming pools are strictly a modern supplement to apartment buildings. Not so, since the original Portner Flats included a swimming pool and tennis courts—the first for an apartment house in Washington. The first section of the building was put up in 1897 at the corner of 15th and U streets, N.W.; the second at 15th and V streets, N.W., in 1899. Demand necessitated construction of a central section in 1902 on space between the original two sections that had been occupied by the pool and tennis courts.

With a range of projecting bays and corner towers, the architect of the flat-roofed six-story structure at-tempted to accentuate its main entrance by raising the center section to seven stories and erecting an open, arched balcony on the top two floors, crowned with a conservative spire and pair of vases. After the center section was constructed, Portner compensated the tenants for the loss of the swimming pool and tennis courts by designing a large public dining room on the first floor. It could easily be converted for use for debutante parties and cotillions. Adjoining were four new public parlors, frequently used for private parties by residents who chose not to entertain in their apartments.

Like the nearby 1898 Olympia Flats and the 1901 Mendota, two rare extant apartment houses of this style, the Portner Flats was an example of an apartment house designed during the transitional phase of development of Washington apartment houses in which Victorian elements were combined with the newly fashionable classical mode. It was not until the Iowa was designed by T. Franklin Schneider in 1900 that a truly sophisticated classical facade appeared on a new apartment house—without any trace of Victorian elements. The three street facades of the Portner included a total of thirteen projecting Victorian bays, with the most prominent, located at the two corners, supporting turrets. Each of the three sections, with its early Beaux Arts tripartite divided fa-

The 1897 Portner Flats was the city's largest apartment house until Stoneleigh Court was built in 1901.

cade (including curious flat pilasters extending from the third through the fifth stories), had its own entrance facing 15th Street. The most interesting part of this enormous building was the corner at 15th and U streets, N.W. Here five metal caryatids, with upraised arms, supported the shallow circular brick balcony above the drugstore entrance. The drugstore remained at this location from the time the Portner Flats opened until the building closed in 1970.

CONVERSION TO DUNBAR HOTEL

After World War II many of the long-time residents of this 15th Street corridor, which marked the boundary of the Shaw neighborhood to the east and the Dupont Circle neighborhood to the west, began to move to the Virginia and Maryland suburbs to acquire detached houses with lawns and ample space for gardens. During the late 1940s the area between 14th and 15th streets, N.W., slowly began to change from a white to a black residential neighborhood. As part of this trend, the Portner Flats was sold in 1945 by the Portner family to several investors of whom Harvey H. Warwick, Sr., was a principal partner. They reopened the Portner Flats as a black apartment-hotel named for the distinguished black poet and short story writer, Paul Laurence Dunbar.

The elaborate Beaux Arts entrance to the drugstore at the Portner Flats was embellished with metal caryatids painted to resemble stone.

At the time of conversion, the Portner had 123 large apartments and thirty small suites in the center section for use as hotel units, each with a bedroom, sitting room, and bath. Permanent residents occupied the two end sections of the building, which included mostly three-bedroom units. Many prominent Washingtonians in World War I lived there, including Congressman Henry D. Flood, the chairman of the House Foreign Affairs Committee, who wrote the Declaration of War against Germany in 1917.

In the new Dunbar, the large apartments were remodeled into 485 bedrooms with baths. Under poor management at first, the hotel lost its liquor license in 1950 and received a great deal of bad publicity because of the prostitutes, narcotics dealers, and gamblers who frequented its nightclub. Conditions were promptly improved under experienced management, however, and the Dunbar became Washington's leading black hotel, frequented by many famous sport and entertainment figures. Howard University's faculty, as well as others in the black professional stratum in the nation's capital, also frequented it. Known at one time as the largest black hotel in the nation, the Dunbar slowly declined after 1956, when the city's major hotels were integrated. Unable to face the competition, it began to deteriorate rapidly about 1964. Sold to the city government in 1970, the Dunbar was closed and eventually demolished in 1974 despite efforts by preservationists to find alternative uses for the historic structure. The vacant lot was used to construct the new seven-story, concrete Campbell Heights apartment house in 1978, which replaced the beautiful mellow rose tones of the Portner's pressed brick and sandstone facade.

10

BALFOUR, formerly the WESTOVER

2000 16th Street, N.W.; northwest corner of 16th and U streets

ARCHITECT: George S. Cooper, 1900

ORIGINAL APARTMENTS: 36 (12 efficiencies; 24 three-bedrooms)

STATUS: opened as rental in 1901

One of the first successful Beaux Arts apartment house facades was the Balfour, designed by architect George S. Cooper in 1900.

The six-story Balfour, first known as the Westover, underwent a name change in 1909, most likely because there was already a small apartment house with the same name at 2501 Pennsylvania Avenue, N.W. It was renamed for Arthur James Balfour, the first Earl of Balfour (1848–1930), who served as British Prime Minister, 1902–05. The renaming reflected growing American interest in Great Britain, stemming from many prominent marriages between American heiresses and titled British noblemen. A great deal of public attention was centered, for instance, on the marriage of Consuelo Vanderbilt to Charles Spencer Churchill, Duke of Marlborough, in 1896. English names were thought to add prestige to buildings. The use of such names for Washington apartment houses began in the 1890s with the Savoy and the Victoria and continued into the 1930s with the Harrowgate and the Westchester, among others.

Designed by Washington architect George S. Cooper early in 1900, the Balfour cost $100,000, indicating that it was one of the most expensive apartment houses of its day. The facade of the Balfour was beautifully designed for the strategically important corner of 16th and U streets, N.W. Few buildings were then located that far north on 16th Street, still a relatively undeveloped area. Due to the efforts of Mrs. John B. Henderson, who resided nearby

Oriel windows like those on the Balfour would become popular on Beaux Arts apartment houses in Washington between 1900 and 1918.

in the great stone Romanesque Revival Boundary Castle, as well as Senator John Sherman of Ohio, who owned extensive land in the neighborhood, 16th Street was extended across Florida Avenue and up steep Meridian Hill to intersect with Columbia Road before 1890. By World War I, the entire length of 16th Street, N.W.—the city's premier boulevard—swept northward 6½ miles to the Maryland line.

The effect of this building is one of quiet but powerful majesty. Architect Cooper demarcated the two street facades of the Balfour by the use of bold quoins set in the three exposed corners above the limestone first story and basement. The U Street or south facade, as well as the now-hidden north facade, includes two octagonal bays that rise to the fifth floor, stopping at the stringcourse. On the front facade, a pair of oriel windows extend from the second through the fourth stories. The classical lime-

stone porch, with its pairs of fluted composite columns, shelters a massive entrance with a wide fan light and side windows. Above, a small, intricately carved Palladian window lights the second-floor hallway, while a wide, richly decorated frieze sweeps around the building just below the cornice. Surprisingly, the facade remains intact except for the loss of ten small iron balcony railings under windows on the third, fourth, and fifth floors of both street facades.

Within, the rectangular lobby floor is laid in off-white ceramic tiles with a Greek-key border of yellow and red tiles. Peculiar to Washington, this floor design is found in the lobbies and public hallways of almost all better apartment houses in the city built between 1900 and 1920. The lobby walls are embellished with paired classical pilasters and 5-foot-high marble wainscoting. The unusual marble staircase balustrade, extending from

Most of the Balfour's original apartments were large five-room units.

the lobby to the first landing, serves as the focal point of the small but richly detailed lobby.

To light the almost square building, Cooper slightly recessed the center of the rear facade facing the alley and included as well two central lightwells or skywells as they were then often called. He was careful to place spaces of secondary importance—kitchens, baths, pantries, and the public staircase—facing the lightwells. Even so, the use of lightwells was archaic. Architects attempted to avoid them in apartment houses since they offered no view and interfered with the residents' privacy. One of the few early surviving apartment houses to have had one was the Beacon, of the same date, at Calvert Street and Adams Mill Road, which was renovated in 1985–86. At that time, the large open lightwell was filled in with an emergency staircase exit and the remainder used to create additional apartments.

Each floor contained six apartments—four large units of five rooms each and two small units perhaps for elderly parents or guests or servants. The parlors contained decorative fireplace mantels, while wide envelope doors separated the parlor from the adjoining library and dining room. Each dining room contained a handsome leaded glass corner china cabinet and 5-foot-high paneled wainscoting. Even though most of the apartments here were spacious, no innovative technology or interior planning was introduced—the old-fashioned long hallway wasted

space in each apartment. The 16th Street, N.W., address, the large apartments, and the marble lobby all enticed affluent renters to come here. With advances elsewhere in interior planning, however, the Balfour was hopelessly outdated within a decade.

Shortly after the interior of the Balfour was photographed in October 1980 for this study, the building was sold and, except for the lobby, completely gutted in March 1981. Because of the recession in 1982, the new owners could not secure adequate financing to continue the conversion to condominiums, and the building remained an empty shell. Repossessed by a bank, the Balfour changed hands again in early 1984, after which reconstruction of the interior was resumed and completed in late 1985, when the units were rerented at much higher rates. During the conversion the two lightwells were filled in to provide additional living space. The Balfour now contains a total of fifty-five apartments, all much smaller one- and two-bedroom units but with new kitchens, bathrooms, wiring, and plumbing.

The handsome corner china cabinets, paneled wainscoting, and decorative fireplace mantels were unfortunately destroyed in the 1980 renovation of the Balfour.

11

HAWARDEN

1419 R Street, N.W.

ARCHITECT: George S. Cooper, 1901

ORIGINAL APARTMENTS: 20 (all two-bedrooms)

STATUS: opened as rental in 1901; converted to co-op in 1949

The Hawarden (1901) and its twin to the west, the Gladstone (1900), were designed by Washington architect George S. Cooper in an eclectic style combining both baroque and Romanesque Revival features. The five-story front facades of these two small apartment buildings are framed by pairs of octagonal bays connected at the first floor by a classical porch with Ionic columns, at the third floor by an iron balcony, and at the fourth floor by a massive porch. The front facade of the Hawarden remains remarkably intact, even though the original stone balustrade, which extended across the top of the projecting bays at the fifth-floor level, and the balustrade across the roof were removed in the 1930s. Designed with three projecting bays on each side, the elongated Hawarden originally possessed functional exterior louvered blinds on its side facades—an unusual feature for a Washington apartment house. The front facade unfortunately is painted, which disguises the rich Victorian composition resulting from the contrasts of brick, stone, and wood.

The Hawarden and the Gladstone were built as identical apartment houses adjacent to one another; each has twenty apartments, four to a floor. Every apartment contains four rooms, kitchen, and bath. Although a small elevator was installed at an early date, the Hawarden

lacks a lobby and is thus considered an apartment building rather than an apartment house.

Almost all of the original interior details survive—transom windows, handsome wood grilles partially shielding the vestibule from the parlor, elaborate decorative fireplace mantels with mirrors above, built-in china closets in the dining rooms, dumbwaiters in the kitchens, paneled wainscoting in the entrance corridors, and the original staircase balustrade. During the renovation of one apartment in 1980, the remains of the original icebox drainage system were revealed. From the stripped interior ceiling, it was obvious that the pantry in each apartment still contains the galvanized plumbing system used to drain the icebox: as the ice melted, the water was drained directly through interior pipes to the outside at ground level. For a middle-income apartment building, the Hawarden was designed with unusually fine detailing. It remains one of the most intact early middle-class Washington apartment buildings.

Immediately after World War II, the corridor between 14th and 15th streets, N.W., bordered by Massachusetts Avenue on the south and Florida Avenue on the north, began to change in its demographic composition. The Hawarden was converted in 1949 from a rental

Shown in this early twentieth-century photograph, the Gladstone, far left, and the
Hawarden were identical apartment houses, named, respectively, for Britain's prime
minister and his country estate in Wales.

The typical floor plan of the Hawarden includes four apartments per floor.

Converted to a co-op in 1949, the Hawarden has preserved most of its original details such as the decorative parlor mantels and the grilles atop the doorjambs. The Hawarden's board of directors, including several of the original shareholders, appears in this portrait taken in 1980.

building for lower-income whites to a cooperative apartment house for middle-income blacks. Still well managed and maintained, it is probably the oldest black co-op in the city. Many of the Hawarden's original purchasers, who paid $9,000 for the front units and $7,000 for the rear units (then an expensive price), remain in residence. They have carefully preserved most of the original architectural details. Such was not the fate of the Hawarden's twin, the Gladstone, still a rental building, which has deteriorated badly both inside and outside.

The Gladstone, erected one year before the Hawarden, was named for William Ewart Gladstone (1809–1898), who served four times as Prime Minister of Great Britain under Queen Victoria. The son of a rich Liverpool merchant, Gladstone began his sixty years of service in Parliament as a conservative. He eventually changed his basic political beliefs to become the country's principal liberal leader for social and political reform. Even though

his efforts to secure home rule for Ireland failed, he is often considered the greatest statesman of nineteenth-century Britain.

Washington's Hawarden apartment house was named for Hawarden Castle (pronounced "Harden" in Britain), Gladstone's country estate near the village of Hawarden, Flintshire, Wales. Hawarden became Gladstone's home when he married its Welsh heiress, Catherine Glynne, in 1839. He once said that through managing such a large estate he gained the experience necessary to manage the finances of Britain. This impressive 1752 stone manor house remains in the Gladstone family today. Why the original owners, L.S. Firstoe and S.G. Cornwell, named these two buildings for William E. Gladstone and his country estate remains a mystery to this day, but the Anglophilia current at the time in Washington may offer an explanation.

12

MENDOTA

2220 20th Street, N.W.; southwest corner of 20th Street and Kalorama Road

ARCHITECT: James G. Hill, 1901

ORIGINAL APARTMENTS: 49 (23 one-bedrooms; 12 two-bedrooms; 7 three-bedrooms; 7 four-bedrooms)

STATUS: opened as rental in 1902; converted to co-op in 1952

The Mendota, two blocks northeast of the intersection of Columbia Road and Connecticut Avenue, N.W., is not only the oldest intact luxury Washington apartment house but also one of the few such buildings that remain from the transitional phase of development—that is, the period between 1897 and 1905 when Washington apartment houses awkwardly combined new classical facades with Victorian features. The buff-brick facade of the Mendota, with its limestone details, combines a Victorian massing with Beaux Arts features and temperament. The former is characterized by a series of alternating rounded and octagonal bays on the 20th Street and Kalorama Road facades. In addition, the partially hidden south facade, facing an adjacent house, has three oriel windows extending from the second floor to the roof cornice. The Beaux Arts influences include the separation of the facade into the classic tripartite division of base, body, and entablature.

The Mendota is designed in a U-shaped plan, embracing a rear court. One enters the seven-story building under a handsome limestone balcony supported by a pair of ornate and massive stone scrolled consoles. Ascending a short flight of steps in the vestibule, one reaches a high-ceilinged lobby, with 6-foot-high marble wainscoting, a terrazzo floor framed by a Greek-key border set in a colorful mosaic, and an impressive iron staircase. The original brass mailboxes are set in the wall to the left of the staircase, while to the right are the small parlor and the elevator with its original faux-mahogany paneled cab, still operated by an attendant.

The forty-nine apartments vary in size from efficiencies to seven-room units. Many of the apartments retain their original details—unpainted birch woodwork, spacious kitchen pantries, corner dining room cupboards, transom windows, envelope doors, and gas-log fireplaces. Many of the original bathrooms also remain—lined in 5-foot-high white tile with corner marble sinks, claw-footed enamel bathtubs, medicine chests built into the thick walls under the window, and a mirror built into the wall above the sink. One is immediately struck with the unusually tall ceilings of 10 feet. The only other apartment house still in operation with such tall ceilings is the Ontario. (The tallest ceilings ever designed for an apartment house were those at the McCormick, measuring 14 feet.) Most of the apartments could be expanded according to the needs of the original renters by using connecting doors inside walk-in closets. The public dining room on the top floor and the drugstore and doctor's office on the first floor (now Nos. 76, 5, and 6, respectively) have long since been converted to residential use.

Top: The lobby of the Mendota—with its 6-foot-high marble wainscoting, wrought-iron staircase, and brass mailboxes—remains in original condition. *Bottom:* The Mendota, shown at completion in 1901, remains the city's oldest surviving intact luxury apartment house.

The Mendota was the first of three Washington apartment houses, including Stoneleigh Court and the Ontario, designed by architect James G. Hill (1841–1913). Both the Mendota and the Ontario were designed for the same client, Archibald McLachlen of the McLachlen National Bank, and their interior detailing is remarkably similar. Hill served as Supervising Architect of the Treasury from 1879 to 1884 before retiring to establish his own practice. His principal buildings in Washington include the old Bureau of Engraving and Printing at 14th Street and Independence Avenue, S.W. (1879), the Main Government Printing Office at North Capitol and H streets, N.W. (1899), the Washington Loan and Trust Branch of the Riggs National Bank, 9th and F streets, N.W. (1891), and the National Bank of Washington, 7th Street and Pennsylvania Avenue, N.W. (1888). In addition, he designed the U.S. courthouses in Albany (1877), Minneapolis (1877), and Baltimore (1881). Perhaps it was while working in the Midwest that Hill became familiar with "Mendota," the name of a suburb in Minneapolis on the

The ends of the U-shaped Mendota contain large three- and four-bedroom apartments.

The handsome built-in corner china cabinets at the Mendota are similar to those at the Ontario; both were designed two years apart by the same architect.

Mississippi River. It is a Sioux Indian word meaning "mouth of the river."

At the time it was built, the Mendota was the most northerly situated apartment house in the city. It was built on part of the grounds of Managasset, the home of Colonel George Truesdell, a prominent developer, who lived in the large Victorian frame "country" house that faced the Mendota across 20th Street. To the rear of the Mendota was the imposing Woodward House, also designed by Hill, belonging to the department store family, which was ultimately razed in 1925 for the site of the large apartment house at 2101 Connecticut Avenue, N.W. Since it was then the tallest building in the Kalorama-Washington Heights area, Mendota residents had unobstructed views of the entire city to the south, of Rock Creek Park to the north, and of the gardens of Colonel Truesdell's estate to the east. Within a few years, however, the neighborhood was to undergo a record-breaking building boom, with dozens of new apartment houses rising on adjacent Columbia Road and Connecticut Avenue.

During its early years the Mendota was one of the most fashionable apartment houses in the city. The lead-

The bathrooms at the Mendota were designed with footed bathtubs, marble corner sinks, narrow radiators, white tile wainscoting, and medicine cabinets beneath the windows.

ing Washington social register in the early twentieth century, the *Elite List*, listed thirty Mendota residents in 1910 and forty-eight in 1918. In the 1920s, however, this social prominence declined as residents moved to larger and newer apartment houses being completed on Connecticut Avenue and on 16th Street, N.W. Prominent early residents of the Mendota included James G. Hill, its architect (before he moved to his third apartment house, the Ontario); George W. Norris, the progressive senator from Nebraska; and Jeanette Rankin of Montana, an ar-

dent pacifist who became the first woman to serve in Congress.

The conversion of the Mendota into a cooperative in 1952 saved it from later alterations. During the condominium craze of the 1970s and early 1980s, several dozen important Washington apartment houses worthy of landmark status were partially or completely gutted in order to create smaller units. Developers often felt it safer to market two- and three-room units rather than the far more expensive five- and six-room original apartments.

13

HIGHLANDS

1914 Connecticut Avenue, N.W.; southwest corner of Connecticut Avenue and California Street

ARCHITECT: Arthur B. Heaton, 1902

ORIGINAL APARTMENTS: 69 (18 one-bedrooms; 51 two-bedrooms)

STATUS: opened as rental in 1903; converted to hotel in 1977

The Highlands in 1903. Its facade design was influenced by McKim, Mead, and White's Villard Houses of 1882 in New York.

The finest of the ten apartment houses that architect Arthur B. Heaton designed in Washington between 1899 and 1937 are the Highlands and the Altamont. Since the original detailed drawings of the Highlands survive intact (preserved in the Prints and Photographs Division of the Library of Congress), we now know more about the interior treatment of this building than any other of its early date. They are useful because major alterations in 1955 and 1977 have almost completely erased any vestige of original interior design.

The Highlands was built by a group of investors in 1902 at a cost of $200,000, making it one of the most expensive apartment houses in the city when it was finished. The average cost of a luxury apartment house at this time was $100,000, and the only other buildings to exceed this figure by 1902 were the Cairo, the Portner Flats, and Stoneleigh Court. The Beaux Arts–inspired eight-story-and-basement structure was designed with an unusual front court. The small circular front driveway led to a flight of steps, framed by a stone balustrade. The electric car entrance was to the left, leading to a small basement garage complete with an electric generator, used to recharge car batteries. The Highlands was the first and only Washington apartment house to provide a basement automobile garage until the late 1920s, when

The front court of the Highlands before it was hidden by a recent tasteless addition.

construction of 1705 Lanier Place, N.W., the Army and Navy, 1661 Crescent Place, N.W., the Broadmoor, and Tilden Gardens included basement parking space. The Highlands' richly detailed classical facade was designed with a heavy rusticated two-story base, while a series of fourteen oriel windows ranged between the third and sixth floors. Elaborate cartouches were set under the wide cornice and between the windows of the top story, which was itself defined by a series of shallow iron balconies on all facades.

Much of the expense of building the Highlands was used on the elaborate paneling for the large first-floor public dining room, ballroom, and marble lobby. One surviving original interior photograph of the Highlands shows part of the lobby design, which consisted of white marble wainscoting and richly embellished gilded arches, panels, and ceilings. Only seventeen of the original sixty-nine apartments included kitchens. A typical floor had eight apartments of three or four rooms, each with re-

ception hall, kitchen, dumbwaiter, and bath. On several upper floors, however, some apartments were combined at an early date, providing larger units with seven to twelve rooms. Because of the fourteen oriel windows, the architect was able to design most parlors and dining rooms in an octagonal shape. The Highlands offered every modern apartment house amenity, including electric elevators, telephones in every apartment connecting to the lobby switchboard, its own electric generation plant, refrigeration and filtration systems, nightwatchman's clock system, and mail chutes.

The Highlands was considered to have the finest apartment house view in the city. The developers of this building emphasized this point in their advertisements and thus introduced a new criterion for desirability in Washington apartment houses. Indeed, the "modern" custom of advancing the rents (or today the sale price for a condo or co-op) according to the height of the apartment began with the Highlands. The early apartment houses built before the Highlands were chosen for their location, preferably either in the downtown neighborhood or on a major streetcar route. In contrast, the Highlands' site was selected solely for its view, which indicates a major shift in apartment house planning.

Another unusual development occurred in 1905 with the construction of a tunnel containing steam pipes between the basement of the Highlands and that of the Westmoreland, the apartment house to the rear. To economize in the operations of both apartment houses, a common boiler was used.

Both buildings were purchased in 1907 by Stilson Hutchins, a prominent local real estate investor, the founder and former owner of the *Washington Post*, and the developer of the immensely profitable linotype machine. The two buildings were jointly owned and managed for many years by Hutchins and later by his estate. When the Westmoreland's dining room closed in 1932 because of the Depression, an enclosed pedestrian passageway was constructed at ground level between the two apartment houses to allow Westmoreland residents convenient access to the Highlands' dining room.

In 1955 the Highlands was sold to a syndicate of five businessmen headed by Charles S. Howard, a Washington builder. At that time the long-term tenants were moved out and the building was completely gutted. When rebuilt, it contained 104 efficiency and 40 one-bedroom units. The contractor for the remodeling was amazed to find how well the structure was built. The massive steel frame was set into huge granite slabs in the basement. The brick walls ranged in thickness from 32 inches on the first floor to 12 inches on the eighth floor. The new owners converted the basement into the first floor and filled in the open front court with an inappropriate metal and glass lobby that extended to the front facade line. In 1969 a large house to the south was razed for construction of the present bland Holiday Inn, which now obscures the Highlands' once-famous view of Washington's skyline. Further architectural damage was inflicted when another Washington investor bought the Highlands in 1977 and converted it into a hotel, adding, in order to "keep it modern," a high and insensitive mansard roof above the 1955 entrance.

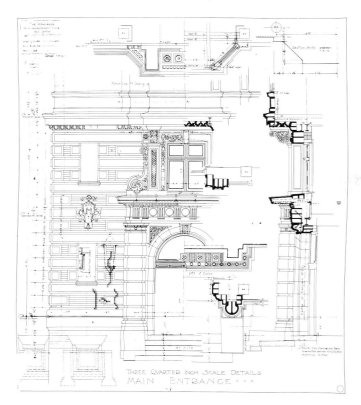

The intricate detailing on the front facade of the Highlands is shown in architect Arthur B. Heaton's original ink-on-linen drawing.

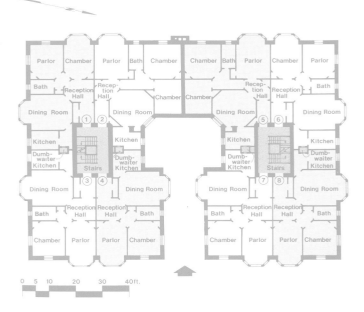

Most of the Highlands' apartments had unusual octagonal dining rooms.

14

STONELEIGH COURT

1025 Connecticut Avenue, N.W.; southeast corner of Connecticut Avenue and L Street

ARCHITECT: James G. Hill, 1902; wing added in forecourt, William I. Deming, 1926

ORIGINAL APARTMENTS: 90 (15 one-bedrooms; 60 two-bedrooms; 8 three-bedrooms; 7 four-bedrooms)

STATUS: opened as rental in 1903; razed in 1965

By 1902 Secretary of State John Hay had assembled various lots occupied by prominent Victorian rowhouses, none more than twenty years old, around the southeast corner of Connecticut Avenue and L Street. He cleared the site and commissioned Washington architect James G. Hill, who had designed the Mendota the previous year, to formulate plans for Stoneleigh Court as the city's largest luxury apartment house.

No expense would be spared in this palace. Stoneleigh Court was designed as an imposing limestone and buff-brick Beaux Arts–fronted eight-story-and-basement apartment house. The entire building was freestanding, with two street facades fronting Connecticut Avenue and L Street (246 by 194 feet, respectively) and the two rear facades facing alleys. Abundant light and air were thus provided. The foundations for Stoneleigh Court were impressive—laid in concrete piers, reinforced with iron, 30 feet below the street grade, and unique for an apartment house of the time.

Another milestone in design involved the elevators of Stoneleigh Court. This was the first apartment house in the city to separate the usual bank of two adjoining elevators. As the *Evening Star* reported in May 1902, "The architect, Mr. James G. Hill, has arranged the interior divisions, with separate elevators, the purpose

being to avoid the delay which comes from having one central place in a large building as a distributing point for all the occupants." This was one of a number of sophisticated improvements made to Washington apartment houses in the early twentieth century, as local architects became more experienced with the design of this relatively new building type. Stoneleigh Court also contained three principal staircases and four service staircases.

The *Evening Star* also reported in October of the same year that the building would open as scheduled on 1 December, even though the national strike of marble workers had delayed installation of the marble wainscoting in the public rooms and corridors. The majority of the ninety apartments were leased six weeks before the opening, indicating the early success of this apartment house. A decade would pass before another apartment house equaled the $1 million cost of Stoneleigh Court.

Stoneleigh Court was set back from Connecticut Avenue and L Street, N.W., with wide lawns and a graceful circular driveway around a wide, shallow fountain in the forecourt. Above the limestone rusticated two-story base rose eight tiers of small iron balconies framing the French windows of the various apartments. The top floor was set off by its prominent stringcourse and wide cornice. From

Resembling a large Italian palazzo, Stoneleigh Court dominated the intersection of
Connecticut Avenue and L Street for sixty years.

this vantage point, the residents could clearly observe
the construction of the Lincoln Memorial during and after
World War I.

The ground floor of Stoneleigh Court resembled a
hotel in many ways, with its large public parlor, dining
rooms for small parties, enormous public cafe, drugstore,
and smoking room for gentlemen. Most of the apartments
were large—the grandest had a foyer, parlor, dining room,
four bedrooms, two baths, kitchen, pantry, servant's room,
and servant's bath. Projecting bays on all facades except
the front allowed for increased light and space.

CHANGE FROM RESIDENTIAL TO COMMERCIAL

At the time Stoneleigh Court was built in 1902, both
lower Connecticut Avenue and nearby K Street were prestigious residential addresses. Even at this early date,
however, pressure from developers was growing to expand
the old business district of the city, then centered on F
Street between 7th and 15th streets, N.W. The lack of

zoning regulations, which were not enacted until 1920,
was also a factor in this development. Almost all of the
recently built Victorian rowhouses on lower Connecticut
Avenue were either demolished or converted to commercial use between 1900 and 1917. By World War I
only a few prominent residential buildings were left on
lower Connecticut Avenue: the Rochambeau (Connecticut
Avenue near H Street, N.W.), the Connecticut apartment
house (Connecticut Avenue and M Street, N.W.), Stoneleigh Court (Connecticut Avenue and L Street, N.W.),
the Grafton Hotel (Connecticut Avenue and DeSales Street,
N.W.), the British Embassy (Connecticut Avenue and N
Street, N.W.), and the Convent of the Visitation (Connecticut Avenue and DeSales Street, N.W.). More than
fifty important Victorian rowhouses were demolished in
the process.

After Hay's heirs sold Stoneleigh Court in 1926, this
once-ornate and elegantly maintained apartment house
began to deteriorate. At that time the open courtyard was
enclosed by a one-story addition, which, along with all
of the adjacent ground-floor rooms, was used for stores

The ground-floor plan of Stoneleigh Court, showing the large amount of public space.

and offices. In an article relating to the sale of Stoneleigh Court, the *Evening Star* reported on 27 February 1926:

> To those who remember Connecticut Avenue but a few years ago its present skyline is a change nothing short of astounding. From a street of magnificent residences, the homes of national society leaders, embassies, and the residences of internationally famous men and women, it has changed into a thoroughfare of beautiful stores.
>
> In place of the quiet old convent, with its spacious ground, stands one of the most magnificent hotels in the country (Mayflower Hotel). On every corner that was once the site of the home of a noted person is a store, an apartment, or a building running from three to eleven stories.
>
> Instead of the quiet avenue where once strolled the elite of the National Capital and high personages of foreign lands for their afternoon and Sunday promenades, and in place of the high broughams, with their high-stepping horses, there is today a bustling crowd of business people, shoppers and others engaged in commerce, who arrive in the street cars, in fast moving automobiles and commercial trucks.

Thus the rapid development of this once-residential enclave into the city's smartest shopping and office area

spelled the end of most of the old downtown luxury apartment houses. Only a few of the twenty such structures remain in use today. The 1922 Presidential at 16th and L streets, for example, survives only because it continues in operation as a co-op.

The commercialization of lower Connecticut Avenue affected Stoneleigh Court at an early date. In April 1927, shortly after sixteen new stores had been located on the ground floor and a one-story addition, it was purchased by developer Harry Wardman for $1.6 million. By careful promotion and advertising, Wardman was able to resell Stoneleigh Court five months later to out-of-town investors for $2.6 million. The new owners, however, lost the landmark after the stock crash of 1929, and it was sold at public auction for only $800,000 in 1933 to the Metropolitan Life Insurance Company.

Because of the Depression and the difficulty of renting many of the 3,000-square-foot apartments, the new owners embarked on the first major project in Washington to remodel actual apartments themselves. The once-massive lobby was reduced in size and remodeled in classical motif with the new streamlined look. The marble Corinthian pilasters gave way to Deco fluted pillars, and the ceiling fixtures and wall sconces were replaced by a coved ceiling with indirect lighting. The floor plans of four massive apartments in the central section of each floor were redesigned and rebuilt into seven small apartments of one and two rooms each. The architect for the interior remodeling, in Colonial and Empire design, was Jarrett C. White.

Because of its strategic location in what was slowly becoming the core of the city's new commercial district, Stoneleigh Court was resold to investors a number of times—in 1941 for $1.5 million, in 1953 for $2 million, in 1957 for $3 million, and in 1962 for $4.5 million. In the last sale the 30,000-square-foot building sold for $150 per square foot, setting a record for Washington real estate at the time. This landmark finally succumbed to the wrecker's ball in 1965 when it was cleared for the site of the Blake Building, a massive concrete International Style office building with strip windows.

LIFE AT STONELEIGH COURT

Stoneleigh Court's first resident manager, George Stephan, lived in an apartment there with his family from 1903 to 1927. His daughter, Alice Stephan Joyce, recently provided an insight into what life was like in one of Washington's premier early-twentieth-century apartment houses:

> My father, son of a German immigrant carpenter, pulled himself up by the bootstraps. After graduation from [Washington] Business High School, he clerked at the Grafton Hotel and went to night school at Washington Columbia Law School and the Lewis Hotel Training School. At the age of 25 he applied for and got the job of manager of Stoneleigh Court, Washington's newly opened eight-story apartment house. He remained there twenty-five years, during which time he married and sired four sons and a daughter.
>
> One of his "perks" as apartment house manager was our apartment, which expanded as our family increased. Eventually, it included a long entrance hall which gave onto a middle hall separating the dining room from the living room, both of which had fireplaces. Four bedrooms and two baths flanked one side of this living area, and a kitchen, butler's pantry, and maid's room and bath flanked the other side, opening onto a service hall and

freight elevator. Like many families of that era, we had a fulltime maid. But in addition we were tended by the chambermaids and kitchen help which formed the domestic staff of the apartment house.

> Such easy living for his children made my hard-working father uncomfortable. Hence, each son, as he became old enough, worked in the hotel office after school, printing the menus for the dining room. I was the youngest child and only girl and was given a handful of domestic duties around the apartment, such as helping our maid dry the dishes and empty the pan under the ice box.

> Two Supreme Court justices, Brandeis and Sutherland, were our neighbors on the eighth floor. Senators Burton, of Ohio, and Shipstead, of Minnesota, and Naval Historian Sims took the time to talk to the manager's young sons. Mrs. William Henry Fitzhugh Lee, the daughter-in-law of Robert E., occupied a large apartment alone, and liked to have my brother Edward sit and visit with her when her servants were off. She was an ancient lady, as I remember her, wrapped in elegant black widow's weeds and never without her large silver ear trumpet. Brother Edward also recalls standing in the elevator between the German and French military attaches on the day war was declared between Germany and France.

> Unfortunately, except for the occasional visiting grandchild, there were very few young children in residence at Stoneleigh Court. The absence of companionship for me concerned my parents, particularly since my youngest brother was five years my senior. Our remedy, to provide me at least with exercise, was arranged by my father and an in-house carpenter. A trapeze was installed into the dark oak door frame between the reception hall and the dining room. By some clever shift of ropes and a portable mat, I could adjust my trapeze to accommodate hanging by the heels or swinging out over the dining room table. I was also allowed to skate around the block or ride my "Irish mule" (a kind of toy which I have never seen since), which was sat upon and pumped away to propel it forward while I exercised our collie dog on the spare lawn on the Connecticut Avenue side of the building. Crossing K Street to get to Farragut Park was forbidden unless I was accompanied by an all-too-often-reluctant brother.

> While I do recall my parents' worries about my dearth of playmates, I don't remember feeling lonely. I was provided with music, dancing, and elocution lessons, all arrived at via the Mount Pleasant streetcar which stopped in front of Stoneleigh. The staff of the apartment house

took more than a passing interest in getting along with the boss's children. There was Mac on the freight elevator, and Nicholas on No. 1 elevator, and Mr. Fritz, the chief clerk. They were all good for a game of catch, or to help out when bats came down through our fireplaces, or to keep us away from such troublesome engagements as spitting down the eight-story stairwell in the main hall so that we could compare the resonance of the "plops."

I spent more time indoors than most children who lived in houses. It was no dreary pastime, however, to sit on the window seat of our eighth floor apartment and watch the comings and goings of Connecticut Avenue below—the horse-drawn milk wagons and vegetable carts, the uniformed street cleaners, and occasionally a fire engine ensemble from the K Street firehouse around the corner. With any luck, the engines were drawn by white horses because of a failure in a fire truck's motor. On other good days the hurdy-gurdy man came by. When spring began to blow through our opened windows, his coming was announced by the music from his hand-cranked organ. Almost always he had with him his monkey, dressed in a cap and a military coat with brass buttons. Sometimes we threw coins to him from the apartment. For pennies, a nickel, or a dime the hurdy-gurdy man pumped out his repertoire of serenades while the monkey scrambled around or made deep bows of gratitude for the coins in his cap.

Mostly, my brothers and I walked from Stoneleigh to Force School on Massachusetts Avenue, to the YMCA swimming pool for early morning swims in the summer, to Foundry Methodist Church on Sunday, and downtown to F Street for shopping. Everybody walked, even Presidents.

While not a frequent occurrence, neither was it rare for one of us to find ourselves walking behind President Harding or Coolidge as we made our way "downtown" via Lafayette Square and along Pennsylvania Avenue. As I recall, the President was always accompanied, but never visibly guarded.

I have no idea when gas lamps on Connecticut Avenue were replaced by electric street lights. I do recall it happening, however, and the wonderment and awe when the entire Avenue brightened at the flick of some invisible switch. Gone forever, then, was the solitary figure of the lamplighter. The image in my memory is of his making his way in the dusk from lamp to lamp, a small ladder in one hand and a long rod in the other. At each lamp he set his ladder down, climbed the steps and pushed the rod into the fixture, turning it until the lamp flickered and began to glow. Did he also come along to turn them off in the morning? He must have. But it is the evening image that comes back whenever I run across Robert Louis Stevenson's poem about O'Leary, the lamplighter.

15

KENESAW, now LA RENAISSANCE

3060 16th Street, N.W.; southwest corner of 16th and Irving streets

ARCHITECT: George W. Stone, Sr., 1903

ORIGINAL APARTMENTS: 65 (12 efficiencies; 8 one-bedrooms; 31 two-bedrooms; 14 three-bedrooms)

STATUS: opened as rental in 1906; converted to condo in 1984

Located two miles north of the White House on a triangular block of land on 16th Street near Columbia Road, the seven-story Kenesaw dominated this neighborhood when it was built in 1905. Although the Kenesaw was designed when the land was acquired in January 1903, construction was delayed for two years because of opposition in Congress. Senators William Morris Stewart of Nevada and Jacob H. Gallinger of New Hampshire and Congressman Roswell P. Bishop of Michigan introduced joint bills to take this triangular block by eminent domain. They felt that this important elevated site should be reserved for a public park to encourage the development of 16th Street, N.W., as the city's most elegant and fashionable residential corridor. The seven original investors in the Kenesaw project (including former Senator John B. Henderson of nearby Boundary Castle) lobbied Congress to prevent government seizure of the site, which is bordered by 16th Street, Mount Pleasant Street, and Irving Street (then Kenesaw Avenue, after which the apartment house took its name). They were successful in blocking the bill and construction commenced in 1905. From 1906 when it opened until 1964, the Kenesaw was owned and operated by the original investors and their heirs.

The Kenesaw was designed in an unusual F-shape plan. It was the second apartment house in the city to be built with all facades finished and exposed to public view (the first being the 1903 Ontario). Each occupies its entire block, which allows good views from all apartments. This concept of a "good view" had originated the previous year with the Highlands. Both the Kenesaw and the Ontario are important examples of new apartment houses offering major improvements in site planning.

The Kenesaw's buff-brick and limestone front facade, facing 16th Street, N.W., is enlivened with three slightly projecting pavilions, shallow iron balconies at the third-floor level, and an oriel window above the entrance, which is sheltered by a robust iron and glass radial marquee. Each of the three wings includes projecting bays.

On the first floor were the manager's office, lobby, vault for valuables, two public parlors, two public dining rooms, and a spacious cafe. The high English basement facing Mount Pleasant Street to the rear included an entrance leading to three shops, while a second side entrance faced Irving Street. The sixty-five apartments varied in size from efficiencies to six-room units.

Because of the prominent residences built nearby, the Kenesaw owners gave the city the apex of their triangular block for a city park in 1913. Here in 1924 was erected the equestrian statue of Francis Asbury (1745–1816), the first Methodist bishop in the United States.

The Kenesaw was the first apartment house designed on its own block of land with all
facades exposed to the streets.

Both the engineer, Frank L. Averill, and the architect, George Winchester Stone, Sr., were paid for their services in shares of stock in the Kenesaw Apartment House Company, which owned the building. Stone was an 1889 graduate of the architecture school of the Massachusetts Institute of Technology. After working for Boston architects Wheelwright and Haven as a draftsman, he moved to Washington in 1901 to serve in the Office of the Supervising Architect of the Department of the Treasury, where he remained until his retirement in 1935. In addition to designing numerous government buildings across the country, he was responsible for additions to several Washington churches, including the Immanuel Baptist and the Chevy Chase Presbyterian. Mr. Stone continued to serve faithfully on the board of directors of the Kenesaw until he resigned in 1957 at the age of ninety-two.

RECENT HISTORY

During the early 1960s the steady profit margin realized by the Kenesaw for her owners began to decline for the first time. The owners needed to choose between making major renovations to the aging building to meet the new District of Columbia fire code and selling the apartment house. Rising expenses, coupled with the steady decline in the character of the neighborhood, resulted in the sale of the Kenesaw in 1964. With the change in ownership, the Kenesaw began to deteriorate rapidly. After a decade of physical decline, the Kenesaw was given to Antioch College of Yellow Springs, Ohio, by its owner, Dr. Aaron H. Gerber, for tax benefits.

The Kenesaw was given to the college for the use of its School of Law, which had been established in Washington, D.C., in 1965 to provide legal training for students from low-income families. Located several blocks south of the Kenesaw in the old Warder House and Meyer House on 16th Street, N.W., Antioch College was faced with either converting the Kenesaw into a classroom building or selling it to establish an endowment for the college. Because of the enormous number of building-code violations that came with the structure, Antioch elected to sell the building in 1977. By that time conditions had become almost unbearable for the seventy-eight tenants (most of whom had refused to pay rent for months): heat and electricity were not functioning and the elevator and janitorial service had been discontinued. After fifty tenants moved out, the remainder formed the Kenesaw Cooperative Association and began a long but futile drive to buy the building themselves.

In the context of the extensive local conversion of

The Kenesaw's triangular site led to its F-shaped plan.

rental apartment houses to condos in the 1970s, the Kenesaw became a symbol of the fight to save housing for the poor. Antioch law students themselves sided with the Kenesaw tenants against the Antioch administration. After considerable turmoil, including court battles, demonstrations, and sit-ins, the District of Columbia Development Corporation, a bureau of the city government, purchased the Kenesaw from Antioch College for $800,000 in 1978. The city planned to renovate the Kenesaw and then sell the apartments to the tenants at a low interest rate.

Consequently the city government began extensive renovations to the Kenesaw in 1979. The contractor selected by the city government for the job unfortunately proved to be the wrong choice, and much of the $2 million-plus renovation had to be redone by a second contractor, at the expense of Washington taxpayers. In the end, the tenants were unable to afford to buy their units. As a result of these futile and ill-managed renovation efforts, the city in 1984 sold the Kenesaw to private developers. At that time an iron fence with stone piers was added on the front lawn and the building renamed La Renaissance.

LIFE AT THE KENESAW

Many of the sons of the original owners followed their fathers' footsteps as members of the board, including Senator Henderson's son, John B. Henderson, Jr., and the architect's son, George W. Stone, Jr. The latter remembers with fondness the golden age of the Kenesaw, before World War II, when the neighborhood remained one of the most desirable in the city—and when the Kenesaw was beautifully managed. Dr. George W. Stone,

Jr., recalled what life was like at the Kenesaw fifty years ago in this 1984 letter:

The site in 1903 had great potential as the city pushed north, but at the time was largely open to fields and free of much building. Florida Avenue was still called "the boundary" and not much further beyond Kenesaw Avenue the land was still farmed. Within two decades, however, the site was proving a happy one for the tenants. Wide and beautiful 16th Street had, of course, zoned-out stores which customarily provide for the routines of daily living, but Mount Pleasant Street had not. Shops began to come with the upsurge of half a dozen smaller apartment buildings—the Amherst, the Cavendish, the Chesterfield, the Winston, the Bloomfield, and the Monticello. By 1911 the car barn at 14th and Park Road had moved up to Decatur, and the structure had been converted to a spacious arcade market, one of the finest in the city, complete with such outlets as a roller skating rink. A comfortable cinema, the Tivoli, bloomed nearby. The Johnson and Powell public schools flourished, a library branch came into being, and churches also began to abound.

Kenesaw tenants from the upper floors watched this neighborhood grow. Also they could and did on a warm summer night hear the not too distant cries of birds and animals from the National Zoo. Cool Rock Creek Park lay just down the hill to the west. Down Columbia Road on leafy Ontario Place the Ontario apartment had come into being as early as 1903, and the Argonne and Harvard Hall would come. Down 16th Street fashionable "2400" [now the Envoy] sprang up, where high school tea dances and social events came to be staples. The modest Earlington House came into being diagonally across 16th Street from the Kenesaw. But when one views the architecture of any or all of these, it becomes apparent that the Kenesaw, in dignified and elegant tradition, set the tone for the neighborhood for fifty years.

16

ONTARIO

2853 Ontario Road, N.W.; northeast corner of Ontario Road and 18th Street

ARCHITECT: James G. Hill, 1903; Hill and Kendall, 1905 addition

ORIGINAL APARTMENTS: 120 (1 efficiency; 73 one-bedrooms; 34 two-bedrooms; 6 three-bedrooms; 6 four-bedrooms)

STATUS: opened as rental in 1904; converted to co-op in 1953

The six-story Ontario is situated on three acres of land on its own elevated triangular block near Columbia Road in the Adams-Morgan neighborhood. The Ontario opened as the city's first freestanding apartment house, with facades designed to be seen from all sides. The earlier luxury Washington apartment houses had been built mostly on corners with only two facades exposed. The tall ceilings and elegant original woodwork make the Ontario's apartments especially desirable. Another reason for the Ontario's popularity when it opened in 1904 was its quiet

Surrounded by open fields when built in 1903–1905 in the Adams-Morgan neighborhood,
the Ontario was first advertised for its lofty and rural location "free from malaria."

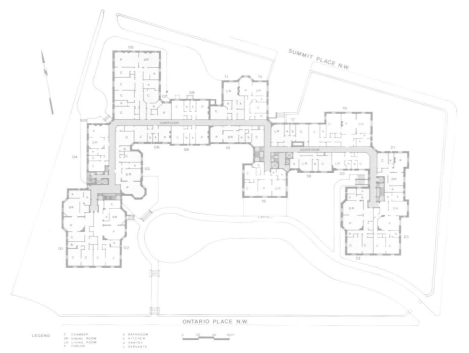

Much of the Ontario's 3-acre site consists of landscaped lawns.

Board member Douglas Robinson poses in the Ontario's rooftop summer pavilion, the first of six Washington apartment houses designed with them.

semirural location. The original brochure promoting the building by the McLachlen Company boasted: "The elevation of 180 feet above tide-level insures pure air and freedom from malaria." Indeed, the Ontario today has five residents who have lived there for more than forty years and one resident for more than sixty years. It remains basically intact because of the original care given it by the McLachlen family who built it as a rental building and later because of its conversion to a co-op in 1953.

The Ontario was developed by Archibald M. McLachlen, a banker and real estate developer who owned much of Lanier Heights, an area defined by Quarry Road, Columbia Road, and Adams Mills Road. In fact, McLachlen demolished his own imposing house to clear the site for the Ontario in 1903. The architect of the Ontario, James G. Hill, who had previously designed Stoneleigh Court and the Mendota, resided here from 1904 until his death in 1913.

To save money on the enormous Beaux Arts facade, the Ontario was designed with a rusticated first-story base of pressed buff brick (rather than the much more expen-

sive limestone), while the upper stories were set in pebbledash, pebbles set in stucco (in place of costly finished brick). The sixth or top story is defined by a stone stringcourse below, recessed brick arches around the windows, and a classical cornice above. The original entrance and lobby were located to the left or north, under an impressive octagonal Victorian tower. This transitional element remains surmounted at the roof level by a classical octagonal "summer pavilion." Perhaps to test the market for rental apartments then so far removed from downtown, McLachlen waited two years before beginning the south or right half of the Ontario. The otherwise bland pebbledash facades are enlivened by buff-brick quoins, keystones over the windows, and several tiers of French-inspired wrought-iron classical balconies above the level of the two original entrance porches with their Ionic columns. Additional light and ventilation are provided by projecting wings on both the front and rear facades.

Arriving through the "new" 1905 entrance to the south or right, one encounters a small but richly appointed entrance hall with marble pilasters, arched openings, and

ONTARIO

60

Elaborate iron staircase in the Ontario lobby.

a terrazzo floor bordered by the Greek-key design that enjoyed great popularity in Washington apartment houses from 1900 to 1920. After passing by the small public parlor and office to the right, one finds a handsome public staircase with a wrought-iron balustrade and marble treads on the left. Opposite are the highly polished original brass letterboxes set into the wall. The Ontario was originally equipped with both gas and electric lighting, telephone service, and electric elevators.

The Ontario's first residents included such prominent members of Congress as Senators Robert La Follette of Wisconsin and Moses E. Clapp of Minnesota. With many other government officials and professionals, more than 60 percent of the residents were listed in the 1907 *Elite List*. The Ontario was particularly popular with Southerners, including, for instance, Mrs. George Pickett, the widow of the famous general of Pickett's Charge at the Battle of Gettysburg. During her residency there from 1905 until 1929, the Confederate widow Pickett supported herself by writing a number of books and magazine articles relating to Civil War history. Among the

nationally prominent residents was Douglas MacArthur, the most controversial American general of the twentieth century, who lived with his mother, Mary Pinckney MacArthur, in No. 305 in 1916–17 while assigned as a captain to the War Department. Another young officer, also in his mid-thirties, resided at the Ontario during World War I, Chester Nimitz (1885–1966). Years later, Fleet Admiral Nimitz became one of the highest ranking officers of the U.S. Navy throughout World War II. He and General MacArthur signed the Japanese surrender document for the United States in 1945 in Tokyo Bay aboard the *U.S.S. Missouri*.

The Ontario, like almost all large first-class apartment houses before the Great Depression, maintained a public dining room. Known as the Ontario Cafe, this facility was located in the large basement; the space today is known as the Assembly Room, in which meetings and parties are held. At one time in the early years, residents could take three meals a day for the monthly charge of $30. An extra charge of 25 cents was required for each meal served in an apartment.

This rare 1905 photograph shows an original resident of the Ontario, Mrs. Marian Lee Patterson Smith, serving tea in her parlor.

Before 1915 the apartment doors in many first-class Washington apartment houses were designed with curtained glass windows, as in this example at the Ontario. For security reasons, the glass has been replaced with wood in almost all of these doors.

When government salaries were cut 10 percent in 1933, during the Great Depression, many apartment house landlords followed suit in reducing rental costs. The McLachlen family, owners of the Ontario, maintained the 10-percent reduction until the late 1930s. By the 1930s the Lanier Heights neighborhood had become completely built up, with the highest concentration of apartment houses in the city. The Ontario had by then become a close-in neighborhood. Columbia Road remained a fashionable area, with the convenient streetcar connecting Mount Pleasant with downtown. Ontario residents could enjoy elegant luncheons at the nearby Avignone Frères, buy furs at Gartenhaus Furriers at 18th Street and Columbia Road, N.W., and enjoy first-run movies across the street at the Ambassador Theatre.

In addition to the Ontario, Archibald McLachlen built two other of the city's early, prominent apartment houses—the Iowa in 1900 and the Mendota in 1901. The McLachlen family continued to own the three investment buildings for more than fifty years. The Mendota and the Ontario were sold in 1952 and 1953, respectively, to a local businessman, Lea Willson, who immediately employed the Edmund J. Flynn Company to convert them to cooperatives. The terms for purchase of the Ontario apartments, priced from $4,700 to $16,500, were 45 percent in cash, with a note on the balance at 4½ percent over a ten-year period. Approximately half of the renters purchased units. No architectural or decorative changes were made to the building at the time of conversion except for the installation of a new automatic elevator in the west wing.

Major demographic changes in the area around the Ontario began to take place in the early 1950s. By 1958 the District of Columbia government was considering expanding the urban renewal program then underway in the southwest part of the city to include Lanier Heights. Much of the area was to be razed and replaced with a new shopping center at 18th Street and Columbia Road. This proposed plan fortunately was never carried out.

With conditions in the neighborhood stabilizing and more progressive boards of directors, much-needed improvements to the Ontario were undertaken from the mid-1970s to the late 1980s. Public parlors were redecorated, corridors painted, renting restricted, new boilers and roof installed, and a long-range major improvements fund established to avoid sudden large-scale assessments. In addition, the Edwardian summerhouse on the front lawn was restored, the driveway and parking lot repaved, the iron balconies repaired, a new bicycle room created, and the antique pool table in the recreation room restored. One of the significant accomplishments of this "renaissance" was the preparation and publication of a history of the building by a group of enthusiastic residents—the best history yet prepared on any individual Washington apartment house.

The Ontario's Victorian octagonal tower, even though partially disguised with its classical roof pavilion and entrance porch, was not fully integrated into the overall Beaux Arts facade design. The innovative and progressive feature of the Ontario, however, was its site plan. Built on a high elevation, the building was surrounded by its own spacious grounds. Like the owners of the Highlands, built the previous year, the developers of the Ontario were quick to promote the views from the apartments, as well as the aspect of cleaner air at a building so far removed from downtown. Its prestige was established in part because it dominated all of its much smaller architectural neighbors.

Although the nearby Kenesaw was designed the same year as the Ontario, also on its own triangular block of land facing 16th Street, it was built much closer to the three streets that bordered it, occupying a much greater density of its site. Even though the Ontario still dominates the area, it was even more striking in the early twentieth century when it stood alone towering over its parklike setting. Its spacious grounds would become a model for later and much larger apartment houses, which, like Cathedral Mansions and the Broadmoor, would be built at an ever-increasing pace during the boom period of the 1920s.

Top: The oldest surviving Washington apartment house coal boiler, handsome and impressive in its unaltered original design but no longer in use, is in the basement of the Ontario. *Bottom:* The simplicity of the Ontario's early boiler, originally operated by the janitor, stands in marked contrast to the sophisticated heating and cooling systems in such large modern apartment houses as those shown at 4000 Massachusetts Avenue.

17

BACHELOR FLATS

1737 H Street, N.W.

ARCHITECT: Wood, Donn, and Deming, 1904

ORIGINAL APARTMENTS: 24 (1 efficiency; 23 one-bedrooms)

STATUS: opened as rental in 1904; converted to an office building ca. 1950

Although converted to an office building, most of the handsome original exterior and interior dealing at the Bachelor Flats remains intact.

The Bachelor Flats is Washington's only surviving early luxury apartment house for single men. The essential feature of a bachelor apartment house, designed for permanent residents, was the absence of kitchens. Residents also expected to receive the considerable amount of service that the Bachelor offered. (A hotel, on the other hand, intended for transients, usually offered one furnished bedroom rather than an apartment suite.)

All of the city's pre–World War I luxury bachelor apartment houses were located in the old residential neighborhood downtown—near Lafayette Square—because of its proximity to prominent men's clubs, such as the Cosmos, the Metropolitan, and the Army and Navy. They were also within walking distance to most offices and shops. The earliest known was the Everett at 1731 Eye Street, N.W. Designed in 1883 by Joseph Hornblower, this five-story building had one apartment of three rooms (without kitchens) on each floor above the ground floor. Another was located on the northeast corner of 18th and Eye streets, N.W. (seven stories with twenty-eight apartments). A third example was the Benedict, built in 1905 at 1808 Eye Street, N.W.

Opposite: The Bachelor Flats had no grand lobby—but the finest vestibule of any early Washington apartment building.

Detail of the intricate cast-iron newel post at the Bachelor Flats.

The five-story Bachelor Flats was designed in the Georgian Revival style, with a rusticated first-story base, pair of oriel windows, wide cornice, and pergola embellishing the roof. The Bachelor Flats' original design as a seven-story, mansard-roofed building, also by Wood, Donn, and Deming, was shown at the 1904 exhibition of the Washington Architectural Club at the Corcoran Gallery of Art. Because of financial restraints, however, the height of the Bachelor Flats was lowered two floors before construction began and the facade treatment reworked. This structure was one of the first apartment houses in the city to be designed with a Georgian Revival facade. Although many other apartments would be built in this style during the following decade, the Beaux Arts influence would continue to dominate apartment house design until the early 1920s.

Shortly after World War II, when this area of the city had evolved from a fashionable residential neighborhood into a commercial district, the Bachelor Flats was converted to an office building. In 1962 it was purchased by local attorney Henry Glassie, who used it as offices for his law firm, Glassie, Pewett, Dudley, Beebe, and Shanks. Sensitive to the good architectural design and quality workmanship, Glassie had both the front facade and most of the interior details carefully restored. He was also responsible for nominating the Bachelor Flats in the National Register of Historic Places—the first apartment house in the city to receive an individual listing (as opposed to inclusion in an historic district). One can still see the richly detailed vestibule, with its colorful mosaic floor and elaborately paneled walls and plastered ceiling. The original staircase—with its Beaux Arts–inspired iron balustrade, newel post, and marble steps—remains intact. The living rooms of the apartments, now offices, still contain the old decorative wooden fireplace mantels, some with the same gas fire logs, and their handsome plaster cornices.

ARCHITECT WADDY BUTLER WOOD

Waddy Butler Wood (1869–1944) became one of the leading architects in Washington between 1892 and his retirement in 1936. He came to Washington from Ivy Depot, Virginia, after working three years on a railroad survey in his native state. Anxious to become an architect, Wood worked as a draftsman for several firms while studying at night at the Library of Congress. He formed the firm of Wood, Donn, and Deming, which existed from 1903 to 1914. The two partners were Edward W. Donn, Jr., a Washington native, who was professionally trained in architecture at the Massachusetts Institute of Technology and at Cornell University, and William L. Deming, a graduate in engineering from George Washington University. While Wood got the jobs, Donn was often the major designer and Deming the engineer. Wood obtained many of the commissions from his active social connections in the city.

After the partnership was dissolved in 1914, Wood practiced architecture alone until the late 1930s when he retired. Wood became the major architect for the early houses in the Kalorama Circle neighborhood, including the Fairbanks house at 2340 S Street, N.W.; the Fitzhugh

house at 2253 R Street, N.W.; the Delano house at 2244 S Street, N.W.; the Barney Studio house at 2306 Massachusetts Avenue, N.W. (now part of the Smithsonian); and the Tucker house (now the Textile Museum) at 2320 S Street, N.W. Other of his buildings in the area northwest of Dupont Circle include the old Chinese Legation at 19th and Vernon streets, N.W.; the Gunston Hall School for Girls at 19th and T streets, N.W. (now demolished); and the Cordova apartment house at Florida Avenue and T Street, N.W.

Waddy Wood worked in many building types in addition to houses and apartment houses. Some of his major works include the Capitol Traction Company (Car Barn) at 3600 M Street, N.W., in Georgetown; the Masonic temple at 801 13th Street, N.W.; the Department of the Interior building on C between 18th and 19th streets, N.W.; the Southern Railway building at 920 15th Street, N.W.; St. Patrick's Church parish house and school at 924 G Street, N.W.; the East Capitol Car Barn at 1400 East Capitol Street, N.E.; and the Union Trust Company at 15th and H streets, N.W.

In a competition in the late 1930s, Wood was selected to redesign the facade of the old State, War, and Navy Building (now the Old Executive Office Building) to match that of the Department of the Treasury Building. The outbreak of World War II fortunately prevented the proposed change. He was also responsible for designing the 1933 and 1937 presidential reviewing stands for Roosevelt's inaugurations. One of the many prominent buildings he designed on his own was the All States Hotel for women at 19th and E streets, N.W. (now demolished). Wood designed seven Washington apartment houses between 1899 and 1927. Today the Wood drawings are lost, but many of his papers have been preserved at the Library of Congress.

Most units in the once-exclusive Bachelor Flats included a living room, bedroom, and bath. Meals were prepared in the basement and served in the apartments.

LIFE AT THE BACHELOR FLATS

Very little information has been found on many of the early apartment houses of Washington, including the half-dozen bachelor apartment houses that existed in the early twentieth century. One of the most valuable accounts is the original 1905 pamphlet on the Bachelor Flats published by the developer, which presents a very good description of what life was intended to be there and of the services available. Particular attention was given to the desirable location of the building—adjacent to clubs and government offices, but still in a prestigious residential area. Technological improvements were also emphasized, such as the electric elevator, mail chutes, showers (the first mentioned in a Washington apartment house), and wall safes in each unit, as well as the availability of apartments with both good light and views. The high rent charged limited the Bachelor Flats to only the most affluent. The developers described the new apartment house as follows:

> The Bachelor was designed to meet a long-felt want. There have been, in the past, no chambers for men in Washington that were up-to-date in every particular. There have been none that were so well conducted that the occupants could have their needs as well supplied as if they were in their own homes. "The Bachelor" fills these requirements. It has a corps of efficient servants. It is absolutely fireproof. It has the best finish of woodwork, decorating, etc., that can be obtained. Particular care is given to the service.
>
> The plumbing, heating, and ventilation have been made a special feature. All the plumbing fixtures are of the latest standard. In addition to the tub, every bath has a shower. The showers are supplied with anti-scalding, mixing valves, and rubber curtains. All exposed plumbing is heavily nickeled and all valves and faucets are of the most approved designs. A special heater in the basement furnishes an ample supply of hot and cold water at all hours, both summer and winter.
>
> Suites have roomy, well-proportioned closets, provided with electric lights on the ceiling. Each suite consists of a large reception hall (or vestibule), of sufficient size to receive the casual visitor; a living room with built-in bookcases; a bed-room; and a bath.
>
> The location of the lot is open on three sides and admits ample light to all rooms. Most of the rooms face east

on a wide alley, or south on H Street. In purchasing the lot for "The Bachelor" special care was taken to select a good location. Being on the north side of H Street, between Seventeenth and Eighteenth Streets, it is within two or three blocks of the most important clubs in town. It is in the same block as the Metropolitan Club, and is one block from the two principal street-car lines of the city. Its location is especially accessible to the State, War, and Navy Departments. It is near the foreign legations and is in the fashionable, residential portion of the city.

> The elevator is an "Otis" of the latest electric type. It will run night and day. There are mail chutes on each floor. On top of the building is a roof-garden with a tiled floor and rustic seats. Built in the form of a pergola and arranged for awning coverings, it provides an excellent opportunity for occupants of "The Bachelor" to sit out of doors and enjoy a charming view.
>
> Each suite in "The Bachelor" is provided with a long-distance telephone. A "central," downstairs, takes any messages that come during the absence of an occupant from the building. The customary charge of five cents for every out going message will be made. Iced spring water, clothes pressing, shoe polishing, and attendance on rooms, is free of charge. This is a distinct feature.
>
> Breakfasts will be served in each suite, if desired, from service pantries, situated on each floor. These connect with a dumb-waiter which runs to every floor, and is in turn connected with a small serving room. Here is a gas-stove, sink, and dresser. It is the aim of "The Bachelor" to make its service as perfect as possible. Criticisms and suggestions of tenants will be gladly received. Each suite contains a fireproof safe. It is built into the wall and is of sufficient size to hold valuables, books, papers, and silverware.
>
> Apartments will be leased, furnished or unfurnished, and tenants taking long leases can have doors cut and suites thrown together, if desired. The prices of apartments range from thirty to sixty dollars a month, according to size and location.

18

CORDOVA, now PRESIDENT MADISON

1908 Florida Avenue, N.W.; southeast corner of Florida Avenue and 20th Street

ARCHITECT: Wood, Donn, and Deming, 1905; A.H. Sonnemann, 1915 addition

ORIGINAL APARTMENTS: 40 (11 one-bedrooms; 24 two-bedrooms; 5 three-bedroom duplexes)

STATUS: opened as rental in 1906

The Cordova was designed in 1905 by architect Waddy B. Wood in an unusual bent T-shape to accommodate the intersection of Florida Avenue and 20th Street, N.W. It is significant both as the city's largest Spanish Colonial style apartment house and as the earliest example incorporating duplex apartments.

Both the central section and the two wings of this sprawling, three-story, stuccoed residence possess aus-

The three-story Spanish Colonial style Cordova was designed with two summer pavilions and a pergola on the roof.

CORDOVA
70

Opposite: Still intact, the lobby of the
Cordova features an elaborate inlaid mosaic
floor and a double staircase.

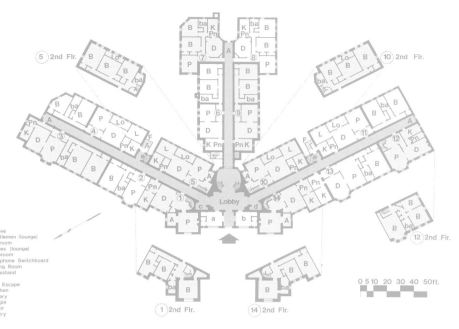

Legend
A   Alcove
a   Gentlemen (lounge)
B   Bedroom
b   Ladies (lounge)
ba   bathroom
c   Telephone Switchboard
D   Dining Room
d   newsstand
e   lift
F   Fire Escape
K   Kitchen
L   Library
Lo   Loggia
P   Parlor
Pn   Pantry

Included within the irregular T-shaped Cordova were five two-story apartments,
Washington's first duplexes.

tere street facades. The front of the Cordova is embellished, however, with two roof pavilions, crowned with
red-tile hipped roofs; the original handsome wood pergolas that connected them are now missing. The main
entrance below still has intact its elaborate rusticated
baroque entablature, a typical element of the Spanish
Colonial style, with engaged columns and a rounded pediment surmounted by stone vases. The two flanking wings
are enlivened by red-tile hipped roofs with wide eaves,
pierced by baroque dormers with two-story projecting bays
below.

The Cordova originally was designed with forty apartments, including five duplex units. The largest contained
a parlor, dining room, library, loggia, kitchen, and pantry
on the lower level and three bedrooms, loggia, and bath
on the upper level. Although the front facade of the Cordova was situated close to the street, extensive gardens
and two tennis courts were placed in the rear of its one-
acre site.

Today, as over eighty years ago, one enters the building through a graceful coffered and arched vestibule with
brass mailboxes recessed in the two long marble walls.
The rectangular lobby with its elaborately patterned mosaic floor connects the two wings, each with its elevator.
The focal point of the lobby is the pair of semicircular

marble stairs with Beaux Arts–inspired cast-iron balustrades opposite the entrance. The two lounges, one for
ladies and the other for gentlemen, opening off the lobby
and flanking the entrance, have long since been converted
into efficiency apartments. The only other apartment house
with this unusual arrangement of a pair of lounges in the
lobby was 2029 Connecticut Avenue, N.W., where the
lounges also have become efficiency apartments. Because
of the success of the Cordova, a four-story annex with
thirty-three additional apartments was erected at 1809
20th Street in 1915. Today the annex is separately owned
and no longer connected to the Cordova.

In 1952 the Cordova was sold to investor Leo M.
Bernstein, who renovated the building, subdividing the
apartments, including the duplexes, into 103 units, to
produce increased revenue. Bernstein renamed the apartment house the President Madison after he acquired several original furnishings that reportedly belonged to James
Madison. When the renovation was completed, he placed
these items on display in the lobby for several years.
Although most of the interior detailing and floor plans
have been obliterated, the facade and the lobby remain
in a fairly good state of preservation, even if somewhat
shabby.

19

WARDER

1155 16th Street, N.W.; southeast corner of 16th and M streets

ARCHITECT: Bruce Price and Jules H. de Sibour, New York and Washington, D.C., 1905

ORIGINAL APARTMENTS: 6 (2 two-bedrooms and 4 four-bedrooms)

STATUS: opened as rental in 1906; converted to an office building in 1940; razed in 1958

Considered Washington's most sophisticated apartment house at the time it was built in 1905, the five-story Warder resembled a first-class Paris apartment house because of its finely detailed low-scale classical facade and its sophisticated floor plan. The carved garlands and keystones of the window lintels, the pedimented attic windows, slate mansard roof, and top floor balcony were beautifully proportioned to one another. When originally constructed by the estate of Benjamin F. Warder, a former leading Washington real estate investor and developer, this apartment house fit into the neighborhood of large houses without drawing attention to itself. Its small domestic scale, resembling a private mansion rather than an apartment house, was its most unusual feature. The closest apartment houses to it still standing today, in scale, design, and quality of construction, would be the McCormick, now in use as the headquarters of the National Trust for Historic Preservation, four blocks away at Massachusetts Avenue and 18th Street, N.W., and Wendell Mansions at Massachusetts Avenue and Decatur Place, N.W.

In addition to its small domestic scale, the other significant feature of the Warder was its floor plan, the first sophisticated apartment house floor plan to appear in Washington. Based on those in Paris, it featured the distinct separation of the three classes of space in each apartment—public rooms, bedrooms, and service rooms. The building's architect, Jules H. de Sibour, had received architectural training at an atelier in Paris for a year before practicing architecture in Washington. The interior was arranged with two apartments on the first floor and one on each of the four floors above. In the typical apartment, the dining room, salon, and library, all with wood-burning fireplaces, faced 16th Street and opened into each other to facilitate large-scale entertaining. The four master bedrooms, with generous closet space, opened onto M Street, which provided abundant light. The service area—including the serving room, four servants' bedrooms, servants' bath, laundry, servants' hall, kitchen, pantry, and service elevator—was carefully contained on the east and south sides of each apartment for privacy.

The building, officially named by its address, 1155 16th Street, N.W., was nevertheless known locally as "the Warder" after the family that built and owned it. The use of the Warder as an apartment house ended in 1940 when the American Chemical Society bought it for its national headquarters. Because of rapid growth, this society razed both the Warder and adjoining historic houses in 1958 for its present large International Style office building. At that time the District of Columbia had no

b   Bathroom   S   Servant's Room

Bedroom

b   Sewing   S   S   S   S

b

Bedroom

Laundry

Bedroom

Servants Hall

b

Kitchen

Bedroom

ELEV   Pantry   ELEV

DN   UP

Foyer

Library

Dining Room

Salon

The elegant French-inspired Warder was unfortunately demolished for an office building by the American Chemical Society shortly after World War II, when the city had few preservation laws.

Each floor of the Warder consisted of one apartment, skillfully designed with complete separation of public, private, and service areas.

historic preservation laws to protect such outstanding, privately owned architectural landmarks, except in Georgetown, which had been made an historic district in 1950. The Warder's beautiful facade, well-designed floor plan, sensitive domestic scale, and excellence of construction made it one of the most successful apartment houses ever built in the city. Its demolition was a distinct loss to Washington's collection of early luxury apartment houses.

The architects of record of the Warder were Bruce Price and Jules H. de Sibour, although Price, the senior partner, had died two years earlier. Both were outstanding American designers in the late nineteenth and early twentieth centuries. Shortly after the Warder was built, Jules H. de Sibour moved from New York to Washington and practiced under his own name. Architect de Sibour, re-

sponsible for designing many of Washington's finest Beaux Arts houses as well as four of its finest apartment houses, was quite capable of continuing what Price had begun, that is, a firm accepted as stylish by the very polite and very wealthy. Certainly de Sibour's position as junior partner to Price helped establish his own practice after Price died. [Bruce Price, a native of Cumberland, Maryland, is noted for his design of Tuxedo Park (1885–90), an exclusive summer colony one hour north of New York City developed by Pierre Lorillard IV. Price's design of dozens of important Shingle Style houses there was influential on other architects, especially Frank Lloyd Wright. Price's other outstanding projects include the Windsor (railroad) Station in Montreal of 1888 and his twenty-story American Surety Company Building of 1894 in New York.]

20

FLORENCE COURT, now CALIFORNIA COURT and CALIFORNIA HOUSE

2153 California Street, N.W. (California Court) and 2205 California Street, N.W. (California House)

ARCHITECT: T. Franklin Schneider, 1905

ORIGINAL APARTMENTS: 46 (the west and east halves of the building form two separate apartment houses, each with 23 apartments, all two-bedrooms)

STATUS: both apartment houses opened as rental in 1905; west half, or No. 2205, converted to condo in 1978; east half, or No. 2153, converted to condo in 1985

Florence Court is divided in the center into two separate apartment houses.

The handsome front porch of Florence Court connects the two separate lobbies.

The small but imposing six-story Florence Court, now known as California Court and California House, was designed and built by Washington architect T. Franklin Schneider in 1905. Schneider, who was also the developer and half-owner, named it Florence Court in honor of his eleven-year-old daughter. Florence Court is unique in Washington in that it contains two apartment houses with separate addresses—even though they were built under the same roof, at the same time, and made to look like one apartment house. They share the same front court and porch but have separate entrances and lobbies. The only interior connection is a small locked basement door between the two apartment houses. When the building was completed, each partner took separate title to half of the building.

It was not until 1965 that a new owner, Stuart Bernstein, changed the name of Florence Court to California House. A few years later the entire building (both sets of apartments) was purchased by another developer, Malcolm E. Peabody. The two adjoining but separate apartment houses have continued. In 1978 the left or west half, No. 2205 (still called California House), was converted by Peabody to twenty-three condominiums; the east half, No. 2153, remained rental until he converted it into a separate condominium in 1985 and named it California Court. While No. 2205 remains in almost perfect original condition with its same floor plan and interior detailing, No. 2153 has been subdivided into fifty-three much smaller apartments.

One enters the front court of the Beaux Arts complex,

Each original apartment at Florence Court had either five or six rooms; the windowless dining rooms were awkward, however.

An unusual feature of Florence Court is the white marble used for both doorjambs and wainscoting in the public corridors.

with its classic buff-brick and limestone tripartite facade and small fountain, through an elaborate iron fence and gate. The unusual square lobby of No. 2205 still contains its original mirrored doors, brass mailboxes, and elaborate terrazzo floor decorated with mosaic borders and central medallions. The walls are richly treated with marble pilasters and elaborate plaster panels and cornice. This theme is continued through the public corridors with marble wainscoting, unusual marble doorjambs, and full-length mirrors set into the corridor ends to create a more spacious feeling. The landing on the marble staircase between the first and second floors with its Beaux Arts cast-iron balustrade is embellished with an elaborate leaded glass window with a stained glass cartouche.

Each apartment has either four or five rooms with kitchen and bath, four apartments to a floor. Most of these units were designed with a long corridor that led into a large square reception hall, which was partially screened from the living room by a pair of engaged columns. The original hardwood floors and envelope doors remain intact.

Florence Court and its neighboring apartment houses on these two blocks of California Street—including the Highlands, the Westmoreland, the Brighton, the St. Nicholas, and the St. Regis—were all fashionable addresses before World War I, enjoying excellent views of the entire city from this high elevation. Among the best-known residents of Florence Court were Supreme Court Justice Louis D. Brandeis and artist Marc Chagall. Several prominent local real estate developers, including Bates Warren and Gerson Nordlinger, Sr., lived at Florence Court in the early years as well.

21

WESTMORELAND

2122 California Street, N.W.

ARCHITECT: Edgar S. Kennedy and Harry Blake, 1905

ORIGINAL APARTMENTS: 55 (32 one-bedrooms; 23 two-bedrooms)

STATUS: opened as rental in 1906; converted to co-op in 1948

When this site was purchased by developers for a new apartment house, the view to the east was already blocked by the slightly earlier Highlands apartment house. With the rapid development of apartments in this area, it was expected that another apartment house would also occupy the lot to the west (as happened when the Lonsdale was built here in 1909). The architects therefore designed the Westmoreland in an unusual double E shape to provide as much light and air circulation on the restricted site as possible. Resembling a Maltese cross, the six-story buff-brick and limestone Beaux Arts Westmoreland was one of several early apartment houses erected on California Street with a commanding view of the city from the crest of Kalorama Heights. Because of conversion to condominiums or hotel use, most of these early apartment house landmarks have lost their original features, detailing, and plans. On California Street the best preserved remain the Westmoreland and the St. Regis.

The most important original feature in the Westmoreland is the impressive classical lobby with its Ionic columns and pilasters and beamed ceiling. The lobby is further embellished with marble wainscoting. By surmounting it with recessed blind arches, the architects created an unusual visual rhythm that unites the lofty space. The handsome mosaic floor, worn by use, is un-

The front facade of the Westmoreland.

fortunately now hidden by wall-to-wall carpeting. The interior detailing of the Westmoreland's apartments, which range from two to five rooms, is rather plain, as was typical of all but the most expensive apartment houses in 1905. Within a year, however, a number of new apartment houses would possess unusual and fine interior detailing—a trend that began with the Warder in 1905 and continued until World War I. The few unusual details in the Westmoreland apartments are found mostly in the large units at the front and rear corners of the building. In the dining rooms in these rear apartments, the architect camouflaged two protruding structural steel beams on one wall by building a leaded glass china cabinet between them. Originally sliding doors were used only in the middle-sized units (Nos. 3 and 5 tiers); in the larger apartments (Nos. 1, 2, 7, and 12 tiers), the dining and living rooms are separated by a hallway.

The Westmoreland's plan has a total of ten tiers (a vertical section of apartments of identical floor plans), with the largest apartments located in the No. 7 and No. 2 tiers. These have large porches facing the rear as well as projecting bays. Two former public spaces have since disappeared: the public parlor behind the first-floor lobby (now apartment No. 161) and the top-floor dining room on the central east wing (in what would normally constitute the Nos. 4, 6, 8, and 10 tiers). The Nos. 9 and 11 tiers were omitted when the architects originally assigned tier numbers because they were not needed, since the west side of the building has odd numbers and the east side even numbers. Thus the tier numbers range from No. 1

A resident of the Westmoreland searches for her front door key under the Beaux Arts portico on a humid August afternoon.

to No. 12 although there are only ten tiers. Another peculiarity is the original numbering system used by the architects for tiers. All tiers here are preceded by the number five—what would normally be the No. 1 tier was originally and still is called the No. 51 tier. To prevent confusion, the normal tier number designation has been used on the adjacent typical floor plan for the Westmoreland.

At the time the Westmoreland was built, its southern views of the city from these apartments were unsurpassed. The sweeping panorama has unfortunately been partially blocked by the uninspired eight-story Holiday Inn, constructed in the early 1960s on Connecticut Avenue and Leroy Place, N.W. The Westmoreland residents and other neighbors had successfully blocked plans for an even

Located on an inside lot, the Westmoreland takes maximum advantage of light and air by means of this irregular double-E plan.

The handsome lobby of the Westmoreland is unified by a series of blind classical arches encircling the room.

Wide balconies offer an added amenity for residents of rear apartments at the Westmoreland.

larger, if better-designed, apartment house by architects A. R. Clas and George H. Riggs in 1955.

The developers originally planned to call the building the Waverly but changed the name before construction was completed. When it opened in 1906 the Westmoreland contained fifty-five apartments. From the beginning, a public dining room, the Westmoreland Cafe, was operated on the top floor of the east central wing, serving three meals a day. The manager often lived in an adjoining apartment until the cafe closed in 1932, during the Great Depression. At that time a covered passageway was built between the Westmoreland and the adjoining Highlands, so that Westmoreland residents could use the public dining room there without needing protection from the weather. The old passageway was torn down in 1948 when the Westmoreland became a co-op, although the Highlands dining room continued operation until about 1955. Today the Westmoreland has fifty-nine apartments; four additional units resulted in 1935 from the closing of the cafe, and a fourth when the old parlor, adjacent to the lobby, was converted in 1949.

When changed from rental to cooperative status in 1948, the building included a lawn with a rose garden on the west side. This gave way in 1962 to a parking lot for the residents, now holding thirty cars.

Because of the building's high elevation on California Street, the city water system was originally not powerful enough to furnish water pressure to the top three floors. As a result, a large iron storage tank was built at the top of the staircase in the rooftop penthouse. It remains in place, more than eighty years later, as a reminder of the original Edwardian engineering system. Although a number of early apartment houses in American cities are known to have had water storage tanks, this is the only one to survive in Washington.

The Westmoreland was built and originally owned by Edgar S. Kennedy, who later built the spectacular Meridian Mansions in 1916, and Harry L. Rust, who founded the H. L. Rust Company in 1889. The latter named the building for his rural birthplace, Westmoreland County, Virginia. In 1907, soon after the Westmoreland was completed, it was sold to real estate investor

Stilson Hutchins (1838–1912). Hutchins had earlier bought the adjacent newly built Highlands as well as other property on nearby Leroy Place. A longtime newspaper editor, Hutchins had moved to Washington from St. Louis in 1877 and founded the *Washington Post*. He ultimately sold the paper in 1889 to devote his time to his investments. In addition to buying a great deal of Washington real estate, Hutchins made a considerable fortune as the principal financial backer of the newly invented linotype machine in 1885. His National Typographic Company manufactured the machines, which revolutionized the printing industry. At Hutchins's death in 1912, he left an estate of more than $3 million. Both the Westmoreland and the Highlands remained part of the Hutchins estate until it was settled in 1924, after which they were held in trust for most of the remaining period before 1948 by the National Savings and Trust Company. The Westmoreland became a cooperative in 1948.

The roof of the Westmoreland contains a penthouse with this original water tank, necessitated because city water pressure would not reach this high elevation in 1905.

LIFE AT THE WESTMORELAND

This 1986 letter from Mary Calvert Conger of Lovettsville, Virginia, provides important insight into a girl's life at the Westmoreland during the late 1930s and 1940s:

There was a time when apartment living became a desirable alternative: it coincided with a time when many families chose to be small families (one child or two). I had as many friends who grew up in apartments, as those who grew up in houses. I grew up at the Westmoreland on California Street, because Cleveland Park was a longer commute than my father wanted, Chevy Chase was so far out in the country it was never even considered, Westmoreland Circle was surrounded by fields. California Street seemed just right: convenient and congenial—the many large apartment buildings provided friends and family nearby. Children could walk to visit, not needing an adult to accompany or drive them. The Mount Pleasant streetcar was nearby to whisk young people, unaccompanied, to F Street for the Saturday lunch and movie preoccupation.

My aunt and uncle lived down the street at Florence Court, another next to that at 2219, and a third in a house in the next block, so there was a lot of visiting that went on. I walked to school with a friend who lived at the Highlands, and another who lived at the Brighton. Halfway down Connecticut Avenue we met another schoolmate who lived on Bancroft Place, and then continued on to Gunston Hall at 19th Street and Florida Avenue.

The Westmoreland lobby was white marble with a big red velvet sofa on each side, the switchboard and mailboxes in one corner and a small public writing desk in another corner. Further on, beyond the elevator, and up about six marble steps, was a comfortably furnished sitting room, or parlor, for the use of the residents receiving visitors, but it was seldom used. Neither was the small penthouse room on the roof, which was furnished with wicker. The benches on the roof itself were used quite a bit in those days before air conditioning: there was always a cool breeze on a warm evening, a panoramic view of the city, and a great place to view the July 4th fireworks at the Washington Monument. On summer days, two friends who lived at the Wyoming and I would use the roof gardens of the two buildings, for suntanning, in addition to walking over to the Wardman Park pool for more of the same, or journeying further to a club pool.

Another fair weather bonus of the Westmoreland was the large, fenced-in, shady yard on the west side. Its benches were also enjoyed by the residents on warm evenings. About ten residents asked for and received permission to have their own individual flower beds along one side of the yard. They were lovely and provided much interest and promoted lasting friendships. Many happy hours were spent working in those gardens, cultivating climbing roses, delphinium, zinnias, petunias, lobelia, heliotrope, nicotiana, and much more.

Each spring the janitor would put in the window screens and the window awnings in all the apartments to provide shelter from the summer sun. The oriental rugs would be rolled up and sent away for cleaning and summer storage, white slipcovers appeared on the chairs and sofas, and sheer summer curtains replaced the winter draperies. How shady and cool and pleasant those summer rooms were with the awnings lowered. Bowls of fresh flowers were around, picked in the side garden or purchased on the weekly jaunt to the outdoor country stands at the K Street Market [21st and K streets, N.W.] or the Farm Women's Market in Bethesda.

There was no special dress code for apartment dwelling young people. These were the days when adequately "proper" dress seems to have been well known by all ages, and adhered to. And apartment children learned early of the need to greet politely the residents that one ran into constantly on the front steps, in the lobby, on the elevator, in the garden, on the roof, as well as in the dining room at the Highlands.

There was an enclosed passageway between the Westmoreland and the Highlands. From the Westmoreland you got to it by the back door of the elevator, a half flight down from the first floor. The dining room consisted of three fairly large rooms, one of which was reserved for residents of the Highlands and the Westmoreland only. California Street was "home" for so many retired admirals, generals, colonels, etc., that one resident jokingly called it "the last stop before Arlington Cemetery"! Many of these were regulars in the Highlands dining room and had their special tables. There were white tablecloths,

flowers, polite waiters. Everyone knew and greeted everyone else. The very good three-course dinners were 50 cents and 55 cents, when I first became aware of prices. Across the street, the Brighton Hotel had an equally nice dining room, but I think the dinners were more expensive, maybe 65 cents!

All during my era at the Westmoreland, Rowe was our full-time caretaker; he and his family lived in an apartment in the basement. In addition, Jeanette and Marie took turns at the switchboard; visitors were always "announced" . . . a convenient "warning" before the elevator deposited him/her at your door. Various "elevator men" and "old Ernest" and "young Ernest" (janitors) were always around. A familiar early morning sight all along California Street in fair weather was Rowe in front of the Westmoreland (and other janitors in front of their buildings) watering the small lawns with a hose and shooting (with the hose) the minimal collection of dust, trash, and leaves off the sidewalk.

The front doors of the apartment buildings were never locked. One could come in at any hour freely; "old Ernest" (on duty from midnight to eight A.M. supposedly at the switchboard) was always on the red velvet sofa catnapping. He would jump right up, though, upon the entrance of a resident to take them upstairs on the elevator. The elevator never became self-service [during her time]. It was a large airy cage, and even contained a wooden bench with arms.

Apartment houses didn't have washing machines. Everyone sent their laundry "out": in our case, Page Laundry picked up and delivered weekly. Milk was delivered to our door in the early morning by Chestnut Farms Dairy. The *Evening Star* was at our door promptly each afternoon. Garfinckel's, Woodies, Hecht's, etc., delivered anything and everything promptly and free of charge. When we went downtown shopping, if we bought a pocketbook or a dress or whatever, we usually did not want to carry it home. We had it charged and sent! The smart shops on Connecticut Avenue were nearby and always interesting during an afternoon stroll.

22

WYOMING

2022 Columbia Road, N.W.; southeast corner of Columbia Road and Connecticut Avenue

ARCHITECT: B. Stanley Simmons, 1905; 1909 addition; 1911 addition

ORIGINAL APARTMENTS: 105 (34 one-bedrooms; 42 two-bedrooms; 28 three-bedrooms; 1 four-bedroom)

STATUS: opened as rental in 1906; converted to condo in 1982

The Wyoming was built in three stages between 1905 and 1911 by Lester A. Barr, a noted Washington real estate developer. Looking at the Wyoming today, one can clearly recognize the three sections: the original 1905 I-shaped building forms the present right front wing, the 1909 addition forms the right rear wing, and the final 1911 addition forms the left wing and central entrance pavilion. A fourth addition, designed by Simmons in 1922 to include seventy-five additional apartments on the left rear, was never built. Construction of the Wyoming in stages was not unique in Washington at this time. Investors were cautious in building large apartment houses that would not rent promptly, and additional sections were built only after earlier ones proved successful. Other examples of apartment houses built in sections include the Portland Flats, the Concord, the Portner Flats, the Ontario, and the Cordova (now the President Madison).

The architect of the Wyoming, B. Stanley Simmons (1871–1931), was a native of Charles County, Maryland, who moved to Washington at the age of ten with his family. When Simmons graduated from the Massachusetts Institute of Technology, he became one of the first native Washingtonians to be academically trained in architecture. The normal practice at that time was to apprentice in the office of a local architect. Practicing architecture

The original entrance to the Wyoming was through the large arch on the right. It was converted to two apartment windows when the present portico and central entrance were completed in 1911.

The intricate classical plasterwork in the lobby of the
Wyoming is the best of any Washington apartment house.

The original ground-floor plan of the Wyoming, showing the
location of the elaborate lobby and public dining room as well as a
number of large three- and four-bedroom apartments.

in the nation's capital for forty years, Simmons designed
a number of banks, office buildings, and schools. More
than sixty apartment houses came from his drafting board
between 1890 and 1926. Among his best-known Washington buildings were the Elks Club (now demolished),
Sacred Heart Catholic Church, National Metropolitan
Bank, the Barr Building, and the Columbia Country Club
in Chevy Chase. His more prominent apartment houses
included the DeSoto (demolished), the Mount Vernon
(demolished), the Embassy (1616 16th Street, N.W.), the
Cumberland (demolished), 1870 Wyoming Avenue, N.W.,
the Fairfax (originally an apartment-hotel, now the Ritz-
Carlton Hotel), and the Wyoming. He worked successfully
in a number of styles, including Romanesque, Colonial
Revival, classical, and Art Deco.

The Wyoming entrance pavilion, with its elaborate
iron and glass Beaux Arts–inspired marquee and its arched

porch, is framed by two pairs of massive stone columns
and crowned by a stone balustrade with four urns. Upon
entering, the visitor will today discover the finest surviving
Beaux Arts apartment house lobby in the city. Colors,
textures, forms, and materials, especially the plasterwork, were skillfully used by the architect and artisans
to create a unique space. This public space comprises a
long entrance hall that connects perpendicularly with the
lobby. The rear lobby includes a large square reception
room or public parlor, also embellished with an elaborately plastered ceiling. At each end of the lobby is located
one of the two passenger elevators. A public dining room,
the Wyoming Cafe, originally opened onto the west or
right side of the lobby. It was in operation from 1912
until the late 1940s, then converted into a large apartment. The impressive entrance hall, 22 feet wide by 29
feet long, with a 15-foot ceiling, has a delicate mosaic
floor with tiles of gold, rust, and green on a light gray
background. The hall is dominated by massive freestanding and engaged marble columns on each side. The walls
are covered with 9-foot-high oyster-colored marble wainscoting. The elaborate plaster ceiling design of garlands,
festoons, tobacco leaves, strings and tassels, modillions,
rosettes, and highly decorated escutcheons creates an air
of robust elegance. The same rich design continues through
the 19-by-73-foot-long lobby and the adjacent 26-by-32-
foot reception room, where many dances and debuts were
held before the Depression.

When completed in 1912, the 105 apartments in the
Wyoming ranged from two rooms and bath, with no kitchen,
to six rooms, reception hall, kitchen, and bath. Most of
the thirty-five large apartments, some 2,000 square feet
each, had three exposures. Although the rooms in many
apartments are spacious, their plans are often awkward
and there is little interior detailing of note. The one
exception is No. 702, an elegant six-room unit, originally
designed for Lester A. Barr, the builder and original
owner, as his residence. His family lived here from 1912
to 1939. This unit, intact today, has an elaborate foyer,
drawing room, and dining room, with beamed ceilings in
both rooms, parquet floors, and refined molding. It was
later occupied by the builder's son, John L. Barr, Sr.,
from 1946 until his death in 1969.

Before World War II many prominent political and

The most elaborately detailed apartment at the Wyoming is this top-floor unit, originally occupied by the builder and owner, Lester Barr.

military figures made their homes here, including Senators Albert B. Cummins and Walter F. George, Major and Mrs. Dwight D. Eisenhower, and Admirals Charles D. Sigsbee and William S. Benson. In the late 1940s it was the home of General Anthony C. McAuliffe, the hero of the Battle of the Bulge in World War II.

The Wyoming was threatened with demolition in 1979 when John L. Barr, Jr., attempted to sell it and two adjacent apartment houses, the Oakland and the Schuyler Arms. The three apartment houses were to be razed for expansion of the adjacent Washington Hilton Hotel. Numerous citizens groups, including the Kalorama Citizens Association, as well as many of the tenants, organized and lobbied against the sale. The District of Columbia Zoning Commission ruled against the Hilton's expansion, and the Wyoming was ultimately designated as an historic landmark, the exterior in 1981 and the lobby in 1983. The listing of interior spaces in the National Register is very unusual. Among Washington apartment houses, only the lobbies of the Wyoming and the Northumberland are so listed. Soon after, the Wyoming was sold to the development firm of Segerman, Keats, and Polinger for conversion to condominium ownership. The developers offered the apartments for sale to the public in 1982. During the process of development the interiors of approximately one-third of the apartments were renovated, with new kitchens and closets being added.

LIFE AT THE WYOMING

The most famous residents in its long history were Dwight and Mamie Eisenhower, who resided here in 1927–28 and again from 1929 to 1936, while Ike was stationed in Washington as an Army major. It was the Eisenhowers' longest full-time home until they left the White House for retirement to their farm in Gettysburg, Pennsylvania, in 1961. The biography of Eisenhower by Kenneth S. Davis, *Soldier of Democracy*, contains the following description of the Wyoming:

> He, Mamie and John were living at the Wyoming Apartments on the corner of Columbia Road and Connecticut Avenue. Quite a clique of army people lived here at the Wyoming, including Dwight's good friend Leonard Gerow whenever the latter had a Washington assignment. It was not one of the ultra-modern buildings which were springing up all over Washington in those years. On the contrary, it was a product of an earlier era and gave the impression of being much lived-in. The apartments were made up of unusually large comfortable, well-lighted rooms which pleased Mamie greatly. She had three bedrooms, a living room, a dining room, a large kitchen and bath—plenty of space for the heavy, beautiful furniture which she had by this time acquired (partly with Dwight's subsistence allowance, partly with her own money) and for Dwight's collection of oriental carpets.

23

WENDELL MANSIONS

2339 Massachusetts Avenue, N.W.; northeast corner of Massachusetts Avenue and Decatur Place

ARCHITECT: Edward H. Glidden, Sr., Baltimore, 1906

ORIGINAL APARTMENTS: 4 (each three-bedrooms)

STATUS: opened as rental in 1907; converted to co-op in 1968

Wendell Mansions was designed by Baltimore's leading apartment house architect, Edward Glidden, Sr.

Wendell Mansions, or simply "2339" as the residents of this co-op prefer today, contains four apartments above the ground floor, one per floor. The building is situated on Embassy Row and abuts the rear garden of the Woodrow Wilson House on S Street, N.W. The handsome facade of 2339 has a rusticated limestone base and a handsome shallow classical porch crowned by a balustrade. To the left, upon entering, is a small public parlor, which includes a beamed ceiling and a Beaux Arts–inspired stone fireplace, fluted pilasters, and paneled wainscoting. Opposite the main entrance is a spacious hallway, with paneled doors and intricate classical doorjambs, which leads directly back to the stairwell and the 1907 Otis elevator. This manually operated cab, enclosed in the original cast- and wrought-iron grille, is the oldest surviving example of its type in the city. A simple marble staircase encircles the elevator shaft. The janitor's apartment, with its separate entrance from Decatur Place, occupies the rear of the ground floor.

The apartments are carefully laid out with a clear separation of public space, master bedrooms, and service rooms. The public rooms in each apartment include an oval foyer, reception room, parlor, dining room, and library. To the rear of this space are three large master bedrooms, three baths, sitting room, and sun room. The

The dining room in each apartment at Wendell Mansions includes handsome paneled wainscoting, a decorative fireplace mantel, a beamed ceiling, and sliding or envelope doors.

This well-laid-out eighty-year-old plan of an apartment at Wendell Mansions, occupying one entire floor, still ranks among the best in the city.

rear wing, which is screened from the master bedrooms by a long narrow hall, contains the kitchen, pantry, three small servants' bedrooms, and servants' bath. The interior detailing found in the parlor and dining room are among the best in Washington for an apartment house—beamed ceilings, handsome mantels, wide cornice, paneled wainscoting, and French and envelope doors.

ARCHITECT EDWARD H. GLIDDEN, SR.

The architect, Edward H. Glidden, Sr., a native of Baltimore, was a son of William Glidden, founder of the Glidden Varnish Works. After studying architecture at the Ecole des Beaux Arts in Paris for four years, he returned to practice architecture in Baltimore in 1903. His career and style were similar to those of Washington's outstanding architect of the period, Jules H. de Sibour. Glidden designed a number of important buildings in Baltimore—houses, churches, schools, commercial buildings, and hospitals. He became a specialist, however, in first-class apartment houses, designing more than thirty in Baltimore before his death in 1924. These include the Homewood, the Washington, Canterbury Hall, Calvert Court, and the Wentworth. Wendell Mansions is his only known Washington building. His son, Edward H. Glidden, Jr., also an architect, was noted for his design of many impressive houses in the Baltimore neighborhoods of Guilford, Homeland, and Ruxton.

Opposite: A view from the front entrance hall into the lobby of Wendell Mansions.

24

CHEVY CHASE

5863 Chevy Chase Parkway, N.W.; northeast corner of Chevy Chase Circle and Chevy Chase Parkway

ARCHITECT: Leon E. Dessez, 1909

APARTMENTS: 16 (8 one-bedrooms; 8 two-bedrooms)

STATUS: opened as rental in 1910

Prominently located on the east side of Chevy Chase Circle, only fifty feet from the Maryland state line, the Chevy Chase is one of the smaller of the dozen Spanish Colonial style apartment buildings erected in the city before World War I. As such, it has a stucco facade, wide eaves, red-tile roof, and an elaborate plaster baroque entablature over the main entrance and the staircase hall window above. These features are the most expressive of

The Chevy Chase remains one of the best-designed four-story walk-up apartment buildings in Washington.

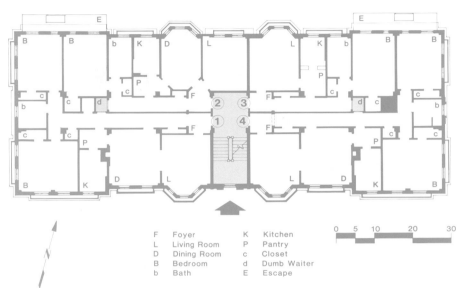

The two large apartments on each floor of the Chevy Chase have three exposures.

F	Foyer	K	Kitchen
L	Living Room	P	Pantry
D	Dining Room	c	Closet
B	Bedroom	d	Dumb Waiter
b	Bath	E	Escape

0 5 10   20   30

the Spanish Colonial style for a Washington apartment building of the period. It was designed in 1909 as a freestanding suburban apartment building with spacious lawns on all sides. At the time it was built, very few residences existed in this immediate neighborhood. It was the first true suburban Washington apartment building.

Even though this residence has no public lobby or elevator, it is important for its handsome facade design as well as for its floor plan. Half of the sixteen apartments are large four-room units, each with three exposures. Additional light fills apartments above the first floor through the pair of oriel windows designed for both the front and rear facades. The windows on the second and fourth floors, with their handsome balconies, are considerably taller than those on the first and third floors. Apartments at the west end of the building overlook Chevy Chase Circle, with its elegant circular fountain and abundance of trees.

The Chevy Chase's two entrances, opposite one another, bisect the center of the building. The staircase hall and landings have marble floors and marble wainscoting throughout. Each floor has four apartments; the larger two-bedroom units face the front, onto Chevy Chase Parkway, while the two one-bedroom units face Western Avenue in the rear. The handsome chestnut woodwork in all of the apartments was originally stained a dark walnut color. Only one apartment, No. 21, occupied by Miss Louise O'Neal since 1929, remains with this original

finish. The remainder have been painted white, a custom that first became standard in Washington apartment houses in the early 1920s. The dumbwaiters, with their vertically sliding doors, are still located in the long hall opposite the kitchen door in each unit. The basement has the standard laundry, storage rooms, and janitor's apartment. Although Miss O'Neal's residence in the Chevy Chase exceeds fifty-five years, that of the janitor, Ralph Crawford, sets the record for the building. He was born here before World War I when his father, Emmet, was the first janitor. Ralph Crawford succeeded his father in 1935 and remains in charge of the building today.

The land adjacent to the Chevy Chase to the east was purchased in 1911 by the newly formed Catholic church, the Shrine of the Most Blessed Sacrament. The congregation, half in Washington and half in Maryland, compromised on a location, building a small wooden chapel next to Chevy Chase Circle as close to the boundary line as possible. This early building was replaced by the present handsome stone church in 1925. The congregation purchased the Chevy Chase apartment building in 1962 in order to protect the church property against possible future development. Blessed Sacrament, which continues to operate the Chevy Chase, is dedicated to preserving its important original exterior and interior architectural design.

The second-floor units at the Chevy Chase have the added advantage of French windows.

ARCHITECT LEON E. DESSEZ

The architect of the Chevy Chase, Leon E. Dessez (1858–1918), was born to European immigrants—a French father and a German mother, who settled in Washington in the 1850s. His father, an engineer and builder, worked for the Confederacy on military fortifications, but the family remained in Washington during the Civil War years. Young Dessez entered a career in architecture at the age of 19, in 1877, when he began work in the office of Hornblower and Poindexter, soon to become Hornblower and Marshall and one of the city's most prominent late-Victorian architectural firms. He worked as an architectural assistant on the completion of the Washington Monument and then on architectural projects at the Washington Navy Yard. After nine years of architectural work in other offices, he opened his own firm in 1886, in the Corcoran Building at 15th Street and Pennsylvania Avenue, N.W., where many Washington architects were located. In that year he and a handful of other local architects founded the Washington chapter of the American Institute of Architects.

Dessez left a marked impact on Washington as the leading architect in the newly developing Maryland suburb of Chevy Chase. He was the director and chief architect of the Chevy Chase Land Company for twenty-five years, from its founding in 1893 until his death. Although he specialized in large houses, such as the Francis Newlands house on Chevy Chase Circle and the Admiral's House (now the Vice President's House) on Observatory Circle, he designed many other building types.

Before his death in 1918, Dessez designed a variety of important buildings, including the Raleigh Hotel, the D.C. Prison in Occoquan, Virginia, Gallinger Hospital, the hospital at the Soldiers Home, and many fire stations, such as Engine Company No. 2 at 719 12th Street, N.W. (razed in 1986), as well as numerous freestanding houses. Dessez's four Washington apartment houses were designed between 1899 and 1901.

25

DRESDEN

2126 Connecticut Avenue, N.W.; southwest corner of Connecticut Avenue and Kalorama Road

ARCHITECT: Albert H. Beers, 1909

ORIGINAL APARTMENTS: 56 (7 one-bedrooms; 22 two-bedrooms; 14 three-bedrooms; 13 four-bedrooms)

STATUS: opened as rental in 1910; converted to condo in 1974

In 1909 developer Harry Wardman built the Dresden and its sister building, the Northumberland—his two most elaborate apartment houses—in the Georgian Revival style. Both boast outstanding woodwork and plasterwork. The elaborate parquet floors, intricate door and windowjambs, and plaster moldings were so expensive that Wardman never attempted such fine interiors on any of his many subsequent apartment houses.

The outstanding feature of the Dresden is its "rounded" facade, which ranks as one of the most distinctive and handsome in the city. Actually, the building is U-shaped—not rounded—with a rear court. Although the northeast corner of the Dresden is curved, the floor plan indicates that the other corners are square. Because of the curve, the rooms in three of the eight tiers of apartments in the building are slightly pie-shaped.

The first-floor facades on Connecticut Avenue and Kalorama Road are delineated by richly rusticated limestone, pierced by a range of eighteen massive recessed arched windows accentuated by bold scroll keystones. The rhythm of these windows successfully carries the front facade facing Connecticut Avenue around the corner to the side facade, opposite the Chinese Embassy on Kalorama Road. The verticality of the Dresden is established by the tiers of single and paired windows that rise above the great arched first-floor windows. The limestone window surrounds set against the red brick simulate a lacework pattern when seen from a distance. The bold stone stringcourse above the sixth floor defines the top story with its shallow cornice and roofdeck railing and lamp posts. The lack of a cornice at the roof level was unusual for any apartment house at this time, and although it may look today as if something is missing, the facade was actually designed without the cornice. Perhaps the architect felt that the elaborate windows were adequate decoration and that a wide cornice would be "too much icing on the cake."

The visitor ascends a short flight of steps to arrive at the front desk in the small low-ceilinged lobby with handsome marble wainscoting. The adjacent modest parlor is located opposite the two passenger elevators. Immediately in view are the extremely wide public halls, their floors laid in white tile with maroon Greek-key borders—a standard Wardman design feature. As in the Northumberland, the largest apartments were located at the ends of the U-shaped residence. The most impressive apartments were located in the No. 5 tier, with seven rooms, two baths, a large reception hall, kitchen, and servant's room and bath. The No. 2 tier apartments have the best exposure because they are located on the south-

The "rounded" facade of the Dresden, with its unusual Georgian Revival stone window surrounds, remains one of the most handsome in Washington.

Detail of one of the arched windows set into the first-floor rusticated limestone base of the Dresden.

west corner. The residents of several of these apartments have opened the wall between the parlor and the chamber to create a spectacular space with the dining room and two drawing rooms opening into one another.

The fifty-six-unit Dresden, which cost $250,000 to build in 1909, was sold by Harry Wardman for $500,000 in 1910. In 1916 it was sold for the same amount to the American Security and Trust Company, as trustees of the Benjamin H. Warder estate. The Dresden remained relatively unchanged until it was converted from rental to condominium status in 1974. At that time Washington architect Peter Voghi made a number of changes to the floor plan. Space was taken from the rear bedroom of the No. 2 tier on each floor to create a small communal laundry room and trash room. All but one of the largest apartments, located in the No. 5 tier, were subdivided into two apartments. The original brass dining room chandeliers, similar to those still in place at the Northumberland, were unfortunately removed and discarded. At the time of conversion the small apartments, with 874 square feet, sold for $37,500, while the largest unit, with 3,175 square feet, sold for $135,000.

Since the Dresden's property included a small lawn in the rear, it was possible to convert this area into a parking lot for eighteen cars, a rare feature for a pre–World War I apartment house. During the conversion to condominium ownership, the roof garden was rebuilt into one of the most handsome of any Washington apartment house. Further changes were made by the Dresden's board of directors in 1983 when the public halls and lobby were redecorated and recarpeted.

ILLUSTRIOUS RESIDENTS

Many of the long-time residents bought their apartments and stayed when conversion to condominiums occurred. These included Mrs. Nellie Tayloe Ross, the nation's first woman governor (Wyoming, 1925–27) and later the director of the United States Mint for twenty years during the administrations of Franklin D. Roosevelt and Harry S. Truman. Others included Mrs. Helen McCain Smith, social secretary to Mrs. Richard M. Nixon, and Colonel and Mrs. George H. Millholland. Mrs. Millholland was the former Alice Wardman, elder daughter of the builder and original owner of the Dresden, Harry Wardman.

Another interesting long-term resident who still lives at the Dresden is Helen J. Sioussat. Her great-great-grandfather, Jean Pierre Sioussat, was brought to Washington from Paris by President James Madison in 1812 to become the first manager (today called the "chief usher") of the White House. While in this position, he helped Dolley Madison save the Gilbert Stuart portrait of George Washington when the British burned the mansion in 1814. Following several years in business, as well as a year on the stage headlining with a partner doing Spanish adagio dancing, Mrs. Sioussat, as she is now known, embarked on a career in radio. She became assistant to Phillip H. Lord, radio personality and producer of the "G-Men" and "Gang Busters" radio series. The following year she moved to CBS, becoming the first woman executive of an American broadcasting network, where she remained for twenty-six years. She succeeded Edward R. Murrow as director of the department of public affairs, which maintained contact for CBS with Congress and the White House. She also edited the CBS quarterly digest *Talks*. Mrs. Sioussat,

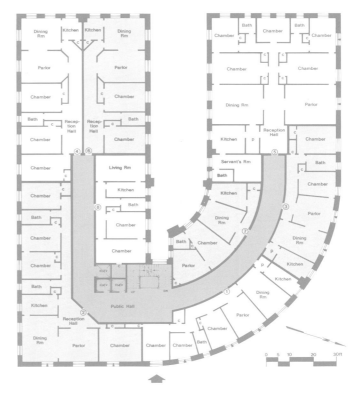

Although it appears to be round, the Dresden is actually U-shaped with a rear court.

author of *Mikes Don't Bite*, has lived at the Dresden since 1958 and currently serves as chairman of the board of directors.

Among the most interesting of all Dresden residents was Julia Grant Cantacuzene, the granddaughter of President U. S. Grant, who died at the Dresden in 1975 at the age of ninety-nine. Born in the White House in 1876, while her father, Major General Frederick Dent Grant, was fighting in the Indian Wars in the West, she grew up in Vienna where her father later served as the American minister to the Court of Emperor Franz Joseph. In 1899 at the Newport home of her aunt, Mrs. Potter Palmer of Chicago, Julia Grant was married to Prince Michael Cantacuzene, chief military adjutant to Grand Duke Nicholas, the grandson of Tsar Nicholas I. For the following eighteen years she lived on her husband's vast estates near St. Petersburg and in the Crimea until the Russian Revolution forced them to escape to Sweden.

In this Dresden apartment, double drawing rooms open onto the dining room (in the distance) to create an impressive open space.

Princess Cantacuzene became a frequent lecturer and the author of three books, all relating to her life in Russia before and during the Revolution. As a popular lecturer, she was an outspoken foe of Communism as well as of the New Deal during the 1930s and 1940s. In 1934, Madame Cantacuzene (sometimes also addressed as Princess, which she preferred) regained the American citizenship she had given up at her marriage thirty-five years earlier.

ARCHITECT ALBERT H. BEERS

During the last seven years of his life, 1904–11, Albert H. Beers resided in Washington and served as the chief architect for Harry Wardman. Before coming to Washington he lived in Fairfield, Connecticut, and worked in Bridgeport. His seventy-one apartment houses are located in many sections of the city, including Georgetown, 16th Street, Kalorama Heights, Mount Pleasant, the Columbia Road area, and Capitol Hill. In addition to the Dresden, he designed its sister building, the Northumberland, and many other apartment houses, including the Toronto, the Brighton, the Carlton at 2101 N Street, N.W., and another at 2131 California Street, N.W. Seven unusual small four-story walk-up apartment houses that he designed in 1909 are the Ohio, the Rochester, and the Detroit at 1436–1440 Meridian Place, N.W., and on the same block, the Marguerite, the Isabella, the Duquesne, and the Clarion at 1477–1495 Newton Street, N.W. Designed for Harry Wardman, these eclectic apartment houses combine elements of both the Arts and Crafts movement and the Mediterranean style.

26

DUMBARTON COURT

1657 31st Street, N.W.; east side of 31st Street between Que and R streets

ARCHITECT: George S. Cooper, 1909

ORIGINAL APARTMENTS: 35 (8 efficiencies without kitchens; 3 efficiencies with kitchens; 8 one-bedrooms without dining rooms; 12 one-bedrooms with dining rooms; 4 two-bedrooms)

STATUS: opened as rental in 1910; converted to co-op in 1920

In the late nineteenth and early twentieth centuries, more than a dozen small apartment buildings were erected in Georgetown. None were first-class "apartment houses," since they lacked lobbies and elevators. At the same time, in the 1890s, several large Victorian houses, such as the Dodge House on the southeast corner of 30th and Que streets, N.W., were converted into flats. A former antebellum private school for girls at 1305–1311 30th Street, N.W., had been converted into flats as early as 1870. Now known as the Colonial Apartments, this structure is the oldest building in the city that has been continuously used for apartments. None of these structures, however, could ever compete in either size or prestige with the great apartment houses erected before World War I on upper 14th Street (in the vicinity of Florida Avenue), lower Connecticut Avenue (south of the Taft Bridge), Columbia Road (between 16th Street and Connecticut Avenue, N.W.), or in the Dupont Circle neighborhood.

Georgetown at that time was not considered a fashionable location for smart apartment houses. Those built before 1940 were all middle class and could not be considered luxury buildings. They lacked grand lobbies, elevators, and large units. Of the ones built in this early period, however, there is no question that Dumbarton Court stands out as the best surviving example, preserved in its basic original condition.

Dumbarton Court was planned and originally built as an investment by Washington architect George S. Cooper. For its site Cooper purchased the old Herr estate on the east side of 31st Street midway between two great historic Georgetown mansions, Tudor Place to the southwest and the Linthicum estate, now Dumbarton Oaks, to the north.

Within weeks after Cooper acquired this spacious lot, 100 feet wide and 200 feet deep, he demolished the abandoned brick Herr House for the site of his new four-story Mediterranean-inspired apartment house. Abundant light and air were provided by his H-shaped design with front and rear courts. The austerity of its facade is partially relieved by four features: the red-tile hipped roof with its wide bracketed eaves, the rusticated first-floor base, the slightly projecting central pavilion, and the splayed lintels over the windows. The spacious front and rear lawns were unusual features at a time when most Washington apartment houses had little open space around them.

The interior had neither a lobby nor an elevator. Entrance was to a small vestibule with brass mailboxes and speaking tubes (all still in original condition). The thirty-five apartments ranged in size from two to four rooms. Corner apartments had the advantage of sleeping porches, which have all now been enclosed. Many of the original features, such as decorative fireplace mantels

Front facade of Dumbarton Court with its red-tile Spanish Colonial hipped roof.

and dumbwaiters, remain in place. Although originally built as a walk-up, Dumbarton Court now has a small elevator, located in the north hallway. The building converted from rental to cooperative status in 1920.

ARCHITECT GEORGE S. COOPER

Practically unknown today, architect George S. Cooper (1864–1929) was a prominent and prolific local architect between 1884 and 1910 when he retired from practice to manage his extensive real estate holdings. Born in Washington, Cooper served as a draftsman for several local architectural firms—including Gray and Page, Hornblower and Marshall, and A. B. Mullett—before opening his own practice in 1884. In 1885 he joined with B. Carlyle Fenwick to form the firm of Cooper and Fenwick. After three years the partnership was dissolved and Cooper resumed his architectural practice alone.

Cooper designed a number of important commercial buildings, including the Washington Riding Academy at 22nd and P streets, N.W., the Davidson Office Building at 1413 G Street, N.W., and the Bond Building at New York Avenue and 14th Street, N.W., one of the city's most important early Beaux Arts office buildings. He was noted for designing dozens of important rowhouses in the Dupont Circle and Logan Circle areas in the 1890s. These include the Burnett House at 1205 New Hampshire Avenue, N.W., the Bulkley House at 1216 16th Street, N.W., and his own house at 1807 R Street, N.W. Cooper was also the architect, developer, and owner of many houses along Bradley Lane in Chevy Chase. He was best known, however, for designing twenty-four apartment houses between 1892 and 1909, of which the Balfour is the most prominent. Many of these were three stories with two flats per floor. In addition to Dumbarton Court, these include the Lafayette, the Berwyn, the Oregon, the Helena, the Onondaga, the Oneida, the Montrose, the Peb-

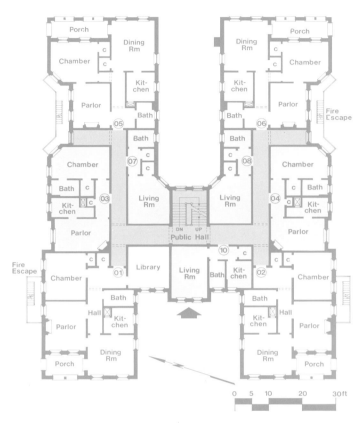

Dumbarton Court was one of the first Washington apartment buildings designed with an H-shaped plan.

have this view!" The owner, a lady whom we privately called "Hettie Green," was asking $7,000, an outrageous price for a four-room apartment in those days. We bought it and never regretted it. Later my father was to buy two other apartments in the building as an investment.

On a summer night when we were allowed to stay up until after dark, we all gathered around the black janitor who told us ghost stories with such dramatic flair and terrifying intensity that we practically flew through the halls and up the steps when it was time for bed.

As in all cooperative apartment buildings and modern-day condominiums, there is a certain intimacy among owners brought about by their common investment and interest in the welfare of the building. At Dumbarton Court each owner took his or her turn in various offices on the board of directors. There were regular meetings of the board, and occasional special meetings when the need arose for majority vote on a large expenditure or when a new tenant sought approval. I remember my parents speculating as to whether or not the prospective tenant might "throw wild parties."

One time my father settled a particular problem without benefit of a board meeting. One of the tenants (an owner would never have done this!) moved and left a cat which had become wild and lived in the basement where kind ladies threw it a daily ration of scraps. This went on

bleton Flats, the Marietta, the Gladstone, the Hawarden, and the Analoston. Most were located in the 14th Street, N.W., apartment house corridor.

LIFE AT DUMBARTON COURT

An early resident of the building, Mrs. Katharine Brown Ivison, provided information on life there between the two World Wars:

I went to live at Dumbarton Court when I was six years old. I remember my parents taking me with them to look at an apartment which had come up for sale on the fourth floor in front overlooking beautiful Tudor Place, the estate belonging to Armistead Peter III. I remember my mother saying, "I don't care what this apartment costs, I've got to

Many pre–World War I apartment buildings in Washington, such as Dumbarton Court, possess elaborate bathroom tiles.

for weeks until there were more fleas in the basement than one cat could accommodate. This meant that all who ventured down the basement steps returned covered with fleas. The SPCA was called, but never could get near the cat. I am sure that in these present times there would be some efficient, legal way of getting rid of a wild cat in the basement, but my father—a lover of animals, let me hasten to add—solved it his way. He shot it. Practically every occupant in the building rushed out into the halls simultaneously calling "What was that!" Dad was an excellent shot, and the cat was mercifully relieved of its miserable existence, but it took my father a long time to live it down. The elderly ladies who had been feeding the cat ignored him for months.

As I grew up I often had the feeling that there was more interest in my welfare than I needed. I could handle one set of parents, but a whole building full of well-meaning Dutch uncles and aunts was sometimes too much. An innocent good-night kiss after a date was not enhanced by a squeaking door down the hall. But that very same intimacy made us all rally to each other's support when the need arose, a death in the family, financial problems, etc.

I can remember when electric refrigeration came to Dumbarton Court, a unique system in which all the refrigerators were hooked into a common compressor in the basement. Initially, this must have been very expensive to install, but I suppose it was ultimately more economical than individual compressors.

I shall always remember that neighborhood as one of the most ideal locations in Georgetown. With Montrose Park nearby for tennis and recreation, and what was then an excellent public school system within walking distance, what better place could there be for bringing up a child during the Depression. My own children were brought up in a comfortable home in Chevy Chase with more material advantages than I ever had, but I'm sure they never had more fun!

27

1509 16TH STREET, N.W.

East side of 16th Street between P and Church streets

ARCHITECT: Averill, Hall, and Adams, 1909

ORIGINAL APARTMENTS: 7 (2 three-bedrooms; 5 four-bedrooms)

STATUS: opened as rental in 1910; converted to rooming house in 1932; converted to hotel in 1939;
converted to youth hostel in 1971; converted to office building in 1981

An early view of 1509 16th Street, ca. 1915.

This very narrow seven-story red-brick and limestone apartment house was designed in the Georgian Revival style with one apartment per floor. This feature was unusual but not unique for Washington apartment houses. Other luxury apartment houses had one apartment per floor, including the Warder, Wendell Mansions, the McCormick, and, later, 2120 Kalorama Road, N.W. But the plan was considered of sufficient importance that the *American Architect* magazine carried a photograph and three pages of drawings of 1509 16th Street, N.W., in an article in 1911. The handsome facade has a rusticated limestone first-floor base. The body of the front facade between the second and sixth floors is embellished with massive tripartite windows with bold limestone surrounds, while the top floor is emphasized by a limestone face and a bold cornice with classical detailing. As a major luxury building, 1509 is unusual for Washington in that it was situated within the block rather than on a corner.

Upon entering, the visitor passed through a small entrance hall trimmed in Caen stone (a very soft stone secured from Caen, in southwest France), with a vaulted ceiling in gold and fresco. The main staircase, with marble steps and cast-iron balustrade, was located on the left and the elaborate elevator cage of iron and bronze grillwork on the right. Servants used a centrally located ser-

Detail of one of the limestone and terra cotta window surrounds on the front facade of 1509 16th Street.

Each of the drawing rooms in the apartments at 1509 16th Street has a handsome mantel featuring a sunflower-motif frieze.

vice elevator and servants' stairs that connected to the pantry of each apartment.

The single apartment on each floor contained a large foyer, a drawing room and a dining room separated by mahogany envelope doors, a library, four principal bedrooms, two baths, balcony, kitchen, two pantries, three servants' rooms, and servants' bath. Although the shape of the building dictated a long hall, the three areas of the apartment were skillfully isolated—public rooms facing 16th Street, principal bedrooms facing north, and the service core facing south.

The most interesting surviving rooms in terms of interior detailing are the drawing room, 22 by 17 feet, and the dining room, each with an ornamental plaster

cornice and elaborate classical fireplace with gas logs. Both of these rooms were prominently located on the front facing 16th Street. Of almost equal interest was the library, located on the north or left central side of each apartment. Each included a gas log fireplace, built-in glazed cabinets, a wall safe, elaborate beamed ceiling, and wrought-iron Arts and Crafts chandelier and wall sconces. The two pantries were also unusual even in large apartments: one reserved for serving and the other for storage of china and glassware.

In 1931 the effects of the Depression began the slow but constant decline of 16th Street as a prime residential address in the city. Many owners could no longer afford to maintain the large houses or renters the expense of extra-large apartments. This mood is mirrored in the fate of 1509. Its original affluent residents, such as Senator John B. Foraker, had long since departed; however, the original owner, the once-famous painter and etcher John Taylor Arms, continued to live nearby during most of the decade at 1800 New Hampshire Avenue. Because of the Depression, the building became a rooming house in 1932 and, during World War II, the Alturos Hotel. It further deteriorated, becoming a youth hostel—the Christian Inn—in 1971. After forty-seven years of neglect, the landmark building was sold in 1979. Ironically, lower 16th Street, between Scott Circle on the south and Meridian Hill Park on the north, had by then started its slow but steady comeback as a revitalized historic residential district, close to the downtown commercial area. The old maxim that "poverty is the best friend of preservation" is epitomized along the 16th Street corridor: almost all of it remains intact.

The new owner, Jeffrey Cohen, commissioned the Washington architectural firm of Mariani and Associates to convert the building to offices. Changes involved complete removal of the service stairs and elevator, as well as the main public staircase from the lobby to the second floor, and construction of a new brick-enclosed elevator and stairs on the north central facade facing the alley to the left of the entrance. Residential neighbors pressured the new owner into using an exterior red-brick elevator shaft, more harmonious with the original design than a proposed all-glass structure. The new elevator was installed to open into the library of each apartment. Mariani and Associates restored the fireplace mantels, cornices, and other details in the drawing room and dining room as well as part of the details of the library of each apartment. The remainder of each floor was gutted for new office space. The front facade, with its elaborate iron and glass marquee and cornice, was completely restored in compliance with regulations pertaining to the 16th Street, N.W., historic district, which now extends from Massachusetts Avenue to Florida Avenue. Even though all rooms of each apartment became office space, the developer and his architect sensitively saved the most important elements of original design in their modern conversion.

Each floor of 1509 16th Street consisted of one ten-room apartment.

28

NORTHUMBERLAND

2039 New Hampshire Avenue, N.W.; southeast corner of New Hampshire Avenue and V Street

ARCHITECT: Albert H. Beers, 1909

ORIGINAL APARTMENTS: 68 (14 efficiencies; 33 one-bedrooms; 7 two-bedrooms; 14 three-bedrooms)

STATUS: opened as rental in 1910; converted to co-op in 1920

The Northumberland remains one of the best-preserved pre–World War I apartment houses in Washington. Because of its notable exterior and interior design, it was listed in the National Register in 1980. The principal feature of the Northumberland's Georgian Revival facade is its three horizontal bands. This treatment, with the lower and upper bands in buff brick and the middle band in red brick, is unique in Washington. On the front facade each of the buff-brick bands includes a two-story-high range of arched windows, termed "Florentine windows," embellished with Gibbs surrounds, on the ground and top floors. The central body of the facade, which includes the third through the fifth floors, is laid in a contrasting dark red tapestry brick, emphasizing the horizontality of the structure. A second notable feature on the front facade is the handsome recessed classical porch, with its two pairs of Doric columns and simple entablature crowned by a pair of urns, and the pair of cast-iron wall sconces mounted on the sides of the porch.

The 14-foot-high rectangular lobby is marbleized in a muted yellow resembling Siena marble. A massive decorative fireplace mantel is located at each end. Beside each fireplace a short flight of steps leads to the first-floor apartments. A cast-iron staircase with iron balustrades, opposite the front entrance, sweeps upward from the cen-

The Renaissance-inspired facade of the Northumberland with its Georgian Revival details is divided into three horizontal levels with the lower and upper buff-brick bands embellished with Florentine windows—that is, two-story arched window surrounds.

An unusual feature among Washington apartment houses is the Northumberland's recessed entrance porch, framed by its classical portico.

ter rear of the lobby to the seventh floor. The semicircular staircase branches to each side from landings set midway between each floor. The first landing, visible from the lobby, is embellished with three large stained glass windows, each with the letter N set in the center of a shield which is flanked by a pair of torches. To the left of the staircase in the lobby is the front desk with a switchboard, which has been operated twenty-four hours a day since the Northumberland opened in 1910. Behind the front desk is a small mail-sorting room with a large standing safe.

This U-shaped residence with a rear courtyard originally contained sixty-eight apartments ranging in size from efficiencies to six-room units, each with kitchen and bath. The curving public corridors have unique plaster coved ceilings and white tile floors defined by maroon Greek-key borders. The apartments themselves have a number of unusual features. All living rooms, including the efficiencies, originally included decorative fireplace mantels, but with the passage of time most have been removed and only three remain. Every room, including the kitchens, has parquet floors laid in red and white oak with mahogany borders. Each kitchen originally had a trash chute—now all long closed off—that connected to the basement. The original solid brass four-light chandeliers with crystal prisms remain in place in most of the

View from the lower landing of the massive iron staircase of the Northumberland into the
lobby with its marbleized columns and walls decorated for Christmas 1981.

dining rooms. All apartments contain wall safes, usually found in the bedrooms and next to the window jamb for concealment by the curtains, located in the thick outer wall that would survive the longest in a serious fire.

The windows are 6 feet square on the two street facades, and 5 feet square elsewhere, providing an abundance of light and excellent circulation. Large, flat-headed arches in many apartments connect the long hall with the

living room and often the living room with the dining room. The living rooms are embellished with wide, coved plaster cornices of varying designs. Most of the white tiled bathrooms still contain their original massive nickel-plated showerheads set over paw-foot tubs, the oldest surviving examples in a Washington apartment house.

Named after the county bordering Scotland in builder Harry Wardman's native England, the Northumberland

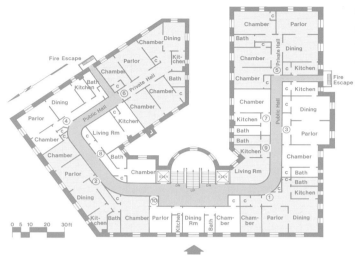

Each of the ten tiers of apartments at the Northumberland varies in plan and size, with the largest units at the ends of the two wings. Most of the early, U-shaped apartment houses had their principal staircase in the center of the curve, to provide better air circulation throughout the building during the humid summer months.

was built just one block east of 16th Street, N.W., then the city's Embassy Row. Today the neighborhood remains architecturally intact—rich in important Romanesque Revival and Beaux Arts houses. When the Northumberland opened in 1910, however, the area was only lightly built up. The principal building was Boundary Castle, the imposing 1888 Victorian stone house of Senator and Mrs. John Henderson a block northwest at 16th Street and Florida Avenue. It was Mrs. Henderson who built some dozen great classical houses in the neighborhood and rented them to foreign governments as embassies so that 16th Street would be the most elegant thoroughfare in the nation's capital.

Although both the nearby Boundary Castle and the Portner Flats have been replaced with more modern buildings, the other landmarks remain intact. At 16th and V streets, N.W., one block west, stands the 1908 red-brick Georgian Revival mansion of Chief Justice Charles Evans Hughes, many years later the Bulgarian Embassy, and converted to an office building in 1984. At the corner of 15th and V streets, still in a state of perfect preservation, is the impressive granite Gothic Revival St. Paul's Roman

Catholic Church (now St. Paul's and St. Augustine's), which was known originally as "the church of the diplomats" since most Catholic diplomats worshiped here before World War I. Another important landmark is the Congressional Club, a social club for wives of senators and members of Congress, at 16th and U streets, an elegant Beaux Arts structure built in 1914 on land donated by Mrs. Henderson.

In 1914, only four years after the Northumberland was completed, it was sold by Wardman to William J. Kehoe for $375,000. The following year Kehoe purchased the five vacant lots on New Hampshire Avenue to the southwest of the Northumberland for $23,000. Following World War I he employed architect George N. Ray to prepare plans for a new seven-story Georgian Revival apartment house, Hampton Court, for this site. In 1925, the same year that Hampton Court was under construction, another large apartment house, in the Tudor Revival style, was built on the vacant triangular block on the northeast side of the Northumberland. Known as Wakefield Hall, the latter building effectively filled the last vacant land in the area.

In 1920, following rapid inflation and rent increases after World War I, at least twenty-six luxury rental apartment houses in Washington were converted to co-ops. The Northumberland was among the first, converted by the building's third owners, developers Clarence C. Calhoun and James Sharp. They sold the building to the residents for $480,000. The original prices ranged from $4,000 for efficiency apartments to $11,800 for the largest six-room units. At that time the public dining room was closed and sold as a residential apartment, No. 106.

Located along Embassy Row, the Northumberland remained a fashionable address until the Great Depression. The neighborhood's slow, almost imperceptible decline remained unnoticed by most Washingtonians. Because of demographic changes in the 1950s and riots nearby in 1968, a number of embassies on 16th Street and Meridian Hill Park moved to Massachusetts Avenue, N.W. As a result of all of these changes, the prices of co-op apartments at the Northumberland continued to decline. In 1970, for instance, the largest apartments were selling for only $15,000 each.

Conditions in the neighborhood slowly began to im-

The elaborate 1909 parquet flooring in the Northumberland is red and white oak with mahogany borders that provide contrast in texture and color, as seen in the wide hallway of an apartment in the No. 6 tier.

prove about 1975, when many young couples and singles started moving into the Dupont Circle neighborhood to purchase, restore, and enjoy life in the historic Victorian and Edwardian rowhouses. Rehabilitation of a number of historic apartment houses near the Northumberland—such as the Brittany in 1980, the Balfour in 1985, and Haddon Hall in 1986—also improved the area. By 1986 the preservation movement that had spread outward from Dupont Circle in the mid-1970s reached this neighborhood. The opening of the new municipal office building at 14th and U streets, N.W., in 1986 also helped generate renewed prosperity for an old neighborhood. Throughout the period of decline, however, most of the shareholders stayed at the Northumberland, so that the building itself remained stable and escaped unsympathetic remodeling.

The few physical changes to the Northumberland occurred between 1957 and 1964 with implementation of the new District of Columbia fire code. At that time the original revolving front door was replaced, the staircase landings on each floor were enclosed with walls to prevent the spread of smoke, the glass panels on the upper half

of each apartment door were replaced with wood, and the louvered outer doors of the main entrances to most apartments were removed. During this same period the original hand-operated wrought-iron passenger elevator cab designed with open grilles was replaced by a new automatic cab. Summer canvas window awnings disappeared, as most residents had installed air conditioning units.

Before World War II, the Northumberland had many prominent residents—six members of Congress; several judges; Theodore Tate, Treasurer of the United States under President Coolidge; noted explorer Colonel Ashley McKinley, who accompanied Admiral Richard Byrd to the Antarctic and wrote two books about the expedition; and General Lacey Murrow, brother of newscaster Edward R. Murrow. Louisiana Senator Allen J. Ellender (1890–1972) resided there from 1936 to 1943. During his thirty-five years in Congress, Ellender became chairman of the Senate Agriculture and Appropriations committees and president pro tempore of the Senate. He indulged in his favorite hobby of Creole cooking in his Northumberland galley kitchen for his many guests.

Many Northumberland apartments have arches between the dining and living rooms, lighted by unusual 6-foot-square windows.

One of the most interesting events to take place in the Northumberland in recent years was the use of the front facade and lobby for filming by director Francis Ford Coppola for the movie *Gardens of Stone* in July 1986. Based on the novel of the same name, the movie portrays an Army sergeant, played by James Caan, who is reas-

The original stock certificate for an apartment in the Northumberland, which, along with more than twenty-five other rental apartment houses, was converted to co-op status in 1920 because of post–World War I inflation.

signed from Viet Nam to the honor guard at Arlington Cemetery. He resides in an old-fashioned Washington apartment house, where he falls in love with another resident, a reporter for the *Washington Post* played by Anjelica Huston. Another historic building on the same block, the 1914 Congressional Club, was used for filming the ballroom scene in the movie. A second film, *Broadcast News*, starring William Hurt, was shot in apartment No. 301 at the Northumberland in the summer of 1987.

[Several other films have included scenes from Washington apartment houses. The Carlyn was included in the 1962 film *Advise and Consent* starring Henry Fonda and directed by Otto Preminger. In 1949 the Biltmore was included in *All the King's Men* with actors Broderick Crawford and Mercedes McCambridge. Paramount Pictures included the Carlton at the southeast corner of Connecticut and Cathedral avenues, N.W., in *The Man Who Wasn't There* in 1983. In 1987 *The Assassination* was filmed at the Watergate. Usually the facade and the lobby are actually filmed on location, while the apartment unit itself is built on the set.]

29

2852 ONTARIO ROAD, N.W.

Southwest corner of Ontario Road and Ontario Place

ARCHITECT: Appleton P. Clark, Jr., 1909

ORIGINAL APARTMENTS: 6 (6 three-bedrooms)

STATUS: opened as co-op in 1910; converted to rental ca. 1948; converted to co-op in 1975

This three-story V-shaped residence located at the corner of Ontario Road and Ontario Place has the distinction of being the second apartment house built as a cooperative in Washington, preceded only by the 1891 Concord at New Hampshire Avenue and Swann Street, N.W. (The 1891 Concord was razed in 1962 for the present mundane International Style apartment house of the same name.) The earliest mention of 2852 Ontario Road, N.W., appeared in the *Evening Star* on 16 August 1909:

> Carrying out a novel co-operative building scheme, a coterie of prominent Washington folk are engaged in constructing an apartment house in Ontario Street, opposite the Ontario apartments, in which they plan to live in peaceful seclusion from the harrying landlord and the bumptious janitor. The building will be ready for occupancy about 1 October. Members of the company, who will also be tenants of the apartments, are: George F. Bowerman, Dr. L. A. Bauer, Charles E. Edgerton, Dr. Victor E. Clark, Mrs. G. T. Summer, and L. D. Underwood. The building will cost about $40,000 and the details of arrangement and of the decorating of each apartment will be under the direction of the respective tenants. Each occupant will pay rent to the company, and in turn will participate in any dividends which may accrue from profits.

This solemn, dark red building, with its low-hung hipped roof, contains six apartments, two to a floor. It combines elements of both the Georgian Revival and Craftsman styles and resembles a large private house rather than an apartment house. The small public entrance hall, with a wide, dark-stained wooden staircase and balustrade, is well lighted by a fanlight over large glass French doors. Although the building has never had an elevator, it must be considered a first-class apartment house because of the quality of construction as well as the uniformly large units. Each five-room apartment has a parlor with a wood-burning corner fireplace separated from the library by a pair of sliding doors, a dining room, two bedrooms, bath, large kitchen, and pantry. The one awkward feature of the layout is the placement of the parlor and library at the opposite end of the long hall from the entrance. Unusual features of each apartment include the separate entrance from one bedroom into the public hall and the cabinets located above the bedroom closet doors. The first-floor apartments are particularly elegant with round-headed French doors opening to stone balconies. Each apartment also has a small rear porch connecting to an exposed iron staircase.

This co-op converted to a rental building about 1948. Following the civil disturbances between 1968 and 1971,

Resembling a large house more than an apartment building, 2852 Ontario Road contains two spacious apartments per floor.

it rapidly deteriorated. In 1975 five friends and members of the Church of the Saviour privately purchased the entire building from the landlord for $84,000, renovated the interior, and reestablished it as a co-op for themselves.

The church, at 2025 Massachusetts Avenue, N.W., is a private nondenominational, ecumenical church of 110 members. It was established in Washington in 1947 by Gorden Crosby, still the pastor, to help improve the community through social work. The Church of the Saviour has been a major force for change in the Columbia Road neighborhood near the apartment house. In 1960 the church established the Potter's House, a coffee house and bookstore at 1658 Columbia Road, N.W. Later, in 1973, this church established Jubilee Housing, Inc., to provide low-income residences in the same area. For this project four nearby apartment houses—the Ritz, the Mozart, the Marietta, and the Sorrento—were purchased, renovated, and rented. The tenants are trained to manage and maintain these buildings. Continuing their role of civic service, the Church of the Saviour founded Columbia Road Health Services, Inc., in 1979 to provide low-cost medical service and counseling for families in the area. A number of residents of 2852 Ontario Road, N.W., including Dr. Janelle Goetcheus, donate several days of their free time each week to serve in the health unit, the apartment houses, or other forms of social work.

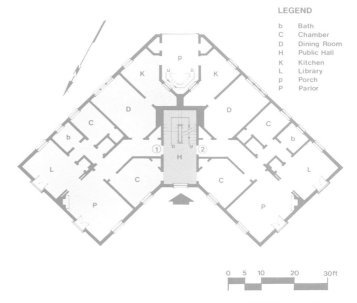

LEGEND

b Bath
C Chamber
D Dining Room
H Public Hall
K Kitchen
L Library
p Porch
P Parlor

0   5   10   20   30ft

An unusual feature of each apartment's plan at 2852 Ontario Road is the second entrance from the public hall into a bedroom.

30

WOODWARD

2311 Connecticut Avenue, N.W.; northeast corner of Connecticut Avenue and Ashmead Place

ARCHITECT: Harding and Upman, 1909

ORIGINAL APARTMENTS: 45 (14 one-bedrooms; 14 two-bedrooms; 17 three-bedrooms)

STATUS: opened as rental in 1910; converted to condo in 1973

Of the handful of Spanish Colonial apartment houses built in Washington prior to World War I when this style was fashionable, the Woodward remains the most exuberant. It was designed in a modified U shape to fit the site at Connecticut Avenue and Ashmead Place adjacent to the Taft Bridge, which had been completed only two years before the Woodward opened in 1910. The most striking feature is the elaborate baroque, three-story-high poly-chromed terra cotta entrance entablature with pairs of columns crowned by the third-floor window surround. The slightly projecting corner pavilions on the front facade are embellished with prominent hipped roofs; the left corner serves as an open summer house or roof pavilion, with a sweeping view of Rock Creek Park.

The Woodward was built as an investment by Samuel Walter Woodward, a native of Damariscotta, Maine, who had come to Washington in 1880 from Chelsea, Massachusetts, a suburb of Boston, with his partner, Alvin Mason Lothrop. They were seeking a recession-proof economy for their dry goods operation, originally known as the Boston Dry Goods Store. Woodward and Lothrop believed in the long-range possibilities of the Washington market not only for their department store but for real estate as well. Mr. and Mrs. Woodward reared their six children in a house on the northeast corner of Connecticut

The Woodward was one of six apartment houses built as investments by Samuel W. Woodward, founder of the Boston Dry Goods Store, now known as Woodward and Lothrop.

The Woodward's elaborate Spanish Colonial entrance, shown here, and other details, including the summer pavilion on the roof, were based on the design of a New York apartment house, the Hendrik Hudson, built in 1906 at Riverside Drive and 110th Street.

and Wyoming avenues near his two luxury apartment houses, the Woodward and the Woodley. Woodward built four other smaller apartment houses elsewhere in the city—two with names derived from his own, the Wood and the Ward, plus the Damariscotta and the Eckington. He also built several commercial buildings for investments, the largest of which was the Woodward Office Building at 15th and H streets, N.W.

The Woodward's forty-five apartments ranged from two to six rooms, each with kitchen and bath. The most prominent apartments are the set of three duplex units over the entrance, which form the No. 7 tier. They were designed with the dining room, kitchen, pantry, parlor, and library on the lower level and the bath and three bedrooms above. The largest flats are found in the No. 2 tier, in the right rear, with parlor, dining room, three bedrooms, bath, kitchen, and pantry. Perhaps the most

unusual original design feature was the bank of four elevators—a large number for a medium-sized building. Two passenger elevators faced the lobby, while behind were located a servants' elevator and a freight elevator.

The rectangular lobby, with the office to the right and parlor and telephone room to the left, was designed with mosaic floors, buff Caen stone walls, and white marble wainscoting. The original woodwork in the apartments varied from mahogany to oak, according to the original rental price. Tile floors and walls originally lined each bathroom and kitchen. Amenities included a roof garden with a summer pavilion, a mail chute on each floor connecting to a public mailbox in the lobby, an outlet in each apartment leading to a central vacuum system, a room to the left of the lobby arranged as a doctor's office, and a wall safe in each apartment. The spacious basement contained a "social hall" for parties, a billiard room, barber shop, servants' bath, and individual storage lockers.

The Woodward was basically unchanged until it was sold in 1968–69 by the trustees of the Alonzo O. Bliss Estate to the Landmark Companies, owned by J.E. Bindeman and his son, David P. Bindeman. The Bindemans renovated the entire building and reopened it in September 1970. Apartments remained spacious, and a second bathroom, created from a large closet, was added to many. The small public parlor was detached from the lobby and added to the adjacent doctor's office. The servants' hall on each floor—with its toilet, elevator, and janitor's closet—was converted to a laundry. In addition, four new apartments were developed from unused basement space. The Woodward has no garage but provides eight parking spaces behind the building.

The Bindemans were the first real estate firm to buy pre–World War I Washington apartment houses for renovation. They chose only buildings in good locations. The cost of renovations—rewiring, new plumbing, new elevators, new roofs, new heating systems, and new baths and kitchens—usually equalled the purchase cost. By doubling the rents, the cost of remodeling was repaid in three years. In 1973 they converted the Woodward to a condominium, one of the earliest in Washington. Since then the Woodward's board of directors has made significant improvements, including restoring the red-tile

One of the most elegant classical apartment house lobbies in Washington is at the Woodward; note the unique elevator-cab entablatures.

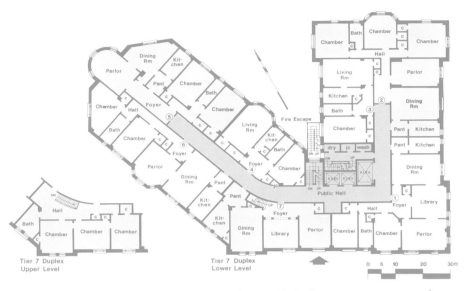

The 1909 Woodward was the second apartment house with duplex apartments—unpopular and rare in Washington until the 1960s.

ARCHITECTS HARDING AND UPMAN

Harding and Upman were Samuel N. Woodward's favorite architects, designing not only the Woodward apartments but the Woodward Building at 15th and H streets, N.W., and the Woodward and Lothrop department store as well. A native of Rochester, Minnesota, Frank Upman practiced architecture in Washington from 1903 until close to his death in 1948. He was associated with architect Henry Ives Cobb before forming a partnership with Clarence L. Harding in 1904. While a partner with Percy C. Adams (Upman and Adams) from 1924 to 1948, his firm designed the Chevy Chase Theatre (now the Avalon) on Connecticut Avenue, a number of important public schools in Washington suburbs, hospitals for the Army and Navy departments, and post offices across the country. In ad-

roof, repointing the exterior brickwork, and restoring the ceilings of the public corridors, which had unfortunately been lowered during the first remodeling.

dition to serving as president of the Washington chapter of the American Institute of Architects and president of the Allied Architects, he supervised the drawing of plans for the Longworth House Office Building on Capitol Hill.

There is no doubt that the facade of the Woodward was influenced by earlier buildings in both Washington and New York. Perhaps the most influential predecessor was the Hendrik Hudson apartment house at Riverside Drive and 110th Street in Manhattan, designed in 1906 by the architectural firm of Rouse and Sloan. Remarkably similar to the Woodward in massing and general features, it too had a Spanish red-tile roof and a pair of hipped roof summer pavilions that served as part of the roof garden. An account of the Hendrik Hudson, with numerous photographs, which Harding and Upman must have seen, was published in *Apartments of the Metropolis* in 1908. Two other local pre–World War I buildings also feature elaborate Spanish Colonial doorways—the Cordova apartment house by Waddy B. Wood, at Florida Avenue and 20th Street, N.W., and the Spanish Embassy, by George Oakley Totten, at 2801 16th Street, N.W.

31

WINDSOR LODGE, now the CHANCELLERY

2139–2141 Wyoming Avenue, N.W.; northeast corner of Wyoming Avenue and Thornton Place

ARCHITECT: Merrill T. Vaughn, 1910–11

ORIGINAL APARTMENTS: 16 (16 three-bedrooms)

STATUS: opened as rental in 1911–12; converted to co-op in 1972; converted to condo in 1976

One block west of Connecticut Avenue on Wyoming Avenue at Thornton Place, Windsor Lodge consists of two four-story buildings, each designed with eight apartments, two per floor. The original east building, 2139 Wyoming Avenue, was built in 1910 by Leo Simmons, president of Simmons Properties. His son, Berkeley L. Simmons, built the west building, 2141 Wyoming Avenue, the following year. These two luxury apartment houses, each with its own small lobby and elevator, originally were separated by a one-story garage. This small structure was removed and the space between the buildings filled in before World War I to provide dining rooms for the No. 1 tier of apartments in the west building.

The facades of the two buildings are eclectic. The round-headed windows reflect the influence of the Victorian rowhouse; the cornices are classical, while other elements could be classified as Craftsman in style. The most prominent feature of the east building is the spacious porte-cochère, now serving pedestrian rather than vehicular traffic. The plain west building facade is relieved by a massive iron balcony over the entrance and an extremely wide three-story hexagonal bay.

Most of the sixteen apartments of Windsor Lodge were designed as railroad flats, meaning that all rooms open onto a long hall. The largest apartments, in the No.

1 tier of the east building, offer 2,900 square feet of space, with a large reception hall, double parlor, dining room, balcony, three bedrooms, three baths, den, kitchen, sleeping porch, pantry, servant's room, and servant's bath. In the center of each building is a curiously designed lightwell and service stair, covered by a skylight.

Although the two buildings were built next to each other, and both are operated today as one condominium association, they remain separate apartment houses with their own small lobbies. The lobby of the east building has a delicate wooden stair balustrade, with paneled wainscoting, built-in upholstered bench, and a circular stained glass window opening onto the interior service and light court. The entrances to individual apartments are recessed, with handsome paneled molding, but their original glass transoms and side lights have long since been replaced with wooden inserts to meet revised city fire codes.

In 1972 developer Alex Laurins converted Windsor Lodge from rental to co-op status. Converted into a condominium in 1976, it remains one of the most desirable apartment houses in the Kalorama neighborhood because of its spacious units and its location among large houses in a quiet neighborhood away from the traffic on Connecticut Avenue. Today Windsor Lodge is known as the

Windsor Lodge consists of two adjacent apartment buildings with separate lobbies built a year apart, 1910–11.

Chancellery—not to be confused with another Washington apartment house, the Chancery on Wisconsin Avenue opposite the Washington Cathedral.

SENATOR BORAH'S APARTMENT

Prior to World War II Windsor Lodge was occupied primarily by members of Congress, army and navy officers, and chief clerks of various government bureaus. Perhaps the most notable resident was William E. Borah, Republican senator from Idaho, who lived in apartment No. 21, in the east building, from 1913 until 1929. A native of Illinois, Borah began his career as an attorney representing mining and lumber companies in Boise in the 1890s. He then served as a progressive U.S. senator from Idaho from 1907 until his death in 1940. A powerful force in foreign affairs, he was a major opponent of President Wilson's policies and a decisive factor in keeping America out of the League of Nations. The isolationist Borah op-

posed international regulations that required political or military sanctions. During the 1930s as World War II approached, he was a leading advocate of neutrality legislation.

Borah was very frugal regarding his personal expenditures. He demanded lower rents in the apartment houses he lived in, and he got them, since many Washington landlords wanted the prestige of a senator's residing in their building. Although he bitterly opposed a rent increase in 1920, he ultimately paid it. It appears, however, that when the rent was increased again—in 1929—he moved to a nearby apartment house of even grander dimensions, 2101 Connecticut Avenue. Because of Borah's long residence at Windsor Lodge, the American Association of State and Local History nominated his apartment, No. 21, to the National Register of Historic Places in 1976. In this rare designation, one apartment was placed in the National Register, while the building itself was not listed.

The east half of Windsor Lodge, at 2139 Wyoming Avenue, was one of the first apartment buildings in the city with a porte-cochère, as shown on this original elevation drawing of 1911.

The rooms in each apartment in the two Windsor Lodge buildings are arranged along a long hall; the longest extends 114 feet.

LIFE AT WINDSOR LODGE

One of the most emotional features of life in a rental apartment house is the subject of rent increases. It is the same today as it was two generations ago. Although Senator Borah's letter of opposition to the 1920 Windsor Lodge rent increase has not survived, the reply to it by the landlord, Leo Simmons, has been preserved in the Borah Papers at the Library of Congress:

I have been expecting you in to see me, as you have not done so, I deem it my duty to notify you that your rent after October first will be one hundred and sixty ($160.00) dollars per month, the same rate I receive for other similar apartments. The increase might seem high over what you are now paying, without considering the facts; this building was built in 1911, and the rate was then fixed for the apartment you are now occupying at one hundred and fifty ($150.00) dollars per month. It was calculated that it would then pay only about 7%. Finding that the neighborhood at that time, and for a few years thereafter, was considered *far out*, I deemed it advisable to let the apartments at much less than I expected to receive, consequently I have had only a very small return on my investment.

Since my expenses of maintenance have more than doubled, taxes have likewise doubled, so there is nothing left for me to do after this year, but to join with my son, who owns the building next door, and convert them into one building so as to cut down expenses—we intended to do so this fall, but refrained because of the inconvenience that it would cause the tenants.

Moreover, as you know I have always allowed you to have your rent under that paid by any other tenant. The parties occupying the apartment similar to yours are paying at the rate of $140.00 per month, and so it will be noticed that my increase in the apartment made necessary to meet the enormous increase of expenses and taxes is only $20.00 over what it should have been last year, which is less than $2.50 per room not taking into consideration the baths and porches.

As there are only eight apartments in this building you will readily realize that the amount of the increase will scarcely take care of the increased cost. Slight calculation will show you that the rental that I have charged you as compared with the rate I have received for the other

Mr. and Mrs. Sidney Zabludoff are seated in the living room of their Windsor Lodge apartment. In the left background is the long rear hall.

apartments is considerable and I do not feel justified in continuing the same condition further. It is not fair to any other tenants or myself, and I believe that you will realize this.

Of course you know that the apartment is extra large with the unusual feature of three baths and extra lavatory and two porches, and extra large bed-rooms. The price asked for the space occupied is at least 30% less than anyone else would demand for same, even if it were not in the very best residential section of Washington. I am very sorry that I have to raise the rent at all, for I assure you that it is a very disagreeable thing for me to do, and hope that you will appreciate my position in the matter, and advise me of your desire at an early date.

32

ST. REGIS

2219 California Street, N.W.; north side of California Street between Phelps Place and 23rd Street

ARCHITECT: Merrill T. Vaughn, 1912

ORIGINAL APARTMENTS: 20 (20 three-bedrooms)

STATUS: opened as rental in 1915

One of the finest of the surviving pre–World War I Washington apartment houses is the St. Regis. A small building with twenty units, located on California Street two blocks west of Connecticut Avenue, the St. Regis is not widely known because of its small size. For some unexplained reason, perhaps because of a lack of financing, construction went on for three years between the date the building permit was issued and the date the building opened. This restrained Beaux Arts–inspired building with its tripartite facade division includes elements of the Craftsman style. The almost square building has slightly projecting corner pavilions and plain casement windows. The stark facade is relieved, however, by a robust stringcourse with three balconies at the third-floor level. There is also a simple but wide cornice "supported" by pairs of prominent decorative brackets. The original iron and glass marquee is unfortunately missing from the front entrance. The garage, built as a separate structure to house nine cars, is in the rear alley, the city's oldest apartment house garage still in use.

Upon entering the St. Regis, one finds a spacious lobby raised by a flight of steps above the vestibule. This space is simple, decorated only by fluted pilasters and a handsome wrought-iron and marble staircase. The distinguishing feature of each apartment is its large size, with parlor, dining room, library, two bedrooms, bath, kitchen, and pantry. All kitchens open onto a convenient iron fire escape landing that also serves as a narrow porch, while the rear apartments have screened porches. Although they lack entry foyers, the apartments function well for entertaining, since the parlor opens into the dining room and library via large flat-headed arches.

In an awkward arrangement, the prime view from the front apartments, facing California Street, is curiously given to the bedrooms, rather than to the parlor and dining room. It is both remarkable and fortunate that many original interior details remain intact, including the brass hardware, living room fireplaces, handsome 6-foot-high paneled wainscoting in the dining rooms, and even dumbwaiters in the kitchen pantries that are still in use. Each evening between six and seven o'clock, the janitor signals each apartment in turn by an electric bell before sending the dumbwaiter up to receive trash: the dumbwaiter is used instead of a freight elevator.

Because of the spacious apartments and excellent location, very few tenants move away from the St. Regis, still a rental building owned by the families of the original builders, R. W. Bolling, brother of the second Mrs. Woodrow Wilson, and Bruce Clark. Members of the Bolling and Clark families have always occupied apartments

The simplicity of the facade of the St. Regis is typical of the Arts and Crafts style that was popular in Washington between 1905 and 1918.

here, and the St. Regis "record" goes to a daughter of R. W. Bolling, Mrs. Gertrude Lutz, who moved into her apartment in 1915 when the building opened and lived there until 1978. She elected to move to a smaller apartment at the Westchester and use the public dining room there.

Other long-term residents have included Thomas Knowland, director of the United States Geodetic Survey (forty-three years), and Huntington Cairns of the National Gallery of Art (forty-two years). Mr. Cairns was required to take out a special insurance policy to protect the building because his library, housed in built-in bookcases in every room, exceeded 22,000 volumes. One of the Bolling residents entertained her sister, Mrs. Woodrow Wilson, at the St. Regis for more than thirty years at weekly bridge parties. Mrs. Wilson gave the building several White House hydrangeas that still grow in the small side garden at the St. Regis.

The tradition of interesting residents continues. For instance, Wilhem de Looper, the Dutch-born curator of

Although all of the apartments at the St. Regis are spacious, the interior locations of the dining room (on the side) and the parlor (on the inside) are awkward; the bedrooms have the prime front view.

Six-foot-high paneled wainscoting survives in the dining rooms of only three apartments at the St. Regis.

paintings at the Phillips Collection and one of Washington's most talented contemporary artists, lives here. Another well-known artist, Frederick Hart, the sculptor of The Creation tympanum on the Washington Cathedral and the handsome figural sculpture for the Vietnam Veterans Memorial, lived on the fifth floor with his wife and two children for a decade while he was creating these major works. Because of the large apartments and location in a quiet intown residential area, there is a long waiting list for new tenants.

33

AVONDALE

1726 P Street, N.W.

ARCHITECT: Frank R. White, 1913

ORIGINAL APARTMENTS: 39 (12 one-bedrooms; 14 two-bedrooms; 13 three-bedrooms)

STATUS: opened as rental in 1914; converted to co-op in 1920; converted to rental in 1940; reconverted to co-op in 1949

Conveniently located only one and a half blocks east of Dupont Circle, the Avondale was one of Harry Wardman's important early luxury apartment houses. Its severe tan-brick facade suggests the Craftsman style; nevertheless, limestone stringcourses above the first and fourth floors, the iron and glass marquee, and the heavy cornice indicate Beaux Arts influence. The same facade treatment is reflected in several other Washington apartment houses built just before World War I, such as 2001 16th Street, N.W. (now the Brittany), the Farnsboro on the southwest corner of Florida Avenue and Decatur Place, N.W. (also by architect Frank R. White), and the St. Regis, just discussed. This Craftsman style, extremely simple with very little detail, was a harbinger of the decline in the 1920s of the classical style. An exuberant original iron and glass marquee and a pair of lamp standards, however, still embellish the front entrance. The unusual, extremely large windows on the front facade of the Avondale are reminiscent of another Wardman apartment house, the Northumberland, built four years previously.

The five-story Avondale has thirty-nine apartments, varying from two to five rooms, each with kitchen and bath. Designed in a U shape, its open court faces west, on the right side. Through iron grille doors is a massive classical lobby with fluted pilasters, cornice, and paneled

Another apartment house influenced by the Arts and Crafts movement was the Avondale, built by developer Harry Wardman in 1913.

The Avondale's plan is U-shaped, typical of the period, but the courtyard faces west, to the side, rather than traditionally to the rear.

LEGEND
F   FOYER
P   PARLOR
D   DINING ROOM
K   KITCHEN
PA PANTRY
C   CHAMBER
B   BATHROOM
Z   BALCONY

ceiling. The original office, entered through a flat-headed arch at the east (left) end, has the same plaster detail. A tier of marble steps at each end of the lobby, with marble wainscoting and original solid brass handrails, leads to the first-floor apartments. The original white-tile lobby floor, with its Greek-inspired maroon and white border, survives under black and white linoleum squares; the design can still be seen in the public corridors, which remain uncovered. Some of the original Colonial Revival lobby furniture—ladderback chairs, bench, and stool—remains in place.

Although most decorative wooden mantels have been removed, the Avondale still possesses several unusual design features. One tier, No. 7, has working fireplaces with 7-foot-wide mantels, the largest ever designed for a Washington apartment house. The Avondale was one of the first buildings with walk-in shower stalls—in the largest apartments. Just one survives intact; the others have long since been remodeled.

Just after the Avondale was completed, Harry Wardman traded it to Mrs. E. J. Walter for a number of her downtown properties. This was typical of the way that he built his real estate empire; in one year Wardman realized

a $100,000 profit on the Avondale. He built it for $175,000 and exchanged it for properties worth in excess of $275,000. In 1920, because of the dramatic increase in rents during World War I, the Avondale was one of more than two dozen apartment houses converted from rental to cooperative: residents were eagerly seeking co-ops to avoid inflation and constantly escalating rents.

It remained a co-op for two decades, until 1940, when the shareholders (or resident owners) disbanded the co-op and sold the building to an investor, Charles Headden, who reopened the Avondale as rental. The reasons for this change remain unclear. The Depression may have forced the co-op owners to sell; more likely, the residents sold out because they were offered a very high price for the building. It proved a poor investment for Headden, however, since the government imposed rent controls on all Washington apartment houses within a year after he bought it.

In 1949, with rent controls still in force, Headden decided to dispose of the building. Rather than sell it to another investor, he evidently found it far more profitable to convert it back to a co-op. He commissioned the real estate firm of Edmund J. Flynn Co. to sell the units. The Avondale has been successfully operated as a co-op since then. These changes from rental to co-op to rental to co-op were highly unusual, although not unique, for a Washington apartment house. No similar record exists in the city for a condominium, since that form of ownership is relatively new, having first been introduced in the 1960s. There have been several instances, however, of Washington apartment houses converting from rental to co-op to condo.

Over the years the value of the Avondale apartments has fluctuated because of a number of factors. According to advertisements in both the *Washington Post* and the *Evening Star* in 1920, the largest apartment, five rooms with kitchen and bath, sold for $13,500. In comparison, new brick eight-room rowhouses near the Taft Bridge were selling for exactly the same price that year. The Avondale's location near Dupont Circle was then very desirable as a residential address. An intown residence was then still preferred to the suburbs.

Three decades later this had changed. When the Avondale apartments were put back on the market as co-

The classical lobby of the Avondale, with its fluted pilasters and paneled ceiling and walls, remains in original condition. Only the elaborate mosaic floor is missing; it was covered with linoleum in the 1950s.

The apartments in one tier of the Avondale have working fireplaces with the longest mantels in any apartment house in the city.

ops in 1949, the same large apartment was sold for only $11,500. At the same time a renovated rowhouse in Georgetown was bringing $25,000. Why the difference? First, Dupont Circle had changed drastically between 1920 and 1949, from a residential area to primarily a commercial area. Second, the Avondale was not at that time considered particularly desirable since it was an old-fashioned building with no central air conditioning and outdated kitchens and bathrooms. In addition, no parking garage existed in such an early building. And demographics had changed, with the flight to the suburbs in full swing, making a downtown address less appealing.

In 1985 the same large apartment that was $13,500 in 1920 and $11,500 in 1949 cost $150,000, the price of a large new apartment in the suburbs or a new tract house in Rockville. The location of the Avondale had become very desirable once again, with the Dupont Circle subway station only a four-minute walk away. Furthermore, the neighborhood has recently been declared an historic district, protecting it from additional commercial encroachment or destruction of adjacent historic houses. A third important reason is the interest generated by quality construction. Wood floors, fine plasterwork, high ceilings, and large rooms are desirable even in apartments with old-fashioned kitchens. The Avondale could compete with the new apartment houses built with 8-foot ceilings, concrete floors requiring wall-to-wall carpeting, and rooms of small dimensions.

34

ALTAMONT

1901 Wyoming Avenue, N.W.; northeast corner of Wyoming Avenue and Columbia Road

ARCHITECT: Arthur B. Heaton, 1915

ORIGINAL APARTMENTS: 27 (4 efficiencies; 14 one-bedrooms; 3 two-bedrooms; 6 four-bedrooms)

STATUS: opened as rental in 1916; converted to co-op in 1949

Many of the original interior details of the Altamont remain in pristine condition, including the façade, lobby, summer pavilions (or "roof houses" as they were first called), and even laundry room. The Altamont was one of the great luxury apartments of Washington when it opened in 1916. Its history and design remain among the most interesting of any apartment house standing in the city today.

The Altamont was developed by Colonel George Truesdell on an irregularly shaped large lot originally bounded by Columbia Road, Wyoming Avenue, Kalorama Road, and 19th and 20th streets. The edge of this block had been occupied by a large three-story frame Victorian house erected in the 1890s as Colonel Truesdell's residence. Formerly a District commissioner, Truesdell was a well-known real estate developer who as early as 1901 had built a number of Washington apartment houses, including three groups of two- and three-story apartment houses on Lincoln Road and R Street, N.E., adjacent to North Capitol Street. The seven-story Altamont—with a horizontally rusticated limestone base, marble entrance porch, and roof pavilions—was built of tan brick, basically in a ∪ shape. Influenced by the Italian Renaissance, all of the Altamont's facades were completed in a finished design, since the building at the time could be seen from all angles.

The Altamont still has two summer pavilions on the roof. The public dining room on the top floor and the billiard room, barber shop, beauty parlor, and servants' dining hall in the basement have long since disappeared—all converted to apartments during the Depression.

Colonel George Truesdell used part of the extensive grounds of his own 1880s country house, Managasett, at Columbia Road and Wyoming Avenue for the Altamont, to which he and his family moved after it opened in 1916.

Just inside the main Wyoming Avenue entrance is found a spectacular lobby, with oak floors laid in a herringbone pattern embellished with mahogany borders, a richly paneled plaster ceiling, and a prominent decorative Renaissance-inspired fireplace of marble and tile, with a tapered hood above, surmounted by a gilt cartouche. The collection of Tudor Revival chairs, sofa, library table, wall sconces, and Oriental carpet dating from 1916 are still in place. Truesdell's instruction to his builder, the Davis Construction Co., to spare no expense in buying the finest materials for the Altamont is still reflected in the brick, wood, fireplace mantels, and other features.

The size of the apartments varied from floor to floor.

The first through third floors contained small apartments of one to four rooms. In a well-conceived design, the architect isolated the two centrally located elevators on all floors by surrounding them with public corridor, service rooms, public stairs, and servants' stairs, so that no noise from their operation would disturb any apartment.

The fourth through sixth floors consisted of only three apartments per floor. In the center, above the main public entrance to the building, was one small apartment. On each side of it was a very large twelve-room apartment, beautifully designed with the ideal separation of public rooms, private rooms, and service rooms. These large units contained a drawing room, library, dining room, four bedrooms, three bathrooms, sleeping porch, kitchen, pantry, servants' hall, two servants' bedrooms, and servants' bath. There were elegant circular reception rooms, and an elliptical drawing room in the eastern apartment. Each of these suites had two working fireplaces, one in the dining room and one in the library or reception room.

While the bedrooms throughout the Altamont were papered, the other rooms had painted canvas-covered walls, an expensive procedure that created the smoothest possible surface. Wooden strips of molding were then applied over the canvas. Every room in the building had a circular outlet in the baseboard that connected to a vacuum machine in the basement.

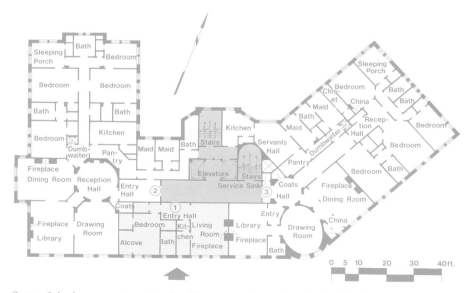

Some of the large apartments in the Altamont, such as these in the No. 2 tier on the upper floors, shown on this plan, had the rare feature of four exposures.

The elaborate lobby of the Altamont remains in pristine condition, even to its original 1916 furniture.

The seventh floor had a cafe, a room for private parties known as the Palm Room, a loggia, and a tiled roof garden with a pergola between the two summer pavilions. In a unique arrangement, this top floor rather than the customary basement also included an individual storeroom for each of the twenty-seven apartments. Apartments on the sixth floor were thus protected from extreme heat in the summer and cold in the winter. The basement contained a billiard room, barber shop, beauty parlor, servants' dining room, and laundry, which still has a massive clothes dryer with racks once heated by gas— one of only two remaining in the city from the pre–World War I era. By limiting the Altamont to six rather than seven floors of apartments, Colonel Truesdell was able to increase the ceiling height to 10 feet rather than 9 feet, 2 inches, which was then standard in first-class apart-

The unusual oval dining room of this current three-room apartment at the Altamont was formerly part of one of the large twelve-room units, all of which were subdivided by a new owner in 1926 to produce increased revenue.

ments. The seventh-floor ceilings consequently were lower than those in the residences below in order to stay within the city's 1894 height-limit law.

Even though the apartments were expensive, they were all rented when the Altamont opened late in 1916. In 1919, when Colonel Truesdell sold the building to another investor, James O'Donnell, more than 100 applicants were on the waiting list to rent units. Seeking increased return on his investment, the new owner in 1926 subdivided the large apartments into one- and two-bedroom units, which made a total of fifty-eight units. No additional major changes were made until 1949 when it was converted to a cooperative. The new owners of four of the co-op apartments had to resort to lawsuits to remove renters in the summer of 1949. At the time of conversion, the cafe, party room, and loggia on the seventh floor were converted to a four-room apartment, while the billiard room in the basement, with its separate outside entrance, became a one-bedroom unit. Today the Altamont contains sixty-one apartments: fifteen efficiencies, forty-two one-bedrooms, and four two-bedrooms. The large rose garden in the rear has become a parking lot for twenty-three cars.

ARCHITECT ARTHUR B. HEATON

The designer of the Altamont, Arthur B. Heaton (1875–1951), practiced architecture in Washington from 1900 to 1950. A native of the city, he graduated from Central High School and worked as a draftsman for the local architectural firms of Paul J. Pelz and Marsh and Peter before opening his own office in 1900. His education continued when he studied for a year at the Sorbonne in Paris and participated in a study tour of cathedrals in Europe before World War I. In the first two years of his practice, he designed four Washington apartment houses—the Highlands, the Montgomery, the Marlborough, and

This pre–World War I gas-fired clothes dryer in the basement of the Altamont is one of only two surviving examples in Washington.

the Augusta. Of the twenty-eight apartment houses he designed between 1900 and 1940, the Altamont remains his most important. Heaton was among the most prolific of any architect in Washington history. More than a thousand projects came from his office, including houses, commercial buildings, office buildings, apartment houses, and theaters.

Heaton designed a number of important houses for prominent local residents, including William S. Corby, David Lawrence, and Rudolph Kauffmann, and the Rockville country house of Gilbert Grosvenor. A number of his houses won architectural awards, such as 3324 Newark Street, N.W., and others in Cleveland Park. During the 1920s he designed more than 500 houses in the Burleith area for the firm of Shannon and Luchs. One of his most innovative groups of houses was designed on a cul-de-sac at Rittenhouse Street and Broad Branch Road in Chevy Chase, D.C., in 1931.

The architect was particularly interested in Georgian Revival architecture and made a number of trips to Williamsburg to study its eighteenth-century buildings. His prominent designs also include the second National Geographic Society Building, the Capital Garage, the Methodist Home for the Aged, the former YWCA building at 17th and K streets, N.W., the Washington Loan and Trust Building at 17th and G streets, N.W., and the Park and Shop complex at Connecticut Avenue and Ordway Street, N.W. The latter is important as the first planned neighborhood shopping center where a substantial amount of offstreet parking was provided as an integral part of the original scheme.

The winner of many design awards, Heaton was elected a fellow of the American Institute of Architects and was voted membership in the Cosmos Club. He founded and served as president of the Washington Building Congress during the Great Depression to promote the local building industry. Heaton served as the first supervising architect on the construction of the Washington Cathedral from 1908 to 1928. Fortunately, the son of his former colleague, Leon Chatelain III, donated all of Heaton's 20,000 architectural drawings to the Library of Congress in 1982. This collection, mostly ink-on-linen Beaux Arts–inspired drawings, is the most voluminous archive of any Washington architect.

35

McCORMICK

1785 Massachusetts Avenue, N.W.; northeast corner of Massachusetts Avenue and 18th Street

ARCHITECT: Jules H. de Sibour, 1915

ORIGINAL APARTMENTS: 6 (2 three-bedrooms; 4 six-bedrooms)

STATUS: opened as rental in 1917; converted to office building in 1940

The five-story classical McCormick, located one block east of Dupont Circle on Massachusetts Avenue across 18th Street from the Sulgrave Club, was the finest apartment house erected in Washington. Not only were the apartments the largest that existed in the city, 11,000 square feet each, but the facade, interior detailing, and floor plan were superbly designed. The balance and proportion in the arrangement of elements throughout were in excellent taste and done without regard to cost. No other apartment house in Washington equalled its quality of construction.

The site was first developed when a massive Romanesque Revival brick turreted house with Gothic and Queen Anne elements was built in 1880 by a rich New York merchant, Belden Noble. This property was purchased as an investment from Noble's aged widow in 1906 by Chicago businessman Stanley F. McCormick, son of Cyrus McCormick, who invented the reaper and founded the firm that was to become the International Harvester Company. Stanley McCormick served as an officer in the firm and invested in real estate until he was declared mentally incompetent, after which the Chicago courts managed his $36 million estate for his heirs.

The estate of Chicago investor Stanley McCormick commissioned Washington architect Jules H. de Sibour to design the McCormick in 1915. It was the finest apartment house ever built in the city.

Detail of the marquee of the McCormick.

ARCHITECT JULES H. DE SIBOUR

It was not until 1915 that the McCormick interests elected to clear the site for a monumental Beaux Arts–inspired building costing $600,000, then the most expensive apartment house in the city. It was designed by master Washington architect Jules H. de Sibour, who also designed five other Washington apartment houses—1155

16th Street, N.W. (known as the Warder); the Jefferson; the Hotel Martinique, 1209 16th Street, N.W., built as an apartment house for W.E. Fowler in 1920; the Anchorage; and the Lee House, an apartment-hotel. Only three are left—the Warder and the Martinique were demolished in the 1950s and the Lee House in 1983.

Jules H. de Sibour (1872–1938) was born in Paris to a patrician father, Count Gabriel de Sibour, a direct

Based on the style of Louis XVI, the McCormick's limestone facade includes handsome balconies, pedimented window surrounds, and beltcourses.

descendant of King Louis XI of France, and an American mother from Belfast, Maine. After attending schools in Paris he was sent to St. Paul's School in Concord, New Hampshire, and then to Yale University where he was graduated in 1896. De Sibour studied architecture in the offices of Ernest Flagg and then Bruce Price in New York before returning to Paris for further study at the Ecole des Beaux Arts. Just before departing for Europe, he married Margaret Claggett of Washington who resided with him in Paris. De Sibour returned to New York where he formed a partnership with Bruce Price under the name Bruce Price and de Sibour. After Price died in 1903 de Sibour kept the firm name until 1909, when it was changed to his alone. Although he continued to live in New York, his architectural commissions in Washington steadily increased. His first building in the nation's capital was the Howard House at 1164 19th Street, N.W., followed by Freedman's Hospital in 1904. Five years later de Sibour gave up his New York office and moved permanently to Washington. Socially prominent, de Sibour specialized in large town houses, mostly for his friends.

More than fifty important Beaux Arts–inspired mansions were built in the city before World War I, mostly on Massachusetts and New Hampshire avenues, 16th Street, and Dupont Circle. The nationally known architects of these important buildings included Carrere and Hastings; Little and Brown; McKim, Mead, and White; and John Russell Pope, but many were the work of the best Washington architects, such as Glenn Brown, Waddy Wood, George Oakley Totten, Horace Peaslee, and de Sibour. The latter's distinguished residences include the Guggenheim House, 1201 16th Street, N.W.; Mulligan House, 1601 R Street, N.W.; and the Lawrence House, 2221 Kalorama Road, N.W. (now the French Embassy). Those on Massachusetts Avenue, N.W., include the Stewart House at 2200, the Moore House at 1746, and the Wilkins House at 1700.

His prominent commercial commissions include the Keith-Albee Building, the Investment Building, the McLachlen Building, Hotel Hamilton, the Racquet Club (now the University Club), and the Chevy Chase Club. One of his last great houses was Oxon Hill Manor in Prince George's County, Maryland—designed for Sumner Welles as his second or country home in 1927.

FRENCH INSPIRATION

The French-inspired facade of the McCormick was based on the style of Louis XVI. It resembles as well the better Paris apartment houses of the late nineteenth century because of its limestone facing, five-story height, and mansard roof. The McCormick was not an intrusion on its neighbors but a complement to the streetscape of stately single-family residences.

Handsome details are evident on all sections of the facade where, for instance, the rusticated first story is capped by a handsome carved stringcourse. French windows on the second and third stories are embellished with paneled false balustrades, while decorative carved foliated panels embellish the space below the fourth-floor windows. The slate mansard roof is punctuated by massive pedimented dormer windows, framed by a shallow iron balcony and by the nine chimneys that served the forty-five fireplaces in the six apartments within. The most prominent exterior feature is the rounded corner bay with its elegant iron and glass marquee and great tripartite windows above.

One enters the McCormick at the corner of Mas-

The circular lobby of the McCormick with its domed ceiling.

Each apartment above the first floor at the McCormick occupied an entire floor with twenty-five rooms totaling 11,000 square feet.

sachusetts Avenue and 18th Street, N.W., through a circular public foyer. Here a breathtaking segmental plaster dome, subdivided by radial bellflower ribs, sets the stage for the eventual entrance into the six grand apartments. The restrained floor is laid in simple black-and-white marble squares that create a diamond pattern. The walls are decorated with vertical sections separated from the pie-shaped paneled ceiling by a wide but delicate dentiled cornice. The focal point is the black marble fireplace surround, framed by a pair of fluted Ionic pilasters and surmounted by an oval panel and a broken Georgian pediment. The elevator is in the raised rectangular vestibule to the rear.

The first floor contained two duplex apartments with their service rooms in the English basement below. Each of the four apartments above, one to a floor, contained an elliptical reception hall, two coatrooms, two foyers, a large salon, an enormous 24-by-45-foot living room, a 24-by-35-foot dining room, six bedrooms, and four bathrooms. Two spectacular ranges of eleven cedar-lined closets with mahogany doors lined each of the private hallways. These apartments were comparable to the finest then being built in New York.

The carefully thought-out floor plan completely isolated the service area, comprising 30 percent of each apartment, from the private and public areas. A separate system of corridors connected the five servants' bedrooms and bath, located on the eight mezzanine levels, adjacent to the five major floors and facing the rear light court. This design of a mezzanine for servants was first used in the United States by Hubert, Pirsson, and Company in their Central Park Apartments in New York in 1883, and even earlier, in 1879, by Richard Norman Shaw for his Albert Hall Mansions in London. Through this secondary system of traffic corridors, the servants could reach their own bedrooms without entering the family quarters, and also could bypass the formal family rooms enroute to the family bedroom area. The service area also included a servants' stairway and elevator, servants' dining hall, kitchen, pantry, butler's pantry with walk-in silver safes, and a large storeroom.

All of the apartments' principal public rooms, with 14-foot ceilings, were ornamented with applied plaster wall moldings, wainscoting, chair rails, and elaborate classical cornices featuring egg-and-dart, Greek-key, or floral designs. Each of the upper apartments had nine principal rooms and seven smaller servants' rooms. The basement had a separate laundry with an ironing and drying room for each of the six apartments, as well as a central refrigeration room with compressors to cool the refrigerators of the apartments. Rent for the typical apartment was $15,000 a year in 1917. In the early 1930s, however, because of the Great Depression, rents were lowered to $12,000 per annum.

In 1917, six families with forty servants moved into the McCormick. In an age before air conditioning, year-round residence in Washington was rare, as many of the affluent went to New England or Europe to escape the unbearable Washington summer heat and humidity. During the twenty-three years that the McCormick remained an operating apartment house, its tenants were mainly diplomats, financiers, and socialites from New York, Boston, and Pittsburgh. During the 1920s and 1930s the residents were some of the city's best known. Diplomat Robert Woods Bliss, the first important American collector of pre-Columbian art, lived here before his marriage to Mildred Barnes, the Castoria heiress. They later purchased and renovated the Dumbarton Oaks estate in Georgetown. Another diplomat, Sumner Welles, who became Franklin Roosevelt's Under Secretary of State and the originator of his Good Neighbor Policy toward Latin America, lived here during the late 1920s. After his marriage he moved into his late mother-in-law's mansion, the Townsend House at Massachusetts and Florida avenues, N.W., now the home of the Cosmos Club.

Another tenant from 1930 to 1934, Alanson B. Houghton, whose family owned the Corning Glass Works, was away most of the time as President Hoover's ambassador to Great Britain and later Germany. He eventually built his own house on Massachusetts Avenue, N.W., across from the British Embassy. Oil- and machine-tools heiress Perle Mesta, who became one of Washington's most famous hostesses, also lived here in the early 1930s. (While minister to Luxembourg, she inspired the popular Irving Berlin musical *Call Me Madam*, in which Ethel Merman portrayed her on the New York stage.)

ANDREW W. MELLON: MOST EMINENT RESIDENT

The most famous of all residents was Pittsburgh banker Andrew W. Mellon (1855–1937), among the foremost financial figures in the United States for many years. Mellon expanded a small private bank into a significant institution and played a critical role in the financing and development of Alcoa, Gulf Oil, and other major industrial corporations. Mellon rented the top-floor apartment from 1921 to 1937 while he served as Secretary of the Treasury under Presidents Harding, Coolidge, and Hoover and then, briefly, ambassador to Great Britain. Until the onset of the Great Depression, he was notably influential in reducing both tax rates and the federal debt.

The concept for a National Gallery of Art in Washington was formed at the McCormick. Mellon's acquisitions for his impressive art collection there form one of the most important series of events ever to occur in a Washington apartment house. His infatuation with paintings began in his twenties. Accompanied by his close friend, steel magnate Henry Clay Frick, he made his "grand tour" of Europe in 1882 and acquired his first

Pittsburgh industrialist and financier Andrew Mellon stands at a fireplace in his apartment on the top floor of the McCormick, while he was Secretary of the Treasury about 1929.

View of one of the 55-foot-long drawing rooms in an apartment at the McCormick in the 1930s.

One of the many unusual features found in each apartment at the McCormick was a row of massive cedar-lined storage closets, each with a solid mahogany door. The 14½-foot-tall ceilings set a record for Washington apartment houses.

important painting for $1,000—a price at that time that astounded his friends.

When as the Secretary of the Treasury he moved into the McCormick from his palatial house in Pittsburgh in 1921, the sixty-seven-year-old Mellon brought with him a fine collection of art. During his residence there he bought only the finest paintings and only from two firms, Knoedler and Company of New York and the Duveen Brothers of London. By this time he had developed a distinct taste in paintings. He disliked dark pictures, those depicting unpleasant scenes (such as crucifixions), and nudes. Even though he did purchase Titian's semiclad *Venus with a Mirror*, it remained permanently in storage. Paintings with religious scenes were never hung in the public rooms of his McCormick apartment, where cocktail parties were given. Despite these quirks, however, Mellon's collection of paintings during the 1920s was very impressive, and his interest in this "hobby" increased with time. At one point he found a particularly desirable

collection of eighteenth-century English portraits in the collection of a New York bank. When the bank directors politely but firmly declined to sell him the paintings, he ultimately acquired them—by buying the bank.

It was Mellon's custom to take paintings "on approval" for three or four months. For many years he collected seventeenth- and eighteenth-century Dutch and English paintings. On the advice of his personal lawyer, David Finley, whom he later designated as the first director of the National Gallery of Art, Mellon also began to collect the great masters of the Italian Renaissance. No painting was purchased without considerable business negotiations by Mellon—not a dollar was wasted—and the dealers respected him not for his frugality but for his business acumen in dealing with them, even though he was considered the richest man in America by the time of his death in 1937.

His greatest single purchase was made in 1932 while he was ambassador to Great Britain. Through the London

A current view of a drawing room at the McCormick after conversion to an office by the National Trust.

dealer Duveen he paid $6.5 million for twenty-one Old Master paintings from the Hermitage Collection in Leningrad. To finance industrial development, the Soviets sold superb paintings by Raphael, Titian, Rembrandt, Botticelli, and others. For security reasons Mellon kept much of his collection in storage at the Corcoran Gallery of Art, where he viewed them frequently.

The idea of establishing a National Gallery of Art in Washington entered Mellon's thinking as early as 1923. Embarrassed that European diplomats could find no "national collection" in Washington, then a charming but provincial Southern city, Mellon would often have them to lunch at the McCormick to view his own paintings. The public first learned of Mellon's plan for establishing the National Gallery when he was brought to court in 1934 on federal charges of tax evasion. After his acquittal two years later, Mellon formally offered his entire art collection to the nation in December 1936 and agreed to pay for the gallery building.

At that time Lord Duveen wrote Mellon that he was planning to retire and offered his extensive inventory of paintings in storage to Mellon before they were offered to the public. Too weak to travel to either London or New York, Mellon sent Finley to inspect them. Arrangements were then made to move the paintings to the fourth-floor apartment in the McCormick, below Mellon's, for leisurely viewing. After hanging the Van Dycks and Lawrences, Mellon's favorites, and the paintings needed to round out Mellon's collection of European works from the thirteenth to eighteenth centuries, Duveen returned to New York, leaving a caretaker and guards. With Duveen's key in hand, Mellon inspected the collection almost every day for three months before making a decision. Finally Mellon invited Duveen for lunch at the McCormick and, after haggling for two hours, bought everything Duveen had sent to 1785 Massachusetts Avenue, N.W.—twenty-four paintings and eighteen sculptures. The $21 million paid by Mellon startled even the international art world.

Working frantically against time, the eighty-one-year-old Mellon selected as his architect John Russell Pope and chose both the materials and the design of the National Gallery of Art building. He also established a large endowment to maintain the collection. Mellon unfortunately never saw any of the dream fulfilled, for he died in Washington a few months after ground had been broken for the National Gallery building.

CONVERSION

Because of the acute office-space shortage in Washington as a result of the defense preparations made by President Roosevelt just prior to America's entry into World War II, the fate of the McCormick was irrevocably changed. Officials of the Department of State convinced the McCormick estate to lease the building to the British Embassy. It was immediately converted to office space in February 1941 for the British Purchasing Commission, which was buying weapons to fight the Axis powers. The McCormick was subsequently to change hands three times: in 1950 the McCormick estate sold it to the American Council on Education, in 1970 it was bought by the Brookings Institution, and last it was purchased by the National Trust for Historic Preservation in 1977. The last purchase was a relief to Washington preservationists, since Brookings had already torn down more than a dozen richly detailed late Victorian houses to the east of the McCormick in the 1950s to clear the site for their present overscaled office building. But in the 1950s there was little public respect for nineteenth- and early twentieth-century buildings or for preserving historic inner-city neighborhoods.

RESTORATION

The National Trust immediately began a $4.5 million program to restore and renovate the landmark. Yerkes, Pappas, and Parker, Washington architects, were commissioned to prepare the landmark for the National Trust headquarters. Nicholas A. Pappas, the partner-in-charge, elected to restore the principal rooms and alter the plain service core of the building. Thus new electrical ducts, plumbing, and mechanical equipment were run through the old servants' rooms without disrupting the elaborate plasterwork and parquet floors in the old family quarters. Because of the sensitive and high-quality restoration work, this project won the first prize for historic preservation awarded by the Washington chapter of the American Institute of Architects in 1980. Today the National Trust occupies the basement and first two floors and rents the space above to various organizations, including law firms and the Chancellery of Gambia. The visitor today can thus still admire the exceptional original interior design. It remains a monument to the skill of local architects and builders—and as the premier example of a Washington apartment house.

36

2029 CONNECTICUT AVENUE, N.W.

Southeast corner of Connecticut and Wyoming avenues

ARCHITECT: Hunter and Bell, 1915

ORIGINAL APARTMENTS: 22 (1 one-bedroom; 2 two-bedrooms; 6 three-bedrooms; 7 four-bedrooms; 6 five-bedrooms)

STATUS: opened as rental in 1916; converted to condo in 1977

Washington developer Bates Warren selected this site on Connecticut Avenue for both its high elevation and its proximity to other stylish apartment houses, such as the Highlands, the Wyoming, the Dresden, and the Woodward. Ivory-colored terra cotta is used extensively on the facade, especially on the two porches, window surrounds, and on the first, second, and seventh floors.

Projecting from the rusticated base are two prominent entrances, an octagonal porch facing Connecticut Avenue and a circular porch on Wyoming Avenue. Designed in Renaissance style, the porches are richly detailed with decorated pilasters, fleurs-de-lis, and salamanders. They are based on the well-publicized corner entrance porch of the Alwyn Court designed by Herbert S. Harde and R. Thomas Short and built in 1907 at 180 West 58th Street in New York. The two street facades of the Alwyn Court are completely faced with terra cotta, making it the most elaborate terra cotta New York apartment house ever built. Both the twelve-story Alwyn Court, which still stands, and 2029 Connecticut Avenue, N.W., are Renaissance-inspired buildings with an overlay of Francis I ornament, though in fact they had nothing in common with a true French building of the sixteenth century.

The tripartite facade division of 2029 Connecticut Avenue includes the extensive application of terra cotta on the base and top floor.

Both Connecticut and Wyoming avenue entrances to 2029 Connecticut Avenue have ornate terra cotta porches featuring the fleur-de-lis and salamander, symbols used by Francis I.

The design of the two rounded porches of 2029 Connecticut Avenue was based on the main entrance of the Alwyn Court apartment house in New York, shown here.

Certain architectural details of 2029 Connecticut Avenue, N.W., such as the pilasters, spandrels, panels, and salamanders, are closely associated with the French monarch Francis I. The salamander, for example, is a dominant feature on the porches of 2029. It was used as a badge or emblem by Francis I, reportedly selected for him by his mother when he was ten. A heraldic device was then commonly used to identify the property of a lord as well as that of his retainers, soldiers, and vassals. The salamander symbolized endurance: it was commonly believed that it could survive both fire and water. It was depicted as a fierce fire-breathing lizard. Francis had the salamander, topped with a crown, carved on the staircases and fireplaces of many of his châteaux, including Chambord, Blois, Villers-Cotterets, and Fontainebleau.

Francis I (1494–1547) influenced the development of French civilization more than any previous ruler since Charlemagne. He introduced into France Mannerism, a school of art first developed in Italy, and made it fashionable throughout Europe. Through Francis's influence as well, French architects were made aware of the ar-

The dining rooms at 2029 Connecticut Avenue were designed with strapwork ceilings suggestive of the Tudor style.

A resident of 2029 Connecticut Avenue, John Peters Irelan, relaxes in one of the pair of public retiring rooms adjacent to the lobby. Each of these lounges was recently converted to an efficiency apartment.

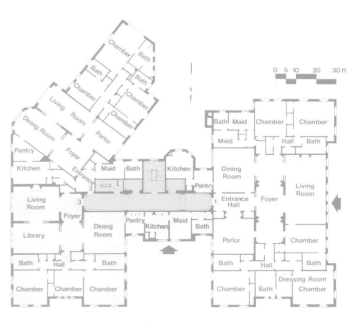

The typical floor plan at 2029 Connecticut Avenue includes three apartments per floor with the largest in the front, facing Connecticut Avenue (right).

All apartments at 2029 Connecticut Avenue have spacious foyers or galleries; the largest
are in the front apartments facing Connecticut Avenue in tier No. 1, shown here.

Mrs. Sidney Kent Legare, a resident at
2029 Connecticut Avenue since 1940,
poses in her drawing room. The long gallery
appears in the background.

chitecture of the High Renaissance in Italy. He not only rebuilt and redecorated the old French palaces of Blois and Fontainebleau, but also erected a number of new châteaux across France, such as the one at Saint-Germain in the 1530s.

The spacious lobby included an unusual feature—richly detailed parlors, or "retiring rooms," for men and women, with lavatories, where arriving guests could freshen up before proceeding upstairs. In addition to the four apartments originally located on the entrance floor, there were three per floor above, totaling twenty-two. A mahogany revolving door was at each of the two lobby entrances. One is still in use on Wyoming Avenue. Only two of the revolving doors in luxury pre–World War I apartment houses survive—one here and one in the lobby of the Altamont, built at the same time one block to the east. A major revision of the District of Columbia fire code in 1961 forced the removal of most of them.

On each typical floor, the largest and best-laid-out apartment faces Connecticut Avenue. Here a 19-foot entrance hall leads the visitor to a spectacular 13-by-43-foot foyer or gallery, which runs the central length of the unit, clearly dividing the space into public, private, and service areas. Each of the six 5,400-square-foot apartments in this tier has a 19-by-33-foot living room, a parlor, dining room, five bedrooms, four baths, two servants' rooms and servants' bath, kitchen, and pantry. There are parquet floors, handsome paneled walls, pairs of fluted Corinthian plaster columns, a plaster strapwork dining room ceiling reminiscent of the Tudor period, and elaborate classical plaster cornices.

The basement originally housed the building's refrigeration plant, which operated the refrigerators in each apartment, plus dumbwaiters and an early gas-fired clothes dryer. The latter was removed in 1977 when 2029 was purchased by Conrad Cafritz and converted into condominiums. The interior details of each apartment, with 9-foot, 6-inch ceilings, fortunately were preserved. The original annunciator bell system installed in all apartments, with the call box in the kitchen for summoning the servants, was left intact and is still used. The selling price for these large units in 1977 ranged from $150,000 to $240,000. Half of the tenants bought their apartments. At that time the two retiring rooms off the lobby were

The elaborate Beaux Arts–inspired plasterwork in the apartments at 2029 Connecticut Avenue even extends into the master dressing room.

made into efficiencies, certainly the most elegant in the city today, and a convenient two-level parking structure was added on the former lawn to the rear of the building.

The original residents constituted an impressive list, and the tradition continues. In 1917–18 former President William Howard Taft lived here while serving as co-chairman of the National War Labor Board. From the time he became Chief Justice in 1921 until his death in 1930, he lived two blocks west in an imposing house at 2215 Wyoming Avenue, N.W. That landmark is now the Embassy of Syria. Another notable resident was General John J. Pershing, commander of the American Expeditionary Forces in Europe during World War I; he lived here from 1922 until 1926, then moved to the Metropolitan Club at 17th and H streets, N.W., where he lived until 1936. The widow of Supreme Court Chief Justice Harlan Fiske Stone moved here when she sold her house near Kalorama Circle in the 1950s. Recent residents have included Senator George McGovern, Congresswoman Lindy Boggs, consumer advocate Virginia Knauer, and entertainer Lena Horne.

ARCHITECTS HUNTER AND BELL

Ernest C. Hunter and G. Neal Bell were specialists in designing Washington apartment houses between 1905 and 1925. Most of their work was commissioned by either John L. Warren or Bates Warren, then major developers. Between 1904 and 1912, Hunter and Bell also designed several detached houses in Cleveland Park. In 1915 they designed a number of rowhouses, such as the group of eight three-story examples at Irving Street and Park Place, N.W. Earlier, in 1905, they designed small apartment houses, including a four-story walk-up at the northeast corner of California and 18th streets, N.W. Several of their major apartment houses include the New Berne at Massachusetts Avenue and 12th Street, N.W. (now the New Plaza), in 1905; the Stafford at 1789 Lanier Place, N.W., in 1910; the Netherlands at 1860 Columbia Road, N.W., in 1909; and 1868 Columbia Road, N.W. (now the Norwood), in 1916. In 1919 Bell and his partner at that time, A. S. Rich, designed 2301 Connecticut Avenue, N.W. (now the Carthage).

37

1870 WYOMING AVENUE, N.W.

Southwest corner of Wyoming Avenue and 19th Street

ARCHITECT: B. Stanley Simmons, 1916

ORIGINAL APARTMENTS: 28 (9 two-bedrooms; 19 three-bedrooms)

STATUS: opened as rental in 1917; converted to co-op in 1951

Built by Lester Barr, one of Washington's best-known real estate developers in the early twentieth century, 1870 Wyoming Avenue, N.W., was completed only a few weeks before entry of the United States into World War I restricted nonessential uses of building materials. This restrained seven-story buff-brick Beaux Arts residence was designed by B. Stanley Simmons, a Washington architect who, along with T. Franklin Schneider, became an early specialist in apartment houses. Simmons served as the principal architect for all of Barr's projects. Professionally trained, Simmons designed increasingly sophisticated facades and interior plans: his floor plan for 1870 is much more sophisticated than his earlier plan for the nearby Wyoming. The irregularly shaped lot resulting from the diagonal angle of Wyoming Avenue and 19th Street dictated the unusual design. The front facade, facing Wyoming Avenue, is distinguished by two projecting, massive, square pavilions, while the 19th Street facade includes a unique series of six setbacks, to conform to the street line.

The twenty-eight apartments are unusually large, many of them more than 2,000 square feet. A typical floor contains four apartments—one apartment of five rooms plus one bathroom, kitchen, and pantry, and three apartments of six rooms with two bathrooms, kitchen, and

The tan-brick 1870 Wyoming Avenue apartment house was designed by architect B. Stanley Simmons for developer Lester Barr.

pantry. The dumbwaiters in each apartment were used as trash chutes until 1980. Since the bathrooms in the Nos. 2, 3, and 4 tiers do not have outside windows, each is ventilated and lighted by two lightwells.

Miss Josephine Burke is shown with her dog in the lobby of 1870 Wyoming Avenue, one of only two surviving examples of marbleized walls in Washington.

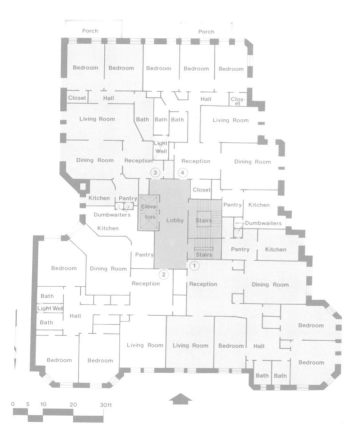

Most of the apartments at 1870 Wyoming Avenue contain two bathrooms, unusual in pre–World War I Washington apartment buildings.

The most striking feature of 1870 Wyoming Avenue, N.W., is its gray and cream marbleized lobby. Only one other such example survives in a Washington apartment house, the yellow and cream lobby at the Northumberland. An elaborate polychrome mosaic floor, massive classical cornice, shallow paneled pilasters, plaster strapwork ceiling reminiscent of the Tudor period, and original bronze wall sconces complete the decoration of the 1870 Wyoming lobby.

Unusual in these spacious apartments are their large, square reception halls. Two wide, square-headed arches open from the reception hall into the living room and dining room—ideal for entertaining. In all of the apartments, the public rooms are completely separated from the bedrooms and bathrooms, a sophisticated arrangement uncommon in most Washington apartment houses of the period. This building was one of the first, if not the first, luxury apartment house without Victorian decorative fireplace mantels in the living rooms. Because the earliest Washington apartment houses were based on the rowhouse design, they always included decorative fireplaces to create a domestic feeling. It was not until the 1930s that this feature was finally eliminated to permit freer placement of furniture.

The two passenger elevators have their original cabs and are still operated manually. In 1951 the building was converted to a cooperative, as were many others in Washington as a result of the inflation caused by World War II.

38

MERIDIAN MANSIONS, now the ENVOY

2400 16th Street, N.W.; northwest corner of 16th Street and Crescent Place, N.W.

ARCHITECT: Alexander H. Sonnemann (plans), F. W. Fitzpatrick (elevations), and Reginald W. Geare (interior detailing), 1916

ORIGINAL APARTMENTS: 190 (112 efficiencies and one-bedrooms for transients;

78 two-bedrooms and three-bedrooms for permanent tenants)

STATUS: opened as rental in 1918

Because of its spacious apartments, elegant public rooms, and location in the midst of Washington's old Embassy Row, Meridian Mansions, now the Envoy, was for many years one of the truly great apartment houses in the nation's capital. This apartment-hotel, built by William and Edgar Kennedy, offered large apartments for permanent residents and furnished bedrooms and small suites for transients. The landmark included a large lobby, intact today, and other important features that are now lost— two ballrooms, both on the right rear of the first floor, a spacious public dining room on the left rear, and prominent roof pavilions. Built at a cost of $950,000, it was the most expensive apartment house in the city when constructed in 1916–18. Meridian Mansions had its own power plant and a large three-story garage for three hundred cars plus chauffeurs' and servants' quarters above. Tennis courts were on the garage roof. The 560-room building included public spaces on the first floor and apartments on the six floors above.

At the time Meridian Mansions was built, the neighborhood was one of the most exclusive in the city. Down the steep hill to the south stood Boundary Castle, the great Seneca sandstone Romanesque Revival mansion built in 1888 by Senator and Mrs. John Henderson of Missouri. Mrs. Henderson was the astute businesswoman who developed 16th Street, N.W., into Embassy Row between 1900 and 1930. She built and rented more than a half dozen great Beaux Arts houses on or adjacent to 16th Street to foreign governments for their embassies and legations. Additional prestige came to this section of 16th Street, N.W., when such prominent leaders as Chief Justice Charles Evans Hughes arrived. He built a house nearby at the northwest corner of 16th and V streets, N.W., in 1911.

Meridian Mansions faced the new Meridian Hill Park, which was developed on an 11-acre tract across 16th Street between 1914 and 1936. The area received its name because it lies directly on the meridian of Washington, two miles due north of the White House. The land for the park was purchased from Mrs. Henderson by the federal government in 1910 for $490,000. The original landscape scheme of 1914 by George Burnap was completely revised by architect Horace Peaslee during the 1920s. In developing this Italian Renaissance park, Peaslee spent several months studying formal gardens in Italy. Peaslee divided the park, located on a steep hill, into three sections—an upper garden and terrace, a lower garden and pool, and a stepped cascade of water in between. Most of the plantings were prepared by the New York landscape firm of Vitale, Bonickeroff, and Geiffert.

Top: In the first extensive remodeling of Meridian Mansions—in the 1960s—the original summer pavilions on the roof, shown in this 1923 photograph, were unfortunately removed. *Bottom:* Meridian Mansions took its name from Meridian Hill, home of Meridian Hill Park across 16th Street, as shown in this mid-1930s photograph when the park was completed.

Over the years the Meridian Hill area has served a variety of purposes. In 1819 Meridian Hill, a federal mansion, was built here by John Porter. Located just outside the city limits, the mansion was later used as a residence by President John Quincy Adams when he left the White House. The first buildings for Columbian College (now George Washington University) were erected in the 1820s on what is now the upper terrace of Meridian Hill Park. During the Civil War the college buildings were used as a hospital by the Union army. A black college, Wayland Seminary, was located on part of the land from 1865 until it was moved to Richmond, Virginia, in 1890. A number of important outdoor sculptures are located in the park, including an equestrian statue of Joan of Arc by Paul Dubois (1922), a standing figure representing Dante by Ettore Ximenes (1921), and a seated bronze statue of President James Buchanan by Hans Schuler (1930). Under the control of the National Park Service, it remains one of the great urban park designs in the United States.

The land for Meridian Mansions was purchased from Mrs. Henderson by William M. and Edgar S. Kennedy, who formed the real estate firm of Kennedy Brothers. They were natives of Orange County, Virginia, who came to Washington in the late nineteenth century to build and sell rowhouses. They were very successful, because the population of the city was expanding rapidly. Many of their pre–World War I rowhouses were built in the Northwest section on Lamont, Irving, and 17th streets, and on Rock Creek Church Road. The Kennedy brothers were also involved in building two other early apartment houses, the Park Regent at Park Road and Mount Pleasant Street, N.W., and the Westmoreland on California Street, N.W.

The buff-brick front facade of Meridian Mansions, described at the time as Italian Renaissance, featured two tiers of terra cotta balconies, six on each side of the main entrance, which was framed by a dignified iron and glass marquee. At the front of the roof two handsome pavilions were joined by a brick colonnade. The massive building extended deep into the block with four pairs of wings, providing abundant light and air, and a total of six roof pavilions.

Meridian Mansions originally contained 112 small units and 78 large apartments, many with five or six rooms plus a kitchen and two baths. The building was the setting for many notable gatherings and was the home of numerous members of Congress and diplomats. As early as 1921 the Bolivian Legation was in Meridian Mansions, while as late as 1956 representatives of thirty-two foreign governments rented apartments.

Meridian Mansions has unfortunately been beset with problems since its construction. When the city's leading electric company proposed charging the Kennedy brothers top rates for power in the building, the owners decided to build their own power plant on the grounds. The requisitioning of the two large iron boilers by the federal government for the war effort delayed the opening of the new apartment house for six months. In 1920 the Kennedy brothers learned of the federal government's proposed development at Meridian Hill Park. They bitterly opposed architect Horace Peaslee's design for the park, as he oriented its access toward residential 15th Street rather than 16th Street, which was a far grander boulevard. The Kennedys wanted the park redesigned with terraces to the west, extending greenery down to the sidewalk. Their efforts failed and the present massive stone retaining wall was built directly across the street from Meridian Mansions.

In spite of these difficulties, during the first twelve years every apartment was filled, and a long waiting list developed. When William Kennedy died in the mid-1920s, his widow inherited his share of the building. Many of the residents, including the widow Kennedy, were ruined by the stock crash of 1929. Both she and her brother-in-law Edgar Kennedy were forced to move to much smaller apartments on Connecticut Avenue. Half of the large Meridian Mansions apartments consequently became vacant in the early 1930s.

Edgar Kennedy formed a partnership in 1930 with a much younger developer, Monroe Warren, to build a second great Washington apartment house, the Kennedy-Warren. It was more than they could handle during those difficult years, and they lost the Kennedy-Warren to the holder of their mortgage, the B. F. Saul Company, midway during construction in 1932. In addition, the Park Bank, at 14th Street and Park Road, N.W., which served many Washington developers, including the Kennedy brothers, failed in 1933. The Kennedy family lost most of its capital. Meridian Mansions was taken over by the holder of the first trust, the Metropolitan Life Insurance Company, and the Kennedys struggled to retain what was left of their real estate holdings, mainly four small apartment houses on Connecticut Avenue. In addition to building Meridian Mansions, Edgar Kennedy, along with Donald L. Chamberlain, achieved much acclaim for their development of suburban Kenwood, Maryland, before the crash.

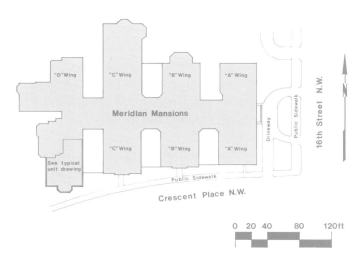

To provide abundant light and air, Meridian Mansions was designed with a total of eight wings, ranged along its north and south sides.

Unit plan of an apartment in the "D" wing of Meridian Mansions.

The only remaining original interior feature in the once-elaborate Meridian Mansions, renovated twice and gutted once, is the lobby, shown in this 1935 photograph.

RECENT HISTORY

In 1936 when Meridian Mansions was sold, most of the public space was redecorated and a fashionable Art Deco nightclub added. Life at Meridian Mansions, by now known as the Hotel 2400, evidently continued at an even keel. Then the penthouse controversy began. Even though Congress had authorized the nine-room penthouse on the roof in 1918 by an amendment to the 1916 building permit, the structure exceeded the height limit for residences. The city government attempted to ban use of this penthouse during World War II, claiming that it violated an 1894 law prohibiting human habitation above the roof line. The dispute was not settled until 1952 when Congress authorized its use only as an office—and not as a luxury apartment.

Meridian Mansions (Hotel 2400) changed hands again in 1956, when the neighborhood began to deteriorate. Two years later the property, subject to a lien for local taxes, was seized. Soon afterwards it became one of the city's first integrated apartment-hotels. When black New York Congressman Adam Clayton Powell attempted to buy the building in 1962 for use as a retirement home for elderly poor, many groups opposed the plan. The Department of State asked Congressman Powell to cancel the attempted purchase because Meridian Mansions was one of the few "badly needed" apartment houses available to African diplomats. Because of a number of allegations concerning the congressman's financial associations, he abandoned the attempt in March 1963.

This landmark was sold for $2.2 million in 1964 to three New York investors who changed the name from Hotel 2400 to the Envoy Towers. Their $2.5 million renovation included reducing the size of the apartments and gutting much of the public space. New floor plans, totaling 334 apartments, were devised by the Washington architectural firm of Mills, Petticord, and Mills. When the new owners defaulted on their payments, the mortgage was foreclosed in 1967 by the Manufacturers Hanover Trust Company of New York. It was sold at public auction

The original public dining room at Meridian Mansions.

Residents are shown having their breakfast on the balcony of their Meridian Mansions apartment overlooking 16th Street, still Embassy Row when photographed about 1935. The photographer posed the maid (her arm is just visible at right) with a silver tray to reflect sunlight onto the face of the woman pouring coffee—to improve the lighting for the photograph.

to the federal government only ten days later, a sad comedown for what was once Washington's finest apartment-hotel. The subsequent 1968 riots, centered only two blocks east, plunged the neighborhood into further decline. As federal government property, the building was used as temporary housing for persons displaced by the riots. Briefly owned by a California investor between 1972 and 1977, Envoy Towers reverted to the federal government once again when he did not make the mortgage payments.

The government sold the building in 1979 to another developer, David Clark of North Carolina, who had recently achieved two remarkable successes with his conversions of the Iowa and Fairfax Gardens apartments into condominiums. Clark employed Melvin Mitchell Architects of Washington to completely renovate Envoy Towers, now renamed the Envoy (not to be confused with a 1960 International Style apartment house by the same name at 2144 California Street, N.W.). During this renovation the entire building was gutted, except for the lobby, which was handsomely restored and redecorated by Washington designer C. Dudley Brown, and the apartment units were redesigned again, with even smaller rooms. In the process the two ballrooms and dining room were eliminated. The impressive original roof pavilions had long since disappeared, so the architect created an elegant new roofdeck. The large penthouse, such a source of controversy thirty years before, was converted into an exercise room, solarium, sauna, greenhouse, and bar. The 303 new condominium apartments were completed in the fall of 1981 and placed on the market just as extremely high interest rates were contributing to the decline of the condominium boom. When no individual units sold, the Envoy was purchased by investors, who manage it today as a rental building.

LIFE AT MERIDIAN MANSIONS

Published accounts of life in Washington apartment houses are rare. One of the most complete such tales was written by the prominent novelist, Frances Parkinson Keyes, in her autobiography, *All Flags Flying*. She describes in considerable detail her life as the wife of the junior senator from New Hampshire, Henry Wilder Keyes, at Meridian Mansions in the 1920s. While at Meridian Mansions, Mrs. Keyes assumed the burden of extensive entertaining, including the constant rounds of official calls on the wives of high government officials and diplomats—a part of Washington etiquette that did not disappear until the outbreak of World War II. Mrs. Keyes recalled her first year at Meridian Mansions in 1919–20:

My tardiness in meeting the obligations of a new senator's wife weighed rather heavily on my conscience, unavoidable as it had been. I tried to make up for it by plunging with all the vim and vigor of which I was capable into the multiple stereotyped activities of the following autumn.

We had at last found a small, well-located, furnished apartment at Meridian Mansions—later known only by a number and street as 2400 Sixteenth Street—in Washington itself. For our needs this was a great improvement on a crowded, inconvenient house in the suburbs, though it was even more of a strain on our budget—five hundred dollars a month—and it required a formidable amount of cleaning to render it fit to live in, from my viewpoint. This took a good deal of my time and strength. The pre-

vious tenants had evidently departed in some haste and with little thought to their successors' comfort. We found soiled linen on the beds, rubbish in the bureau drawers and even spoiled food in the refrigerator. Quantities of boiling water, antiseptic soap and disinfectant were indicated, and all were unsparingly used. Harry, Peter, Carrie, and I took possession early one Saturday afternoon, and my first caller arrived about ten minutes after we did and climbed unconcernedly over the clutter in the front hall. It had not occurred to me to leave word at the desk that I was not receiving, since this was not the day of the week when I was supposed to do so, but thereafter I was more careful. The following Thursday I had my first "At Home." It was not as well organized as I would have liked, but I was right in believing that I would not have to provide for as many visitors then as later in the season; and I did not commit the almost unforgivable sin of declining to receive all callers who did come (unless I was sick in bed or out making calls myself) if they presented themselves between four and six Thursday. From then until April, except when completely incapacitated or prevented by some emergency, I faithfully received every other Thursday, making calls on the alternate Thursday and on every other day of the week.

These were then officially allotted, with a degree of rigidity which would have done credit to the laws of the Medes and Persians: Supreme Court ladies received on Mondays, congressional ladies on Tuesdays, Cabinet ladies on Wednesdays, Senate ladies on Thursdays, diplomatic ladies on Fridays, resident society—"cave dwellers"—on Saturdays and Sundays. . . .

There were a few loopholes in following the code for the calling system and a few compensations for it. It was not unusual for a large number of congressional ladies who all lived in the same apartment house to pool their resources and receive together. When this was done, the visitor who had called on one could consider that she had called on all, unless each had provided a basket labeled with her name in the entrance hall for the cards left on her. Some doormen had their favorites, and it was not uncommon to see them take a fistful of cards from one basket and drop them in another, permitting their pet tenants to brag the next day that they had more visitors than their fellow hostesses. Two senators' wives sometimes received together, and when they did, there was no question: the call was made on both. And calls could be very brief, especially if the drawing room led into the dining room;

View of an apartment in the "D" wing at Meridian Mansions about 1935.

then the visitor could go in one door and, quite unobserved by her hostess, out another. She did not need to stop for tea at more than one place, and no matter how voracious her appetite, she could not possibly drink it everywhere she went. Mrs. Charles Hamlin, whose husband was a member of the Federal Reserve Board, told me she had once made seventy calls in one afternoon; I think that must have been a record, but it was no great achievement to polish off twenty or thirty. . . .

Indeed, without stepping out of Meridian Mansions, I soon found that I was surrounded with friends—it had actually been nicknamed "The Senatorial Beehive," for eleven senatorial families lived there during the postwar period. The ladies in this group were constantly in and out of each other's apartments; they played a great deal of bridge together; they cooperated in calling and entertaining. I became very fond of my fellow tenants in the "Beehive" . . . and look back with fond memories to those carefree housekeeping years spent there within the great world of Washington.

ARCHITECT ALEXANDER H. SONNEMANN

One of the most productive Washington architects of the early twentieth century was Alexander H. Sonnemann (1872–1956), a native of Chevy Chase, Maryland, who practiced for sixty years in Washington. He was the son of Karl Sonnemann, a German architect and engineer who immigrated to Washington to work on the dome of the United States Capitol in 1858 and later the main building of the Library of Congress. His parents were one of the first families to settle in what is now Chevy Chase, Maryland. Young Sonnemann was trained as an architect by his father and established his own office at the age of twenty-three in 1895. While a partner with Louis Justement, 1919–24, his firm won an architectural award of honor from the Washington Board of Trade for a group of houses on Ogden Street, N.W. His extensive practice included the design of houses in all sections of the Washington area—including Kenwood, Maryland—and numerous commercial buildings. Many of the best-designed rowhouses in Mount Pleasant came from his drawing board. Between 1905 and 1935 he designed more than forty apartment houses, among them Kew Gardens and the large 1935 annex to the Kennedy-Warren, as well as Meridian Mansions. Other major works include the Kenwood Golf and Country Club and the Capital Cemetery. Sonnemann designed many rowhouses for the Kennedy brothers, including a group at 3644–3658 Warder Street, N.W., in 1909 as well as those at 3639–3649 Georgia Avenue, N.W., and 706–764 Rock Creek Church Road, N.W. His son, Karl O. Sonnemann, also became an architect, working for the General Services Administration of the federal government before his death in 1967.

39

WHITELAW

1839 13th Street, N.W.; southeast corner of 13th and T streets
ARCHITECT: Isaiah T. Hatton, 1918
ORIGINAL APARTMENTS: 25 (25 one-bedrooms) plus 22 hotel rooms
STATUS: opened as rental in 1919; closed ca. 1970

The Whitelaw was the first black apartment-hotel in the nation's capital and one of the first in the United States. Erected at a cost of $158,000, the Whitelaw opened in November 1919 as the pride of Washington's black community. It was one of the few large buildings at that time completely developed, financed, designed, and built by blacks. Erected when segregation was practiced in all Washington hotels and restaurants, the Whitelaw became the center for social functions of the city's black intellectual and professional elite. It served as a bold statement that the city's blacks had the money and ability to create a major building of sophistication and good taste. Not only did the hotel offer public accommodations, which provided a dignified and gracious setting for entertainment, but the apartments furnished first-class permanent housing as well.

The Whitelaw was developed by John Whitelaw Lewis, a black laborer who came to Washington in 1894 with Coxey's Army of the unemployed. Two marches on Washington, one in 1894 and another in 1914, were led by a Pennsylvania quarryman, Jacob S. Coxey, who tried to persuade Congress to furnish funds to enable all American communities to hire the unemployed for public works. He was considered a radical at the time, but many of his proposals were adopted by President Franklin D. Roose-

The Whitelaw opened in 1919 as Washington's first apartment-hotel for blacks.

158

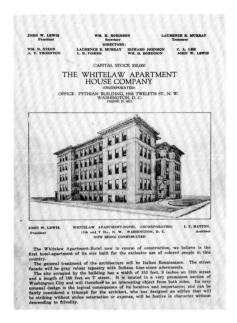

The original 1918 broadside advertising the Whitelaw Hotel.

velt during the Great Depression. After the first demonstration, John Whitelaw Lewis remained to develop a realty company and later founded the highly successful Industrial Savings Bank, which is one of the oldest black-owned banks in the United States.

The Whitelaw was designed by Isaiah T. Hatton, a black architect of considerable talent until his untimely death in 1921 at the age of thirty-three. Hatton was graduated from Washington's M Street High School and is thought to have apprenticed under the city's leading black architect of the early twentieth century, John Lankford. Hatton's work also included the city's Industrial Bank Building, the Murray Palace Casino, and the Southern Aid Insurance Company building.

The exterior of the U-shaped Whitelaw is in a restrained Beaux Arts design. The four-and-a-half-story buff-brick building includes a front court occupied by a one-story section of public rooms. To add interest to the front facade, the architect framed the nine central windows on each projecting pavilion with raised bands of brick and limestone sills. Although the bracketed cornice and two stringcourses help to relieve the severity of the building, the entrance remains an elaborate focal point. The front doors are housed within a recessed portico with a limestone arch, or "Serliana," above and a pair of rusticated brick pilasters on each side. Below the stepped pediment, the name *Whitelaw* is incised in a Doric frieze.

The principal public rooms were on the first floor—lobby, parlor, and, in the center of the building and embellished with an elaborate art glass ceiling, a dining room that was also used as a ballroom. The Georgian Revival detailing in the public rooms was well designed and remained in good condition for fifty years. A cafe and barbershop were provided in the English basement, which was entered from T Street. In the upper three stories, housed in separate wings, were the twenty-five small apartments and twenty-two hotel suites. The Whitelaw would remain the only luxury apartment house for blacks until 1949 when the Portner Flats, renamed the Dunbar Hotel, was converted to the city's largest apartment-hotel for blacks.

After the Whitelaw closed in the early 1970s, much of the interior was badly vandalized—but might have been saved had plans materialized in 1980–81 for its conversion to a condominium. This project was abandoned when soaring interest rates in 1981 kept local

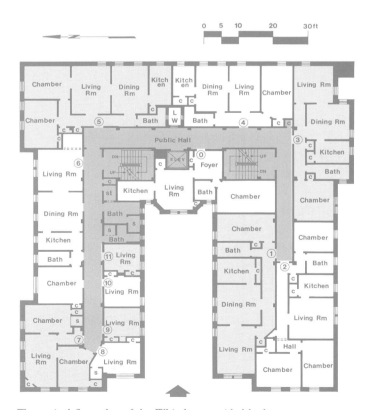

The typical floor plan of the Whitelaw provided both apartments and hotel suites.

developers from financing the project. It remains a vacant shell after a serious fire that gutted much of the interior in late 1981.

Apartment houses for blacks were first built about 1900 in Washington. The dozen that existed before 1920 were small, with only two to six units per building. During the 1920s black apartment houses increased dramatically, however. Although most remained small, a dozen were six- and seven-story buildings. Half of these were built as rental apartment houses by the Cafritz Company and the B. F. Saul Company, while the other half were taken over by blacks as they moved into formerly all-white neighborhoods. (As early as the 1890s, as the black population swelled, a number of white neighborhoods adjacent to black residential areas changed racial composition very quickly. One of the earliest white middle-income neighborhoods to change to black housing was LeDroit Park, a group of Victorian detached houses built in the 1870s near Florida Avenue and 5th Street, N.W. The expansion of nearby Howard University and the need for adequate housing for its black faculty initiated this development.)

The black population of Washington greatly increased immediately after the Civil War. Many freedmen felt that their rights would be better protected if they lived in the capital city that gave them their freedom, but there was a serious lack of adequate housing. Many lived in alley dwellings, small rowhouses built in the alleys in the middle of blocks of white housing. (Washington was unlike most Southern cities with clearly demarcated black ghettoes.) Developers purchased back halves of the long lots behind white rowhouses and built ranges of small two-story brick rowhouses, which they rented to blacks at considerable profit. Often squalid and unhealthful, the alley dwellings housed more than 20,000 blacks on more than 300 blocks of the city by 1900. Most had no indoor plumbing or electricity. The first attempt to eliminate these dwellings was initiated by the first Mrs. Woodrow (Ellen Louise Axson) Wilson as early as 1913. Efforts were intensified by Eleanor Roosevelt during the 1930s to replace them with healthful and pleasant garden apartments, such as Langston Dwellings, built as part of the federal government's first public housing program. It was not until the late 1940s that the last alley dwellings were abolished. The significant numbers of black apartment houses during the mid- and late 1920s were thus a welcome improvement to the shortage of decent housing for blacks.

In her crusade to remove the obnoxious alley dwellings throughout the city, Eleanor Roosevelt was joined by Agnes E. Meyer. In an article in her husband's newspaper, the *Washington Post*, in 1944 Mrs. Meyer wrote:

> In my journey through the war centers I have visited the worst possible housing. But not in the Negro slums of Detroit, not even in the Southern cities, have I seen human beings subjected to such unalleviated wretchedness as in the alleys of our city of Washington. Altogether there are more than 20,000 substandard houses in Washington having neither toilet nor bath and about 6,800 are without running water. Five or six persons to a room, occupying at times a single bed, is commonplace. The outdoor toilets are frequently stopped up, so that several neighboring houses, as well as the passerby, use the nearest obtainable facilities.
>
> How can such uncivilized things happen in Washington? Is there no inspection? Of course there is, by six different departments. But what can, for instance, our very competent Health Department do about it? The only thing it can do is put the tenants on the street because there is not, and has not been for six months, a single available Negro dwelling in Washington, except a few for immigrant war workers.

One of the most important accounts of the origin and development of apartment houses for blacks in Washington was William Henry Jones's *The Housing of Negroes in Washington, D.C.*, published in 1929 by Howard University where he was a professor of sociology. Jones's description of the process of the conversion of white apartment houses to black residency in the 1920s is worth quoting:

> About 1924 a few genuine apartment buildings were constructed [for blacks] and several formerly occupied by white people—because of the shifting of the Negro population—passed unexpectedly into the hands of Negroes. It is significant to note that, in the transition of a community from white to Negro inhabitants, the apartment house plays a conservative role—being, in nearly every instance, the last stronghold of white residency to give way to Negro invasion. There is a definite reason why the

This 1922 photograph by Scurlock Studio of Washington shows a ball held in the ground-floor dining room of the Whitelaw.

apartment is slow in passing over to Negro occupancy for it constitutes a sort of neighborhood in and of itself. Its life is more or less independent of that of its immediate environment. The neighbors of the apartment dweller are primarily the persons who live in the other apartments of the building; more specifically, those who occupy the same floor. Hence, the apartment building constitutes the physical boundaries of a more or less distinct neighborhood, dissociated—except for location—from the rest of the community.

A careful study of the life of the apartment house established the fact that it is quite aloof from the general life of the immediate geographical area in which it is situated. The highly transient nature of its residents, their pronounced outside interests, and their freedom from community responsibility cause them to disregard, more or less, even the changes in the racial composition of the population of the surrounding neighborhood, as long as these changes are not extending to the internal life of the apartment [house]. White occupants of apartment houses do not usually experience the same kind of feelings that white persons who live in the surrounding private residences experience when confronted by a Negro invasion, because they are not in danger of having Negroes as neighbors across the hall or on the other floors of the building. As long as an apartment house is occupied by white people, there exists, within, a white neighborhood with its own life and with likemindedness, consciousness-of-kind, and common interests.

Hence, the apartment houses tend to remain as the last vestiges of white tenure in communities which have become "colored." But, in due time, they too, are surrendered to the invaders. During the past five years, about forty apartment houses have "gone over" to Negroes, and almost as many have been constructed for their occupancy. These new dwellings are proving extremely attractive to blacks and are being rented as fast as they can be built. They are especially popular because of their newness, and the fact that they are equipped with modern conveniences.

This tendency of blacks to move into white neighborhoods bordering on their own districts was particularly prevalent between 1945 and 1970 when the black population again greatly increased in Washington. Just after World War II the black neighborhood expanded westward rapidly beyond its traditional boundary of 13th Street, N.W., to 19th Street, N.W. Many of the apartment houses in this area changed from white to black residences by 1970, partly because black housing was being depleted by the destruction of old housing for expensive renovations in Georgetown and for new buildings in the Southwest. In 1949, during these demographic changes, several white rental apartment houses were converted to black cooperatives, notably the Hawarden and the much larger first-class apartment house at 1916 16th Street, N.W. They remain the oldest black co-ops in the city.

40. ALBEMARLE
1700 T Street, N.W.
ARCHITECT: T. Franklin Schneider, 1900
STATUS: opened as rental in 1900; converted to condo in 1980

41. IOWA
1325 13th Street, N.W.
ARCHITECT: T. Franklin Schneider, 1900
STATUS: opened as rental in 1900; converted to condo in 1979

42. MARLBOROUGH

917 18th Street, N.W.

ARCHITECT: Arthur B. Heaton, 1901

STATUS: opened as rental in 1901;
converted to offices ca. 1950; razed in 1979

43. FARRAGUT

900 17th Street, N.W.

ARCHITECT: T. Franklin Schneider, 1901

STATUS: opened as rental in 1901; converted to offices in 1938; razed in 1959

44. SHERMAN

1101 15th Street, N.W.

ARCHITECT: T. Franklin Schneider, 1901

STATUS: opened as rental in 1901; razed in 1958

45. CECIL

1026 15th Street, N.W.

ARCHITECT: T. Franklin Schneider, 1903

STATUS: opened as rental in 1903; razed in 1958

46. PLYMOUTH

1236 11th Street, N.W.

ARCHITECT: Frederick G. Atkinson, 1903

STATUS: opened as rental in 1904; converted to condo in 1986

47. ROCHAMBEAU

815 Connecticut Avenue, N.W.

ARCHITECT: T. Franklin Schneider, 1903

STATUS: opened as rental in 1904; converted to offices ca. 1938; razed in 1962

49. CHAMPLAIN

1424 K Street, N.W.

ARCHITECT: Clinton Smith, 1905

STATUS: opened as rental in 1905; converted to offices ca. 1955

48. WOODLEY

1851 Columbia Road, N.W.

ARCHITECT: T. Franklin Schneider, 1903

STATUS: opened as rental in 1903; converted to condo ca. 1979

51. TORONTO

2004 P Street, N.W.

ARCHITECT: Albert H. Beers, 1908

STATUS: opened as rental in 1908; converted to co-op in 1920; converted to offices ca. 1956

50. PORTSMOUTH

1735 New Hampshire Avenue, N.W.

ARCHITECT: T. Franklin Schneider, 1906

STATUS: opened as rental in 1906; converted to condo in 1980

52. NETHERLANDS

1860 Columbia Road, N.W.

ARCHITECT: Averill, Hall, and Adams, 1909

STATUS: opened as rental in 1909; converted to co-op ca. 1920

53. STAFFORD

1789 Lanier Place, N.W.

ARCHITECT: Hunter and Bell, 1910

STATUS: opened as rental in 1910; converted to co-op ca. 1920

54. COVINGTON

1858 Columbia Road, N.W.

ARCHITECT: Ralph Healy, 1901

STATUS: opened as rental in 1901; converted to low-yield (nonprofit) co-op in 1980

55. BILTMORE

1940 Biltmore Street, N.W.

ARCHITECT: Claughton West, 1913

STATUS: opened as rental in 1913

56. 2001 16TH STREET, N.W.,
now the BRITTANY
ARCHITECT: A. M. Schneider, 1914
STATUS: opened as rental in 1915; converted to condo in 1980

57. 1868 COLUMBIA ROAD, N.W.,
now the NORWOOD
ARCHITECT: Hunter and Bell, 1916
STATUS: opened as rental in 1917

58. SOMERSET HOUSE
1801 16th Street, N.W.
ARCHITECT: Frank R. White, 1916
STATUS: opened as rental in 1916

59. 1424 16TH STREET, N.W.

ARCHITECT: Appleton P. Clark, Jr., 1917
STATUS: opened as rental in 1917;
converted to offices ca. 1958

60. NORTHBROOK COURT

3420–3426 16th Street, N.W.
ARCHITECT: Frank R. White, 1917
STATUS: opened as rental in 1917; converted to condo in 1980–81

3

THE BOOM PERIOD, 1919–1931

INTRODUCTION

THE BOOM PERIOD

81.

BROADMOOR, 3601 Connecticut Avenue, N.W.

82.

HARVARD HALL, 1650 Harvard Street, N.W.

83.

WARDMAN TOWER, 2600 Woodley Road, N.W.

84.

HAMPSHIRE GARDENS, 4912 New Hampshire Avenue, N.W.;
block bounded by Emerson, Farragut, and 3rd streets, and New Hampshire Avenue, N.W.

85.

WOODLEY PARK TOWERS, 2737 Devonshire Place, N.W.

86.

SHOREHAM HOTEL, 2500 Calvert Street, N.W.

87.

WESTCHESTER, 4000 Cathedral Avenue, N.W.

88.

KENNEDY-WARREN, 3133 Connecticut Avenue, N.W.

89.

SEDGWICK GARDENS, 3726 Connecticut Avenue, N.W.

NOTABLE ADDITIONS

Although Washington's most distinguished apartment houses were constructed in the decade before World War I, the development of this building type in the 1920s stands out for other reasons. This decade was a boom period—not unlike the 1980s and the ambitious construction of new office buildings at that time. More luxury apartment houses were being built than ever before in the city's history. With the expansion of the federal government during World War I, thousands of workers arrived to staff the new agencies. Federal civilian employment in Washington almost tripled between 1916 and 1918, growing from 41,804 government workers to 120,835. These numbers fell after the war, but they remained significantly higher than prewar employment. Developers worked around the clock to build new apartment houses to shelter the new Washingtonians. Other significant changes during these years included the advent of freestanding apartment houses with large amounts of open space as an integral part of the scheme. The variety in housing forms and plans proliferated during this postwar period.

Beaux Arts decorative motifs, which had been the leading influence for Washington apartment houses for twenty years, began to be abandoned in the early 1920s. Architects of the era began adapting traditional architecture to modern requirements, feeling the need to inject new life into old styles. The result was often eclectic, combining classical with Tudor, Moorish, or even Art Deco motifs. The introduction of such technological advancements as push-button elevators and electric dishwashers had a major impact as well in the 1920s.

Along with facade changes, apartment houses were built larger to accommodate the growing population. The typical apartment during this period, however, was smaller, with far less detailing and lower ceilings than had been the norm. Much higher prices and increased scarcity of skilled workers discouraged developers from using parquet floors, elaborate plasterwork, and other expensive refinements. Changes in technology affected floor plans in many ways: the popularity of the automobile led to basement garages, and push-button elevators permitted a greater freedom in planning because of their economy of operation. Developers could therefore afford to install

three or four automatic elevators in several areas, rather than clinging to the tradition of a single bank of two hand-operated elevators in the main lobby.

Cooperatives now became very popular, and by 1924 developers began to build apartment houses intended for that purpose. The important architects and developers who specialized in apartment house design during this period left a lasting mark on the city's character and physical appearance. Another significant development of this era was the establishment of zoning laws in 1920. Opposition to apartment houses by owners of detached houses, who claimed they increased traffic and noise and reduced light and air for smaller adjacent structures, forced the city government to concentrate many apartments in restricted areas of the city, such as along Connecticut Avenue.

Apartment house popularity immediately following World War I was due largely to inflation. Because of the billions of dollars spent by the federal government to finance America's military role in World War I, the value of the dollar declined 51 percent between 1914 and 1920. And, according to the Bureau of Labor Statistics, the price of building materials for houses nearly tripled during those six years. The greatest increase in the cost of living in the United States in any year in the twentieth century occurred in 1920.

Because government salaries had not kept pace with inflation, half of the federal employees in Washington could not afford to purchase houses. The cost of houses in the capital was exceeded only by the price structure in New York until 1928, when Washington overtook New York as the most expensive city. In that year the average cost of a Washington house climbed to $8,600, as compared with an average of $5,200 for the thirteen other largest American cities. Washington was subject to such high cost figures partially because the city had far fewer working class dwellings than were found in all other major American cities.

Rental apartments helped solve the problem by offering less expensive housing for salaried people. While the advantages of a private house were lost, one gained certain freedom from the responsibilities of maintaining a house. Apartment living was far better than the alter-

Architect Appleton P. Clark, Jr., as he appeared when he began his architectural practice in the 1880s. Clark designed more than two dozen Washington apartment houses, including 2852 Ontario Road, the Roosevelt Hotel, and the Presidential, as well as 1424 16th Street.

Between 1905 and 1925 Frank Russell White, above, served as one of developer Harry Wardman's principal apartment house architects.

native—a crowded noisy boarding house (for which Washington had been famous since 1800) with little privacy and no individual housekeeping facilities.

CO-OP CONVERSIONS

The serious inflation caused by World War I resulted in a massive building boom in rental apartment houses throughout the 1920s; it also made co-ops extremely popular for both upper- and middle-income populations. Although co-ops had existed in principle since the early eighteenth century in France and since 1880 in New York, only two had appeared in Washington before 1920—the Concord at New Hampshire Avenue and Oregon Avenue (now Swann Street), N.W. (1891, razed in 1962), and 2852 Ontario Road, N.W. (1909). Both had been organized, built, and owned by the original residents. By 1929 the city had more than seventy-five co-ops; almost fifty of these are still in operation, with the others either returned to rental status or demolished.

The first co-ops of the 1920s consisted of converted rental buildings. More than two dozen rental apartment houses were converted in 1920 alone—a record for one year that has never been exceeded. The fact that the World War I rent control law was still in effect in 1920 was an incentive for apartment house landlords to convert to co-op status, since their investments were not producing adequate returns.

The man credited with making the first co-op conversions in 1920 was Allan E. Walker, who modeled his on those of New York. The apartment house involved was legally converted into a corporation (usually incorporated in the state of Delaware to reduce taxes), and shares of stock were sold. The purchasers of the stock, known as shareholders, were issued shares according to the square footage of their apartments. The shareholder also received a proprietary lease for the apartment that he or she occupied. The apartments thus were not owned outright by the residents, as are houses or condominiums (which were introduced to Washington only in 1963). The co-op building instead was owned by a corporation, and each resident was a shareholder in that corporation. The shareholder was a part-owner of the building, with exclusive rights to occupy one or more apartments according to the shares owned.

Early cooperative apartment buildings used shares of stock to represent the owner's interest in the cooperative corporation. A block of stock was allocated to each apartment unit, based primarily on size, but reflecting other, less tangible factors, including its location in the building, view, elevation, room arrangement, and unusual amenities like fireplaces or balconies. Stock was then divided into two types—preferred and common. The percentage interest between the two types was always the same for every apartment and was based on the developer's original request for a down-payment percentage. If the developer advertised apartments to be purchased with 25 percent down, 25 percent of the stock for each unit would be preferred, the remainder common. The preferred stock would represent one's equity (cash down payment at settlement), and the common stock would represent his or her share of the building's corporate mortgage.

In the case of liquidation of the cooperative (by either foreclosure or voluntary liquidation), it was advertised that preferred stock would be paid off first to try to ensure that purchasers would recover their original down payments. After this stock was paid back to the purchasers, whatever remained of corporate assets would be distributed among the shares of common stock. In reality, there is no difference between distribution of common and preferred stock. All owners would receive proceeds from liquidation of corporate stock based on their proportionate interest in the corporation, regardless of how much common or preferred stock they owned. But in order to calm potential purchasers in this new form of home ownership, "preferred and common stock" was used as a marketing tool.

Today only common stock is held in almost all of the early co-ops, inasmuch as their mortgages have long since been paid off. In all co-ops, regardless of whether they had one or two classes of stock, the proprietary lease was about the same. It established the legal relationship between the shareholder and the corporation.. The owner would be guaranteed the right to vote at annual and special meetings of the shareholders. The charter and bylaws dictated frequency of meetings, procedure of electing the board (which managed the apartment house), and the manner in which the corporation would be dissolved, should it ever be liquidated.

Based on New York practice, it was customary for the shareholder to possess one vote per share of stock held: the owners of large apartments had more votes than the owners of small ones. The co-op owner paid a monthly maintenance fee, based on an amount per share of stock multiplied by the number of shares. The fee included any mortgage payments on the building, taxes, operating costs (fuel, water, wages of staff, and repairs), and any extra expenses incurred by the co-op corporation. A special reserve fund for major improvements was often maintained in older buildings. All co-ops in Washington were stock cooperatives until 1948, when the first membership co-operatives were established at the Westmoreland and the Broadmoor. This more democratic arrangement provided for one vote per apartment, regardless of the size of the unit. Almost all co-ops established since then have been set up as membership co-ops.

In addition to the Allan E. Walker Company, at least seven other real estate firms were involved in converting rental apartment houses to co-ops in 1920. They included the Gatewood S. Bennett Company, the H. B. Tribby Company, the Wardman Construction Company, the William H. Lanham Company, Highie and Richardson, the Union Realty Company, and the F. H. Smith Company. The Smith firm advertised in the [Washington] *Evening Star* on 26 June 1920, for instance, that it was converting the Dupont apartment house at 1717 20th Street, N.W., into a co-op. Most of the nineteen high-ceilinged apartments there were large (five or six rooms plus a maid's room). The Dupont was later converted back to rental status, and the large apartments were subdivided in the 1950s.

Although it was unusual, at least twenty local co-op apartment houses are known to have been converted back to rental status. Most resulted from demographic changes in the neighborhood. For instance, most of the co-ops created in the 1920s along the old 14th Street, N.W., apartment house corridor were reconverted to rental status in the 1950s and the early 1960s when this area was racially integrated. These included the Adelphia, 1427 Chapin Street, N.W.; the Maxwell, 1419 Clifton Street, N.W.; the Kensington, 2501 14th Street, N.W.; the Leamington, 2503 14th Street, N.W.; the Creston, 1475 Columbia Road, N.W.; the Hoyt, 1330 Belmont Street, N.W.; and the Savoy, 14th and Girard streets, N.W. A few years later many of these early apartment houses were destroyed or badly damaged in the riots of 1968. In several other cases the co-op form of ownership was liquidated, and the apartment house was converted to an office building as the neighborhood changed from residential to commercial. This occurred to the Toronto, 20th and P streets, N.W., and the Parkwood, 1746 K Street, N.W., in the 1950s.

POPULARITY OF THE COOPERATIVE APARTMENT HOUSE

The leading co-op apartment house realtor to emerge in the 1920s was Edmund J. Flynn (1889–1983) who, after two years with the Allan E. Walker Company, established his own business, the Edmund J. Flynn Company, in 1923. Still in operation, it specialized in both selling co-op units and converting rental apartment houses to co-op status. Because of strict adherence to sound business practices and conservative management, none of the fifty-eight apartment houses that the Flynn Company converted during the past sixty-three years has failed.

Flynn's success was due in part to his two iron-clad rules: the land must be owned by the co-op, not held on a ground lease, and the apartment's unit price must include the building's mortgage, not just the down payment. In addition, Flynn always opposed setting aside part of the co-op building for rental space. A number of early co-ops in New York had done this, expecting that the income from several rental apartments or shops on the ground floor would pay the co-op's maintenance costs. With recessions and depressions, this space often became vacant, and the co-op apartment house frequently was forced to liquidate. Flynn believed also that it was unwise to establish initial down payments that were too low when converting rental apartments to co-ops. The subsequent monthly maintenance fees invariably were above the units' rental values and ultimately affected the apartments' marketability.

Because converted co-ops were so successful in the early 1920s, a number of new ones were planned and built as such by Washington developers between 1923 and 1929. In 1923, soon after developers Monroe and R. Bates Warren began the construction of 1705 Lanier Place, N.W., a modest four-story walk-up apartment house adjacent to Columbia Road, Edmund J. Flynn suggested they try to sell the units as co-ops. Intrigued, the Warren brothers commissioned Flynn to attempt the sale of the apartments while the apartment house was under construction. Because of Flynn's success in selling all of the apartments before the roof was on, the Warren brothers became the first developers to begin building co-op apartment houses.

Encouraged by the success of 1705 Lanier Place, the Warrens immediately embarked on a much larger middle-class co-op, the 1924 Cleveland Park apartments on Porter Street. After selling out again, the Warrens decided to construct and market three luxury co-ops—the Army and Navy, now 2540 Massachusetts Avenue, N.W., and 1661 Crescent Place, N.W., both in 1925, and the largest complex of all, Tilden Gardens, in 1927. Unlike the Lanier Place and Cleveland Park buildings, these later three were considered luxury apartment houses because they had elevators, elaborate lobbies, switchboards, receptionists, and large staffs. Indeed, the most luxurious co-op in the city before World War II remained 1661 Crescent Place, with enormous seven-room suites of 2,500 square feet or more.

The success of the Warrens influenced several other Washington developers to undertake co-op apartment houses during the 1920s. Morris Cafritz built the Porter at Connecticut Avenue and Porter Street, N.W., in 1925. In 1926 he built two more, the Clydesdale at Clydesdale Place and Adams Mill Road, N.W., and Hilltop Manor, at 14th and Ogden streets, N.W. Although the Clydesdale was successful, Hilltop Manor (later the Cavalier) was not, and subsequently opened as a rental building. After this experience Cafritz's subsequent apartment houses were rental buildings. One of the most unusual groups he built extends from 1433 through 1445 Spring Road, N.W. Erected in 1923, these seven buildings were given names that spelled out C-A-F-R-I-T-Z. The modest three-story walk-ups include the Cromwell, Aberdeen, Fernbrook, Rosedale, Isleworth, Traymore, and Zeldwood. Cafritz was influenced by Harry Wardman, who built a group of seven rental apartment houses at 15th and R streets, N.W., in 1914 with names that spelled out W-A-R-D-M-A-N.

Architect Horace W. Peaslee, shown here with his family, designed the innovative Moorings with nautical themes.

The city's largest developer, Wardman built a complex of five middle-class co-op apartment houses at New York Avenue, 1st and M streets, N.W., in 1925. Totaling 152 apartments and nine stores, this project was touted as the largest co-op complex outside New York City at the time. These modestly designed walk-ups, originally named Alcova Heights Apartments, are still intact. They went from co-op to rental in the 1950s, and back to co-op in the late 1970s. The modest one-bedrooms there originally sold for $6,500, then the same price as a modest suburban house. Wardman built few other co-ops during his career, because he found them less profitable than rental buildings.

Real estate developers were careful to build their better cooperative apartment houses in good residential neighborhoods. Most also soon learned, in the 1920s, to avoid designing co-ops with too many different sizes of apartments. It was felt that apartment houses in which all units were large would attract harmonious residents of the same basic social and financial backgrounds. Washington developer R. Bates Warren, at a realtors meeting in 1927, advised his colleagues to follow certain rules in designing and selling co-ops:

> The promoter of any co-operative apartment project can eliminate many of the snares of selling by properly planning and locating his building. It is a mistake to mingle two widely different kinds of apartments in the same building. This tempts two classes of purchasers. Then, again, to place a building in the wrong neighborhood tends to bring a conflict of class, particularly a reasonably priced apartment in a good neighborhood. In such a building the realtor will have applicants who can afford to purchase but yet who would lower the general standard of

the neighborhood. Here the salesman must be very tactful and careful. The role is not an easy one. The salesman is tempted to sell in order to earn a commission, yet he knows to take a chance will result eventually in dissatisfaction on the part of the employer and other purchasers in the building. This in the long run will hurt his earning power.

> To sum up the situation in selling co-operative apartments, the selling agent must bear in mind that the success of the project depends on the harmony in which the different purchasers live. This is best secured by placing people with as nearly the same tastes and standards of living in the same building as possible.

GUIDING THE INDUSTRY

Although the Warrens, Cafritz, Wardman, and Flynn were reliable businessmen, an unhappy incident in 1928 cast doubt on the integrity of co-op sales in general. A large co-op apartment house, the Parkway at 3220 Connecticut Avenue, N.W., then just finished, went bankrupt. The developer, Arthur M. Suit, had sold only twenty-five of a total eighty-three apartments in the building when he legally established it as a co-op. He ran through the $25,000 down payment made on the twenty-five, then left town when the building went under. The Parkway went bankrupt in mid–1928, heavily encumbered by a $340,000 first trust and a $100,000 second trust. Shortly thereafter it was auctioned off. All twenty-five purchasers lost their down payments, and the eighteen "shareholders" who had already occupied their units were evicted by court order.

The furor over this situation put a damper on the sale of other co-op apartment houses throughout the city, including, for example, disposing of the last co-op apartments at Tilden Gardens. In 1929 the District of Columbia Committee of the United States House of Representatives held hearings on the Parkway case and the entire subject of the formation and operation of cooperatives. Many developers, including the Warrens and Flynn, were called to testify. R. Bates Warren testified that the Parkway was the first and only co-op apartment house of the seventy then in operation that had failed. The twelve hundred co-op apartments in the city were then worth $10 million and were managed soundly. As a result of the hearings the developer of the Parkway was arrested for fraud, and the twenty-five shareholders were reprimanded by the court for capriciously investing in an unsound project. The hearings also led to a regulation that no co-op be incorporated until at least 80 percent of the units had been sold, and future developers were required to place all deposits on co-op apartments in escrow in a sound local bank. Only after the co-op had been incorporated and the first meeting held by the new board of directors were the deposits to be withdrawn from the bank by the developer.

Ironically, in April 1928, shortly before the failure of the Parkway, the National Association of Real Estate Boards (headquartered in Chicago) was taking steps to protect the public from fraudulent or poorly conceived co-op projects. A plan was devised by the realtors association's Co-operative Apartment Bureau, which had been established in 1925 through the efforts of R. Bates Warren, to certify the soundness of all new co-op apartment houses. Upon the application of a co-op builder, this bureau would investigate the financial, legal, architectural, and sale plans. It was thought that once this service became widespread it would be impossible for a developer to market his co-op project without a certificate of approval. The Depression began unfortunately before the system was adopted nationwide. Since very few new co-op apartment houses were built in American cities during the 1930s, the bureau ceased operations.

During the 1925–29 period, however, the activities of the Co-operative Apartment Bureau were significant. The realtors met annually in a variety of cities and toured new co-op apartment houses. The resulting exchange of information among developers helped to refine and standardize co-op development. The leaders of this bureau came from cities with the largest number of co-ops in the 1920s—New York, Chicago, and Washington.

At a bureau meeting in December 1925 in New York, eighteen Washington realtors, including B. F. Saul, Monroe and R. Bates Warren, Rufus Lusk, Waverly Taylor, and Edmund J. Flynn, were in attendance. At this important meeting, the New York hosts led a tour of recently completed apartment houses in the city and its Westchester County suburbs. Two of the architecturally out-standing suburban apartment houses visited were the Blind Brook Lodge in Rye, by architects Van Wait and Wein, and the Fleetwood Hills Country Club apartments, by architect C. C. Wendehack, in Fleetwood Hills. Both were in the newly fashionable Tudor Revival style. Built of red tapestry brick with rough texture and variegated coloration, and with limestone trim, these two co-ops were designed to imitate large private country houses. An atmosphere of quaint domesticity was provided by their gabled roofs, asymmetrical massing, bays, dormers, towers, and chimneys. A parklike setting with spacious landscaped grounds, footpaths, tennis courts, and playgrounds was essential to set the desired tone.

One year later, the Warren brothers used the two New York projects—especially the facade and landscaping of Blind Brook Lodge—as prototypes for Washington's first Tudor Revival "suburban" co-op apartment house, Tilden Gardens. The Washington realtors also were greatly influenced by their tour the following year of Alden Park, an important suburban apartment complex designed by Edwin Rorke in Philadelphia. The cross-shaped plan of the three massive towers at Alden Park, constructed in 1920–24, was copied in a number of Washington apartment houses, including Tilden Gardens in 1927; 4701 Connecticut Avenue, N.W., in 1926; Wardman Tower in 1928; and the Shoreham Hotel in 1930.

AN APARTMENT HOUSE CITY

Apartment houses became extremely popular in Washington during the 1920s with the continuing growth of the federal bureaucracy. The housing shortage begun in 1917 led to a boom period between 1919 and 1931, when more than a thousand new apartment houses were built, ranging in size from modest four-unit walk-ups to opulent complexes with more than three hundred apartments. The vast majority were rentals; most of them are still in use.

Another striking change occurred during this period when the number of new apartments far exceeded the number of new houses. In 1922, 70 percent of new residential construction involved houses, as compared with 30 percent apartment units. By 1928 the figures were exactly reversed. So much of the city's population lived

Architect George F. Santmyers is most noted for his design of several hundred Art Deco apartment houses in the 1930s. Some of his best include 3901 Connecticut Avenue, 4701 Connecticut Avenue, the Delano, and the Normandie. He collaborated with Joseph Abel in designing 2101 Connecticut Avenue.

The [Washington] *Evening Star* on 30 August 1930 cited these eight men as the most prominent apartment house developers in Washington. Left to right in the upper row are Harry Wardman, Edgar S. Kennedy, Monroe Warren, and R. Bates Warren. In the lower row appear Harry M. Bralove, Morris Cafritz, David L. Stern, and Gustave Ring.

in apartment houses by 1926 that the commissioner of the Bureau of Labor Statistics referred to Washington as "a city of cliff dwellers." Because of the high cost of living in Washington, this trend has continued. By 1930 an estimated 50 percent of Washington's population was living in apartment houses.

DEVELOPERS OF APARTMENT HOUSES

During the 1920s dozens of developers made fortunes through the construction of apartment houses in Washington. Although the co-op was important during this decade, the vast majority of new apartment houses offered rental facilities. The most prominent figures were Edgar S. Kennedy, Monroe and R. Bates Warren, Harry M. Bralove, Morris Cafritz, David L. Stern, Frank Tomlinson, Gustave Ring, Goldsmith and Keller, Baer and Scholz, A. Joseph Howar, William S. Phillips, the Ell and Kay Company, and Harry Wardman.

The Kennedy brothers had already established themselves when they built and opened the majestic Meridian Mansions (now the Envoy) in 1918. Edgar S. Kennedy, the surviving brother, went on to build four apartment houses at the northeast corner of Connecticut and Ca-

thedral avenues during the 1920s. His ill-fated Kennedy-Warren, started in 1931 (but not finished because of bankruptcy), remains the city's finest Art Deco apartment house.

Most of the Warren brothers' important 1920s apartment houses were built as co-ops—1705 Lanier Place, N.W.; the Cleveland Park; 3000 Porter Street, N.W.; the Army and Navy; 1661 Crescent Place; and Tilden Gardens. Harry M. Bralove was responsible for the Broadmoor; 2101, 3901, and 4707 Connecticut Avenue, N.W.; the Shoreham Hotel; and a number of smaller apartment houses. Morris Cafritz, although active mainly in house construction during the 1920s, built five large Washington apartment houses—Corcoran Courts (23rd and D streets, N.W., later demolished to make way for the Department of State building), Hilltop Manor (later the Cavalier), the Park Central, the Park Lane, and the Miramar. In addition to building its own apartment houses, the Cafritz Construction Company was employed by other developers; one such project involved the Pershing at 16th Street and Spring Road, N.W., for McKeever and Goss in 1924. During the 1920s, Cafritz employed and trained Gustave Ring, who set out on a spectacular building career of his own in 1930.

Two important post—World War I developers were

Architect Harvey H. Warwick, Sr., active in the 1920s and 1930s, designed the Chalfonte, Hilltop Manor, the Park Central at 1900 F Street, and with Francis L. Koenig both Colonial Village and the Marlyn.

Architect Louis T. Rouleau designed Woodley Park Towers, an important Art Deco apartment house.

David L. Stern and Frank Tomlinson, who together built fifteen apartment houses in the city between 1922 and 1926. Both partners surprisingly were also practicing architects. Two of their largest apartment houses were 1915 16th Street, N.W., and 1830 K Street, N.W. After the firm dissolved in 1926, each developer established his own company and continued to build apartment houses.

Another developer, Joseph Howar, was responsible for a number of important large apartment houses in the 1920s, including two Tudor style buildings, the Windemere at 1825 New Hampshire Avenue, N.W., and the adjacent Harrowgate. He also built the Clyde at 1122 10th Street, N.W.; the Lombardy at 2019 Eye Street, N.W.; 736 22nd Street, N.W.; and 2115 Pennsylvania Avenue, N.W.

William S. Phillips commissioned Stern and Tomlinson in 1922 to design his prestigious Argonne, now the Park Plaza, at 16th Street and Columbia Road, N.W. This once-luxurious apartment house has now fallen on hard times. Phillips also built and owned the innovative Harvard Hall as well as Phillips Terrace (soon renamed the Chalfonte) and the Valley Vista.

The firm of Baer and Scholz constructed the enormous Alban Towers, as well as 2310 Connecticut Avenue, N.W., and the Greystone at 815 18th Street, N.W. The

Ell and Kay Company completed a number of large apartment houses shortly before the stock market crash in October 1929, including the Woodley Park Towers; 5420 Connecticut Avenue, N.W.; and 2800 Ontario Road, N.W. The firm of Goldsmith and Keller built the well-publicized Park Towers, opposite Meridian Hill Park on 16th Street, N.W., in 1928—one of the first Washington apartment houses to incorporate Art Deco facade detailing. (After being closed for many years, the Park Towers was renovated and reopened by Jonathan Woodner in 1987.) They also built the Schuyler Arms at 1954 Columbia Road, N.W.; La Reine at 5425 Connecticut Avenue, N.W.; 1437 Rhode Island Avenue, N.W.; a pair of large apartment houses at 4105–4115 Wisconsin Avenue, N.W.; and the Chamberlain at 1425 Rhode Island Avenue, N.W.

THE INFLUENCE OF HARRY WARDMAN

Certainly the most important real estate developer of the twenties was Harry Wardman (1871–1938), who amassed a fortune of $30 million between the time he entered the construction business in Washington in 1897 and the beginning of the Depression thirty-three years later. The son of a dry goods merchant in England, the seventeen-year-old Wardman immigrated to New York in 1889. After a few years he moved to Philadelphia, where he worked for John Wanamaker's department store and at night learned the art of building staircases.

Arriving in Washington in 1895, Wardman practiced his trade as a skilled carpenter, working as a staircase carpenter for the many small builders of Washington's brick rowhouses. He also laid floors in many buildings in the late 1890s, including the famous Willard Hotel. His first success in the construction business came in 1897, when he built six wooden detached houses at 900–908 Longfellow Street, N.W., and 5520 9th Street, N.W. Soon afterwards his career as the city's most successful builder was launched as he began to construct dozens upon dozens of rows of modest, but highly profitable, two-story flat buildings.

During the following three decades Wardman built an enormous number of Washington buildings, including four thousand houses (freestanding, semidetached, and rowhouses), twelve office buildings, eight hotels, two clubs, two important hospital annexes, two embassies, one large parking garage, and four hundred apartment buildings. Indeed, the development of the modern Washington apartment house was considered Wardman's most important contribution to his adopted city. His first two important luxury apartment houses—the Dresden and the Northumberland—were built simultaneously in 1909. Many other important examples followed: the Avondale in 1913; 2001 16th Street, N.W. (now the Brittany), in 1914; and Wardman Courts (now Clifton Terrace) at 14th and Clifton streets, N.W., in 1914–15. His three principal architects, Albert H. Beers, Frank Russell White, and Mihran Mesrobian, created innovative and trend-setting apartment houses for other builders to follow.

As early as 1915 Wardman planned Woodley Courts, a massive cluster of luxury apartment buildings on Connecticut Avenue between Woodley Road and Calvert Street. Because of the approach of World War I and the expected restriction of building materials, he abandoned the proposed Woodley Courts in place of the Wardman Park Hotel, which opened in 1918 as the city's largest apartment-hotel. Wardman's apartment houses became progressively larger during the 1920s. In another grandiose but ill-fated scheme, he planned Wardman Gardens in 1926, a series of five high-rise apartment towers on the 12-acre site now occupied by the Shoreham Hotel at Calvert and 24th streets, N.W. This complex would have housed five thousand residents and would have been the largest apartment house in the world, but lack of adequate financing prevented him from carrying out the project. Many other large apartment houses were built during the 1920s, however. His Cathedral Mansions of 1922–23, a complex of three large apartment buildings at Connecticut and Cathedral avenues, was considered the largest luxury apartment house south of New York at the time. In 1928 he built two of his largest apartment houses on Connecticut Avenue—the Wardman Tower and Davenport Terrace.

While Wardman concentrated his attention on construction projects, he failed to maintain close inspection of his financial affairs. Through the unprofessional financial management of his real estate empire by his two principal assistants, Thomas P. Bones and James D. Hobbs, Wardman found himself land rich but short of cash by 1927. By publicly selling stock in the Wardman Construction Company and by mortgaging part of his real estate holdings, he raised $13 million the following year. This allowed Wardman to continue building at a frantic pace. Even with these warning signs, his second wife, Lillian Wardman, continued to live on an extravagant scale, dividing her time between Paris, London, and Washington in the late 1920s.

Financially overextended when the stock crash came in late 1929, Wardman lost his fortune of more than $30 million. At that time he was credited with having built one-tenth of the residences of Washingtonians. After enduring an embarrassing congressional investigation into his financial affairs in the early thirties, he resumed building on the extensive land he still owned (saved, because it was in his wife's name). His reputation was so solid among members of the business community that he was able to resume business operations and build more than a thousand small houses during the Depression. Wardman was on the way to making a complete financial recovery when he died of cancer in 1938.

a

b

c

d

Porte-cochères became popular with apartment house developers in the late 1920s and early 1930s as the automobile became more prominent. Examples of the revival styles used include the Tudor Revival at Alban Towers (a), the Colonial Revival at the Wardman Tower (b), and the Moorish Revival at the Westchester (c). The best example of an Art Deco apartment house porte-cochère is at Sedgwick Gardens (d).

NEW DESIGN CONCEPTS

Important design improvements appeared in Washington apartment houses between 1919 and 1931. During the preceding traditionalist period in architecture, 1897–1918, most first-class apartment houses resembled overblown classical palazzi, often U-shaped with rear courtyards, and with almost no vacant grounds around them. Although some pre–World War I apartment house plans did vary, such as the Warder with its interior court, and 1509 16th Street, N.W., with its rectangular inner block plan, most occupied 60 percent of their sites.

In the early 1920s this sort of plan was abandoned increasingly for a new design concept, the "suburban" apartment house. Based more on resort hotels than on traditional apartment house design, it had spacious grounds, was set back well from the street, and was often irregular in plan. The first such building was the Wardman Park Hotel, which opened in 1918 at Connecticut Avenue and Woodley Road, N.W. With five spokelike radiating wings, the hotel was designed with half its space for permanent apartment residents. Its location on 10 acres of landscaped grounds was influenced by Harry Wardman's frequent visits to the Homestead resort at Hot Springs, Virginia. This spoke plan would become the model for all future, large luxury apartment houses in the city. Wardman's Cathedral Mansions of 1922–23 followed this plan. Other notable examples designed in the suburban ideal between 1926 and 1931 included the Broadmoor, Tilden Gardens, the Westchester, and the Kennedy-Warren.

Increased open space around the much larger apartment houses of the 1920s led to improved air circulation, better views, and greatly increased light. Although the U-shaped plan almost disappeared, the V shape continued—traditionally used on triangular lots formed by the city's diagonal avenues. The new shapes of the 1920s included the X plans of the Shoreham Hotel, Tilden Gardens, Wardman Tower, and 4701 Connecticut Avenue, N.W. In addition, a few square or rectangular buildings with spacious interior courtyards, such as Kew Gardens, were designed to conform to the new zoning regulations.

GARDEN APARTMENTS

The 1920s brought garden apartments to Washington. Defined as a group of three or more two- or three-story buildings without lobbies or elevators, garden apartments are arranged together in a landscaped setting. The first two garden apartments in Washington were unsuccessful architecturally, because their elements were poorly related to one another. The idea works best when the buildings are grouped together harmoniously around a spacious landscaped courtyard. Developer Allan E. Walker built the first such project in 1921–22 at 124–130 and 131–133 Webster Street, N.W., one block from the Soldiers Home. Named Petworth Gardens (now Webster Gardens), the complex consists of six rectangular two-story red-brick walk-ups, arranged so that their ends face the street. Domesticity is suggested by the projecting end pavilions and bays, hipped roofs, decorative dormer windows, glazed sleeping porches, arched doors, and wide eaves. Four are on the south side of the street and the other two on the north side. Landscaping is provided by narrow rectangular lawns between the identical buildings. They were designed by architect Robert F. Beresford and were based on the Pomander Walk apartment complex recently built in London.

The second garden apartment development was built at 3018–3028 Porter Street, N.W., just west of Connecticut Avenue, in 1924–25 by Monroe and R. Bates Warren. Known as the Cleveland Park, these six three-story cooperative buildings are of more expensive construction, larger, and on a much more spacious site than Petworth Gardens. Although situated in a row facing Porter Street, Cleveland Park also has more open landscaped grounds and garages in the rear.

Inspired by the suburban luxury apartment house, the city's first successful and sophisticated garden apartment, Hampshire Gardens, was built by developer Edmund J. Flynn as a cooperative in 1929. The facades of each of the eight cross-shaped two-story buildings vary in their cross-timbering, crenelation, and door treatment. The buildings are skillfully arranged around a very large oval park with abundant plantings and connecting walkways. Only one block of eight buildings was completed because of the Great Depression: the original plan had called for more than ten city blocks.

Garden apartments did not become popular in Washington until after the Great Depression. Thus, between 1935 and 1942, more than three hundred garden apartment complexes were built in Washington and its suburbs, constituting one of the most important collections of this type of apartment house in the United States.

INTERIOR CHANGES

A dramatic change occurred in apartment house design immediately after World War I because of major changes in floor plans, technological innovations, improved site planning, the introduction of zoning, and other factors. The introduction of the "modern" apartment house in Washington in the 1920s also brought a number of interior changes. Because of the city's building height restriction, few first-class Washington apartment houses exceeded seven stories in 1910. The rooms usually had ceilings about 9 feet, 2 inches high. After the war, to economize, ceilings were often dropped so that a standard-height building could accommodate eight stories. As a further means of creating an additional floor within the height limit, some apartment houses were built with step-down lobbies. Several developers found another way to stretch the height law by building apartment houses on steep slopes with the allowable height at street grade but with an additional one or two stories below grade in the rear. Two early examples are 1705 Lanier Place, N.W., and the Kennedy-Warren.

First used to establish the prestige of the apartment house about 1909, the large lobby was well established by the beginning of World War I. During the 1920s the lobbies in first-class Washington apartment houses became even larger to increase air circulation during the hot, humid summer months. Before air conditioning, the large lobby became an established domestic institution where residents could gather during the day for conversation in a relatively cool atmosphere. The most impressively large and ornate lobbies of the 1920s are in the Broadmoor, Sedgwick Gardens, and 2101 Connecticut

Avenue, N.W. Because the price of land has never been as high as in New York or Chicago, Washington developers could afford larger lobbies than those generally found in apartment houses in other American cities. Large elegant lobbies have continued to be a standard feature of Washington apartment houses. On the other hand, in other cities they were generally abandoned in the 1950s when central air conditioning was introduced. As the size of the Washington lobby increased, however, the average size of apartments decreased. Not only were families smaller in the 1920s, but the cost of living had risen dramatically. To keep pace, the average new Washington apartment decreased from four to three rooms.

Other interior changes included garages in apartment house basements, although some were along alleys behind the buildings, such as at Cleveland Park. The earliest known garage of any type dates to 1902 at the Highlands, which had a ground entrance from Connecticut Avenue for electric cars. They were housed in the basement, where an electric battery charger was available. The first modern basement garages were at 1705 Lanier Place, N.W. (1924); the Army and Navy (1925); 1661 Crescent Place, N.W. (1925); 4701 Connecticut Avenue, N.W. (1927); the Broadmoor (1928); Harvard Hall (1928); and Woodley Park Towers (1928). Garages were becoming common in large apartment houses (those with more than a hundred units).

Features within the apartment also changed rapidly during the 1920s. The breakfast alcove or "nook," separated from the kitchen by a pair of china cabinets, became a hallmark everywhere. The crown molding, parquet floors, and elaborate wainscoting popular in luxury apartment houses before World War I largely disappeared. (By the early 1930s the formal dining room was replaced by a dining ell or recess, which opened off the living room to conserve space.) The high cost of skilled labor in inflationary times limited embellishments. On the other hand, applied molding "panels" on the walls of public rooms became standard in many of the better apartment houses of the 1920s, such as the Broadmoor, 2101 Connecticut Avenue, and Woodley Park Towers. These too would disappear in the more economically minded—and streamlined—1930s. Metal casement windows, used in only a few apartment houses of the 1920s, came into general use between 1935 and 1950. Since the goal of apartment houses of the 1920s was to appear domestic, most of their windows were in the narrow, sash style, made of wood.

Although a number of Washington apartment houses had telephone switchboards by 1910, they did not become standard until the 1920s. They were familiar features until the 1970s, when rent control resulted in their removal in many buildings to cut operating costs. Also popular during the 1920s were interior French doors, which separated dining and living rooms. When dining alcoves replaced dining rooms during the 1930s, however, they were discontinued. Harvard Hall in 1929 was the first apartment house with electric dishwashers in every kitchen, as well as the first major building to include in its original design an indoor swimming pool, located in the sub-basement.

Public dining rooms were usually continued in the plans of luxury apartment houses during the 1920s and early 1930s. They either occupied a standard apartment, such as at Somerset House at 16th and S streets, N.W., or constituted a much larger formal dining area on the ground floor, such as in the Kennedy-Warren, Woodley Park Towers, and the Westchester. Most of the seventy public dining rooms in Washington apartments closed during the Depression. Only a dozen are left now. Older apartment houses with restaurants today include the Westchester, the Kennedy-Warren, the Broadmoor, Alban Towers, and the Woodner. Newer examples include several mixed-use buildings in the city—the Watergate, Georgetown Park, and Washington Harbour—and the Promenade and Prospect House in the suburbs. These projects differ, however, from the older apartment house dining rooms, as their restaurant facilities are designed to serve the general public.

The sleeping porch appeared here and there during the early 1920s, before air conditioning and in a time when personal safety was taken for granted. Several original open porches remain at the Army and Navy as well as at 4701 Connecticut Avenue. Even a few apartment houses built later in the 1930s, such as the Normandy, continued to have them. By the late 1920s, however, most new apartment houses had been built with the sleeping porch glassed in—later renamed a solarium—so that it

could be used in the winter; among them are Tilden Gardens and 2101 Connecticut Avenue.

Many apartment kitchens included cabinets with outer doors opening onto the public hall, from which the resident janitor would remove trash. This system, first used as early as 1903 in the Plymouth, did not become common until the 1920s. For security reasons trash doors were not designed for new apartment houses after the late 1960s. In some apartment houses, such as at Harbour Square in 1966, trash doors were discontinued and replaced by hallway trash chutes. Some buildings, such as the St. Regis, used the dumbwaiter before World War I, and, in the Cleveland Park, during the 1920s. The janitor would send the dumbwaiter up to each apartment for the trash at an established time every day (always by hand, with a rope). A system of bells signaled when the dumbwaiter was coming and when the trash was ready to be removed. While several early Washington apartment houses still use dumbwaiters for trash removal, they have not been built into new buildings since the 1930s. As early as 1910, the Northumberland had a trash chute in each kitchen that connected to the basement. In many of the older buildings, such as the Ontario, trash has always been deposited outside the apartment door between 6 A.M. and 8 A.M. and removed by the resident janitor. When the burning of trash in incinerators was outlawed in Washington in the early 1970s, many buildings installed compactors to conserve storage space until the garbage truck could arrive.

ZONING INFLUENCE

The establishment of zoning in Washington in 1920 had a major impact on apartment house development. The nation's capital was only four years behind New York, the first American city to pass zoning ordinances. The Washington zoning law, enacted to enhance the special character of the city, was based on recommendations of a prominent St. Louis city planner, Harland Bartholomew.

Before 1920, few regulations governed the location and design of Washington apartment houses. The first height-limit law affecting apartment houses, passed in 1894 in reaction to the 156-foot-high Cairo apartment house, limited apartment houses to 90 feet and office buildings to 110 feet. The second regulation governing apartment houses came in 1905, requiring new ones to maintain open space around their facades to "give sufficient light and air independent of any use that any other property owner may make of the adjoining or neighboring lots." Apartment houses on corner lots had to maintain 10 percent of the site open, while those built within the block were required to keep 35 percent of the lot free of construction. In addition, all apartment houses more than 50 feet high, regardless of their location within a block, had to keep 12 feet of open space in front of each facade.

The 1920 zoning law had a major impact on several aspects of apartment house development in Washington. This law with its subsequent amendments during the 1920s designated neighborhoods that were restricted to single-family houses. It allowed apartment houses in these neighborhoods by confining them to one street. The best example of this regulation is evident along Connecticut Avenue. In this area apartment houses were allowed to extend only 100 feet back from the sidewalk. Five commercial strips were allowed along the length of upper Connecticut Avenue between the Taft Bridge and Chevy Chase Circle. The new regulations also required a far greater percentage of open land around new buildings.

These zoning regulations furthermore resulted in a major change in traditional apartment house design, particularly in the shape of the building. Before 1920 most first-class apartment houses were built close to the lot line with little adjacent open land. Their design usually included a narrow rear court, which resulted in the U-shaped plan. Although new apartment houses built after 1920 were permitted public restaurants, exterior signs to advertise for patrons were no longer allowed in order to preserve the private residential character of the neighborhood. Furthermore, the restaurant could have an entrance only in the building lobby, not a separate street entrance.

During the early 1920s new apartment houses in single-family neighborhoods were not allowed to have garages without the consent of a majority of the neighboring property owners. By the early 1930s, however, developers could build garages without this consent. The zoning law as amended in 1931 allowed eight-story apart-ment houses with garages where only five-story buildings had formerly been permitted on Connecticut Avenue. In return for the increased height, the developer was required to maintain more open landscaping around the building, which could now occupy only 51 percent of the lot. As a result, a more uniform skyline was created and parking congestion was reduced.

The 1920 zoning law also affected the fate of many outstanding landmark residences. One of the earliest implementations was to zone the old downtown residential areas, still mostly intact, for commercial use. Developers applied for permission to expand the traditional commercial area from F Street between 7th and 15th streets, N.W., outward toward the northwest. At a time when little regard was given to the preservation of historic buildings, the zoning commission approved developers' applications to construct office buildings in major historic residential areas. Consequently the dozens of surviving stately antebellum Greek Revival rowhouses in the neighborhoods around Lafayette and Farragut squares—as well as the elegant Second Empire and Beaux Arts houses along K Street, N.W., and Franklin Park—were rapidly demolished during the 1920s and 1930s for commercial development.

Zoning officials, like those in many cities, felt that the new tax revenue from the office buildings would be of great benefit to the city. Good planning should have directed commercial expansion to the east instead, between 7th and F streets, N.W., and Union Station, a then-blighted area that needed development. As a result of the city's first zoning laws, the most important old residential area of Washington fell. Not only were the houses lost, but most of the city's elegant early apartment houses from the 1880s and 1890s disappeared as well. Some of them are described at length in newspapers of the time, but few photographs have survived as a record of their actual design. Perhaps the zoning commissioners of the era never really understood the long-term implications of their rulings. Their unfortunate decision is still felt today.

As the 1930s and 1940s progressed, many minor changes were made in the zoning code that affected apartment house design. A 1942 amendment, for instance, required all new apartment houses to provide offstreet parking. So many puzzling amendments were added to the zoning law that most citizens and even their real estate attorneys found them difficult to understand. A new zoning study consequently was undertaken in the mid-1950s by the prominent New York city planner Harold M. Lewis. In 1958 the city repealed the original Zoning Act of 1920, with its hundreds of amendments. The Zoning Act of 1958 is still in force.

ZONING BATTLES

Since the initial opposition to the Cairo in 1894, more than two dozen major battles have been fought against apartment house projects. In 1914 Mrs. John B. Henderson opposed the construction of apartment houses facing the proposed Meridian Hill Park. Indeed, Mrs. Henderson's objections between 1914 and 1919 were a contributing factor in the adoption of Washington's Zoning Act of 1920.

In late 1914 Harry Wardman announced plans to build three apartment houses on land he owned at the corner of 15th and Euclid streets, N.W., facing the proposed park site. Since the resolute Mrs. Henderson was the principal force behind the federal government's development of the park, which eventually took more than twenty years to build, she immediately negotiated with Wardman to acquire his land. In January 1915 Mrs. Henderson traded several of her lots at the corner of 17th and Willard streets, N.W., for Wardman's lots at 15th and Euclid streets, N.W. Mrs. Henderson already owned extensive real estate facing the proposed park, and she built a half-dozen houses there for sale or rent to embassies. Indeed, she created the first Embassy Row, which remained intact along 16th Street until her death in 1932. After World War II the principal location for embassies shifted to Massachusetts Avenue, N.W., between Dupont Circle and Observatory Circle. Following her victory over Wardman in January 1915, Mrs. Henderson stated: "Meridian Hill Park, which is planned to be one of the most beautiful small parks in the whole country, is now protected from any surroundings which could fall below a certain standard of beauty."

A few years later, in 1919, Mrs. Henderson became embroiled in a second well-publicized fight to limit the height of an apartment-hotel, the Roosevelt, which was already under construction on 16th Street between V and W streets, N.W. The owners of the Roosevelt, at the foot of Meridian Hill Park, had already obtained a building permit and begun construction before Mrs. Henderson learned that its height would interfere with the view of the city from the top of the park. In a barrage of letters from her summer home in Bar Harbor, Maine, she secured the endorsement of the Commission of Fine Arts to reduce the Roosevelt's height to seven stories. Consequently a bill was passed in Congress requiring the Roosevelt owners to remove the rooftop pergola.

During the 1920s many other important battles were waged by citizens groups against the construction of apartment houses in prominent residential areas. Apartment house construction was prohibited in many areas of Northwest Washington. For instance, new apartment houses were prohibited in 1923–24 in most of Cleveland Park and in Georgetown, except for a small strip on Que Street between 27th Street and Dumbarton Bridge. During this decade zoning and planning officials in Washington, New York, and other American cities made a concerted effort to keep apartment houses out of new neighborhoods of freestanding homes. Edward M. Bassett, counsel to the New York City Zoning Commission, stated in 1928: "The kind of apartment which seeks to locate in a private home district because of the high rents obtainable is an evil in that it simply capitalizes on the parklike character of the district while destroying that character at the same time."

Another important zoning case in 1925 involved Washington apartment houses. Dozens of prominent citizens testified for and against apartment houses on Massachusetts Avenue, N.W. Opposition was voiced before the zoning commission by a formidable array of citizens, including Chief Justice and former President William Howard Taft, Colonel Henry A. duPont, and Bishop C. F. Bratenahl of the Washington Cathedral. Likewise, numerous other influential citizens argued for apartment houses on Massachusetts Avenue.

Prominent architect Waddy B. Wood, who had designed a number of important houses on or adjacent to that section of the avenue, argued that the addition of first-class classical limestone-faced five-story apartment houses "such as are erected in Paris" would add to the beauty of this thoroughfare. In additional testimony, Rufus Lusk, secretary of the Operative Builders Association, declared: "But if you come down as far as Fifteenth street and prohibit apartment houses, it will not be long before the people on Rhode Island avenue, New Hampshire avenue and similar thoroughfares will say, 'We don't want apartments.'" Other residents of Massachusetts Avenue, N.W., near Thomas Circle argued that they supported well-designed apartment houses in their neighborhood in preference to boarding houses, which were already beginning to mar the prestige of their area.

Opposition to and concern over apartment houses continued long after the 1920s, however. Groups other than private owners have protested as well. Proposed plans to build a large $1.7 million eight-story apartment

Beginning in the 1890s many apartment houses were named for the wives or daughters of the developers. Two were named for the daughters of T. Franklin Schneider—Ethel (left) and Florence: the 1902 Ethelhurst (now offices at 1025 15th Street) and Florence Court (now known as California Court and California House).

house at the northwest corner of Connecticut Avenue and Leroy Place, N.W., was halted through opposition by the residents of two adjacent apartment buildings, the Westmoreland and the Highlands, who contended that the new apartment house would block their light, air, and view. Residents of single-family rowhouses on both Leroy and Bancroft places also objected because of worry over traffic and parking.

In 1965 the Greater Washington Council of Churches issued a statement indicating that it was alarmed to find that only 5 percent of apartment dwellers attended church, as compared with 60 percent of residents of single-family houses. The report urged Washington-area clergy to change their orientation from family life in order to adjust to the apartment house resident. The author of this study, the Rev. Charles Ellett, wrote: "The big problem in this area lately is the rich untapped lode of potential church membership that determined clerical prospectors could be chipping loose from the luxurious pools and patios of high-rise urban apartment buildings."

Residents of Cleveland Park vigorously opposed a petition before the zoning commission to allow new apartment houses at Wisconsin Avenue and Newark Street, N.W., in 1968. One resident of the area described apartment dwellers as "transient people who are ruthless and don't care about the neighborhood, who will drive out many of us who want to stay."

APARTMENT HOUSES NEVER BUILT

Many grand schemes to build large apartment house projects that were broached in the 1920s fell victim to unavailable financing and/or the Depression. Only a small section of Hampshire Gardens (1929) was built because of the Depression. Harry Wardman's proposed Wardman Gardens, described as the largest apartment house in the country, was never built in the late 1920s because of lack of financing.

Another grand suburban apartment house was planned in June 1929 by developer B. X. Warner, Jr., for a site in Montgomery County, Maryland, abutting Rock Creek Park. Designed as a fifteen-story tower with two thousand rooms, the luxury residence—never even named—was to begin rising in the spring of 1930. Underground driveway approaches would preserve the gardenlike atmosphere. The basement garage was to hold five hundred cars. Two playgrounds—one for younger and one for older children—with trained supervisors were planned. An adjacent large building was to house a swimming pool, gymnasium, drugstore, grocery store, and five other shops. Affluent residents could avail themselves of the planned golf course and adjacent landing field for privately owned airplanes, all part of the 30-acre complex. The Great Depression caused the project to be abandoned. Both of these elaborate schemes were based in part on the plans of Alden Park in Philadelphia.

Perhaps the most bizarre plans of all concerned the proposed congressional apartment house. Members of Congress, on fixed salaries, were not the least to feel the effect of inflation during World War I and through 1920. As a result, Congressman John W. Langley, chairman of the Committee on Public Buildings and Grounds of the U.S. House of Representatives, conceived the idea of a special apartment house reserved for members of Congress and their families and suited to congressional salaries. After sending a form letter to members of Congress, he found 60 percent interested in living in the proposed apartment house. The planned 1928 building, which would also have been available to cabinet officers and Supreme Court justices, was to have included three hundred apartments, ranging from three to ten rooms. The rent would have been sufficient to pay both the maintenance and eventually the construction cost, but the proposed bill never came up for vote.

A second attempt was made in 1935 to erect a congressional apartment house. Congressman Adolph J. Sabath, Democrat of Illinois, called Washington rents "extremely excessive" and asked the District of Columbia commissioners for work-relief funds to construct a special apartment house for members of Congress and their staffs. When Congressman Sabath's proposal was ignored, the battle was resumed by Congressman Alfred F. Beiter, Democrat of New York, in January 1937. Beiter drafted a bill to provide $6 million of federal funds—amortized over forty years—for the project, now greatly enlarged. The new proposal was for buildings near the Capitol in the southwest section, bounded by Independence and Virginia avenues, South Capitol and 7th streets. Ten streets in this area would be closed. The project, to be in Tudor Revival style, would have included a twenty-story hotel tower (federal government buildings are exempt from the height law), four smaller apartment towers, and sixty-six brick rowhouses. The hotel, with fifteen hundred rooms, was to include an auditorium, swimming pool, and two dining rooms—one for members of Congress and one for their employees. The large grounds would be landscaped with a reflecting pool, parks, and a sunken garden. Beiter's bill did not reach the floor for a vote in 1937, however, because of attention in Congress on legislation to combat the Depression.

The acute housing shortage caused by World War II and inflation prompted a fourth attempt for a congressional apartment house. Congressman Sabath, now chairman of the House Rules Committee, came back on the campaign for it. He charged on the House floor in January 1945 that many new members of Congress seeking homes in Washington were being "held up and robbed" through high rentals by Washington landlords. Sabath urged prompt action on a bill that he introduced, calling for $3 million for two buildings near the Capitol for members of Congress and their staffs. This fourth attempt also failed, and the matter was never considered again.

APARTMENT HOUSE NAMES

The practice of naming apartment houses rather than simply using the street address became more widespread in Washington than in any other American city. Of the many kinds of names used, the most fashionable before World War II were British, which were thought to denote aristocratic Anglo-Saxon heritage, respectability, and prestige. Although used constantly between 1880 and 1940, English names enjoyed their greatest popularity during the 1920s. A few of the many in Washington include Albemarle, Cavendish, Cecil, Devonshire, Effingham, Haddington, Marlborough, Monmouth, Northumberland, Rockingham, Somerset, Stratford, Westchester, Wimbledon, and York.

Other foreign place names also became popular during the 1920s. Mostly European but some North African, they included such exotic names as Algiers, Berlin, Monterey, Netherlands, Panama, Sorrento, Touraine, and Turin. Elegance and romance were the connotations. Even prominent World War I battles (all Allied victories) were used as apartment house names in the 1920s, such as the Argonne, Château Thierry, and the Marne. Of the twenty-two apartment houses named for states of the Union, the Iowa and the Wyoming remain the most architecturally prominent. These two were actually named, respectively, for the circle and the avenue in their immediate vicinity.

Other apartment houses were named for women, presidents, statesmen, military heroes, Indians, literary figures, and other American cities. Early twentieth-century Washington apartment houses with Indian names included the Kenesaw, Seneca, Oneida, Huron, and Mendota. Another two hundred carry female names, after the spouses or daughters of the builders, developers, or architects. T. Franklin Schneider named two of his Beaux Arts apartment houses for his daughters: Florence Court (now known as California House and California Court) and the Ethelhurst (now an office building at the southeast corner of 15th and L streets, N.W.).

Usually the grander the name, the less pretentious the apartment house, as is the case with the Premier, Majestic, Royal, La Reine, Le Marquis, Castle, Congress, Senate, Paramount, and Elite. Most apartment houses bearing the name Park—including the Park, Park Plaza, Park Terrace, Park Crescent, Park Wood, Park Lane, Park East, Park Place, Park Lee, Park View, Park Vista, Park Central, Park Manor, Park Meridian, Park Pleasant, and Park Imperial—do not face parks. Even though 80 percent of Washington apartment houses have names, the city's two finest apartment houses today are not named—2029 and 2101 Connecticut Avenue, N.W. The psychological effect of an apartment house's name on its popularity would be a valuable study in twentieth-century social history.

MOVING DAY

One of the peculiarities of life in Washington apartment houses before World War II was moving day, so-called because leases traditionally expired on 1 May and 1 October. The practice of so scheduling leases began in the 1890s in most major American cities, including New York, Chicago, Washington, and New Orleans, and continued in Washington until the early 1940s, when leases became randomly staggered throughout the year.

The May and October moving days created an enormous strain on moving companies. Horse-drawn and motorized vans in Washington were overworked for two weeks; as a result, even department stores could not deliver purchases promptly because of the lack of vans. Moving was costly, because the laborers and drivers were required to work overtime. Real estate agents, decorators, and the telephone and electric companies were rushed. Conditions had deteriorated to such an extent that in August 1929 the National Association of Real Estate Boards urged realtors in all American cities involved to begin staggering apartment leases.

APARTMENT-HOTELS

One of the new types of apartment houses to appear during this boom period was the apartment-hotel, with notable examples being the Mayflower, the Roosevelt, and the Shoreham. At the Mayflower, the eastern half of the building was set aside for small apartments of two or three rooms. There the permanent residents had their own private entrance and lobby. In another arrangement, the permanent apartments at the Roosevelt were located on the top three floors to provide privacy from transients. The opening of the enormous Wardman Park Hotel in 1918, which was 50 percent apartments, no doubt influenced the construction of the others. The apartment-hotel was very popular in Washington; it was ideal for members of Congress who often wanted a small furnished apartment along with hotel services for only part of the year.

THE BRINK OF DISASTER

The Great Depression did not really affect Washington apartment houses until early 1932, when all construction ceased. Several large apartment houses were built during the early years of the Depression, 1930–31—the Shoreham Hotel, the Westchester, Sedgwick Gardens, and the Kennedy-Warren. Failure to secure additional financing, however, resulted in only half of the Westchester and the Kennedy-Warren being built. Not only did Edgar Kennedy and Monroe Warren lose the Kennedy-Warren by bankruptcy in 1931, but a number of other real estate developers were ruined. The most spectacular loss was the collapse of Harry Wardman's real estate empire. Construction of apartment houses would not be resumed until 1934 when economic conditions improved. During the next period of development, lasting until 1945, the apartment house would change again in many ways.

61

CHASTLETON

1701 16th Street, N.W.; northeast corner of 16th and R streets

ARCHITECT: Philip M. Jullien, 1919

ORIGINAL APARTMENTS: 310 (approximately 77 efficiencies; 191 one-bedrooms; 42 two-bedrooms)

STATUS: opened as rental in 1920

The facade of the Chastleton makes it perhaps the most impressive apartment house on the entire six-and-one-half-mile length of 16th Street, N.W. No other great Washington apartment house, however, with the exception of Meridian Mansions (now the Envoy), has undergone so many trials and tribulations in the past sixty-five years. This imposing Gothic-inspired residence was built by the S. W. Strauss Company of New York (not, as is popularly thought, by Harry Wardman, who was one of its later owners). Its distinguished facade, handsome public rooms, and long history make it one of the most prominent early twentieth-century Washington apartment houses.

The Chastleton is the largest and most ornate Gothic Revival apartment house ever built in the nation's capital. Its original design included only the southern half of the present building and contained 155 apartments. When the construction was finished in August 1920, the owner had architect Philip M. Jullien double its size by adding the northern half, adjacent to the Scottish Rite Temple. This expanded the total number of apartments to 310, ranging from efficiencies to two-bedrooms. The Chastleton cost $1.7 million to build and until Cathedral Mansions was built three years later was the city's largest apartment house. It was a response to the tremendous demand for

The Chastleton, also known as Sixteenth Street Mansions in the 1920s, is Washington's best Gothic Revival apartment house.

Detail of the carved Gothic tracery over the main entrance of the Chastleton.

small apartments in first-class buildings that accompanied the capital's high rents and expensive living conditions.

The eight-story buff-brick Chastleton covers an acre of land. The vertical thrust of its facade is reminiscent of both Tudor and Gothic architecture. Slightly projecting bays, faced with terra cotta, break the massiveness of the facade. The two entrances, facing 16th Street, are separated by a massive two-story-high arched Gothic window, complete with stone gargoyles, tracery, and pseudo-buttresses. The interior hallways are richly decorated with pilasters, flagstone floors, brass Gothic sconces, and gilded strapwork ceilings. Much of the first floor consists of public space, including an impressive two-story-high lobby with balconies on three sides, a lounge, and a large dining room. The intricate Tudor plaster ceilings in the first floor corridors, lobby, lounge, and dining room are the most elaborate of any Washington apartment house. Most of the apartments above the first floor have porches off the living room.

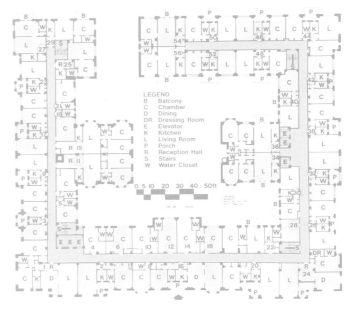

The articulated plan of the Chastleton includes a large courtyard opening to the alley in the rear.

The lobby of the Chastleton with its Gothic strapwork ceiling and balconies was restored in 1986.

The original New York investors and builders sold the Chastleton only months after it was completely finished in 1921 to Washington investor Felix Lake for $3 million. Lake sold the building to Mr. and Mrs. Alfred I. du Pont of Wilmington, Delaware, the following year. Several months later the du Ponts sued Lake for misrepresenting the true value of the building and the actual rentals at the time of sale. The du Ponts lost the case and sold the Chastleton. The building, with its large mortgage, changed hands many times after 1921. One owner changed its name in 1923 to Sixteenth Street Mansions, but three owners and three years later it was changed back to the Chastleton. ("Mansions" was a term used in Victorian and Edwardian London to denote a first-class apartment house.) In March 1926 it was purchased by Harry Wardman, who rented one-fourth of the building as hotel rooms and the remainder as apartments. He also converted space near the R Street entrance into a drugstore. By the late 1920s Wardman owned six fashionable apartment-hotels—the Wardman Park, the Chastleton, the Carlton, the Somerset House, the Hay-Adams, and the Roosevelt—but lost them all in 1932.

The fashionable Chastleton survived the Depression with little change, housing many congressmen and other notables, including Mrs. Wallis Simpson (later the Duchess of Windsor) and General Douglas MacArthur. In 1943 the Navy attempted to seize the building to house WAVES. At that time 11,500 women officers and enlisted personnel in the Navy were stationed in Washington, including WAVES, Spars, and women Marines. Because the eight hundred tenants of the Chastleton held almost nightly protest meetings, Secretary of the Navy Frank Knox decided to seek military housing elsewhere.

In early 1946 the Chastleton was again sold and converted into a 623-suite transient hotel. By 1958 it had been converted back to an apartment house with 309 apartments, but the once-popular dining room was then closed. The Chastleton was purchased in 1960 by Washington real estate investor Norman Bernstein, who renovated it in 1966, installing new bathrooms, kitchens, plumbing, wiring, and carpeting. In the process the 2,410 original wooden casement windows were replaced with new aluminum sash windows.

By the early 1970s the Chastleton was home to a wide ethnic, cultural, and economic range of residents. The building was sold once again in 1979 for $4 million to developer Virginia Page, who planned to convert it into a hotel and then possibly to luxury condominium units. Not only did the tenants oppose the conversion, but within weeks the city government passed emergency legislation to prevent rental units from converting to either condominium or hotel status. Most tenants were willing

Elaborate plaster ceilings are found throughout the public rooms on the ground floor of the Chastleton.

to move when Mrs. Page offered each a $4,000 subsidy, five months' free rent in an apartment house in Southwest Washington, and a color television. Twelve, however, refused the offer and stayed in the building until they were evicted in 1984. Mrs. Page soon joined the partnership of Interstate General Corporation of St. Charles, Maryland, which began to renovate the apartments, installing new bathrooms and kitchens, and to restore the facade and public spaces. The renovation was completed in 1986, when the apartments were placed on the market for rental once again.

ARCHITECT PHILIP M. JULLIEN

Philip M. Jullien (1875–1963), a native of Washington, taught architecture during the 1920s and 1930s at Catholic University. He was a specialist in the design of hotels and particularly of industrial plants in Philadelphia, Pittsburgh, Buffalo, and Atlantic City. In addition to the Chastleton, Jullien designed the Kenmore apartment house in suburban Bethesda, Maryland, the Congressional Country Club, and the Bowen Building. It is known that Jullien designed eleven apartment houses in Washington between 1919 and 1938.

62

ROOSEVELT HOTEL

2101 16th Street, N.W.; east side of 16th Street between V and W streets

ARCHITECT: Appleton P. Clark, Jr., 1919

ORIGINAL APARTMENTS: 126 (99 efficiencies; 15 one-bedrooms; 6 two-bedrooms; 6 three-bedrooms) and 168 hotel suites

STATUS: opened as rental in 1920; converted to senior citizens home in 1963

The first plans for the Roosevelt Hotel, an apartment-hotel that once ranked among the finest in Washington, were made by developer John W. Weaver in August 1918. He commissioned the well-known New York architectural firm of Carrère and Hastings to design a $1.6 million five-story apartment-hotel for the intersection of 16th and W streets, N.W. Construction was delayed for one year due to the shortage of building materials caused by World War I. In late 1919 Weaver decided to increase the size of the building. He abandoned the earlier plans and commissioned Washington architect Appleton P. Clark, Jr., to design a $2 million eight-story apartment-hotel. Architect Clark planned five identical wings extending out from the rectangular body of the building toward 16th Street, N.W.

The new plan called for an elaborate roof garden with vine-covered pergolas on the three central wings of the apartment-hotel. The District of Columbia government had already issued a building permit in August 1919 that allowed the roof garden when an influential neighbor, Mrs. John B. Henderson, claimed it would block the view of the city from the proposed Meridian Hill Park then being planned across W Street. As a result of her objection, in November 1919 Congress overruled the D.C. building permit—unless the roof garden was eliminated.

This action was unfortunate, for the proposed roof garden, requiring only 10 additional feet, would have added greatly to the design of the front facade and would never have interfered with the park vista.

Construction proceeded rapidly. The Roosevelt offered 126 small apartments, ranging from one to three rooms, on the top three floors. Reserved for permanent residents, they provided privacy as well as good views. When the Roosevelt opened in the summer of 1920, it was considered the finest apartment-hotel south of New York. Originally called the Hadleigh, in 1924 it was renamed for President Theodore Roosevelt, the name it has retained ever since.

In 1926 developer Harry Wardman purchased the Roosevelt for $2.5 million. Two years later, however, in need of cash for his ever-expanding real estate empire, Wardman sold the Roosevelt to a syndicate headed by Frank B. Banks for the same price he had paid for it.

The classical facade of the Roosevelt is impressive. Although an enormous structure that extends the length of the block, the wings and facade elements are well balanced, especially in their verticality. The red-brick facade is relieved by the pleasantly contrasting limestone used for the first-floor area, as well as by the massive quoins—the corner blocks on each wing—and by the

The Roosevelt Hotel was designed with five massive wings projecting toward 16th Street.

handsome baroque-inspired balconies on the top two floors on all three street facades. The space between the five wings was decorated with limestone screens (similar to those at 1661 Crescent Place, N.W.) that partially hid the first-floor level. The two south or right wings on the first floor and the body behind them were arranged for apartments. The remaining two-thirds of the first floor was given over to public space—a spacious lobby, cafe, parlor, office, ballroom, large dining room seating three hundred guests, and numerous service rooms. Convenient shops were located on the ground floor of the V Street, N.W., facade including a grocery, optician, and beauty parlor.

The apartments were especially popular with members of Congress, many of whom moved here when the old Congress Hall apartment-hotel on Capitol Hill was demolished in 1926 for the Longworth House Office Building. According to Congressman and Mrs. George H. Mahon of Texas, who lived at the Roosevelt from 1936 to 1939, rents were high for the Depression. Two-room unfurnished apartments cost $140 a month. Most apartments had Murphy beds, which folded into closets or swung out on metal brackets from dressing rooms. Other features included "servidors," shallow metal cabinets attached to the outerside of the apartment doors, where residents could leave their suits or dresses, to be picked up for dry cleaning and returned the same day. Fashionable dances and concerts were held in the Roosevelt's ballroom from 1920

until the mid-1950s. Legendary entertainers such as Ray Charles, Benny Goodman, The Three Sons Trio, and Nat King Cole performed here in the early 1950s.

CONDITION IN 1941

The Roosevelt was offered for sale in 1941 to several New York investors for $1 million. Negotiations were underway in early 1941 between the owners and Sam Husbands, president of the federal Defense Homes Corporation. The government was seeking a purchaser for the Roosevelt who would in turn lease it to the government for emergency housing. The following letter of 25 February 1941 from Washington realtor Charles H. Hillegeist to Alfred T. Jenkins of New York describes the condition of the building:

Yesterday Mr. Smythe and I thoroughly inspected the Roosevelt Hotel and had a long talk with the Assistant Manager. The following may be helpful to you.

The physical property is really in excellent condition. There are two new boilers with "Iron Firemen" stokers. The elevators have ample speed for the height of the building. The rugs and furniture appear to be in excellent condition and there is almost no apparent need for painting.

The earnings record of the last few years is amply explained in the phrase "insurance company management."

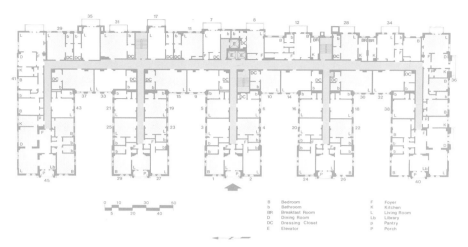

The Roosevelt Hotel was designed with apartments on the top two floors, shown here, and hotel rooms on the lower floors.

All of the rental rates are absurdly high in comparison with the rates of other hotels here and undoubtedly do much to explain the low percentage of occupancy. Considerable heat is being wasted in vacant apartments since all of those that we visited had the radiators turned full on. The hotel, of course, does no advertising, has no liquor license, and it is impossible even to purchase a bottle of beer on the premises. This naturally explains the operating loss in the restaurant department.

A great deal of space is being wasted and undoubtedly the low percentage of occupancy reacts on the price which can be charged for the various stores and concessions in the building. In my opinion, a skillful and aggressive management could, in the next four or five years, greatly exceed the 1935, 1936, and 1937 earnings, which were, respectively, $40,966.75, $24,963.42, and $37,511.07.

The building was originally planned for a roof garden but this plan was blocked by a wealthy land owner whose private residence was on the adjacent corner. This person has since died and her estate would interpose no objections. In Washington, particularly, a roof garden can be extremely profitable, and the view from the roof of the Roosevelt is altogether exceptional.

The dining room is not air-conditioned and in Washington today air-conditioning of any dining room is a competitive necessity. I am quite sure that Prudential Co., holding the first mortgage, would waive amortization payments in an amount sufficient to permit the installation of air-conditioning in the dining room and a cocktail lounge should it be desired to open one.

Having studied the place I can only conclude that it is a splendid opportunity for any aggressive, experienced hotel management organization.

This letter is important in showing why the Roosevelt was losing money during the 1930s. Careful management of any apartment house is essential for a successful profit. Perhaps Mr. Hillegeist should not have been so candid, for, despite months of correspondence and telegrams between the owner's real estate agent and the three prospective New York buyers, there was no sale. With entry of the United States into World War II in December 1941, Washington was in the grip of a shortage of both permanent and temporary housing. Every room and suite in the Roosevelt was filled, providing a large profit for the owners. During the war, and for a decade later, the old-fashioned high standards of the Roosevelt were maintained. The doormen, white-gloved waiters, and entire staff took great pride in the reputation of the Roosevelt. Although air conditioning did not come until much later, many distinguished guests continued to stay here because of the service and attention they received.

RECENT HISTORY

The Roosevelt's fortunes declined rapidly in the mid-1950s, and the building was closed by the city building inspector in 1956 because of defective plumbing. It was sold by Mrs. Marie Kramer to Sylvan Lawrence of New York in 1961. He remodeled the interior, covering all of the handsome ornate plaster columns and ceilings with wallboard, so that only a small portion of the elaborate wood paneling of the former public parlor is now visible. A pleasant flagstone terrace with umbrellas and garden

On the 16th and V street facades of the Roosevelt Hotel are these dramatic terra cotta balconies surmounted by two-story entablatures.

furniture had extended to the rear, along W Street to New Hampshire Avenue, and provided a place where luncheon was served from spring to fall. The new owner sold this large garden for development of a mundane massive apartment house, which cuts off light, air, and a view of Meridian Hill Park for the neighboring older apartment houses on New Hampshire Avenue. At the same time Fred Safran of New York remodeled all of the original hotel suites to create more small apartments.

The building reopened in 1963 as the Roosevelt Hotel for Senior Citizens. Sold to Mrs. Frances Hayes of Florida in 1965, it continued in this capacity until 1986. At that time it was purchased as an investment by Stanley Boucree, an oral surgeon, who offered the remaining residents joint partnership with him, with 5-percent interest in the ownership. This plan fell through, and the city government purchased the building in 1987 for continued use as a residence for senior citizens.

63

CATHEDRAL MANSIONS

2900, 3000, and 3100 Connecticut Avenue, N.W.;
west side of Connecticut Avenue between Cathedral Avenue and Devonshire Place

ARCHITECT: Wardman and Waggaman, 1922–23

ORIGINAL APARTMENTS: 492 (mostly one- and two-bedrooms)

STATUS: opened as rental in 1923–24; Cathedral Mansions Center partially converted to office building in 1962;
Cathedral Mansions North (now Cathedral Park) converted to condo in 1974

Cathedral Mansions, a complex of three massive buildings extending nearly a quarter of a mile along Connecticut Avenue, was the largest of more than four hundred Washington apartment houses that developer Harry Wardman constructed between 1905 and 1929. Indeed, when completed in 1924, the $4 million project was considered the largest apartment house south of New York. As was

his custom, Wardman sold Cathedral Mansions only two years after it was built to other real estate developers and realized a handsome profit. This was Wardman's secret to success: build quality apartment houses, sell within three years of construction, and free capital for new and larger real estate projects.

The complex of 492 apartments, ranging from two

The first apartment house modeled after a resort hotel, with spacious lawns, was Cathedral Mansions, in 1922.

Georgian Revival detailing was used throughout the three buildings comprising Cathedral Mansions, including the handsome east entrance and stairtower at Cathedral Mansions South.

rooms with kitchen and bath to five rooms with kitchen and two baths, was housed in three separate but adjacent large buildings—Cathedral Mansions South, Cathedral Mansions Center, and Cathedral Mansions North. The original plan to name each for an adjacent street—Cathedral, Jewett, and Klingle—was never carried out. They were all designed in the Georgian Revival style, with limestone quoins and dark-faced red brick. The four-story buildings, with gabled and hipped roofs embellished by decorative dormer windows as well as third-story limestone stringcourses, created a domestic appearance. Because the site was a steep hill, 40 feet above street level, Wardman had to remove more than 125,000 tons of earth and rock before construction began. The buildings, es-

View from the fifth floor of the east staircase at Cathedral Mansions South.

Developer Harry Wardman and his daughter Helen shortly before World War I, on the lawn of the Homestead, the famous resort hotel in Hot Springs, Virginia, which was a major influence on the site plans of both his Wardman Park Hotel and Cathedral Mansions apartment house.

pecially the south one, were surrounded by spacious lawns and were patterned after the recently built Wardman Park Hotel. Just after the turn of the century, the site had been considered for the Washington Cathedral, but its final location on Wisconsin Avenue was selected because of the higher elevation there, and because the owner of that land finally agreed to sell it.

Construction on the 8-acre site began with the south building at the northwest corner of Connecticut and Cathedral avenues. This building, with its irregular T shape, three entrances, and unusually shaped main lobby, is the most interesting in the complex. Almost all of the 152 apartments have sunrooms and three exposures. The south entrance, designed as a circular portico, and the east entrance, consisting of a circular five-story rounded tower with a Palladian window above the door, are particularly striking. In this building, as in the other two before their renovation, most apartments have four large rooms plus kitchen and bath. The centrally located living room has no outside windows and, though enclosed by the bedroom and dining room on two sides, it is also adjacent to the apartment's entrance and on a direct line with the sunroom.

The U-shaped center building, originally with 170 apartments, had a front court enclosed by a one-story colonnaded range of shops. Amenities included a public dining room, garage, grocery store, drugstore, beauty shop, delicatessen, pastry shop, and caterer. Zoning restrictions presented considerable difficulty in opening these shops. Finally, after a number of appeals, the D.C. Zoning Commission allowed them in the center building. (Although most of Connecticut Avenue was zoned for residential use, several commercial strips, such as the cluster in Cathedral Mansions Center, were allowed as the avenue developed in the 1920s.) The north building is shaped as an irregular L and, like the other two buildings, has many projecting wings that provided maximum light and air circulation for its 170 apartment units.

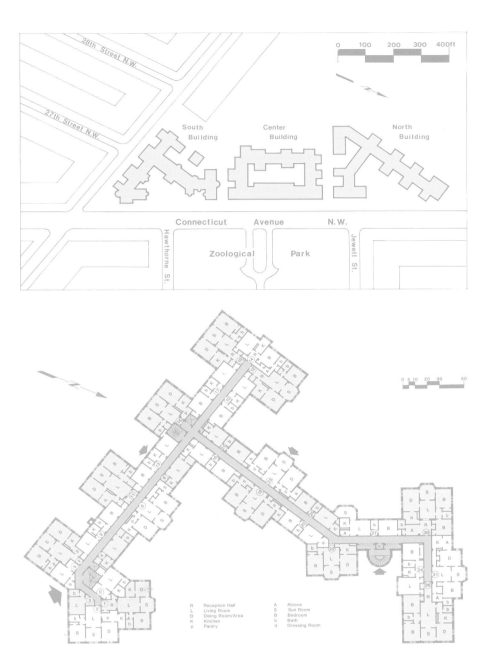

Top: The rambling irregularly shaped buildings comprising Cathedral Mansions allow considerable air circulation and light, innovative for their time. *Bottom:* Typical floor plan of Cathedral Mansions South.

The original twenty-seven hundred residents of Cathedral Mansions enjoyed a full service staff. The buildings are opposite the Smithsonian's National Zoological Park, which, except for an occasional lion's roar, afforded added peace and quiet. Within the complex were nine elevators and three telephone switchboards. Added conveniences included a large public dining room and a children's playground with a "competent instructress in charge." Originally a private bus took residents from the front door to the downtown shopping district, a custom that continues elsewhere in a few of the area's largest apartment houses.

During the 1970s amenities in Cathedral Mansions slowly declined. Here, as in many other Washington rental apartment houses, the owner removed the switchboards and reduced the size of the staff because of inflation and

Two tenants of Cathedral Mansions South, Margaret Leidler Fisher and Joseph Morgan, on an apartment terrace there on a summer evening in 1981.

rent control. In 1974 Cathedral Mansions North was purchased by a group of investors and converted into a condominium. The extensive modernization and renovation included new kitchens, bathrooms, plumbing, heating systems, wiring, redecoration of the lobby, a new roof, carpeting, laundry rooms, and a security system. Prices then for the condo units varied from $20,000 for an efficiency to $52,100 for two-bedroom units. The building was subsequently renamed Cathedral Park.

Forced to move, many of the moderate-income Hispanics living there as renters petitioned the city council to prevent the building's conversion to a condominium. This petition and other similar ones resulted both in rent control laws and in new regulations to retard or prevent such conversions. Beginning in the mid-1970s, tenants were given the right of first refusal to purchase the whole building when a conversion to condominiums was planned. In addition, a majority of the tenants had to approve the conversion. This law has prevented a number of rental buildings, such as Van Ness South, from being converted.

More than a decade before Cathedral Mansions North was converted, a major change had taken place in Cathedral Mansions Center. In 1962 developer Norman Bernstein purchased this building and undertook a major renovation in which many of the apartments as well as the shops were converted to office space. Today Cathedral Mansions Center remains rental and contains 115 apartments, 55 offices (mostly occupied by psychiatrists), and 9 stores. Cathedral Mansions South still consists entirely of rental apartments and is the best preserved and least changed of the three buildings.

64

KEW GARDENS

2700 Que Street, N.W.; southwest corner of Que and 27th streets

ARCHITECT: Alexander H. Sonnemann, 1922

ORIGINAL APARTMENTS: 112 (varied from efficiencies to two-bedrooms)

STATUS: opened as rental in 1923

Designed in the Georgian Revival style, Kew Gardens was erected for $1 million just after World War I by developer Harry A. Kite, noted as a prolific builder of Washington rowhouses during the 1920s. Built of red brick with gabled slate roofs and decorative dormer windows, this apartment house varies from two to four stories because of its location on a steeply sloping lot of approximately 84,000 square feet. The body of Kew Gardens is symmetrical and consists of a rectangular block with a spacious open central court. The advantage of this arrangement is that all of the rooms open to the outside. Its disadvantage is seen in the resulting long and boring public hallways. Originally designed by a New York landscape architect, the building's open courtyard is unique in Washington. Paved walkways are laid out around a handsome stone lily pond. Now more than sixty years old, the trees and shrubbery are fully developed and offer the residents a tranquil and peaceful space, far removed from the traffic noises of busy Que Street. The court is decorated on the north by a handsome latticed wall; on the south a large arch opens to the alley beyond—to improve air circulation.

The imposing main lobby at the Que Street entrance, designed in Adamesque style (based on the late eighteenth-century neoclassical designs of the English archi-

The east entrance to Kew Gardens, on 27th Street.

The main Que Street lobby of Kew Gardens is designed in the Adamesque style with a pair of gracefully curved stairs leading to the second floor.

Many apartments at Kew Gardens contain spacious sun rooms, such as this example facing 27th Street.

tects Robert and James Adam), includes striking pairs of fluted pilasters and a ceiling with delicate plastered medallions and foliated plastered beams. Also within the lobby graceful arches open onto the original office, the two public hallways (one on each side), and the centrally located main staircase. A pair of curving stairs, with delicate iron balusters and handrails—much lighter in scale than those in pre–World War I apartment houses—rise to meet at the landing above. Today they frame a large plate glass window, which unfortunately replaced the original French doors, set in front of an iron balcony overlooking the large courtyard beyond.

Kew Gardens—its name a double pun for both its address and the famous public park in London—was originally designed with 112 apartments, ranging in size from efficiencies to two-bedroom units. During several renovations, beginning in the late 1930s and continuing during the housing shortage of World War II, all of the two-bedroom apartments were subdivided so that the building now contains more than 150 apartments. Most have two rooms, but some three-room units with kitchen and bath have survived. Because of the many changes, it has not been possible to recreate here the original floor plans, which have been lost, although the adjacent site plan has been included. The original developer included such amenities as a large public cafe adjacent to the imposing porticoed 27th Street entrance. Many of the large apartments had spacious glazed sleeping porches that opened through French doors into the living rooms. A playground for children was on the west side of the building.

Even though Kew Gardens no longer offers many of its original amenities, scores of residents have stayed on. For instance, Mrs. Mildred Trimble, the widow of a former congressman from Kansas who later served for many years as Clerk of the U.S. House of Representatives, lived here from 1940 until her death in 1986.

Another long-term renter was artist Samuel Bookatz, a native of Philadelphia who rented the 4,000-square-foot public dining room after it closed in 1942 (because

The landscaped enclosed courtyard of Kew Gardens is the largest of any Washington apartment house.

of the labor shortage caused by World War II). This space was still used by Bookatz as his studio at the time of his death in 1987. One of the first combat artists commissioned in World War II, Bookatz left the Navy with the rank of commander in 1945. His distinguished career as a painter was seen in the hundreds of paintings that were crammed into this space. In 1942 President Franklin D. Roosevelt assigned him the Lincoln Room in the White House as a studio for several months, where he painted a number of noted Americans. Commander Bookatz's portraits created at his Kew Gardens studio are included in the collection of several prominent museums, including the Corcoran Gallery.

In an age before "tenant associations," most of the residents of Kew Gardens banded together in 1946 and wrote the owner, then Jack G. Leo of New York, of the need to replace their resident manager. The tenants accused him of slovenly—and at times illegal—management: allegedly stealing items belonging to the tenants from the storage room, refusing to allow tenants into the

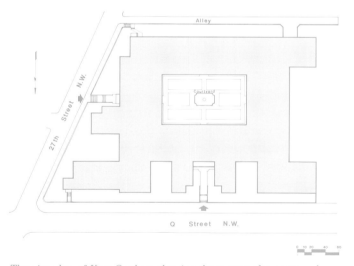

The site plan of Kew Gardens showing the rectangular courtyard.

storage room at reasonable times, moving them at inconvenient times, refusing to allow them to borrow the duplicate key to their apartments when they were locked out, and—most of all—maintaining a surly attitude in relations with the tenants. As a result, a new resident manager was soon employed.

65

MAYFLOWER HOTEL

1127 Connecticut Avenue, N.W.; southeast corner of Connecticut Avenue and DeSales Street

ARCHITECT: Warren and Wetmore, New York; Robert F. Beresford, associate architect, 1922–23

ORIGINAL APARTMENTS: 100 (mostly one-bedrooms) and 440 hotel rooms

STATUS: opened in 1925; apartments converted to hotel rooms ca. 1958

For three decades after it opened in 1925, the Mayflower Hotel was considered Washington's most elegant large downtown hotel. When first built, it easily surpassed all of its Washington rivals, including the famous Willard Hotel. The Mayflower offered more ballrooms, with space for conventions and meetings. It had modern technological improvements, such as outlets for radio reception, shower stalls, improved lighting, modern ventilation systems, and an unusually efficient floor plan. Extending from Connecticut Avenue along the south side of DeSales Street to 17th Street, the block-long building included 440 hotel rooms and 100 apartments. The latter were grouped together in the east end, extending from the center of DeSales Street to the corner of 17th Street. Apartment house residents had their own private entrance and lobby on DeSales Street, while transient hotel guests used the main entrances on Connecticut Avenue and 17th Street, N.W. Apartment sizes varied from one room with bath and kitchenette to three rooms, bath, and kitchenette. The larger apartments, facing DeSales Street, located at the ends of the four wings, boasted working fireplaces as well.

The Mayflower occupies the site of the Academy of the Visitation, which was responsible for the side street's name, "DeSales." The Catholic sisters commissioned Washington architect Adolph Cluss to design a spacious four-story day school on the site in 1877. By the early twentieth century, however, the southern end of Connecticut Avenue as well as nearby K Street were changing rapidly from a residential to a commercial neighborhood. As early as 1910 the sisters made plans to sell their property because of its greatly increased value. At that time Goldwin, Starrett, and Van Vleck of New York designed the "George Washington Hotel" for this location. This massive structure, which was also to have apartments, never materialized when adequate financing could not be obtained.

In 1919 the academy was sold to developer Allan E. Walker. Three years later he commissioned the New York architectural firm of Warren and Wetmore, already noted for a number of famous hotels, and Washington architect Robert F. Beresford to design the Mayflower. The resulting ten-story classically inspired hotel was built of buff-colored brick set above a limestone base, with terra cotta trim and quoins. The most striking feature of this apartment-hotel is the pair of curved "towers" that face Connecticut Avenue and frame the principal hotel entrance. While the building was under construction in 1923, the architect designed a two-bay-wide addition to the south side of the south tower, known at various times as the Annex or the Piedmont Annex.

From beneath the richly detailed metal marquee on

The original marquee of the Mayflower Hotel, about 1930.

The Mayflower Hotel, designed by the New York firm of Warren and Wetmore, as it appeared in 1940.

Connecticut Avenue, with its elegantly notched corners and cresting of classical urns, cornucopias, wreaths, and palmettes, guests enter a spacious public lobby from which a wide hall extends through the building to 17th Street, N.W. Known as the Promenade, this massive corridor is decorated with a slightly coved plaster ceiling, walls with marble wainscoting, and pilasters with gilded capitals.

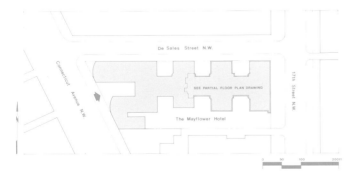

Site plan of the Mayflower Hotel. The east half of the building was originally designed for apartments.

The wide variety of marble that sheaths the walls of the lobby and adjacent ballrooms and dining rooms is complemented by finely cast, low-relief plaster decorations, often embellished with gold leaf. Since its opening, the Mayflower has held inaugural balls for every president beginning with Calvin Coolidge in 1925. Its guest list has included such distinguished national and international figures as Sir Winston Churchill, General Charles de Gaulle, Amelia Earhart, Charles Lindbergh, Igor Stravinsky, John Wayne, and Norman Mailer.

An important description of the apartments here is contained in the original promotional booklet printed by the Mayflower in 1926. The unnamed author was not noted for either modesty or understatement:

> The repute of the Mayflower as the ideal domicile for the sojourner of a few days or a few weeks in Washington has been spread to the four corners of the earth by its guests. By reason of the permanency of its semi-housekeeping guests, however, the facilities of this department of the Mayflower are not so widely known.
>
> The standard semi-housekeeping suites comprise a

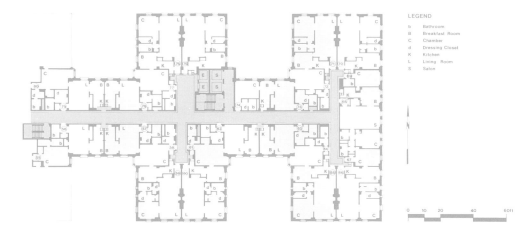

LEGEND

b   Bathroom
B   Breakfast Room
C   Chamber
d   Dressing Closet
K   Kitchen
L   Living Room
S   Salon

Typical floor plan of the apartment section of the Mayflower Hotel, which was converted to hotel use in the mid–1950s.

large living room with a separate bedroom, dressing closet and bathroom, and breakfast room with kitchenette. There are also smaller suites consisting of a living room provided with twin beds which fold into a bed closet, a roomy dressing closet, bathroom, and breakfast room with kitchenette. All apartments are so situated that an adjoining bedroom may be connected.

In the furnishings of these apartments is continued the same note of elegance and richness characteristic of the public quarters. While carefully preserving and honoring the Colonial tradition, the Mayflower has departed from the austerity and stiffness of that period. There is an inviting atmosphere of solid comfort and luxury in the apartments. Deeply upholstered davenports, oscillating fans, circulating ice-water, ventilated closets, cater to the physical comfort of the guest.

Additional to the genuine comfort of the apartments, there is that subtle element of charm arising from the perfect taste and harmony of the furnishings. Every apartment on each floor has its own individuality—no two are furnished alike. The furniture collector will recognize many beautiful and interesting reproductions. The dignity and luxury of the furnishings, the pleasing color combinations of the silk draperies, furniture upholstering, and floor coverings produces a soothing sense of restfulness and harmony pleasing to the most critical connoisseur.

The term "semi-housekeeping" is used advisedly. The apartments are primarily designed for that class of guests who desire the maximum relief from the responsibilities and annoyances of the individual household but who do not wish to lose contact altogether with their own culinary department. The chintz-draped and tastefully furnished breakfast rooms are most inviting. The kitchenettes, which are small editions of model culinary establish-

ments, will delight every housekeeper. Equipped with electric ranges, porcelain iceboxes artificially cooled, a set of decoratively-colored agate ware, and a full complement of cooking utensils, china, glassware, silver, and table linen, the breakfast room and kitchenette are perfectly adapted for the breakfast or luncheon for which they were intended. And in fact the skilled housewife who cares to do so, can prepare and serve successfully a family dinner. For the family not caring to prepare its own dinners, or who may have dinner guests, as elaborate a dinner as may be desired can be ordered from the main dining room, which will be perfectly served in the breakfast room.

Many householders would like to have released for other uses the large proportion of their time which is absorbed by the almost mechanical processes of living—the furnishing and maintenance of a separate household; the hiring and supervision of servants; the never-ending problem of catering. To many such, the usual hotel "housekeeping" apartments connote small, barrenly and uncomfortably furnished rooms, inadequate service, odors of cooking, and the feeling of a crowded environment.

To such persons the semi-housekeeping apartments at The Mayflower will be a revelation. So far as the routine processes of living are concerned, the relief is complete; nor is such relief achieved at the cost of loss of elegance and individuality in one's mode of living. The atmosphere of refinement and elegance with which a family of means and culture surrounds itself in its own home is not lost upon moving to The Mayflower.

When living in an apartment at The Mayflower, there is none of the usual discomfort of hotel life. Residents in The Mayflower apartments are not required to come into contact with the occasional congestion and activity around the hotel due to large social functions and gatherings of various kinds which center there. An entirely separate entrance lobby for the semi-housekeeping apartments is maintained on DeSales Street, a block from the main entrance on Connecticut Avenue. It is provided with its own passenger and freight elevators, its own desk clerks, bell-boys, doormen, etc. But when desired, the apartment elevators may be reached by way of the beautiful gallery or promenade from the main entrance.

In the mild serenity of the semi-housekeeping apartments, the guest can enjoy an individual, personal detachment and privacy in living. But, if interested, he can observe, as from a quiet backwater off the main stream, the vivid fashionable, diplomatic, and political life of the nation and the world, which courses, as through a great artery, through The Mayflower. Here he finds a brilliant cross-section of the ultra-smart life of the nation—swiftly-changing, ever-fascinating. In its stately promenades, he recognizes celebrities of political life; he catches the picturesque flavor lent by a foreign uniform; he detects the accents of polyglot tongues and finds a diverting touch of cosmopolitanism. The famous Presidential Restaurant, with its fine orchestra, the subdued hum of conversation,

interesting groups of diners, provides as fascinating a picture as may be found in any world famed eating place.

The sumptuousness of the public quarters and the exquisiteness and dignity of the furnishings and appointments of the apartments, although important, comprise the least part of the real charm of living at The Mayflower. The ideal of The Mayflower goes far beyond merely providing lodgings of a luxurious type. It is in its human relations that this great institution is at its best. Its huge organization is dedicated to the single purpose of the comfort of the guest.

Mayflower service is not mere obsequiousness—not a gesture. It is the natural outgrowth of a standard which does not tolerate the merest suggestion of mediocrity. Like good breeding in the individual, service is innate in this hotel. A guest could not imagine a discourtesy, a reluctancy, a jarring note, in the unobtrusive but efficient service which is ever at his command.

The availability of the great cuisine of The Mayflower for service in the semi-housekeeping apartments is in itself a noteworthy service. Under the roof of The Mayflower the guest finds a perfection and a comprehensiveness of service instantly available, which would be

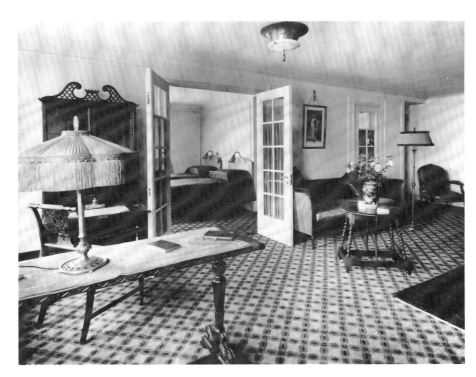

An apartment in the Mayflower Hotel about 1925.

absolutely unattainable in any private home. But only by scanning the House Directory appended does the guest realize the superlative service furnished by The Mayflower organization.

That which is called 'atmosphere' is an indefinable quality. Though difficult to phrase, it is very real at The Mayflower. Like the fragrance of a flower, it cannot be described but can be sensed only through contact. It is the result of the perfect coordination of all the qualities that make a single home successful. Good taste in furnishings and appointments, the finest quality in the cuisine, a watchful and silent anticipation of a guest's every need—which is the essence of a genuine hospitality—all contribute to produce that harmonious, restful quality called atmosphere. In the restrained elegance of the main lobby, in the graceful beauty of the airy Palm Court, in the impressive richness and dignity of the main restaurant and in the magnificence of the great Galerie, wherein are found tapestries, statuary, and rare pieces of furniture which would arouse admiration as museum specimens, is found an expression of elegance and luxury surpassed in no other hotel in the world.

The apartments at the Mayflower remained in great demand until the hotel management decided to convert most of them to single hotel rooms in the late 1950s. (The same decision was made at about the same time by the owners of the Shoreham Hotel.) The greater number of hotel rooms provided a higher rate of return than the apartments, and only two apartments survive today at the Mayflower. Its public rooms remain in remarkably original condition, however. The Mayflower was recently listed in the National Register of Historic Places. Any tax deductions relating to restoration efforts or facade changes consequently must be approved and monitored by the National Register.

During the period 1981–84 the Mayflower underwent an extensive $60 million renovation and restoration project. This work was made feasible by the 1980 federal tax law granting an owner a 25-percent tax credit for rehabilitation expenditures if the rehabilitation meets the Department of the Interior's standards for rehabilitation. While most of the upper floors were gutted to improve the floor plans and to install new plumbing and mechanical equipment, the first-floor public rooms were carefully restored by the present owners, May-Wash Associates. Interior designer Louis Cataffo of Los Angeles and architect Vlastimil Koubek of Washington, D.C., effected extensive renovations and restoration of many public areas, retaining the Mayflower's reputation as one of the city's premier hotels.

66

MERIDIAN HILL STUDIO

2633 15th Street, N.W.; east side of 15th Street between Euclid and Fuller streets

ARCHITECT: George Oakley Totten, Jr., 1922

ORIGINAL APARTMENTS: 12 (2 one-bedrooms; 6 two-bedrooms; 4 three-bedrooms)

STATUS: opened as rental in 1923; converted to co-op in 1941

The thirteen-unit Meridian Hill Studio resembles an Arts and Crafts version of a French château. Its E shape was one of the most popular plans of the 1920s. With a large semicircular drive in the landscaped forecourt, the stucco-covered facade is picturesque and eclectic in design. Each of the gable ends of the three wings is embellished with quaint rounded baroque-inspired window pediments, as well as a pair of blind baroque windows at the attic level. A number of shallow balconies with iron balustrades and French doors are at the second-floor level. Above the principal entrance, with its small but elegant iron and glass marquee, are two oriel windows at the third-floor level. A series of chimneys pierces the roofs of all three wings; those on the central wing rise a full 30 feet and are supported by iron tie-rods connected to the gabled roof. All of these angles add a charming sense of domesticity to this small apartment building.

Meridian Hill Studio has several other unique design features, beginning with the construction of the building, which was supervised by Snowden Ashford, later municipal architect of Washington. Following a technique originated by the U.S. Army Corps of Engineers in World War I, Ashford had all of the two- and three-story walls poured in concrete in wooden forms lying flat on the ground. After the concrete forms hardened, the walls were

One of the most unusually designed apartment houses in Washington is the Meridian Hill Studio, which vaguely resembles a small French château.

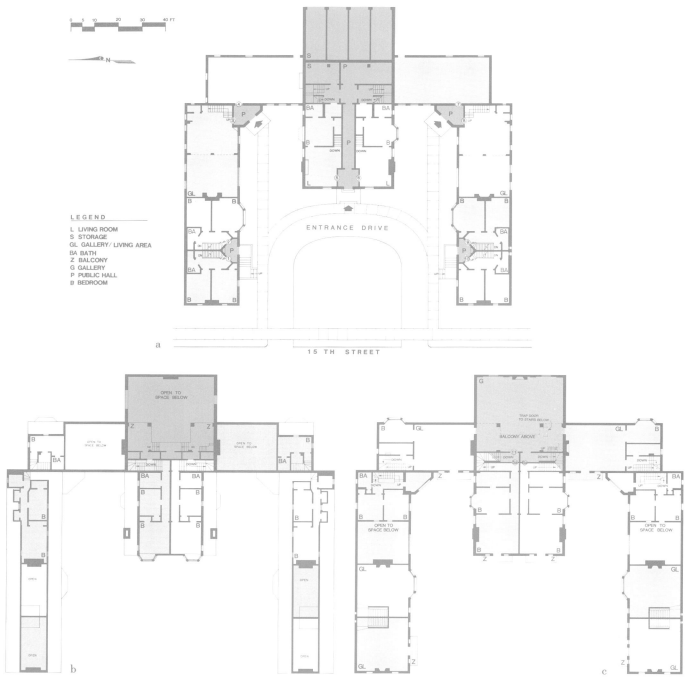

LEGEND

L LIVING ROOM
S STORAGE
GL GALLERY/ LIVING AREA
BA BATH
Z BALCONY
G GALLERY
P PUBLIC HALL
B BEDROOM

The design of Meridian Hill Studio is unique in Washington. Its E shape accommodates eleven units, including simplex, duplex, and triplex apartments. Shown here are plans of the (a) first, (b) second, and (c) third floors.

raised to the vertical; steel rods reinforced the concrete. The entire south wall, which varied in thickness from 8 to 12 inches, measured 88 by 25 feet when it was raised by workmen using cranks and pulleys in January 1923. It was the city's first "prefab" apartment building.

Meridian Hill Studio was owned by Mary Foote Henderson, widow of Senator John B. Henderson, who wanted to enrich the neighborhood with an expensive apartment building designed for artists and bachelor diplomats. It was the only luxury apartment building ever designed for artists in Washington—although a number had been built in Manhattan at the turn of the century for affluent artists. Originally known as studio apartments, those at Meridian Hill had two-floor-high living rooms, with the kitchen and bath on the lower level and two bedrooms that opened onto a balcony overlooking the living room on the upper level. Living only three blocks away in her own Roman-

esque Revival mansion at 16th Street and Florida Avenue, N.W., Mrs. Henderson could easily survey the dozen or so important residences she built on the 16th Street corridor adjacent to the magnificent Renaissance-inspired Meridian Hill Park then under construction. A shrewd businesswoman, she forced the development of the neighborhood to enhance the value of her extensive land holdings there.

Most of the nearby embassies, as well as Meridian Hill Studio, were designed by Mrs. Henderson's favorite architect, George Oakley Totten, Jr. His own studio house, with its facade suggesting a sixteenth-century baroque Spanish villa, still stands across the street from Meridian Hill Studio. Built in an eclectic style, his residence housed both antique furniture and antique architectural fragments he had collected on his many travels in Europe and Asia. Mrs. Henderson must have been fond of the Totten House,

Detail of the balustrade of the main staircase of Meridian Hill Studio.

Two residents of Meridian Hill Studio, Mr. and Mrs. Erik Hillman, both concert pianists, practice in the first-floor living room of their triplex apartment.

since her Meridian Hill Studio also features many baroque details.

Also across the street from Meridian Hill Studio is the imposing Warder House. It was Totten who purchased the walls and interior detailing of the famous 1884 Warder House at 15th and K streets, N.W., in 1924. This landmark was to be demolished by developer Harry Wardman for a new office building, even though it had been designed by one of the country's finest architects, Henry Hobson Richardson. Totten purchased and disassembled the building and had the interior components carefully numbered. The original entrance and the principal fireplace mantel were donated to the Smithsonian Institution at the time, where they remain in storage in the National Museum of American Art. He then reerected the landmark on 16th Street in the spacious garden of his studio house. Numerous changes were made in the reconstruction, however, such as widening each courtyard entrance 15 feet to accommodate cars. He converted the relocated man-

sion—one of the first attempts at historic preservation in Washington—into three spacious apartments, one to a floor. The adjacent Warder House and Totten House were both later acquired by Antioch College's School of Law and sadly allowed to deteriorate during the 1970s and 1980s.

The plan of Meridian Hill Studio includes a series of duplex and triplex apartments in the two outer wings. The triplex units have their own outside entrances. Each of the enormous ceramic murals above the fireplace mantels in the apartments was designed differently by Mrs. George Oakley Totten and fired in her own kiln across the street. Still intact, they are Washington's best surviving example of Arts and Crafts ceramic murals. The building now includes a huge efficiency apartment (the former art gallery), two one-bedroom apartments, six two-bedroom duplex units, and four triplex units.

The apartment floor plans vary considerably. Two of the triplex apartments, Nos. 4 and 7, contain a large

This large gallery on the second floor (rear) of Meridian Hill Studio was used by the original residents, mostly artists, for their private exhibitions. The gallery is now Washington's largest efficiency apartment.

gallery, or open living-dining space, and kitchen on the first floor; two bedrooms and bath on the second floor; and two bedrooms on the third floor. One of these three-story apartments, common in New York but rare in Washington, was owned by Mr. and Mrs. Erik Hillman, both concert pianists. Shown in the 1982 photograph, they gave piano lessons at home and had four grand pianos in their apartment; students were graduated to the better pianos as their skills improved.

Parking for five cars is provided in a garage on the ground-floor rear of the central wing, entered through the rear alley. Above the garage is the most interesting unit of all, the "gallery": a large room 30 by 40 feet with a 22-foot ceiling. It was transformed to an enviable efficiency apartment by adding a kitchen and bath when the building was converted to a co-op in 1941. Originally intended as a working painting studio and exhibition gallery, this unit contains the most beautiful of all of Mrs. Totten's Arts and Crafts-style mosaic fireplace murals.

On the opposite wall, two open staircases, which rise to balconies where musicians once entertained at parties, provide access to the smaller third-floor apartments with skylights. On the floor of the gallery, now an efficiency apartment, a trap door opens to reveal a hidden staircase leading to the garage and service room on the ground floor below. The many other unusual features include the wrought-iron stair balustrade in the first-floor public hallway, skylights, and unusual dormer windows. Meridian Hill Studio is the only known apartment house to have been designed by Totten.

Had Meridian Hill Studio not been converted to a co-op, it is doubtful the building would have survived the rapid demographic changes that began in 1953. A number of interesting residents have lived here, including Totten himself. One of the longest-term residents is William Howard Payne, an attorney for Oklahoma Indians for many years and also the secretary to Will Rogers in the 1920s.

67

PRESIDENTIAL

1026 16th Street, N.W.; southwest corner of 16th and L streets

ARCHITECT: Appleton P. Clark, Jr., 1922

ORIGINAL APARTMENTS: 46 (16 bachelors; 16 one-bedrooms; 14 two-bedrooms)

STATUS: opened as rental in 1923; converted to
co-op in 1959

Within weeks of the District of Columbia Zoning Board's vote in 1922 to allow apartment houses on 16th Street, N.W., south of Scott Circle, two were begun—the Presidential and the Jefferson. Both were of classical design, faced with limestone. They remained fashionable addresses until the dignified mansions that surrounded them were replaced by office buildings during the 1940s and 1950s. The Jefferson was converted to a hotel in the 1950s and elegantly renovated in the early 1980s. Of the numerous apartment houses that once graced the old downtown neighborhoods of Lafayette, Franklin, and Farragut squares, only the Presidential still stands. The last holdout against commercialization in this neighborhood, the Presidential is maintained today in remarkably good condition as a co-op. Although neither design included a public dining room, both the Presidential and the Jefferson offered a high degree of service, with doormen, twenty-four-hour elevator operators, and maid service.

The Presidential was built as an investment by a wealthy widow, Mrs. Clara R. Dennis, for $350,000. The principal 16th Street front facade was designed with octagonal eight-story bays on each side. The entrance is emphasized by an elaborate Adamesque porch with two pairs of fluted Corinthian marble columns resting on plinths and crowned by an elaborate cornice and balcony. An

Front facade of the Presidential.

octagonal oriel window extending between the fourth and seventh floors above was designed to match the corner projecting bays. Of additional interest on the street fa-

The doorman stands under the imposing stone portico of the Presidential.

cades are the rusticated two-story base, the tripartite windows, the roof's marble urns (since removed), and the shallow second-floor iron window balconies.

The lobby, low-ceilinged by 1922 standards, remains in original condition. The floor is laid with black and white marble squares, while the walls are paneled and embellished with a pair of fluted Doric columns. The most spectacular feature is the elaborate plaster ceiling in the Adamesque design, typical of those in great late eighteenth-century English country houses.

The Presidential was designed with a total of forty-six apartments—four on the first floor and six on each floor above—ranging in size from one to four rooms. On most floors two units were bachelor apartments containing one room and bathroom but no kitchen. The two tiers of the largest apartments, both facing the front, have large foyers, with columns and French doors. The Presidential was designed so that an entire floor could be converted to a single fourteen-room apartment.

Several of the long-term, forty-year residents explained the reason for naming the apartment house the Presidential. In a grandiose scheme, the original owner, Clara Dennis, wanted most of President Harding's cabinet members and their families to live here, one to a floor. Even though the Presidential was only three blocks from the White House, the plan never worked. It is not known if any one floor was ever converted to a single apartment,

although it was so advertised when the Presidential opened in 1923.

Because of its location, as well as its service features, the Presidential was one of the most desirable Washington apartment houses in 1929. A random sample of two-bedroom apartments advertised in the [Washington] *Evening Star* that year shows that monthly rents ranged from $100 at the Argonne and the Chastleton to $200 at the Presidential and Meridian Mansions—then among the most costly in the city.

In 1959 the Edmund J. Flynn Company converted the Presidential to a cooperative apartment house. The four first-floor apartments were sold separately as medical office suites. Because of its location, the land value of the Presidential far exceeds the value of the building today.

The typical floor plan of the Presidential contains six units, including two bachelor apartments without kitchens.

The lobby of the Presidential is one of five in Washington designed in the Adamesque style.

ARCHITECT APPLETON P. CLARK, JR.

The Presidential is an excellent example of the design skill of architect Appleton P. Clark, Jr. (1865–1955), who, through his sense of scale, proportion, and context, skillfully blended this high-rise into the original residential neighborhood. His other apartment houses on 16th Street, N.W., include No. 1424 (now an office building), No. 2001 (now the Brittany), and the Roosevelt Hotel. Among Clark's twenty-seven local apartment houses are two early examples in Georgetown, 3014 and 3020 Dent Place, N.W., designed in 1902–03. A native of Washington, D.C., Clark was trained in architecture in the office of A. B. Mullett for a three-year period after he graduated from high school in 1883. At the age of twenty, Clark opened his own architectural office, where he designed a wide variety of building types over the next sixty years. His prominent office buildings include the Herman Building at 901 7th Street, N.W., of 1885; the Barrister Building of 1909 at 635 F Street, N.W., now demolished; and the Homer Building at 601 13th Street, N.W., of 1914. Other notable commercial buildings that came from his drafting board included the Home Savings Bank of 1902 at 7th Street and Massachusetts Avenue, N.W., and the Washington Post Building at 1337 E Street, N.W., of 1893, both of which have been demolished. Clark's residential buildings included rowhouses such as those at 1644–1666 Park Road, N.W., and a number of mansions such as the 1911 Craftsman style house built for H. Cornell Wilson at 1609 16th Street, N.W. His institutional buildings include the Foundry Methodist Church and the Central Presbyterian Church as well as two buildings for Garfield Hospital and the Hillcrest orphanage on Nebraska Avenue, N.W. After designing two other orphanages, Clark produced a book, *Institutional Homes for Children* (1945), in which he urged the use of cottages for orphanages to create a more domestic ambiance.

All apartments in the No. 2 tier at the Presidential have a pair of fluted columns set in a wide classical arch between the living room and the foyer.

68

2500 MASSACHUSETTS AVENUE, N.W.

West side of Massachusetts Avenue between S Street and Decatur Place

ARCHITECT: Louis E. Sholtes, 1922

ORIGINAL APARTMENTS: 8 (8 three-bedrooms)

STATUS: opened as rental in 1923; converted to co-op in 1948

Protected by both its diplomatic neighbors and Rock Creek Park, 2500 Massachusetts Avenue, N.W., has remained a fashionable address since it first opened for tenants in 1923. The architect and original owner, Louis E. Sholtes, faced the front facade, with its eclectic classical detailing, with Indiana limestone. The building's most prominent external features are the two octagonal bays that extend from the ground to the third floor. The facade remains in original condition, although one wishes that the current co-op owners would restore the iron and glass marquee, now covered with aluminum.

A small foyer with steps leads up to the elevator landing, originally decorated with marble wainscoting, a pair of Ionic columns, and paneled walls. The U-shaped building is laid out with two apartments on each of the four floors. The living room and conservatory of each apartment face the street and connect to the dining room through folding French doors. Working fireplaces, which became fashionable in Washington apartment houses in the 1920s, are the focus of every living room and dining room. The long hall leading to the rear provides access in each apartment to three bedrooms, three baths, sunroom, kitchen, pantry, and maid's room and bath. The only flaw in the plan is that neither the kitchen nor the pantry connects directly to the dining room, which is across the hall.

Each apartment at 2500 Massachusetts Avenue (two to a floor) has a conservatory or sun room, located at the sides of the building.

The dining room in the apartment of Mrs. Johnson Garrett at 2500 Massachusetts Avenue.

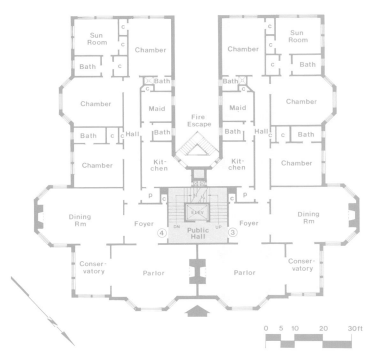

Typical floor plan of 2500 Massachusetts Avenue.

Maxwell Taylor, who served as U.S. ambassador to Vietnam and chairman of the Joint Chiefs of Staff of the Department of Defense, in his living room at 2500 Massachusetts Avenue, in 1982.

The interior detailing in these apartments is relatively simple, consisting primarily of the mantels and handsome plaster crown molding in the living and dining rooms. The original applied panels on their walls were removed when the building was converted to a co-op in 1948. Behind the building is a freestanding garage with spaces for eight cars. A delightful small private garden extends beyond, facing Rock Creek Park. Over the years 2500 Massachusetts Avenue, N.W., has provided a comfortable home for a number of distinguished military and diplomatic leaders, including General Maxwell Taylor, who lived here in retirement until his death in 1987.

69

METHODIST BUILDING,
now the UNITED METHODIST BUILDING

100 Maryland Avenue, N.E.; northeast corner of Maryland Avenue and 1st Street

ARCHITECT: Walter F. Ballinger, Philadelphia, 1923; Edward L. Bullock, Jr., Philadelphia, 1931 addition

ORIGINAL APARTMENTS: main building: 15 (6 one-bedrooms; 9 two-bedrooms); annex: 54 (mostly one-bedrooms)

STATUS: opened as rental in 1924; apartments in main building converted to offices in 1975–85

To support the Prohibition movement in the United States, the Methodist Episcopal Church (Northern branch) purchased a lot on Capitol Hill in 1916 for the site of a new building. Church leaders believed that the impressive physical presence of a structure close to the U.S. Capitol, built by church members who were also voters, would enhance their lobbying for Prohibition. The building would house church offices on the two lower floors; rental apartments above would produce income. It was assumed correctly that all or almost all of the apartments would be rented to members of Congress and their staffs, and the church would thus exert its influence in a variety of ways.

First known as the Methodist Building, the new structure had fifteen apartments on the upper three floors—nine four-room units and six three-room units, each with kitchen and bath. The lower two floors were used by the Methodist Board of Temperance, Prohibition, and Public Morals—a title to strike terror into the heart of any free spirit. Established in Chicago in 1888 to publish tracts and leaflets against alcohol, the Board of Temperance eventually moved to Washington to make its presence felt on the national scene. Its temporary location was in a large Victorian house at 110 Maryland Avenue, N.E., just behind the present Methodist Building.

The 1917 plans for a six-story marble-faced classical

An early mixed-use structure was the Methodist Building, erected in 1923 with offices, a public dining room, a chapel, and apartments.

225

Detail of the rusticated limestone first-floor facade of the Methodist Building.

structure by Ballinger and Perrot of Philadelphia were never carried out, because the entry of the United States into World War I restricted most building materials to defense purposes. Construction was also delayed because the District of Columbia Zoning Board required the Methodist Church to reduce the height to five stories in respect for the Capitol. Redrawn by Ballinger in 1922, plans for the new building were quite similar to the original concept, with these changes: the building would have only five stories, faced in limestone; one main entrance at the corner of Maryland Avenue and 1st Street replaced the two principal entrances of the earlier design; and five limestone balconies on the fourth floor were substituted for the twenty iron ones originally intended for the third and fifth floors. The most distinguished single feature of the Methodist Building, however, is the range of great arched French windows on the rusticated first floor on both street facades.

Although the Eighteenth Amendment mandating prohibition went into effect in 1920, the Methodist Building was nonetheless erected in 1923. The Board of Temperance aimed to work actively to block the new movement to bring back the sale of wine and beer. As noted in its newsletter, *The Voice*, in the early 1920s, the board also campaigned against dancing, motion pictures, boxing,

tobacco, immigration, and the Roman Catholic Church. During the Roaring Twenties the board indeed needed every inch of space. With other evangelical groups, it succeeded in preventing the voiding of the Volstead or Prohibition Act until 1933, when the Twenty-first Amendment was ratified, repealing the Eighteenth and making liquor, wine, and beer available again.

Because of the McMillan Commission Plan of 1901, both city and federal governments strongly encouraged classical design for new major buildings in Washington. This mode was especially appropriate for the Methodist Building, as it faced the Capitol. In planning the new building, the Methodist Church consulted frequently with both Congress and the Commission of Fine Arts, and the design of the building was carefully developed over a period of seven years.

Interior plans for the Methodist Building included an elegant, elliptical lobby decorated with blind arches, handsome black marble columns, and pilasters. Although the Tudor Revival furniture and chandeliers are gone now, the lobby still has the elegant bronze floor lamps installed in 1924. The west side of the original building, facing 1st Street, N.E., had a paneled conference room adjoining the lobby and an excellent cafeteria that became popular on Capitol Hill. Daily services for the two floors of Methodist office workers were held in the paneled chapel in the east wing of the original building along Maryland Avenue. The best apartments were on the apex, with the view of the Capitol to the west and, after 1935, of the new U.S. Supreme Court building across Maryland Avenue to the south.

With revenue generated from the fifteen rental apartments, the church built an annex with an additional fifty-four apartments in 1931. The Annex, at 110 Maryland Avenue, N.E., extended through the block to Constitution Avenue. Although ten fine Victorian brick houses were razed to make way for the new structure, this was an age when Victorian architecture was considered less than desirable. The Annex added 150 percent to the original building's space. In the tightly restricted basement garage of the Annex, a turntable, then called an auto-turnable, was installed to aid in parking the cars in the thirty-five spaces available. The design of the Annex was reviewed by the Commission of Fine Arts, the first building for

Lobby of the Methodist Building.

The diagonal angle of Maryland Avenue dictated the wedge-shaped design of the Methodist Building, which included apartments on the top three floors, as shown here.

The clerical staff of the Board of Temperance, Prohibition, and Public Morals of the Methodist Church prepares a mailing in the Methodist Building in 1925.

which approval was required, under the terms of the Shipstead-Luce Act of 1930. This law authorizes the Commission of Fine Arts to review the exterior design and height of all private buildings erected near major government buildings in Washington. The church's original plan for a 72-foot-high annex was not approved because of its proximity to the proposed Supreme Court building. One can clearly see today the abrupt drop in the cornice line between the two Methodist buildings; the ceilings in the Annex consequently are much lower than those in the original building.

Strenuous efforts were made at that time to restrict any further building adjacent to the Capitol. William H. Taft, as Chief Justice, was in 1930 planning the new Supreme Court building. He wanted the federal government to seize the Methodist Building's entire block under the power of eminent domain and close Maryland Avenue between 1st and 2nd streets, N.E. (which the Annex was to front). He failed, as did a bill introduced by Senator

Henry W. Keyes of New Hampshire for the government to acquire this block.

The interior appointments of the Annex were far less spectacular than those in the original building. Following the dictates of then-current taste, there were no decorative fireplaces, no mantels, no gas logs like those that embellished the 1923 Methodist Building. Both buildings were expensively and handsomely erected, however, and were extremely popular with members of Congress; the apartments always had a waiting list. During the 1960s, congressional residents included Senators Carl Hayden, Sam J. Ervin, Jr., Albert Gore, George D. Aiken, and Ralph W. Yarborough.

Unification of three major Methodist denominations in 1939 brought together the Northern and Southern churches, which had parted before the Civil War over the issue of slavery. This merger increased the need for office space, as did new efforts by the Board of Temperance. The need increased further in the 1960s when the

The only two apartment houses in Washington with private chapels are the Methodist Building, shown here, and the Army Distaff Hall.

church expanded its activities in the areas of civil rights, world peace, drug abuse, women's rights, welfare, and health care. Still more administrative space was required when the Evangelical United Brethren and the Methodist churches merged to form the United Methodist Church in 1969. The building was then renamed the United Methodist Building.

These mergers led to a policy in 1969 (prior to rent control) to gradually convert the entire building into offices. Some were rented to outside groups—all educa-

tional or charitable organizations, in conformity with D.C. law since this area is not zoned commercial. The dining room was closed, and by 1984 only one apartment in the original building and a dozen in the Annex remained as residences. Both the original Methodist Building and its Annex deserve to be preserved, not only for the quality of their construction and the elegance of their classical design, but also for their appropriate scale: both complement the Capitol and Supreme Court and are assets to the streetscape of Capitol Hill.

70

ANCHORAGE

1900 Que Street, N.W.; southeast corner of Que Street and Connecticut Avenue

ARCHITECT: Jules H. de Sibour, 1924

ORIGINAL APARTMENTS: 12 (one-bedrooms and two-bedrooms)

STATUS: opened as rental in 1925; converted to offices in 1964

Mrs. John R. Williams—Ma Williams, as she was affectionately known by her friends—built this exclusive bachelor apartment house as an investment. The Anchorage was home to many distinguished residents until it was converted to offices in 1964. It was across the street from three other fashionable apartment houses that Mrs. Williams also owned and managed herself—the Galleon, the Caravel, and the Moorings. All four had not only nautical names but also many nautical motifs. It is unclear why she was fond of the ocean; the widow of an Army officer, Mrs. Williams was known to become seasick every time she sailed.

Her first two apartment houses were the Galleon, on the northeast corner, and the adjoining Caravel on Connecticut Avenue. A caravel was a light sailing ship used by the Spanish and Portuguese in the fifteenth and sixteenth centuries. Nautical terms are unusual for Washington apartment houses because the city has no major harbor. One of the few other local apartment houses named for a ship is the 1898 Olympia Flats, on the southeast corner of Euclid and 14th streets, N.W. Its developer, in a fit of patriotic fervor, named it for Admiral Dewey's flagship, the *U.S.S. Olympia,* to commemorate the U.S. victory at Manila Bay during the Spanish-American War. Both the Galleon and the Caravel were Beaux Arts-

inspired buildings dating from the turn of the century and intended for commercial use. The imposing five-story Galleon had originally been a fashionable sanitarium operated by Dr. Henry D. Fry, and the Caravel had housed shops and offices. Spurred by the financial success of her first two apartment "ports," Mrs. Williams commissioned Washington architect Jules H. de Sibour to design the Anchorage in 1924, and Horace Peaslee to design the Moorings in 1926. Impeccable service was the hallmark of all four apartment houses. For four decades the Anchorage housed Pierre's Restaurant, famous for its French cuisine. Inasmuch as Pierre's delivered and served meals to residents—including Mrs. Williams, the apartments in the four buildings had only kitchenettes.

The four-story Anchorage was designed in the classical mode and built of tan brick with limestone trim. The lobby, entered through the slightly projecting central pavilion on Que Street, had a switchboard and elevator; the remaining space on the first floor was used for shops. The twelve apartments above varied in size from two to four rooms, and all had high ceilings, working fireplaces, and handsome woodwork. The nautical theme flourishes in both the exterior and the interior. On the facade are wrought-iron balconies with an anchor design in front of the third-floor French doors. Under the name *Anchorage*

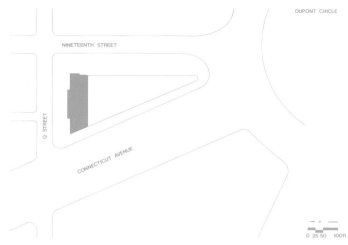

Site plan of the Anchorage.

on the Connecticut Avenue facade is a 6-foot-high metal anchor. Mounted between four pairs of Ionic stone pilasters flanking the two main entrances on Que Street were four handsome bronze lamps designed like the projecting bay window on the captain's cabin on the stern of an eighteenth-century ship. Many of the original wrought-iron wall sconces, decorated with sailing ships, remain in the Anchorage's rooms. Each apartment also had a brass door knocker in the shape of a ship, a ship's clock on the wall, a seascape mural in the living room, and chintz curtains printed with whales and dashing waves.

The Anchorage was considered the most desirable of the four buildings because it had the largest apartments, with the most spacious rooms, highest ceilings, and finest detailing. During its thirty-nine years as an apartment house, more than two dozen members of Congress lived here. The longest-term resident was Sam Rayburn of Texas, House Speaker (longer than any other man), 1940–47,

Top left: Architect Jules H. de Sibour's Beaux Arts design of the Anchorage included unusually large windows. *Middle:* The west facade of the Anchorage is embellished with a large bronze anchor, while the balustrades of the third-floor balconies incorporate a design of crossed anchors. *Bottom:* Continuing the nautical motif, architect de Sibour designed a pair of ship lanterns for the main entrance of the Anchorage on Que Street.

Mrs. John Williams, a socially prominent
Washington businesswoman, managed her
four apartment buildings located near the
intersection of Connecticut Avenue and Que
Street. She gave them all nautical names—
Anchorage, Moorings, Galleon, and
Caravelle.

Massachusetts Avenue, N.W.—she sold it the next year to Gladys Vanderbilt. During most of her life in Washington, up to her death in 1945, "Ma" Williams lived in one of her four apartment houses at Connecticut Avenue and Que Street to better supervise their operation. The secrets to her success as a businesswoman were her good taste, her careful and discreet attention to the management of her apartment houses, and her role in society. She was so well liked that her apartments would have been sought after even if they were not so well managed.

Eventually, in 1962, the Williams estate sold all four apartment houses to Washington attorney and real estate investor Clifford J. Hynning for a total of $680,000. The new owner converted the Anchorage and the Moorings to offices in 1964, retaining most of the intriguing original details in the rooms. The Galleon and the Caravel were unfortunately demolished in 1969 for a mediocre highrise, the Caravel Office Building, completely out of scale with the streetscape.

1949–53, and 1955–61, who occupied a third-floor apartment for twenty-five years, until his death in 1961. Others who stayed here briefly included Charles A. Lindbergh, Tallulah Bankhead, General and Mrs. George C. Marshall, Frances Parkinson Keyes, and Robert F. Kennedy.

The owner of the Anchorage, Marie Hewitt Williams of St. Louis, was the widow of Colonel John R. Williams, an 1876 graduate of West Point. Mrs. Williams (also called Ma and Maie by her friends) conceived of her Washington apartment-hotels after living for several months in a London mansion flat that provided full service. She moved to Washington after her husband's death in 1919, probably to be near her eldest daughter, Juliette Leiter. The Leiter House was just south of the Anchorage, on New Hampshire Avenue at Dupont Circle. The socially prominent Mrs. Williams was famous as a hostess; she was also a major force behind the Thrift Shop, which raised funds for children's charities, and the Sulgrave Club, of which she was a founder. Although she built one of the great houses of Washington in 1921—2929

The Anchorage's architectural detailing includes handsome
fireplace mantels and built-in china cabinets in all dining rooms.

71

CLEVELAND PARK,
now known by individual addresses

3018–3028 Porter Street, N.W.

ARCHITECT: James E. Cooper, 1924–25

ORIGINAL APARTMENTS: 72 (one-bedrooms and two-bedrooms)

STATUS: opened as six separate co-ops in 1925

Encouraged by the rapid sale of the thirty apartments in their first co-op apartment house, 1705 Lanier Place, N.W., the brothers Monroe and R. Bates Warren began construction of the Cleveland Park apartments in 1924. The six Georgian Revival buildings, extending along the south side of Porter Street west of Connecticut Avenue, are of identical size but vary in facade treatment. Each has twelve apartments. Although built at the same time, the buildings were designed as and remain separate co-operatives.

Their floor plan was much like 1705 Lanier Place, with four apartments per floor, some with two rooms, kitchen, and bath and some with three rooms, kitchen, and bath. Each has a galley kitchen, with a dining alcove at one end. The stairs are in the center of each building. To the rear, facing the public alley, extend a range of thirty-six garages, designed in groups of six, one for every other apartment. The original cost of these modest apartments varied from $5,800 to $7,500, with a 20-percent cash deposit. Sales of the apartments, conducted by the Edmund J. Flynn Company, were brisk and highly successful. They were the first co-op apartments that were frequently and extensively advertised in the local newspapers—thereby providing an important record of the advantages associated with co-op ownership and life.

One of the six three-story buildings that comprise the Cleveland Park apartments.

A 1924 advertisement for the Cleveland Park, one of the first Washington apartment houses built as a co-op.

Residents of the Cleveland Park were provided with small individual garages in the alley behind the complex.

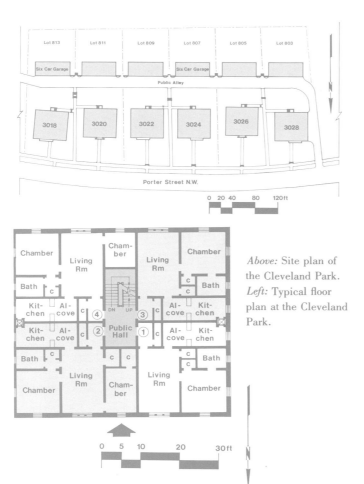

Above: Site plan of the Cleveland Park. *Left:* Typical floor plan at the Cleveland Park.

The spacious lawns on all sides of the Cleveland Park, as well as the three-story height and hipped and gabled roofs of each building, create a highly domestic appearance. The Cleveland Park—a forerunner of a new building form, the garden apartment—was the second Washington apartment project with a cluster of low-rise buildings related to one another by landscaping. (The first was the 1922 Petworth Gardens, now Webster Gardens, near the Soldiers Home.)

The eclectic Cleveland Park buildings, with Georgian Revival detailing, remain in remarkably original condition; even the lattice-work screens connecting the garage buildings survive. Although originally called Cleveland Park, each of the six buildings is known today only by its address.

72

ARMY AND NAVY,
now known by its address

2540 Massachusetts Avenue, N.W.; west side of Massachusetts Avenue between Belmont Road and Waterside Drive

ARCHITECT: Harry L. Edwards, 1925

ORIGINAL APARTMENTS: 38 (14 one-bedrooms; 12 two-bedrooms; 10 three-bedrooms; 2 four-bedrooms)

STATUS: opened as co-op in 1926

When it opened in 1926, this thirty-eight unit apartment house was considered the finest cooperative in Washington. Its success spurred the development of ever-larger and grander co-ops until the Depression halted all new luxury apartment house construction in 1932. Known today only by its address, the building was called the Army and Navy for many decades because seventeen of the original shareholders were military officers, most members of the United States Army. Many, including six generals and seven colonels, were assigned to the general staff of the Department of War. These officers commissioned developers Monroe and R. Bates Warren to erect the building shortly after their successful construction of two earlier co-op apartment houses—1705 Lanier Place, N.W., and the Cleveland Park. At that time there were some three dozen cooperative apartment houses in Washington, but most had originally been built as rentals. Before the Warren brothers began to build co-ops in 1923, only two Washington apartment houses had been actually built as co-ops—the Concord in 1891 and 2852 Ontario Road in 1909—and they remained the only ones until 1920. Postwar inflation prompted scores more in the 1920s.

The officers who organized 2540 first considered buying a site at the southwest corner of Wisconsin and Massachusetts Avenues, N.W., but decided on a location

The 1925 Army and Navy was designed in the Georgian Revival style.

The Army and Navy was one of the first Washington apartment
houses with a step-down lobby.

The apartments at the Army and Navy vary considerably in design,
but two floors have this plan.

adjacent to Rock Creek Park. Monroe Warren worked with the group. The committee of officers made many design decisions themselves—sleeping porches on the rear wings, for instance. The H. L. Rust Company, as the loan company that financed the building, chose Harry L. Edwards as its architect. Although Edwards designed the facade, lobby, and detailing, the floor plan was produced by the Edmund J. Flynn Company, working with the military officers. Because of its experience as a co-op specialist, this real estate firm was employed by the loan company as consultant for the floor plan and as sales representative when the building was completed.

The restrained Georgian Revival facade is appropriate in this neighborhood of large houses built in the 1920s in the same style. The two most prominent features are the imposing entrance, with its rusticated limestone surround and iron and glass marquee, and the pair of projecting pavilions. Each pavilion has a limestone base, rusticated-brick second floor, and a pair of soaring pilasters that "supports" a richly sculptured entablature. The sixth, or top, floor is finished off with an arched pediment set on line with the prominent limestone belt-course encircling the entire building. A semicircular front driveway planted with boxwood complements the symmetry of this steel-frame residence. By setting the ground floor below street grade, the architect reduced the bulk of the structure. The plan's U shape gives on to an open rear courtyard facing Rock Creek Park.

The ground floor includes a spacious and richly detailed step-down lobby, office, garage for seventeen cars, a mail room (originally designated the "baby carriage room"), a storage room with lockers for each apartment, laundry room, boiler room, and the resident manager's apartment. The typical plan included nine apartments per floor, ranging from two rooms to six rooms. The No. 5 tier has both the largest and the best planned apartments, with the bedrooms and baths carefully separated from the public rooms.

An unusual aspect of the Army and Navy was that many of the original co-op owners helped to plan their own apartments. With few exceptions, it was not until the 1960s that Washington developers offered options in apartment plans to purchasers of co-ops before construction began. Because so many original owners, working

with the architect and the Edmund J. Flynn Company, were involved in the initial plans for Army and Navy, apartments vary considerably in their details. One unit has walls finished in a rough plaster, with plaster cornices designed in a rope motif. In half the apartments, applied rectangular moldings decorated living room walls, fairly typical of detailing in principal public rooms in first-class apartments between 1915 and 1929. Most such moldings have since been removed because of the difficulty they cause with picture hanging. Several of the largest apartments have two entrances, one into the foyer and another to the kitchen. The apartments on the second through fourth floors originally had decorative fireplace mantels, designed to the original owner's preference. The fifth- and sixth-floor apartments have working fireplaces. While the building was under construction, some of the original owners of adjacent apartments arranged for the reassignment of rooms from one apartment to another. Thus there are only two "typical floor plans," with the other three floors having various configurations.

Over the years residents have made other changes that have improved the original designs. All open sleeping porches but one have been enclosed. Each of the ten front corner apartments originally had an enclosed sunroom with casement windows adjacent to the living room. The walls dividing the sunrooms from the living rooms have since been removed to admit more light into the living rooms and to provide more open space for entertaining. Such alteration of interior walls has been possible because all walls, including exterior ones, are non-load-bearing, due to the building's steel frame. Other changes were made to conform to revisions in the city code. Originally a trash chute was provided on each floor; trash was burned in the basement incinerator until 1972, when new air pollution control laws prohibited this practice. The incinerator was replaced by a compactor into which trash is fed via the original chutes.

By established custom and courtesy, and to avoid confusion, Washington developers have usually refrained from giving one apartment house the same name as another. On the building permit for the Army and Navy issued in 1925, the official name was listed as 2540 Massachusetts Avenue, N.W. From the very beginning, however, it was called the Army and Navy because of

A resident of the Army and Navy in her handsome sun room. This feature was most popular in local apartment house design in the 1920s.

the unusually high number of military families who lived there. Soon after 2540 opened, a new twelve-story apartment-hotel at 820 Connecticut Avenue, N.W. (designed by architect Matthew G. Lepley in 1927), was officially named the Army and Navy Apartments. This new building, together with its proximity to the Army and Navy Club, created confusion among letter carriers, taxicab drivers, and others heading for any of the three. Thus, the owners of the apartment-hotel on Connecticut Avenue changed its name to the Claridge in 1934. [Although unusual, even today there are buildings of the same name, and the resulting confusion. Two Envoys are found—one on 16th Street, N.W., and the other on California Street, N.W. There are also two Somerset Houses; again the original is on 16th Street, N.W., and the second is now under construction in Somerset, Maryland.]

Besides the Army officers who initially lived at 2540 Massachusetts Avenue, N.W., the building has housed businessmen, authors, university presidents, clergy, members of Congress, and diplomats. The distinguished residents included the three maiden daughters of General Philip Henry Sheridan—Mary, Irene, and Louise. Before moving to 2540, they lived nearby in a house at Sheridan Circle overlooking their Civil War hero-father's equestrian statue. The youngest daughter of General Sheridan died at the Army and Navy in the late 1960s. [The three Sheridan sisters were well known in Washington, but their fame was eclipsed by three others, the Patten sisters, who lived a block away in a Romanesque Revival house on the southeast corner of Massachusetts and Florida avenues, N.W. The two sets of sisters were friends and often visited one another for bridge parties or teas. Because the three Patten sisters were extremely social and out constantly for luncheons and dinners, they heard most of the gossip in the city and exchanged it among themselves and their friends, the Sheridan sisters, the following day. It was said in the 1920s and 1930s that the fastest way to get a message across town was "Not to telephone or to telegraph but to 'tell-a-Patten.' "]

73

CHALFONTE

1601 Argonne Place, N.W.

ARCHITECT: Harvey H. Warwick, Sr., 1925

ORIGINAL APARTMENTS: 200 (93 efficiencies; 95 one-bedrooms; 12 two-bedrooms)

STATUS: opened as rental in 1926

Site frequently dictates the basic configuration of an apartment house—especially in the inner city where land is expensive and the neighborhood densely populated. This is certainly the case at the Chalfonte, which occupies the entire triangular block bounded by Argonne Place, Harvard Street, and Lanier Place, N.W. Location required an irregular E-shape plan for the Chalfonte. The five large wings, with their projecting pavilions and bays, provide maximum air and light for the tightly constrained building of two hundred apartments. The Chalfonte has a width of 470 feet and a depth of 240 feet.

The building was designed by architect Harvey H. Warwick, Sr., a native of Kansas City, who opened his own architectural practice in Washington in 1922. He worked as a partner of Louis Justement briefly between 1927 and 1930. Of the thirty-six Washington apartment houses that Warwick designed between 1922 and 1941, the monumental Westchester and Colonial Village were his most important. Warwick lived briefly at the Chalfonte in 1927 and later in two other apartment houses that he had designed, the Valley Vista in 1929 and the Westchester throughout the 1930s.

The developer of the Chalfonte, William S. Phillips, was a prominent builder in pre-Depression Washington who constructed more than nine hundred rowhouses in addition to the Valley Vista, Harvard Hall, and Argonne apartment houses. Originally Phillips planned for the Chalfonte to have six stories. When he announced this in May 1923, the Mount Pleasant Citizens Association attacked the plan bitterly, charging that its height would keep light and air from the surrounding rowhouses and mar the entrance to the zoo. Subsequently, the zoning commission required Phillips to drop the height to four stories and to set the building 30 feet back from Harvard Street in case that street had to be widened. This is why the rear or Harvard Street side of the building has a wide lawn, while the other facades extend to within a few feet of the sidewalks. The bill then pending before Congress to widen Harvard Street was never passed, however.

The design of the Chalfonte is eclectic, a curious blend of classical and Mediterranean features typical of the 1920s. The tan-brick facades crowned by gabled, hipped, and flat tile roofs form a picturesque ensemble that adds variety to the neighborhood. Of all Washington apartment houses, its facade is perhaps the closest in style to several hundred Mediterranean-influenced apartment houses built in Los Angeles during the 1920s.

Early advertising represented the Chalfonte as a refuge from Washington's summer heat. About 25 percent of the apartments included screened sleeping porches that

The eclectic facade of the Chalfonte includes elements borrowed from Mediterranean architecture, such as the hipped tile roofs, arched windows, and engaged spiral columns.

Site plan of the Chalfonte, showing the numerous wings designed by architect Harvey H. Warwick, Jr.

in later years were enclosed with casement windows. A second important contribution to summer comfort was the Johnson Ventilating System. A. S. Johnson's patented design consists of air shafts approximately 4 by 8 feet, connecting tiers of apartment bathrooms from the basement to the open roof. Fresh air thus circulates within the apartments through the bathroom windows, which open onto the shafts, and passes from the shafts into public corridors through metal grates in the corridor walls. This system, in conjunction with the outer louvered apartment doors and open apartment windows shaded by canvas awnings, circulated cool air throughout the building.

The Chalfonte was known for a variety of features and services that included a telephone in every apartment linked to a twenty-four-hour switchboard. A private lounge for ladies originally opened onto the main lobby. Although the 100-foot-long swimming pool proposed for the sub-basement was never built, a cafe, beauty parlor, and valet shop—all situated on the ground floor near the east door—remained in operation for several decades.

Originally known as Phillips Terrace after its developer, the million-dollar apartment house was renamed the Chalfonte in 1930 by the second owner, who selected the French-sounding name to establish a stylish atmosphere. The name was actually English, however, taken from the town of Chalfont in Buckinghamshire. This change at Phillips Terrace caused confusion, however, because an earlier Chalfonte apartment house already existed— a four-story twenty-four-unit building at 2116 P Street, N.W., built about 1914; it became part of the Hartnett Hall boarding house complex in the 1950s and was razed in the early 1980s.

The later Chalfonte limped through the Great Depression in receivership until 1941, when it was purchased by the Goldwyn Realty and Management firm of New York City. Within eighteen months after paying $850,000 for it, Irving Goldwyn spent $50,000 more on improvements. He outfitted all four lobbies with wingback chairs and traditional furnishings, and the main lobby with paintings. During the 1940s and 1950s the wife of resident manager Marian Reeves, Florence, helped to create a showplace by her constant supervision of the planting and maintenance of large beds of roses, iris, and azaleas on the immaculate lawn.

After the Chalfonte was sold in 1962, conditions in the building slowly but surely deteriorated. To gain more income, additional apartments were constructed in the east lobby and in the former cafe and beauty shop. The marble baseboards and hardwood trim in the south lobby were painted chartreuse. Such amenities as the switchboard, doorman, and lobby furnishings were eliminated, while the seven resident janitors were reduced to three. Nevertheless the building today remains basically intact and an important architectural addition to the Adams-Morgan neighborhood.

Plan of an apartment in the No. 21 tier of the Chalfonte.

74

1661 CRESCENT PLACE, N.W.

North side of Crescent Place between 16th and 17th streets

ARCHITECT: Joseph Younger, 1925

ORIGINAL APARTMENTS: 50 (5 efficiencies; 25 two-bedrooms; 5 three-bedrooms; 15 four-bedrooms)

STATUS: opened as co-op in 1926

A Georgian Revival red-brick six-story E-shaped apartment house with limestone trim, built as a cooperative, 1661 Crescent Place, N.W., is located on a charming short side street opposite Meridian Hill Park. It is surrounded by three important Beaux Arts buildings—the White-Meyer House, Meridian House, and Meridian Mansions (now the Envoy). Monroe Warren, the developer of 1661 Crescent Place, N.W., selected this site in 1925 because of its high elevation and its proximity to then-fashionable 16th Street, N.W.

Originally, 1661 had fifty apartments in ten tiers of varying sizes. Almost half of the apartments were unusually spacious with as many as four bedrooms. As can be seen in the typical floor plan, the three largest tiers form the front ends of the wings extending out to Crescent Place. With three exposures and large central foyers, these are particularly desirable. The apartments were planned for entertaining, with access through arches from foyer to drawing room to dining room. They are also embellished with a number of interesting details—wain-

The original perspective drawing of 1661 Crescent Place.

Detail of the entrance to 1661 Crescent Place, showing the blind arches and pedimented windows above.

The large four-bedroom apartments at 1661 Crescent Place are on the front ends of the three wings.

The lawns between the wings of 1661 Crescent Place are embellished with these handsome classical screens of columns.

An interior view of an apartment at 1661 Crescent Place when it opened as a co-op in 1926.

scoting, crown molding, French doors, and working fireplaces. This building lacks sleeping porches, which were voguish during the 1920s and 1930s: the developer found that few people used the ones he had built in the Army and Navy the year before, so he omitted them here.

The original prices for the apartments, then the city's costliest, varied from $6,000 for the efficiencies to $29,000 for the largest seven-room apartments. Over the years several large apartments have been modified to make second apartments. A duplex apartment was created by joining apartment Nos. 209 and 309 via a curving stair with an unusual birdcage elevator cab in the middle of it. Later this unit belonged to William K. Ryan, concert pianist and grandson of financier Thomas Fortune Ryan. He remodeled a bedroom into a ship's cabin, and the entire room, intact today, remains mahogany paneled with built-in leather chairs and leaded glass cabinets. This "cocktail room" has spiraled columns painted in blue and gold.

A noteworthy feature of 1661 is its large step-down lobby—with rows of piers and columns leading to the two passenger elevators in the rear, and its many original Jacobean-style chairs and sofas from the 1920s. Monroe Warren built step-down lobbies here and at the Army and Navy because both buildings were on a hill. This feature allowed the addition of another story and yet stayed within the height limit.

Most of the first owners or shareholders at 1661 were military officers, foreign service officers, writers, and other notables such as Senator Elmer Thomas of Indiana, Senator Thomas J. Walsh of Montana, and Mrs. Marie Doughty Gorgas, the widow of Major General William Crawford Gorgas, who developed the method for controlling yellow fever in Cuba and Panama. In 1939 Senator Claude Pepper of Florida lived here, as did Dr. Charles Pergler, the Czech minister to Japan later chosen by Syngman Rhee to draft South Korea's constitution. According to the extensive co-op records preserved in the office at 1661,

Senator Thomas P. Gore of Oklahoma lived here in 1943; Elmer H. Davis, Director of the Office of War Information during World War II and prominent author and journalist, in 1945; Walter K. Bachrach, a famous portrait photographer, in 1961; Ambassador Wilton T. Beale, Jr., in 1964; Mary Jane McCaffrie, White House social secretary during the Eisenhower administration, in 1967; and Edith Kermit Roosevelt, journalist and granddaughter of President Theodore Roosevelt, in 1973.

For many years the two handsomely landscaped front lawns created by the E-shape design, partially screened from the street by two colonnades, have been a delight to the residents. In 1947 the cooperative board, in an unusual move, purchased the Crescent, a small adjacent walk-up apartment building to the west. They acquired this modest 1930s red-brick building both to protect 1661 from possible future development and to put desirable renters in the neighboring building. Although sold in 1987, this arrangement of forty years' duration is the only one in Washington in which a cooperative apartment house owned a rental building as an investment.

Today 1661 remains in excellent condition, although much of the adjacent area declined rapidly following the riots of 1968. Improvements began in the neighborhood in 1977, however, with the construction of the Beekman Place condominiums and the renovation of two adjacent historic apartment houses—Meridian Mansions (now the Envoy) in 1984 and the Park Tower in 1987.

This apartment at 1661 Crescent Place was enlarged into a duplex unit with its own private elevator.

Infatuated with nautical themes, the owner of this apartment at 1661 Crescent Place remodeled her study in the 1950s to resemble the captain's cabin in an eighteenth-century ship.

75

2120 KALORAMA ROAD, N.W.

South side of Kalorama Road, between Connecticut Avenue and Thornton Place

ARCHITECT: Louis Justement, Jr., 1925

ORIGINAL APARTMENTS: 4 (4 three-bedrooms)

STATUS: opened as co-op in 1926

Each floor above the ground level at 2120 Kalorama Road consists of a single apartment.

This restrained red-brick Georgian Revival residence, a cooperative apartment house, was built by close friends—Mr. and Mrs. Clifford Bangs and Mr. and Mrs. Walter Grey. They selected the site, worked with architect Louis Justement, Jr., to plan it, and reserved their own apartments on the top two floors before the remaining two were sold to others. Because of its small scale, 2120 Kalorama Road, N.W., is seldom recognized as an apartment house and thus is successfully integrated into the inner-city Kalorama neighborhood of large houses without calling attention to itself.

The facade of 2120 is divided into two parts—the three-bay-wide principal section on the right and the shallow wing on the left. Facade decoration consists mainly of the richly detailed limestone door surround, the three blind arches into which the second-floor windows are set, and the limestone beltcourses above the first and fifth floors. The plainness of the body of the building is relieved on the left wing by the great expanse of windows with iron railings. The open driveway passage at the street level leads to a courtyard in the rear. Above it are the original open front balconies, now glass-enclosed and used as studios. The dining room of each apartment is behind this room. The long narrow lot thus dictated the plan of 2120, in which each apartment is two rooms wide and five rooms deep.

This view of an apartment at 2120 Kalorama Road shows the folding French doors between the dining room and the sun room, on the right, and the foyer, on the left, with its black and white marble floor.

Because no other small apartment house in Washington quite matches the urbane design of 2120, the plan of the ground floor has been shown in addition to the typical floor plan. As in the earlier Wendell Mansions, the entire ground floor was designed for utilitarian purposes. One enters a spacious, square lobby. Here, under the stairs, are the original mailboxes, as well as the curious 1926 speaking tubes that still work. The small passenger elevator is a few feet to the left. Each of the four apartments above has its own storeroom and maid's bedroom on this level; here too are the boiler room, janitor's bedroom, a single bathroom for the five staff members, laundry room, large storage room, and a garage with

space for eight cars—two per apartment. Today the servants' rooms, although no longer in use, remain in original condition.

Each apartment has a generous-sized living room and dining room, with wide double doors opening onto the square foyer floored in black and white marble squares. The woodwork in each dining room is beautifully designed with folding French doors crowned by a high entablature. Two of the three bedrooms open onto a wide sleeping porch in the rear, providing extra air circulation. Residents now use the sleeping porches, with their casement windows, as dens, reserving the front living rooms for formal entertaining.

Plans of the ground floor and a typical upper floor at 2120 Kalorama Road.

The rear courtyard at 2120 Kalorama Road showing the garage for eight cars as well as the driveway entrance (right background).

76

4701 CONNECTICUT AVENUE, N.W.

Northeast corner of Connecticut Avenue and Chesapeake Street

ARCHITECT: George T. Santmyers, 1927

ORIGINAL APARTMENTS: 49 (1 efficiency; 1 one-bedroom; 47 two-bedrooms)

STATUS: opened as rental in 1928; converted to condo in 1977

The architectural style of the five-story 4701 Connecticut Avenue, N.W., apartment house could be called "Twenties Eclectic." On the rather plain facades of this unusual X-shaped building are such classical details as balustrades on the corner sleeping porches, finials on fourth-floor balconies and roof, and carved swags over the entrance. The architect has skillfully handled the mass of the building, creating an interesting plasticity through the play of shadow and light. This was achieved with both projecting pavilions on each side of the wings and projecting sleeping porches on the corners of the wings. The projections not only increased air circulation but also provided additional space. By substituting open porches for the sleeping porches on fifth-floor corner apartments, architect George T. Santmyers visually decreased the bulk of 4701. At the same time, by siting the building diagonally on the corner rather than facing it directly onto Connecticut Avenue, the architect gave 4701 a much more commanding and imposing presence.

The semicircular front driveway leads to the projecting entrance, which opens into a large rectangular lobby embellished with an elaborate gilded strapwork ceiling, decorative fireplace mantel, iron balustrade, and pair of short stairs leading to the open first-floor hall. All original forty-nine apartments are spacious. Of the ten

The 1927 apartment house at 4701 Connecticut Avenue was designed with screened corner sleeping porches; most have since been enclosed in glass.

tiers, eight are located in the four wings, where each apartment has four rooms plus a large reception hall, porch, kitchen, and bath. The apartments in the remaining two tiers, in the body of the building, are smaller.

The developer of 4701, Harry M. Bralove, whose most famous building was the Shoreham Hotel, included

Above: The eclectic design of the lobby of 4701 Connecticut Avenue includes an elaborate strapwork plaster ceiling, decorative fireplace, and openings to the step-up first-floor public corridor. *Left:* The corner apartments on the top floor of 4701 Connecticut Avenue have open porches rather than screened sleeping porches.

a basement garage for sixteen cars. At the rear ground level, there is a separate exterior door for each garage space, rather than the usual single or common garage entrance for all cars. (The design of apartment house garages was still in its infancy in 1927, and Washington architects continued to experiment with different plans.)

THE TRUMAN RESIDENCE

Residing in 4701 from January 1941 until April 1945 were Senator and Mrs. Harry S. Truman and their daughter Margaret. When Truman first moved to 4701, he was the junior senator from Missouri. Four years later, in January 1945, he was vice president. While living there, on 12 April 1945, following the sudden death of President Franklin D. Roosevelt, Harry S. Truman took the oath as president of the United States. The family moved to Blair House four days later and from there into the White House on 7 May 1945.

Truman lived in more Washington apartment houses than any other president: at Tilden Gardens in 1935–36; at Sedgwick Gardens part of 1936; at the Carroll Arms, 301 1st Street, N.E., in 1937; at the Warwick, at 3051 Idaho Avenue, N.W., in 1938; back to Tilden Gardens in 1939; at 3930 Connecticut Avenue, N.W., in 1940; and then at 4701. When Senator Truman first came to Washington, he was shocked by the high rents of both houses and apartments. Constantly looking for a bargain, he wrote his wife on 17 July 1935:

> . . . I have been out apartment looking this morning. The one at 1821 Nineteenth was directly across from the school [Gunston Hall at Florida Avenue and T Street, where Margaret Truman was enrolled in 1938] but wouldn't do. They were remodeling an old house—one of the three-story kind—and making an apartment of each floor. No private entrance or anything.
>
> There was one at 1726 Massachusetts that's a dandy but the rent's too much. It had a grand hall, living room and a dining room, two bedrooms, two baths, and closets galore, two-car garage and a Missouri [black] for a janitor—graduate of Lincoln University at Jefferson City. They asked $160 per month. I fell out of there in a hurry. Found a rather nice place at 1921 Kalorama Road.

Top: Senator and Mrs. Harry S. Truman pose for a photographer early in the morning on 15 April 1942 in the kitchen of their 4701 Connecticut Avenue apartment. Both were habitual early risers. *Bottom:* The "Truman photograph" was recreated by photographer Jim Tetro in 1983 for this study. Shown in the kitchen of the same apartment at 4701 Connecticut Avenue is the present resident, Vicky Baker. A neighbor, Jim Lacy, was borrowed to fill in for Truman. The only major change in the apartment in more than forty years has been the removal of the rear pantry to create a longer kitchen.

It was a northwest corner, fifth-floor apartment—two bedrooms, two baths, living room, small dining room, large hall, $125 per month. NO garage. Then I looked at a house at 2218 Cathedral, a block north of Connecticut. It was a house like Pete Allen's. They were painting and papering it from cellar to attic. It had a two-car garage and was just the same size and kind as Pete's house. They wanted $90 per month. I then went down to the Highlands at California and Connecticut. They had a nice two-bedroom apartment on the southeast corner, fourth floor, at $125—better I think than 1921 Kalorama Road. Then I looked at the Westmoreland, right behind the Highlands on California. They wanted $100 for a two-

bedroom apartment on sixth floor, and $79.50 for one on fourth floor that had four rooms. It is an old place but the location and rooms were very nice. You'll notice that all these places are within two or three blocks of the school. I am going to look at 2400 Sixteenth Street and the Jefferson tomorrow and a couple of houses. I bet I find something that'll suit before I quit. Margey owes me a letter. Kiss her anyway. Love to you, Harry

The apartment at 4701 proved to be their favorite private residence in Washington. In a brief ceremony there in November 1947, Major General Harry H. Vaughan, military aide to President Truman, unveiled the brass plaque on the door of apartment No. 209, which still commemorates Truman's residency there.

A major renovation was undertaken in 1973–74 by The Landmark Companies and the new owners, J. E. Bindeman and his son. Rents then doubled. The Bindemans saved as much as possible of the moldings, arches, doors, windows, railings, and brass fixtures; however, they upgraded each apartment with a new kitchen that included a dishwasher, a second bathroom, an air conditioner in every room, and all new wiring and plumbing. During the renovation seven new apartments were added in the ground or basement level. (Since 1964 the Bindemans have remodeled more than twenty early Washington apartment houses, including the Woodward and 3014–3020 Dent Place, N.W.) In 1977, the Bindemans sold 4701 to the Holland and Lyons realty company, which converted it to condominium ownership. At that time, apartment prices ranged from $54,000 to $74,000.

LEGEND

ba	Bathroom	E	Elevator	LS	Light Shaft
C	Closet	F	Foyer	Par	Parlor
Ch	Chamber	H	Hall	Ph	Porch
D	Dining Room	jc	Janitor Closet	r	Refuse Closet
DA	Dining Alcove	K	Kitchen	S	Shaft

The X-shaped plan of 4701 Connecticut Avenue provides most apartments with abundant light.

77

MOORINGS

1909 Que Street, N.W.; northwest corner of Que and 19th streets

ARCHITECT: Horace W. Peaslee, 1927

ORIGINAL APARTMENTS: 8 (8 one-bedrooms)

STATUS: opened as rental in 1928; converted to offices in 1964

During the 1920s a dozen large and grand apartment houses were built in Washington—all well known to the public and nearly every taxi driver in the city. Less familiar are the small but beautifully designed apartment houses with fewer than twenty units each. Of this small, select group, and perhaps the most charming, are the Meridian Hill Studio by George Oakley Totten, Jr., and the Moorings by Horace W. Peaslee. Even though the former has suffered from the deterioration of the surrounding neighborhood following the riots of 1968 and the latter was converted to offices during the same decade, *Best Addresses* would not be complete without them both.

The Moorings was built by the eccentric social arbiter Mrs. John R. Williams as one of her complex of four adjacent "smart flats" designed with nautical themes near Connecticut Avenue and Que Street, N.W. The best, and the two surviving, are the Anchorage and the Moorings. The five-story limestone-faced Moorings, with eight apartments, cost $70,000 to build in 1927. Peaslee designed it in one of the most avant-garde styles of the 1920s: a cubist form, with plain walls and undecorated window openings. That an architect of Peaslee's conservative tastes would design such an unconventional building demonstrates how rapidly the Beaux Arts influence was going out of fashion. Nevertheless, he kept the tra-

ditional, tripartite facade with a rusticated ground floor, three-story body, and a stringcourse above to define the fifth or top floor.

Because of the density of the neighborhood and the high land values, the ground floor was devoted to commercial use. The original smart metal and plate glass shop windows, with a limestone base, that project in the center of the first floor, remain in place today. The simplicity and overall streamlined feeling were harbingers of the Art Deco and International styles of the next decade.

As previously noted, Washington architecture between World Wars I and II was often eclectic, combining elements of two or even three styles. Many of these buildings were most successful in their massing, proportion, and detailing. Even though they cannot be neatly pigeonholed into specific categories of design, many are just as significant as the purest Beaux Arts or International Style apartment house. (This misunderstanding of "style" was unfortunately one of the major reasons the city government allowed the architecturally significant Governor Shepherd apartment house to be demolished in 1985.)

The nautical motifs on the exterior and interior of the Moorings are so subtle that few Washingtonians notice them. The two principal entrances, one at each end of the front facade, are designed with handsome baroque

The Moorings was designed by architect Horace W. Peaslee with nautical themes.

One of the two front entrances at the Moorings with a rope border and a "shell" light fixture above the architrave.

limestone surrounds. The inner molding consists of a rope motif with the overhead light hidden by a shell cover. On the roof a series of paired stone bollards (posts on which a ship's ropes are secured to a wharf) connect and define the original low iron fence on the roofdeck. The present high iron fence on the roof, incompatible with the building's original proportions, was erected later to meet the current building code. Crowning the ensemble is an octagonal elevator tower designed like a lighthouse with a beacon light in its lantern roof.

The original floor plans and a description of the interior of the Moorings were fortunately published in the *Architectural Record* in March 1928:

> The apartment building with an individuality of its own, or a personality derived from its locality, is rarest among the genus, particularly in the first mentioned class. One such building, however, "The Moorings," at Washington, D.C., is here illustrated. Upon a lot of very restricted area (the structure is only 63 by 28 feet in dimensions), a number of compact bachelor apartments—especially appealing to naval officers, of whom there are always a number about the Capital—have been provided. Several of them are duplex in type.
>
> The fifth floor has two suites consisting of a living room termed "salon" or "cabin" upon the plans, with

Even the original floor plans of the Moorings included nautical terms for the rooms.

"bunkroom," bath and a very limited "galley" adjacent. The large "salon" with "galley" is shown at the rear connected with a "stateroom" and bath upon the floor below. Beside this fourth floor "stateroom" is another, serving a full size "salon" upon the third floor. The middle apartment on each floor is complete in itself in each instance, but the end spaces are divided upon alternate floors into two "staterooms," used with an upper and under "salon."

In further carrying out the nautical idea suggested by the name, bathrooms and "galleys" are ventilated by "portholes." The roof is developed as a promenade pier, with penthouse camouflaged as a lighthouse; smokestacks and vents are also handled in a maritime manner. As a result, the exterior has achieved a definite character all its own, perhaps suggesting some of the modern Continental architecture while being actually no more than a straight-forward solution of an unusual architectural problem, endeavoring to combine land and water motifs, consistently bearing out the same nautical idea.

The furnishings of the apartments continue to follow the same line. Cheerful curtains and covers and a few antique pieces are mixed in with informal comfortable furniture of other kinds, which make the quarters seem attractive and desirable. The "galleys" contain only a small icebox, an electric plate large enough for coffee and eggs, and enough unobstructed area to shake a container vertically if not horizontally. Service is furnished the occupants, and a tea room equipped with miscellaneous maritime paraphernalia is upon the premises. This venture, along with another companion building, "The Anchorage," has been in great demand. The fact that the areas of the rooms are quite limited is often lost sight of in the comfort of their equipment and the idea of spaciousness they give in contrast to the even more circumscribed nautical rooms whose appearance they simulate, and in which, probably, the tenants have spent many years.

As can be seen in the adjacent plans, the fifth floor contained three apartments, a two-room flat on the right, a two-room flat in the center, and [a part of] a large duplex of two rooms on the left. The latter contained a working fireplace in its "salon" or living room-dining room. On

The elevator penthouse on the Moorings roof resembles a miniature lighthouse.

the fourth floor the center flat remained the same, whereas the left and right apartments were reversed in basic design from the upper floor . . . [in other words, on the left or west end of the building, one duplex extended from the fifth to the fourth floor and another extended from the fourth floor to the third floor, while on the right or east end of the building, a duplex extended between the fourth and third floors]. The interior detailing carried out the nautical theme. The plaster walls of the apartments were scored to resemble plank boards, while the elevator doors included circular porthole windows.

The last person to own the Moorings while it was still an apartment house was Washington attorney Clifford Hynnings. Soon after he sold it in 1964, it was converted into an office building by the Institute for Policy Studies.

78

TILDEN GARDENS

3000 Tilden Street, N.W.; triangular block bounded by Connecticut Avenue and Tilden and Sedgwick streets

ARCHITECT: Parks and Baxter; Harry L. Edwards, associate architect, 1927–29

ORIGINAL APARTMENTS: 200 (63 one-bedrooms; 65 two-bedrooms; 72 three-bedrooms)

STATUS: buildings A and B opened as separate co-ops in 1927–28; buildings C, D-E, F-G, and H-I opened as rental in 1929–30, and the four buildings converted to a single co-op in 1939

Tilden Gardens was the city's most innovative large apartment house constructed in the 1920s. A six-building complex of two hundred units on a 5-acre triangular block on Connecticut Avenue, just above Porter Street, it was noted not only for its unique landscaping plan but also as the city's largest luxury apartment house built as a co-op—until the Watergate was constructed in the 1960s. The developers of Tilden Gardens, Monroe and R. Bates Warren, were pioneers in the construction of Washington's cooperative apartment houses. Although more than thirty-five rental apartment houses were converted to co-ops between 1920 and 1924, Washington real estate developers were skeptical about building a co-op apartment house. The city's first two co-ops, the Concord (1891, now demolished) and 2852 Ontario Road, N.W. (1909), were not built by developers but by groups of friends. The Warren brothers eventually risked building the first new co-op, 1705 Lanier Place, N.W., in 1924. When its units sold in record time, an important precedent was established for other developers for the rest of the decade.

This 1930 photograph of the main building (H-I) of Tilden Gardens shows part of the complex just after it was finished.

Opposite: Gabled roofs and numerous chimneys were employed by the architects to produce a domestic ambiance for Tilden Gardens. This animated roofscape is reminiscent of a miniature skyscraper, with the setbacks common in this period.

The grounds of Tilden Gardens are the most elaborately landscaped of any Washington apartment house.

THE WARREN BROTHERS

The firm of Monroe and R. B. Warren, Inc., which developed Tilden Gardens, was founded by the elder of the two brothers, Monroe Warren, Sr., quite by accident. Following in the footsteps of his father and grandfather, young Monroe Warren (1895–1983), of Clayton, Alabama, planned to enter the medical profession when he enrolled in the University of Virginia shortly before World War I. His future career, however, was dramatically changed through a part-time job. During the summer vacation of 1916, he worked in Washington as timekeeper for his uncle, Bates Warren, an established local builder who was then constructing one of the city's finest apartment houses, 2029 Connecticut Avenue, N.W. To his surprise, the young college student found the construction industry fascinating and as a result abandoned plans for a career as a physician. After serving in World War I as a first lieutenant, he permanently settled in Washington in 1919. In that year, another uncle, John Warren, also

a builder, lent him the funds to start his own company, Monroe and R. B. Warren, Inc., in partnership with his younger brother, R. Bates Warren.

At the beginning of the boom period of the 1920s, the younger Warrens were quite successful in building dozens of houses. They are best remembered, however, for pioneering the construction of six Washington co-op apartment houses during the second half of the decade— 1705 Lanier Place, N.W.; Cleveland Park (3018–3028 Porter Street, N.W.); the Army and Navy (2540 Massachusetts Avenue, N.W.); 3001 Porter Street, N.W.; 1661 Crescent Place, N.W.; and Tilden Gardens. Later, after R. Bates Warren left the firm, Monroe Warren and Edgar Kennedy became the builders and brief owners of the beautiful but ill-fated Kennedy-Warren in 1931.

Monroe Warren, Sr., remained a major figure in Washington real estate from 1919 until his retirement in 1966, despite the serious financial loss he suffered when the Kennedy-Warren went into bankruptcy in the early years of the Depression. He was responsible for organizing the Home Builders Association in Washington in 1926 and was active in promoting co-op apartments, both locally and nationally, during the 1920s. During the 1930s he became one of the most active builders of low-cost housing on a grand scale in the Washington area.

His second firm, known as Meadowbrook, Inc., was based in Chevy Chase, Maryland, and existed from 1932 to 1966. This firm built more than five hundred low-cost houses in Landover Hills, Maryland, in 1936. Other projects in the Maryland suburbs included houses in Rockville (Rockcrest) as well as Woodley Gardens, Hamlet Place, the Chevy Chase Lake Apartments, and many others in Chevy Chase. Within Northwest Washington he built Woodley Hills and Ordway Gardens, the latter as wartime housing for civilian defense workers in 1942. The Federal Housing Administration called his 750 "track houses," built in Arlington Forest, Virginia, in 1939, the best buildings for their price in the United States. It was the first detached housing development financed by the FHA, and buyers of the $6,000 houses had to deposit only $600 with a mortgage for 25 years.

During the 1920s R. Bates Warren, the younger brother in the original partnership, was equally influential in the co-op apartment house movement. He was instrumental in founding the Cooperative Apartment House Bureau of the National Real Estate Board, headquartered in Chicago, in 1925.

Because of their significant success in constructing and marketing five co-op apartment houses between 1924 and 1926, the Warrens embarked on their largest and most expensive co-op undertaking, Tilden Gardens, in 1927. Built at a cost of $3 million, Tilden Gardens ranked—along with Cathedral Mansions (1922–23), the Broadmoor (1928), the Westchester (1930), and the Kennedy-Warren (1931)—among the city's five largest and most luxurious apartment houses (with at least two hundred units) until the 1950s, when prosperity brought even larger apartment houses.

THE SIX-BUILDING COMPLEX

After purchasing the site from the Chevy Chase Land Company, the Warrens cut Sedgwick Street through on

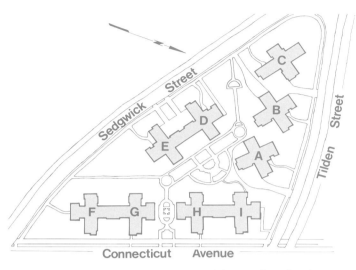

The complex of Tilden Gardens consists of three X-shaped and three double-X-shaped apartment buildings. The typical long halls were eliminated in the larger apartment houses, which were divided into two separate sections by a solid wall down the center of each building.

Typical floor plan of the H-I building at Tilden Gardens where the main lobby is located.

the south and Tilden Street through on the north to form a triangular 5-acre block that connected to Reno Road on the west. In an age before air conditioning, this location on upper Connecticut Avenue was particularly desirable as its elevation was 300 feet higher than downtown and thus noticeably cooler in summer. The site was protected from any future encroachment to the south by a new public park. The grounds of the U.S. Bureau of Standards occupied space to the north. In order to secure building permits, the Warrens were required to obtain an exemption from the zoning commission. Under the original 1920 Zoning Act, as amended, apartment house construction on upper Connecticut Avenue was restricted to a narrow 100-foot corridor bordering both sides of the avenue. The unusual exemption was granted for Tilden Gardens because most of the site was to be developed as parkland, partially obscuring the six buildings.

The architects, Parks and Baxter, based their cross-shaped floor plan for Tilden Gardens on Philadelphia's Alden Park, designed by architect Edwin Rorke in 1920. Much of the facade treatment of Tilden Gardens was influenced by the Blind Brook Lodge apartment house in Rye and the Fleetwood Country Club apartment house in Fleetwood, both in Westchester County, New York. The surburban feeling of Tilden Gardens was further enhanced by the extensive landscaped gardens covering 3 of the site's 5 acres. Gravel walks connected the six apartment house buildings, which were originally surrounded by fountains, pools, pergolas, terraces, and many stately trees that were preserved during construction. Only the east side of the site, the steepest part of the hill, was graded so the two large buildings would be level with Connecticut Avenue.

After more than fifty-five years of growth and proper care, these grounds are among the most charming of any apartment house in the city, although most of the pools and pergolas have been removed. There is nothing else like it, because no developer today would devote so much expensive land within the city to so attractive but unprofitable a use. When completed in 1930, the design of Tilden Gardens actually surpassed its three prototypes in architectural excellence; Tilden Gardens' buildings were lower in scale, its basement garages more cleverly concealed, and its landscaping more elaborate. The steeply

The facades of the six buildings of Tilden Gardens are built of tapestry brick, often laid in unusual patterns, with limestone trim.

sloping site also offered greater privacy, seclusion, and better vistas for the residents of the various buildings.

The original 1927 plan for Tilden Gardens called for a total of seven buildings. Five small ones were designed in the shape of a cross [+], while two large buildings consisted of a double cross [++] formed by joining a wing of each of two crosses. Two small buildings and one large one were to have faced Connecticut Avenue. After construction of the first building had begun, the site plan was altered in favor of two large buildings facing Connecticut Avenue. Not only would the larger buildings present a more imposing appearance facing Connecticut Avenue, but their large scale would more effectively block traffic noises for the other four buildings in the enclave to the west. Correspondingly, landscape architect Henry Bauer redesigned the connecting paths and other landscape features. In the process the original design for an elaborate Japanese bridge was omitted.

Construction of the six buildings was planned in sequence, starting with the small "A" building on Tilden Street and running counterclockwise around the block to the "H-I" building on Connecticut Avenue (see the site plan). The "H-I" was started several months before the "F-G" building, since "H-I" was the main building with the largest lobby, main telephone switchboard, and the public dining room. The average construction time for each building was less than a year, with the "A" building beginning in April 1927. The final building, "F-G," was begun in February 1930 shortly before the actual effects of the Depression forced almost all construction in Washington to come to an abrupt halt.

In addition to the cross-shaped plans and the elaborate landscaping, Tilden Gardens offered other desirable features. Most of the two hundred apartments have three exposures, ensuring maximum light and ventilation. The six buildings are set apart from one another on the sloped site, allowing privacy, good light and ventilation, and varied views of the parklike setting. The careful design permitted the three small buildings facing Tilden Street to be set at an angle to create a picturesque setting and to provide for good lighting all year round.

DESIGN SPECIFICS

The apartments at Tilden Gardens vary in size from three to seven rooms. A few include a private walled terrace. Each unit was designed with an enclosed sunroom, which connected through French doors to the living room. All apartments were originally planned with decorative fireplaces, but many were omitted when the financial realities of the Depression necessitated greater economy. Many units had leaded glass Tudor-inspired windows. To ensure quiet and privacy, a solid wall divides the center of each of the three large buildings, with separate elevators and staircases in each half. In addition, the six buildings all have garages, and some had automatic electric doors, the first in Washington. Parking varied from fourteen spaces in the "A" building to twenty-nine in "F-G."

The public dining room in "H-I" seated a hundred, and two smaller private dining rooms seating thirty could be rented for parties. The staff delivered meals and ca-

tered parties in all six buildings. There was also a small 20-by-50-foot "ballroom" south of the dining room for private parties. Original plans specified that this room could be converted to a golf practice driving range by installing a net and mat. This feature, as well as the more elaborate plans for a swimming pool, tennis courts, outdoor cafe, and gymnasium, was omitted as the Depression's economic effects were felt.

Each of the six buildings was supposed to be converted and sold as a separate cooperative when completed. The first two buildings completed, "A" and "B," on Tilden Street, were indeed organized and incorporated as separate co-ops—3016 Tilden Street, Northwest, Inc., and 3020 Tilden Street, Northwest, Inc. They still have their own separate boards of directors. Originally, apartments in these two buildings cost from $10,600 to $16,165, about the same as the average Cleveland Park house. The Great Depression prevented sales in the four other buildings, which were then rented from 1930 to 1939. The most famous tenants included Senator and Mrs. Harry Truman, who rented a four-room apartment here during the congressional session of 1935–36 and again in 1939. In the latter year, with the improved economy, the four buildings constituting "C," "D-E," "F-G," and "H-I," along with the extensive central garden, were converted to a single co-op corporation, Tilden Gardens, Inc. This corporation is managed by a board of directors to which the stockholders of each of the four member buildings elect one director. In 1955 all of the mortgages were retired.

The facades of the six buildings were designed with considerable sensitivity to detail. Quality construction was a hallmark of the Warrens and is seen in all their early apartment houses. Rough textured "tapestry" brick, with Indiana limestone trim, was used in combination with half-timber and stucco to create the eclectic Tudor Revival style popular in American domestic architecture in the 1920s and 1930s. To simulate the scale of domestic buildings, the architects employed hipped roofs, often broken with gables and dormers, and numerous chimneys. Exposed copper down-spout boxes were handmade. All of the exterior window trim was painted light green, a distinctive shade that Washingtonians characterized for many years as Tilden Gardens green. Many of the front

In the private canopied terrace of her apartment at Tilden Gardens, Jo Lucille Ageton, left, entertains William Savin, a neighbor, and a house guest from New York.

facades have slightly projecting pavilions. These features and the excellent massing make the buildings look asymmetrical, although they are actually symmetrical. The jagged roof lines and projecting wings produce a skyscraper effect, even though the buildings are only five stories high (plus a basement).

As Tilden Gardens neared completion, large half-page advertisements appeared in the Washington newspapers expounding on its unusual design. Most dealt in particular with its Art Deco or "Moderne" design. An example is this ad that appeared in the [Washington] *Evening Star* of 21 September 1929 entitled "Moderne!":

> Startling . . . bizarre, perhaps . . . but certainly unique and interesting as well . . . today's modern note in interiors, as disclosed in the newly designed, decorated and furnished model apartment home at Tilden Gardens. Expressive of the new age, this creation is a revelation of the stark simplicity, the daring innovations in color and form, the harmony of line and tone that can be achieved with an intelligent interpretation of the new motif in interior decoration . . . radically different, but utterly intriguing. Description would be futile . . . only by inspection can it be appreciated. Moderns will be charmed. And even those of more conservative tastes will be interested in seeing this unusual home. Afterward . . . or before . . . they will be quite delighted with the other model home, furnished in the Colonial style, conventional and restrained.

Perhaps the "bizarre" elements refer to the unusual Art Deco ziggurat doorways in the shape of terraced pyramids—which have long since been filled in!

Over the years few alterations have been made. The public dining room closed in 1970, and the switchboard serving the entire complex was removed in 1979. The dining room is now rented as a meeting room to the Daughters of the American Revolution, and the adjacent vacant space converted to five bedrooms and baths that residents can rent at modest prices for visiting guests. Regrettable indeed is the closing of the dining room, a cherished Washington institution during its forty years of operation. Today Tilden Gardens, which is convenient to the Cleveland Park subway station, continues to carry out its purpose as described in the original sales brochure— "providing pleasant homes in a happy mean between urban and suburban life."

LIFE AT TILDEN GARDENS

An interesting account of the public dining room at Tilden Gardens appeared in an informal guide published in 1970 describing Washington's better restaurants. Judith and Milton Viorst recalled their visit as follows:

> Old-fashioned American cooking, harking back to the days of the front-porch swings and no freezers, is alive and well at the Tilden Gardens restaurant. If your definition of gourmet foods includes a beautiful pot roast or a homemade custard pie (and ours does! We don't believe good food is always *pate de foie gras*), then you'll be thoroughly impressed with the splendid selection of high-quality dishes available at this restaurant.
>
> Let me caution you, however, that Tilden Gardens wins, hands down, our most-genteel-restaurant-in-this-book award. Its atmosphere is so proper that the ashtrays seem almost to be labeled For Gentlemen Only, so hushed that a modest clearing of the throat thunders through the room like a jet transport.
>
> The restaurant, lodged on the ground floor of an old brick apartment building on upper Connecticut Avenue, is decorated in early Senior Citizen. It looks like a place where no liquor is served, and no liquor is. The dining room, however, is spacious and clean, with sparkling white cloths, pretty china, and fresh daisies at each table. The black line drawings of serene garden vistas that decorate the walls are perhaps the best summary of the goals and aspirations of this gentle place.

79

2101 CONNECTICUT AVENUE, N.W.

East side of Connecticut Avenue between Wyoming Avenue and Kalorama Road

ARCHITECT: Joseph Abel and George T. Santmyers, 1927

ORIGINAL APARTMENTS: 64 (64 three-bedrooms)

STATUS: opened as rental in 1928; converted to co-op in 1976

Built by developer Harry M. Bralove and his partners, Edward C. Ernst and John J. McInerney, this finest apartment house to appear in Washington between the two World Wars was remarkable not only for the quality of its construction but also for the spaciousness of its sixty-four units. Several large houses had to be demolished for 2101, including Samuel W. Woodward's imposing Georgian Revival residence, designed by James G. Hill at the turn of the century. The eight-story apartment house fitted neatly into the streetscape, however, as other large apartment houses had already been built nearby—2029 Connecticut Avenue, N.W., to the south, the Altamont to the east, the Dresden to the west, and the Woodward to the north. Every effort was made to ensure dignity and quiet for the residents of 2101, as was clearly emphasized in the brochure in which Bralove first advertised the apartments for rent in 1928:

Front facade of 2101 Connecticut Avenue.

> Occupying the entire frontage on Connecticut Avenue between Wyoming Avenue and Kalorama Road, 2101 Connecticut Avenue is located in Washington's most fashionable residential and apartment center. It crowns one of the highest points in the city of Washington and is so designed that each unit has three exposures, thus assuring a maximum of light and ventilation. The character of the tenancy is assured through careful selection of guests. The elimination of small apartments carries with it assurance of a permanent, quiet, and socially attractive atmosphere.
>
> These apartments were inspired and created because it was believed that an ideal, permanent home atmosphere

The eclectic detailing on the facade of 2101 Connecticut Avenue includes elements taken from Gothic, Moorish, and Spanish Colonial architecture.

The main entrance of 2101 Connecticut Avenue.

could be obtained and maintained within an apartment. It was endeavored not only to design comfortable living quarters but to incorporate many details that would aid the resident in establishing a home atmosphere, one possessing a charm and dignity usually found only in a private house. Infinite thought and care have been given to reduce household responsibilities to a minimum. In this direction a new standard has been established for the perfect apartment-home which is now offered to the Washington public. These residential apartment-homes are divided into units of seven and nine rooms—each unit having three baths, and are available either *furnished* or *unfurnished*. The rooms are large and well planned, lending themselves admirably to any decorative theme; they have been designed with such artistry that when the large foyer and heated enclosed porch are included in the reception rooms the host and hostess will find ample space perfectly adapted for large and formal gatherings.

This original description is significant because it indicates the features that the original owner and developer felt were the best. The wide gallery in each unit is ideal for formal entertaining of large groups. It allows circulation within all of the public rooms and, furthermore, divides the three bedrooms on one side from the public rooms on the other side and at the end. Also emphasized are the three exposures of each apartment that admit sun and breezes: there are no "bad units" in the entire building. The neighboring well-established luxury apartment houses are also noted to establish the "right location" for the discriminating resident.

The apartments vary from 2,600 to 3,200 square feet, the size of an average house. Along with five or six principal rooms, each unit has an enormous amount of additional space, including a sunporch, gallery, two baths, kitchen, pantry, one or two maid's rooms, and a maid's bathroom. Every room in the building has an outside exposure except the pantries and maids' bathrooms, and even these are adjacent to air shafts. This access to light and air is effected by the eight wings, four facing Connecticut Avenue and four facing the rear. The typical floor plan shows eight apartments, with 9 foot, 2 inch ceilings, one to a wing. Only two apartments have been

The public corridors of 2101 Connecticut Avenue are unusually long.

altered—No. 87 took one room from No. 88, and No. 72 took one room from No. 71. Most living rooms in the top three stories have working fireplaces. The walls in the wide gallery, living room, and dining room in the majority of the apartments originally had decorative wall molding—but it was removed in most units because it made picture hanging difficult.

There is parking for sixty-eight cars behind the building in a two-level garage built in 1954. These spaces are separately owned by the residents, an unusual arrangement for a co-op where parking spaces are usually rented.

The step-down lobby of 2101 with its 16-foot ceiling is situated in the space between the two central wings, much like the spacious lobby Joseph Younger, Jr., designed for 1661 Crescent Place, N.W., in 1925, but on an even grander scale. Entering the lobby, one finds a large meeting room with double doors (usually kept closed) on the front left. The reception desk to the left rear is adjacent to a bank of two elevators. Within the lobby the two rows of six steel beams supporting the eight-story

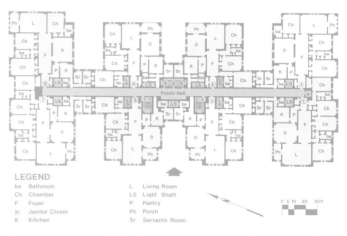

LEGEND

ba	Bathroom	L	Living Room
Ch	Chamber	LS	Light Shaft
F	Foyer	P	Pantry
jc	Janitor Closet	Ph	Porch
K	Kitchen	Sr	Servants Room

Typical floor plan of 2101 Connecticut Avenue: all apartments have either three or four bedrooms.

The step-down lobby of 2101 Connecticut Avenue.

building are sheathed in mahogany with elaborate carved capitals. These mahogany piers divide the ceiling into three massive square sections, each ornately decorated and gilded in the Adamesque style. The central ceiling section includes a shallow recessed dome with a crystal chandelier. The lobby floor, laid in pearl gray marble squares, is covered by a large Oriental carpet, 30 by 40 feet. Adjacent to the lobby are apartments for the manager, assistant manager, and engineer. The lobby roof creates a garden terrace, with potted plants and lawn

furniture, for residents of the Nos. 3 and 5 apartments, whose French doors open onto it.

One of the unusual features of 2101 is the private deck on the southwest corner of the roof above apartment No. 81, built by the developer, Bralove, as the residence for one of his partners. It was occupied for many years by Washington realtor H. L. Rust. Stairs from the entry hall to the roof and a private dumbwaiter, installed in 1977 by the current residents, facilitate entertaining on this 3,000-square-foot private roofdeck. The present residents of the apartment, former Congressman and Mrs. William S. Mailliard, have redesigned the deck with a redwood floor and created a series of three large outdoor "rooms." Mrs. Mailliard based the design for the stair railing, trellises, and benches on historical patterns, including Chinese Chippendale. During the summer, wooden boxes and large earthenware pots are filled with alyssum and petunias as well as a pine tree, Japanese cutleaf maples, a tall Russian olive tree, and a white oleander. More than a hundred guests can be entertained here in the summer for cocktails or fifty for a seated dinner. The deck is especially popular for the Mailliards' annual Fourth of July party because of the spectacular view of the fireworks on the Mall.

A full year of extensive renovations began at 2101 in 1976 as the building was converted to a co-op by the B. F. Saul Company. New elevator cabs, roof, risers, kitchens, and pantries were installed. Central air conditioning was optional, to avoid disturbing those residents who did not want it; later, however, most units were connected to the central system. The ornate lobby was restored and regilded by students from the Corcoran Gallery of Art. Approximately 50 percent of the residents bought apartments at reduced rates during the conversion. The original selling prices, from $70,000 to $100,000 per apartment, soon proved to be a bargain: by 1987 the upper-floor apartments were selling for $800,000.

The list of notables who have lived at 2101 during the past half-century includes Senator William E. Borah (who moved here from the Windsor Lodge), Vice President Alben Barkley, Ambassador Douglas MacArthur II (nephew of the general), Supreme Court Justice Tom Clark,

Looking from the foyer into the long gallery found in all apartments at 2101 Connecticut Avenue.

The principal feature of the apartments at 2101 Connecticut Avenue is the long central hall or gallery, from which all public rooms radiate.

Apartments on the top two floors of 2101 Connecticut Avenue have working fireplaces, as in this drawing room.

and J. Harry Covington of the Washington law firm of Covington and Burling. Lively gossip columnist Evelyn Peyton Gordon (Mrs. H. Wells March) lived here for more than twenty-five years prior to her death in 1984. Many of the apartments have had but two or three residents since the building opened in 1928. Apartment No. 62, for instance, has housed only Senator and Mrs. Borah and the present resident, Harry Hoskinson, for many years chairman of the building's board of directors.

Each of the wings on the tan-brick front facade of 2101 is enhanced by a slightly projecting central pavilion that includes a pair of French windows with limestone balconies at its base. Two limestone beltcourses, a holdover from the Beaux Arts influence prior to World War I, encircle 2101 above the first and sixth floors, effectively dividing the facade into base, shaft, and capital. All decoration is on the base and capital zones. The principal entrance has a semicircular driveway, defined by a pair of handsome limestone piers, each decorated with a baroque scroll at one side and a pineapple finial. The most prominent feature of the building, this entrance is designed as a colonnade of five arches, the central three of which house the three doors, which are protected by an

iron and glass marquee. The entrance entablature is decorated by four parrot gargoyles in the spandrels, and six lion heads are set into the frieze above. The building's exterior represents a good example of eclectic 1920s architecture, exhibiting in form and detail an urbane sophistication then unusual in Washington. The architects of 2101 based many of their design details—including the entrance and rooftop pavilions—on New York's 1924 Shelton Club Hotel.

Above the quiet and dignified entrance, Joseph Abel, the architect, played with myriad delightful decorations on the top two floors and roof. He relieved the monotony of the four symmetrical wings by several devices, including terra cotta decorative balconies with arched brackets and terra cotta window surrounds and panels. The elevator shaft is cleverly concealed in a central tower with a terra cotta cornice and tall arched glass windows. Each of the elevations on the two adjacent rooftop pavilions includes a pair of terra cotta arched openings with a Byzantine-style spiral column, a balcony with four trefoil medallions, and an owl gargoyle. All three hipped roofs of these "towers" are laid in red tile and defined by onion-shaped finials on their corners. These summer pavilions are now rarely used, as the principal roofdeck for 2101 has been moved to the northwest corner of the building. Four open balconies (replacing the enclosed sunrooms) at the eighth-floor level—two in the front and two in the rear—provide additional interest at the center of the front facade.

Advertisements by numerous terra cotta producers appeared in most of the American architectural journals of the 1920s. The work on 2101 was most likely manufactured by the Atlantic Terra Cotta Company of New York and Atlanta, the world's largest producer, which made many figures and motifs almost identical to those at 2101 during the 1920s. Two New York buildings of the same period have identical details—the Farmers Loan and Trust Company Building by Starrett and Van Vleck, architects, and the Shelton Club Hotel, designed by Arthur Loomis Harmon. Advertisements by Atlantic Terra Cotta in 1924 and 1926 illustrate identical cornices, arches, grotesques, and roof treatment. Atlantic Terra Cotta's role in the construction of all types of large buildings before the Depression is indicated in this firm's advertisement in *Pencil Points* magazine in May 1924:

The New York Zoning Law, by curtailing floor space in plan, has started a new type of American architecture. Buildings go higher, and the required breaks in the ascent, saved from abruptness by detail, give the architect an opportunity to use Atlantic Terra Cotta with interesting originality.

In the lower stories of the Shelton Club Hotel brick was equal to the repressed detail of the first and second cornices; Terra Cotta defines the ornament only slightly. On the upper stories, where bolder and more open detail was demanded, Atlantic Terra Cotta is prominent.

Winged griffins of Terra Cotta with eight foot projection are placed at the corners just below the last break in the shaft. Gargoyles of almost equal projection appear just below the coping. A Terra Cotta balustrade surmounted by Terra Cotta grotesques [similar to 2101 and reminiscent of Notre Dame Cathedral in Paris] occurs in the breaks of the parapet, and Terra Cotta ornament tops the penthouse corner piers. The windows and stack are outlined in Terra Cotta. Atlantic Terra Cotta ornament springs naturally from a brick surface. The two burnt clay materials have natural harmony and there is no contrast in color or texture.

Top: Many of the bathrooms at 2101 Connecticut Avenue remain in original condition with handsome white tilework, pedestal sinks, and porcelain bathtubs. *Bottom:* The private roofdeck on the right front corner of 2101 Connecticut Avenue spans 3,000 square feet.

The manufacture and use of terra cotta on new buildings in the United States today are almost lost arts. Only one company in California still produces it, primarily for restorations of early twentieth-century American landmark buildings.

The most charming and whimsical features at 2101 are the sixteen original 5-foot-high "guardians" [some have been blown over] perched above the cornice of the front four wings. Designed as horned grinning demons, each holds a massive ball over his head—"threatening" to toss down a stone boulder on intruders to protect the fortunate residents within.

80

ALBAN TOWERS

3700 Massachusetts Avenue, N.W.; southwest corner of Massachusetts and Wisconsin avenues

ARCHITECT: Robert O. Scholz, 1928–29

ORIGINAL APARTMENTS: 216 (mostly one-bedrooms and two-bedrooms)

STATUS: opened as rental in 1929; converted to student housing by Georgetown University in 1973

The five-story Alban Towers was the city's largest apartment-hotel when it opened in 1929. It was designed in Gothic Revival to complement the Washington Cathedral and St. Alban's School, diagonally across the street. Two other important Gothic Revival apartment houses had been built during the preceding decade, the Chastleton and the Embassy. The developer of Alban Towers purchased this block of vacant land from the Washington Cathedral, whose trustees needed additional funds for construction costs.

The apartment house is basically a bent L, with eight staggered and projecting wings—each with a spacious balcony—to take maximum advantage of light and air. The principal entrance on Massachusetts Avenue is defined by a crenelated Gothic tower, set back from the tier of porches below and framed by a pair of gabled roofs. The handsome limestone porte-cochère is embellished with carved spandrels and panels, corbel stones "supporting" the Gothic arches and carved with Gothic motifs—five medieval male heads and the sixth contemporary, an aviator, doubtless inspired by Charles A. Lindbergh's famous solo flight from New York to Paris in 1927.

A double pair of leaded glass Gothic doors (since removed) led from Massachusetts Avenue into the spacious main lobby with its Tudor strapwork, plaster ceiling,

and short flight of stairs to the lower lobby and its Jacobean Revival furniture. Here was the main desk, and nearby were the bank of three elevators, public dining room, and public hallway. The Gothic-inspired hallways throughout Alban Towers are designed with rough plaster finish, pointed arches, and sculptural plaster pilasters and brackets. Sculptured plaster arch panels and friezes in the public corridors resemble the signs of the zodiac.

The main section of Alban Towers was built in 1928 with 132 apartments. Because the building was so popular, the owners, Robert O. Scholz and David A. Baer, enlarged it a year after it opened with 84 more units in the rear, at the corner of Wisconsin Avenue and Garfield Street, N.W., now the two most southern wings. When completed in the summer of 1930, most of Alban Towers' 216 apartments were small one-bedroom units. The numerous projecting wings allowed 90 percent of them to have porches. The heated basement garage—one of the first large apartment house garages in Washington—accommodates 125 cars. The bank of three centrally located elevators was built in the original section, while a single elevator served the residents in the addition. Unusual were the maids' spacious lounges with lockers and a bathroom adjacent to the elevators on each floor. The apartment house was named for Mount St. Alban, the hill

Five of the six corbels on the porte-cochère of Alban Towers were designed as medieval figures, but the sixth depicts an airplane pilot. It honors Charles Lindbergh, who made his historic flight to Paris in 1927 shortly before this apartment house was completed.

Top: Alban Towers, originally an apartment-hotel, is now a dormitory for Georgetown University. *Bottom:* Detail of the Gothic Revival stonework above the front entrance of Alban Towers.

Top: A 1930 view of the original lobby of Alban Towers, showing the Tudor-inspired strapwork ceiling and the leaded glass doors with stained glass coat of arms. *Bottom:* Detail of the elaborate plasterwork in the public corridors at Alban Towers.

on which the Washington Cathedral, one block north, was being built. The hill had taken its name from an early nineteenth-century house (Mount Alban), built by Joseph Nourse. This location and that of the Soldiers Home near the head of the present North Capitol Street are among the highest points of land in the District of Columbia. When it was built, no tall buildings were south

of Alban Towers, so the residents enjoyed a panoramic view of the entire city as well as of the Potomac River.

In addition to the public dining room, other hotel-like features included a beauty shop, travel agency, valet shop, grocery, and lunch counter. A minority of the small apartments served as hotel suites and were used by well-known visitors over the years. During the inauguration of

When Georgetown University purchased Alban Towers for use as a dormitory, a few of the former residents such as Mary Lee Nissley were permitted to remain.

Top: Site plan of Alban Towers. *Bottom:* Plan of three-bedroom apartments in the No. 1 tier at Alban Towers.

President John F. Kennedy in January 1961, a number of entertainment stars including Bette Davis and Frank Sinatra stayed here. Several embassies, including those of Great Britain, Canada, Australia, and South Africa, leased apartments for their diplomats.

Without proper care and maintenance, the public areas of Alban Towers slowly declined during the late 1960s. Now still somewhat shabby compared with its original elegance, Alban Towers was purchased by Georgetown University in 1973 for use as student housing. About twenty apartments are still occupied by long-time residents living there at the time of conversion. More than 450 college students occupy the remaining apartments, many of which have been subdivided. One note from the past still survives—a snappy eatery named Primavera, in the old public dining room. It is one of only a dozen restaurants remaining in Washington area apartment houses today.

81

BROADMOOR

3601 Connecticut Avenue, N.W.; northeast corner of Connecticut Avenue and Porter Street

ARCHITECT: Joseph Abel, 1928

ORIGINAL APARTMENTS: 179 (mostly one-bedrooms and two-bedrooms) and a dozen hotel rooms

STATUS: opened as rental in 1929; converted to co-op in 1948

Similar to Cathedral Mansions, the Broadmoor was designed like a resort hotel surrounded
by spacious grounds.

When the Broadmoor opened in October 1929, its location was considered somewhat remote from downtown Washington, for much of upper Connecticut Avenue was still undeveloped. Porter Street, only two lanes wide, wound its way down to Rock Creek Park. Dense woods surrounded the building on three sides. Built as an apartment-hotel by the Washington firm of Bralove, Ernst and McInerney at a cost of more than $2 million, the Broadmoor was named for the famous luxury resort hotel in Colorado Springs, Colorado.

This landmark building was unusual in that it occupied only 15 percent of its 5-acre site, being set well back from the intersection of Connecticut Avenue and Porter Street. Open land around luxury apartment houses was almost nonexistent before World War I when most were built downtown on expensive lots. After World War I construction of luxurious apartment houses began in outlying sections, often wooded, such as Connecticut Avenue, where land was much cheaper. Between 1932 and 1945 most new intown apartment houses were relatively small compared with most of the grand buildings of the preceding decade. It was not until just after World War II that building of luxury apartment houses resumed on large sites with spacious lawns, gardens, and wooded

areas; the use of large tracts for apartments reflected good economic times.

The irregular L-shaped eight-story Broadmoor is built of rough tapestry brick. As at other stylish Washington apartment houses of the 1920s, such as Tilden Gardens a block north, many of the bricks in the facade were laid to protrude from the surface at irregular intervals. This elaborate "tapestry" brickwork, of variegated color, adds to the surface texture and contrast. During this decade architects explored ways in which to make both the masses and the silhouettes of their buildings more interesting. Their goal was domestic appearance and ambiance, and the detail on the eclectic facades during the 1920s did much to achieve this effect.

Prominent at the Broadmoor are the stepped, projecting towers and bays with carved limestone panels and window surrounds. Many of these decorative elements are heraldic, such as the cross motifs on the balconies, which relate the building to the Gothic Revival. Slightly raised cornices on many of the projecting pavilions suggest a skyscraper. A massive porte-cochère defines the principal entrance at the apex of the building, similar in scale and massing to those on several other large Washington apartment houses of the 1920s and early 1930s—Alban Tow-

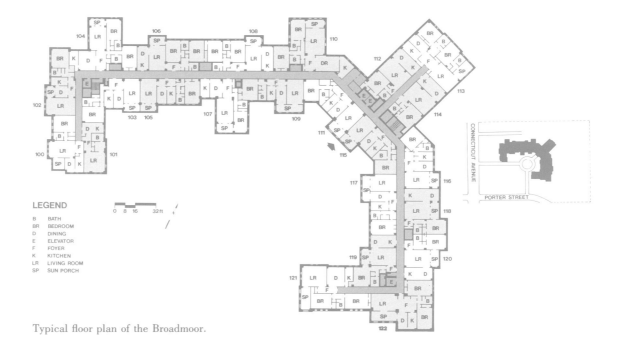

Typical floor plan of the Broadmoor.

The original 1928 Tudor Revival lobby of the Broadmoor was remodeled in 1939 in the Art Deco style shown here.

ers, Sedgwick Gardens, the Westchester, and the Wardman Tower. A semicircular driveway and a herringbone brick sidewalk are defined by brick gateposts on both Connecticut Avenue and Porter Street and lead to the porte-cochère. The outer edge of the driveway is bordered by a curvilinear brick wall. The basic style of the facade might be termed modern Tudor.

The Broadmoor featured many elements associated with a full-service apartment house: the impressive two-story lobby with a switchboard and front desk; a spacious ground-floor public dining room, in the shape of an elongated Y, originally called the Silver Grill, adjacent to the lobby; and a two-level basement garage for 118 cars. Today the residents use ninety-seven spaces, the staff two spaces, and the guests and dining room patrons, nineteen. In the 1930s part of the roof over the garage and adjacent to the public dining room was used as a terrace for cocktail parties.

A small number of hotel rooms and suites, less than 10 percent of the building, were available for public rental during the 1930s and 1940s, ranging from $3 to $6 a night. Other services included a barber shop, pastry shop, newsstand, valet and laundry service, and beauty shop; the valet shop, beauty shop, and dining room remain in operation. Maid service is also available: three maids work full-time at the Broadmoor and are booked at hourly rates through the front desk. Since 1969 the dining room has been leased to Csikos Restaurant, offering among the best Hungarian cuisine in Washington.

The Broadmoor originally contained 179 apartments and a dozen hotel rooms. Because of changes over the years, there are today 194 apartments, including 32 efficiencies, 105 one-bedrooms, 55 two-bedrooms, and 2 three-bedrooms. In addition Broadmoor residents may rent three bedrooms for the use of their guests. Most apartments originally had an open sun porch, but all of them were later enclosed with glass. Almost all bedrooms have attached baths, a rare feature in pre–World War II apartment houses. Instead of separate dining rooms, most apartments have small dining alcoves separated from the kitchens by pairs of small china cabinets—popular in Washington apartment houses during the 1920s and 1930s. Each unit also contains a small kitchen cabinet with a door opening to the public hall for daily trash removal.

Many major changes have been made inside the Broadmoor over the years. In 1938–39 both the public dining room and the lobby were renovated. The Tudor-style lobby, with open balcony, was changed to streamlined Art Deco with some Colonial Revival elements included. In 1942, when Washington had a serious housing shortage, the Broadmoor converted unused space in the public corridors on the ground floor into eighteen bedrooms and baths for women officers of the Army and Navy.

The front desk of the Broadmoor, showing the safe, mailboxes, and switchboard operator.

In 1949 these became hobby rooms that are now rented by the residents.

LIFE AT THE BROADMOOR

Much of the history of the Broadmoor appears in a booklet written by a committee of residents chaired by Stephen Kent in 1983:

> Unfortunately, there are no written records available of the many distinguished or extraordinary people who have stayed in this building. A few individuals with long memories have been able to recall some of them. Among the families prominent in the business world of the city who made their homes here were the Hechingers, the Mazors, and the Zlotnicks. At any time prior to conversion to co-operative status, there were a number of members of Congress in residence. The flamboyant Senator Huey Long of Louisiana moved here from the Mayflower Hotel in March 1934, and maintained his Washington residence in apart-

ment No. 601 until his assassination the following year. His three bodyguards were in constant attendance wherever he was. Senator John Sparkman of Alabama and Senator Prentiss Brown of Michigan were long-time residents. Representative and Mrs. Richard Nixon of California stayed here temporarily while house-hunting [January-June 1947]. In the late thirties, the coach and nearly the entire Washington Senators baseball team lived in the building for about three years during the baseball seasons. The bar, in the Silver Grill, is reputed to have been their principal watering hole during that time. Japanese Minister Isoda, General Suma, and Secretary of Embassy Iguchi were residents until their apartments were confiscated by the State Department and they were sent to internment at the Bedford Springs Hotel in Pennsylvania in 1941. Mr. George Meany, the labor leader, lived in apartment No. 419 for several years, and Hephzibah Menuhin, a well-known concert pianist, resided in apartment No. 308 for a year or two during which time her brother, Yehudi, one of the leading violinists of the 20th century, was a frequent visitor. Throughout the war and until 1950, Archduke Otto of Hapsburg, then claimant to the Austro-Hungarian throne, lived in apartment No. 315. His younger brother, Archduke Felix, also resided here until he was drafted into the U.S. Army. Secretary of Labor and Mrs. Mitchell were resident members in apartment No. 213 from 1956 to 1960. The last living descendant of President Lincoln, Robert Todd Lincoln Beckwith, resided in apartment No. 108 in the early 1960s.

The president of the board of directors at the Broadmoor, Claudius Easley, has lived there since before it was converted to a co-op in 1948.

CO-OP CONVERSION

A watershed year for the Broadmoor was 1948, when the rental apartment-hotel was converted to a cooperative apartment house. The federal government's failure to remove World War II rent controls after the war resulted in a rash of such conversions. During this inflationary period apartment house owners were not receiving adequate returns on their investments. The same conditions of inflation had prevailed immediately after World War I.

The Broadmoor was the largest and most prestigious apartment house to become a co-op up to 1948. It was also the city's second co-op organized on a membership basis: each owner had one vote at special and annual shareholders meetings rather than the traditional prorated votes based on the number of shares of stock owned in the co-op (computed by the size of the apartment).

The Broadmoor Cooperative Apartments, Inc., became a reality on 16 August 1948. The new corporation purchased the building and the land from the original builders and owners, the firm of Bralove, Ernst and McInerney, for $2.375 million. The cost to the members was $2.5 million, however, because they also needed to pay a commission of $125,000 to the Flynn Company. Edmund J. Flynn, the city's oldest and leading co-op apartment house specialist at that time, organized the Broadmoor as a co-op and served as the first president of the board. In order to legally establish this co-op, Flynn was required to sell 60 percent of the apartments by 15 November 1948. Although no public announcement of the conversion was made until 21 August, during the first week 100 apartments were sold, and most of the remaining 94 units were sold by early September. Because all of the apartments were occupied, many outside purchasers had to buy from floor plans without inspecting the actual units; this was unusual, as one would normally inspect at close range an apartment before purchasing it. The settlement and transfer of title occurred on 1 November 1948.

The reaction to the co-op conversion was varied. Some residents welcomed it, others were resigned to it, a minority were vehemently opposed. A group of thirty-six residents brought suit against the original owners and the Broadmoor Cooperative Corporation, claiming that the conversion violated the rent control law. The court decided in favor of the co-op on 9 December 1948 and allowed the board to evict those renters who refused to move. The Edmund J. Flynn Company turned over the management of the board to the newly elected officers at the first annual meeting in April 1950.

A reminder of World War II at the Broadmoor are these decals still attached to a few of the outer louvered apartment doors.

82

HARVARD HALL

1650 Harvard Street, N.W.; southwest corner of Harvard Street and Lanier Place

ARCHITECT: Louis Justement, Jr., 1928

ORIGINAL APARTMENTS: 153 (42 efficiencies; 92 one-bedrooms; 19 two-bedrooms)

STATUS: opened as rental in 1929

The facade of Harvard Hall was designed in a mixture of Art Deco and classical details.

Despite its comparatively small apartments, Harvard Hall was considered very desirable when it opened in September 1929 because of its many amenities. Built by developer William S. Phillips at a cost of $1.1 million, the seven-story tan-brick residence with limestone trim included a number of unusual features. It was the first standard apartment house in the city with an indoor swimming pool; it had a basement garage with space for one car for each apartment, radios built into each living room wall, and kitchens with electric dishwashers—the first provided in any apartment house in the city. A small receptacle next to each apartment door was provided for daily delivery of newspapers and milk. Most of the 153 apartments—which ranged in size from one room, plus kitchen and bath, to three rooms, plus kitchen and bath— had enclosed porches located in the building's twelve projecting bays. A convenient cafe (long since closed) was located at the south end of the first floor, adjacent to Lanier Place.

The unusual plan of the apartments offered kitchens with dining alcoves that faced directly—through glassed walls—onto glassed-in porches, thereby providing natural light to the porch, dining alcove, and kitchen. Even though the kitchens were distant from the facade wall of the building, the natural light satisfied a law requiring

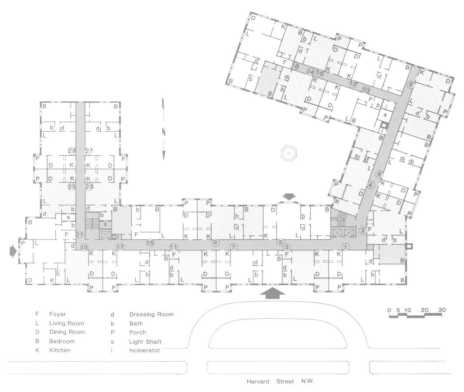

F   Foyer   d   Dressing Room
L   Living Room   b   Bath
D   Dining Room   P   Porch
B   Bedroom   s   Light Shaft
K   Kitchen   i   Incinerator

Harvard   Street   N.W.

Typical floor plan of Harvard Hall.

all kitchens to have outside windows. This plan was so unusual that the architect patented it—the only such patent known for the floor plan of a Washington apartment house.

The facade is embellished with restrained Art Deco detailing—geometric limestone carvings at the front and side entrances and in the bases of the projecting bays. The ribbed upper story of the projecting bays produces a feeling of height. Within the spacious 34-by-60-foot two-story marble lobby one can still find the original pair of Art Deco chandeliers and four wall sconces. The impressive coved-ceilinged lobby with its elegant French doors looks out onto the garage roof, which is cleverly disguised as a landscaped rear lawn with an octagonal stone fountain.

Following the trend of the late 1920s, the apartments have no formal dining rooms. A pair of china cabinets separates the small dining alcove from the kitchen. Even though the adjacent projecting sun porch is shallow, it has three exposures. A bathroom and dressing room separate most bedrooms from the living room.

Today Harvard Hall remains relatively unaltered. Gone, however, are most of the amenities that made life so comfortable there forty years ago: the public dining room and indoor swimming pool are closed, the staff depleted, and even the lobby furniture removed.

THE ZIONCHECK AFFAIR

The Zioncheck Affair at Harvard Hall in 1936 is vividly remembered by the one original resident still living there fifty years later. The incident, as it unfolded, was reported on the front pages of all Washington newspapers as well as the *New York Times* almost daily from May to July 1936.

It began when a middle-aged widow and resident, Pamela Schuyler Young, who supported herself by freelance writing for popular magazines, left on an extended tour of South America to gather fresh material. In December 1935, while she was away, a local real estate agent leased her furnished Harvard Hall apartment to Marion A. Zioncheck, a thirty-four-year-old Polish-American freshman congressman from Seattle, Washington. The eccentric bachelor had just arrived in Washington. His residence at Harvard Hall during the following seven months became the most famous brouhaha caused by the subletting of an apartment in the city's history.

Within weeks after the congressman moved in, trouble began: at 3 A.M. on New Year's Day 1936 he commandeered the switchboard of a fashionable nearby Connecticut Avenue apartment house, tied up the receptionist, and called more than two dozen sleeping residents to wish them a happy new year. When she read the account of the incident in the newspapers the following day, the Harvard Hall resident manager began to have doubts about the emotional stability of her new tenant. During the following three months, Congressman Zioncheck gave a number of boisterous all-night parties in his apartment. Shortly thereafter, he was involved in various other cases of misconduct around the city. He was arrested for speeding, drunk driving, and even assaulting a police officer. When the Zioncheck problem grew worse, the resident manager wired Mrs. Young to return as soon as possible to protect her furnishings for her own good and to retrieve her apartment for the general peace and quiet of the other residents.

Mrs. Young left South America immediately and returned to Washington in May 1936. She entered the sublet apartment with her own key—unchallenged since the congressman was away on a three-week wedding trip to the Virgin Islands. A bevy of reporters watching the apartment house learned of Mrs. Young's return and quoted the unsavory conditions she found in her sublet apartment:

> A broken genuine Sheraton antique table, missing silverware, whereabouts of a Bokara oriental rug and a bedstead [unknown], inch-deep dirt in corners, two broken windows, some 100 strewn-about empty [liquor] bottles, buttermilk on the walls and furniture, broken china (some of which was tossed out a window), a paisley bed cover used as a rug under the dining room table, the door off the latch and all windows open, many white rings apparently left by tumblers decorating table tops, a dead herring in a green-rimmed glass set in the middle of the floor, etc., etc., ad infinitum.

Mrs. Young immediately reoccupied the apartment, began legal action with a damage suit for $2,000, and prepared to move the Zionchecks' personal belongings out of the building. A battle royal ensued for possession of the apartment when the Zionchecks returned from their honeymoon several days later. The [Washington] *Evening Star* reported the results of their confrontation with Mrs. Young on their return to Harvard Hall on 30 May 1936:

> Mrs. Benjamin Scott (Pamela Schuyler) Young was under treatment at Emergency Hospital today after she had been forcibly ejected twice in her battle to oust Representative

The architect of Harvard Hall patented his design of a kitchen set behind the sleeping porch but connected by three wide windows (shown in the right distance). This design allowed direct light into the kitchen through the sleeping porch.

and Mrs. Zioncheck from the Harvard Hall apartment she sublet to Zioncheck last December. The magazine writer was carried from the "battle-ground" after receiving first aid in the corridor outside Zioncheck's door. Police had called for an ambulance from Emergency Hospital. Splints were placed on Mrs. Young's leg by Dr. George Lemeshewsky, who responded with the ambulance. The semi-hysterical woman then was removed to the hospital where she was treated for nervous shock while awaiting her private physician, Dr. Curtis Lee Hall. Dr. Lemeshewsky said Mrs. Young displayed symptoms of having a fractured hip. She was to undergo an X-ray examination later today. Mrs. Young's right arm was bruised and swollen.

Mrs. Young said she would ask her lawyer to obtain a warrant for Zioncheck on a charge of assault. The author then took another tack in her grim determination to save her "antiques" from what she describes as Zioncheck's "wanton destructiveness." Her determination was strengthened by the sight of half a dozen cases of rum deposited here and there. She sought aid of the United States attorney's office without result and returned to the disputed apartment. There Zioncheck found her confronting his wife when he came home about 9 o'clock last night. At first, Zioncheck was amiable. He showed Mrs. Young how his pet turtle could dance to the tune, "I Can't Give You Anything But Love, Baby."

The strife started about midnight when Mrs. Zioncheck told Mrs. Young she would have to leave. Mrs. Young refused, and the two women began to tussle. Zioncheck cheered his wife on. "She's making a touchdown!" he shouted. Then Zioncheck entered the play and grabbed Mrs. Young by the feet, while his wife took her head and arms. In a few seconds, Mrs. Young was in the corridor. She had lost her shoes in the shuffle, and they were thrown after her into the hall.

The battle over the sublet Harvard Hall apartment continued for ten additional days. Zioncheck's clashes with the Washington police were reported regularly in local and national news stories. Mrs. Young took out warrants for the arrest of both Marion and Rubye Zioncheck for assault by forcibly evicting her from the apartment. The final episode occurred in early June 1936 when the congressman drove his new roadster on the wrong side of Connecticut Avenue and on the sidewalk. He then de-

This 1929 indoor swimming pool at Harvard Hall is the earliest surviving example in any Washington apartment house.

livered a satchel of empty beer bottles to the White House as a present to President Roosevelt. Zioncheck was arrested for lunacy and placed in Gallinger (now D.C. General) Hospital for observation. Shortly thereafter Mrs. Zioncheck had him committed to a private sanitarium in Baltimore to prevent his detention by Washington police on Mrs. Young's warrant.

Zioncheck escaped from the Baltimore sanitarium by scaling a 7-foot wire fence surrounding an exercise yard, outdistanced attendants in a running race, and hid all night in the woods. The *Evening Star* further reported that he eluded a search party by hitchhiking a ride into Washington and hid in his Capitol Hill office for several hours before he was discovered. Capitol police prevented Washington police from arresting him, asserting congressional immunity. It was not until House Sergeant at Arms Kenneth Romney arrived and acted as a mediator that the impasse was solved. Capitol Hill police then escorted Zioncheck to Union Station the same day for safe conduct to his native Seattle, where he planned to begin his campaign for reelection. His mother was hospitalized there, suffering from shock over her son's clashes with the law.

In a final mad act, Zioncheck, depressed with the uphill fight to win reelection against seventeen candidates for his House seat, ended his life by jumping from his fifth-floor office window, coincidentally landing on the running board of the family car, where his wife was waiting to take him home to dinner.

As a postscript, Mrs. Young did receive compensation for her wrecked apartment after Washington police seized Zioncheck's property and sold it at auction in September 1936. Thus ended the most bizarre case in Washington history of a sublet apartment.

While apartment subletting is fairly common in New York, it is forbidden in most Washington apartment houses today. Certainly the Zioncheck affair contributed to this local custom. Indeed, disruptive problems may occur when the owners or board of directors of an apartment house, regardless of its type—rental, condo, or co-op— fail to screen new residents properly to ensure their financial dependability and to ascertain their compatibility with other residents. The screening of apartment house tenants is not new: Roman landlords required references from their tenants more than two thousand years ago.

83

WARDMAN TOWER

2600 Woodley Road, N.W.; southwest corner of Woodley Road and Connecticut Avenue

ARCHITECT: Mihran Mesrobian, 1928

ORIGINAL APARTMENTS: approximately 55 (mostly three-bedrooms)

STATUS: opened as rental in 1929; gradually converted to hotel rooms, beginning in 1973

The X-shaped plan of the Wardman Tower was influenced by Alden Park, a first-class Philadelphia apartment house complex of three buildings that had been built slightly earlier.

The Wardman Tower is distinguished by its prominent location, its unique design, and its many past famous residents. It was built in 1928 by Harry Wardman as the luxury apartment house wing of his adjacent apartment-hotel, the Wardman Park, which had opened a decade earlier. Originally known as the Annex, then the Eastern Wing, and later the Congressional Wing, it was finally renamed the Wardman Tower in 1973 in honor of its original owner and developer.

WOODLEY ROAD PROJECTS

Harry Wardman, Washington's premier builder in the 1920s, had just completed the city's largest luxury apartment complex in 1915—three buildings called Wardman Courts (now Clifton Terrace) at Clifton and 14th streets, N.W., totaling 270 units—when he conceived of Woodley Courts, which was to be the largest apartment development in the United States. He bought and consolidated 20 acres of undeveloped woodland on Connecticut Avenue between Woodley Road and Calvert Street for a complex of ten apartment houses, arranged around a central court. Wardman told the press that his Wardman Courts would "look like a baby" when compared with Woodley Courts.

Detail of the Georgian Revival facade of the Wardman Tower.

Each building was to be seven stories high and contain 125 apartments, for a total of 1,250 apartments. The $5 million plan included parks, tennis courts, playgrounds, ballroom, library, gymnasium, and public dining room. The project got underway in 1916 when the city government agreed to extend Calvert Street west of Connecticut Avenue.

In early 1917 Wardman abandoned his grandiose plans for Woodley Courts. In July construction began instead on the smaller Wardman Park Hotel, which nevertheless was the city's largest and one of the country's ten largest apartment-hotels when completed in 1918. It is not clear why Wardman changed his plans (most of his papers have been destroyed), but wartime restrictions on construction materials may have been responsible. Although guests began moving in by November 1918, construction was not completed until mid–1919. Because of the housing shortage at the time, the Wardman Park was

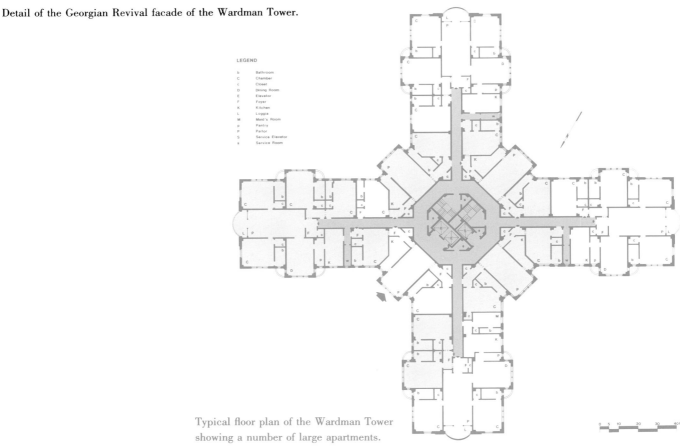

LEGEND

b   Bathroom
C   Chamber
c   Closet
D   Dining Room
E   Elevator
F   Foyer
K   Kitchen
L   Loggia
M   Maid's Room
p   Pantry
P   Parlor
S   Service Elevator
s   Service Room

Typical floor plan of the Wardman Tower showing a number of large apartments.

an immediate success, filled to capacity. Completely un-founded were the fears that it was too far removed from downtown Washington, although it was called Wardman's Folly while under construction.

The design of the hotel—by architect Frank R. White—was directly influenced by that of the luxurious Homestead in Hot Springs, Virginia. Both were enormous red-brick buildings with spokelike wings, set in land-scaped parks. The U-shaped Wardman Park Hotel faced Woodley Road, while the four large wings radiated from the rear toward Rock Creek Park. It was approached from a large semicircular driveway; a three-story garage was at the rear. The building was designed so that 90 percent of the rooms received direct sun at some time during the day. Other features included a 200-by-45-foot lobby, a roof garden, dining room seating five hundred, tearoom seating a hundred, Turkish bath, billiard room, drugstore, and grocery. One end of the lobby was used as a dance floor in the evenings. Because of the Spanish influenza epidemic, public meetings were banned and no grand opening was held. Approximately one-sixth of the Ward-man Park was originally reserved for hotel guests with the remainder for permanent apartment residents.

As early as 1921 Wardman had contemplated a sep-arate luxury apartment wing with extra-large units, but it was not until 1928 that he built it. The resulting eight-story Wardman Tower was constructed on the site of Wardman's own imposing eighteen-year-old house, which was demolished in April 1928. Because of its location on a steep hill, parts of the new luxury apartment house were submerged. Architect Mihran Mesrobian, who worked on a number of important Washington hotels and apart-ment houses for Wardman in the 1920s, designed the Georgian Revival-style Wardman Tower in a cross plan. He was directly influenced by the recently built Alden Park apartments in the Germantown section of Philadel-phia. That large luxury complex, designed by architect Edwyn Rorke in the early 1920s, had three separate cross-plan buildings—the Kenilworth, the Manor, and the Cambridge.

Like Alden Park, the Wardman Tower employed red brick with white stone trim, quoins in the wings to strengthen the design, and tiers of balconies at intervals on the sides of the arms and at their ends.

The $2 million Wardman Tower was designed so that almost all rooms on each floor were connected. Thus an apartment could be enlarged to any size, although most varied from five to seven rooms. The intersection of the four wings produced a core that was used for service facilities, including the stairways and elevators.

The main entrance to the Wardman Tower was through an imposing Georgian porte-cochère with a gabled roof supported by a pair of columns and piers. A long sem-icircular drive connected the porte-cochère to Woodley Road. Radiating from the west side was a long narrow arcade or corridor that connected to the Wardman Park Hotel. Known as the promenade, the arcade has massive Georgian arched windows on each side; both ends are framed by columns and fan lights. Still intact, it is used today as a sun room and an informal lounge by both hotel guests and apartment residents—as well as for a con-necting corridor to the newly built Sheraton-Washington Hotel.

Mihran Mesrobian skillfully designed the facades of the Wardman Tower to produce a rich plasticity, avoiding the boxlike massing usually found on cross-shaped build-ings. Wide projecting bays, framed by small rounded balconies on the sides of each wing, produce a strong vertical feeling. There is also a tier of prominent rounded balconies at the end of each wing. The otherwise boring facade of the square core has similarly been enlivened by projecting bays at each apex, where two wings meet. The facades are divided into three horizontal sections by the beltcourse above the second floor and the prominent cornice that defines the mansard roof housing the eighth-floor apartments. The eighteenth-century Georgian do-mestic style is further emphasized by the rich combination of Palladian, arched, and dormer windows; Ionic pilas-ters; decorative urns; brick quoining; single and paired chimneys; and even gabled porches. The rich limestone trim is as successful as that on the Dresden, also built by Wardman. The city's most distinctive Georgian apart-ment house facades are found on these two structures.

Opposite: This long public corridor, designed in the Georgian Revival style with French windows, originally connected the Wardman Tower to the Wardman Park Hotel, now the Sheraton-Washington Hotel.

The irregularly shaped lobby is punctuated by a row of exposed steel beams in the ceiling. The beams themselves and the space between them are richly decorated with neoclassical plaster detailing reproduced from the 1773 edition of *Works in Architecture* by Robert and James Adam. The ceiling is based on two in London, both designed by the Adam brothers: the drawing room of a house built by the Earl of Derby in 1773 and the ballroom of the 1766 Shelburne House. The other notable feature of the Wardman Tower lobby is the series of arches that unify the room and establish a formal rhythm reminiscent of the Georgian period. Some are windows, others are mirrored, while still others open onto corridors, staircases, and elevators.

One of many famous residents of the Wardman Tower was Perle Mesta, shown here at a party at her apartment about 1968 with guests Charles Robb, Washington Mayor Walter Washington, and Lynda Bird Johnson Robb.

FAMOUS RESIDENTS

The Wardman Tower was most famous as the home of high-ranking government officials. No other Washington apartment house has equaled its record. More presidents, vice presidents, and cabinet members have lived here than at any other Washington apartment house. They preferred this building because of its excellent hotel service in combination with spacious apartments. Some lived here before their terms of office and others during or afterwards. These celebrated residents included the following:

Spiro T. Agnew—*Vice President*
Robert B. Anderson—*Secretary of the Treasury*
Hugo Black—*Associate Justice*
Walter Brown—*Postmaster General*
Tom C. Clark—*Associate Justice, Attorney General*
John B. Connally—*Secretary of the Navy, Secretary of the Treasury*
Charles Curtis—*Vice President*
Robert J. Dole—*Senator*
John Foster Dulles—*Secretary of State*
Dwight D. Eisenhower—*President*
Albert Fall—*Senator*
Henry H. Fowler—*Secretary of the Treasury*
Barry M. Goldwater—*Senator*
Will Hays—*Postmaster General*
Herbert Hoover—*President, Secretary of Commerce*
Cordell Hull—*Secretary of State*
Robert H. Jackson—*Associate Justice, Attorney General*

Lyndon B. Johnson—*President*
Frank Knox—*Secretary of the Navy*
Henry Cabot Lodge, Jr.—*Senator, U.S. Ambassador to the United Nations*
Clare Boothe Luce—*Representative*
William Gibbs McAdoo—*Senator, Secretary of the Treasury*
Neil McElroy—*Secretary of Defense*
Joseph W. Martin, Jr.—*Representative*
Thruston Morton—*Senator*
Lawrence O'Brien—*Postmaster General*
Dean Rusk—*Secretary of State*
Lewis Schwellenbach—*Secretary of Labor*
John Snyder—*Secretary of State*
Adlai Stevenson—*U.S. Ambassador to the United Nations*
Henry Stimson—*Secretary of State*
Arthur Summerfield—*Postmaster General*
Robert A. Taft—*Senator*
Millard E. Tydings—*Senator*
Arthur Vandenberg—*Senator*
Frederick M. Vinson—*Chief Justice, Secretary of the Treasury*
Henry A. Wallace—*Vice President, Secretary of Agriculture, Secretary of Commerce*
Earl Warren—*Chief Justice*
Marvin Watson—*Postmaster General*
Caspar Weinberger—*Secretary of Defense, Secretary of Health, Education, and Welfare*
Charles E. Wilson—*Secretary of Defense*

One of the longest-term residents was Cordell Hull, Franklin D. Roosevelt's Secretary of State, who lived in the Annex from 1935 to 1955. Other prominent residents here included authors Mary Roberts Rinehart and Temple Bailey, as well as hostess Perle Mesta. Mrs. Mesta moved to a large ten-room apartment in the Wardman Tower in the mid-1960s from her large penthouse at 3900 Watson Place, N.W., when it was converted from rental to a co-op.

Mrs. Perle Shirvin Mesta, often referred to as "The Hostess with the Mostest," was the most prominent resident socially. She left her mark on Washington social history for the hundreds of lively parties she gave in the nation's capital from the early 1920s until she moved back to her native Oklahoma in 1973. In addition to her legendary parties, the former U.S. Minister to Luxembourg was an astute businesswoman and a shrewd politician. She was born into a wealthy family that owned extensive Texas oil fields, Oklahoma City real estate, and a large Western hotel chain.

After studying music and voice in Paris and New York, she married George Mesta, owner of the Mesta Machine Company of Pittsburgh. Beginning in the early 1920s, they maintained an apartment in the Willard Hotel in Washington in addition to their Pittsburgh home. After her husband died in 1926, she managed the large steel-making equipment company in Pittsburgh.

With the election of Franklin D. Roosevelt, Perle became an active Democratic fund-raiser and good friends with many members of Congress, including then-Senator Harry S. Truman. Because of her ability to make friends easily as well as her practical business sense, she was nominated by President Truman in 1949 as the first U.S. Minister to Luxembourg. She was the perfect choice for these qualities, especially since Luxembourg was a major steel producer in Europe and she understood the business.

Upon her return to Washington in 1953 she bought, with her sister and brother-in-law, Marguerite and George Typson, Les Ormes, a handsome estate in the Spring Valley section of Washington, where she entertained. After eight years there she rented and joined together four adjacent penthouse apartments at 3900 Watson Place, N.W., selling Les Ormes to Vice President Lyndon B. Johnson. After Perle's beloved sister died in 1963, she moved to another large rental apartment at the Wardman Tower, then the apartment annex of the Sheraton-Park Hotel, now the Sheraton-Washington Hotel. The last two years of her life were spent in her native Oklahoma City with her brother, William B. Shirvin, where she died in 1975.

She is remembered for Irving Berlin's Broadway musical *Call Me Madam*, which opened in New York in 1950 with Ethel Merman as its star. A huge hit, the show had as its main character Sally Adams, a party-loving Washington hostess and ambassador to a tiny European duchy, whose escapades were based on Perle Mesta's life. Mrs. Mesta wrote her own memories of her fabulous life, *Call Me Perle*, in collaboration with Robert Cahn.

The Sheraton Corporation purchased the Wardman Park Hotel and its adjacent luxury apartment house annex in 1953, renaming the famous hostelry the Sheraton-Park Hotel. At that time the thirty-two large apartments, with five to ten rooms each, were redecorated, and some were subdivided into two-bedroom units. Conversion of the apartment suites to hotel use began slowly in 1973, as permanent residents gradually left. With rent control the Sheraton could profit far more from this space as hotel rooms than as apartments. By 1983 only about a dozen permanent residents remained, including Mrs. Earl Warren, widow of the chief justice, and Lieutenant General Robert Le Baron, whose long and prominent military and civilian service began with his appointment as military aide to President Wilson during World War I.

Construction of an even larger hotel, designed by the architectural firm of Hellmuth, Obata, and Kassabaum, was built adjacent to the original Wardman Park Hotel building in 1978–80. When it opened in 1980 as the Sheraton-Washington Hotel, the original Wardman Park Hotel was demolished. Because of the Wardman Tower's prominent location and excellent design and construction, the Sheraton Corporation fortunately decided to preserve and restore it. On the sixtieth anniversary of the old Wardman Park Hotel—and just before construction of the new building in 1978—the Sheraton Hotel chain gave a gala banquet for more than two hundred former permanent residents of both the old Wardman Park Hotel and the Wardman Tower. They came from across the country to pay tribute to the passing of the old Wardman Park Hotel building and the start of restoration of the Wardman Tower.

84

HAMPSHIRE GARDENS

4912 New Hampshire Avenue, N.W.; block bounded by Emerson, Farragut, and 3rd streets and New Hampshire Avenue, N.W.

ARCHITECT: James E. Cooper (facade design) and George T. Santmyers (plan and interior design);
Parks and Baxter, associate architects (landscape design), 1929

ORIGINAL APARTMENTS: 102 (4 efficiencies; 64 one-bedrooms; 28 two-bedrooms; 6 three-bedrooms)

STATUS: opened as co-op in 1930

The two-story buildings that comprise Hampshire Gardens were designed in the Tudor Revival style.

When designed in early 1929, Hampshire Gardens, Washington's first true garden apartment complex, was to have been the largest such project in the nation. Developers J. B. Shapiro and Edmund J. Flynn planned to spend $15 million to build a total of twenty-five hundred apartments housing seventy-five hundred people on a 50-acre site between Rock Creek Park and the Soldiers Home. This location near the Maryland boundary, although largely farmland, was adjacent to recently extended bus lines. The concept was bold and the plan exceptionally well conceived. Had it been completed as first planned, Hampshire Gardens would have been both the largest garden apartment project and the largest co-op in the United States. Hampshire Gardens, however, like the Kennedy-Warren and the Westchester, was caught in the beginning of the Depression and never completed. Only one of twenty-five proposed city blocks of apartment houses was finished, because the developers could not obtain additional financing after the stock crash of October 1929.

The single completed block, measuring 360 by 83 feet, contains nine two-story Tudor Revival apartment buildings that cost a total of $500,000 to build. The nine buildings, eight designed in irregular cross plans, contain 102 apartments—the smallest: two rooms, kitchen, and bath; the largest: five rooms, kitchen, and bath. All build-

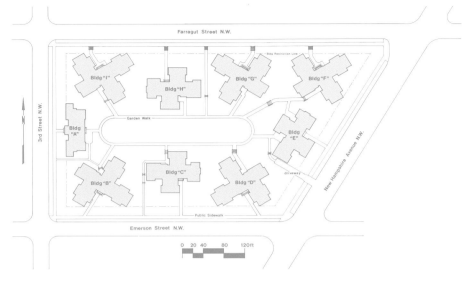

Hampshire Gardens was the first successful garden apartment house. Its nine buildings, all connected by sidewalks, are skillfully arranged around a large inner courtyard.

The spacious inner courtyard of Hampshire Gardens was well landscaped when completed in 1929.

ings are connected with sidewalks and arranged around a spacious interior oval park. The grounds, landscaped by Parks and Baxter, occupy two-thirds of the site. James E. Cooper designed the exteriors and George T. Santmyers the interiors. In addition to a street address, the nine buildings are designated by letters A through I. Several buildings had small gymnasiums, showers, and locker rooms in their basements—rare in Washington at that time. Even though these gyms have long since been closed, the complete facilities remain preserved in one building, forgotten by time.

The high-quality construction and attention to detail were unusual for middle-class apartment buildings—those without lobby, receptionist, elevator, or garage. No two buildings are identical. Variety and a domestic feeling are lent by dark red-brick facades, punctuated with recessed arched stone portals, half-timbering, crenelated cornices, stone finials, and gabled and hipped slate roofs. The small scale and lack of elevators belie the spaciousness within. The nine buildings vary in size, with eight to fifteen apartments each. The entire complex is heated by a central power plant, unique in 1930 in multibuilding

Washington apartment complexes. This plan was soon followed by such other early garden apartments in the suburbs as Colonial Village in Arlington, Virginia, and the Falkland in Silver Spring, Maryland.

At the time Hampshire Gardens was Washington's only multibuilding cooperative in which all buildings were administered as one co-op. The few other multibuilding co-ops in the city in 1929, such as the Cleveland Park and Tilden Gardens, were organized with each building as a separate legal corporation. At Hampshire Gardens the residents of each building have always elected a three-member house committee, whose chairman represents that building on the co-op board for the entire complex.

Hampshire Gardens was the first co-op on the east coast to be certified by the National Association of Real Estate Boards through its consultation bureau. Such certification held that the financing, organization, and construction met the high standards of a sound cooperative apartment project. Apartments sold rapidly, with only six

Air circulation was excellent at Hampshire Gardens because of the wide arches between the public rooms in each apartment.

Typical floor plan for one building—C-E-H—at Hampshire Gardens.

unsold by June 1930. The original price of the largest unit—a five-room, kitchen, and bath apartment—was $8,900. The down payment was $1,335, and monthly payments $74.75. Most original residents were young married couples. They held many social events in the basement clubroom at 250 Farragut Street, N.W., such as monthly dances with prizes for the couple who performed the best waltz and the best fox-trot. The original developer, Edmund J. Flynn, lived here with his family from 1929 to 1948.

The co-op managed to weather the Depression by careful management. When some residents fell behind in their shareholder payments, the board of directors had them move out, rather than foreclose. Their apartments were then rented for them, and after the owners were financially back on their feet, they were allowed to return. Hampshire Gardens remains in its original state with little or no change in either interior or exterior design. Many of the interior details found here, such as the rough plaster walls, Moorish arches, and porcelain ceiling fixtures, were hallmarks of many apartment houses designed in the 1920s, including Alban Towers and 4701 Connecticut Avenue, N.W.

85

WOODLEY PARK TOWERS

2737 Devonshire Place, N.W.; northwest corner of Devonshire Place and Connecticut Avenue

ARCHITECT: Louis T. Rouleau, Sr., 1929

ORIGINAL APARTMENTS: 163 (12 efficiencies; 78 one-bedrooms; 68 two-bedrooms; 5 three-bedrooms)

STATUS: opened as rental in 1930; converted to condo in 1973

Front facade of Woodley Park Towers.

Detail of the Art Deco driveway canopy at Woodley Park Towers.

The most striking feature of Woodley Park Towers is its unusual outline and shape. Built of tan brick, with restrained Art Deco geometric detailing, the six-story building is on a site with 100 feet fronting on Connecticut Avenue and 500 feet facing Devonshire Place. Its irregular V shape includes a radial plan with four wings projecting from the rear of the building overlooking Rock Creek Park and Klingle Road. Wide space was left in both the front and the rear to allow for extensive landscaping and to provide for a circular driveway to the front entrance (with its rakish marquee) and another driveway to the garage.

Accommodating the rambling design of the 163-unit Woodley Park Towers, the architect conveniently included six entrances and six passenger elevators, which avoided walking down seemingly endless corridors. The two-level garage has space for sixty-five cars. Other amenities originally included a spacious two-story-high lobby with a front desk and switchboard, balcony, public parlor, and maids' quarters in the basement. The first floor originally included a hundred-seat public dining room, but this operated only from December 1929 when the building opened until early 1931. Zoning laws prohibited the restaurant from advertising, and its location at the left (west) end of the building placed it too far from Connecticut Avenue to attract customers.

Woodley Park Towers was built by four developers

Plan of three-bedroom apartments in the No. 20 tier at Woodley Park Towers.

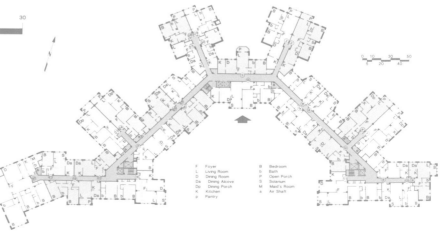

Typical floor plan at Woodley Park Towers.

View from the front desk across the lobby to the public parlor at Woodley Park Towers.
Like the Kennedy-Warren, the geometric Art Deco detailing was carried out in the Aztec
motif.

who were related—Abraham and Barney Liebman and Sydney C. and Joseph C. Kaufman. All but Joseph Kaufman lived with their families in the No. 20 tier (far left), the most spacious apartment tier in the building. The 3,000-square-foot units are beautifully laid out: a wide centrally located gallery leads directly from the entrance to a large living room with a working fireplace and then to the connecting sun porch. On the left of the gallery, or entrance hall, are three bedrooms and two baths, while on the right are the dining room and connecting pantry,

Apartments in the No. 20 tier at Woodley Park Towers have a wide central gallery from which all rooms radiate.

Double paneled doors open from the long gallery into the dining room in apartments in the No. 20 tier at Woodley Park Towers.

kitchen, and maid's room and bath. Applied molding was used on the walls in the entrance hall, living room, and master bedroom. Unusual features include two massive arches with double doors that connect the dining room to the gallery and the living room to the sun porch, and parquet flooring throughout. The design of the five apartments of this tier is much like that of the units in 2101 Connecticut Avenue, N.W.

Among the prominent residents of Woodley Park Towers in the early years was a freshman congressman from Texas, Lyndon Baines Johnson, and his wife, Lady Bird, who occupied apartment No. 224 from January 1941 to November 1942. [During three months of 1942, however, when Congressman Johnson was on active duty with the Navy, Mrs. Johnson sublet their Woodley Park Towers apartment and moved in with Mrs. John (Nellie) Connally in the Buckingham Apartments in Arlington.] The Liebman and Kaufman heirs sold the building in 1973 when it was converted to a condominium, with prices from $27,500 for an efficiency to $160,000 for the three-bedroom units in the No. 20 tier.

ARCHITECT LOUIS T. ROULEAU, SR.

The architect of Woodley Park Towers, Louis T. Rouleau, Sr. (1895–1937), a native Washingtonian, received his architecture degree from Catholic University in Washington in 1916. After serving as a fighter pilot for the U.S. Navy in World War I, he began his seventeen-year practice of architecture. Rouleau designed many houses in Washington, including his own at 2021 Massachusetts Avenue, N.W., in 1930, and many others in suburban Silver Spring and Chevy Chase. His work, however, also included more than twenty-six Washington apartment houses between 1923 and 1937—3051 Idaho Avenue, N.W.; 1921 Kalorama Road, N.W.; 2517 K Street, N.W.; 1725 New Hampshire Avenue, N.W.; 4007 and 5420 Connecticut Avenue, N.W.; and the impressive Century at 1620 Fuller Street, N.W. His most important apartment house was the Ambassador, an eleven-story Tudor-style luxury building in Baltimore at Canterbury Road and 39th Street, built in 1931. Rouleau died of pneumonia in Washington at the age of 42.

86

SHOREHAM HOTEL

2500 Calvert Street, N.W.; southwest corner of Calvert and 24th streets

ARCHITECT: Joseph Abel, 1930; Dillon and Abel, 1935 addition

ORIGINAL APARTMENTS: 132 (varied from one-bedrooms to three-bedrooms) and 250 hotel rooms

STATUS: opened as rental in 1931; apartments converted to hotel rooms in 1950–55

When the Presbyterians decided not to build their national church on the south side of Calvert Street between 24th and 28th streets, N.W., the 11-acre site was sold to developer Harry Wardman in early 1929. Late in that year, however, because of the stock crash and Wardman's impending bankruptcy, the land was sold to the Washington banking firm of Swartzell, Rheem, and Hensey. The new owners immediately commissioned a young local architect, Joseph Abel, to prepare plans for an apartment-hotel half as large as the $6 million thousand-apartment complex that Wardman had planned but never built. Apartment-hotels were popular in Washington from the early 1880s through the mid–1950s. By then apartments were being replaced by far more profitable hotel rooms. A number of other famous examples built during the 1920s included the Mayflower Hotel, the Roosevelt Hotel, the Broadmoor, and the Chastleton.

Construction began on the new Shoreham Hotel in January 1930. The original design included two eight-story cross-shaped buildings joined by a one-story connecting wing. The latter was to house the public spaces—large lobby, public dining room, several private dining rooms, ballroom, nightclub, swimming pool, and miniature golf course (miniature golf was a new sport that had become extremely popular). Just weeks after the con-

struction firm of Bralove, Ernst, and McInerney broke ground, the Shoreham Hotel plans were enlarged by raising the two cross-shaped buildings and the connecting structure to a full nine stories. Bad luck plagued these owners, however, who declared bankruptcy midway through construction in 1930.

Exercising an option in his original contract, Harry M. Bralove purchased the Shoreham and completed the landmark building. Born in 1891 in Philadelphia, Bralove settled in Washington after graduating from Ohio State University and the Georgetown Law School. He first worked as a secretary for Franklin D. Roosevelt, then assistant secretary of the Navy, before becoming a Senate reporter and then opening his own law firm. In 1926 he founded his construction company, with Edward C. Ernst and John J. McInerney as junior partners. The firm enjoyed immediate success in the four years before the Shoreham was built—constructing four large apartment houses on Connecticut Avenue: the Broadmoor and Nos. 2101, 4701, and 4707.

The new building was named after an earlier Shoreham Hotel on the northeast corner of 15th and H streets, N.W., a once-famous landmark built in 1889 for Vice President Levi P. Morton of New York, who named it for his birthplace, Shoreham, Vermont. The original Shoreham Hotel on 15th Street, N.W., had been purchased by Harry Wardman and razed in 1928–29 for the present handsome Shoreham Office Building.

The new Shoreham was surrounded by spacious lawns on all sides and adjacent to Rock Creek Park. The buff-brick building, designed in an eclectic style, included 132 apartments and 250 hotel rooms. The largest apartments, on the ends of the wings, had 2,600 square feet of space, with a foyer, living room, dining room, sun parlor, three bedrooms, two baths, kitchen, and pantry. They could even be enlarged by connecting additional bedrooms and baths—a feature previously employed at the Wardman Tower. All living rooms had working fireplaces and built-in bookcases. The Shoreham offered many advanced features, including a two-hundred-car garage beneath the front lawn, self-leveling elevators recently perfected by General Electric, glass-enclosed bathroom shower stalls, an indoor and outdoor playground, and the newly introduced solaria and balconies in most of the apartments. One of the most beautiful features of the Shoreham was the Renaissance-inspired vaulted lobby. Other public rooms on the first floor were decorated in Art Deco style, as were many apartments.

ENTERTAINMENT AT THE SHOREHAM

Notable guests who have stayed at the Shoreham since 1930, in either the apartments or the hotel rooms, have included every president since Franklin D. Roosevelt, as well as Ethiopian Emperor Haile Selassie, Henry Ford, August Busch, Clark Gable and Carole Lombard, Marlene Dietrich, Gary Cooper, Marilyn Monroe, Gene Autry, Robert Taylor, Robert Mitchum, and Jimmy Hoffa. Many of the famous guests were artists who performed at the hotel: Bing Crosby, Ed Sullivan, Jimmy Durante, Bob Hope, Eddie Duchin, Jack Benny, Mitch Miller, and Rudy Vallee. For many years the entertainment in the Shoreham nightclub, terrace dancing pavilion, and ballrooms was considered the city's best. On opening night, 30 October 1930, the program featured Harry Richman, stage star; Lisa Basquette, screen star; the Dave Gould Girls; several adagio teams; and dance music by Paul Fidelman and his orchestra, joined by the star of the day,

Half of the Shoreham Hotel originally consisted of apartments for permanent residents.

Rudy Vallee. The Shoreham Hotel's newsletter recently recalled the event:

The hotel had booked numerous diversions for its maiden floor show in 1930, but, as a piece de resistance, it went after the biggest drawing card of the era, the crooner, Rudy Vallee. Vallee was booked solidly for theatre and night-club engagements in New York City, but by dangling $9,000 in front of him, the Shoreham persuaded Rudy to cancel one New York performance and to load his Connecticut Yankees into a trimotored airplane.

A press agent with unlimited funds couldn't have arranged events better. Vallee's plane was caught in a thunderstorm and for several hours the wires were crackling with reports that the high-priced crooner was missing. Since bootlegged liquor was much in evidence the crowd stayed on. Miss Amelia Earhart, operator of the air line that owned the plane, was herself at the Shoreham, bringing periodic bulletins to the titillated [sic] guests. Actually the plane had been forced down at Camden, New Jersey. The weather lifted in time for Vallee and his Yankees to arrive at the Shoreham at 4:15 A.M., where the crowd still awaited them. He played a few numbers, then headed his air-weary Yankees down to Union Station to take a slow train back to New York. In a recent broadcast, Vallee reminisced with nostalgic awe about the time he was paid the "fabulous sum of $9,000 for fifteen minutes of music." The Shoreham always figured it got its money's worth in publicity and excitement.

Coping with the unexpected has become commonplace over the years at the Shoreham. When the Democrats gave their 1948 victory party for President Truman and Vice President Barkley, food and drinks were ordered for

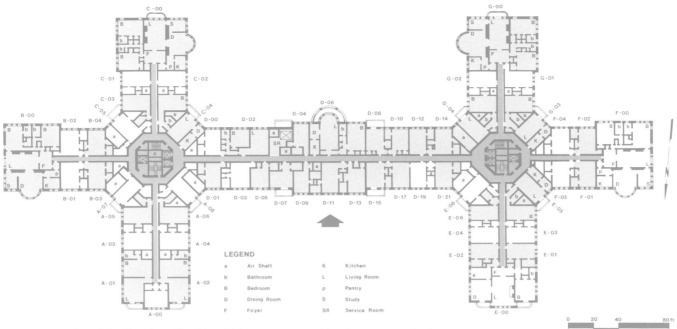

Typical floor plan of the Shoreham Hotel in which apartments and hotel rooms are mixed.

five thousand guests, but more than eight thousand showed up. The traffic outside was paralyzed for blocks. After Truman was smuggled in by a back door, it took Barkley another hour to drive to the hotel from his nearby apartment at 2101 Connecticut Avenue.

Anticipating America's entry into World War II, the Shoreham owners purchased the entire stock of a Scottish distillery and were prepared to serve Scotch throughout the war. Other wartime measures included converting the hotel's riding stable into a chicken ranch where thousands of broilers were raised for Shoreham tables.

ADDITIONS

The popularity of the Shoreham caused the Bralove family to add addition after addition to the original building. As a result, the elegant lines of the 1930 structure, with its spacious front and rear lawns, unfortunately are now mostly hidden by an incongruous mixture of driveway ramps, new wings, and other additions. The first expansion was a $190,000 eight-story addition to the west, containing 153 new hotel rooms, designed by Dillon and Abel in 1935. In 1946 the stylish original glassed-in swimming pool was replaced with a cocktail lounge, dining room, and sun room. Then, in 1949, the Shoreham built another hundred-room addition in a five-story sprawling "motor inn" on the southeast corner of the property. In 1979 New York developer William Zeckendorf, Jr., attempted to purchase the Shoreham. He planned to refurbish the hotel and to build several large condominium buildings on part of the Shoreham tract. Because of opposition from

a number of quarters, including the National Park Service, these plans were never approved by the government and Zeckendorf never bought the Shoreham.

Realizing that the profits from the hotel rooms far outweighed the rents from the apartments, as early as 1938 the Bralove family stopped renting apartments when tenants left. Finally, in 1950, the Shoreham asked most of the permanent apartment residents, including a number of senators and congressmen, to move so that the units could be broken up for hotel use. By the end of the year only twenty-five apartments were left, and these were slowly phased out during the following five years. Many of the apartment residents moved into apartments at the nearby Wardman Park Hotel, which in 1950 still housed approximately a thousand permanent residents.

Following the death of the builder and owner, Harry Bralove, in 1961, the Shoreham came under the management of his son, Bernard R. Bralove. His outstanding accomplishment was planning and building the adjacent Shoreham West in the early 1960s—still one of the five best-designed and best-managed luxury apartment houses in the city.

The Shoreham has changed ownership several times during the 1970s and 1980s. When owned by the Dunfey Hotels, a subsidiary of Aer Lingus, the Irish airline, the 775-room Shoreham underwent extensive renovation in 1984–85, costing more than $15 million. The landmark was purchased by the Omni hotel chain in late 1985. Fittingly, the Shoreham was used in the mid-1980s as the monthly meeting place of the Art Deco Society of Washington, devoted to the study and preservation of the city's Art Deco landmarks.

87

WESTCHESTER

4000 Cathedral Avenue, N.W.; southwest corner of Cathedral Avenue and 29th Street

ARCHITECT: Harvey H. Warwick, Sr., 1930

ORIGINAL APARTMENTS: 556 (86 efficiencies; 324 one-bedrooms; 110 two-bedrooms; 36 three-bedrooms)

STATUS: opened as rental in 1931; converted to co-op in 1953

Planned to cover twenty-eight acres on Cathedral Avenue, this large apartment house complex was conceived in 1929 by Washington developer Gustave Ring. He recruited his former employer, Morris Cafritz, and architect, Harvey H. Warwick, Sr., as junior partners.

The first Westchester building was begun in March 1930, but the financial pressure of the Depression permanently halted the master plan midway through construction. Nonetheless, the four completed buildings made the Westchester the largest luxury apartment house in Washington for twenty years until the slightly larger Woodner was completed on 16th Street in 1951. While the Woodner has fallen on hard times and can no longer be considered prestigious, the Westchester has never lost its footing. Although a number of even larger luxury apartment houses succeeded the Westchester in the 1950s and 1960s—such as the Westchester's neighbor, the Towers, the famous Watergate on the Potomac, and others in the suburbs, including the Rotonda in McLean, Virginia, and the Grosvenor Park in Rockville, Maryland—they can never quite equal the character of the Westchester.

The site of the Westchester had been the cattle farm of the Kengla family, Georgetown butchers, who kept animals there until ready for slaughter. In 1921 developer William M. Kennedy bought the farm, with its simple

This 1931 photograph shows the OB building at the Westchester, the first section completed.

Victorian frame house, as the site for an apartment house. After his sudden death in 1927, the Kennedy estate rented the Victorian house there for two years to Mrs. Albert J. Myer, nee Baroness Irene Ungern, who used it as a finishing school for girls. Although Kennedy did not live to

300

This rare aerial view of the Westchester shows the complex in 1933 with the imposing alley of cedar trees and sunken fountain in the center. The Great Depression stopped plans to construct three additional buildings on the grounds shown at the upper left.

1   "A" Building
2   "OB" Building
3   Center Building
4   Main Building
5   Terraced Garden
   With Central Fountain

Site plan of the Westchester showing the relationship of the four buildings, named A, OB, Center, and Main.

This massive pair of eighteenth-century English gates was added to the Westchester driveway entrance shortly after World War II.

This centrally located sunken garden and fountain make up the focal point of the Westchester complex.

develop the site, he was responsible for having the address changed from Jewett Street to the more imposing Cathedral Avenue.

When Gustave Ring bought the site in 1929 from the Kennedy estate, Cathedral Avenue was still largely undeveloped, and land in the area was relatively cheap. The immense scope intended for the Westchester was unique in Washington. It was to have been the largest apartment house south of New York, with eight buildings—containing 23 million cubic feet and costing more

F   Foyer
R   Reception Hall
L   Living Room
D   Dining Room
K   Kitchen
C   Chamber
b   Bath
S   Sun Room (open porch on eighth floor)
M   Maids Quarters
A   Air Shaft

Typical floor plan of the OB building at the Westchester.

than $10 million—designed around a spacious quadrangle with its front end open to Cathedral Avenue. Ring pointed out when construction began that the depth of the quadrangle would be equivalent to two long city blocks. The Depression, however, interrupted construction and only four buildings were built.

PLANS AND CONSTRUCTION

The original plans for the Westchester called for more than a thousand apartments. The proposed (unbuilt) principal building, to be located at the far end of the entrance drive or apex of the quadrangle, was to have a ballroom, public dining room, rooftop swimming pool (glass-enclosed in winter), gymnasium, and a little theater. A two-story passageway would connect all of the eight buildings.

Located on the edge of a steep hill 300 feet above downtown Washington, this building would offer a broad view of the entire cityscape and the Potomac River. A serene parklike setting was ensured for the original residents, since the four buildings occupied less than 10 percent of the 28-acre site. Landscape architects assisted with the planning from the beginning, leaving intact the original contours of the area. Although the Victorian farmhouse and the trees on the plateau were leveled for construction of the various Westchester buildings, the trees on the three steep slopes surrounding the quadrangle were spared.

Construction began in early 1930 with two similar eight-story freestanding buildings, one on each side of the entrance driveway—the "OB" building (meaning old building) to the right or west, and the "A" building to the left or east. Each is rectangular with four projecting wings and has a prominent red-gray brick-and-limestone tower with a red-tile hipped roof that houses the elevator machinery. There are no unfinished rear sides to any of the Westchester buildings, since all facades were designed with finished tapestry brick and full limestone detailing. The facade design is eclectic and typical of the fashion of the late 1920s and early 1930s.

A number of architectural elements from various historical styles were carefully integrated into the composition of the Westchester. For instance, the recessed plaster arches surrounding a number of second-floor windows, surmounted by limestone keystones, are Georgian. The shallow limestone balconies randomly placed on the upper floors, with their prominent corbels, are of Tudor derivation. Moorish influence can be seen in the elaborate limestone cornice of the elevator towers, the crenelation of the facade cornice, and the massive porte-cochère of the main building. The geometric carved spandrel panels scattered throughout the facades show a distinct Art Deco influence. Although none of these foreign elements is authentic to its original source, the architect, Harvey H. Warwick, Sr., adapted and blended them in his own unique, and often charming, manner.

Although the third and fourth buildings—Main and Center—adjoin one another, each has its own entrance and lobby. To provide maximum light and air and to avoid a great flat facade, Main is H-shaped and the attached smaller Center is an irregular L shape. Main is the most important apartment house in the complex, since it contains the principal reception desk, the largest lobby, the manager's office, and the public dining room. Its entrance

The Westchester is the only Washington apartment house with a full-time chauffeur and its own gas pump.

One corner of the large lobby of the Main building at the Westchester.

scrap plans for the other four buildings. Indeed, he stopped all construction of Main and Center between January and April 1931 after his financial backers, the local mortgage house of Swartzell, Rheem, and Hensey, collapsed. After herculean efforts, he found funds to finish these buildings.

Even though the landscape work continued until 1933, the four buildings, with a total of 556 apartments, were opened for occupancy in October 1931. Rooms are spacious, with some living rooms 25 by 15 feet, bedrooms 18 by 14 feet. Many apartments have glassed porches with two exposures, since they are located in the projecting pavilions. Contemporary features included step-down living rooms and indirect lighting. Throughout the 1930s and 1940s, the Westchester maintained approximately forty hotel rooms and suites for transients, guests of permanent residents. Today ten of these furnished rooms still provide convenient accommodations for guests of the residents. Because some apartments have been combined with others, there now are 521 units.

MANAGEMENT AND OWNERSHIP

Because the Westchester opened during the worst of the Depression, Gustave Ring had a serious problem in renting the expensive apartments. For the first two years he offered three months' free rent to people who would sign a one-year lease. This approach worked, for by 1934 all apartments were rented and the Westchester "family" totaled 1,800 residents (many of whom were children), 700 nonresident servants, and a staff of 135. (The Depression left a number of apartments vacant in the most expensive apartment houses in Washington, such as Meridian Mansions and 2101 Connecticut Avenue. The problem was not solved in many until 1934–35 when the city experienced a serious housing shortage.) Throughout the 1930s and 1940s the Westchester and the Wardman Tower reigned as the two Washington apartment houses with the greatest concentration of distinguished residents. At the beginning of World War II, for instance, the Westchester's residents included two cabinet members, thirty-one congressmen, twelve senators, and fourteen judges.

Because the burden of managing such a large enterprise hindered his ability to develop the area's largest

is accented by a massive porte-cochère and promenade that lead to the step-down lobby measuring 150 by 35 feet. This building has the principal garage with facilities for changing tires, washing cars, and an outside gas pump for the exclusive use of the residents. Other facilities located in Main include a grocery store, drugstore, beauty shop, barbershop, and valet shop. The Westchester's own uniformed chauffeur can be booked to drive one's car.

One of the unusual features of the Westchester is the elliptical sunken garden, 150 by 200 feet, in front of Center. Designed on three levels, four flights of ornamental brick and limestone steps lead to the fountain and pool in the center. The original landscape design called for a border of fifty cedar trees arranged in two rows, one on each side of the entrance drive. The transplanting of these seventy-five-year-old trees from a Maryland estate was one of the most ambitious landscape projects ever undertaken for a Washington apartment house.

The Depression made it impossible to obtain additional financing in early 1931, and Ring was forced to

The public dining room off the lobby of the Westchester Main building.

garden apartment project, Colonial Village, Ring sold the Westchester in 1937 to a Dutch investment company, Amsinck, Sonne, and Company, for the original construction cost of $4 million. Ring and his partners, Warwick and Cafritz, thus realized a profit. Because Queen Wilhelmina of the Netherlands owned stock in the Dutch corporation, which held hundreds of properties in Europe as well as in North America, it was erroneously believed that she personally owned the Westchester.

In need of funds for rebuilding war-torn Holland, the Dutch company sold the Westchester for $4.3 million in 1947 to the City Investing Company of New York, a holding company of the Realest Corporation. During the following seven years the president of this company, Robert W. Dowling, took a personal interest in the Westchester and made a number of improvements. For instance, while traveling in England in 1952, he located and purchased the two pairs of massive Georgian carriage gates that now stand guard at the Westchester's front driveways. They had been left intact on the Essex estate of Copped Hall even though the manor house had been destroyed

in the Blitz. Purchased for $10,000, the four great carved stone pillars and the pairs of massive wrought-iron gates dating from 1760 were shipped back to Washington in thirty-eight crates weighing eight tons and erected the following year. Soon afterwards, Dowling commissioned the notable American interior designer Dorothy Draper to refurbish all four lobbies.

CO-OP CONVERSION

Because of the continuation of the city's rent control law as well as high inflation, a number of owners of Washington apartment houses converted their buildings to co-operatives in the decade following World War II. At this time the Westchester rents, which ranged from $65 for efficiencies to $247 for three-bedroom units, did not produce an adequate return on the investment. Unlike tenants at the Broadmoor, however, Westchester residents were almost unanimously opposed to the conversion proposed in 1950 and voted against buying the buildings

Residents of the Westchester play cards in the basement recreation room, which also houses the lending library.

A number of Westchester apartments have step-down living rooms, which first became popular in the 1930s.

and land for $7.5 million. The sale prices of the units then varied from $4,000 for efficiencies up to $25,000 for the three-bedroom apartments. After three years of negotiations between the tenants and the owner, however, the Westchester became a co-op in December 1953, and 75 percent of the residents purchased their apartments. The monthly maintenance fees are higher than normal at the Westchester mainly because of the large staff and to a lesser degree the ground rent that must be paid to the owner of the land—since 1962 the Mutual Benefit Life Insurance Company of Newark, New Jersey.

By leasing the 12 acres occupied by the four Westchester buildings for ninety-nine years and by entirely giving up the remaining vacant 16 acres, the owners were able to offer the Westchester to the tenants for only $6 million. This development occurred to reduce the purchase price in the face of tenant opposition to the sale. The City Investing Company also was allowed to retain title to the dining room, stores, guest suites, and garage space. The failure of the tenants to buy the entire property at the time of conversion proved to be a serious mistake, however.

The Westchester co-op board of directors bought back the public spaces in the buildings from the City Investing Company, but at a much greater expense than would have been necessary in 1953. During the ten years

following the co-op conversion, the owners of the 16 adjacent wooded acres on three sides of the Westchester made a considerable profit on their sale as the sites for 3900 Watson Place, N.W., the Colonnade, and Cathedral West. The Westchester tried to block construction of these adjacent luxury apartment houses, fearing traffic congestion and blockage of views, but lost in court. Under the terms of the land lease, however, the Westchester retains the right-of-way of its rear driveway, cutting through the grounds of the Colonnade down to Fulton Street, N.W.

Cooperation among the Westchester residents has always been noteworthy. The Westchester Club organizes a tour of ten apartments within the complex every two or three years, for instance. The funds raised go toward improvement of the club room in Main, new gardens on the grounds, and other projects. These tours are particularly popular, since few apartments are identical. Although six basic floor plans were originally used, architect Harvey H. Warwick, Sr., made numerous variations in different buildings and different tiers. In addition, many owners have joined two apartments, so that a single floor plan on one floor may be almost unrecognizable in another. Some five apartments on the top floors have their own private roofdecks—an unusual design in any apartment house. But then, the Westchester has never been typical.

88

KENNEDY-WARREN

3133 Connecticut Avenue, N.W.; east side of Connecticut Avenue between the National Zoo and Klingle Road

ARCHITECT: Joseph Younger, 1930; Alexander H. Sonnemann, supervising architect for 1935 addition

ORIGINAL APARTMENTS (including 1935 addition): 317 (109 efficiencies; 80 one-bedrooms; 120 two-bedrooms; 8 three-bedrooms)

STATUS: opened as rental in 1931

Of the seven thousand apartment houses in the Washington metropolitan area, only a handful stand out because of their combination of excellence in architectural design, innovative features, and long-time social prominence of their residents. The Kennedy-Warren easily remains among the top ten apartment houses in this distinguished category. Not only is it still the finest Art Deco apartment house ever built in the city, but it was the earliest example in the nation to have a forced natural air cooling system when it opened in October 1931. It was also the first building in Washington in which aluminum was extensively used on both the exterior and the interior. Because both dull and highly burnished finishes are mixed, the aluminum detailing at the Kennedy-Warren is strikingly beautiful.

The enormous front facade of the Kennedy-Warren is a successfully unified and handsome Art Deco composition. Although a number of local apartment houses were built in the late 1920s with Art Deco detailing, such as the Moorings, the Park Central, Harvard Hall, and the Senate Courts, the Kennedy-Warren is the city's most dramatic full-blown example of Art Deco apartment house architecture. In many of the other buildings, Art Deco carvings were inserted around the entrances but not carried through the facade to unite the entire structure as at the Kennedy-Warren.

Front facade of the Kennedy-Warren, Washington's finest Art Deco apartment house.

On the exterior of the Kennedy-Warren, verticality is stressed by the use of handsome aluminum spandrels set in two vertical rows on the left front (northwest) wing closest to Connecticut Avenue. The focal point of the building, however, is the central entrance "tower" with its pyramid copper tile roof, embellished with a pair of

Architect Joseph Younger's original perspective of the Kennedy-Warren. The large wing to the right of the circular drive was never built because of the Great Depression.

The entrance pavilion at the Kennedy-Warren, with its aluminum marquee and copper tower, is a familiar landmark on Connecticut Avenue.

limestone griffins just below the cornice. Again two vertical rows of geometric aluminum panels (produced by Alcoa) soar above the elegant streamlined aluminum marquee. Both exterior and interior motifs might be described as Aztec Art Deco.

Most of the trim on the buff-colored front brick facade is on the left or northernmost projecting pavilion and on the entrance pavilion; together these provide the principal focus of the entire structure. Framing the sleek aluminum rounded marquee are two windows surmounted by pairs of geometric carved birds set into the two-story rusticated limestone base. All of the decorative stonework was produced by the Edmonds Art Stone Company of Washington.

INTERIOR DETAILS

The Aztec motif is continued in the interior on the elevator doors, lobby ceiling, ballroom columns and ceiling, and hardware. Even the door knockers are excellent examples of Aztec Deco. The 20-foot-high lobby was embellished with ceiling beams painted in zigzag patterns in dull gold and pastel colors, geometric aluminum balcony and staircase railings, fluted and rounded marble-faced pilasters, and indirect lighting. Originally the north and south walls were paneled in Prima Vera, a rare wood, framed with marble trim. Even though the paneling has since been

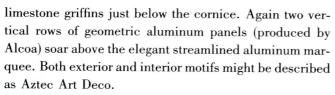

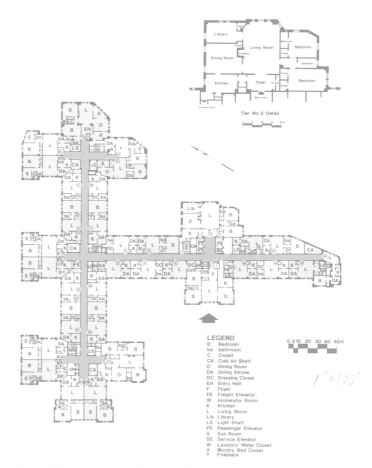

Typical floor plan of the Kennedy-Warren. The left rear wing was added by the B. F. Saul Company in 1935. The most important tiers in this building, according to size, are Nos. 1, 2, 14, and 27—all large four- or five-room units.

The painted Aztec beamed ceiling and the aluminum balustrades, shown in this 1933 photograph, were the principal Art Deco features in the Kennedy-Warren lobby.

removed, the lobby remains remarkably intact today. The adjacent elevator doors are decorated with geometric copper "trees" set into a field of black metal. The architect's original perspective drawing for the lobby shows the Moderne chairs and sofas as well as the group of torchères and pair of large ceramic vases. Within the lobby, on each side of the main entrance, which is crowned with a curved bay of imported cathedral glass windows, are spacious step-down parlors, originally used for bridge parties or private gatherings.

Architect Joseph Younger's original perspective of the Kennedy-Warren lobby.

The Kennedy-Warren is one of the few Washington apartment houses with a ballroom. It follows the building's Aztec Art Deco style.

The second important public space is the dining room, seating two hundred, just north of the lobby. Today its only surviving decorative elements are the Art Deco fluted round columns with curious Art Deco square capitals, set in the arches on the north side of the room. Long gone are the dining room's geometric silver and gold ceiling and the set of "picturesque Japanese mirrors" that covered the walls. Located below the dining room, the ballroom complements the lobby design with its fluted round columns, aluminum rails, Aztec mirrored and fluted piers, painted beamed ceiling, and Art Deco wall sconces.

Only 50 percent of the original design conceived by the owners and builders, Edgar S. Kennedy and Monroe Warren, Sr., and their architect, Joseph Younger, was completed at the time of their sudden bankruptcy in late 1931. Missing were the left rear (northeast) wing and the large south wing. Because of the Depression, it was not until 1935 that the left rear wing was completed (still referred to by Kennedy-Warren residents as the "new wing"). Most of the impressive principal public rooms,

however, including the main lobby, dining room, and ballroom, were completed. Had the original plans been realized, at the full cost of $3.2 million, the Kennedy-Warren would then have been the city's largest single apartment building under one roof, with 442 apartments and 50 hotel rooms and baths.

Located on the edge of Rock Creek Park, which drops away rather precipitously from Connecticut Avenue, the Kennedy-Warren is nine stories tall in front and fifteen in the rear. The original plans called for the building to be 478 feet wide and 325 feet deep. Because the Kennedy-Warren was built on a steep hill, it was possible to add six stories below the main lobby or street level. Below that level are the following floors in descending order: the second floor, which includes the entrance to the two-story ballroom, beauty shop, apartments, and storerooms; the first floor, with the lower half of the ballroom and apartments; and the B level, which includes twenty maids' rooms (long since closed), laundry, storerooms, garage space, and the loading dock. Continuing to descend, garage space is found on the 1B and 2B levels, while the boiler room, fans, and mechanical rooms are located on the lowest level, 3B. The garage includes space for 220 cars.

Most of the thirty-four tiers of apartments contain small units of one, two, and three rooms. Each efficiency unit originally had a Murphy bed that swung out into the living room from a dressing closet. Four tiers, however, Nos. 01, 02, 14, and 27, have handsomely designed large apartments of four and five rooms, each with its own entrance hall and three exposures. The apartments on the top three floors of these tiers all have working fireplaces. The monthly rents in 1931 ranged from $65 for efficiencies to $259 for the largest five-room apartments.

EARLY "AIR CONDITIONING"

One of the innovative features of the Kennedy-Warren was the use of five huge metal fans, "squirrel cage" design (each 8 feet wide), set in the sub-basement to pull the cool air from adjacent Rock Creek Park into the building. The fans are capable of moving 32 million cubic feet of cool air per hour. Because they are so effective, only three are used today. The air, ten degrees cooler than on Connecticut Avenue, circulates through airshafts into vents in the corridors of each floor. The air then passes through the apartments via the metal louvered panels over the door on each unit. This early "forced natural air" cooling system was soon copied in approximately a dozen other

The public dining room at the Kennedy-Warren is one of only six still in operation in Washington apartment houses.

Washington apartment houses between 1935 and 1941, before central air conditioning was introduced on a large scale in the late forties.

EXTENSIVE USE OF ALUMINUM

While the exterior aluminum spandrels for the Kennedy-Warren were designed and made by Alcoa in Pittsburgh, all of the interior aluminum work and the elaborate marquee were produced by A. F. Jorss Iron Works of Washington. In a number of places, burnished bronze was used in conjunction with the aluminum to produce a gold and silver effect. The marquee and the balustrades remain the finest Art Deco examples of any private building in Washington and are not surpassed by any other structure in the country. They are equal to the superb Art Deco aluminum detailing found in the famous Biltmore Hotel built in 1929 in Scottsdale, Arizona. Karl Jorss, now head of A. F. Jorss Iron Works, remembers that the original drawings sent to his father by architect Joseph Younger failed to include any design for the aluminum newel posts in 1930. A week after fabrication had begun on the aluminum work, the architect hit upon the design of the newel posts over breakfast. He directed A. F. Jorss to purchase the best-quality aluminum orange juice squeezer, prepare a mold, and cast elongated examples for mounting on the dining room and balcony staircases. They remain in place today. Aluminum foil, now missing, was originally used for the barrel arch ceilings in the two lobby corridors and in the ceiling niches and beams in the dining room.

NEW WING BUILT

With the bankruptcy of Edgar Kennedy and Monroe Warren, Sr., in 1931, ownership of the Kennedy-Warren was assumed by the B. F. Saul Company since it held the mortgage. This firm continues to own and manage the building as rental property. Although apartments were hard to rent in the early years of the Depression, the situation abruptly changed in 1934 with the increase in the size of the federal government. New Deal agencies

Apartment doors at the Kennedy-Warren still retain their original 1932 Art Deco knockers and peepholes.

brought thousands of new employees to Washington. The resulting housing shortage caused the B. F. Saul Company in 1935 to commission architect Alexander H. Sonnemann to complete the T-shaped left rear (northeast) wing after original plans of Joseph Younger. As a result 107 new apartments were added, increasing the current total to 317. It also marked the revival of major apartment house construction in Washington, which had ceased between 1932 and 1934. In Washington more than a dozen major apartment houses were auctioned when their owners declared bankruptcy in 1931–32, the worst years of the Depression.

The Kennedy-Warren always maintained a distinguished roster of residents, such as Harry Hopkins, close personal adviser to President Franklin D. Roosevelt. Congressman and Mrs. Lyndon B. Johnson lived here from May to August 1937 and during most of 1940. During World War II the Kennedy-Warren was the home of the wives of twenty-nine generals and admirals then stationed overseas.

UNBUILT SOUTH WING

From a twelve-page supplement relating exclusively to the opening of the Kennedy-Warren in the *Washington Post* of 30 September 1931, a great deal is known about the original design, construction history, and planned operation of this landmark apartment house. Even though the massive south wing was never built, the steel supports were constructed. They can still be seen extending 3 feet above the lawn, long since capped with concrete. Even though the garage below was completed in 1931, it has been sealed and never used. In one storeroom in a sub-basement are dozens of large cast-concrete decorative Art Deco panels that were intended for the cornice of the south wing. The south wing was planned to have a large "assembly room," 52 by 66 feet, for meetings and receptions, as well as an elevator extending to an elaborate roofdeck. Had the south wing been completed as planned, the Kennedy-Warren would have occupied only 51 percent of the site. At present it occupies only 35 percent of its land.

In 1987 the B. F. Saul Company located dozens of original, elegant pencil-on-tissue plans for the Kennedy-Warren in an abandoned storeroom. It would be a unique and noteworthy project if the current owners would consider completing this landmark according to its original design.

B. F. SAUL COMPANY

Perhaps even more interesting than the residents is the history of the Saul family, which has figured prominently in the nation's capital since John O'Hennesy Saul immigrated to Washington in 1851. Born in County Cork, Ireland, he was working as a nurseryman for the Earl of Shannon on the Isle of Wight off southern England when he was discovered by prominent U.S. landscape architect Andrew Jackson Downing on a tour of British gardens in 1850. Downing owned a nursery at Newburgh, New York, one of the country's largest, and had written several influential books on landscape architecture and architecture. Soon after Congress commissioned him to landscape the Mall in Washington, he met Saul and hired him to supervise the work. After Downing's tragic death in a steamboat accident on the Hudson River in 1852, Saul completed much of Downing's design of the Mall as a romantic English park, with winding asymmetrical carriage drives and groves of evergreen trees. He remained

Many Kennedy-Warren kitchens remain in original condition with a pair of china cabinets dividing the kitchen from the dining alcove.

in Washington, where he started two nurseries—one in Petworth and the second on 16th Street, N.W., on the present site of Walter Reed Hospital. Saul served for many years as chairman of the "Parking Commission" of the District of Columbia, which was responsible for planning and maintaining the city's parks as well as planting thousands of trees along city streets.

His son, Benjamin Francis Saul, established the family's real estate business by developing the nursery site on upper 16th Street, N.W., as an early Washington suburb in the 1890s. He cut streets through the nursery, naming them for flowers, and sold off the land as building lots. Saul's further success as a mortgage broker resulted in his establishment of the Home Savings Bank, which was absorbed into the American Security Bank in 1916. B. F. Saul was a member of the board of directors of many Washington businesses, served on the executive council of the American Bankers Association, and was president of the D.C. Bankers Association and director of the Washington Board of Trade. One of his seven children was Rose Saul Zalles, a long-term resident of the Kennedy-Warren until her death in 1987. Following the death of B. F. Saul in 1931, the B. F. Saul Company, established in 1892 for mortgage loans and property management, was headed by his son, Andrew Saul. His grandson, B. Francis Saul II, now directs the firm.

89

SEDGWICK GARDENS

3726 Connecticut Avenue, N.W.; southwest corner of Connecticut Avenue and Sedgwick Street

ARCHITECT: Mihran Mesrobian, 1931

ORIGINAL APARTMENTS: 120 (29 efficiencies; 76 one-bedrooms; 15 two-bedrooms)

STATUS: opened as rental in 1932

The success of the eclectic and exuberantly designed Sedgwick Gardens facade is due partly to its plan, a double U with the apex as the corner entrance. Within this apex area is the handsome Art Deco porte-cochère, while beyond is a wonderfully eclectic Moorish-inspired octagonal lobby. Standing before the entrance, the eye of the viewer is carried backward and upward by a pair of high-relief female figures above the entrance, a pair of carved low-relief male figures, and the rose window on the massive square elevator tower in the background. Interest is increased by use of white-brick bands in the red-brick facade under the corner wings, by the white-brick beltcourses at the base and top, and by a peculiar cornice treatment that is interrupted by triangular projecting sculptured panels and niches holding wrought-iron Deco railings.

The main facade of Sedgwick Gardens incorporates Art Deco and Moorish elements in its eclectic design.

Sedgwick Gardens has one of the most important Art Deco lobbies in Washington.

Photographed about 1935, this view shows the original garden and playground behind Sedgwick Gardens.

Popular in Washington apartment houses during the 1920s and 1930s, Murphy beds closed into either closets or dressing rooms of efficiency apartments. This example at Sedgwick Gardens swings out of a closet with double doors in an efficiency unit occupied by Violet Faulkner, a longtime resident.

The two dozen projecting bays that encircle the building provide additional light and air for most of the apartments. Many of the enclosed porches are set into these projecting bays; others are on the corners. The myriad sculptured panels, many executed in zigzag patterns, relate to Byzantine, medieval, and Islamic elements.

Max Gorin of the Southern Construction Company built Sedgwick Gardens for $500,000. The interior of the building includes such fine materials as solid mahogany doors, solid brass hardware, and abundant limestone and marble in the spectacular octagonal lobby. It has intriguing angles and spaces formed by the two dozen Moorish-style arches and columns, the six-sided skylight, and the octagonal fountain (now used as a planter). A short staircase in the center rear of the lobby leads up half a story to the first floor. In the style of the 1930s, dinettes replace large formal dining rooms in the 120 apartments. All

Typical floor plan of Sedgwick Gardens.

efficiencies and many of the one-bedrooms originally contained Murphy beds (see photographs); only a few have survived.

Amenities include a sixteen-car basement garage with additional outdoor spaces in the rear, a playground on the side, adjacent parkland to the rear, and a sprinkler system on the roof for cooling top-floor apartments in summer. Increased labor costs have not been offset by greater revenue, due to the current rent control law; therefore, the building no longer has the doorman, valet parking attendant, switchboard operators, or twenty-four-hour porters of its early days. Still a rental building, Sedgwick Gardens has an interesting mix of young professionals and old-timers.

LIFE AT SEDGWICK GARDENS

One of the original residents, Judy Catlin, who came to the building as a child of seven, vividly remembers life there during the 1940s:

World War II brought change to Sedgwick Gardens as it did to all of America. The Victory Gardens behind the building were begun, and a basement storeroom was cleared to make an air raid shelter. Tenants donated carpets, furniture, and canned goods to fix up the shelter, and first aid was taught to everyone by a Red Cross nurse. My mother learned to deliver a baby and splint a leg, while my father donned the helmet and armband of an air raid warden. We kids went from door to door collecting scrap metal and rubber in the form of old silverware, flattened tin cans, galoshes, and balls of foil rolled by candy and cigarette wrappers.

Soon after the war we received our first self-service elevator (a thrilling machine which I promptly jammed between floors while showing off to a friend). This was but the first of many changes which came to Sedgwick Gardens in the years to follow, and it is a vastly different apartment house today. But though the "Queen" may be a bit faded now, much of the old charm survives in its lobby, exterior, and original furnishings. It is still home to many of the early tenants as well as to an excitingly diverse group of newer residents. And for most of us, who seem in no hurry to move on, it is still a great place to live.

90. ARGONNE, now the
PARK PLAZA
1629 Columbia Road, N.W.
ARCHITECT: Stern and Tomlinson, 1922
STATUS: opened as rental in 1923

91. JEFFERSON, now the
JEFFERSON HOTEL
1200 16th Street, N.W.
ARCHITECT: Jules H. de Sibour, 1922
STATUS: opened as rental in 1923;
converted to hotel in 1955

92. BELVEDERE

1301 Massachusetts Avenue, N.W.
ARCHITECT: B. Stanley Simmons, 1923
STATUS: opened as rental in 1924

93. 1705 LANIER PLACE, N.W.

ARCHITECT: James E. Cooper, 1923
STATUS: opened as co-op in 1923

94. EMBASSY

1613 Harvard Street, N.W.
ARCHITECT: B. Stanley Simmons, 1924
STATUS: opened as rental in 1925

96. DUPONT CIRCLE

1332–1366 Connecticut Avenue, N.W.

ARCHITECT: Mirhan Mesrobian, 1926 and 1931 addition

STATUS: opened as rental in 1932; converted to offices in 1942

95. 1700 CONNECTICUT AVENUE, N.W.

ARCHITECT: George N. Ray, 1925

STATUS: opened as rental in 1925; converted to offices in 1978

97. HILLTOP MANOR, now the CAVALIER

3500 14th Street, N.W.

ARCHITECT: Harvey H. Warwick, Sr., 1926

STATUS: opened as rental in 1927

98. **3901 CONNECTICUT AVENUE, N.W.**
ARCHITECT: George T. Santmyers, 1927
STATUS: opened as rental in 1928

99. **PARK TOWER**
2440 16th Street, N.W.
ARCHITECT: William Harris, 1928
STATUS: opened as rental in 1929

4

TIGHTENING THE BELT, 1932–1945

INTRODUCTION

100.

COLONIAL VILLAGE, 1913 Wilson Boulevard, Arlington, Virginia

101.

LANGSTON TERRACE, 2101 G Street, N.E.

102.

2929 CONNECTICUT AVENUE, N.W.

103.

MAJESTIC, 3200 16th Street, N.W.

104.

GOVERNOR SHEPHERD, 2121 Virginia Avenue, N.W.

105.

GWENWOOD, 1020 19th Street, N.W.

106.

MARLYN, 3901 Cathedral Avenue, N.W.

107.

CRYSTAL HEIGHTS, northeast corner of Connecticut and Florida avenues, N.W.

108.

GENERAL SCOTT, 1 Scott Circle, N.W.

109.

CARLYN, now GATEWAY GEORGETOWN, 2500 Que Street, N.W.

110.

DELANO, 2745 29th Street, N.W.

111.

DORCHESTER HOUSE, 2480 16th Street, N.W.

112.

McLEAN GARDENS, 3811 Porter Street, N.W.

113.

PARKFAIRFAX, 3360 Gunston Road, Alexandria, Virginia

NOTABLE ADDITIONS

The building boom that followed World War I continued throughout the 1920s, terminating finally in 1931. The last of the city's luxury apartment houses—Sedgwick Gardens, the Westchester, and the Kennedy-Warren—were built that year. Financial arrangements and plans for these buildings had all been made in 1929 before the stock market crash. Economic conditions deteriorated so rapidly in 1931, however, that only half of the Westchester and the Kennedy-Warren were completed, and all construction of luxury apartment houses was halted for the next three years.

EFFECTS OF GOVERNMENT EXPANSION

By 1935 President Franklin D. Roosevelt's efforts to curtail the Depression had a marked effect on improving Washington's economy. The city experienced a housing shortage as the population swelled with the continuing arrival of thousands of new federal workers. In the apartment building industry, this change was heralded by the construction of two massive new garden apartments, Langston Terrace and Colonial Village, and the addition of a large rear wing to the Kennedy-Warren. Private construction amounted to $21 million in 1935, an increase of 140 percent over 1934 and 300 percent over 1933, the lowest year in twenty-five for Washington's building industry.

While new apartment house construction remained depressed in most American cities (no new luxury apartment houses were built in Chicago until after World War II), Washington and New York were leading the country in new apartment houses from 1935 to 1941. Rents increased in Washington by 25 percent in 1935, but apartment houses stayed fully occupied. Both housing and office space were hard to find. An article in the [Washington] *Evening Star* of 28 December 1935, entitled "D.C. Building Activities Show Boom-Like Gains," suggests several reasons:

> Increased rentals for both apartment units and houses, coming in wake of the largest federal payrolls since the World War, were the primary reason for the great revival of home building [in 1935] in the Capital. Thousands of

new employees of New Deal agencies rapidly took up the slack in residential space, causing rentals to increase 25 percent and more. Hundreds of families that had been renters found they could purchase small homes on favorable long-term financing plans where monthly payments could be less than or the same as rental and consequently entered the market. Government agencies obtained large blocks of space in a hundred downtown office buildings. A hotel, the Arlington, two large apartments and numerous residences, a number of them Washington landmarks, were converted into offices when no more normal commercial space could be obtained.

The two factors of rising rents and the availability of long-term, low-interest mortgages on new houses caused hundreds of families to move from the city to the Virginia and Maryland suburbs. While most of Washington's pre–World War I housing consisted of either apartment houses or rowhouses, these new suburbs of the 1930s and afterwards offered detached houses with garages and grassy lawns. Arlington County, Virginia, and Montgomery County, Maryland, witnessed the greatest construction activity in their history, exceeding even the building boom years that Washington had enjoyed in 1925–26. Alexandria, likewise, had new buildings and modernization—"restoration"—of numerous early houses, many of which had been unoccupied for years.

Beginning in 1935, more new homes were built in the Washington suburbs than in the city proper, a pattern that has continued. The federal government started the trend by constantly expanding its New Deal agencies and staffs beginning in 1934. To provide space the government then established a peacetime policy of leasing privately owned office buildings. Even though private developers built a number of new office buildings during the late 1930s, the situation was not markedly improved. Many of Washington's great houses were leased by the government for office purposes, including the McLean House on the south side of McPherson Square and the Walsh House at Massachusetts Avenue and 21st Street, N.W. The government also leased such apartment houses as the Rochambeau and converted them to offices, and in 1935 bought the Potomac Park, 21st and C streets, N.W., for the Public Works Administration. The prominent residents, given a thirty-day notice to vacate, complained bitterly that they had no recourse but to move. One of the tenants most vocal in opposition was Arthur Godfrey, who conducted his morning radio broadcast from Washington.

POPULARITY OF GARDEN APARTMENTS

The most prolific period in the development of garden apartments occurred between 1935 and 1945. During the Depression and war years, garden apartments were considered a practical alternative for the middle class. Although the term itself did not come into general use until the late–1920s, the history of garden apartments in Washington actually began in 1914, when the [Washington] *Evening Star* published an interview with Richard B. Watrous, secretary of the American Civic Association. Just back from a study of the "garden city" movement in England, he had viewed a dozen new model towns on the outskirts of such industrial urban centers as London, Liverpool, and Birmingham. The low density, parklike setting, and clean air in these places provided greatly improved, inexpensive living for workers. The concept impressed Watrous as an idea he might bring back across the Atlantic.

He felt that Washington was the ideal American locale for the first "garden city" in the United States. Because of the relatively low—if constant—incomes of government employees, Washington's high cost of living, and the traditional preference for rowhouses, most residents could not afford detached houses in town. The lower priced homes in the garden city would thus be ideal for Washington clerks, the middle and most numerous level of federal workers. Although the garden city would not come to Washington until the mid–1930s with the construction of Greenbelt in the Maryland suburbs, another important, and related, housing development occurred. The garden apartment arrived in the 1920s when the first three were built—Webster Gardens, the Cleveland Park, and Hampshire Gardens. Each was consecutively more sophisticated in design, but further development of the garden apartment in Washington was aborted by the early years of the Great Depression.

The construction of the massive Colonial Village

Architect Francis L. Koenig, above, with Harvey H. Warwick, Sr., designed Colonial Village and the Marlyn. In the early 1940s Koenig also designed the Carlyn and the Dorchester House.

complex in Arlington, Virginia, beginning in 1935 marked the arrival of garden apartment popularity in Washington in a big way. Rented at low rates, Colonial Village used less than 20 percent of the 40-acre site for buildings. The generous landscaping and siting of these buildings provided abundant parkland for children, plenty of fresh air, and open space. Though adjacent to busy Wilson Boulevard, within the development there was ample parking and no traffic congestion.

Colonial Village was the first of many garden apartment complexes to receive financial backing from the Federal Housing Administration, the New Deal agency established to promote inexpensive housing for the average worker. The enormous local and national publicity given to Colonial Village during the mid–1930s made it a model for dozens of other similar developments across the nation during the following decade. It was a direct influence, for example, on the design and construction of the massive Falkland garden apartments in 1936 in suburban Silver Spring—still Maryland's best landscaped and most innovative garden apartment complex.

While Colonial Village and the Falkland were still under construction, the federal government was building Washington's first "garden city," Greenbelt, Maryland. Here a number of garden apartments were set within clusters of rowhouses, and the model community center included a school, library, theater, and shops—all carefully landscaped and placed in logical relationship to one another.

Because garden apartments required much more space than the intown luxury apartment house, most were built in the Virginia and Maryland suburbs where vacant land was much cheaper and more readily available. Notable examples in the Virginia suburbs during this period include Colonial Village, Buckingham, Arlington Village, Shirlington, Parkfairfax, and Fairlington. Others built within the city before and during the war include Langston Terrace, Brentwood Village, Fairfax Village, Belleview, Naylor Gardens, and McLean Gardens. The last two were built by the federal government in 1942–43 to house civilian war workers.

EFFECT OF WORLD WAR II ON HOUSING

Even with the construction of these dozens upon dozens of garden apartment complexes during the late 1930s and early 1940s, the Washington area continued to have a housing shortage. The situation was not helped by the leasing of apartment houses for office space by the government, a practice that was not without precedent. During World War I the federal government had rented several—one apartment house, for example, at 15th and M streets, N.W., was used in 1917–18 for the newly created Aero Corps of the War Department. Available housing became even more scarce in 1940 as the government began to prepare for war and took even more apartment houses for conversion to offices. The Lend-Lease Act of 1941 brought hundreds of Allied military and civilian officers to Washington to coordinate the sale of American arms. Because virtually all possible office space was already in use, the government declared an emergency and began to seize apartment houses by eminent domain, forcing the owners to lease them for defense purposes.

One of the first apartment houses to go was the city's finest, the McCormick, which was taken in 1940 over the outraged protests of its wealthy occupants. Within a month it was occupied by the staff of the British Purchasing

The staff of the architectural firm of Berla and Abel is shown in its Connecticut Avenue office in 1948. Left to right, seated, are George Agron, Julian Berla, Joseph Abel, Nick Satterlee, and standing, Mayhew Seiss and Jessie Weinstein.

Commission. Shortly afterwards this agency as well as the British Admiralty Commission were provided with at least four other apartment houses adjacent to one another: the Kedrick at 1801 K Street, N.W.; the John Marshall at 1910 K Street, N.W.; the Bradford at 1800 K Street, N.W.; and the Vancouver at 1825 K Street, N.W. When even more space was needed, the government began to take hotels for office use, including the Grafton, the Prince Karl, and part of the Willard. By 1942 more than thirty-four hundred British were working in these former residences, and other foreign governments used other seized apartment houses. The Soviet Purchasing Commission occupied six, including the Yorkshire at 3355 16th Street, N.W., and another at 1610 Park Road, N.W.

The government sometimes seized new apartment houses just being completed, such as Rock Creek Gardens at 2501 Que Street, N.W. By October 1941 the federal government had acquired more than two dozen apartment houses with more than two thousand units, displacing seven thousand residents. Some of these buildings were torn down to make way for offices. In 1940 the Boulevard in Foggy Bottom was razed for the new building of the War Department, which two years later moved again into the much larger Pentagon in Arlington. The seizure of apartment houses continued throughout the war, including three taken in 1944 in the 2600 block of 13th Street, N.W., to provide housing for civilian war workers. Other buildings served as barracks for WAVES and other American military personnel.

By 1942 civilians in apartment houses began to organize tenants associations to oppose government takeovers. The Federation of Citizens Associations blocked the seizure of an apartment house at 1809 G Street, N.W., as did the tenants of the Chastleton in 1942–43. The most dramatic fight involved the government's seizure of the Dupont Circle apartment-hotel at 1346 Connecticut Avenue, N.W., in 1941. A number of the six hundred tenants of this twelve-story building sued the owners for agreeing to lease the building to the government. At the fair market rent, it was a good deal for the owners. A prominent resident there, journalist George E. Reedy, Sr., represented his fellow tenants at a congressional hearing on the takeover. The case continued to make newspaper headlines during the summer and fall of 1941. In one emotional scene, Congressman Newt Hill of Louisiana struck Reedy, a World War I veteran with an artificial leg, while he was testifying. The tenants lost their case and finally vacated, except for one seventy-year-old holdout, Mrs. Valta Parma. She remained in her top-floor apartment while her six-year legal battle continued, leaving only when her original lease terminated in 1948.

Most of the government-occupied apartment houses in Washington were not returned to private use until late 1946 or 1947 because of delays in demobilization of various wartime agencies. A number of the buildings, such as the Dupont Circle and the McCormick, never again became residential.

INSTITUTION OF RENT CONTROL

Constantly rising rents for both apartments and houses in Washington prompted a congressional hearing in July 1941. The federal price administrator testified that Washington rents were the highest in any American city—consuming about 35 percent of the average tenant's income compared with the national average for other large cities of 20 percent. The average Washington government worker earned $150 monthly, of which $52 went for rent. Rent control advocates maintained that controls were particularly necessary in Washington, where the largest number of workers on fixed incomes resided.

The price administrator stated that federal workers in Washington were the "hardest hit by the rising cost of living." As a result of the 1941 hearings, most congressmen determined that rent control was necessary to prevent the 15- to 20-percent surge in housing costs that occurred during World War I. Congress was slow in acting at that time and did not impose rent control until May 1918, late in the war. The World War I law was not completely effective, however, as it did not apply to houses, new construction, or apartments that became vacant. It was amended in October 1919 to control the rent of new apartment houses. Rates were then set, allowing a 6- to 10-percent profit for landlords, who constantly questioned the rent control commission's evaluation of property and brought long-running law suits. The controls remained in effect, however, until 1926 when Congress ended them over the objections of President Coolidge; rents then skyrocketed.

Not long after the July 1941 hearings, a bill introduced by Congressman Jennings Randolph was passed and took effect on 1 January 1942. Rents for all houses, hotel rooms, boarding house rooms, and apartments were frozen at their 1 January 1941 level—and were enforced. As a result, more than a thousand apartment tenants petitioned for rent decreases, and 75 percent were successful. After the end of World War II Congress continued to extend rent control in Washington on a yearly basis, despite local landlords' fruitless petitions to end the controls. Beginning in 1946, however, landlords could receive permission to raise rents by showing that their taxes and operating costs had increased. It was not until the end of the Korean War in 1953 that rent control was lifted in the city.

WARTIME SCARCITY OF APARTMENTS

Rental apartments became so scarce that many dubious tactics were used to obtain them. During the war apartment hunters voluntarily offered a year's rent in advance. A number of advertisers in local newspapers in 1942 offered to rent two-bedroom apartments in first-class buildings for $7,500, double the previous year's normal rent. Other would-be renters offered a commission to anyone who could find them an apartment. Some relied on the sympathy of the public, as "four young career women plead with some kind soul to rent them furnished apartment; we prefer Dupont Circle vic. so we can walk to work as we need the exercise." One couple quickly rented a small Georgetown house in 1942 when a friend rewrote their advertisement from "Couple with two children want unfurnished house N.W. section" to "Cultured, conservative family desires residence in refined, exclusive neighborhood. Exchange references." At the Kennedy-Warren the manager reported a waiting list of five thousand people in May 1943!

Even though private construction in Washington and its suburbs continued to escalate each year between 1935 and 1941, the supply failed to meet the demand. The new construction was due to the enormous increase in federal civilian employment in Washington, first caused by the new agencies to relieve the Depression and then by the defense buildup. Federal jobs swelled by fifty-one thousand in the second half of 1940 and by eighty-seven thousand in 1941. In 1941 alone private residential construction broke all previous yearly records with a total value of $102 million (providing a hundred thousand new residences—60 percent apartments and 40 percent houses).

WARTIME APARTMENT CONSTRUCTION

By late 1941 Congress had restricted building materials for defense purposes, but insurance companies were encouraged to build modest rental apartment house complexes for war workers in Washington. Two of the most significant were large garden apartment developments built in 1942 by the Metropolitan Life Insurance Company— Parkfairfax and Fairlington. Although most garden apartments were erected in the suburbs, a number were also built in the city, such as the Jonathan Woodner Apartments, erected for blacks in 1944 in Northeast Washington, and the 720-unit Naylor Gardens in Southeast Washington. Private developers also built a number of apartment-hotels for war workers, including the Meridian Hotel at 16th and Euclid streets, N.W., in 1942.

Permission to construct several peculiar, experimental apartment houses was granted during the war. A circular building on R Street, N.W., just east of Florida Avenue, was designed in 1944 by W. Wadsworth Wood, architect and editor of *Small Homes Guides*. Designed for naval officers, it was constructed of brick, steel, and concrete. A winding stairway led from the side entrance through the three floors to the roof. Each floor had a circular hall around the stairway. Wedge-shaped bedrooms opened from this hall. Each room had a connecting bathroom with shower. The basement contained a large open recreation room with a communal kitchen.

The war affected life in Washington apartment houses in many ways. Most had their own air-raid wardens, who made sure each apartment had blackout curtains for nighttime drills. Resident managers also helped with the Salvage for Victory campaigns in which critical materials— metal, rubber, and rags—were collected. One serious problem was the shortage of elevator operators caused by the draft. Women were substituted, but some large buildings operated only half of their elevators because many women preferred better-paying government jobs.

Architects Alvin L. Aubinoe, Sr., shown here, and Harry L. Edwards designed both the Majestic and the Hightowers for developer Morris Cafritz.

INTRODUCTION OF MODERNISM

The style of apartment houses changed markedly from the 1920s to the 1930s. The many eclectic styles, including the geometric phase of Art Deco, of the 1920s and early 1930s gave way for the new streamlined phase of Art Deco, as well as the early International Style, in the mid- and late 1930s. The geometric or early phase of Art Deco design was usually expressed in incised overdoor or window panels filled with geometric forms; this is found at Harvard Hall and the Kennedy-Warren. The lobbies feature carved geometric reliefs, like those at the Woodley Park Towers. Even though the geometric Art Deco phase was centered in the decade 1925–35, it lingered for several years with pyramid cornices such as those on the Hightowers and the Gwenwood.

The streamlined or second phase of Art Deco extended from around 1935 to 1945. Called Moderne, it was characterized by simple bold curved walls, glass blocks in the lobbies, and an absence of facade detailing. One of the best is the Majestic. Closely related to streamlined Art Deco was the early International Style, which is reflected in numerous apartments built in the 1935–38 period: Langston Terrace; Greenbelt, Maryland; 2929 Connecticut Avenue; the Governor Shepherd; and 2407 15th Street, N.W.

Often streamlined Art Deco was incorporated into the design of many of these early International Style buildings, such as the lobbies in the last three examples. It was not until immediately after World War II that Washington apartment houses were built in the pure International Style, with a complete absence of ornament and streamlined Art Deco influence. Good versions of this are the Woodner, the Greenbriar, and Potomac Plaza. Indeed, even today the appropriate terminology for such work of the late 1930s and 1940s is debatable. In Washington apartment houses the various modern phases were always mixed during this period, with several examples even incorporating all three—geometric Art Deco, streamlined Art Deco, and early International Style. Even though the Moderne was employed in the design of some garden apartment complexes, most built in Washington between 1935 and 1945 were the safer Colonial Revival, including Colonial Village, the Falkland, Parkfairfax,

Architect Hilyard R. Robinson with his associate architect, Paul Williams, survey the plans for Langston Terrace, the city's first Art Deco garden apartment house complex, in 1936.

Fairlington, McLean Gardens, and Fairfax Village.

Perhaps the most successful builder of streamlined Art Deco apartment houses was Morris Cafritz. In a number of his buildings, such as the Gwenwood, the Hightowers, and the Majestic, Art Deco detailing was focused on the double entrance doors with their large round window, framed by glass blocks and aluminum. One of the most successful streamlined Art Deco marquees was designed for the entrance to 4801 Connecticut Avenue, N.W., by architect David Stern. The same style is featured in the handsome round lobby vestibule, with its glass block walls and terrazzo floor laid in a sunburst pattern. Many of the streamlined Art Deco apartment houses had step-down lobbies with recessed lighting. Examples are the General Scott, the Delano, the Normandie, and the Empire—buildings that are still well preserved. Another streamlined Art Deco feature was the placement of the lobby between two floors, with stairs leading up and down to the two levels, as in both the Marlyn and the Carlyn.

A major proponent of the International Style during the 1930s and afterwards was Washington architect Joseph Abel. Early forerunners were his 2929 Connecticut Avenue, as well as his Governor Shepherd, which both included Art Deco elements. His other pre–World War II apartment houses, more purely International Style—with their ribbon windows, unadorned facades, and glass block detailing around their entrances—include 2407 15th Street, N.W.; the Washington House, at 2020 16th Street, N.W.; and 2100 Connecticut Avenue.

Often the plain facades of Washington's many Art Deco apartment houses belie their elaborate lobbies, such as this striking circular glass-block lobby vestibule at 4801 Connecticut Avenue.

During the Depression and war years, the interiors of new apartments included little decoration, reflecting the practicality of the times. A traditional Washington embellishment since the Victorian period—the decorative, nonfunctioning fireplace mantel in the living room—at last disappeared in the mid–1930s. The rooms became even smaller than during the 1920s. The dining room and the breakfast nook disappeared in favor of a dining alcove opening directly onto the living room. Many apartment houses during the late 1930s were designed with only small units—mostly efficiencies with some one-bedrooms, such as the Gwenwood and the General Scott.

Another feature typical of this period was the solarium, in which a drawbridge-like Murphy bed was often housed. The Murphy bed of the 1930s, when up and not in use, was stored in the dressing room between the living room and bathroom. Rather than being pulled directly out of the wall, it was swung around first on a metal pivot into the living room, where it was dropped to its horizontal position.

TECHNOLOGICAL IMPROVEMENTS

Perhaps the most important of the many new technological improvements introduced in Washington apartment houses during the 1930s was air conditioning. Attempts to cool apartment houses in Washington actually began in the late 1920s when several apartment houses on Connecticut Avenue had water sprinkler systems installed on their roofs to keep the top-floor apartments cool. The first cool air system was designed by the developers of the Kennedy-Warren in 1931. It incorporated five giant fans at the sub-basement level, blowing cool air from the ground level up through iron grilles into the public corridors of the various floors. The apartments were equipped with a louvered panel above the door to allow a free passage of air into each apartment in the summer months. From 1935 until 1940 at least a dozen other Washington apartment houses copied this system, including the Governor Shepherd, the Normandie, and the Delano. Large fans on the Delano roof pulled air into the building. Two apartment houses from this era, the Kennedy-Warren and 2001 Connecticut Avenue, were still using the original fans to blow natural air through their public corridors in 1988. They are still quite effective!

The second air-cooling system was central air conditioning involving chilled air. It had been used in Washington from May 1933 in several bedrooms in the White House and since 1936 at both the United States Capitol and the Trans-Lux and other movie theaters. A revolutionary change occurred in 1938 when it was introduced into the Marlyn—the first apartment house in the United States with *central* air conditioning. Its success caused at least six new apartment houses in the city to copy it before World War II, including the Carlyn, the General Scott, and the Dorchester House.

During most of the Depression and World War II years, Washington enjoyed a building boom in apartment houses unequaled in any other American city. The city's population swelled from 500,000 in 1930 to 950,000 at the end of World War II. It was a period of innovation and change—garden apartments, automatic elevators and air conditioning, and a pared-down modern architecture came into general acceptance. Most of the best apartment houses from this era remain well preserved.

100

COLONIAL VILLAGE

1913 Wilson Boulevard, Arlington, Virginia (resident manager's office); originally 24 freestanding clusters of buildings bounded by Wilson Boulevard, Queens Lane, Veitch Street, and Lee Highway

ARCHITECT: Harvey H. Warwick, Sr., 1935–37; Francis L. Koenig, 1940

ORIGINAL APARTMENTS: 1,059 (approximately 10 percent efficiencies; 60 percent one-bedrooms; 20 percent two-bedrooms; 10 percent three-bedrooms)

STATUS: opened as rental in 1935–40; one-tenth demolished; remaining: rental, 50 percent; condominiums, 25 percent; co-ops, 12½ percent; public housing, 12½ percent

One of the many varying designs of the Colonial Revival buildings that form the garden apartment complex of Colonial Village.

Although unable to finish his first major apartment house, the elegant Westchester, because of the adverse early economic effects of the Great Depression, developer Gustave Ring (1904–1983) managed to avoid bankruptcy by frugal and careful management when the building did open in 1931. Ring's next major real estate project, Colonial Village, 1935–40, was an outstanding success that established him as a nationally prominent real estate developer. Because of its excellence of design and construction, Colonial Village became a prototype for dozens of other large garden apartment complexes in other states.

A shrewd businessman, Ring was among the first local developers who survived the lean Depression years and sensed a rapidly forthcoming change in housing. His 1934 plans to build the area's largest garden complex, Colonial Village, met with immediate success because of the acute housing shortage in the mid–1930s. After Franklin D. Roosevelt became president in 1933, thousands of additional civil servants came to Washington to administer the burgeoning New Deal agencies. As a result, the apartment vacancy rate dropped from 12.5 percent in mid-1933 to 0.5 percent in late 1934. The success of Colonial Village spurred dozens of similar developments, mostly in the suburbs where land was cheap and available. Construction increased 1,000 percent in Ar-

Living room and dining room of a duplex apartment at Colonial Village.

Site plan of Colonial Village.

lington County, Virginia, between 1933 and 1934, and 300 percent in Montgomery County, Maryland.

[Ring was familiar with three of the country's pioneering garden housing complexes—Sunnyside Garden Apartments in Queens, New York (1924–28); Radburn, New Jersey (1929); and Chatham Village, Pittsburgh (1932)—all the work of town planners Clarence S. Stein and Henry Wright. At Sunnyside Gardens, Stein and Wright introduced the concept of superblocks—large, plainly designed brick apartment houses facing a common green. Because of the existing gridiron streetplan, however, each superblock unfortunately bore little relationship to its neighbor. Radburn, even though never completed because of the Depression, was more successful than Sunnyside Gardens. Less rigid in plan, Radburn was designed as a garden community complete with commercial, residential, and recreational facilities. Detached houses were placed within superblock developments both in loose rows and along cul-de-sacs. The superblocks were united by a greenbelt that completely separated pedestrian and vehicular traffic. By contrast, Chatham Village was surrounded on three sides by greenbelts that followed the sloping contours of the land. The houses fronted on an interior grass mall and were arranged in parallel rows set back slightly.]

Ring found a fairly inexpensive undeveloped 46-acre tract of land adjacent to the Arlington County Court House in Clarendon, conveniently near Rosslyn Circle and the Key Bridge leading into Georgetown. A Colonial Village resident could then drive to the Capitol in only fifteen minutes. The site had first been used by members of the Metropolitan Club of Washington in 1894 when they converted a 165-acre farm into the Washington Golf and Country Club with a nine-hole golf course. The club required its playing members to wear knickers and scarlet coats with green lapels. Golf became so popular that the club sold this property in 1908 and built an eighteen-hole course on a larger tract farther out North Glebe Road.

Not only was Colonial Village conveniently close to the city, but its design was an improvement on all previous garden housing projects. Ring always worked closely with his architects, Harvey H. Warwick, Sr., and Francis L. Koenig. The apartment buildings were built in clusters and grouped about spacious courts, some courtyards being almost enclosed and others open but set back from the street. Each court was designed as a park within a park and differed one from another through various patterns of walkways, landscaping, and the subtle variety of building detailing.

Colonial Village was well publicized in more than two dozen national architectural, urban planning, and banking journals, not only for its excellent design but also for its innovative financing. Its construction was made possible by the first issue of an apartment house insurance loan from the newly created Federal Housing Administration (FHA). Acting cautiously and remembering the failure of Hampshire Gardens, Washington's first true garden apartment house, Ring decided to build Colonial Village in four stages. Events moved rapidly. In February

The careful siting of Colonial Village includes the many sidewalks that connect dozens of apartment buildings. Some pass through basements.

1935 the FHA approved mortgage insurance, lent by New York Life Insurance Company, for the first phase at 4.5 percent interest. Construction began two months later on 20 April 1935.

Between 1935 and 1940, Ring built twenty-four free-standing clusters of buildings in the garden apartment complex, in four phases, with a total of 1,059 apartments. During phase one, April to December 1935, 276 units were built on 25 acres of land flanking North Rhodes Street. Phase two, December 1935 to November 1936, produced 462 units along Key Boulevard and west of phase one to North Uhle Street, while in phase three, February to July 1937, 236 units were completed west of North Uhle Street. Within the first phase was Queens Lane, the only nonvehicular accessible street in Arlington. Architect Harvey H. Warwick, Sr., designed all of these plans. The remaining land was used for the last phase designed by Francis L. Koenig and offered 12 apartment houses with 85 units built in the summer of 1940. The two- and three-story apartment buildings cost a total of slightly more than $4 million to build.

Colonial Village had 18 basements, 9 laundries, 130 garage spaces, 720 onstreet parking spaces (Ring retained ownership of some of the streets to deter public use), 24 heating plants, and a community center with a lounge, social hall, and kitchen. Designed in the Colonial Revival style, which became the prototype for almost all other Washington area garden apartments during the 1930s and 1940s, the buildings have a variety of alternating roof lines, door designs, and wing treatments. Abundant light and air were ensured, since every apartment had two or three exposures. Materials and construction quality were outstanding. Slate was used to roof the gabled buildings. Soundproof floors had 6 inches of concrete overlaid with hardwood.

UNUSUAL AMENITIES

Ring built a shopping center adjacent to Colonial Village on Wilson Boulevard in April 1936—eight stores, with two groceries, bakery, laundry, hardware store, drugstore, beauty parlor, and barbershop. He also designed playgrounds away from the street, since most of the units were for families with one or two children. Lawns were abundant. With more than four-fifths of the acreage unspoiled, the two streams that ran through the hilly tract were retained, as were the existing trees and terrain. Garbage collection points were carefully screened by enclosed brick walls, and rules relating to common areas were strictly enforced. Clotheslines, for instance, were allowed behind the apartment houses, but all clothes had to be removed by a certain hour. The nine basement laundry rooms also provided additional clotheslines in bad weather.

Another rule allowed only one child in a one-bedroom apartment. If two children were discovered, the family was forced to move. Surprise inspections were made regularly. In a walk-through of the grounds in 1982, the surviving architect, Francis L. Koenig, explained that steam on the bathroom window was a sure sign of a baby since the parents were secretly washing diapers in the apartment. Most residents welcomed the rules because they provided a well-maintained and orderly environment.

The detailing used by the two architects was subtly different. Warwick, for instance, extended his brick quoins through the cornice to the roofline, while Koenig stopped

his quoins at the cornice. Koenig's buildings often featured wooden Chinese Chippendale fretwork railings between the pairs of decorative chimneys at the ends of the gables.

A NATIONAL PROTOTYPE

The ideal living conditions of Colonial Village and its modest monthly rents during the 1930s ($36.50 for an efficiency, $50 for a one-bedroom, and $62.50 for a two-bedroom) insured success. In fact, Colonial Village's popularity exceeded the most optimistic hopes of the developer, the insurance company that lent the construction funds, and the FHA. The New York Life Insurance Company originally backed Colonial Village with some trepidation in early 1935 and later that year rejected a similar request from the Blair family for mortgage money for the Falkland Apartments in Silver Spring, Maryland. But once Colonial Village's financial success was established, New York Life began actively to seek investments in

One of the large basement laundry rooms designed for Colonial Village.

similar projects. By 1939 it had more than $18 million in mortgage funds in twenty-two large-scale rental housing projects across the country. When Colonial Village's first phase of 276 apartments was completed in December 1935, there were ten thousand people on the waiting list. Under Ring's ownership, the vacancy rate of Colonial Village remained at zero because of excellent management and reasonable rents.

The success of Colonial Village was widely touted by the FHA. Agency administrators invited Ring to write a series of articles on how the complex was designed and on his concept of garden apartments. One of his principal guidelines was that a successful garden apartment complex should occupy only 20 to 25 percent of its land. (Colonial Village had only 18 percent occupied by buildings.) Ring felt that two-story garden apartment buildings were preferable and that four-story walk-up apartment houses were hard to rent; elevators were too expensive to purchase and maintain unless the apartment house was five or more stories high. He advocated the efficient location of stairs, elimination of lobbies for small public foyers, and units with two exposures. A separate dining room was considered wasteful: Ring preferred a dining alcove next to the kitchen. He also believed that the garden apartment buildings should be designed so that most bedrooms faced any direction but west, which was too hot in late summer afternoons and nights. All rooms, including kitchens and baths, should have windows. Ring believed that any garage should be carefully screened from the street. All buildings should be connected by sidewalks. At Colonial Village, several walkways even passed through a series of buildings at the basement level. The garden apartment buildings should be set off from the street in deeply staggered setbacks and should face onto spacious, well-landscaped courtyards.

The site plans and description of Colonial Village were widely published and copied by developers across the United States. The Federal Housing Administration was indeed one of the most successful of the New Deal agencies, and between 1934 and 1944 backed construction of eleven thousand apartment buildings and other housing projects in twenty-four states. As a result, five million Americans were housed in 1.25 million new apartment units and houses. The FHA advised developers and owners and even helped plan buildings.

In addition to Colonial Village, Gustave Ring built three other important garden apartments in the late 1930s—Arlington Village and Brentwood Village in the Washington area and Northwood in Baltimore. All were successful financially and were well designed. Approximately three hundred garden apartments were built in the capital area by other developers during the 1930s and 1940s following the success of Colonial Village. A few important examples are the Falkland and Rock Creek Gardens in Maryland, and Fairlington, Parkfairfax, and Buckingham in Virginia.

A LANDMARK PRESERVED

A major change came to Colonial Village when Ring sold the complex to the Mobil Corporation in 1977 for $17 million. The land became particularly valuable a few years later because of the opening of the nearby Courthouse Metro subway station. Tenants immediately organized the Colonial Village Tenants Association and fought to place the complex in the National Register of Historic Places after learning that Mobil planned to demolish half the apartment houses for commercial development. In a compromise reached in 1979, Mobil agreed to raze only one-tenth of the apartment buildings on an 8-acre site on the top of the hill nearest the courthouse. Here three twelve-story "Colonial Place" office buildings were planned.

The remaining body of Colonial Village was divided into rental, cooperative, and condominium sections. Because a number of the tenants were elderly and lived on modest incomes, a rental section was set aside for fifteen years before conversion to either condos or co-ops. All tenants living at Colonial Village prior to 11 December 1979 were guaranteed rental apartments if they chose to stay. Colonial Village fortunately was listed in the National Register. While that honorific designation does not prevent proposed changes to the buildings, Mobil's sale of the condominiums and cooperatives and its establishment of the public housing units here ensure preservation of the site.

101

LANGSTON TERRACE

2101 G Street, N.E. (resident manager's office); 20 clusters of buildings centered around the square bounded by H, G, 21st, and 24th streets, N.E.

ARCHITECT: Hilyard R. Robinson; Paul Williams, Los Angeles, associate architect, 1935

ORIGINAL APARTMENTS: 273 (mostly two-bedrooms)

STATUS: opened as rental in 1938

Conceived in 1934 by President Franklin D. Roosevelt's Works Progress Administration (WPA) as a model, low-income housing project for local blacks, Langston Terrace received national publicity because of its progressive design when completed in 1938. Its 273 apartments were in twenty clusters of buildings, ranging from three- and four-story small apartment houses to two-story rowhouses. The buildings occupied only 25 percent of the 14-acre site overlooking the Anacostia River. Architect Hilyard R. Robinson could thus provide a spacious central court-yard and much greenspace—which provided an unu-sually large area for playgrounds at the time. The complex was built as a social experiment—demonstrating how well-designed but low-cost public housing could improve the lives of low-income Americans. At that time this project was considered by many to constitute a radical concept for the federal government. Its detractors, how-ever, were soon silenced by its outstanding success.

At that time more than ten thousand of Washington's poor blacks were living in "alley dwellings." Most were small, poorly built rowhouses without plumbing or elec-tricity interspersed along two hundred of the city's alleys located within residential blocks. More than half of the alley houses were indeed eliminated by the Alley Dwelling Authority, a federal bureau that existed between 1934 and 1943, when it was reorganized and renamed the National Capital Housing Authority.

Secretary of the Interior Harold D. Ickes laid the cornerstone for the $1.8 million Langston Terrace, also known as Langston Dwellings. It became a showplace for demonstrating the success of public housing and was visited by such famous White House guests as Queen Wilhelmina of the Netherlands in 1940. The original monthly rents, which ranged from $19.50 for a two-room apartment to $31.20 for a five-room apartment (including utilities), prompted more than four thousand applications for the 273 units. Tenants were carefully chosen; re-quirements included a record of steady employment, pay-ing rent on schedule, and living on low incomes in the worst slums. The original WPA plan to build a comparable large garden apartment house for low-income whites was never carried out because of inadequate public funds, but the proportion of whites in substandard housing was only 7 percent in comparison with 35 percent of blacks. The federal government's 1937 experiment in public housing in Greenbelt, Maryland, was, in contrast, for medium-income whites.

Hailed by the local press as a "planned utopia" and a "model community for the reclamation of human lives," Langston Terrace was named for John Mercer Langston

The principal decorative feature of the main building of Langston Terrace is this sculptural frieze, "The Progress of the Negro Race."

Langston Terrace was named for noted educator John M. Langston, founder of the law school at Howard University and the first black congressman from Virginia during Reconstruction.

(1829–97), one of the most important and respected black crusaders for racial justice and freedom during the second half of the nineteenth century. Born in Virginia, Langston spent most of his childhood in Ohio. He attended Oberlin College, was admitted to the Ohio bar, and was elected clerk of the city council in Brownhelm, Ohio. During the Civil War he recruited black soldiers for the Union Army. Active in Republican politics during Reconstruction, he was elected to Congress from Virginia, appointed by President Ulysses S. Grant as minister to Haiti, and served on the D.C. Board of Health. Especially interested in increasing the opportunity for blacks in education, Langston became president of Virginia State College in Petersburg, Virginia, and later the first dean of the law school at Howard University in Washington.

The first residents did not move into Langston Terrace until the entire complex was finished in April 1938. At that time they elected a resident council to organize adult social clubs, special field trips, playgrounds, a nursery, a food cooperative, a credit union, scout troops for boys and girls, a children's band, dancing classes, outdoor movies, and athletic programs. For many years the resident council nurtured pride of occupancy and a wholesome environment. The seventeen hundred residents neatly maintained the red and muted orange brick apartment buildings with their clean, straightforward lines. The restrained architecture included such simple embellishments as curved Art Deco handrails at the doors, entry overhangs, and concrete house numbers produced by Washington architectural sculptor John Joseph Early. These details might be referred to as a stripped Deco mode.

Entrance to the main Langston Terrace building is through an open concourse leading from the street to the inner courtyard. The facing of this inner arch is decorated with a frieze by several sculptors including Daniel G. Olney of "The Progress of the Negro Race." The nearly life-size terra cotta figures were a WPA project produced under the supervision of the Procurement Division of the Department of the Treasury. A native of New York, Olney had worked under Gutzon Borglum and Paul Manship before studying sculpture in Munich in the early 1930s. After completing a number of garden sculptures for the Robert Woods Bliss family at Dumbarton Oaks, he was awarded the Langston Terrace commission. In addition to the entrance frieze, several large concrete sculptures of animals were designed for the main open courtyard.

ARCHITECT HILYARD R. ROBINSON

The progressive design of Langston Terrace was primarily the work of Hilyard R. Robinson (1899–1986), at the time Washington's most prominent black architect. A native Washingtonian, Robinson graduated from the M Street High School before studying architecture at the University of Pennsylvania, Columbia University, and the University of Berlin. He then served in World War I as an artillery lieutenant in the U.S. Army. In 1930 Robinson returned to Europe to study the recent development of modern architecture in Holland, Denmark, Germany, and Russia. He was particularly influenced by several Bauhaus architects, including Walter Gropius, Marcel Breuer, and Erich Mendelsohn. Robinson became interested in the new concept of public housing in Europe and, along with such others as Clarence Wright and Catherine Bauer, became an authority in America on the subject during the late 1930s. After teaching architecture at Howard University in 1934, Robinson became a Department of the Interior architect in charge of designing public housing projects for blacks. In addition to selecting sites for slum clearance, he designed the Frederick Douglass Dwellings as well as Langston Terrace in Washington. During World War II he planned several large defense housing projects for the federal government at Sparrows Point, Maryland; Tuskegee, Alabama; and Ypsilanti, Michigan. He also designed Carver Hall and Slowe Hall, the first government hotels for black war workers in the nation's capital. In Washington today Robinson is most noted for his design of a number of buildings at Howard University.

Perhaps the most famous of his many noteworthy architectural projects, however, remains Langston Terrace, which architecture critic Lewis Mumford termed in 1938 "vigorous and positive works . . . that set a high standard of exterior design, and the use of sculpture against the flat walls of the buildings . . . looks better than the best modern work in Hamburg and Vienna that I can recall. . . ." Even though Langston Terrace remains standing today, many of Robinson's design elements have been seriously damaged. Not only have the handsome original dark steel casement windows been replaced with glaring aluminum, but the chaste Art Deco porchlights have disappeared for a motley collection of indifferent new fixtures. In addition, the once-immaculate landscaping has deteriorated into an eyesore. The listing of Langston Terrace in the National Register in 1987, however, will help prevent any further architectural alterations.

Site plan of Langston Terrace.

2929 CONNECTICUT AVENUE, N.W.

East side of Connecticut Avenue just south of the National Zoo

ARCHITECT: Dillon and Abel, 1936

ORIGINAL APARTMENTS: 96 (24 efficiencies; 64 one-bedrooms; 8 two-bedrooms)

STATUS: opened as rental in 1937

Just south of the National Zoo and adjacent to Rock Creek Park, this nine-story apartment house is of special interest as a forerunner of the International Style of architecture in Washington. The red-brick facade with white concrete trim contains elements from three styles—International, Art Deco, and Prairie, as practiced by Frank Lloyd Wright during his early years in Chicago. The chief decorative feature of the front facade of this U-shaped residence, with its open south-side courtyard, is a projecting pavilion counterbalanced by a tier of wide balconies.

A strong horizontal feeling is produced by the ribbed brickwork found on both the left projecting pavilion and the right tier of balconies. While the left pavilion is almost entirely enclosed, with narrow balconies terminating its right side on each level, the right end of the facade has wide open balconies fronting directly onto Connecticut Avenue. By leaving the top right balcony uncovered, the architect has emphasized the feeling of asymmetry.

Horizontality is further emphasized at the top-floor level, where the windows are bordered by strips of concrete, echoed above by a white concrete cornice strip. The horizontal, flat, low-hung marquee, framed by a pair of massive square "pillars," anchors the base while complementing the horizontal top-floor window treatment. The facade is one of the most successful of any Washington

The front facade of 2929 Connecticut Avenue reflects both the style of the Prairie School and the International Style, new in 1936.

The streamlined Art Deco lobby of 2929 Connecticut Avenue. All early International Style–inspired Washington apartment houses of the late 1930s and early 1940s included Art Deco lobbies, a local architectural peculiarity.

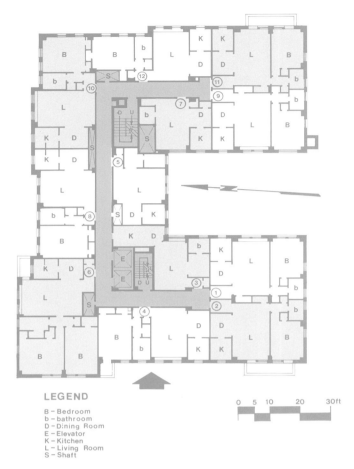

LEGEND

B – Bedroom
b – bathroom
D – Dining Room
E – Elevator
K – Kitchen
L – Living Room
S – Shaft

0 5 10   20   30ft

Typical floor plan of 2929 Connecticut Avenue.

Two large fans in the basement sucked cool air from Rock Creek Park into conduits from which it was blown through grilles into the public corridors of each floor. A vent in the lower half of each apartment door provided access to the steady stream of relatively cool air during the summer.

Originally built by Gustave Ring and Henry K. Jawish, 2929 was purchased by real estate investor Dunbar Rosenthal (1891–1982) in 1961. A native of Washington, Rosenthal was a very successful businessman who established a large paper mill in Chambersburg, Pennsylvania, and acquired a total of twelve large Washington apartment houses as personal investments. In addition to 2929 he owned the Parkway (3220 Connecticut Avenue, N.W.), Sedgwick Gardens, Tilden Hall (3945 Connecticut Avenue, N.W.), Cathedral Court (3701 Massachusetts Avenue, N.W.), and the Rodney (1900 R Street, N.W.). Since Rosenthal's death, his apartment houses have been managed by Daro Realty, Inc. Because of its good state of preservation, excellent location near a shopping center and the subway, and the low rents guaranteed by rent control, 2929 remains a desirable residence.

apartment house designed in the 1930s. The simplicity of its elements produces clean lines, but their arrangement also results in a rich plasticity that does credit to the streetscape. One can never be bored with this facade.

The majority of the ninety-six apartments here are one-bedrooms. The eight more desirable two-bedroom units are all in the sixth tier, located on the left front of the building. A striking feature is the perfectly preserved step-down Art Deco lobby with rounded pillars, indirect lighting, and glass-block wall. The roof was designed with a large deck as well as a penthouse handball court, the only example ever built on an apartment house roof in Washington. Another unusual feature for a medium-sized apartment house (fifty to a hundred units) of this period was the large restaurant in the basement. Facing the courtyard garden and fountain, it is now rented to two social clubs, the Dupont Circle and the Capital Chess clubs.

Following the example of the Kennedy-Warren, the design of 2929 also included a forced-air cooling system.

The builder of 2929 Connecticut Avenue, Gustave Ring, enjoyed handball—thus the handball court on the roof, unusual for a Washington apartment house.

103

MAJESTIC

3200 16th Street, N.W.; west side of 16th Street, diagonally opposite the Roman Catholic Church of the Sacred Heart

ARCHITECT: Alvin L. Aubinoe, Sr., and Harry L. Edwards, 1937

ORIGINAL APARTMENTS: 151 (111 efficiencies; 32 one-bedrooms; 8 two-bedrooms)

STATUS: opened as rental in 1938

Another important Washington apartment house influenced by New York design was the Art
Deco Majestic, built by Morris Cafritz in 1937.

Detail of rounded bays with windows opposite one another at the Rockefeller apartment house in New York—a major influence on Washington's Majestic.

The Majestic is one of a dozen significant Art Deco apartment houses built by developer Morris Cafritz during the 1930s. This building is constructed in an irregular U shape around a front court. The north (right) wing is much shorter than the south wing because of the site.

The building's most conspicuous feature appears on the front ends of the two wings, each with a pair of seven-story-high round bays with ribbon glass windows facing away from one another, toward the edges of the property, to ensure privacy. There is no doubt that these bays were directly influenced by the slightly earlier (1936) Rockefeller Apartments at 17 West 54th Street in New York, designed by J. Andre Fouilhoux and Wallace K. Harrison. The name, however, was borrowed from the Majestic of New York, a thirty-story luxury apartment house at 115 Central Park West, designed in 1930 by Irwin S. Chanin and Jacques Delamarre in the Moderne style, as it was then known.

To increase interest, the facade of Washington's Majestic includes corner wraparound windows and a vertical thrust achieved by the ziggurat cornice, the slightly projecting entrance bay, and the central north bay on the left wing. The aluminum entrance incorporates a large round window set in the pair of doors, which are crowned by a shallow aluminum cornice and framed by fluted half-round pilasters and a glass-block surround.

As suggested, one of the most significant features of the overall design of the Majestic is the impression of soaring verticality. This was achieved by four rounded bays, three slightly projecting pavilions within the front court, vertical brick ribs extending above the roof line, and tiers of glass corner windows. The great height of New York City Art Deco apartment houses, often more than thirty stories, achieved skyscraper effects naturally. But in Washington, height restriction limited apartment houses to only seven or eight stories. To simulate the New York-style verticality, many Washington architects resorted to the devices used on the Majestic. It, along with the Hightowers, also on 16th Street, N.W., and also designed by architects Alvin L. Aubinoe, Sr., and Harry L. Edwards for the Cafritz Company, are among the finest streamlined Art Deco buildings in the city.

Responding to the need for economy even in new luxury apartment houses during the Depression years,

This 1937 photograph shows the model apartment at the Majestic with its Art Deco glass-block decorative fireplace mantel and modernistic lighting.

Typical floor plan of the Majestic.

most apartments were efficiencies. Their interiors had almost no detailing, except, as in the Majestic, aluminum casement windows and wood-block floors. When the Majestic opened in 1938, several photographs were taken of the model apartment by Theodor Horydczak, the city's most prolific apartment house photographer during the 1930s and 1940s. The designer placed the dining alcove in the rounded bay and furnished the two rooms in the Art Deco mode. The views from the roofdeck of the Majestic, located on one of the highest points of the city, are truly majestic. Today the building remains remarkably intact, even though its neighborhood is no longer fashionable.

ARCHITECTS AUBINOE AND EDWARDS

One of the most important teams of designers of Art Deco apartment houses in Washington during the 1930s and early 1940s was Alvin L. Aubinoe (1903–74) and Harry L. Edwards (1902–58). Aubinoe, born in Washington, was a son and grandson of local builders. Following his education as an engineer at the University of Maryland, he began his career in 1923 with the Rust Engineering

Company in Washington as an engineer, architect, and builder. He became active as an architect during his years with the Cafritz Construction Company, 1926–38. While with Cafritz, he and Harry L. Edwards jointly designed both the Majestic and the Hightowers. They also shared responsibility for four other Cafritz apartment houses, including 2000 Connecticut Avenue, N.W., in 1936, and in 1937, Park Crescent, 2901 18th Street, N.W.; Ogden Gardens, 1445 Ogden Street, N.W.; and Otis Gardens, 1445 Otis Place, N.W. One of their finest private residences was Morris Cafritz's house at 2301 Foxhall Road, N.W. (1936).

Born in Florida, Harry Edwards spent his youth in Alabama before coming to Washington at the age of eighteen with his mother. After studying architecture at George Washington University, 1920–23, he remained in Washington where he worked for a number of firms as a draftsman. Before joining Cafritz in 1930, Edwards was employed by Monroe Warren to assist the principal architects in the design of both Tilden Gardens and the Kennedy-Warren. After Aubinoe left the Cafritz Construction Company to start his own firm in 1938, Edwards continued to work for Cafritz, designing such apartment houses as the Empire, 2000 F Street, N.W., in 1939; 1660 Lanier Place, N.W., in 1940; and the Greenway, at Minnesota Avenue and Ridge Road, S.E., in 1940–41.

Meanwhile, Aubinoe became a very successful developer of his own buildings. He alone was responsible for designing the Congressional Apartments, 215 Constitution Avenue, N.E., in 1939 and the Winthrop House, 1727 Massachusetts Avenue, N.W., in 1940. When he became extremely busy supervising construction, he employed other architects as designers, including David L. Stern and Joseph Abel for his apartment house at 4801 Connecticut Avenue, N.W., in 1938 and Harvey H. Warwick, Sr., for the Commonwealth Building, 1625 K Street, N.W., in 1941.

Following World War II Edwards left Cafritz and rejoined Aubinoe, forming Aubinoe, Edwards, and Beery. Two of their major buildings include the Wire Building, 1000 Vermont Avenue, N.W., in 1948 and a luxury International Style apartment house for the Belgian government in Leopoldville, the capital of the Belgian Congo (now Zaire) in 1951. The latter was a twelve-story apartment house designed for visiting European scientists. Built at a cost of $4 million, these unusually elegant hundred-apartment "guest quarters" included a swimming pool, rooftop restaurant, sun deck, large rooms, and servants' quarters. This firm won awards for three buildings from the Washington Board of Trade—the Wire Building, the Hotel Dupont Plaza (originally an apartment-hotel) at Dupont Circle, and the Abingdon Apartments in Arlington, Virginia. Active in civic affairs, Aubinoe was a board member of many Washington organizations, president of the Home Builders Association of Metropolitan Washington, and a long-term member of the D.C. Commissioners Zoning Advisory Committee. A number of his Art Deco buildings are now owned and managed by his son, Alvin L. Aubinoe, Jr., of Bethesda.

104

GOVERNOR SHEPHERD

2121 Virginia Avenue, N.W.

ARCHITECT: Dillon and Abel, 1938

ORIGINAL APARTMENTS: 128 (112 efficiencies; 16 one-bedrooms)

STATUS: opened as rental in 1939; demolished in 1985

One of the greatest losses to Washington's legacy of distinguished apartment houses occurred in 1985 when the Governor Shepherd was demolished to make way for an office building for the World Health Organization. It was one of the earliest International Style buildings in Washington and widely praised for its excellence of design by both the Museum of Modern Art and the editors of *Architectural Forum* magazine.

The Governor Shepherd's facade was primarily International Style, with streamlined Art Deco detailing on the first floor and in the lobby. It was built two years before William Lescaze's Longfellow Office Building (northeast corner of Connecticut and Rhode Island avenues, N.W.), which is often mistakenly cited as the city's earliest International Style structure. The Governor Shepherd actually was one of the three earliest International Style buildings in Washington, all designed by architect Joseph Abel between 1936 and 1939.

The International Style was developed in the 1920s by a group of European architects, including Walter Gropius and Mies van der Rohe, working in the German Bauhaus school of design, as well as Le Corbusier, working in France. Devoid of ornamentation, the new style was to be completely functional. The term was first coined by architectural historian Henry-Russell Hitchcock and

The Governor Shepherd was one of the earliest International Style apartment houses in Washington when built in 1938.

The streamlined Art Deco lobby of the Governor Shepherd was one of the best in the city until the building was unfortunately razed in 1985 for a new office building.

architect Philip Johnson in their 1932 book, *The International Style*. Washington accepted the style slowly. Privately erected buildings were changed to streamlined Art Deco in the mid-1930s but were not truly International Style, since they were embellished with curved bays and carved or cast spandrels, highly decorative entrances, or projecting vertical ribbed brickwork.

Perhaps Washington's slow acceptance of the International Style was due partly to the federal government's policy to continue the Beaux Arts tradition recommended by the McMillan Commission back in 1901. Only the last building of the Federal Triangle, the Apex Building or Federal Trade Commission Building, incorporated "stripped classicism" in its facade—that is, the use of the tripartite facade division but with a minimum of ornament or detailing. Other late 1930s federal buildings, including the Department of the Interior building and the Department of War building (now used by the Department of State), both on Virginia Avenue, employed the stripped classical mode. Because of its severe facade design, the adjacent Governor Shepherd apartment house thus harmonized with its prominent new neighbors.

DESIGN SPECIFICS

The buff-brick-faced nine-story, steel-framed Governor Shepherd had four tiers of balconies, each protected by a top-floor concrete canopy, embellished and defined by slightly projecting front corner pavilions. The ground-floor facade was faced with polished black marble. The central bays of the building, above the front entrance, were decorated with three blue porcelain enamel spandrels per floor.

A large lobby, beauty parlor, and pharmacy occupied much of the first floor. The pharmacy was converted in the 1940s into the Governor Shepherd Restaurant, which became a rendezvous for State Department officials for more than three decades. The lobby was one of the last important interior Art Deco spaces built in the city, with a black terrazzo floor, rounded and sleek Moderne corners on the dropped ceiling, mirrored side walls, aluminum elevator doors and jambs, and two wood-veneered counters with black marble tops. A pair of massive square, fluted aluminum piers supported a plaster drop ceiling at the rear of the lobby adjacent to the pair of elevators. Two illuminated disks were set into the deep ceiling and surrounded each of the aluminum piers. They served as streamlined "capitals" for the "columns." Another Art Deco lighting scheme was composed of an elongated illuminated band set into the ceiling of the vestibule. It extended outside the lobby entrance, terminating on the bottom edge of the marquee, lighting the door and the Art Deco lettering above: *Governor Shepherd 2121*.

Most of the 128 apartments in the Governor Shepherd were small. Only two of the seventeen tiers of apartments were one-bedrooms (located on the front two projecting

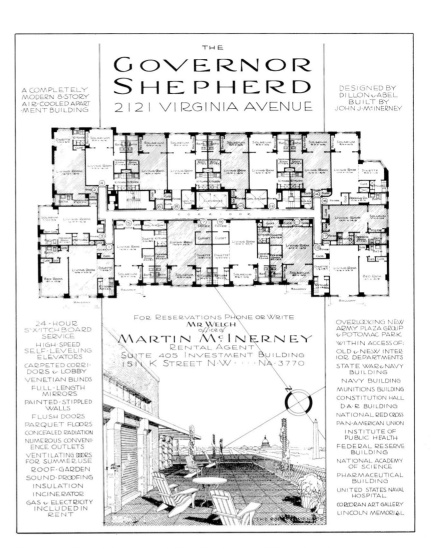

This original hand-drawn broadside, with the typical floor plan of the Governor Shepherd, hung in the manager's office for many years.

pavilions); the remainder were efficiencies. The typical efficiency consisted of a living room and a glass-partitioned solarium with a Murphy bed. The building was cooled by a large fan on the ground floor next to the alley on the east; it blew air through grilles into the public corridor of each floor. The residents could open their apartment doors but leave their outer louvered doors closed while receiving a steady stream of cool, fresh air.

The developer and owner of the Governor Shepherd was John J. McInerney, who in association with earlier partnerships was involved in the construction of the Shoreham Hotel, 2101 Connecticut Avenue, and the Broadmoor. McInerney reserved a top-floor one-bedroom apartment, No. 815, for his own use. This unit was air-conditioned, with machinery located in the small penthouse above. Still in place at the time of demolition, it was the oldest air-conditioning equipment still operating in the city. Not knowing of its historic importance, it was scrapped by the demolition crew in mid-1985.

The Governor Shepherd was one of ten Washington apartment houses designed in the 1930s and early 1940s with a forced-air cooling system. This large fan pulled cool air from the outside ground level and blew it through ducts into the public corridors.

Over the years the Governor Shepherd apartments had consistently been in great demand because of their convenient downtown location, especially for foreign service officers working at the Department of State, just one block to the south. After the building was purchased by the World Health Organization in 1968, the apartments were converted slowly but consistently to offices as residents left. At the time it was demolished, only a dozen residents remained.

ARCHITECT JOSEPH H. ABEL

The architect of the Governor Shepherd was Joseph H. Abel (1905–85), a pioneer in modernist design in Washington. His remarkable career began while he was still in architecture school at George Washington University. At the age of twenty-two, he designed one of the city's finest apartment houses, 2101 Connecticut Avenue, N.W. Before his last building, the Van Ness Centre in 1962, Abel—either alone or with his various three partners—was to design more than a hundred Washington apartment houses, employing many styles, including Tudor Revival, Art Deco, and International Style. Born in Washington, he first worked as an apprentice draftsman for George T.

Santmyers during the late 1920s and later as a draftsman for Arthur B. Heaton, one of the city's important Beaux Arts architects. Abel and Charles Dillon established their own firm, Dillon and Abel, in 1935. They were the first Washington architects to follow the guidelines of the International Style—lack of ornament, severe facades, and functionalism.

The many modernistic apartment houses of the late 1930s and 1940s that they created included 2407 15th Street, N.W.; 2929 Connecticut Avenue, N.W.; the Croydon at 1815 17th Street, N.W.; the Washington House at 16th Street and Florida Avenue, N.W.; and the Highview at 2700 Wisconsin Avenue, N.W. Light tan brick and abundant use of glass blocks in the entrance, lobby, and cantilevered projecting bays characterized these buildings. Their apartments were informal, with the dining alcove completely open to the living room. Glass walls usually divided the living room from the solarium, which was used as either a bedroom or a dining alcove. Abel's best-known apartment houses are 2101 Connecticut Avenue, the Broadmoor, the Shoreham Hotel, the Irene, and Van Ness Centre. In addition to dozens of apartment houses, Abel's firm designed a number of commercial structures. In 1947 Abel and Fred N. Severud were coauthors of *Apartment Houses*. Long out of print, it is one of the few American books ever written as a guide for the design of apartment houses.

In 1941 Abel took in a partner, Julian E. Berla, and changed the name of the firm to Berla and Abel. Berla had studied at Harvard University and taken his graduate degree in architecture from the Massachusetts Institute of Technology. He served as the president of the Washington Chapter of the American Institute of Architects, 1946–48. The most prolific work of Abel and his partners occurred in the boom years after World War II when they designed dozens of important apartment houses, such as the Towers, the Canterbury House, and the Irene, in addition to the Van Ness Centre. The first apartment house in the city with a rooftop swimming pool, the James, was designed in 1960 by his firm. When Berla retired in 1972 following a serious automobile accident, the firm became Abel and Weinstein. Shortly afterwards Abel retired. After the death of Abel in 1985, the firm continued in operation under the charge of Jesse Weinstein.

105

GWENWOOD

1020 19th Street, N.W.; west side of 19th Street midway between L and K streets

ARCHITECT: Harry L. Edwards, 1938

ORIGINAL APARTMENTS: 192 (176 efficiencies; 16 one-bedrooms)

STATUS: opened as rental in 1939; razed in 1981

Built by developer Morris Cafritz in 1939 as a birthday present namesake for his wife, Gwendolyn, the eight-story Gwenwood apartment house boasted one of Washington's most spirited Art Deco facades. An elegant skyscraper effect was created by the pair of pyramid-shaped finials atop the two prominent front bays and the interesting range of bold vertical piers in which the narrow bathroom windows were inserted. The otherwise restrained facade featured an ornate pair of heavy aluminum doors, each with a crescent-shaped window and circular marquee. It was not until 1956 that the glass blocks between the pair of black marble pilasters, which framed the entrance, were covered with six vertical bands of brilliant red mosaics.

Like many apartment houses built in Washington between 1936 and 1941, the Gwenwood was designed primarily with efficiency apartments because of the Depression. Washingtonians had little choice, because the cost of living in the nation's capital, then as now, was much higher than the national average.

There were so many efficiencies at the Gwenwood that they were available in three sizes and priced accordingly. To conserve space, each included a folding dining table with matching benches, as well as a Murphy bed. The bed, which hung vertically on a metal bracket

Vertical ribbons of brickwork created a skyscraper effect on the front facade of the Gwenwood.

in the dressing room in the daytime, swung out at night into the living room. Shortly before the building was demolished in 1981, examples of the Gwenwood's 1930s built-in furniture—a bed, a table, and an accompanying pair of benches—were salvaged by the author and preserved at the Smithsonian Institution. (Cafritz had been using folding beds since 1927 when he built the Pershing apartment house at 16th Street and Spring Road, N.W. He was not the first to do so, however, for they were recorded in a newly built Washington apartment house as early as 1922.)

The simple small step-up lobby (designed to accommodate the loading platform in the rear) had Art Deco aluminum stair rails, an office, switchboard, and indirect lighting—typical in the 1930s. Several shops occupied the left front basement corner of the Gwenwood. When it was built, this neighborhood was still primarily residential, with many nearby Victorian rowhouses. By 1980, however, the area had become almost exclusively commercial, and the land occupied by the Gwenwood was extremely valuable. The apartment house was unfortunately demolished in 1981 for a new office building.

MORRIS CAFRITZ

Along with Harry Wardman, Morris Cafritz was one of the two most prodigious builders in Washington during the twentieth century. The son of Russian immigrants, the young Cafritz came with them to Washington from New York in 1898. He began his career as a fledgling businessman in 1904, when he borrowed $1,400 from his father to open a wholesale coal yard. Within a few years he had branched into other enterprises, including a bowling alley, and by 1915 owned a chain and had become the city's bowling alley king. Five years later he opened a real estate office, beginning a spectacular career that was to last until his death forty-four years later in 1964. His first important venture was the construction of more than two thousand low-cost rowhouses on the former site of the Columbia Golf Club in the Petworth section of the city. Because of convenient financing and the quality of construction, the project was a notable success.

A conservative businessman, Cafritz survived the Depression while such competitors and friends as Harry Wardman lost their entire fortunes in 1930–32. Cafritz

Most of the Gwenwood apartments were efficiency units.

Each efficiency apartment in the Gwenwood included a Murphy bed as well as a Murphy dinette—a table and pair of benches that folded into a cabinet in the wall.

resumed construction as the city's economy began to revive rapidly with the implementation of Franklin D. Roosevelt's New Deal programs. Working from his modest office in the Ambassador Hotel (14th and K streets, N.W.), which he had built in 1929, Cafritz continued to erect houses throughout the city, especially near Westmoreland Circle and in Bethesda. One of the leading factors in his success was his sense of timing. In 1940 he foresaw the development of K Street, N.W., as the city's leading business artery and built a number of important office buildings there and on adjacent Eye Street, including the Cafritz Building. His most ambitious office building projects were the Universal Building and Universal North Building on the old Temple Heights site at Connecticut and Florida avenues and a concentration of new office buildings at Pentagon City near the National Airport in Virginia.

Cafritz built more than eighty-five apartment houses between 1925 and 1941, including fifteen luxury build-

ings and seventy small examples. His best Art Deco examples include the Majestic, the Hightowers, the Empire, the Park Crescent, Park Terrace, the Gwenwood, and 2000 Connecticut Avenue, N.W. Other prominent examples include the Hilltop Manor; the Miramar at 15th Street and Rhode Island Avenue, N.W.; 3600 Connecticut Avenue, N.W.; and 2025 Eye Street, N.W.

At the time of his death, Cafritz left an estate of $65 million, the largest will ever probated in the District of Columbia. Half of it was willed to the Morris and Gwendolyn Cafritz Foundation, the city's leading philanthropic organization devoted to projects for the improvement of life in Washington. Mrs. Cafritz, one of the city's primary hostesses during the 1940s and 1950s, continues to live in the family's impressive Art Deco house on Foxhall Road, N.W. Following the example of their father, all three Cafritz sons—Calvin, Carter, and Conrad—are involved in real estate development in the Washington area.

106

MARLYN

3901 Cathedral Avenue, N.W.; north side of Cathedral Avenue between 39th Street and Idaho Avenue

ARCHITECT: Francis L. Koenig and Harvey H. Warwick, Sr., 1938

ORIGINAL APARTMENTS: 119 (25 efficiencies; 83 one-bedrooms; 10 two-bedrooms; 1 three-bedroom)

STATUS: opened as rental in 1938; converted to condo in 1974

Built by the highly successful real estate developer Gustave Ring and named jointly for his wife, Marion, and his daughter, Carlyn, the Marlyn is the very model of a first-class apartment house in Washington of the 1930s, with a quietly restrained Art Deco facade and small units within. Although Harvey H. Warwick, Sr., is listed on the building permit as the architect, the Marlyn was actually designed by his assistant architect, Francis L. Koenig, also the architect for the last phase of design of Colonial Village, the Dorchester House, and the Carlyn, now Gateway Georgetown.

The six-story Marlyn, an open-winged U-shaped building with spacious lawns and stately trees, straddles a steep downslope of Mount St. Alban. As a result, the lobby entrance at the corner of Cathedral Avenue and 39th Street, N.W., is midway between the first and second floors. The facade was completed in cream-colored brick with horizontal bands of brown brick, emphasized by black slate strips. Porcelain enamel spandrels with limestone windowsills further decorate the facade. Above the two lobby doors are four Art Deco medallions designed by architect Koenig and executed by Washington sculptor John Joseph Early in concrete and colored stone.

The sophisticated lobby with its streamlined fluted walls and Art Deco frieze was designed by the Walter Ballander Company of New York. The architect, as with

The Marlyn when it opened in 1938. Three apartments on the west facade, shown here, have their own private outside entrances.

Although the Art Deco lobby of the Marlyn is at ground level at the corner of Cathedral Avenue and 39th Street, it is set midway between the first and second floors.

his slightly later Carlyn apartment house, set the lobby midway between two floors so that the staircase from this level is seen both ascending and descending. Other distinctive Art Deco detailing includes the elevator-locator dials and call buttons on each floor. The lobby floor, interrupted in the center by a massive supporting pier, and now covered with carpeting, was laid in black terrazzo with aluminum dividing strips. To reduce traffic and noise in the lobby, located at the east end, the two passenger elevators were placed in the center of the building.

Many of the 119 apartments, mostly one-bedroom units, originally contained Murphy beds in the living rooms that folded into "bed closets" when not in use. In some units, such as the Nos. 18 and 20 tiers, a stylish curved Art Deco wall partially separates the bed alcove from the living room. An innovative feature in these two tiers was the separation of the toilet (adjacent to a ventilating shaft) from the bathtub. The three ground-floor apartments facing Idaho Avenue—Nos. 13, 14, and 15— all have private outside entrances with patios. Other ground-floor units on the north and east facades contain fenced patios. The top floor, facing Cathedral Avenue, offers good views of the gardens of the Westchester and the adjacent wooded parks.

The Marlyn was the first centrally air-conditioned apartment house in the United States, an innovation prominently advertised when the building opened in 1939. The Carrier Company, in an experimental project, installed three central refrigeration machines in the basement, each with a fifty-ton capacity. Cooled water was pumped from the basement to the top floor and distributed downward to all apartments. Steam heat was distributed through the same system of pipes in the winter. It took the Carrier Company eighteen months and three breakdowns to make the air-conditioning system work correctly. Once these mistakes were eliminated, the original air-conditioning machinery worked perfectly from 1940 until it was replaced in 1969 with the present modern basement plant.

Other original amenities included a receiving room for packages, a telephone switchboard, and a receptionist in the lobby. Today the garage, switchboard, and receptionist continue, joined by a sauna, exercise room, and new roof terrace.

The Marlyn was converted from rental to condominium by the Cafritz Company in 1974. Fortunately for its architectural integrity, few changes were made to "modernize" the building. Roof replacement and corridor renovations in 1985–86 stirred considerable unrest among the residents and resulted in steep special assessments. As a result the Marlyn's budget has been returned to its original spirit of economy.

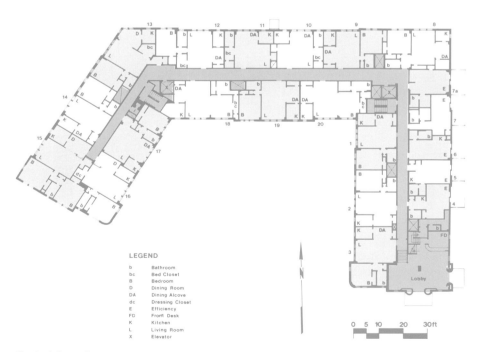

LEGEND

b   Bathroom
bc   Bed Closet
B   Bedroom
D   Dining Room
DA   Dining Alcove
dc   Dressing Closet
E   Efficiency
FD   Front Desk
K   Kitchen
L   Living Room
X   Elevator

Typical floor plan of the Marlyn.

ARCHITECT FRANCIS L. KOENIG

When recently interviewed by the author, the Marlyn's architect, Francis L. Koenig, provided this sketch of his self-made career:

I was born in Chicago in 1910 but grew up on a farm in the Shenandoah Valley of Virginia. In constructing chicken houses and brooding facilities on the farm, I became interested in drafting. I made my own first board and T-square. Construction experience on the farm gave me enough nerve at sixteen to apply for a job as a carpenter's helper on a cold-storage building in Winchester, and I got the job.

One summer day, hot, tired, and grimy from laying steel and pouring concrete (in those days carpenters did everything), I spotted a man getting off the fifth-floor elevator, in an immaculate white linen suit and a Panama hat. The contractor and his entourage were a discreet two steps behind him as he gestured authoritatively with a manicured finger. The contractor's staff obediently, almost reverently, made notes. In a flash they all disappeared to another floor. When I was able to "ungape," and close my jaw, I whispered to the carpenter I was working under, "Who was that?" "Oh," he replied, with deference to my naiveté, "that was the 'arck-ee-teck.' " I said to him, "That's what I'm going to be!" That night I exchanged an almost new subscription to *Popular Mechanics*, which I had just purchased, for Scribners' *Architecture* (a beautiful magazine since merged with old *Pencil Points* and then *Progressive Architecture*). That same week I worked out the financial arrangements for a course from International Correspondence Schools, Scranton, Pennsylvania, in "Architectural Drafting." I think it cost $300, and I remember my number, FBY-1375069.

As I became more proficient, I would draw plans for houses, churches, store remodeling, and restoration of old farm buildings into "hunting boxes" for wealthy Northerners. Some of the work I solicited myself, others came through contractor friends. Much of my work was never built, because the Great Depression was coming on. As usual in such times, the work of the very wealthy did not cease, and I would draw the plans, then put on my carpenter's overalls and get carpenter's wages for working on the jobs I drew the plans for (forty-five cents an hour!). The greatest experience in the world. First to draw, second to build and find out drawing errors, but mostly,

Detail of the Art Deco clock in the lobby of the Marlyn.

what is actually needed in a drawing to pass on ideas accurately to a construction crew whom you didn't know. And finally, to learn the tastes and desires of that part of our society that I could only dream of someday emulating.

In this episode, and as you will see in my later adventures, I have been so much more fortunate than my contemporaries in architecture, because I was intimately involved in the execution of my drawings and my ideas. Others feel that they were spared the onus of the sweat and lunch boxes of the proletariat. I say I was blessed a thousandfold through participation. I learned construction techniques and, importantly, workers' limitations. Most architects *never* learn this.

In 1935 I left the farm and went to the big city, Washington, D.C. I found a job as a designer for a "spec-builder." This was a new phase of the industry to me, and I again profited by my closeness to the inside of the operations. I really learned here more of what *not* to do, than what to do! I found out later that the entrepreneur I worked for almost went to jail for hidden fourth trusts on the houses he sold.

My next move was as designer-in-residence for Kennedy-Chamberlain, the duo responsible for the development of Kenwood in Montgomery County. I designed a few houses here but was fired when I returned from my honeymoon in May 1936, I guess for having assumed too much authority while the permanent architect was having a hemorrhoid operation. This disaster proved to be the best break I ever got. After two weeks of pavement pounding, I landed a drafting job with Harvey Warwick, chief architect for Gustave Ring, the fabled developer of the Westchester and Colonial Village. My thirty- to sixty-day temporary appointment at a dollar an hour lasted four

This unusual curved streamlined Art Deco arch opens the bedroom to the living room in a number of small apartments at the Marlyn.

years, by which time I was a one-third partner in the firm. Harvey held the other two-thirds.

Next, in 1940, Gustave Ring himself seduced me with an offer of $750 per month and the vice presidency of Ring Engineering Company. Here again I learned by doing it all. I would design, then build the design, then handle the rentals or sales as the case may be, and if rented, operate the facility for our own account. One sinks or swims under these conditions. Any mistakes are your own, there is no one else to pin it on. This is the dream education!

My great good fortune is that I worked for two great men, Harvey Warwick and Gustave Ring, who not only gave me the benefit of their vast knowledge of architecture, construction, finance, and management but allowed me practically a free hand in accomplishing assignments. I am fully aware of what the consequences of mediocrity would have been, but how could one fail with the opportunities I had been granted?

LIFE AT THE MARLYN

Because of its prime location, the Marlyn was and still is a best address with its share of notable residents. In the early years of World War II, it attracted noted economist John Kenneth Galbraith, who recalled that:

> It was an exceedingly pleasant place of residence and very much a center of discussion of mobilization policy at that time. That was because David Ginsberg, a major architect of wartime economic policy, and Eric Roll, later Lord Roll, a dominant figure in British procurement policy, were fellow residents. I suppose we had some discussion of the problem of wartime price and procurement policy almost every evening.

For many years neighbors believed that FBI Director J. Edgar Hoover lived in the Marlyn, because of his frequent appearance there and because his armor-plated bullet-proof limousine, attended by his driver Crawford, was seen almost daily in the driveway. In point of fact, Hoover was visiting his close friend and alter ego, Clyde A. Tolson, special assistant to the director of the FBI, who lived there in apartment No. 515 from 1940 to 1960. Hoover lived in a house at 4936 30th Place in Cleveland Park until his death in 1964. They were inseparable for five decades and are buried adjacent to one another at Congressional Cemetery.

In another curious insight into private life at the Marlyn, the right of tenants to keep pets became a cause célèbre during World War II. The trouble began on 17 March 1942 when the manager of the Marlyn orally informed tenants that dogs would no longer be allowed in the building. He confirmed the new rule by letter on 2 April. The three tenants with dogs claimed that the ban on dogs violated the D.C. Emergency Rent Act, which went into effect on 1 January 1942, freezing rents at their level as of 1 January 1941. This law also stipulated that the landlord must continue to supply the same services to which the tenant was formerly entitled on that date. The courts, however, upheld the landlord when the appeal was decided in March 1943, and the three tenants chose to vacate their apartments rather than give up their pets. The [Washington] *Evening Star* reported the case on 21 October 1942:

> Tonia, Coffee, and Barber, a pair of cocker spaniels and a dachshund, today were the central figures of a stormy

eviction suit that will be heard soon in the Municipal Court of Appeals.

Their owners, residents of the Marlyn Apartments, 3901 Cathedral Avenue, N.W., have been ordered by the Municipal Court to get rid of the dogs, or seek other quarters. Determined to fight to the last, they have appealed.

Defendants in the eviction suit, brought by the apartment house management, are Whitney P. Mee, engineering examiner of the RFC, owner of Tonia, Samuel L. Samuel, an attorney, owner of Coffee, and Philip W. Copelin, War Department civilian employee, now out of the country, owner of Barber.

On September 20, Judge Armond W. Scott dismissed the eviction suit but a new trial was granted, and Judge Brice Clagett upheld the contentions of the apartment house management that a clause in the lease held on the apartment prohibited the keeping of pets.

The tenants declared that the resident manager permitted them to move in with the dogs in early 1941 and no objection was made until a notice was sent them in April stating they would have to move by May 1 unless they gave up the dogs. They refused to move on the ground that the resident manager had let them come in originally with the dogs.

Mrs. Mee said she had already made several concessions in the matter and declares that she will not give in a mite further. She sent three cockatoos she brought from Mexico to the Zoo for Director William Mann to keep, and she gave another cocker, Joe Lewis, to a friend to keep for her.

107

CRYSTAL HEIGHTS

Northeast corner of Connecticut and Florida avenues, N.W.
ARCHITECT: Frank Lloyd Wright, Scottsdale, Arizona, and Spring Green, Wisconsin, 1940
ORIGINAL PLANNED UNITS: 138 apartments (efficiencies and one-bedrooms) and 1,230 hotel rooms
STATUS: designed in 1940; never built

One of the tragedies in the history of Washington apartment houses is that Frank Lloyd Wright, partly through his own braggadocio, sealed the doom of his controversial design for the Crystal Heights apartment-hotel. At the request of Washington developer Roy S. Thurman, the famous architect designed a spectacular self-contained community for the northeast corner of Connecticut and Florida avenues, N.W., in 1940. (Although the drawings for the project were labeled "Crystal Heights," it was always referred to as "Crystal City" in Washington newspapers at the time.) An apartment-hotel designed with 138 small apartments and 1,230 hotel rooms, Crystal Heights was also to include a garage for fifteen hundred cars, roof gardens, terraces, fountains, a cocktail lounge extending 400 by 32 feet, a restaurant, ballroom, thousand-seat theater plus several smaller theaters, and a shopping center. During the summer of 1940 Wright and Thurman corresponded continually concerning the project, refining all of the details. Wright wrote in one letter:

> The whole thing should be worked out in white marble, verdigris bronze and crystal, and show up the Capitol for a fallen dumpling and Washington hotels as insufferable. And this is to suggest that you change Temple Heights to Crystal Heights because of the crystalline character of the whole edifice. It will be an iridescent fabric with every

surface showing of the finest quality. I have assumed that you wanted to make a clean sweep of the success of Crystal Heights and I am proceeding accordingly with a thoroughbred. After all, no half-way measures, or men either, are ever greatly successful. This calls for protective administration of what it has to give to Washington, and that ought to mean the world.

The design called for twenty-one square glass towers, with tiers of triangular rooms, grouped together to form an irregular U shape at the crest of this steep hill. Motorists would park in the garage entered from Florida Avenue or on the parking terrace above. The latter extended from the glass towers, forming an apex at Connecticut and Florida avenues, N.W.

Most of the apartments designed for these towers, the tallest of which was to have been 135 feet, were to have balconies and working fireplaces. Although each room was to have two glass walls, no windows were to open. Many of the hotel rooms could be joined to form additional apartments.

The 10-acre site of Crystal Heights was then known both as the Dean Tract and as Temple Heights. Located on a steep hill, it was the site of the 1873 Second Empire brick house called Oak Lawn, formerly owned by Edward C. Dean, a prominent Washington businessman. The es-

Architect Frank Lloyd Wright designed Crystal Heights, also known as Crystal City (not to be confused with present-day Crystal City in Arlington), for the site now occupied by the Washington Hilton Hotel at Connecticut and Florida avenues in 1940, but it was unfortunately never built.

tate was sold to the Grand Lodge of Masons by the Dean family in 1922 as the proposed location of their national temple. Because of the Depression the Masons were unable to build, and the land was offered for sale for $1 million. The developers of Crystal Heights signed a contract to purchase the site for that amount, pending the city's approval of the project, in April 1940.

Wright announced plans for Crystal Heights at a press conference in Washington on 23 September 1940 in developer Roy S. Thurman's office at 1643 Connecticut Avenue, N.W. Wright described the project in glowing terms: built of steel, bronze, white marble, and glass, Crystal Heights would command dramatic views of the entire city. Many of the giant oak trees, including the four-hundred-year-old Treaty Oak, a local landmark, were to be saved and become part of the complex. According to Wright, a line of cars eight miles long could be parked within Crystal Heights in twenty minutes. The twenty-

one vertical concrete shafts, all of varying heights, that comprised the building would fit the natural contours of the land.

When questioned about the design of Crystal Heights, Wright said: "But it will not be built on the heights, rather, it will be of the heights. As the land rises and falls, so will the twenty-one parts vary in height. Crystal City will have all the virtues of standardization but none of its drawbacks." Wright further compared the cantilevered suspension of the floors from the central shaft with "the branches of a tree." The architect claimed it would combine economy, lightness, and beauty, and would be fireproof, earthquake proof, and vermin proof. Compared with New York's Radio City, Crystal Heights would be Washington's showplace. The developer equated the project to Wright's famous Imperial Hotel in Tokyo, which had become that city's "social clearing house for official life such as it never has had." The seventy-one-year-old architect claimed "Versailles won't look like much compared to this when it is finished."

Both the architect and the developer had to obtain approval from the city government. Not only the three District commissioners (who then governed the city) but the D.C. Zoning Commission and the National Capital Planning Commission opposed Crystal Heights. In the winter of 1940 all three groups rejected Wright's scheme, technically refusing to allow an exception to the 110-foot building height law. They also declined to change the site's zoning from residential to commercial, although this was permitted for another project twenty years later.

There is no question that Frank Lloyd Wright's personality was the factor that ultimately determined the fate of Crystal Heights. True to form, the irascible Wright denounced the quality of design of all existing buildings in Washington as well as the professional ability of the architects then practicing in the city. Wright had already created many enemies in 1938 when he addressed a meeting of local architects. The [Washington] *Evening Star* reported it under the headline: "Wright's Lance Hurled at D.C.":

> Fresh from his dialectical assault on the colonial architecture of restored Williamsburg, Frank Lloyd Wright appeared in Washington last night to "place a verbal tombstone on the old order of architecture" and to toss his verbal darts of scorn at architecture as the Government practices it.
>
> Striding with aplomb into the enemy's camp, Mr. Wright told a special meeting of the federal architects that federal "buildings are not built to serve the people, but to satisfy a kind of grandomania utterly obsolete. Grandomania has given most buildings the symbols of authority, pillars, cornices and the pontifical past. The Jefferson Memorial is obviously across the grain of indigenous American feeling for architecture. It is the greatest insult yet."

Wright again attacked local architecture at the press conference announcing plans for Crystal Heights. He then declared: "The term modernity covers a multitude of sins and we're trying to avoid some of the sins. But to say that in the capital of the United States anything modern would be an anachronism is pretty bad. We feel Washington

Frank Lloyd Wright explains the design of his ill-fated Crystal Heights at a press conference in Washington in 1940.

has a sufficiency of the deadly conventional. There is plenty here of the commonplace elegance. None of that for us." He went on to suggest that one of the benefits of World War II would be the bombing of Washington by the German air force so that the city could be rebuilt with decent architecture.

ARCHITECT FRANK LLOYD WRIGHT

During his seventy-year career, Frank Lloyd Wright (1867–1959) designed more than a thousand structures, of which four hundred were built. After a childhood in Wisconsin, Wright was trained in architecture by the firm of Adler and Sullivan in Chicago. He exemplified the Prairie School, the philosophy of Chicago architects at the turn of the century who aimed to integrate their buildings with the landscape, and to simplify construction and architectural detail. Because of his innovative designs (he was as much an engineer as an architect), Wright had already become internationally famous by World War I. He had designed several dozen famous buildings such as the Coonley House in Riverside, Illinois (1904), the

Larkin Administration Building in Buffalo, New York (1904), and the Unity Temple in Oak Park, Illinois (1906), as well as the Imperial Hotel in Tokyo, Japan (1916). Wright lived in his own self-made environment, complementary to nature, at his summer home, Taliesin, near Spring Green, Wisconsin (1911), and his winter home, Taliesin West, near Scottsdale, Arizona (1937). In 1932 he established the Taliesin Fellowship, which enabled up to forty apprentices to live and study under his direction.

During the 1930s Wright's creativity continued in spite of a turbulent personal life. During that decade he wrote a number of influential books, including *An Autobiography* (1932), *The Disappearing City* (1932), and *An Organic Architecture* (1939). Wright believed that his buildings should be elegant and powerful, and represent the philosophy of "space over matter." Often of arbitrary shapes, his architecture always harmonized with the land. His designs encompassed many building types, including houses, hotels, commercial and industrial structures, offices, and civic buildings. During his later years he continued to design such award-winning buildings as Fallingwater, the Kaufmann house near Mill Run, Pennsylvania (1936), the Johnson Wax corporate headquarters at Racine, Wisconsin (1936), the Guggenheim Museum in New York (1947), and the Marin County Civic Center in California (1957). In addition, his inexpensive, modest, and practical "Usonian" houses, first conceived in 1937, were widely heralded.

Although he designed several apartment houses, only one was ever built—the Price Tower in Bartlesville, Oklahoma, in 1953, a mixed-use apartment-office complex. His other apartment house designs included one for St. Mark's-in-the-Bowery (three glass towers surrounding the church) in New York (1929), another for Chicago (1930), and one for Ellis Island in New York Harbor (1959). These three were related to the design of Crystal Heights, in that a grouping of glass towers was the principal feature.

Wright's innovations included steel and concrete cantilevers, variations of poured concrete, and concrete block. Demanding and arrogant, he expected all or nothing. His personality got the better of his architectural creativity in 1940, and unfortunately his Crystal Heights site finally became the present Universal and Universal North buildings and the Washington Hilton Hotel (1960s).

Crystal Heights would have been the largest apartment-hotel in the country. A stunning design, it would have been one of the great works of architecture in the city. Unfortunately only two buildings in the Washington area were built from Wright's designs, both small houses—the 1940 Pope-Leighey House in Falls Church, Virginia (since moved to Woodlawn Plantation, near Mount Vernon, Virginia), and the 1958 Robert L. Wright House in Bethesda, Maryland. Not until Grosvenor Park in Rockville and the Watergate complex in Foggy Bottom were constructed in the 1960s were any apartment houses to equal the size of Crystal Heights.

108

GENERAL SCOTT

1 Scott Circle, N.W.; northeast corner of 16th Street and Massachusetts Avenue
ARCHITECT: Robert O. Scholz, 1940
ORIGINAL APARTMENTS: 175 (151 efficiencies; 24 one-bedrooms)
STATUS: opened as rental in 1941; converted to condo in 1982

Front facade of the General Scott.

Several important streamlined Art Deco apartment houses were built on 16th Street, N.W., immediately before World War II. Good examples include the General Scott, the Hightowers, the Washington House, the Dorchester House, and the Majestic. The General Scott was built by Robert O. Scholz, also the architect, and E. C. Ernst, and was named for General Winfield B. Scott, commanding general of the United States Army from 1841 to 1861, whose equestrian statue stands in the circle in front.

The Art Deco detailing on the two street facades includes a streamlined aluminum marquee, five projecting pavilions with black panels, and strip windows on the prominent rounded bay at the corner of 16th Street and Scott Circle. The most impressive interior feature is the sleek step-down lobby, with its original linoleum floor, bowed front desk, recessed circular domed ceiling with indirect lighting, and handsome aluminum elevator doors. The building originally had 175 apartments, but 6 more were added when unused space in the basement was renovated in 1982. All are small: eighteen of the twenty-one tiers were designed for efficiencies averaging 500 square feet. Most featured a solarium, screened from the living room by glass walls, and a Murphy bed, either concealed in the solarium in all efficiencies or hidden in the dressing closets adjacent to the bathrooms in the one-

The streamlined Art Deco step-down lobby of the General Scott includes this bowed desk and a circular recessed ceiling with indirect lighting.

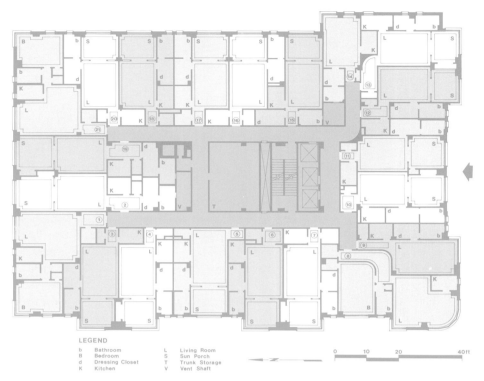

LEGEND

b	Bathroom	L	Living Room
B	Bedroom	S	Sun Porch
d	Dressing Closet	T	Trunk Storage
K	Kitchen	V	Vent Shaft

0 10 20 40ft

Typical floor plan of the General Scott.

bedrooms. The handsomely tiled bathrooms and wood-block floors remain in good condition. The abundant light in these units, as well as their convenient downtown location, have always made the General Scott desirable.

As a first-class apartment house, the General Scott provided central air conditioning, a switchboard, and a glass-enclosed solarium for tenants on the roof (since converted into a penthouse apartment). Built as a rental building, the General Scott was converted to a condominium in 1982.

LIFE AT THE GENERAL SCOTT: FROM RENTAL TO CONDO

Condominium conversion is usually a traumatic experience for tenants. The law now allows residents over sixty-two whose income is below a specified level to continue to rent their apartments even if the building is converted. Furthermore, under a District of Columbia law passed in 1977, the tenants have the right to purchase the building from the owner if a conversion is planned. A tenant-sponsored conversion is an uphill battle and rarely successful, but the General Scott's tenants, after herculean efforts over two and a half years, carried the day. Bill

Black wrote of the General Scott condo conversion battle in the *Washington Post* on 6 November 1982:

What does it take to pull off a successful condo conversion in these tight economic times? While the answer to that question seems to have eluded many experienced Washington area developers over the last several years, one D.C. tenant group has found it to be a combination of tight organization, luck, good business sense, sound advice, and perhaps most important, a willingness to take significant risks.

Early last month, the tenants' association at the General Scott Apartments completed the purchase of their 181-unit building, located at One Scott Circle in Northwest Washington. On Sept. 16, all but two of the eligible tenants voted in favor of converting their property to condominiums. On Oct. 1, the residents signed for a $2.15 million conversion loan on the structure. Those steps capped a struggle by the tenants that had cost them more than $300,000 over 2½ years. During that time, the residents watched in despair as the D.C. condo market deteriorated to a near depression [as a result of very high interest rates], threatening all of their efforts.

In February 1980, the building's occupants were first notified of the owners' intention to sell. Within a few days, one of the renters, Peg Stone, sent a memo to all the other tenants proposing a meeting to discuss alternatives open to them. Stone had lived in the building only a few months and was determined to stay. "I was mad," she explained. "I'd just moved in November. I'd searched for a building with a large apartment that I could afford. It was a personal thing: No, dammit, I'm not going to move."

At that initial meeting, a large crowd of tenants decided to organize an association and set up a nine-member steering committee. Within a short time, more than 80 percent of the residents had joined the group, which elected Stone as its head. The organization began gathering information from the D.C. government, community groups, and other tenants' associations. The group accepted the steering committee's recommendation to have a feasibility study done at a cost of $5,000. Tenants contributed $50 each to finance it. After a series of interviews, the residents selected an attorney and a real estate

consultant who had worked with other tenant groups converting their properties.

The steering committee evolved into the tenants' association's board of directors. That group spent a great deal of time passing information on to other tenants. Much of this liaison work was done by eight floor captains. Some of them had earlier been floor captains for the Christmas fund used to buy gifts for the building's employees. When the feasibility study indicated that a successful conversion might be possible, the residents voted to proceed with their effort to buy the building. Much of the support came from long-term occupants, some of whom have lived in the building since the 1940s. "We have a large population of people 62 and over," said Stone. "I told them, 'stay and join the tenants' association.' There was never any attempt to move them out."

The tenants and their attorneys then began extensive

The elevator doors on the upper floors of the General Scott feature Art Deco monograms.

The efficiency apartments of the General Scott were designed with a solarium; the Murphy bed was kept in a closet.

negotiations with lawyers representing the two estates [of Ernst and Scholz] that owned the property. The high percentage of membership in the tenants' association was a factor in the residents' favor. "Those meetings went on for hours and hours," said Stone. "In them, I said, 'We have 88 percent membership [in the tenants' association] and they'll go along with whatever we okay.'" Despite their length, the negotiations were generally amicable. "I really believe the owners wanted to make it possible for the ten-

ants to purchase the building," commented Emerald Van Buskirk, the tenant association's second chairman. "They saw how serious we were from an early point in the negotiations."

Finally, in April 1981, the residents signed a contract to purchase the property, with settlement scheduled for December of that year. Because of the deteriorating conditions in the Washington condominium market, the tenants were unable to meet that deadline and had to have the contract extended and amended several times. A major decision point came in March of this year. The tenants had already invested an average of $1,400 each for the tenants' association's expenses. Moreover, their professional advisers told them it could cost at least that much more before they could purchase the building and obtain conversion financing. Many banks, however, were already holding in default loans from condo developments. Much of the success of the General Scott conversion depended on whether the tenants could successfully market units to the public, because a lender would be willing to help finance the conversion only if there were a guarantee on the public sales.

John Hoskinson, the real estate consultant advising the tenants, approached several lenders, all of whom were reluctant to make a conversion loan to the residents' group. Through their extended negotiations, however, the tenants' association had been able to persuade the building's owners to take back a $3.1 million loan on the property at 12 percent interest. At the time, the market rate was 18 percent. The tenants had to decide whether they should risk putting up more money for additional development costs and whether they should offer the 12 percent financing to public purchasers, to attract more buyers as quickly as possible. Before they could obtain conversion financing, the lenders wanted the residents to make rehab plans, obtain a fixed-price construction contract, prepare the condo documents, vote in favor of conversion and line up a large percentage of tenant and public purchasers.

Even their real estate consultant wasn't sure of what path the tenants should choose. "At the time their deal wasn't significantly better than the public's," Hoskinson said. "As their professional adviser, I didn't know what they should do." When the vote was taken, the majority decided to go ahead. By offering favorable financing and prices competitive with other projects, the group obtained reservations on 80 percent of the units. With these commitments, the tenants' association again approached several of the reluctant lenders. American Security Bank agreed to provide the financing. On Oct. 1, the residents signed for the $2.15 million conversion loan.

Before they secured the loan, the residents had raised and spent over $300,000 for development costs—an average of $4,000 each—without any assurances they would be able to complete the conversion or that they could get back even a portion of their monies. Of the 181

efficiency and one-bedroom units, 73 were sold to original tenants. Investors have reserved forty-one of the apartments and will continue renting them to their current elderly and low-income residents. Of the sixty-seven public units, only twenty-three remained unsold at the end of last month. The public units went for an average price of $43,000. The original tenants will pay an average of $33,000. The interest rate on the tenant apartments, however, will not be determined until the residents settle on their loans sometime next year, after the renovation of the building is substantially completed.

Tenant advisor Hoskinson is aware of the residents' significant achievement in a real estate market that has confounded many real estate professionals. "They refused to proceed until they had a deal that would work in the most adverse market conditions," he said. "This tenant group has done better than many developers."

As a footnote to this 1982 newspaper article, the conversion of the General Scott was a complete success. During the following year all twenty-three remaining apartments were sold. The tenants' association dissolved itself, and a new board of directors of the condominium was duly elected and has operated smoothly since. Major renovations, completed within two years, included a new roof, new windows, improved electrical service, updating of the original three elevators, a new trash compactor, a redecorated lobby, and major improvements to the heating and cooling system. Each apartment now has individual thermostatic controls. The original 1940 central air-conditioning machinery was overhauled and retained, making it possibly the oldest surviving air-conditioning equipment in any Washington apartment house.

The purchase of the General Scott by its tenants is not unique. Tenants in several other rental apartment houses in Washington purchased their buildings outright, including the Jefferson House and BonWit Plaza in Foggy Bottom and Beverly Court in Adams-Morgan. The tenants' purchase of the General Scott was the most difficult in Washington, however, because interest rates were extremely high then. At that very time, a number of developers attempting to convert other apartment houses to condominium status (involving the Letterman House, the Washington House, the Envoy, and McLean Gardens, for instance) went bankrupt.

109

CARLYN, now GATEWAY GEORGETOWN

2500 Que Street, N.W.; southwest end of Dumbarton Bridge

ARCHITECT: Francis L. Koenig, 1941

ORIGINAL APARTMENTS: 275 (59 efficiencies; 197 one-bedrooms; 17 two-bedrooms; 2 three-bedrooms)

STATUS: opened as rental in 1941; converted to condo in 1973

The severely plain facade of the Carlyn is slightly relieved by the horizontal bands of dark red brick that appear on the left of this photograph.

Built in a record five months for $1 million, the Carlyn opened on a fateful date, 7 December 1941. At the time one of the largest rental luxury apartment houses in Washington, the Carlyn's size is obscured by its irregular U shape. It borders Rock Creek Park and Dumbarton Bridge on the east and extends through the block from Que to P streets. Gustave Ring, the builder and owner, named the seven-story building for his daughter.

The most striking feature of the Carlyn is its stark simplicity. The great length of the front facade and the building's strong horizontal lines produce a rather heavy effect, although seven projecting pavilions on the front, corners, and ends provide some relief. However, the vast brick facade (1.2 million bricks were used) gains subtle interest from the arrangement of contrasting bands of dark tapestry brick, set against the red brick, along part of the top floor and on some of the pavilions. Since the building is located on a hill (the former site of a large streetcar barn), the front entrance is actually on the third floor with the first and second floors facing to the rear on P Street, N.W.

Close inspection of the interior reveals a number of innovative features. Since the Carlyn is situated on a steep hill, the architect placed the street level lobby midway between the second and third floors. The public

Like the Marlyn, the lobby of the Carlyn is midway between the first and second floors.

hallways, visible from the lobby, offer a good review of late Art Deco streamlined design, with such details as an aluminum balustrade, oval columns, dropped ceilings, curved walls, and hard-rubber black borders on each side of the terrazzo floors. The architect's ingenuity is evident in the fire extinguishers set into niches in the hallways, the simple but elegant wrought-iron rails in the staircases, and sliding cabinet doors in the small kitchens to conserve space and prevent accidents. Within the public corridors,

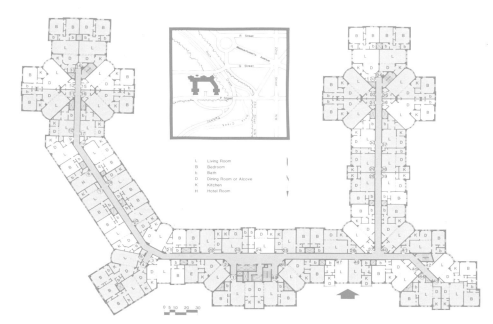

Unusual in the Carlyn is the diagonal arrangement of the living room in a number of tiers.

apartment doors are staggered so that no two doors face one another and thus enhance privacy.

The Carlyn's current 271 apartments range in size from efficiencies to two-bedrooms with two baths. Austerity and economy prevailed through the end of the Great Depression; instead of formal dining rooms, dining alcoves opened directly into the living rooms. Diagonal living rooms in sixteen tiers are particularly unusual and innovative; at the junction of two wings these directly face the apex of the junction. The outer walls of these living rooms (facing the outside) were designed with a projecting bow or curved bay of glass windows, resulting in increased living room floor space, much greater light, and better ventilation. In addition, the curved bays add interest to the rather plain facade of the building. Because of this design, all of the dining alcoves in these units are wedge-shaped. Other odd angles were used for closet space and are thus not noticeable.

A pleasant amenity originally offered involved five furnished "hotel" rooms, without kitchens, which could be rented for short periods by permanent residents as additional quarters for guests. The Carlyn also contains a basement garage on one level, which opens onto P Street, N.W., with space for 120 cars and a doctor's office with a private entrance from Que Street (to the left of the main entrance). Part of the basement space was originally intended as a public dining room, but World War II labor shortages prevented its ever opening. This space was consequently divided into commercial use during the war—drugstore, beauty shop, and barbershop—facilities now long since disappeared. Since the public was expected to use the basement hall, its floor and wainscoting were laid in cheerful yellow and tan ceramic tile, an unusually refined feature for an otherwise neglected area in most apartment houses.

The original owner lived in an apartment on the seventh floor from 1941 until 1951, when he purchased a house on Massachusetts Avenue just west of Sheridan Circle. When Gustave Ring moved out, he sold the building to another local investor, Meyer Siegel, whose careful selection of tenants and management set a model for other rental apartment houses. For the following twenty-two years, Siegel constantly improved and renovated the Carlyn. During this time a number of tenants on the top floor were allowed to add private roofdecks, and tenants on the ground level on the rear courtyard added their own private patios and small gardens. The original marquee was removed and replaced by a simple porte-cochère for cars entering the semicircular driveway. Central air conditioning was added, a new lobby desk was installed, the basement commercial space was closed to reduce noise and traffic, new excavation increased garage parking from 120 to 149 cars, a vestibule was added to the entrance, and the south side of the lobby—which was open to the third-floor corridor—was closed off to provide greater privacy for residents in that area. Siegel's plans for an outdoor swimming pool in the rear courtyard were abandoned, however, when engineers determined that the un-

The architect designed the compact kitchens at the Carlyn with sliding cabinet doors to conserve space and to prevent collision with open doors.

This one-bedroom unit at the Carlyn, owned and occupied by Moya King, has a dining alcove completely open to the living room, a feature that became typical of Washington apartment houses beginning in the late 1930s.

Kenneth Gallaway, the head janitor at the Carlyn, relaxes in his basement office.

derground garage ceiling could not support the added weight.

In 1973 Siegel sold the Carlyn to developers who converted it to a condominium. More than 70 percent of the tenants, an unusually high ratio, elected to buy their units. In the conversion process the developer unfortunately redecorated the lobby, painting over the handsome 6-½-foot-wide Art Deco mural on the west wall, eliminated the five guest bedrooms, and renamed the building "Gateway Georgetown."

Over the years the Carlyn has housed many leading political and military notables, including more than two dozen members of Congress. It was featured in several important scenes when Allen Drury's famous novel about political life in Washington, *Advise and Consent*, was made into a movie. A glittering cocktail party was filmed in a beautiful first-floor apartment, and a second scene in the lobby featured Henry Fonda holding court.

In a recent walk through the Carlyn, its architect, Francis L. Koenig, recounted the many trials and tribulations of its construction. During almost all of 1941 Koenig worked simultaneously as construction superintendent for two large Washington apartment houses, the Carlyn and the Dorchester House (which he also designed). Fearful that America's entry into World War II would cause a severe shortage of building materials, he worked on both buildings at a frantic pace, sixteen hours a day, seven days a week, for several months. Although he developed bleeding ulcers and was hospitalized in late summer 1941, he continued to supervise the construction of both buildings by telephone. As a result both were completed ahead of schedule. The completion of the Carlyn in five months set a record for the construction time for a large Washington apartment house that has never been broken.

110

DELANO

2745 29th Street, N.W.; east side of 29th Street between Calvert Street and Woodley Road

ARCHITECT: George T. Santmyers, 1941

ORIGINAL APARTMENTS: 125 (35 efficiencies; 78 one-bedrooms; 12 two-bedrooms)

STATUS: opened as rental in 1942

Hidden away on 29th Street, N.W., a quiet residential area between Calvert Street and Woodley Road, the Delano remains a delightful surprise to the Art Deco enthusiast. Designed in an H shape, the facade of this six-story tan-brick apartment house includes typical Art Deco detailing such as wraparound corner windows, a pair of rounded bays, ribbed spandrels, and ribbed porch piers on the entrance pavilion. Best of all is the well-preserved lobby with its indirectly lit, circular recessed ceiling, blue mirrors, tufted blue leather "wainscoting," geometric plaster cornice, and wrought-iron swag balustrades.

More than two dozen outstanding Art Deco apartment

The architect's original 1941 perspective of the Delano.

One of the original features of the Delano's Art Deco lobby is the tufted blue leather wainscoting.

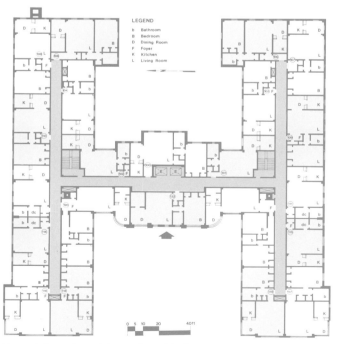

Typical floor plan of the H-shaped Delano.

These two living room arches in a Delano apartment open onto the foyer on the right and a study on the left.

house lobbies survive in Washington. Those built in the 1930s and still intact include the Kennedy-Warren, Sedgwick Gardens, 2929 Connecticut Avenue, N.W., the Marlyn, the Normandie, Park Central, and 4801 Connecticut Avenue, N.W. (Unfortunately, one of the finest of the 1930s was in the Governor Shepherd, razed in 1985.) The best remaining Art Deco lobbies from the early 1940s include the Dorchester House, the General Scott, the Delano, the Bay State, and the Washington House. Many of these are characterized by step-down lobbies, indirect lighting, recessed ceilings, streamlined and curved walls, and aluminum balustrades.

Built on a hill, the Delano is entered on the second floor, with the first floor and basement facing the rear. The building has many amenities, including a lobby switchboard and a basement garage for fifty-one cars. Six fans on the roof originally blew fresh air into the public corridors through a pair of grilles on each floor. This system was unusual, since most of the pre–World War II air-cooling systems in Washington had exterior fans at the ground-floor level rather than on the roof.

A section of the wrought-iron Art Deco balustrade in the lobby of the Delano.

In this roof view of the Delano, the resident manager, Jim Bogley, perches on one of several vents that house fans originally used to blow fresh air into the public corridors. Also shown is the old incinerator smoke-stack and a skylight that provides natural light to the top-floor public corridor.

The majority of the Delano's 125 apartments are one-bedroom units. Within each apartment are a foyer and coat closet, arched openings connecting the living room to the foyer and dining alcove, wood-block floors, and handsome tile bathrooms laid in four colors—black, white, maroon, and beige.

The structure was built by Sidney Brown, a local developer who three years earlier had completed two garden apartment complexes on upper 14th Street, N.W. In the manager's office on the lower level still hangs the original watercolor perspective of the Delano, which is slightly different from the completed building. The Delano is still rental and remains owned by the Brown family.

ARCHITECT GEORGE T. SANTMYERS

The most prolific architect of Washington apartment buildings in the history of the city was George T. Sant-myers, who designed more than four hundred between 1916 and his death in 1960. Born in Front Royal, Virginia, in 1889, he lived mainly in Baltimore before moving to Washington while in high school. He was trained by working as a draftsman under several local architects before opening his own firm in 1914. Although he designed all types of buildings, including houses and commercial structures, he became a specialist in apartment houses. During the late 1920s he designed a number of large eclectic apartment houses, often incorporating the then-popular Tudor, Gothic, or Moorish details in the facades and lobbies. Although many of Santmyers's apartment buildings were small and located in all parts of the city, most were in the Northwest section. His apartment buildings appear on many major streets, such as 3217, 3446, 3901, 4700, 4701, 5130, and 5433 Connecticut Avenue, N.W., and 2200, 3022, 3030, 3110, 3213, 4105, and 4115 Wisconsin Avenue, N.W.

He is best remembered for his many Art Deco apartment houses—mostly garden apartments—from the 1930s and 1940s, but he also designed some elaborate apartment houses during this period, including the Delano, the Normandie, Macomb Gardens, 2800 Woodley Road, N.W., and the Yorkshire on upper 16th Street, N.W. Following World War II he and James Thomen were partners (Santmyers and Thomen). Their prominent modernistic apartment houses from the 1950s include the Tunlaw Park at Tunlaw Road and 39th Street, N.W., the Coronet at 2nd and C streets, S.E., the Wiltshire Crescent at 3801 Connecticut Avenue, N.W., and the Wiltshire Parkway at 3701 Connecticut Avenue, N.W. The last two were built by developers Harry and Morris Lenkin and Meyer Siegel. Santmyers died only six months after he retired from his architectural practice in 1960.

111

DORCHESTER HOUSE

2480 16th Street, N.W.; west side of 16th Street between Kalorama Road and Euclid Street

ARCHITECT: Francis L. Koenig, 1941

ORIGINAL APARTMENTS: 394 (70 efficiencies; 291 one-bedrooms; 33 two-bedrooms)

STATUS: opened as rental in 1941

When constructed between January and October 1941, the Dorchester House was one of the three largest apartment houses in Washington, with a thousand tenants occupying the 394 apartments. The original owners—Herbert Glassman, Morris Gewirz, Harry Viner, and Edward Ostrow—employed the Ring Engineering Company to build the structure, which was completed in a record-breaking nine months. Architect Francis L. Koenig designed the cross-shaped residence to get the maximum number of apartments on the site, which is across the street from then-fashionable Meridian Hill Park.

The streamlined buff-brick facade makes the Dorchester House one of the city's most distinctive Art Deco apartment houses. Interest was added to the vertical bays with brown brick above and below many of the windows. The top (ninth) floor is defined by the black-brick spandrels. As in the Carlyn, also designed by Koenig, the Dorchester House contains so-called diagonal living rooms. In the sixteen tiers of apartments at the intersection of two wings, the living rooms are diagonal to the junction of the two walls. At the ends facing the outside, each of these living rooms includes a wide, protruding curved bay of glass windows, providing additional floor space and good light.

Living rooms in another set of twelve smaller apart-ments on the ground floor facing Euclid Street include glass doors opening directly to the outside, flanked by floor-to-ceiling glass windows, also greatly increasing the light in the living room. In the typical floor plan, three-quarters of the apartments are one-bedroom units; each floor also includes a set of four two-bedroom units and eight efficiencies. In all of the apartments here, as at the Carlyn, dining alcoves opening onto the living rooms replace formal dining rooms, to conserve space and increase natural light.

One enters the Dorchester House under an aluminum marquee at the corner of 16th Street and Kalorama Road, N.W., originally arranged to boast the more prestigious 16th Street address. Passing through a handsome rounded lobby foyer, with indirect lighting and fluted supporting columns (now unfortunately covered), a visitor ascends one of a pair of short stairs to Peacock Alley, which leads to the desk at the far end. A bank of three elevators is in the center of the building. The lobby is thus the longest of any Washington apartment house. Privacy was provided for the six apartments facing the lobby by an additional wall that screens the lobby from their view.

When it opened in 1941 the Dorchester House's amenities included a uniformed doorman, parking space on the grounds, air conditioned public hallways, and a

The main entrance of the Dorchester House was placed in the right wing rather than in the center of the building to secure the more prestigious 16th Street address.

Resident Richard Mancini looks through his Art Deco peephole before admitting a visitor at the Dorchester House.

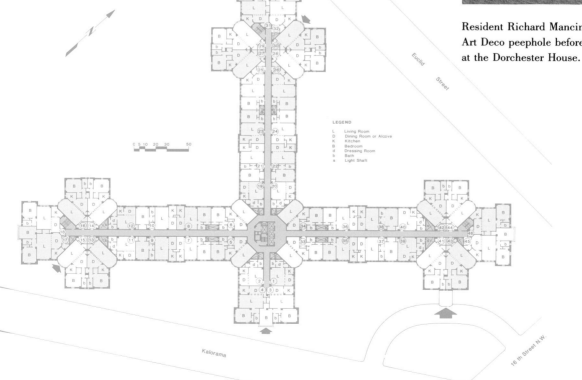

Architect Francis L. Koenig designed diagonal living rooms in the Dorchester House. Their bowed bay windows are in the apexes of the building.

A number of the Dorchester House's ground-floor apartments have private outside entrances and terraces.

roofdeck commanding one of the most sweeping views of the entire city. Five stores—including a drugstore, antique shop, dry cleaner, beauty parlor, and grocery—were located on the basement level.

During World War II numerous prominent residents lived here, including Secretary of Labor Frances Perkins, a dozen members of Congress, and crooner Eddie Fisher, who was then in military service. The most notable resident was a twenty-four-year-old naval ensign, John F. Kennedy, who occupied apartment No. 502 from October 1941 to January 1942. During his brief residence he was romantically involved with a beautiful blonde Danish journalist employed by the *Washington Times Herald*. For this dramatic episode, the Dorchester House is noted in two recent biographies of John F. Kennedy by Herbert S. Parmet and Lynne Taggart.

Already well known as the young author of *Why England Slept*, which he wrote as a Harvard student visiting in London (while Joseph Kennedy was ambassador to the Court of St. James), Jack Kennedy entered the U.S. Navy as an ensign a month before moving into the Dorchester House. After graduating from Harvard in

May 1940, Kennedy had enrolled in summer school at Stanford and then returned to Boston for medical treatment for a severe back disorder. In the spring of 1941 he attempted to enter the Army and then the Navy but was turned down because of his back problem. Consequently he devoted the summer of 1941 to back-strengthening exercises and was finally accepted into the Navy officers training course and commissioned on 25 September 1941.

Assigned to the Office of Naval Intelligence in Washington in October 1941, Kennedy helped prepare intelligence reports, culling information from various foreign sources. Life in Washington was made much more interesting for the young officer by his socially active sister, Kathleen, who worked for the *Washington Times Herald*, then one of the city's largest papers. When young Kennedy was reassigned to the Naval Station in Charleston, South Carolina, in January 1942, his apartment was then occupied by Kathleen. He was later trained for sea duty at Evanston, Illinois, and then shipped to the Solomon Islands in March 1943 as the commander of a PT boat.

112

McLEAN GARDENS

3811 Porter Street, N.W.; west side of Wisconsin Avenue between Porter and Rodman streets

ARCHITECT: Kenneth Franzheim, New York City; Allan B. Mills, associate architect, 1942–43

ORIGINAL APARTMENTS: 721 (60 efficiencies; 441 one-bedrooms; 220 two-bedrooms)
plus 1,152 dormitory rooms (945 singles and 207 doubles)

STATUS: opened as rental in 1942–43; partially demolished in 1974–75; balance converted to condo in 1981

The most famous of all the three hundred garden apartments built in the Washington metropolitan area is McLean Gardens, located on 43 acres of prime real estate just four blocks north of the Washington Cathedral. Like several other large Washington garden apartments, McLean Gardens was built by the Defense Homes Corporation to help house the enormous influx of civilian war workers. After the war the government sold these wartime housing complexes to private developers, who continued to manage them as rental housing.

The federal government purchased a former country estate on the site, Friendship, for $1 million from Evalyn Walsh McLean in late 1941. Although construction began immediately, the original buildings on the estate were not demolished until late summer 1942. The elegant retreat had been created by John R. McLean, an Ohioan who owned both the *Cincinnati Inquirer* and the *Washington Post* as well as numerous Washington properties and business interests. His name survives in fashionable McLean, Virginia, one of the stations on his streetcar line, which extended from Washington into Fairfax County in the early twentieth century.

The Wisconsin Avenue tract of land was originally part of a 3,000-acre land grant made to Colonel John Addison in 1695. Addison's name for his Maryland plantation was Friendship. Although a small Federal house dating from the early nineteenth century was still standing on the grounds, it was not adequate for the McLeans' elaborate formal entertaining. Consequently they commissioned noted New York architect John Russell Pope to design the great Georgian Revival house of 1903. Soon thereafter, Pope was commissioned to remodel the McLeans' townhouse, which was soon expanded to occupy the entire south side of McPherson Square. It was one of two dozen noteworthy Washington area buildings designed by Pope during his long career (the Jefferson Memorial and the National Gallery of Art in 1937 were his last). At the imposing Friendship, John R. McLean entertained such notables as President William Howard Taft, both Theodore Roosevelt's and Taft's military aide Captain Archie Butt, Speaker Joseph Cannon, Nicholas Longworth and his wife, Alice Roosevelt Longworth, and Senator Henry Cabot Lodge.

Following the elder McLean's death, Friendship was inherited by his son, Edward Beale McLean, and his wife, Evalyn Walsh McLean. As heirs of two great fortunes totaling more than $100 million, the young McLeans entertained during the teens and 1920s in a grand style never seen before or since in Washington. By the time of Evalyn McLean's death in 1947, almost the entire

Top: One of the original Colonial Revival buildings at McLean Gardens. *Bottom:*
Friendship, the elegant country house designed by John Russell Pope in 1903 and built for
publisher John R. McLean, is shown in early 1942 shortly before it was razed by the federal
government for McLean Gardens.

inheritance had been spent and the family was destroyed by tragedy—suicide, drug addiction, insanity, and alcoholism.

With the government's purchase of Friendship imminent, Mrs. McLean moved in December 1941 to another historic house on R Street just west of Wisconsin Avenue in Georgetown (which was called New Friendship). An army of workmen descended on the old Friendship to begin construction of the forty large three-story garden apartment buildings. On the rear 30 acres were thirty-one buildings housing 721 apartments—60 efficiencies, 441 one-bedrooms, and 220 two-bedrooms. The front 10 acres bordering Wisconsin Avenue were selected for nine dormitory buildings, in the same Colonial Revival style as the apartment buildings.

The three-story buildings, set on spacious lawns on

winding streets, were an immediate success. Amenities included a nursery school, cafeteria, and weekly dances in the ballroom of the administration building. Nearly four thousand residents occupied McLean Gardens at one time during World War II. Sold by the government in 1948 to the Hartford Insurance Company, McLean Gardens continued to be fully occupied and well managed as a rental property until 1970. Then began one of the longest and most bitter battles between tenants and developers in Washington history.

CHANGING TIMES

The Defense Homes Corporation, which built McLean Gardens, was a federal agency established to help alleviate the serious housing shortage for defense workers that resulted from stepped-up defense production and expansion of military reservations two years before the United States entered World War II. Although first established as part of the Reconstruction Finance Corporation, in 1942 the Defense Homes Corporation became part of the Federal Public Housing Authority. During its eight years of operation, the Defense Homes Corporation built eleven thousand housing units including small houses, dormitories, hotels, and apartment houses in thirteen states and the District of Columbia. In the Washington area during World War II, it built the Meridian Hill Hotel for white women war workers, another for black women war workers, and several large garden apartment complexes in addition to McLean Gardens and Naylor Gardens. (Beginning in 1945, just after the war, the Defense Homes Corporation began to sell its residential real estate holdings and finally closed its operations in 1948.)

The first plans to redevelop McLean Gardens were announced in 1970 by the Hartford Insurance Company, which controlled Fairmac, Inc., owner of both Fairlington Village in Arlington, Virginia, and McLean Gardens ("Fair" plus "Mac"). McLean Gardens was to be razed for a $170 million mini-city that would include office buildings, high-rise apartment houses with twenty-two hundred units, a hotel, hospital, shopping center, and

Evalyn Walsh McLean, wearing the Hope Diamond, with her three children at Friendship several years before it was demolished for McLean Gardens.

private school. In reaction, the alarmed tenants of McLean Gardens immediately formed the McLean Gardens Residents Association and employed lawyers to fight the plan. Weary of the legal delays, the Hartford Insurance Company sold Fairmac, Inc., to the Chicago Bridge and Iron Company (CBI) for $56 million in 1974.

The new owners of McLean Gardens, CBI, announced plans to convert the apartment houses to condominiums. The McLean Gardens Residents Association again organized and, with the help of Ward 3 D.C. Council Member Polly Shackleton, arranged for a moratorium on conversions. CBI meanwhile razed the nine dormitory buildings in 1974–75. This company had encountered little resistance to converting Fairlington Village in Virginia to condos, a project commenced in 1974. Blocked by the condo moratorium in Washington, CBI next announced plans in 1975 to raze the remaining buildings at McLean Gardens and spend $150 million to develop the site for a shopping mall, foreign embassies, offices, and high-rise apartment houses. This project was finally blocked in early 1978, when the District of Columbia Zoning Commission, on the advice of the National Capital

Planning Commission, ruled that the site was inappropriate for a major embassy compound.

Next, the owners of McLean Gardens announced that they could not realize an adequate return on rents because of the D.C. rent control law. They sent eviction notices to the remaining tenants in March 1978, giving them six months to vacate. CBI sold McLean Gardens for $25 million to a California developer, Dwight D. Mize, who announced his plans in April 1978 to convert McLean Gardens to condominiums. By late 1978 the number of tenants had fallen to 205; most had voluntarily left, considering the situation hopeless. As the tenants moved out, Fairmac, Inc., left the units vacant, but beginning in 1977, had spent $740,000 on payments and moving allowances to tenants when eviction notices were served. Most buildings contained eighteen apartments each, six to a floor. By late 1978 many buildings had only two or three occupants. Conditions were depressing, with much of the rubble from the razed dormitories still evident.

Fairmac, Inc., now under Mize's ownership, and abiding by the terms of a new D.C. law, offered to sell McLean Gardens to the remaining two hundred tenants. The Fairmac people were astonished when the tenants raised the down payment of $500,000, most of which had been advanced to the McLean Gardens Residents Association through local real estate developers who planned to have a part in the project if the tenants themselves converted it to condo status. The developers, headed by William P. McCulloch III, had made a deal with the remaining tenants to give them their apartments, which would be renovated, at half their market value, plus 5-percent profit on the entire property and the profits from the sale of sixty apartments. The California developer, Dwight Mize, was paid slightly more than $2 million above his original purchase price by the tenants association and the developers to give up all claims to McLean Gardens.

The tenants converted McLean Gardens into a condominium in 1981. The project was made possible through a $50 million loan from the Continental Illinois Bank and Trust Company of Chicago. Some $31 million was to go for rehabilitation of the existing units before they were sold. The owners included McLean Gardens Residents Association (27.5 percent), Rubloff and Company (51

percent), William P. McCulloch III (7.5 percent), David Marshall (5 percent), and several small investors.

The 1979 conversion plan called for 720 apartments in thirty-one buildings to be rehabilitated and then sold as condominiums in three phases. The first phase contemplated sale of the initial apartments in April 1980. The last phase called for 600 new units to be constructed on the now-vacant land along Wisconsin Avenue, beginning in 1985. Management of the conversion was a disaster, however. The conversion first took too long, with interest on the $50 million loan amounting to $237,000 a month, and then went considerably over budget.

Because of spiraling costs, caused in part by elaborate renovations, prices of the units rose from the original 1978 estimates of $40,000 to $70,000 per apartment up to prices ranging from $95,000 to $215,000 in late 1981. Few of the newly designed luxury duplex apartments sold, especially after the real estate market collapsed in mid–1981. The results were that Rubloff and Company, which owned the controlling share of the stock, fired the project manager, David Marshall; the five-member executive committee; the construction company, Century; and the advertising firm of Words and Company. The representative of Rubloff and Company, Jeffrey Server, had constant fights with the other investors as well.

The Chicago bank, Continental Illinois, as a result foreclosed on McLean Gardens in 1981, acquiring the complex. In July 1982 the bank hired Richard Stein, a Chicago realtor, to supervise sales and conversion of the final apartments, which were now being rehabilitated by the Frederick Construction Company.

THE VILLAGE OF McLEAN GARDENS

In the meantime, the vacant 9.1 acres formerly occupied by the old McLean Gardens dormitories fronting on Wisconsin Avenue and located on both sides of Porter Street was acquired back by CBI, a previous owner. This firm sold the vacant land (including the old Community Building of McLean Gardens) in 1983 to Village of McLean Gardens Associates (VMG). The partners of VMG, Wallace F. Holladay, Terry Eakin, and other officers of the Holladay Corporation, developed the land after the D.C.

government ruled that all new residential construction would be exempt from the city's current rent control law. The drastic drop in interest rates in 1984 was an added incentive to develop this choice intown location as rental apartments.

After approval by the D.C. Zoning Commission, construction began in 1984 on the new $60 million mixed-use building project, designed by the two firms of Keyes, Condon, and Florance and Stinson and Capelli. The project consists of three parts: a nine-story tower housing both residential space (214 apartments) and retail stores, located south of Porter Street; a five-story office building, also on the south side; and 360 apartment units in a series of four-story buildings, located primarily on the portion of the site north of Porter Street. A two-level garage is located below both the residential tower and the office building. VMG also includes a new outdoor swimming pool at ground level on the northern portion of the site. Even though VMG owns the Community Building, the residents of the older buildings within McLean Gardens are allowed full use of it.

LIFE AT McLEAN GARDENS: THE McLEANS

The enormous problems involved with the conversion of McLean Gardens to condominium status (which almost equaled those endured by the tenants of the General Scott) make one wonder if McLean Gardens has permanently fallen under the legendary curse of the Hope Diamond, which Evalyn Walsh McLean proudly owned for half a century. The story of the Hope Diamond and of the McLeans' life-style is an integral part of the history of this site. Through a series of interviews with friends of the family as well as the McLeans' servants, a rare account of life at Friendship was pieced together by [Washington] *Evening Star* journalist George Kennedy in 1951, a few years after the death of Evalyn Walsh McLean:

> John R. McLean died in 1916 and it was then that Friendship entered its living period. The younger McLeans were two of the greatest showoffs in a showy age. The extensive stables became crowded with foreign cars—Fiats, Lancias, Mercedes, and Isotta-Fraschinis.

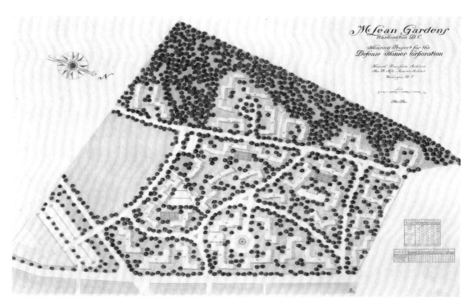

The original site plan for McLean Gardens. Wisconsin Avenue appears in the foreground, while Porter Street bisects it in the center.

When Ned McLean married Evalyn Walsh, daughter of Thomas F. Walsh of the Camp Bird gold mine, both fathers gave them $100,000 each as a wedding present. They spent it on a European honeymoon from which they returned considerably in debt. They started out with a Packard roadster with bucket seat and a rumble space for the chauffeur and a maid. They bought a Mercedes sport car in Paris and let the chauffeur drive the Packard. They had bought one of the largest diamonds in the world, the Star of the East, and soon were to buy the Hope Diamond.

Of all the stories associated with Friendship, the tragic one of the $100 million baby probably will be remembered longest. Vinson McLean, born in 1909, was the most famous American baby of his day. King Leopold of Belgium, who had profited from Thomas F. Walsh's Camp Bird gold mine, gave the baby a $35,000 crib of rosewood decorated with gold.

The baby became so famous through the Sunday supplements that the mother was terrified by crank letters threatening to kidnap or kill the child. The nursemaids were always accompanied by armed bodyguards and the child had a special steel perambulator which attracted so much attention in the press that a crowd of several thousand once assembled on a Hoboken pier to catch a glimpse of it when the McLeans left for Europe.

The child's presents on his fourth Christmas in 1913 were estimated to cost $40,000. One was a scale model of a steam yacht. A special private railway car was built for Vinson with an early air-conditioning system. Vinson's sand box at Friendship was a large one. Two railway gondolas were used to bring sand from Palm Beach. Vinson's parents were afraid to take him to the circus so they had Ringling Bros. Barnum & Bailey come to Friendship and give him a private performance. He had a team of goats, two Great Danes, two Russian wolfhounds, a snow-white Colorado burro and 56 Shropshire sheep.

When the McLeans went to Louisville in 1919 to the Kentucky Derby two more private detectives were hired to guard the boy. That made six. It was then that little Vinson ran out the gate of Friendship across Wisconsin Avenue to greet a gardener with a load of ferns. He snatched a fern and ran back in front of a Model T Ford in which three women from West Virginia were touring Washington. The boy was knocked down, but the car was going very slowly. He jumped up and walked into the house.

The women were assured by the servants that he was all right, no one even took their names, and they had to be located later by the license number of their car. Vinson had a fractured skull and died that evening. The Hope Diamond was blamed for the tragedy by the Sunday supplements, which also laid to it the beheading of Marie Antoinette and the fall of the Caliphate at Constantinople.

During the Harding administration Friendship became a presidential playground. Both Harding and his Vice-President, Calvin Coolidge, played golf on the links, and Harding, Harry Daugherty, Charles Curtis and other administration figures played poker in the house there on summer evenings. Then came the Teapot Dome exposures and McLean's attempt to save Secretary of the Interior Fall by saying he had loaned the cabinet officer $100,000. Called to the witness stand he had to admit it was a lie.

During the remainder of Republican rule in Washington, Friendship had few guests high in administration circles, but in the exciting days of the New Deal it came into its own again. Only the hostess remained. Her husband was in a hospital for years before his death. But it was like the old days. She had almost everybody—except the President. She lionized John L. Lewis and Supreme Court justices and Leon Henderson.

On the last night of 1936 she renewed her New Year's Eve parties—this one in honor of the 21st birthday of Jock, her second son. She built a wing on the house for the party so that there would be room for 600 to dance. Meyer Davis directed his orchestra. That was for the old people. For the youngsters the age of swing was recognized by bringing Benny Goodman and his Hotel Pennsylvania orchestra down from New York. It was one of the biggest parties Grifoni, the butler who had served the elder McLeans, was ever faced with. Three hundred sat down to dinner, and they were served promptly and smoothly.

The last of the parties at Friendship was at the end of 1941, right after Pearl Harbor. The government purchased Friendship, and the big iron gates and the cast-iron pool of the fountain were donated as metal for the military. The house was torn down and buildings began to go up all over the 75 acres. Only the stone wall and the iron mermaids remain today at McLean Gardens.

113

PARKFAIRFAX

3360 Gunston Road, Alexandria, Virginia; intersection of Shirley Highway and Quaker Lane

ARCHITECT: Leonard Schultze and Associates, New York City, 1942

ORIGINAL APARTMENTS: 1,684 (720 one-bedrooms; 863 two-bedrooms; 101 three-bedrooms)

STATUS: opened as rental in 1942–43; converted to condo in 1977–79

Originally covering 201 acres of rolling hills in Alexandria, Virginia, Parkfairfax was built by the Metropolitan Life Insurance Company at the urgent request of the federal government as a rental housing investment in 1942–43. Because Metropolitan Life was thoroughly experienced in planning, building, and even managing large garden apartment projects, Parkfairfax was an exceptional example of good design. By the mid-1920s Metropolitan had built several large garden apartment complexes in the borough of Queens, New York City, and in the late 1930s constructed the renowned Parkchester in the Bronx. The Parkchester, with 12,272 apartments, was then considered the largest single housing project in the world.

Built at a cost of $8.5 million, Parkfairfax consists of 286 separate buildings, many grouped together in connected clusters of two or three that either face or back onto parklike settings. The 1,684 apartments are divided into 720 one-bedrooms, 863 two-bedrooms, and 101 three-bedrooms. The three-bedroom apartments, all duplexes, are placed two to a building with their entrances opening onto an open breezeway running through the center of the building. Most of the largest three-bedroom units are clustered together on "Nob Hill" (Mount Eagle Place).

For variety, two types of brick were used—the cheaper white-painted sand brick and the more expensive finished and exposed red brick. One of Parkfairfax's most desirable features is its separate outside entrances. A second attraction is the small size of the buildings: most are two stories with only four to ten apartments. Both outside entrances and small buildings increase residents' privacy. (Unfortunately, most garden apartments lack these features, which require more land and expense than is practical.)

To further maintain interest, the buildings vary in height, shape, and facade treatment, and the apartments themselves in size and layout. For instance, Building 701, built on a hill, has a total of six apartments: two, facing Valley Drive, occupy the first floor and open onto the rear. The ground-level apartments have their own patios, which extend 20 feet out from the rear of the building. Although the Parkfairfax buildings have no basements, many have attic space under their gabled roofs for storage. Most kitchens and baths are on the fronts of the buildings, while the bedrooms, dining rooms, and living rooms look out on the rear lawns, providing greater privacy.

The developer retained the original rolling contours of the land by arranging the apartment buildings on only one-tenth of the site. All wires are underground. The careful planning included asymmetrical winding streets

Designed in the Colonial Revival style, typical of most Washington garden apartments of the 1930s and 1940s, the buildings comprising Parkfairfax vary considerably in both their plans and their architectural detailing.

Site plan for Parkfairfax.

to keep traffic at 25 mph. At Parkfairfax there are only thirteen apartments per acre, while nearby Fairlington has twenty-seven per acre. (Fairlington, with its thirty-four hundred apartments, was also built by the Metropolitan Life Insurance Company in 1942–43. At the time that Parkfairfax and Fairlington were being constructed, the adjacent Shirley Highway was bulldozed through to connect the newly constructed Pentagon with Fort Belvoir. It greatly improved access to Washington after it was completed in 1944.)

Part of the land in the Parkfairfax complex was donated by Metropolitan Life, along with $50,000, to the city of Alexandria for a new public elementary school. Located on Martha Custis Drive, the Charles Barrett School, named for a Marine Corps general killed in World War II, opened on 25 October 1943, a month after the first resident moved into Parkfairfax. This temporary building was replaced by the present brick school in 1949.

HISTORICAL ROUTES

To complement the Colonial Revival style of the garden apartment buildings, the developers named the fourteen streets in the complex after people (or their houses) associated with eighteenth-century Virginia history. Parkfairfax was of course named for the Fairfax family, the largest eighteenth-century Virginia landowners, who were closely associated with the Washington family. All of the individuals were friends or associates of George Washington, who lived near Alexandria at Mount Vernon. Some of the streets include:

Martha Custis Drive—named after the wife of George Washington.
Gunston Road—after Gunston Hall, the 1758 plantation house of George Mason, the author of the Declaration of Rights and most of the first constitution of the state of Virginia, which greatly influenced the later Bill of Rights of the U.S. Constitution.
Preston Road—after William Preston, the commander of American forces in western Virginia during the Revolutionary War.
Mount Eagle Place—after the house of the Rev. Bryan Fairfax, the eighth Lord Fairfax and Baron of Cameron who lived near Alexandria and was a close friend of George Washington.

Ravensworth Place—after the plantation of William Fitzhugh, whose daughter married George Washington Parke Custis, the grandson of Martha Washington and step-grandson of George Washington.
Greenway Place—after Greenway Court, the Shenandoah Valley estate of Thomas, sixth Lord Fairfax.
Rippon Place—after Rippon Lodge, the house of Richard Blackburn in Prince William County, Virginia.
Wellington Road—after the farm owned by George Washington adjacent to Mount Vernon, used as the home of Tobias Lear, secretary to George Washington.
Coryell Lane—after Cornelius Coryell, owner of the ferry that transported George Washington across the Delaware River at the Battle of Trenton in 1776. His son George, a prominent builder in Alexandria, served as a pallbearer at Washington's funeral.
Fitzgerald Lane—after John Fitzgerald, a prominent Alexandria merchant who served as the aide-de-camp to Washington and who founded the first Catholic church in Alexandria.

Because of its fifteen various floor plans, parklike settings, modest rents, and convenient access to Washington (fifteen minutes by car), Parkfairfax was fully occupied while it was a rental property. It was the home of a number of prominent government officials starting their careers on modest incomes—Richard M. Nixon, Gerald Ford, Dean Rusk, Lyndon Johnson aide Bobby Baker, and Eisenhower aide Sherman Adams. Nixon lived at both 3426 Gunston Road and 3538 Gunston Road in the late 1940s. Ford lived at 1521 Mount Eagle Place during 1951–55.

RECENT HISTORY

Following the war, life at Parkfairfax remained relatively unchanged until 1968, when Metropolitan Life sold the buildings to a New York developer, the Arlen Realty Corporation, for $9.8 million. Between 1970 and 1976 the new owners made a number of improvements at Parkfairfax, including the installation of new kitchen equipment, air conditioning, new boilers, a new gas system, and a swimming pool on Martha Custis Drive.

The good relations between the Arlen firm and the tenants deteriorated rapidly in the early 1970s, however, when plans were announced to demolish part of the Parkfairfax complex for high-rise apartment houses. Arlen

Many Parkfairfax apartments have private terraces.

Realty succeeded in building only one fifteen-story high-rise, the Parc East, on Martha Custis Drive. The tenants, organized as the Parkfairfax Citizens Association, brought considerable political pressure against the project. Ultimately the city of Alexandria refused to grant permits for the high-rise apartment houses because of an inadequate sewage system. The owners consequently lost interest and allowed Parkfairfax to deteriorate.

In 1977 Parkfairfax was sold to International Developers, Inc., headed by a successful Washington developer, Giuseppe Cecchi, who had first made a name for himself as the builder of the Watergate complex in Foggy Bottom. He soon afterwards built several large apartment complexes in the Virginia suburbs, including Watergate at Landmark and the Rotonda in McLean. The $30 million price included the entire Parkfairfax complex (buildings and land) as well as the fifteen-story Parc East high-rise. When Cecchi announced plans to convert Parkfairfax into a condominium in early 1977, many tenants

voiced opposition. Through skillful negotiations with the Parkfairfax Citizens Association, however, Cecchi ultimately gained the confidence and support of the majority of tenants.

Cecchi planned an orderly conversion, dividing the (now 134-acre) complex into four sections, termed "villages," which were to receive minimum renovations before their sale in stages. An unusual feature of the conversion allowed tenants to remain in their apartments during most of the renovations. To minimize disruption, each apartment was renovated in ten days of concentrated work, and the developer was courteous in assisting the residents during the conversion process. Building coordinators notified occupants when work would be performed and the manner in which it would be carried out. While plumbers, painters, and electricians were at work, hospitality suites were available to the residents. Storage boxes and dropcloths were provided; cleaning crews moved in as soon as the work was finished.

The living room and stairs of a duplex unit at Parkfairfax.

The $18 million renovations included new interior plumbing, wiring, storm windows, painting of bathrooms and kitchens, and individual thermostats. The developer combined two adjacent units only when both were empty or would not be purchased by their occupants. To distinguish the fifteen different floor plans, the developer named them for American presidents: a Garfield was a one-bedroom, while a Taft was a four-bedroom combination unit.

Tenants were offered the first option to buy apartments, with discounts ranging from $3,000 to $6,000, before they were offered to the public. Thirty-year residents and ten-year residents over seventy years of age could receive additional discounts of $2,000 off the purchase price. More than 80 percent of the tenants elected to buy units—in marked contrast to a national average of only 25 percent of tenants who remain in apartment houses converted to condos. This may be fairly common in Washington, where living costs greatly exceed the national average. Ownership in the national capital avoids local rents, which are high compared with those in all

nearby cities, such as Baltimore, Philadelphia, and Richmond.

The developer's architect, Wayne Williams, devised a plan to divide Parkfairfax into a community of four villages, each reflecting different general interests of the residents, including performing arts and fine arts, crafts and home arts, culinary arts, and horticulture. In conjunction with this scheme, plans were announced for an amphitheater, hothouse, gourmet kitchen, physical fitness center, and workshops. Although several of Williams's developments similar to the Parkfairfax plan had been well received in his native Los Angeles, these were flatly rejected by Parkfairfax residents. They resented being told what they would enjoy and what their interests would be.

This artificially imposed California life-style plan was ultimately abandoned by Cecchi in favor of a simpler, more sensible idea: two new swimming pools were built, one on Coryell Lane and one on Lyons Lane. In addition, the developer added two volleyball courts and eight tennis courts and converted Building 309 at 3554 Martha Custis

Drive into a woodworking shop and exercise facility. He also installed a sauna. The old rental office was converted to a community center for parties and meetings, complete with a new kitchen and administrative offices.

Part of the conversion involved decorating the model units. Because most of the potential purchasers were on modest budgets, the decorator, Sherman and Associates, spent only $2,500 per apartment in furnishings and accessories. Fabrics were ordered only from a Sears catalog, a standard picnic table and benches were used in one apartment dining area, and bookcases in another were made from chicken crates. All of this worked!

The last Parkfairfax apartment was sold on schedule in 1979, making the conversion a complete success for the developer. It was also a success for the residents who bought in. Prices ranged from $27,000 to $54,000; most units sold for double that a year later. The launching of Parkfairfax as a fully self-governed condo occurred on 24 July 1979, when the first election was held for the board of directors. Why was so much money spent on this modest garden apartment complex, and why did so many residents buy in at the time? The answers are many: quality construction, good site planning, an abundance of trees, lawns, open spaces, swimming pools, quiet, and security.

LIFE AT PARKFAIRFAX: RECOLLECTIONS OF RICHARD M. NIXON

A number of unknown residents came to Parkfairfax in its early days, either because they could not afford to live in an expensive luxury apartment house in Washington during the 1940s or because they could not find one available during the housing shortage. Many were members of Congress. Perhaps the best known was Richard M. Nixon, who was thankful to find lodging and enjoyed the place. In response to an inquiry for this study in December 1985, he wrote the following letter regarding his memories of life at Parkfairfax:

> After my election to Congress in 1946, we came to Washington and it was almost impossible to find an apartment which would be within our budget. The compensation for a Congressman in 1947, incidentally, was $12,500 per year, and I had no outside income. I was fortunate in that one of many supporters in the 12th Congressional District of California was Frank Jorgensen, a Metropolitan Life Insurance salesman who lived in San Marino. I told him of my plight and he contacted the front office of the Metropolitan in New York. According to his account, they moved us up on their long application list and made an apartment available to us at 3538 Gunston Road. It was an excellent apartment in every respect, but most important from my standpoint—the price was right! In 1951, after I was elected to the Senate, we bought a house at 4801 Tilden Street in Washington, D.C.
>
> My most painful recollection of our otherwise very pleasant stay at Parkfairfax was in early February 1947, on a very cold day when I was carrying our year-old daughter, Tricia, down some steps and slipped and fell on the ice. Fortunately, my elbows took the shock and she was unharmed. Otherwise, I had nothing but the most pleasant recollections of the four years we lived in Parkfairfax.

114. FALKLAND

8305 16th Street, Silver Spring, Maryland
ARCHITECT: Louis Justement, 1936–37
STATUS: opened as rental in 1937–38

115. 2407 15TH STREET, N.W.

ARCHITECT: Dillon and Abel, 1937
STATUS: opened as rental in 1937;
converted to dormitory ca. 1979

116. 4801 CONNECTICUT AVENUE, N.W.

ARCHITECT: David L. Stern, 1938

STATUS: opened as rental in 1939

117. HIGHTOWERS

1530 16th Street, N.W.

ARCHITECT: Alvin E. Aubinoe, Sr., and Harry L. Edwards, 1938

STATUS: opened as rental in 1938

5

MODERNISM REIGNS SUPREME,

1946–1973

INTRODUCTION

118.

POTOMAC PLAZA, 2475 Virginia Avenue, N.W.

119.

TOWERS, 4201 Cathedral Avenue, N.W.

120.

ARMY DISTAFF HALL, 6200 Oregon Avenue, N.W.

121.

HARBOUR SQUARE, 500 N Street, S.W.

122.

WATERGATE: WATERGATE EAST, 2500 Virginia Avenue, N.W.; WATERGATE WEST, 2700 Virginia Avenue, N.W.; and WATERGATE SOUTH, 700 New Hampshire Avenue, N.W.

123.

PROSPECT HOUSE, 1200 North Nash Street, Arlington, Virginia

124.

VAN NESS CENTRE: VAN NESS EAST, 2929 Van Ness Street, N.W.; VAN NESS NORTH, 3001 Veazey Terrace, N.W.; and VAN NESS SOUTH, 3003 Van Ness Street, N.W.

125.

IRENE, 4701 Willard Avenue, Chevy Chase, Maryland

126.

SHOREHAM WEST, 2700 Calvert Street, N.W.

127.

CATHEDRAL WEST, 4100 Cathedral Avenue, N.W.

128.

COLONNADE, 2801 New Mexico Avenue, N.W.

129.

FOXHALL, 4200 Massachusetts Avenue, N.W.

130.

SUMNER VILLAGE, 4910 Sentinel Drive, Sumner, Maryland

NOTABLE ADDITIONS

Washington underwent great social, cultural, and architectural changes in the post–World War II years. During the decades after the war, Washington changed from a somewhat slow-paced Southern town to a national city. This change occurred for a number of reasons, including the influx of people from all over the world, the shift from public building to private development, and the move in the city toward greater self-government. In 1945 Washington reached its population peak of 950,000 residents—half of the total metropolitan population. By 1987 the city had declined to 620,000 residents out of 3.6 million in the metropolitan area; construction has mirrored this trend. Most new buildings in the city in the 1980s were commercial, in contrast with the explosion of houses, apartments, and shopping centers, as well as office buildings, under construction in the suburbs.

Many other striking changes surfaced in Washington and its population after World War II. A major demographic change occurred when the black population increased from 30 percent to 70 percent between 1945 and 1970. The federal government continued to expand with construction and ownership of new office buildings. In the 1950s and 1960s, the massive Southwest urban renewal project, masterminded by the federal government but built with private capital, completely changed the face of that section of the city. At the same time private redevelopment similarly transformed Foggy Bottom with the massive Watergate and Columbia Plaza projects, Potomac Plaza, other new apartment houses, a major addition to the State Department building, and, most significantly, the John F. Kennedy Center for the Performing Arts. Probably more than any other single building or factor, the Kennedy Center helped propel the nation's capital from cultural lethargy into prominence.

The character of other sections of the city has changed drastically as well. The area between the White House and Dupont Circle, primarily residential in 1945, became almost completely occupied by International Style office buildings in the following three decades. Hundreds of nineteenth-century landmarks were readily destroyed during the building boom of the 1950s and 1960s, a period when Victorian architecture was largely unappreciated.

Citizens began to organize to try to curb wanton destruction and to save the character of the city. One of

On a return visit in 1982, architect Chloethiel Woodard Smith notes recent changes to the courtyard of Harbour Square, her most prestigious apartment house.

the first such instances occurred in 1971 with picketing to prevent demolition of the old Post Office Building at Pennsylvania Avenue and 13th Street, N.W. At that time citizens formed Don't Tear It Down, a preservation organization named after one of the placards carried in the picket line. Renamed the D.C. Preservation League in 1985, it had more than fifteen hundred active members by 1987 and had succeeded in saving the Willard Hotel and other notable landmarks besides the Post Office Building. Because of growing interest in preservation by Washington citizens, the city government during the 1970s and 1980s established eighteen historic districts. The Cleveland Park, Mount Pleasant, and Kalorama Triangle areas were named historic districts in 1986–87.

The city experienced a major setback with the race riots of 1968, when several major areas—including H Street, N.E., and 14th Street, N.W.—were looted and burned. As a result, construction of Washington's office buildings and apartment houses was retarded for a decade. The establishment of home rule in 1974 helped foster new civic pride in educational and cultural activities.

Transportation was greatly improved, first by Dulles International Airport in 1962 and the outer beltway between 1956 and 1964, and—even more significantly—by the Metrorail (subway) system, begun in the 1960s, with the first section opened in 1976. The efforts of the D.C. Highway Department to raze a large segment of the city in the 1950s to build an inner-city beltway fortunately were blocked by irate citizens who refused to sacrifice their homes and neighborhoods to the domination of the all-powerful automobile. The establishment of the Pennsylvania Avenue Development Corporation in 1961 was important in the eventual development of Pennsylvania Avenue between the White House and the Capitol during the 1970s and 1980s.

One of the first changes following World War II was the conversion of many rental apartment houses to cooperatives. This movement followed a pattern established after World War I: inflation, a housing shortage, and the threat of increased rents encouraged the conversion of dozens of rental buildings to co-ops in both the early 1920s and the late 1940s. The co-op apartment was attractive to investors because the monthly maintenance fee was lower than monthly rent and the owner built up equity during rapidly increasing property values. A num-

Architect Jack Cohen of Cohen and Haft (now CHK Associates), who designed several important apartment houses including Town Square Towers, Market Square (with Hartman-Cox), and Somerset House in Bethesda.

Architects Francis D. Lethbridge, left, David H. Condon, center, and Arthur H. Keyes, Jr., of Keyes, Lethbridge, and Condon (now Keyes, Condon, and Florance) visit Tiber Island in 1982, one of two important Washington apartment houses they designed in Southwest.

ber of residents of these former rental buildings—especially the Broadmoor, the Altamont, the Westchester, and the Westmoreland—unsuccessfully challenged proposed conversions in court between 1948 and 1954.

Each year after 1945 the city extended the rent controls instituted at the beginning of the war. Just when it appeared that the controls would be lifted, in 1950, the Korean War began and ensured their retention for the duration. During these years the rent control board approved small rent increases if an owner could show corresponding increases in operating costs—utilities, taxes, repairs, and staff salaries.

Rent controls were discontinued in 1954, but they were reinstated in 1974 with inflation and rent increases and were still in effect in the late 1980s. Efforts to reform and amend the rent control law in 1985 to allow rent raises on vacant apartments were approved by the city council but were unfortunately overturned by a narrow margin in a general referendum.

The rent control law has had a detrimental effect on the development of housing in the District of Columbia. First, it has halted almost all new construction of rental apartment houses because owners could not realize fair returns on their investments. Second, rent control encouraged the owners of small mixed-use buildings along

Luigi W. Moretti of Rome, principal Watergate architect.

major boulevards, such as those on the blocks on Connecticut Avenue just north of Dupont Circle, to allow the former apartments above the shops to remain vacant or convert them to additional commercial use. A good example is the conversion of the former apartments at 1700 Connecticut Avenue, N.W., to office use. Third, the amenities of many of the once-grand rental apartment houses have all but disappeared. To cut operating costs, switchboards have been removed, valet parking has been discontinued, doormen are no longer employed, fewer janitors tend to buildings, and new carpeting, painting, and general maintenance have been neglected. Those who knew such landmark apartment houses as Cathedral Mansions in 1960 would be shocked to see it in its present condition in 1987. Fourth, rent control established a strong incentive for landlords to convert rental apartment buildings to either condos or co-ops.

At the outbreak of the Korean War, the Defense Department needed office space for seventeen thousand additional civilian workers. In 1951, the Department of Defense leased the newly completed Gelmarc Towers apartment house at 1930 Columbia Road, N.W., as emergency office space for the Civil Defense Administration. Plans were also made that year to lease three large new apartment houses for office space—the Boston House, 1711 Massachusetts Avenue, N.W.; the State House, 2122 Massachusetts Avenue, N.W.; and Hunting Towers in Alexandria, Virginia. Because of the housing shortage,

however, Congress overrode a veto by President Truman, thereby preventing the leasing of these three apartment houses for government offices.

BUILDING BOOM, 1955–69

Following the Korean War, Washington experienced a massive building boom exceeded only by the boom of the 1920s. In both instances most of the construction involved large apartment houses. Several factors facilitated this volume of building: the temporary end of rent control, the continuing housing shortage, availability of construction materials no longer restricted for war use, construction of public housing projects, and general economic prosperity. A very low vacancy rate of 3.5 percent existed in Washington during the late 1950s.

A notable trend of spacious, parklike grounds and large buildings developed, with new apartment houses such as the Rittenhouse, the Towers, 3900 Watson Place,

Economy dictated small lobbies in most Washington apartment houses during the Depression. Immediately after World War II, spacious and elaborate lobbies were again designed, as in Berla and Abel's Crestwood at 3900 16th Street, 1947–49.

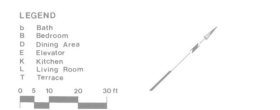

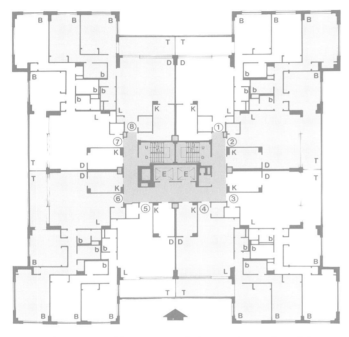

During the 1950s architects resumed the experimentation of the 1920s with innovative new plans for Washington apartment houses. A good example is 3900 Watson Place, designed in 1959, unusual with eight triangular units per floor in two square-shaped towers.

N.W., the Army Distaff Hall, Columbia Plaza, Watergate, the Colonnade, and the Foxhall. At the same time, much of the activity during the second half of the 1950s and the 1960s centered on the new luxury apartment houses in Southwest Washington. The boom ended abruptly with the riots of 1968 and the inflation that followed. Reinstitution of rent control in 1974 helped to paralyze the construction of new apartment houses. Although some were built during the 1970s and 1980s, most were planned as condominiums rather than as rental units. The focus of investors changed from apartment houses to office buildings.

The new public housing projects built during the 1950s and 1960s, many related to urban renewal programs in Southwest and Anacostia, were high-rises. They were not as successful as the earlier public housing projects of the 1930s and 1940s, which were all designed as garden apartments. The small scale of these early projects, usually with courtyards and playgrounds, encouraged more neighborhood participation and lively interchange of the residents.

MODERNISM

Almost all large buildings constructed in the city for more than three decades after the Second World War—apartment houses, office buildings, and public buildings—were in a modified International Style, often referred to simply as Modern. Development of this style began in the 1920s in Europe when a small group of architects, including Walter Gropius and Mies van der Rohe in Germany, J. J. P. Oud in Holland, and Le Corbusier in France, began to design buildings in as functional a manner as possible, without ornament or decoration. These architects sought beauty through discipline, restraint, and a theatrical sort of simplicity. The focus was on smooth and uniform wall surfaces and on horizontality, using ribbon windows and cantilevered balconies. The skin of the building was often emphasized by elegant smooth surfaces of glass, polished metals, and exposed structural members.

During the 1930s many of the most talented European architects of the International Style fled Nazi Germany and emigrated to the United States, where they left a lasting impact on the development of American architecture. Walter Gropius joined the faculty of Harvard University, where he exercised a powerful influence in training a new generation of American architects in his principles. Both he and Le Corbusier in France supported the philosophy of destroying the traditional city and rebuilding it. Their views constituted a major influence in the federal government's later urban renewal program. The attack on nineteenth-century architecture and the proposal to raze American cities to make space for a new, more functional architecture were further buttressed by the publication at Harvard of *Space, Time, and Architecture*, by Siegfried Giedion, which has since become a classic in the field of architectural history. Numerous other European architects were also designing International Style houses and public buildings in the United States during the 1930s, including Mies van der Rohe, Marcel Breuer, George Howe, William Lescaze, Erich Mendelsohn, and Richard Neutra. The style, however, was sharply attacked during this period by many prominent American architects.

It is important to remember that more than 80 percent of the Modern buildings in Washington, from both the late 1930s and the productive three-decade period after World War II, do not fit into any established, labeled style or substyle of Modernism. Nevertheless, Washington does have some prominent examples of many of the subgroups labeled at the time, such as New Formalism (the Kennedy Center), Neo-Expressionism (Dulles International Airport), Miesian (Martin Luther King, Jr., Public Library—actually designed by Mies van der Rohe's office), and Brutalism (the Hoover FBI Building).

Most early Washington examples of Modernism were designed by local architects who were generally more noted for their eclectic work, except for Joseph Abel and his partners, who tended to combine elements associated with the International Style and streamlined Art Deco. Joseph Abel, the first architect to practice Modernism in the city, usually combined Art Deco lobbies with International Style facades, such as the Governor Shepherd.

It was not until immediately after World War II that the International Style became popular, even universal, for apartment houses, hotels, and office buildings in

Architect Milton Fischer of Corning, Moore, Elmore, and Fischer, associate architects of the Watergate. Later, as part of the firm Fischer and Elmore, he designed the Foxhall.

Washington. It never really became popular for houses in a city bounded by Virginia and Maryland and with a preference for the Colonial.

In the boom that followed World War II, many large urban apartment house projects were constructed across the country. Consisting of rows of high-rise apartment houses, many soon became blots on the cityscapes because of poor site planning, density, and lack of adequate playgrounds, shops, schools, or cultural facilities. A good example of these bland projects was Stuyvesant Town, along the East River between 14th and 20th streets in New York City. Built by the Metropolitan Life Insurance Company in 1947, it occupied 75 acres and consisted of eighteen high-rises with a total of eighty-eight hundred apartments for twenty-four thousand residents.

During the 1940s, 1950s, and 1960s several Washington architects stand out as leaders in the local development of Modernism. Their influence and impact on the city were important. The work of Joseph Abel, seen as more significant than that of any other single individual in apartment house design, included more than a hundred apartment houses in the new style. Other leaders at this time included Keyes, Lethbridge, and Florance (now Keyes, Condon, and Florance); Chloethiel Woodard Smith; Charles Goodman; and Nicholas Satterlee. All of these architects contributed by training a new generation of younger local architects in the modern mode.

New directions appeared when President John F. Kennedy began bringing architects from outside of the city to work on local federal government projects in the early 1960s. These architects had not been trained by the old established Washington architectural firms but included San Francisco's John Carl Warnecke, who designed the Lafayette Square "restoration" project, and Nathaniel Owings, for many years with the San Francisco office of Skidmore, Owings, and Merrill, who produced an early design for National Square on Pennsylvania Avenue (happily never carried out). Other notable outside architectural firms that arrived in the city in the 1960s, 1970s, and early 1980s include such great names as Eero Saarinen, who designed Dulles International Airport; Hellmuth, Obata, and Kassabaum, who produced the Smithsonian's National Air and Space Museum; Gordon Bunshaft, of the New York office of Skidmore, Owings, and Merrill, architect of the Hirshhorn Museum; and I. M. Pei, who designed several private buildings and part of the Southwest urban renewal project as well as the National Gallery of Art's East Building—quite a sensation when it opened in 1978.

In the two decades after World War II housing was *the* design problem in architecture schools. Apartment houses were featured prominently in professional architecture magazines with discussions of plans, new construction systems, and new building materials. Discussions were centered on precast concrete, lift-slab construction, curtain walls, new types of glazing (reflective and tinted), hot and cold water circulating systems, and the use of aluminum. The contributions of many foreign architects, such as Le Corbusier's large-scale apartment houses de-

Architect J. Allan MacLane, of MacLane and Chewning, who designed Cathedral West.

Architect Donald Hudson Drayer designed a number of prominent large luxury apartment houses in the 1960s and early 1970s, including Prospect House, the Colonnade, and the Promenade.

a

b

c

g

h

i

m

Following the model of the Portland Flats, which opened in 1880, Washington's luxury apartment houses have for a century provided many hotel-like amenities—public dining rooms, drugstores, and doormen, and—recently—more modern features such as swimming pools, tennis courts, and exercise rooms. Shown here are such particularly desirable services as the receptionist at the Greenbriar (a); the doorman at Albemarle House (b); the beauty parlor at 4000 Massachusetts Avenue (c); the package receiving room (d), meat market (e), and coffee shop (f) in the Berkshire; the valet shop at the Colonnade (g); the car washer at the Westchester (h); the spacious garage at the Washington Park Tower (i); the lending library (j), shopping arcade (k), and security gatehouse (l) at the Promenade; and the spacious balconies at 3900 Watson Place (m).

d

e

f

j

k

l

signed as raised blocks in a parklike setting, were also widely covered by American architectural journals. The interest in apartment house design resulted in part from the housing shortage caused by the postwar baby boom. The government took a lead in trying to solve the housing problem with hundreds of government housing projects and urban renewal across the country.

Although many of the early high-rise Modern or International Style residential complexes for middle- and lower-income residents eventually proved to be failures, a number of superb luxury apartment house towers were built in the 1950s and 1960s. For the first time the design of International Style apartment houses elsewhere greatly affected local tendencies. One of the best early examples is 100 Memorial Drive in Cambridge, Massachusetts, designed in 1950 by Robert Kennedy, Vernon DeMars, and others of the faculty at the Massachusetts Institute of Technology. An eleven-floor slab, the structure has glass walls and balconies overlooking its courtyard and the Charles River. The building was designed with a skip-floor elevator system in which apartment entrances are on every third floor; vestibules in each apartment connect to private stairs leading to the rooms on the floor below or above. This design reduces corridor space, gives cross-ventilation, and provides large, elegant living rooms that connect to balconies. The idea probably came from the slightly earlier plan used by Le Corbusier in his celebrated Marseilles apartment house.

A second important and influential International Style luxury apartment house is the spare, sleek 860 Lake Shore Drive in Chicago, designed in 1951 by Mies van der Rohe. The ground floors of its two glass towers are open space to provide views of the lake. The architect considered the fenestration pattern so important that residents were required to use gray outer curtains in their apartments to preserve the uniformity of the window design. The original rules of the building further required of residents the rather tedious obligation to set their curtains in one of three possible arrangements—fully closed, fully opened, or half-way opened—to maintain the architectural order and uniformity.

During the postwar years, a major influence on

American architecture continued to be Swiss-born French architect Le Corbusier. His 1952 Unite d'Habitation, a massive apartment house for workers in Marseilles, left its mark on American architecture. Designed as a modular slab, it contained two-story apartments, communal rooms, shops, and a roof terrace. Most important, it was raised above the ground, supported by sculptural stilts. This feature was followed a few years later in Southwest Washington with the design of Capitol Park by Chloethiel Woodard Smith and Tiber Island and Carrollsburg Square by Keyes, Lethbridge, and Condon.

In the 1950s the federal government became a major patron of the International Style for the first time. In 1954, the Department of State adopted Modernism for new embassies and chancelleries. During the next decade more than fifteen important U.S. government buildings abroad were designed in the International Style by leading American architects, including Edward Durell Stone (India—the most famous), John Carl Warnecke (Thailand), Paul Rudolph (Jordan), Harry Weese (Ghana), Walter Gropius (Greece), and Marcel Breuer (The Hague). Another major government project in the International Style was the Air Force Academy in Colorado designed by Skidmore, Owings, and Merrill in 1955. This same strong support of the federal government for the International Style in embassies abroad in the 1950s can also be seen in the hundreds of high-rise apartment houses built in Washington and other cities as part of urban renewal.

SOUTHWEST URBAN RENEWAL

Perhaps the boldest attempt to advance the International Style in Washington in the 1950s and 1960s occurred with urban renewal in the Southwest quadrant of the city, which was almost completely leveled for total redevelopment. Unfortunately, part of Pierre Charles L'Enfant's original street pattern was changed as well. More than a dozen apartment house complexes were designed and built over a twelve-year period by many prominent architects, including I. M. Pei.

The 550-acre triangular Southwest area is bordered by the Mall on the north, the Potomac River on the south and west, and South Capitol Street on the east. Since settled in the 1790s, the Southwest has been cut off from the rest of the city. First the Washington Canal (now Constitution Avenue) and the Mall separated it from the main commercial street, Pennsylvania Avenue, N.W., and the main residential area, then F Street between 7th and 15th streets, N.W. After the canal was filled in about 1870, the Baltimore and Ohio Railroad tracks intruded, slicing the Southwest in half.

This was an early nineteenth-century site of spacious Federal houses; originally the province of real estate developers and ship captains, it began to be commercialized after the Civil War. By 1900, however, much though not all of it had become a backwater of warehouses, shipping wharves, and simple rowhouses inhabited by low-income residents. By World War II the Southwest had become the city's worst slum with its alleys, courtyards, and back streets providing most of the housing for the city's poorest inhabitants, who crowded into buildings lacking indoor plumbing and other modern facilities.

In an effort to clean up its worst features, a resolute General U. S. Grant III, chairman of the National Capital Planning Commission, proposed that Congress establish the city's first urban renewal agency in 1945. The D.C. Redevelopment Act of 1946 establishing the Redevelopment Land Agency was a consequence. The first director of the new bureau, Mark Lansburgh, a local department store executive, could do little since no funds had been appropriated. Nevertheless, he remained its head for five years, meeting with city planners, developers, and architects—paying for all costs out of his own pocket. Under his leadership, and with the help of the National Capital Planning Commission, the first urban renewal areas were designated in Marshall Heights and Barry Farms, two deteriorated and neglected low-income residential neighborhoods in far Southeast Washington, adjacent to St. Elizabeths Hospital. The proposed demolition and rebuilding program aroused so much protest and animosity among the residents, however, that in 1950 Congress killed the project.

A major change began with passage of the National Housing Act of 1949, which made funds available to Washington and other cities for urban renewal agencies. The D.C. Redevelopment Land Agency was subsequently reorganized in 1951 with a new executive director, John

R. Searles, Jr., a professional city planner. It selected the entire Southwest section for urban renewal. Demolition began in 1953, and the rebuilding, mostly of large-scale apartment houses, proceeded until 1971. It was to be the largest urban renewal project in the country for middle-class housing and was considered a model for other American cities. The Southwest urban renewal project included 113 blocks, covering more than 450 acres. When it began, 22,539 people lived there—79 percent of them black. The project cost more than $500 million over a period of nineteen years. The new apartments and houses were too expensive for most of the previous residents; they had to find homes elsewhere.

After the Southwest had been selected, the second major decision involved how much to destroy and rebuild. That judgment would concern thousands of low-income residents and would also determine the amount of investment capital needed. In 1983 Mr. Searles, by then retired, recollected the two proposals made for the fate of Southwest in a letter to the author:

The planning in 1951 and 1952 was largely by the National Capital Planning Commission and its consultant Elbert Peets, who had written a book on architecture in the capital and was intrigued by the old red brick rowhouses and apartment houses [over a dozen of which dated from the 1880s and 1890s], whatever their condition might be. Peets felt that minimum treatment should be given to the Southwest and that as many of the old houses as possible should be preserved. He believed that the basic dark red brick texture of the area was priceless and could never be reproduced. At this time we at the Land Agency also felt that the redevelopment should be primarily for families of low and moderate income.

The minimum treatment philosophy and the low income philosophy were severely criticized by certain local architectural groups. Frederick Gutheim, Louis Justement, and others told me that they felt that the Redevelopment Agency and the Planning Commission did not realize the full potential of the Southwest area and were in effect selling it short. Responding to this criticism the Redevelopment Agency requested specially designated funds for planning from the Housing and Home Finance Agency (the predecessor of the Department of Housing and Urban Development) to engage architects to prepare

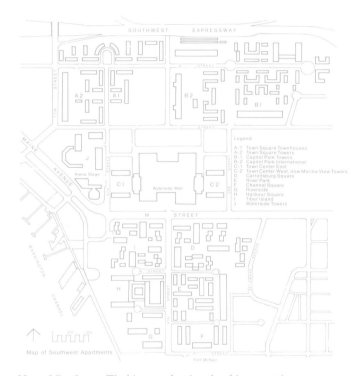

Map of Southwest Washington showing the thirteen major apartment houses built during the urban renewal program, 1954–68.

an alternative plan to that proposed by Mr. Peets. The funds were granted and after interviewing a number of local and out of town architects, we chose Mr. Louis Justement of Justement, Elam, and Darley and Mrs. Chloethiel Woodard Smith of Keyes, Smith, Satterlee, and Lethbridge to work as a team to develop a new plan for the Southwest area.

Mr. Justement and Mrs. Smith prepared a new plan which was a maximum approach to achieve the full potential of the Southwest and involved a complete redoing of the area rather than a minimum approach as had been suggested by Mr. Peets. The Justement-Smith plan was received enthusiastically by the newspapers of the city and others, and received national attention.

After the two plans had been submitted, the National Capital Planning Commission employed an independent firm, Harland Bartholomew and Associates, to study them and recommend action. The conclusion was to support the Justement-Smith plan, which called for the complete removal of existing buildings in the Southwest and the substitution of a new street plan. In contrast to the Peets plan, only a dozen of the two thousand existing rowhouses were to be saved. This decision, which would generate millions of dollars in construction work, was widely applauded by local and national builders.

MASSIVE RECONSTRUCTION

Because of the enormous area involved, the Redevelopment Land Agency first divided the Southwest into sections A through E, to be razed and rebuilt as separate parcels. Area A, at the west end, directly behind the Smithsonian Institution Building, was set aside for development as a major office and commercial center. Redevelopment began with Area B, at the east end (near South Capitol Street), which contained the most slums.

Applications to develop Area B came from more than two dozen major builders. The project was awarded in 1953 to the Bush Construction Company. Architect Milton J. Prassas prepared a plan for an eight-story apartment house, blocks of double duplex apartment houses, and three- and four-bedroom rowhouses. In 1954 William Zeckendorf, a major New York developer, was appointed

to redevelop all of the other areas of Southwest. Thus the "outside" began to appear in this lucrative project. Zeckendorf's plan, developed by I. M. Pei in collaboration with Harry Weese, closely followed the original proposal in the Justement-Smith plan. Included were a complete intown community, rebuilding the Southwest waterfront along Maine Avenue and the Potomac Channel, creating a major boulevard entrance to the Southwest along 10th Street, a mixture of new rowhouses and high-rise apartment blocks, and a shopping center. The blocks and blocks of high-rise apartments represented a new concept for the city. The apartment towers were built in clusters and were separated from the street, since they faced inward toward each other. Thus the residents of these new buildings lived in their own individual fortresses. Newspapers of the time warmly praised this plan as a solution to reviving the decaying city.

When the Bush Construction Company withdrew from Area B, New York developers James Scheuer and Roger Stevens were given the job in 1955. They commissioned Chloethiel Woodard Smith as their architect. Her first building was the Capitol Park apartments, completed in 1959—the first design in the city for a nine-story apartment house with the first floor fully occupied by the lobby and garage. (An exemption was made to the zoning ordinance since the building exceeded the height limit.) No doubt this design was influenced by Le Corbusier's Marseilles apartment house.

A number of apartment houses—such as Tiber Island and Town Square Towers—by other architects in the Southwest urban renewal project followed the same design of using the first floor exclusively for lobby and garage. This rare plan is limited to Southwest buildings except for one apartment house built near Washington Circle twenty year later—Potomac Overlook at 26th and K streets, N.W., where both first and second floors are used exclusively for the lobby and garage. (The site there was too costly to excavate because of solid rock, so the proposed underground garage was located on the first two floors above ground.)

Capitol Park occupied the former site of Dixon's Court, considered the worst slum in the city. Photographs of this slum, with impoverished citizens in the alleys and the dome of the United States Capitol in the background, had been used for three decades in the Soviet Union to illustrate "typical living conditions" in Washington. When Premier Nikita Khrushchev visited in the late 1950s, President Eisenhower personally took him to see Capitol Park, then under construction, to illustrate social improvements.

After Capitol Park was completed, Stevens left the project. Smith continued to design additional rowhouses and apartment houses for this section, but because of increased construction costs, the original proposal to use the apartment houses for low-income residents was dropped. This became a familiar pattern in similar projects in Southwest in the years to follow.

In the meantime the first building to go up in the rest of Southwest (outside of Area B) was the Town Center, a grouping of four high-rise apartment houses with a shopping center, designed by I. M. Pei. Pei was particularly interested in the texture and composition of the concrete for these buildings. The most striking aspect of Pei's buildings, however, is the emphasis on glass, which gives them a beautiful skin. In contrast, the apartment houses designed by Chloethiel Woodard Smith are successful because of a different facade treatment. She used brick, terra cotta, and other materials to produce a domestic feeling rather than a stark aspect. The expense relating to the construction of the facades necessitated rather spartan treatment of the apartments to stay within the FHA cost limitations.

When Zeckendorf realized the enormity of the task of designing and building almost all of Southwest (everything outside of Area B), he agreed to split the project with other developers in 1960. Zeckendorf kept the area north of M Street, including the 10th Street corridor, to develop. His 10th Street, S.W., project, known as L'Enfant Plaza, was centered along the new elevated boulevard running above the site of old 10th Street. When first proposed, L'Enfant Plaza was to have become the cultural core of the entire city, featuring an opera house, concert hall, theaters, convention hall, hotels, restaurants, band shell, ice-skating rink, swimming pool, and garage for twenty-five hundred cars. It was to have been "what the Champs Elysees is to Paris or the Piazza San Marco is to Venice," according to the *Washington Post* of 17 February 1954.

The entrance to L'Enfant Plaza was placed at 10th Street, S.W., because the adjacent railroad tracks dipped the lowest at this point, providing the best location of the elevated entrance drive. That new street was designed to terminate at an elliptical overlook, Banneker Circle, from which one can survey the Southwest waterfront. It was to have connected to a covered bridge, including shops and cafes on both sides, designed by Chloethiel Woodard Smith to cross the Washington Channel to Hains Point, where a proposed national aquarium was to have been built. I. M. Pei's 1959 design for L'Enfant Plaza included a pair of office buildings facing one another and located on the north and south sides of the plaza. They were originally known as the Aviation and Space buildings and housed the government's infant space program. The L'Enfant Hotel was placed to the east and a third large office building, now housing the U.S. Postal Service, to the west. A major feature of the design was an elaborate shopping arcade below the surface of the plaza.

Under the new scheme for Southwest development, the land south of M Street was divided into six areas, each to be designed by different architects and builders. Four were awarded by competition. The first of the six new apartment house complexes was River Park, bounded by 4th, O, and N streets and Delaware Avenue, S.W. John Searles solicited the Reynolds Metals Development Corporation with the idea that it build River Park as a middle-income co-op—and at the same time demonstrate the uses of aluminum in housing.

The Reynolds Corporation accepted the challenge and commissioned Washington architect Charles M. Goodman to design it in early 1961. (Goodman had already received national acclaim for his design of Hollin Hills, a planned suburb of International Style woodland houses in nearby Alexandria.) This uniquely designed River Park housing complex on an 11½-acre site contained 384 apartments in a single high-rise apartment house surrounded by 134 rowhouses with arched barrel roofs. Goodman carefully connected the rowhouses with pedestrian walks and kept all cars outside the inner space. The rowhouses were arranged around courts of different sizes, providing maximum privacy. Another innovative feature was the extensive use of large aluminum grilles on the facades of the high-rise. Designed for both decorative effect and protection from the weather, the balcony grilles admit 75 percent sunlight. Elsewhere in the complex, walls of vertical-ribbed painted aluminum panels were erected between the adjacent rowhouse gardens.

The River Park Mutual Homes complex was widely publicized by Reynolds Aluminum because of the large amount of aluminum on both exterior and interior. *Washington Post* architectural critic Wolf Von Eckardt described it in early 1963 when it was completed:

> River Park, a cooperative sponsored by the Reynolds Metal Company, is by far the most stunning design of its kind not only in this area but probably in the country. It consists of a huge striking ensemble of a black and silver apartment building hovering over a tight cluster of 134 townhouses. There is nothing subdued about it. Like a stage set, and a highly original and creative one, these buildings strive for effect, for emotional impact. But there is no reason why architecture shouldn't do this if it comes off. This does. The apartment is just a bit flashy with all that gleaming aluminum screening. But the compact cluster of townhouses with their white barrel-vault roofs is enchanting and full of surprises. A sudden balcony here, an unexpected vista there. With its pedestrian alleys and cozy, miniature town square it reminds you a little of a medieval town. It is art but it works architecturally, as an environment with a strong character of its own. The cars disappear on the scattered parking lots. Tiny but comfortable patios are fitted into limited space. Everything here has an intimate scale that makes people seem to be as big and important again as they were in the old villages and small towns. The architects' word for this is "human scale." Reynoldsburg-on-the-Potomac will surely and rightly set a new trend in townhouse design.

A second outstanding housing complex, begun in 1961, is Harbour Square, the most important of the twelve apartment house projects designed in Southwest and one of the city's most significant of the 1960s. It is notable not only for its great variety of apartment shapes and sizes but also for its variety of courtyards, roofdecks, reflecting pool, parking arrangements, and the incorporation of a group of historic Federal houses into the complex. Harbour Square was developed as a co-op by Frank Luchs of Shannon and Luchs and by the Edmund J. Flynn

Company. Chloethiel Woodard Smith was the architect.

The well-publicized designs of both River Park and Harbour Square created a great deal of interest in the whole Southwest urban renewal project. It received constant support from the Eisenhower administration as well as the Federal City Council, a group of a hundred prominent local businessmen. The redesign of Maine Avenue, S.W., to remove most of the traffic from the area between the apartment complexes and the riverfront, and the general upgrading of the Southwest did much to create national interest in development of the four remaining parcels, south of M Street. Four design competitions were held in which setbacks from the river, densities, heights, and the number of rowhouses and high-rises were all strictly prescribed. Keyes, Lethbridge, and Condon won the competitions for both Tiber Island and Carrollsburg Square, while Morris Lapidus of New York City won the bid for Chalk House (now Riverside) and Chalk Center.

The Washington architectural firm of Keyes, Lethbridge, and Condon treated the facades of the high-rise buildings of both Tiber Island and Carrollsburg Square similarly. By using the same basic form, with identical colored brick, balconies, and other details in the two projects, the architects helped knit the residential neighborhood together as a cohesive whole. In the case of Tiber Island four 90-foot high-rises and a series of eighty-five two- and three-story rowhouses were designed around a large inner courtyard or plaza. Underlying the design is a two-level 280-car underground garage; its roof forms the central paved pedestrian plaza, thus separating pedestrian and vehicular traffic. In contrast, Carrollsburg contains a central underground garage, with a plaza above of parkland. A small cafe was originally designed for the central paved plaza at Tiber Island, but it was not allowed because of an earlier agreement between developer Zeckendorf and the RLA to restrict commercial development south of M Street, S.W.

Each of the four nine-story apartment houses is set perpendicular to each side of this large 8½-acre square to allow for maximum views and light. Each cluster of varying numbers of rowhouses at Tiber Island has its own common courtyard, while each rowhouse has an intimate walled patio and balcony. Another innovative feature at

Tiber Island is the preservation and incorporation of the historic 1794 three-story Law House, which is now used as a community center.

TRENDS SET, LESSONS LEARNED

The rowhouses of both Tiber Island and the adjacent Carrollsburg Square (which also includes three high-rise apartment houses) were originally marketed in 1965 as condominiums, the first sold in Washington. A special city law had been passed in December 1963, the Horizontal Property Act, to make condominiums legal. Residents of the rowhouses at both Tiber Island and Carrollsburg Square, which originally sold from $40,000 to $75,000, have always shared the same facilities as the apartment residents in their respective complexes—roof-decks, swimming pool, community center, twenty-four-hour secretarial service, package rooms, valet service, laundry rooms, and central garage. Both complexes were developed by the Berens Company and built by the Charles H. Tompkins Construction Company. The high-rise apartment buildings at Carrollsburg are now condominiums and those at Tiber Island cooperatives. Both complexes reflect exceptional quality in their construction.

When completed in 1971 the Southwest urban renewal project included twenty-five new high-rise apartment houses with more than four thousand apartments and a thousand new rowhouses. Although the Southwest project probably received more national publicity than any other, it never overcame several problems. The developers and architects in Southwest tried too hard to be *new*—with new street patterns, new neighborhoods, new building types, new materials, and new parking solutions. They lost many beneficial aspects of the old as a result. One important urban renewal project was the Golden Gateway residential development in San Francisco designed by Wurster, Bernardi, and Emmonds. This complex had more grass and space, no exposed parking. The Washington examples were unlike the Golden Gateway—which included shops and offices to a much greater extent.

Washington's first serious mistake was failing to deal with the poverty problem. The new enclave of luxury apartment houses was adjacent to areas with significant public housing. The pockets of low-income housing adjacent to these luxury buildings resulted in a serious element of crime, which has not been overcome. Moreover, no viable program existed for resettling the original Southwest residents. Second, the master plan did not adequately integrate the designs of the large apartment house complexes because they lacked unity in the use of exterior materials. Designed by different architects and built by different developers, many face away from the street onto their own plazas, forming small enclaves rather than relating to each other.

Other problems with the Southwest urban renewal program involve what was not built. "Ponte Vecchio," Mrs. Smith's brilliantly conceived covered bridge, with its cafes and shops, was one of the most interesting aspects of the whole Southwest design. Her plan was named for the Renaissance example in Florence, the best-known bridge of this type in Europe. It was envisioned to span the Washington Channel and connect to the proposed new national aquarium. Neither the covered bridge nor the national aquarium (which was later built in Baltimore harbor) was ever constructed. Both of these projects would have brought welcomed activity to the area.

Some critics feel that because it is so contrived, Southwest is now bland. In a way, the Southwest project was an attempt to create a suburb in the city, with all of the best and worst aspects of such an environment. The interaction of city life that is found in abundance in such Washington neighborhoods as Georgetown, Dupont Circle, and Capitol Hill was lost. When most of the land was cleared (with the exception of a dozen Federal houses and one church), the neighborhood naturally lost much of its original character. Commerce took far too big a bite: few parks were planned, leaving a vast expanse of masonry and concrete, all looking much the same and with little diversity. The elevated Southwest Expressway, built through the middle of the area, helped once again to divide it from the rest of the city. Finally, the enormous modern government offices built on Independence Avenue along the northern border of Southwest during the 1950s and 1960s are among the most aesthetically mediocre examples in the city.

On the other hand, the residents of Southwest like their proximity to those government offices, the Capitol, and the Mall—as well as the clean lines of the modern buildings. Newcomers to Washington often feel at home there, since many are accustomed to similar high-rise apartment houses in other cities. The most appealing aspect of life there exists in those apartments that face the river, offering exceptional views. Southwest may well become an historic district in another twenty years; it is already a monument to Modernism from the 1950s and 1960s. For all of their drawbacks, the many apartment houses in Southwest constitute the most important urban renewal project in the country.

While the Southwest urban renewal project remains the outstanding International Style complex in Washington, dozens of other important apartment houses in this mode were built throughout the area. Those within the city include the Towers, the Cathedral, and Cathedral West, all on Cathedral Avenue. Three on upper 16th Street are notable—the Woodner, the Crestwood, and the Rittenhouse. The most prominent examples in the Connecticut Avenue corridor are Van Ness Centre and the Shoreham West on adjacent Calvert Street. In Foggy Bottom the outstanding apartment houses from this era include the Watergate, Potomac Plaza, Columbia Plaza, and the Plaza.

Space limitations here have permitted the inclusion of only a few of many more examples found in the suburbs—Prospect House in Virginia and the Irene, the Promenade, and Sumner Village in Maryland. But enough examples are included to indicate the rich variety of International Style apartment houses from the post–World War II era—each with its own site solution and design variation—to the present time. During the 1980s the style had waned and had been reexamined and then reshaped to the Postmodern mode, in a period of architectural transition.

POTOMAC PLAZA

2475 Virginia Avenue, N.W.

ARCHITECT: Dixon and Weppner, 1954–56

ORIGINAL APARTMENTS: 274 (68 efficiencies; 156 one-bedrooms; 34 two-bedrooms; 16 three-bedrooms)

STATUS: opened as co-op in 1957

While the federal government focused its attention on urban renewal in Southwest Washington during the 1950s, private developers initiated redevelopment of Foggy Bottom, the former swampy area between the White House and Georgetown, south of Pennsylvania Avenue, N.W. Private improvement of Foggy Bottom, comprising about forty city blocks, began in 1952 when a group of six investors, headed by John W. Harris of New York City, secured an option to buy a 12-acre tract from the Washington Gas Light Company for $3 million. Besides Harris, other investors were Marvin J. Coles of Washington, Vaughn B. Connelly of Miami, Mark McKee of Detroit, John Hennessey, owner of the Statler Hotels, and George Preston Marshall, owner of the Washington Redskins football team. It was Marshall who first conceived the project.

Located at the intersection of New Hampshire and Virginia avenues, N.W., the site of the present Potomac Plaza was then overshadowed by two large gas storage tanks built in 1898 and 1926. In the late 1940s the Washington Gas Light Company, which had held this land since 1858, began to store its propane and natural gas in a new and more economical underground facility in Rockville, Maryland. The gas company, however, experienced difficulty in selling the old property. At an

Potomac Plaza has an unusual semicircular driveway that passes under the front of the building.

auction in 1950, the highest bid of $4 per square foot was not accepted because it was believed that the land was worth $6 a square foot. In 1952 the developers and investors of the Potomac Plaza Center secured a five-year option to purchase the land for $9 a square foot. Shortly afterwards, in 1954, they bought the part of the tract lying north of Virginia Avenue while continuing to hold the option to buy the southern part.

To the east were blocks of Victorian-era buildings—the Heurich Brewery, which had recently ceased operations, and some three hundred small, dilapidated rowhouses scattered north of the brewery. One of the most notorious slums in this area, Snow's Court, was within the block bounded by 24th, 25th, Eye, and K streets, N.W.

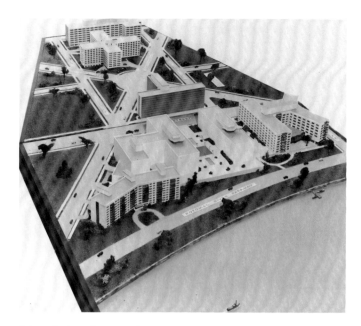

Original 1954 design of Potomac Plaza, then conceived as a much larger complex than the one actually built.

THE AMBITIOUS PLANS

In May 1954, the developers announced their plans to build an enormous complex called Potomac Plaza Center. Constructing the proposed miniature city, covering all of the 12 acres and costing $100 million, would take a decade. The master plan was compared in scale with New York's Rockefeller Center and would include luxury apartment houses, office buildings, a thousand-room hotel, restaurants, shops, a theater, ice skating rink, swimming pool, an underground two-thousand-car garage, bank, outdoor plaza, and yacht basin. Everything would be constructed by the Hegeman-Harris Company of New York. Nationally known, this firm had previously built such important structures as Washington's Statler Hotel (now the Capital Hilton) and the Tomb of the Unknowns at Arlington National Cemetery, as well as Rockefeller Center, the Chicago Daily News Building, and the Chicago Tribune Tower.

The master plan for Potomac Plaza Center was created by a group of city planners and architects, including A. R. Clas of Washington and Chester L. Churchill, John W. Harris, and the firm of Harrison and Abramovitz, all of New York. Potomac Plaza Center was to be built in two sections. The first part, north of Virginia Avenue, was to include a cooperative apartment house, Potomac Plaza, and behind that would stand a smaller cooperative

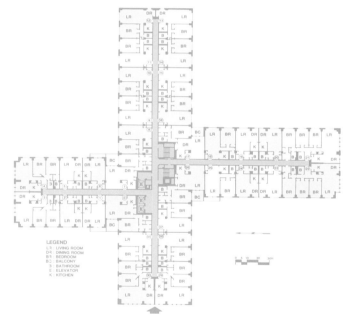

Typical floor plan of Potomac Plaza.

medical office building, Potomac Park Terraces, at 730 24th Street, N.W. The second part, never built, was to include a large complex of mixed-use buildings—apartments, shopping center, hotel, and offices—much like the present-day Watergate, which now occupies this site.

John W. Harris, who was in charge of construction for the entire project, lacked adequate financing to begin the undertaking. The Edmund J. Flynn Company of Washington consequently was brought into the project and commissioned to sell both apartments in the proposed Potomac Plaza and office units in the co-op medical office building. Construction would begin only after Flynn had sold 40 percent of the units in each of the proposed new buildings. Plans for the apartment house were carried out on schedule with half the units sold by 1956 when construction began. The first design of Potomac Plaza was an all-glass apartment house by the noted Boston architect Pietro Belluschi, then dean of the architecture department at Massachusetts Institute of Technology. Rejecting these plans as too radical, avant garde, and expensive to build, the developers next turned to Washington architect Fred Dixon of the firm of Dixon and Weppner, who created the present building.

The owners, known as the Potomac Parkway Plaza Development Company, cleared the 3½-acre square for the first two buildings in the summer of 1954. Other developments were moving rapidly in Foggy Bottom at that time. In July 1954, the National Capital Planning Commission and the D.C. government agreed to the approximate location of a new bridge crossing the Potomac River (the Theodore Roosevelt Bridge). At the same time, the government was planning an inner-city beltway that would cut through the center of the Potomac Plaza Center. Joining forces with officials from George Washington University, the developers convinced the government to redesign the highway in order to place part of it underground. Although the E Street Expressway was built in Foggy Bottom, the rest of the inner-city beltway was abandoned because of strong opposition from Washington residents.

The developers also had to contend with a number of prominent Washingtonians, including Agnes Meyer, wife of the owner of the *Washington Post*, who wanted the south part of the Potomac Plaza Center tract, facing the river, developed as a public park. To complicate

matters further, the federal government began to negotiate for the Heurich Brewery site adjacent to the Potomac Plaza Center project for a national cultural center. Efforts by the Redevelopment Land Agency to start a government-sponsored urban renewal program in Foggy Bottom were blocked by residents and developers in 1955. The developers' need to secure permission from the city to close off a number of streets in the southern parcel facing the river caused additional difficulty.

When construction began, a large circle was built in front of Potomac Plaza at the intersection of New Hampshire and Virginia avenues, N.W., to separate the first, or northern, section of the complex from the second, or southern, section. The southern section, between Virginia Avenue and Rock Creek Parkway, occupying 75 percent of the 12-acre tract, was planned to have a number of apartments, offices, and other buildings and was to be known as Potomac Parkway Plaza.

REVISED PLANS

Only a small fraction of the proposed gigantic Potomac Plaza Center was ever built—the two apartment houses known as Potomac Plaza and Potomac Plaza Terraces. Additional funds to build the remainder of the project could not be obtained after the backers of the effort, the American Securities Corporation of New York, suffered several severe losses in 1959–60. The Potomac Plaza Center project consequently was halted in 1960. At that point, some Italian investors offered to purchase the land behind Potomac Plaza, with the plans for the then-unbuilt Potomac Plaza Terraces, as well as the option to buy the remaining undeveloped land to the south. This land was subsequently purchased for $17 a square foot, and the Potomac Parkway Plaza Development Company realized a handsome profit. Later the same Italian investors would design and construct the Watergate apartment complex in the mid–1960s on the site proposed for the ill-fated Potomac Parkway Plaza. Washington's most famous apartment house, Watergate, is basically similar in concept to the plan for the site a decade earlier.

Designed in the shape of an irregular cross, Potomac Plaza includes 274 apartments, most of them one-bed-

One of the well-thought-out design features of Potomac Plaza involved recessing the elevators along the public corridor on each floor to facilitate the smooth flow of traffic.

room units, originally priced from $9,000 to $34,500 with a down payment of 28 percent required. The two-level basement garage contains space for 106 cars, with additional parking provided on the grounds. Built of off-white brick, the facade of Potomac Plaza is half glass. The semicircular driveway, which connects to both New Hampshire and Virginia avenues, N.W., runs under the front wing to the lobby entrance. The large glass-enclosed lobby has a terrazzo floor and black marble walls and is on two levels with the seating area on the lower level. The upper level, in the center of the building, houses the front desk and two passenger elevators. Since the land had been rezoned commercial, part of the ground floor to the right of the lobby, facing Virginia Avenue, was divided into eight sections or bays and sold as commercial space. These bays first housed a beauty parlor, the Arab American Cultural Foundation, and a branch of the McLachlen National Bank. This was one of the first cases of a mixed-use building, a development that was not to

become popular until the 1970s.

Carefully designed and constructed, Potomac Plaza offered luxury features unusual for its time. Passenger elevators extend to the basement garages, while the service elevator connects to the sundeck on the roof. Apartment units are equipped with oak-block floors, electric dishwashers, and eye-level ovens. Individual storage lockers beside each apartment door are convenient for trash removal. The three-bedroom apartments have the unusual distinction of an additional entry door from the public corridor to the third or guest bedroom, allowing it to be used as an in-law suite or office, if desired. Although the wide central picture windows remain permanently closed, they are flanked by small casement windows that open, permitting fresh air at any time. Four tiers of balconies allow many apartments outdoor access.

When construction was started on Potomac Plaza Terraces, which had originally been designed to house two hundred offices for doctors and dentists, the Edmund

J. Flynn Company had sold only twenty of these office co-ops (for $18,000 each). Sales were slow, primarily because the idea of selling co-op offices was then practically unknown in Washington. Indeed, there was no other co-op office building in the city, although an unsuccessful attempt had been made in 1929 when the Shoreham Building at 15th and H streets, N.W., was built as co-op offices. The Great Depression began just as that landmark was nearing completion, and the proposed co-op offices opened as rental. Furthermore, the site of Potomac Plaza Terraces was not particularly desirable for medical offices, since it was considerably removed from the traditional neighborhood area for doctors' offices centered at Eye and 19th streets, N.W., and because the area was still blighted with dilapidated rowhouses and abandoned commercial buildings. When the proposed offices did not sell, plans for the interior were thus changed. The eight-story building, designed in the International Style, was built as a co-op apartment house, containing efficiency and one-bedroom apartments on the second through eighth floors, with twenty medical offices on the first floor.

During the decades of the 1970s and 1980s, however, a number of co-op office buildings were successfully built and marketed, primarily in the Washington suburbs. They have not been particularly popular, however, since among other things they are sold as empty spaces, or bays in real estate parlance, and the purchaser is required to employ a contractor to finish the space. Far more common and popular are condo office buildings.

A principal result of the construction of Potomac Plaza was that it sparked a major redevelopment of the Foggy Bottom area by other smaller developers. In the process, dozens of Victorian rowhouses in the area were renovated into desirable places to live. Construction of the nearby Kennedy Center and the Watergate and the opening of the Foggy Bottom Metro station have made this a most convenient and attractive residential neighborhood.

119
TOWERS

4201 Cathedral Avenue, N.W.; northeast corner of Cathedral and New Mexico avenues

ARCHITECT: Berla and Abel, 1958

ORIGINAL APARTMENTS: 620 (51 efficiencies; 358 one-bedrooms; 132 two-bedrooms; 78 three-bedrooms; 1 six-bedroom)

STATUS: opened as rental in 1959–60; converted to condo in 1979

The Towers at Cathedral and New Mexico avenues consists of two large buildings joined by
a central lobby.

Visitors are introduced to the 1958 Towers by this exuberant International Style porte-cochère.

The enormous Towers, located on a 12-acre site, was one of Washington's most fashionable apartment houses when completed in 1960. The 620 apartments are contained in two identical thirteen-story irregular T-shaped buildings facing one another and known as Towers East and Towers West. A circular driveway leads to the two-story common lobby, housed in a small, centrally located building connected to the apartment wings by curving glass-enclosed corridors. Behind the lobby (and thus between the East and West buildings) is a large outdoor swimming pool and beyond that, adjacent to Towers East, are the tennis courts.

Built as a luxury rental apartment complex by the Gelman Construction Company and costing $10 million, Towers West opened in 1959 and Towers East in 1960. Each wing has four passenger elevators, which are located in pairs at the two ends of the buildings. The majority of units are one- and two-bedroom apartments. Approximately half the units are provided with wide balconies. The original owner and builder, Melvin Gelman, had difficulty in securing financing in 1957 because most insurance companies and banks questioned the rentability of large units. Gelman was ultimately successful in raising the money to build the Towers from the John Hancock Life Insurance Company and the Greenwich Savings Bank. The developer had purchased the land six years earlier

from Charles Glover II, who lived on his adjacent estate, The Orchards.

The Towers resembled a resort hotel with its extensive landscaping and large public dining room in Towers West. Known as Maurice of the Towers, the restaurant served lunch and dinner and could seat 350 guests. Through its plate glass windows, it faced a putting green in the foreground and the swimming pool and tennis courts in the distance. The restaurant continued in operation under several names and managers until it closed in 1971 and the space was converted to storage. An enormous underground parking garage, located on two levels, provides space for six hundred cars. Other public areas originally included a beauty parlor, a grocery store, and a drugstore, all now closed in part because of the prohibition on street advertising imposed by D.C. zoning regulations. When the Towers was new, according to one long-term resident, patio access to the lobby floor apartments meant that call girls could (and did) rent these units so customers could arrive and depart in privacy.

The Gelman Construction Company was founded in 1925 by Elias Gelman, a Jewish immigrant from Latvia who first settled in New York City. After working as a shoemaker and then a conductor on Manhattan's elevated trains, Gelman thought he could make more money in real estate. He worked part time to learn the construction

Part of the enormous lobby of the Towers.

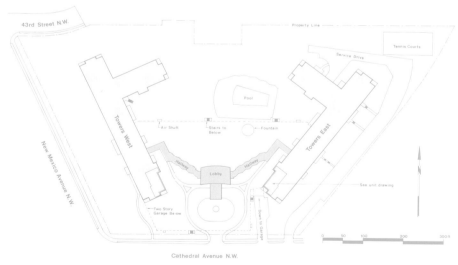

Site plan of the Towers.

Visitors to the Towers must use the intercom in the lobby for entry to the public hallways in the two wings.

trade in New York and then moved to Washington where he entered the real estate business. Elias Gelman built four small apartment houses in the District, the most important being Macomb Gardens at 3725 Macomb Street, N.W., in 1939. His son, Melvin Gelman, expanded the firm enormously in the post–World War II years. He constructed more than two thousand houses in the Maryland suburbs and twelve apartment houses in the Washington area before his death in 1978. Many of his apartment houses were architecturally advanced and innovative for their time, including the Gelmarc Towers at 1930 Columbia Road, N.W. (1950), the Elise at 825 New Hampshire Avenue, N.W. (1956), the Savoy at 1101 New Hampshire Avenue, N.W. (1964), Newport West at 1415 Rhode Island Avenue, N.W. (1966), and the Fountains, 301 North Beauregard Street in Alexandria, Virginia (1968). Almost all the Gelman apartment houses were designed by three architectural firms—George T. Santmyers, Berla and Abel, and Saunders and Pearson. Two Gelman buildings, the Newport West and the Fountains, are unusual because they were the earliest designed with split-level apartments. Only four other local apartment houses offer this arrangement—Prospect House, Sutton Towers, the Envoy of Columbia Plaza, and the Weslie.

After living for a year in Towers West, the younger Gelman and his family moved into their luxurious duplex penthouse in Towers East when that building opened in 1960. The Gelman residence, occupying 9,000 square feet of space, contains sixteen rooms and seven bathrooms and is probably the largest apartment in Washington today, exceeding the size of several 5,500-square-foot penthouse apartments at the Watergate. The most interesting features of the Gelman apartment, redecorated in 1981 by designer Jay Spectre of New York, are the impressive 16-foot-high drawing room and foyer with its mirrored spiral staircase, as well as the elegant terrace on the twelfth floor overlooking the front entrance. A pair of balconies, protected by a cantilevered eave, look down on the apartment's private terrace from the upper level.

Following the death of Melvin Gelman in 1978, the Gelman estate sold the Towers to a developer, Dwight Mize of Dallas, Texas, who converted it to a condominium in 1979. Mrs. Gelman retained the unique apartment as her principal residence, however. During the conversion, the old public dining room was converted to exercise rooms and storage space, roofs were replaced, kitchens modernized, lobby refurnished, public corridors recarpeted, and other features rehabilitated.

The largest apartment at the Towers was designed for the original owner and developer. This fourteen-room duplex is at the top of the east building. Its upper level includes a balcony suspended over a wide terrace.

120

ARMY DISTAFF HALL

6200 Oregon Avenue, N.W.

ARCHITECT: Edwin Weihe and Associates, 1960

ORIGINAL APARTMENTS: 272 (27 bachelors; 106 small efficiencies; 106 large efficiencies; 33 one-bedrooms)

STATUS: opened in 1962 as private retirement club

One of the earliest and best examples of an apartment house serving as a retirement home is the Army Distaff Hall, which opened in 1962 to female Army officers and female dependents of career Army officers. The history of this apartment complex reaches back to the early 1930s with the first attempt to raise funds for a residence for female relatives of Army officers. That effort by a California chapter of the Society of Daughters of the U.S. Army was unsuccessful. The idea was revived in 1950 by the Army Wives Council, composed of representatives of more than thirty Officer's Wives Clubs in the Washington, D.C., area. The Army Distaff Foundation was incorporated in 1959, and a national campaign was initiated to raise funds.

After examining thirty-two possible sites in Washington and its suburbs, the foundation purchased a 16-acre estate known as Blythe Knoll, bordering Rock Creek Park at the junction of Nebraska and Oregon avenues, N.W. The estate had been created in the early 1930s by William Montgomery (1869–1955), president of the Acacia Mutual Life Insurance Company, who built a Tudor Revival residence there.

In 1959 Montgomery's widow, who had recently moved to a Connecticut Avenue apartment, sold Blythe Knoll to the Army Distaff Foundation for $420,000. The

Montgomerys' house, carefully maintained and incorporated into the grounds of the Army Distaff Hall, is now used daily by the residents. After a zoning variance for an apartment house in this restricted residential area was granted, Washington architect Edwin Weihe was commissioned to design the project. His sensitivity to historic buildings led him to incorporate the Oregon Avenue residence, renamed Knoll House, into the master plan for the Army Distaff Hall.

The $4.5 million needed to build it was secured in the early 1960s through numerous fund-raising events, which were strongly supported by President and Mrs. Dwight D. Eisenhower and Army Chief of Staff Maxwell Taylor. In one of the most publicized fund raisers, Mrs. Eisenhower, together with Wernher von Braun, who helped develop German World War II rockets and from 1945 on worked to develop the United States space program, attended the American premier of the Columbia film "I Aim at the Stars," at Washington's Loew's Palace Theatre on 28 September 1960. Following the film, based on Dr. von Braun's life, Perle Mesta entertained the large presidential party at her apartment at 3900 Watson Place, N.W. The Army Distaff Foundation received the first loan from the Federal Housing Administration under its new Housing for the Elderly program in 1960. Fund raising

Army Distaff Hall, right, occupies the grounds of Blythe Knoll, the 1931 Tudor Revival Montgomery family house, shown on the left.

became easier when the foundation was declared tax-exempt in 1963, thus encouraging additional (tax-deductible) gifts, which soon paid off the mortgage.

In the meantime, construction for the complex had begun in November 1960. Because of a severe Washington snowstorm, the scheduled official ground-breaking ceremonies were transferred to the White House. This unique ceremony included Mamie Eisenhower "breaking ground" with a silver-plated infantry trench shovel. Five pounds of earth from the Army Distaff Hall grounds filled a large silver punchbowl held by Lieutenant General Leslie R. Groves, president of the Army Distaff Foundation. Because of Mamie Eisenhower's keen interest in creation of the Army Distaff Hall, where she herself planned to retire, this shovel is now on display at the Eisenhower Library in Abilene, Kansas. When she left the White House in 1961, Mrs. Eisenhower donated her pink hair dryer, pink manicuring table, pink shampoo chair, and pink shampoo basin to the Hall. The home painted the beauty parlor "Mamie pink" in her honor.

The Army Distaff Hall was officially opened in January 1962 with Mrs. Lyndon B. Johnson, wife of the vice president, cutting the ribbon. Fifteen women lived there at the time, but by 1963 all of the original 272 apartments were occupied.

COMFORTS OF HOME

The plan of the building consists of an irregular double Y joined at the stems. Such a layout, which requires a spacious site, allows for a maximum of light, air, and privacy, since no apartment window faces another. The apartments in each tier were identified by letters to indicate their size—"A" units are one-bedrooms, "B" units are large efficiencies, "C" units are small efficiencies, and "D" units are "bachelors," or small efficiency apartments without kitchens. Although all of the apartments are quite small, the Hall contains an enormous amount of public space.

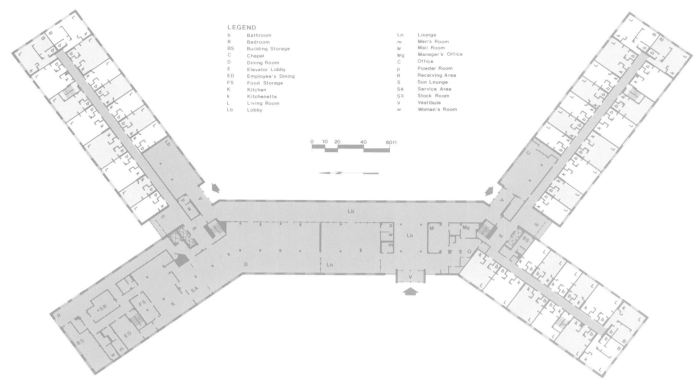

LEGEND

b	Bathroom	Ln	Lounge
B	Bedroom	m	Men's Room
BS	Building Storage	M	Mail Room
C	Chapel	Mg	Manager's Office
D	Dining Room	O	Office
E	Elevator Lobby	p	Powder Room
ED	Employee's Dining	R	Receiving Area
FS	Food Storage	S	Sun Lounge
K	Kitchen	SA	Service Area
k	Kitchenette	SR	Stock Room
L	Living Room	V	Vestibule
Lb	Lobby	w	Women's Room

0 10 20   40   60ft

Ground-floor plan of Army Distaff Hall.

The severely plain brick facade, typical of Modernist architecture after World War II, has large square windows and a canted porte-cochère. Passing through the lobby with its front desk to the right, one finds an extremely long (16 by 200 feet) concourse that looks out upon a rear courtyard, with the Knoll House in the distance. Decorated in silver, white, and gold, the concourse is furnished with lounge chairs and tables; the floor-to-ceiling windows are topped with valances designed with the American eagle and the insignias of Army officers. Adjacent to the concourse is a large dining room seating two hundred and a card room decorated with framed nineteenth-century photographs of American Army officers' quarters.

Two lounges, or solaria, are provided on each of the upper floors, where most apartments are located. Other facilities in the main building include a beauty parlor, a chapel seating eighty, hobby room, director's office, laundry, trunk room, four apartments for staff, a dining room for the medical staff, and an infirmary with thirty-six beds. Most residents eat one meal a day in the dining room and prepare other meals in their own kitchens. The staff of sixty includes maids who clean each apartment once a week. Among the many activities in the hobby room are a painting class, Bible study group, poker club, singing

Mrs. Lyndon Johnson officially opened Army Distaff Hall in 1962.

club, preparation of the monthly newsletter (*The Bugle Call*), and even a whistling club.

Knoll House has a library, music room, and parlor for large-scale private entertaining. William Montgomery had purchased the ornate, fully paneled library from the famous William K. Vanderbilt mansion on Fifth Avenue in New York City shortly before that landmark was razed. The library was installed in Knoll House while it was under construction.

EVOLUTION OF THE IDEA

The word *distaff* refers to a loop used to hold the flax on a spinning wheel. It became synonymous with the wives, daughters, and mothers of British Army officers during the eighteenth century. Following American independence, the term continued to have the same meaning in the new United States Army. While the term is not used in any of the other branches of the American military service, it is still used in civilian life today to mean women, or household women, as "on the distaff side of the family."

Female officers as well as the widows, mothers, and daughters of regular Army officers or reserve officers with at least twenty years of active duty are eligible for residence provided they are single and older than sixty-two. Residents must pay an entrance fee (based on the size of their apartments) and a monthly maintenance fee.

The success of the Army Distaff Hall has led to several similar residence halls for officers and dependents. The Navy has established Vinson Hall in McLean, Virginia, while the Air Force has founded the Air Force Village in San Antonio, Texas. Both of these retirement homes, organized in the early 1970s, differ from the Army Distaff Hall in that they accept married couples as well as single persons.

Privately founded, funded, and managed, the Army Distaff Hall fulfills an important need that became especially evident during the period between the two World Wars when many Army widows were suddenly left without financial support. (It was not until 1974 that Army widows were covered by Social Security.) Today 80 percent of the three hundred residents at the Army Distaff Hall are widows; a number are fully subsidized because of financial needs. Thus the Army Distaff Hall clearly embodies the motto it adopted when it opened: *Colent Arma Militum Uxores*—Let Arms Honor Its Women.

Most of the apartments at Army Distaff Hall are efficiency units with a living room, Pullman kitchen, and bathroom, as shown here.

121

HARBOUR SQUARE

500 N Street, S.W.; north side of N Street between 4th Street and the Washington Channel

ARCHITECT: Chloethiel Woodard Smith, 1963

ORIGINAL APARTMENTS: 448 (140 efficiencies; 172 one-bedrooms; 136 two-bedrooms and larger) and 17 rowhouses

STATUS: opened as co-op in 1966

Because of its innovative design, this $13 million complex of 448 apartments and 17 rowhouses is the most important of the dozen built as part of the Southwest urban renewal program that began in the late 1950s. Fronting the Washington Channel and the Potomac River at Maine Avenue and N Street, S.W., Harbour Square was designed with 134 varying apartment designs. There is no typical floor plan; no other Washington apartment house offers such a multitude of layouts.

Harbour Square occupies a three-block-long rectangular site covering 8 acres. The eight buildings of varying design (named A through H) are grouped around three quadrangles. Operated as a single co-op, they are consolidated as one entity with a single board of directors, resident manager, and heating and cooling system. The various structures within the complex are joined by connecting corridors, footpaths, and an enormous underground garage for 448 cars.

The most prominent of the three sections is the west quadrangle, which faces the Washington Channel. Its three major elements include a pair of ten-story rectangular buildings named A and B, opposite one another, and a 1-acre reflecting pool or water garden separating the two buildings (see site plan). These structures have large balconies and numerous private roof gardens, reached

The principal courtyard and reflecting pool at Harbour Square.

by spiral staircases. Of the eight buildings in Harbour Square, A and B have the best river views and most of the large apartments. Building A has ninety apartments,

426

A number of apartments at Harbour Square have excellent views of the Potomac River with
Hains Point in the distance.

Manager Charles Harker chats with resident Mary Beth Linden on the private roofdeck of her apartment at Harbour Square.

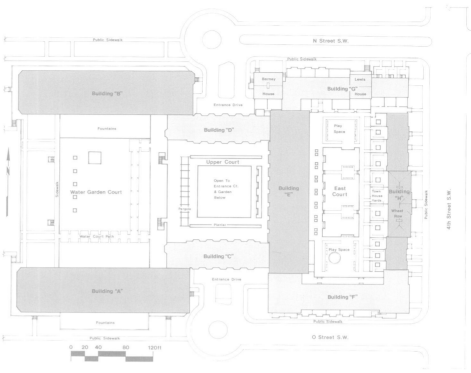

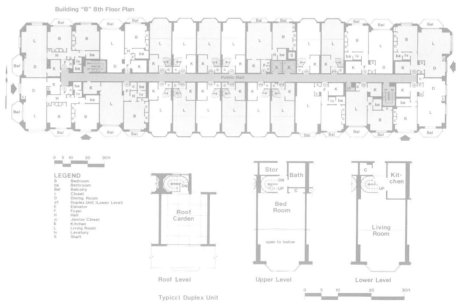

Top: Site plan of Harbour Square. *Bottom:* Eighth-floor plan of the B building at Harbour Square, including the layout of a typical duplex unit there.

thirty-seven of them two-bedroom units, sixteen with three bedrooms, and one four-bedroom.

Only building A has duplex apartments with 20-foot-high living rooms and staircases leading to the single bedrooms on the balcony. The twelve duplex units, faced entirely with glass on one side, offer dramatic views of the water garden. Here also are the only pass-through

apartments, extending the length of the building to both north and south exposures.

Building B offers an Olympic-sized glass-enclosed swimming pool on the ground level. A landscaped park, parallel to the Potomac River, separates the water garden from the Washington Channel.

The central quadrangle, called the tree court, opens

onto the west quadrangle, surrounded by three shorter buildings on the other sides. Two six-story buildings (C and D) border the central quadrangle on the north and south and, like buildings A and B in the west quadrangle, contain private rooftop gardens. The largest number of efficiency apartments are found here—twenty of the thirty units in building C and twenty of the fifty units in building D. The taller, seven-story building E borders the quadrangle to the east. This building includes a large penthouse, with a spectacular river view and spacious promenade, where residents can give private parties for four hundred.

The principal vehicular and pedestrian entrance to the entire complex is through a ramp from N Street, S.W., under building C. Here also are the security gatehouse, the resident manager's office, and guest parking. The guest parking lot, covered on three sides with terraces and pergolas, centers around a square open park. Residents enter the basement garage via two ramps near the main north entrance by building C.

The least obvious of the three sections of Harbour Square is the east quadrangle, known as the English garden, formed by two sets of rowhouses (buildings G and H) and another rectangular high-rise, building F. These three elements plus the E building form the parklike quadrangle.

FEDERAL PRESERVATION

At the time this area of the Southwest was cleared in 1959, three important Federal structures built in the early years of the city's history fortunately were spared. They were renovated and incorporated into the two new sets of rowhouses that form buildings G and H. The largest of the three historic buildings is Wheat Row, a set of four adjoining rowhouses built in 1793 by James Greenleaf, an early Washington developer, and attributed to builder William Lovering. It was named for John Wheat, who owned and occupied the north house. These four rowhouses, united under a single roof and pediment and thought to be the oldest surviving rowhouses in Washington City, form the center section of building G. Each has eight rooms and seven working fireplaces; they are

The spacious indoor swimming pool at Harbour Square.

the largest units within Harbour Square. The rest of building G consists of seven modern rowhouses. Building G is thus a range of seventeen rowhouses, each with a delightful private patio in the rear.

Two other historic Federal houses incorporated into Harbour Square are the Duncanson-Cranch House and the Washington-Lewis House, around the corner on N Street. They form the ends of building H; between them the architect has skillfully incorporated a series of modern rowhouses. The newer ones are faced with brick and are the same height as the adjacent original structures. (The four new rowhouses here were carefully designed with 10-½-foot ceilings to align them with the Federal houses.)

ARCHITECT CHLOETHIEL WOODARD SMITH

Many individuals, working together, were responsible for creating Harbour Square. The major developers included William E. Shannon and Frank J. Luchs of Shannon and Luchs, Inc., and John McShain, the builder who had rebuilt the interior of the White House for President Harry S. Truman, 1948–50. Edmund J. Flynn, the city's leading co-op specialist, sold the units. All suggested ideas to the architect, Chloethiel Woodard Smith.

A native of Oregon, Mrs. Smith was educated at the University of Oregon and Washington University in St. Louis. She served as an assistant for such noted architects

Looking from the bedroom of Mr. and Mrs. Paul Arlt's duplex apartment at Harbour Square
to the living room below. The reflecting pool is in the distance.

as Henry Wright and Clarence Stein before coming to
Washington in 1935. After working for the Federal Housing Administration and for Berla and Abel, Mrs. Smith
started her own firm in Washington in 1946. Her wide
variety of designs included individual dwellings, rowhouses, apartment houses, and commercial buildings.
One of her major projects involved designing a number
of rowhouses at Reston in the 1960s. In 1959 she had
been selected in a competition as the architect for the
first apartment house in the Southwest urban renewal
program. This large complex, Capitol Park, with apartment blocks and adjacent rowhouses, contains seventeen
hundred units. Its success was a major influence in her
development of Harbour Square in 1963.

Mrs. Smith's sensitivity to domestic design was particularly important during an era of "heroic," or heavy
and brutal, architectural design. Her fine sense of scale
and use of refined materials reflected her innate feeling
for domesticity at a time when most Washington apartment
houses were stark and bland. While other architects designed Southwest apartment houses, none surpassed her

variety and innovative designs. Indeed, she was ahead
of her time in several Southwest designs, including her
1966 proposal for a Washington Channel bridge. Not only
did the Southwest ultimately suffer from the failure to
construct this bridge, but the final design of Harbour
Square had to be altered by decision of the Redevelopment
Land Agency. Mrs. Smith's original design for a circular
harbor, with facilities for sailboats, set into the west quadrangle (present site of the water garden) was not approved
because it was thought to be too radical. Twenty years
later Arthur Cotton Moore incorporated this same design
of a circular harbor for his early plan for Washington
Harbour. Although it was never built because of the danger of flooding, the basic concept was used for a large
circular fountain and plaza adjacent to the Potomac River.

A SUCCESSFUL ADDRESS

Much of the success of Harbour Square can also be credited to the Edmund J. Flynn Company. At Harbour Square

A living room in a Harbour Square apartment showing the circular stairs to the private roofdeck.

These two photographs show the custom-designed bed in the Arlt apartment at Harbour Square that partially folds into the wall to provide a table.

the Flynns required one-third down payment and low monthly payments over the remaining thirty-year mortgage. Flynn, a part-owner of the Harbour Square project, had sold two-thirds of the units by October 1963, one month before excavation began. The prices originally ranged from $18,000 for efficiency apartments to $95,000 for rowhouses in Wheat Row.

Dozens of senators, congressmen, judges, and generals have made their homes at Harbour Square. Because of the variety of sizes of units, the complex has housed residents with diverse economic backgrounds. In 1966, for instance, Admiral Arthur W. Radford, retired chairman of the Joint Chiefs of Staff, purchased a three-bedroom apartment in building A, only a few steps from the small apartment of a retired Army sergeant. Two of the most prominent early resident shareholders were Samuel Kauffmann, publisher of the [Washington] *Evening Star*, and Vice President Hubert H. Humphrey. To be nearer the Capitol, the Humphreys sold the house in Chevy Chase where they had lived since 1948 and bought a two-bedroom apartment at Harbour Square.

122

WATERGATE

WATERGATE EAST, 2500 Virginia Avenue, N.W.; WATERGATE WEST, 2700 Virginia Avenue, N.W.;
and WATERGATE SOUTH, 700 New Hampshire Avenue, N.W.

South side of Virginia Avenue between New Hampshire Avenue and Rock Creek Parkway

ARCHITECT: Luigi Moretti, Rome, Italy; Milton Fischer of Corning, Moore, Elmore, and Fischer, associate architects, 1960–69

ORIGINAL APARTMENTS: 641 (Watergate East: 241—23 efficiencies; 71 one-bedrooms; 120 two-bedrooms; 27 three-bedrooms.
Watergate West: 143—80 one-bedrooms; 58 two-bedrooms; 5 three-bedrooms.
Watergate South: 251—122 one-bedrooms; 104 two-bedrooms; 25 three-bedrooms)

STATUS: opened as three separate co-ops in 1965, 1968, 1971, respectively

The three cooperative apartment houses of the Watergate complex are the city's most famous. Indeed, Watergate became a household word and the best-known apartment house in the world after the notorious break-in at the Democratic National Committee offices in the Watergate Office Building during the 1972 presidential campaign. The resulting investigations, which linked high Republican officials to the crime, and a subsequent cover-up attempt led to the resignation of President Richard M. Nixon in August 1974.

The history of Watergate, including its planning, design, and construction, covers seventeen years. To understand Watergate, it is necessary to trace its history step by step.

The name Watergate? It was taken from the first use of the term as it related to the nearby Arlington Memorial Bridge, built in 1926–32, connecting Washington, D.C., and Arlington, Virginia. The bridge design includes a massive semicircular plaza with a monumental flight of forty steps, 206 feet wide, which extend down to Rock Creek Parkway and the edge of the Potomac River. This stairway was named the Water Gate—or ceremonial entrance to the city from the Potomac River—when the bridge opened in 1932. The Water Gate was used as a landing place for boats and as a site for outdoor concerts from 1935 until the noise from jet aircraft approaching and leaving National Airport caused the concerts to be discontinued in the late 1960s.

PREPARING FOR CONSTRUCTION

The Watergate complex was built at a cost of $78 million by one of Europe's largest real estate development companies, the Societa Generale Immobiliare (SGI) of Rome, which bought the 10-acre tract bounded by Virginia and New Hampshire avenues, N.W., F Street, N.W., and Rock Creek Parkway for $10 million in March 1960. Earlier (1955) plans to build another large apartment house complex, Potomac Parkway Plaza, on the site had fallen through because of inadequate financing. The SGI embarked on the enormous Watergate project in 1960–61 after building and selling the nearby co-op, Potomac Plaza Terraces, 730 24th Street, N.W., in 1959–60. The financial success of this much smaller project reinforced the developers' belief that this section of Foggy Bottom held great potential for future co-op apartment house development.

Although first planned and designed in 1960–61, it was not until late 1962 that approval for Watergate was

The East building at Watergate shortly after it was completed.

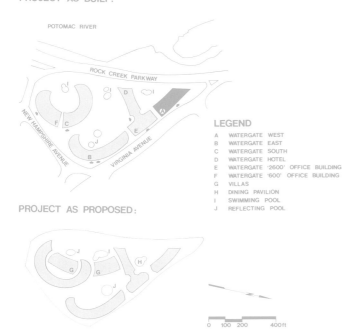

POTOMAC RIVER

ROCK CREEK PARKWAY

NEW HAMPSHIRE AVENUE

VIRGINIA AVENUE

LEGEND

A WATERGATE WEST
B WATERGATE EAST
C WATERGATE SOUTH
D WATERGATE HOTEL
E WATERGATE '2600' OFFICE BUILDING
F WATERGATE '600' OFFICE BUILDING
G VILLAS
H DINING PAVILION
I SWIMMING POOL
J REFLECTING POOL

PROJECT AS PROPOSED:

0   100   200   400ft

Site plans of Watergate, as proposed and as built. The floor plan of Watergate West, building A in the top site plan, appears on the following page.

secured from the Commission of Fine Arts, the National Capital Planning Commission, and the D.C. Zoning Commission. The original concept for Watergate Towne, as it was first named, called for 1,400 apartment units, a 350-room hotel, a shopping mall, nineteen rowhouses (originally called villas), an office building, and a three-level underground garage for 1,250 cars. Construction originally was to start in 1961 and be finished in 1966, but a number of important design changes delayed completion until 1971.

Before construction could finally begin in 1964, the Watergate developers had to solve a number of serious problems. They first needed approval to close portions of 26th, 27th, and G streets, N.W. Next, a variance to the zoning law had to be granted to permit the 130-foot height. Both the Commission of Fine Arts and a number of members of the National Capital Planning Commission opposed the thirteen-story buildings, fearing that their large scale would dwarf the nearby Lincoln Memorial and the proposed national cultural center on the 13-acre site to

The most prominent feature of Watergate's design evolved from the curved balconies with their unusual "toothpick" balusters.

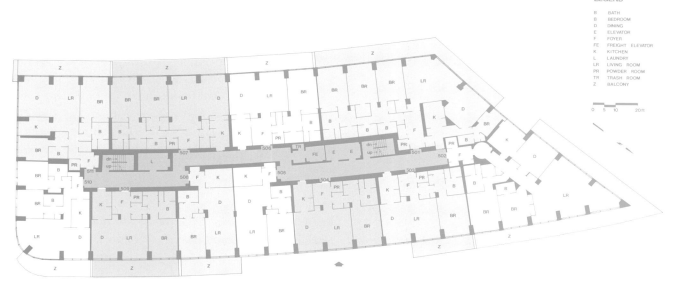

Typical floor plan of Watergate West.

the south. Both commissions ultimately accepted the Watergate design, however, and approved issuance of the necessary building permits in late 1962, requiring the Watergate developers to scale down the size, but not the height, of the four buildings.

The developers also agreed to use only 3 of the 10 acres of the site for buildings; the balance would remain open parkland facing the Potomac River. They also agreed to forgo the proposed nineteen villas or rowhouses originally planned for the courtyard. This was a noteworthy compromise since the law permitted buildings on 75 percent of the land. In addition, only one building would be 130 feet high; the others would rise only to 112 feet. In essence, the compromise involved trading height and density for green space. The developers further agreed to a request from the D.C. Zoning Commission that all office space be limited to professional persons or nonprofit organizations.

Another problem arose when plans for the Watergate were mentioned in a nationally syndicated column by Drew Pearson in August 1962. He wrote mistakenly: "A company financed by the Vatican wants to build a massive apartment house on the Potomac River where it would dwarf the nearby Lincoln Memorial." In response, congressmen received hundreds of letters from irate constituents protesting the design and bulk of Watergate. They argued that a foreign country should not be allowed special privileges that would result in permanent damage to the beauty of Washington. The column further activated efforts of a group known as Protestants and Other Americans United for Separation of Church and State, which incorrectly claimed that the Watergate complex was being built by the Pope. The Vatican actually owned only 20 percent of the stock in the century-old Italian development firm, the Societa Generale Immobiliare. The Vatican's interest in real estate development, as well as its ownership of stock, was enormous and far-flung. In 1965, *The Economist* of London reported that the Vatican owned one-fifteenth of all Italian stocks, worth $613 million. Total holdings in real estate and stock, including European and North and South American investments, at that time exceeded $5.6 billion. The Vatican's interest in Watergate was only one of thousands of real estate investments in which it was involved.

Even though the SGI purchased the site, most of the construction cost came from a $44 million mortgage supplied by an American firm, the John Hancock Mutual Life Insurance Company. A major change occurred in 1968, however, when the Italian Parliament revoked the Catholic Church's long-standing tax exemption on Italian stock. As a result, the following year the Vatican sold its shares in the SGI and reinvested its funds in foreign companies.

THE BASIC PLAN

The most distinctive feature of the four-building complex—Watergate East, Watergate West, Watergate Hotel and Office Building, and Watergate South—is its curvilinear shape. Although some critics objected to the peculiar designs of the balconies—claiming they resembled a fishbone, comb, or sawtooth—members of the National Capital Planning Commission praised the Watergate's overall form. They felt it was an exciting departure from Washington's customary boring rectangular apartment houses and office buildings. The four Watergate buildings are constructed of reinforced concrete. Three are shaped like the letters I, T, and C; the fourth is shaped like a boomerang. The architect, Luigi Moretti of Rome, stated that his design was inspired by the architecture of Bath, England, where many of the eighteenth-century rowhouses were molded into graceful arcs on the crescent streets. Because of the intricate curves of the Watergate facades, a computer was used to figure the exact dimensions of the thousands of concrete panels (each slightly different in size) that had to be cast for the various free-flowing surfaces. The curves permit maximum visibility toward the river and create a spacious interior courtyard with a parklike setting for the residents. Not only the balconies but also the interior apartment walls conform to the curvilinear exteriors.

The drawback to the city is that the courtyard is completely concealed and closed to all vehicular and pedestrian traffic on the two streets it faces on the north and east—Virginia and New Hampshire avenues, N.W. While the peaceful green area away from street noises is

Unusual perspective of Watergate.

beneficial to Watergate residents, the massive wall of concrete hides the view of the river as well as the Watergate's landscaping from other residents of the neighborhood.

Sale of apartments in the first building, Watergate East, began in October 1963, several months before ground was broken. Prices ranged from $17,000 for efficiencies to $200,000 for the largest penthouse apartments. These proved to be bargains, since prices for efficiencies started at $28,000 in Watergate West when it opened in 1969, and $32,000 at Watergate South in 1970. Parking spaces sold for $3,000. Watergate East was constructed between February 1964 and October 1965, when the first shareholders, or owners, moved in. The co-op was officially incorporated in April 1966, when the first officers and board of directors were elected. Watergate East differs from the other two co-ops in that it has two lobbies, north and south, separated by an open concourse that leads to large fountains and a courtyard. The average Watergate East apartment is also larger than those in either Watergate West or Watergate South. Watergate East has 241 apartments on thirteen floors. The lower floors have an open-air shopping mall. Apartments on the top two floors have wood-burning fireplaces; some also have private roof terraces.

STRUGGLES WITH KENNEDY CENTER TRUSTEES

Just before excavation was to begin for Watergate East in 1964, the trustees of the Kennedy Center tried to either block construction of the entire Watergate project or force a major change in its design. Their efforts to enlist the aid of the Commission of Fine Arts and the National Capital Planning Commission in their cause proved fruitless, however, since the necessary compromises had been effected and the building permits issued two years earlier.

Although Washington always had many privately owned theaters, it had never enjoyed a large government-sponsored cultural center for all of the performing arts—drama, opera, concerts, ballet, and film. The genesis of the Kennedy Center dates to 1955 when Congressman Frank Thompson, Democrat of New Jersey, introduced a bill to create a national cultural center in Washington. Congress then appointed a twenty-two-member auditorium committee to study the idea and to recommend its location, scope, and financing. The concept was strongly supported by President Eisenhower.

During the following three years, the auditorium committee considered three possible sites—two in the Southwest section and one in Foggy Bottom. Congressman Thompson's plan to build the center on the northeast corner of 7th Street and Independence Avenue, S.W., was denied because both Secretary Leonard Carmichael of the Smithsonian Institution and Senator Jennings Randolph, Democrat of West Virginia, wanted that site reserved for a national air and space museum. After that issue was settled, events moved rapidly.

Although opposition to Watergate by the Kennedy Center trustees was silenced in 1964, it would resume three years later. In the meantime, construction of the Watergate complex continued in four phases as rapidly as possible. With Watergate East completed, a second phase—the Watergate Hotel and Watergate Office Building—was constructed in 1966 and 1967. The 200,000-square-foot office building fronts on Virginia Avenue, N.W., and is connected to the hotel in the rear by an enclosed colonnade. The two-part building thus forms a T. The Watergate Hotel opened with 213 furnished suites ranging from studios to two-bedroom units. The residents,

Each of the three Watergate apartment buildings, including the West building shown here, has its own outdoor swimming pool.

This oval foyer in a Watergate apartment has a white marble floor.

One of the most dramatic views at Watergate is from the living room of the West building apartments in the tier at the apex; they face the Potomac River.

many of them long-term, and the office building occupants have access to the shopping mall, a health club, and a restaurant.

The third phase of construction produced the second co-op apartment house, Watergate West, built in 1967–68 and first occupied in January 1969. It includes 143 apartments; 19 are ground-floor duplexes, with their own patios. The apartments on the wedge-shaped western end of the building, facing the Potomac River and George-town, are often cited as having the most spectacular views in the entire complex. Even though prices had increased for these apartments, and the developer, Riverside Realty Corporation (a subsidiary of the Societa Generale Im-mobiliare), required a 40-percent down payment, these units sold as rapidly and successfully as those in Wa-tergate East.

The most controversial of the four Watergate build-ings was the last built, Watergate South. The original plans developed in 1961 called for it to be a five-hundred-unit co-op apartment house. In 1967 the developer elected to build it as an office building, however, because of conditions in the market. The residents of Watergate East objected strongly. The new plan was also vigorously at-tacked by Roger L. Stevens and other trustees of the Kennedy Center, then under construction, who tried to enlist the aid of the Commission of Fine Arts and the National Capital Planning Commission to block construc-tion. It was pointed out, however, by the Commission of Fine Arts, that the Kennedy Center officials should have objected to the proximity of Watergate South in 1962 when the zoning commission was considering the building permit. The Kennedy Center trustees received no support, even after arguing that in 1962 the present design of the Kennedy Center had not been conceived. Undaunted, the trustees next tried to push a bill through Congress pro-hibiting any new building more than 60 feet high within 1,500 feet of the Kennedy Center. The bill never passed.

Under threat of suits by both the Watergate residents and the Kennedy Center trustees, the developer compro-mised. The building was redesigned with two parts, Watergate South—a co-op apartment house with 257 units, and Watergate Six Hundred (600 New Hampshire Avenue, N.W.)—an office building with 260,000 square feet of office and commercial space. A second shopping mall, the indoor *Les Champs*, was designed for the ground floor. The project was an immediate success, attracting four thousand persons daily from the Watergate residences and offices, as well as local shoppers and many of the ten thousand daily visitors to the Kennedy Center. The new building was also realigned, turning it to allow more open space opposite the Kennedy Center, only 300 feet away. The compromise plan was mediated in 1967 by Secretary of the Interior Stewart L. Udall. Begun in 1969, Watergate South opened in 1971. Among the notable early tenants of the Watergate Six Hundred office building was the Swedish Chancellery, which occupied the top floor.

DESIGN SPECIFICS

In addition to its unusual curvilinear shapes, the Watergate complex offered other innovative and distinctive features. Although several clusters of large apartment houses had previously been built in Washington, such as Cathedral Mansions (1922), Tilden Gardens (1927), and the Westchester (1930), none had been designed like the Watergate. Facing inward toward an enclosed courtyard, the mixed-use buildings at Watergate constitute a self-contained community within the city. When completed in 1971, it included three apartment houses with a total of 640 cooperative apartments, a hotel, two office buildings, two shopping malls, a health club with an indoor swimming pool, three outdoor swimming pools, a bank, several restaurants, a grocery store, a post office, a drugstore, several doctors' offices, a beauty parlor, a barbershop, a poster shop, dry cleaners, a bakery, a florist, and an indoor parking garage for 1,150 cars. Watergate became a prototype for subsequent large projects, including Columbia Plaza, Van Ness Centre, Grosvenor Park, the Rotonda, and Sutton Towers. Although several of these also contain shops, none can equal the facilities at Watergate, which remains the best example of self-contained living.

Among the most distinctive features of the 640 apartments, designed in 150 variations, are the balconies, some extending 129 feet. At the time they were the largest in the city, exceeded later only by those at the Foxhall. A number of apartments have oval foyers and pie-shaped or round rooms, a distinct break with traditional right-angled rooms. These curves and bends provide ample space for closets.

The balconies have "sawtooth" railings, which provide both air circulation and privacy. And their well-defined horizontal bands counteract the appearance of height. Both the balconies and walls are faced with a light beige quartz and marble aggregate, specifically designed and produced for the Watergate complex. Each panel is unique in curvature and size. At Watergate East, for example, more than twenty-two hundred different panels were installed. When they arrived on the construction site from the Mosaic Building Products Company of Cleveland, each was marked for a specific location. Because the cores are hollow, they weigh half as much as ordinary prefabricated wall panels. Rather than using a crane, the workmen carried the panels by hand to their proper location and installed them in minutes. The new panels were claimed to be durable, easily cleaned, and highly moisture-resistant, and would provide better insulation than normal facade walls. Maximum width of each panel is 12 feet and the height 3 feet.

All buildings have closed circuit television cameras as well as security guards, twenty-four-hour lobby clerks, and doormen. At Watergate East, for instance, fourteen television cameras were installed to constantly monitor the elevators, laundry rooms, and garage.

Soon after construction was completed and both Watergate East and West were occupied, numerous defects were found. When the developer refused to correct the faults, both co-ops sued; the result was that the developers agreed to pay the owners of Watergate East $250,000 and Watergate West $600,000 to correct roof and wall leakage and to prevent water from pouring into the apartments from the balconies. Dozens of balconies were severely damaged during heavy rains. Because balcony drainage was inadequate, water rushed inside under the sliding glass doors.

Other defects were soon evident, as reported in a number of articles in the *Washington Post*. The ventilating system was faulty in a number of apartments, and the air conditioning system cooled from the waist down and heated from the waist up at the same time. Mrs. Maurice Stans, wife of the secretary of commerce, complained that improper air and dehumidifying during the city's humid summers had buckled her parquet floors and spoiled wall-to-wall carpets, almost ruining the seven-room apartment. The outspoken wife of the attorney general, Martha Mitchell, claimed that she had had better living conditions in a $120 rental apartment in New York than at Watergate—without the $1,100 monthly Watergate maintenance fee, of course. Engineering inadequacies required the residents to rush down to their storerooms in the basement to salvage their possessions during periodic floods. In time the balcony and roof leaks and the faulty air conditioning systems were fixed—after $1 million in repairs and untold fraught nerves. Half of the apartments in the adjacent Watergate West were also deficient.

RESIDENT PROFILE

According to the president of Riverview Realty Corporation, which handled the sale of Watergate co-op apartments, the average residents and shareholders were couples, about fifty years of age, with one married child and a second in college. Most were long-time Washington residents who had sold their houses when they moved to Watergate. Many chose to live there for its proximity to downtown, the White House, and the Department of State and for easy access to Capitol Hill via Rock Creek Parkway and the Southwest Freeway. Many sought the superb view. While the newly built Harbour Square, similar to Watergate in many ways, also had a river view of the Southwest waterfront, many preferred the Foggy Bottom area; others liked the convenience of the two shopping malls.

The Watergate has always attracted prominent residents. Several key officials of the Nixon administration lived here, including three cabinet officers: John A. Volpe, as well as Maurice Stans and John Mitchell. Nixon's longtime private secretary, Rose Mary Woods, leased a duplex in Watergate West adjacent to Juanita D. Roberts, former personal secretary to President Lyndon B. Johnson. At least a dozen members of Congress have lived here. Original purchasers in the 1960s included Democratic senators Wayne Morse, Russell B. Long, Alan Cranston, and Abraham Ribicoff, and Republican senator Jacob Javits. Many other high-ranking officials, such as the chief of protocol, director of the Mint, and various undersecretaries, joined them. Another resident frequently in the news is Anna Chennault, a native of Peking and the widow of World War II hero Major General Claire Lee Chennault. A very successful businesswoman, she has been a leader in developing American exports to Asia as well as managing her own freight airline—Flying Tigers. Other well-known Watergate residents include Senator and Mrs. Robert Dole and Mr. and Mrs. Charles Wick.

123

PROSPECT HOUSE

1200 North Nash Street, Arlington, Virginia

ARCHITECT: Donald Hudson Drayer, 1963

ORIGINAL APARTMENTS: 268 (71 efficiencies; 101 one-bedrooms; 96 two-bedrooms)

STATUS: opened as rental in 1965; converted to co-op in 1980

Built on a steep hill, on direct axis with the Mall, this V-shaped eleven-story apartment house boasts two exceptional features—a magnificent view of the city and an unusual floor plan. The apartments near the apex of the building (Nos. 140–150), with their soaring two-story-high floor-to-ceiling angled window walls facing the Potomac River, are particularly dramatic. Many distinguished residents have been attracted to Prospect House—Kate Smith, Anna May Hays (the first American woman general), William Colby (director of the Central Intelligence Agency), Allan Boyd (president of Amtrak), and two dozen members of Congress.

The 268 apartments vary in size from efficiencies to two-bedroom units and have five basic designs. Some are on one level, while others are on two or even three levels. The largest are pass-through apartments, with 32-foot duplex living rooms facing Washington; the kitchen, dining room, two bedrooms, and two baths are on the upper level extending to the front entrance of the building. The front or lobby entrance of Prospect House, with no dramatic view, faces west toward Fort Myer. This unusual plan offers a number of advantages. First, many apartments have both east and west exposures because they extend through the building. Second, because of the arrangement of the apartments, which include flats, walk-

Front facade of Prospect House.

The lobby of Prospect House fortunately remains unchanged with these unusual 1960 chandeliers.

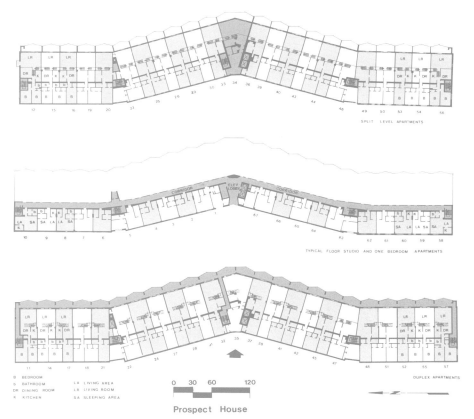

SPLIT LEVEL APARTMENTS

TYPICAL FLOOR STUDIO AND ONE BEDROOM APARTMENTS

B BEDROOM
b BATHROOM
DR DINING ROOM
K KITCHEN

LA LIVING AREA
LR LIVING ROOM
SA SLEEPING AREA

0 30 60 120

DUPLEX APARTMENTS

Prospect House

Prospect House was the first Washington area apartment house designed with a combination of split-level and duplex apartments. The lower-floor plan shows the lower level of the duplex apartments, which are entered from the upper floor. In the middle-floor plan flats are found only on the west side of the building. The upper-floor plan shows the split-level (or tri-level) apartments: each level is equivalent to half a floor in height—except that the living rooms have 13-foot cathedral ceilings.

The entrance of this split-level at Prospect House is on the lower level on the left; the middle-level living room is in the foreground; and the dining room, kitchen, and bedrooms are on the upper level in the background.

ups, and walk-downs, the elevator stops only at every third floor. Valuable space that would normally be used for public corridors thus can be utilized instead for private apartments. The less desirable efficiency apartments face west, while all large units face east with large balconies overlooking the nation's capital. The one-bedroom and two-bedroom units are either split-levels or duplexes. In the duplex apartments, a foyer from the public hall leads to a short (seven-step) staircase to the 13-foot-high living room. A second short (six-step) staircase leads to the upper rooms. Only a half-dozen apartment houses in the Washington area have pass-through apartments.

Two other amenities are an outdoor swimming pool and a rooftop restaurant. Opened in 1966, a year after Prospect House was completed, the Top O'The Town seats 250 for dinner and includes nightly dancing in its lounge. In 1983, when the restaurant was remodeled, part of it became a private club. A glass outside elevator, the first in Washington, was installed at that time to allow public access to the restaurant without passing through the lobby.

The view of the city from Prospect House is considered by many to be the finest of any apartment house in the Washington area. Because Prospect House is on the edge of a steep hill, the former site of the Congressional School, and because all parkland directly below is owned by the federal government as the site for the Marine Corps Memorial and Arlington National Cemetery, the magnificent view of Washington in the distance will always be protected. Most of the major landmarks and monuments in the city are clearly identifiable: the Lincoln Memorial, the Washington Monument, the Smithsonian Institution Building, the U.S. Capitol, and the dome of the Library of Congress.

A number of other apartment houses that were built on high points of land with commanding views have not been as fortunate. Magnificent vistas of the city from the Wyoming, the Highlands, and the Westmoreland—to name only a few—have been partially blocked by large new buildings such as the Holiday Inn, the Washington Hilton Hotel, and the Universal and Universal North buildings. Other apartment houses that still have exceptional views of the city include the Cairo, the Wardman Tower, the Belvedere, the Atrium, the Dorchester House, Wardman Courts (now Clifton Terrace), the Weslie, Meridian Mansions (now the Envoy), Washington Harbour, Watergate, Tiber Island, Town Center West (now Marina View Towers), and Harbour Square. None of these, with the exception of the Weslie, can really match the sweeping vistas from Prospect House, however.

ARCHITECT DONALD HUDSON DRAYER

The architect of Prospect House, Donald Hudson Drayer, became a specialist in designing large luxury Washington apartment houses after World War II. His early designs were so successful with his clients that they and other developers returned repeatedly with more commissions. He studied the problems peculiar to apartment houses and then avoided them. In Drayer's buildings, for instance, apartment doors never were directly opposite one another in the public halls, to ensure privacy. Drayer also learned that residents preferred balconies—rare before World War II—above all other amenities.

After receiving his architecture degree from Washington University in St. Louis in 1931, Drayer served as an architect for the Public Buildings Administration in Washington during the Great Depression and in the Navy Department during World War II. Entering private practice after the war, he was responsible for the design of more than three dozen luxury apartment houses in the Washington area, among them (in the city) the Imperial House, 170 units, 1960; the Bristol House, 200 units, 1961; the Colonnade, 105 units, 1963; and the Carlton House, 105 units, 1963. His many suburban apartment houses include (in Virginia) Arlington Towers, 1,800 units, 1949–54, and River Towers, Alexandria, 490 units, 1961, and (in Maryland) Grosvenor Park, Rockville, 1,700 units, 1962; the Seasons, Bethesda, 247 units, 1969; and the Promenade, Rockville, 1,071 units, 1972. Many of Drayer's apartment houses of the 1960s, his most prolific period, were designed for two local developers—Nathan Landow and Lawrence M. Brandt. Prospect House, perhaps the most innovative of all, was designed for Brandt in 1963. Drayer died in 1973.

Top: The most desirable apartments at Prospect House are the rear units with wide balconies and spectacular views of Washington. *Bottom:* Both Prospect House and the adjacent Weslie, to the north, have exceptionally dramatic views of the city.

124

VAN NESS CENTRE

Van Ness East, 2929 Van Ness Street, N.W.; Van Ness North, 3001 Veazey Terrace, N.W.; and
Van Ness South, 3003 Van Ness Street, N.W.;
east side of Connecticut Avenue between Van Ness and Yuma streets, N.W., opposite the University of the District of Columbia
ARCHITECTS: Van Fossen Schwab and Shanti Singh Sukthankar, Baltimore (Van Ness East);
Berla and Abel (Van Ness North, Van Ness South, Van Ness Office Building, and master plan); 1963–67
ORIGINAL APARTMENTS: 1,524 (Van Ness East: 433—90 efficiencies, 272 one-bedrooms, 60 two-bedrooms, 11 three-bedrooms;
Van Ness North: 466—29 efficiencies, 181 one-bedrooms, 241 two-bedrooms, 15 three-bedrooms;
Van Ness South: 625—79 efficiencies, 461 one-bedrooms, 85 two-bedrooms)
STATUS: Van Ness East—opened as rental in 1964, converted to co-op in 1981;
Van Ness North—opened as rental in 1967, converted to condo in 1979; Van Ness South—opened as rental in 1970

One of the important amenities of Van Ness Centre is this large outdoor swimming pool in the middle of the complex. In a unique arrangement, residents of all three buildings—co-op, condo, and rental—may use it.

Famous as the largest apartment complex along the five-mile length of Connecticut Avenue, N.W., Washington's premier apartment house corridor, Van Ness Centre was built on an 18-acre plot over a six-year period between 1964 and 1970. The $50 million project was developed by Robert I. Silverman, whose Southeast Construction Company was responsible for the residential buildings, and Milton and Howard Polinger, who, in association with Stanley Zupnik, built the commercial building. The Polinger brothers, experienced in apartment house development, had previously built the Whitehall in Bethesda and Suburban Towers on upper 16th Street, N.W. Mr. Silverman had constructed numerous houses, apartment houses, and office buildings in Washington and suburban Maryland. He, more than any other individual, took charge of the construction of Van Ness Centre.

The three apartment houses in the complex—Van Ness East, Van Ness North, and Van Ness South—are adjacent to a large commercial building, originally designed with a spacious underground garage, shopping arcade on the lower two levels, and offices above. The single office building is the only one of the four in the complex that directly faces Connecticut Avenue. Its occupants when it opened in 1967 included Hot Shoppes, Giant Food, Peoples Drug, Boeing Corporation, and Capital City Savings and Loan.

The land occupied by Van Ness Centre was leased for seventy-five years from the Chevy Chase Land Company, formed in 1890 to develop the upper northwest sections of the District of Columbia and adjacent areas of Montgomery County, Maryland. The company cut Connecticut Avenue through the heart of its holdings. In existence today, this firm still owns several apartment houses along the avenue, as well as various office buildings and other real estate.

While very common in Britain and even in certain American cities such as New York and Baltimore, ground leases are relatively unusual in Washington. Nevertheless, more than a dozen local apartment houses now occupy leased land, including the Westchester, Columbia Plaza, 4101 Connecticut Avenue, N.W., the Cathedral, Idaho Terrace, and the Watergate. Under a leased arrangement, the owner of the apartment house pays a yearly rent, which can be fixed or geared to inflation or other factors.

The site of Van Ness Centre is ideal for many, although others would claim it is "too far out." The view to the east is parkland—Soapstone Valley Park, a 24-acre spur of Rock Creek Park. Once an Indian quarry, Soapstone Valley Park now comprises steep wooded banks of a tributary of Rock Creek. Van Ness East, the first building in the complex, directly overlooks this park.

(Other apartment houses with excellent park views include the Woodner, the Westchester, the Cathedral, Cathedral West, the Towers, Sumner Village, the Kennedy-Warren, and Tilden Gardens.)

Despite the presence of the Van Ness Metro station, which opened in 1981, the area has become increasingly congested with automobile traffic following the recent construction of the adjacent Van Ness campus of the University of the District of Columbia and the new Intelsat Building, housing an international consortium that monitors satellites. These buildings, plus a group of new embassies, now occupy the former site of the National Bureau of Standards across Connecticut Avenue from Van Ness Centre.

The fifteen-hundred-unit Van Ness Centre complex offers two outdoor swimming pools—a small one adjacent to Soapstone Valley Park used solely for the residents of Van Ness East, and a much larger 5,400-square-foot pool in the center of the complex, shared by Van Ness North and Van Ness South. The architect, Joseph Abel, emphasized to the developers that a pool of this size would be a major drawing card for Van Ness. He was right. Beautifully designed, this large, unusually shaped pool has an adjacent 15,000-square-foot sundeck, sheltered and bordered on two sides by long ranges of cabanas.

In addition, the complex features several under-

Site plan of Van Ness Centre.

Typical floor plan at Van Ness North.

ground garages—Van Ness East for 200 cars, Van Ness North for 500 cars, Van Ness South for 450 cars, and parking for 750 cars under the office building. The various garages under the three apartment houses and the office building extend from two to four levels underground and were originally all connected to provide overflow space from one building to another. The Van Ness buildings provide more underground parking than any other apartment complex in Washington proper.

The buildings at Van Ness Centre range in height from the six-story office building to the eleven to sixteen floors of the three apartment houses. All of the apartment buildings have doormen, twenty-four-hour secretarial service, valet parking, and package rooms.

VARIETY AND APPEAL

Designed in the International Style, the brick apartment houses are basically identical in facade treatment but markedly different in the size and mix of units within. The percentage of two-bedroom apartments, for instance, is much higher in Van Ness North than in Van Ness South. Most of the units throughout the complex include

balconies, some with open rails and others screened with panels. Many on the ground level have private patios enclosed by brick walls for privacy. All of the buildings are well sited and connected by a large plaza, terraces, driveways, and walkways. Landscaping includes an assortment of fountains and open lawns. Of the 18 acres, 13 are open space.

The newest and largest of the three apartment houses is Van Ness South, which consists of two buildings connected by a centrally located lobby. Although both buildings are considered Van Ness South, they are referred to as the west wing and the south wing. Most of the units in Van Ness South have one bedroom, while Van Ness North has fifteen large three-bedroom apartments and Van Ness East has eleven. Overall, Van Ness East has the largest number of small apartments, while Van Ness North has the most large ones. The complex, a town within itself, houses thirty-five hundred individuals.

Differences exist among all of the buildings, and each has a different configuration, varying from a modified U and L to a T and H. The design and shape of the lobbies also vary considerably. Van Ness South has the most spectacular lobby with a 15-foot ceiling, wide walls of either plate glass or paneled wood, and bold, simple concrete piers. The original International Style furniture from the 1960s complements the architecture. Van Ness East has a smaller lobby, decorated with eighteenth-century reproduction furniture that is out of place in its stark twentieth-century setting. In addition to the variations in their shape, size, and furnishings, the lobbies are on different levels. Since the sixteen-story Van Ness East is built into the grade of a steep hill, the ground-floor lobby, with its handsome porte-cochère, is on the sixth floor.

All three buildings have the same high-quality construction, but the apartments vary in design from building to building. Although efficiency apartments do not have balconies, balconies are included on most one-bedroom and all two- and three-bedroom units. All corner apartment kitchens have outside windows, while all large units have two doors from the public corridor, one for the main

entrance and one for the kitchen. Variations are seen even within a single building. The one-bedroom units in Van Ness East, for instance, range from 801 to 1,015 square feet. Each of the three apartment houses has a laundry room on every floor as well as other amenities like a sauna and a party room. In Van Ness North, residents operate a common lending library in a fourth-floor room.

Van Ness Centre has become particularly popular with diplomats and other professionals. A noteworthy resident was Joseph Abel, the architect of most of the complex, who lived in a three-bedroom unit in Van Ness North from its opening until his death in late 1985. During his remarkable forty-year career, Abel designed more than a hundred luxury apartment houses in Washington. His designs ranged from Tudor Revival and eclectic build-

The balconies of the apartments at Van Ness Centre are separated with glass panels for greater privacy.

ings in the 1920s, to Art Deco and early International Style in the 1930s and 1940s. His last major apartment house project before his retirement was Van Ness Centre. (One of his major contributions to architecture was the publication of his 1947 book, *Apartment Houses*, a critique on how to design good apartment houses.)

OWNERSHIP AND ORIGINS

Although Van Ness Centre was built as a rental complex, two of the three apartment houses have been converted to individual ownership. Van Ness North, including its land, was sold by the original owners for $26 million to a corporation headed by Conrad Cafritz in 1979 for conversion to a cooperative. At the time of the conversion, senior citizens with a low income were allowed by law to rent their apartments for another three years even though they had been sold. Under the D.C. rent control law, tenants in a complex must be offered a chance to match any offer to buy the building. The residents organized a tenants association but failed to buy their building. A majority of the tenants, however, purchased their units at reduced rates.

During the late 1970s the original developers wisely purchased the leased land from the Chevy Chase Land Company. In 1980 Van Ness East and its land were sold to the tenants for $20 million for conversion to a con-

dominium. Efforts to convert Van Ness South, the largest building, into a condo failed in both 1980 and 1983 because of tenant opposition. In 1984 the original owners sold it to the J. M. B. Realty Corporation of Chicago, and it is still a rental apartment house. The office building has been solely owned by Milton Polinger since 1983. Other developments occurred that year when the twenty-unit second-floor shopping mall in the office building, never a success because it was too far from the street, was converted from shops to offices. The street-level stores, including the drugstore, restaurant, and supermarket, were not affected by this conversion.

And the name Van Ness? The complex was named for Van Ness Street, which in turn was derived from the city's ninth mayor, John Peter Van Ness. A native of New York, Van Ness first came to Washington as a member of the House of Representatives shortly after 1800. Accepting a post offered by President Jefferson in the city militia, he was forced to resign his seat in Congress, which interpreted "separation of powers" as meaning that no one in the legislative branch could also hold an executive position. He remained in the city, serving as mayor. Van Ness married heiress Marcia Burns, whose father had owned a small plantation near the present site of the White House at the time the District of Columbia was laid out in 1791. Van Ness, the city's largest land-owner, remained active in civic affairs in Washington until his death in 1846.

125

IRENE

4701 Willard Avenue, Chevy Chase, Maryland

ARCHITECT: Berla and Abel, 1964

ORIGINAL APARTMENTS: 529 (45 efficiencies; 135 one-bedrooms; 274 two-bedrooms; 75 three-bedrooms)

STATUS: opened as rental in 1966

The Irene remains one of the finest luxury rental apartment houses in the Washington area. Located in the Friendship Heights section of Chevy Chase, Maryland, near Wisconsin Avenue and the District of Columbia line, the $15 million Irene was named for the wife of its builder and owner, Abe Pollin. During World War I, the 101,000-square-foot plot was part of a public golf course known as Kirkside. It was frequently used by President Woodrow Wilson in preference to nearby private courses. This sixteen-story International Style apartment house, designed in an irregular E shape, fits tightly into its rectangular site. Although extending to the building line in all four directions, the Irene provides all of its 529 apartments with abundant light and air. It faces Somerset Park on the north and west and two wide streets—Willard Avenue and North Park Avenue—on the south and east.

AN ENVIABLE ADDRESS

The building is noted for its spacious units; most have two bedrooms with 1,300 to 1,710 square feet. The three-bedroom units range from 2,040 to 2,170 square feet. An unusual feature of the Irene is the tenants' name plaque adjacent to each apartment door. Each apartment

Front facade of the Irene.

has its own burglar alarm system, which must be turned off in the hall with a special key. Additional security is provided by a guard who patrols the building during the night. All entrances and public spaces are monitored twenty-four hours a day by closed-circuit television.

No balconies were built at the Irene, since Mr. Pollin felt that year-round solaria would be more useful. The 150 much-sought-after solaria are completely faced with glass on all four sides; in most, two sides have exterior exposures.

All large apartments have two bathrooms and a windowless powder room, a large dining room that opens on one end to the living room, large kitchens with a breakfast room at one end, a separate kitchen entrance from the public hall, and abundant closet space.

Other amenities include a laundry and three large storage rooms on each floor. Four passenger elevators are adjacent to the central lobby, two in the east wing and two in the west wing, while the two freight elevators connect to the street-level loading dock in the west wing. One of the few drawbacks to the Irene's plan is the enormously long and boring central public hallway, which extends uninterrupted for more than 500 feet.

Although the top floor is numbered 17, the Irene actually has sixteen floors because the 13 has been omit-

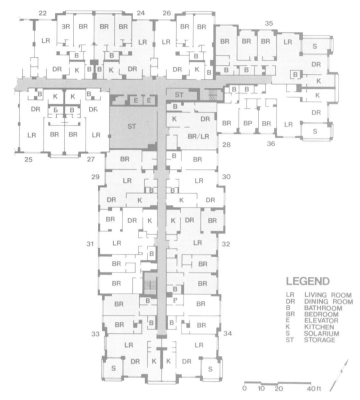

LEGEND

LR LIVING ROOM
DR DINING ROOM
B BATHROOM
BR BEDROOM
E ELEVATOR
K KITCHEN
S SOLARIUM
ST STORAGE

Typical floor plan of the right wing of the Irene.

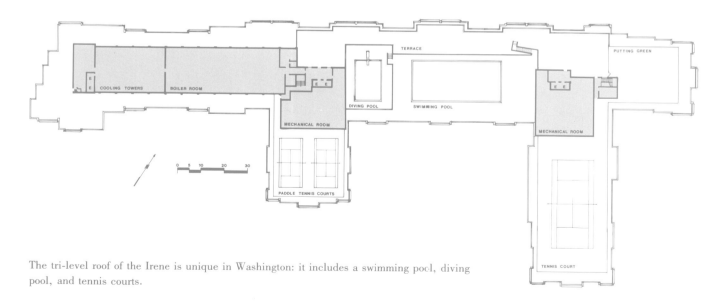

The tri-level roof of the Irene is unique in Washington: it includes a swimming pool, diving pool, and tennis courts.

Lifeguard William Dunning stands in front of the upper-level diving pool; the larger swimming pool is in the background, on the middle-level roof terrace of the Irene.

ted—as in many other American apartment houses and hotels because of superstition that this number bears bad luck. Fifteen floors actually have apartments, since the entire first floor is public space. In addition to the large lobby, the first floor includes a sizable social hall, a beauty shop, the manager's and assistant manager's offices, and a garage. A dozen units on the second floor have been continually rented as offices for physicians, dentists, and a travel agency. The enormous indoor garage has space for 603 cars.

Located near the Friendship Heights Metro station and adjacent to some of the city's finest stores, including Saks Fifth Avenue, Neiman-Marcus, Saks-Jandel, Brooks Brothers, Lord and Taylor, and others, the Irene has sheltered a cosmopolitan group of residents over the past fifteen years. Known as the grande dame of modern rental apartment houses, it has housed such notables as Richard Helms, former director of the Central Intelligence Agency (1968–73), and Luis Herrera, the Chilean ambassador

to the Organization of American States. Present tenants include William Perske, father of Lauren Bacall, and Evelyn Lincoln, personal secretary to John F. Kennedy from 1952 until his assassination. The Israeli Embassy rents a block of apartments for its diplomats. Average time on the waiting list is two years.

Perhaps the most unusual feature of the Irene is its roof plan. Since the apartment house occupied its entire lot, the architect wisely designed the three-level roof with extensive recreational features, including two paddle tennis courts and a tennis court on the east wing. The main section of the large roof includes a square sundeck (originally designed as a putting green), two penthouses (serviced by the four passenger elevators), a 73-foot-long swimming pool, a smaller diving pool, a long rectangular sundeck on the lower terrace level (originally used as a shuttleboard court), and the boiler at the west end. Installing the boiler on the roof allows greater space for the garage in the basement; because of the extra expense, few Washington apartment houses have rooftop boilers. The first one was at 1500 Massachusetts Avenue, N.W., built in 1949.

DEVELOPER ABE POLLIN

The son of real estate developer Morris Pollin, who built the Rittenhouse, Abe Pollin followed his father in building a number of Washington apartment houses. He always used Joseph Abel as his architect because of Abel's innovative ideas and long experience in designing apartment houses. It was Abe Pollin, for instance, who built the James, just north of Thomas Circle at 1425 N Street, N.W., in 1960. This was the first apartment house in Washington designed with a rooftop pool.

Pollin also built Robert Towers in Arlington. This apartment and the James were named for his sons. As a memorial to their sixteen-year-old daughter, who died of congenital heart disease in 1963, the Pollins built the Linda Pollin Memorial Housing Project for low-income residents in Southeast Washington. He also built the Apolline, at New Hampshire Avenue and 20th Street, N.W., named for himself. Pollin is most noted today as the owner of the Washington Bullets basketball team and the Washington Capitals ice hockey team, as well as the builder and owner of the Capital Centre, the large sports arena in suburban Maryland that opened in 1973.

Mrs. Evelyn Lincoln, private secretary to President John F. Kennedy, works on her book on the White House years in this spacious kitchen at the Irene.

126

SHOREHAM WEST

2700 Calvert Street, N.W.; west side of Shoreham Hotel

ARCHITECT: Emery Roth and Sons, New York City; Vlastimil Koubek, associate architect, 1964

ORIGINAL APARTMENTS: 64 (23 one-bedrooms; 32 two-bedrooms; 9 three-bedrooms)

STATUS: opened as rental in 1965; converted to co-op in 1974

One of the finest luxury apartment houses in Washington today, the eight-story buff-brick Shoreham West occupies the southeast corner of Calvert and 28th streets, N.W., adjacent to the Shoreham Hotel. One of its unusual features is that the apartment house is attached via a glass corridor to the Shoreham Hotel; both were originally owned by the Bralove family. The Shoreham West was designed as an adjunct to the hotel to provide such personalized services as twenty-four-hour valet parking; maid, secretarial, laundry, and messenger services; twenty-four-hour security; and catered cocktail and dinner parties. Residents could conveniently put up guests at the hotel and enjoy the year-round swimming pools there. Since Shoreham West has become a cooperative and the hotel has changed ownership, no relationship exists between the two today.

The approach to Shoreham West is by way of a handsome cobblestone-paved circular driveway with a fountain in the center. Passing by the uniformed doorman, one enters a spacious walnut-paneled lobby with a marble floor. The original lobby decoration, since removed, included two murals depicting historic events in seventeenth-century Shoreham, England. These were painted by Philadelphia artist Shirley Tattersfield, who traveled to England for research on Charles II and to see street-

Front facade of Shoreham West.

scapes she ultimately depicted in the murals.

Shoreham West was named after the new Shoreham Hotel (1930–31), which in turn had been named for the original Shoreham Hotel built in 1884 at the northeast

Typical floor plan of Shoreham West.

corner of 15th and H streets, N.W., by Vice President Levi Morton. Morton had named his investment after his birthplace, Shoreham, Vermont, founded in the eighteenth century and named in honor of Shoreham, England.

Shoreham West was originally designed with sixty-four apartments varying from one- to three-bedrooms. All apartments are unusually large: the average is approximately 1,700 square feet—larger than the average house. A typical floor contains eight apartments, most with balconies, which constitute the most prominent feature of the facade. To ensure greater privacy, passenger elevators, each serving only four apartments per floor, are located at each end of the building.

The combination of several adjacent units has decreased the building's total to sixty apartments, each with a large entrance foyer, a 28-foot living room, a 17-foot dining room (which opens onto the living room), and either a private balcony or a patio. The large kitchens in each unit were designed for entertaining, with two refrigerators, two ovens, two broilers, a rotisserie, and a freezer. Each bedroom has its own bath, a large dressing room, and a

wall of closets. Each apartment also has a wall safe, unusual in any Washington apartment house built after World War I. Other amenities include a two-level basement garage for ninety cars, two sauna baths on the terrace level, a sundeck and cocktail area on the roof, a complete central kitchen for room service orders, and well-landscaped grounds.

In recent years Shoreham West has had such distinguished residents as John Pope, director of the Freer Gallery of the Smithsonian Institution, Senator Mark Hatfield, and Governor John B. Connally of Texas. The Connallys' large apartment (a combination of Nos. 813 and 815) was formerly owned by Princess Shams, elder sister of the Shah of Iran. After buying her apartment, she undertook a year-and-a-half-long remodeling job. The princess had built a $5 million palace outside Teheran in 1974 and had two others under construction when the revolution overthrew the Pahlavi royal family in 1978. Princess Shams visited Washington often in the early 1970s when her daughter, Princess Shahrazad, was a student at Mount Vernon College.

Above: Lobby of Shoreham West.
Right: The ground-floor apartment in Shoreham West with its wide windows is occupied by Major General and Mrs. Lawrence R. Dewey.

SHOREHAM WEST

127

CATHEDRAL WEST

4100 Cathedral Avenue, N.W.; west side of the Westchester

ARCHITECT: MacLane and Chewning, 1965

ORIGINAL APARTMENTS: 92 (7 efficiencies; 37 one-bedrooms; 47 two-bedrooms; 1 three-bedroom)

STATUS: opened as rental in 1966; converted to condo in 1977

Located on part of the original grounds of the adjacent Westchester, this T-shaped International Style building is sited in a ravine well below street grade. Cathedral West is bordered on the south and west by Glover-Archbold Park, on the east by the Westchester, and on the north by Cathedral Avenue. The enormous glass windows of all apartments, many of them floor to ceiling, provide views of trees in all four directions.

Entrance to the building is via a curved bridge that connects Cathedral Avenue, N.W., to a below-grade plaza

Cathedral West was built in the ravine below the Westchester adjacent to Glover-Archbold Park. Its lobby entrance is thus well below street level.

Reflecting the style of the 1960s, the split-level lobby of Cathedral West includes glass walls, recessed ceiling lights, and a low stone pool and fountain.

laid in "unistone," a compressed concrete interlocking paving stone that not only provides an economical and practical driveway but is also aesthetically pleasing. A spring-fed stream flows below the entrance bridge adjacent to the plaza. Within the three-level spacious rectangular lobby are floor-to-ceiling plate glass walls, indirect lighting, a large fountain, the front desk, and two passenger elevators. Since the nine-story apartment house was built on a hill, the lobby is on the fourth floor. Much of the first through third floors is occupied by a garage, entered through a ramp on the plaza adjacent to the lobby entrance. At the rear of the first floor, at ground level, is a heated indoor swimming pool. During warm weather, part of the pool area can be opened to an outside sundeck by sliding glass doors.

Cathedral West has nineteen tiers of apartments, numbered 1 through 20 (with No. 13 omitted). The ninety-two apartments range from efficiency units of 736 square feet to 2,070-square-foot apartments with two bedrooms,

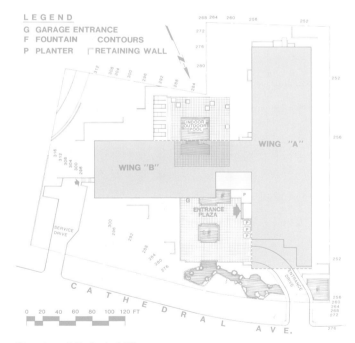

Site plan of Cathedral West.

This indoor-outdoor swimming pool at Cathedral West is unique among Washington apartment houses.

Cathedral West is one of the only two Washington apartment houses with atrium apartments on their top floors.

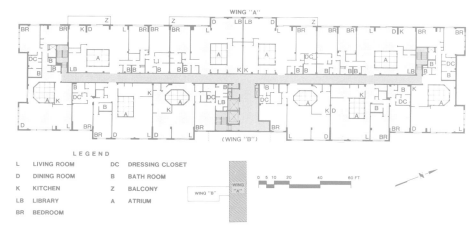

LEGEND

L LIVING ROOM   DC DRESSING CLOSET
D DINING ROOM   B   BATH ROOM
K KITCHEN   Z   BALCONY
LB LIBRARY   A   ATRIUM
BR BEDROOM

Top-floor plan of wing "A" of Cathedral West.

a den, and two and a half baths. The rooms are unusually large: the typical living room measures 14 by 25 feet; the dining room, 12 by 18 feet; and the balcony, 26 feet or longer. Like most post–1960 apartment house construction, the ceilings are only 8 feet, 2 inches high. Abundant storage space with four or five large closets is provided in many units. The main entrances of most apartments have double doors, convenient for entertaining. Although this feature is common in better apartment houses in France, it is rare in America. A dressing room with built-in vanity table and sink is attached to each master bedroom. Many large apartments have two dressing rooms.

The most unusual feature of Cathedral West is the group of seventeen atrium apartments on the top or ninth story, each designed around a private glass-enclosed courtyard open to the sky. Paved and equipped with drainage, each atrium is faced with glass walls on all four sides. The atriums come in various shapes, including octagonal, and sizes, averaging 12 by 14 feet. Some owners furnish their atriums with a few pieces of contemporary lawn furniture; others have elaborately landscaped gardens—often designed in Oriental motifs with moss, ferns, and bonsai. One atrium has been screened because the owner was allergic to bee stings.

The floor plans also vary; for instance, apartment No. 165 is the only unit with neither a balcony nor an atrium. Originally designed as a storeroom, it was first rented as a doctor's office; later, after Cathedral West was converted to a condo, it became a small apartment.

Cathedral West was built by four local investors—Joseph B. Gildenhorn, Donald A. Brown, Melvin Lenkin, and Gerald J. Miller, who formed Cathedral West Associates. The developers purchased the 2½-acre site from the City Investing Company of New York for the $3.3 million apartment house.

The parklike surroundings are seemingly brought indoors in many apartments at Cathedral West because of the extensive use of glass walls.

Today's residents include a number of career women, professors at George Washington University, and State Department officers. Among the prominent government officials who have lived here are Rozanne L. Ridgway, assistant secretary of state for European and Canadian affairs, and William Casey, director of the Central Intelligence Agency from 1981 to 1987.

Life at Cathedral West is made easier than at most Washington apartment houses by excellent service, including a twenty-four-hour doorman, desk clerk, and valet parking.

128

COLONNADE

2801 New Mexico Avenue, N.W.

ARCHITECT: Donald Hudson Drayer, 1965

ORIGINAL APARTMENTS: 283 (24 efficiencies; 137 one-bedrooms; 109 two-bedrooms; 13 three-bedrooms)

STATUS: opened as rental in 1966; converted to condo in 1974

Facing Glover-Archbold Park across New Mexico Avenue, N.W., the Colonnade occupies only 2 acres of its 7½-acre hillside site behind the well-established and much older Westchester. The Colonnade was built by developers Nathan Landow and Lawrence Brandt, who were both experienced in apartment house design and construction: they had previously built a dozen large apartment houses including the Park Sutton on upper 16th Street, N.W.; the Huntington, Chase Plaza, and Carlton Towers on Connecticut Avenue; the Imperial House

The Colonnade was one of three large apartment houses built on the extensive land formerly belonging to the adjacent Westchester.

The large lobby of the Colonnade has both a doorman and a receptionist.

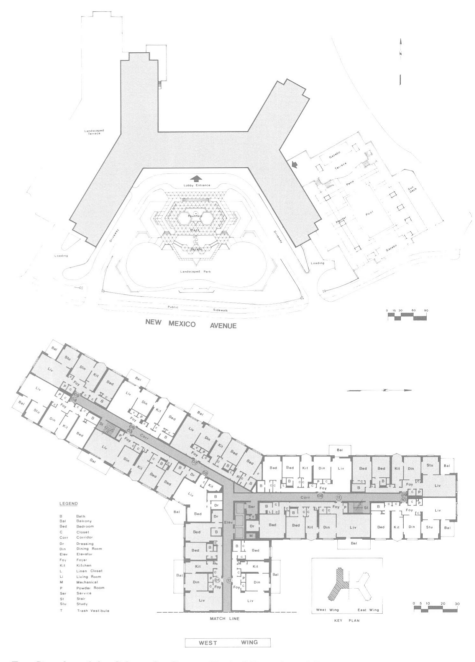

NEW MEXICO AVENUE

LEGEND

B	Bath
Bal	Balcony
Bed	Bedroom
C	Closet
Corr	Corridor
Dr	Dressing
Din	Dining Room
Elev	Elevator
Foy	Foyer
Kit	Kitchen
L	Linen Closet
Li	Living Room
M	Mechanical
P	Powder Room
Ser	Service
St	Stair
Stu	Study
T	Trash Vestibule

MATCH LINE

KEY PLAN

West Wing   East Wing

WEST WING

Top: Site plan of the Colonnade. *Bottom:* Typical floor plan of the west wing of the Colonnade.

at 18th and Que streets, N.W.; and Prospect House, Wakefield Towers, and Arlington House in the Virginia suburbs. The Colonnade, however, remains their most luxurious.

Like a number of notable Washington apartment houses from the 1920s, such as the Broadmoor and Cathedral Mansions, the Colonnade resembles an elegant resort hotel. The grounds are exceptionally well planned. Designed by landscape architect Robert Frost, the front lawn of this double-Y-shaped building includes a formal park complete with fountain, small pavilions, and walk-

ways. It is immediately in front of a porte-cochère with a circular drive. To the east is a large terrace with a rectangular swimming pool with cabanas at its ends.

Because of its hillside location, the floors of the building vary from eight to thirteen levels plus the penthouse floor. The large, centrally located lobby has two banks of elevators, one pair at each end of the two wings. The 283 apartments were designed in forty-two different arrangements ranging from efficiencies to three-bedroom units. The largest are the seventeen penthouse apartments.

Every apartment has a private balcony. Other luxury features include 9-foot ceilings, bathtubs 5½ feet long and 15 inches deep (the standard is 5 feet by 14 inches), foyers in all units, formal dining rooms averaging 13 by 17 feet, and four-pipe separated air conditioning and heating, which permits different rooms to be heated or cooled at the same time. Solidly built with special sound-proofing materials, the Colonnade includes a sauna, grocery store, recreation room, beauty parlor, and valet shop. The five-level underground garage can house 380 cars.

Built at a cost of $7.5 million, the Colonnade has always had a distinguished roster of residents, including Supreme Court Justice Arthur Goldberg; President Carter's chief of staff Hamilton Jordan; the late Irvin Feld, owner of the Ringling Brothers-Barnum and Bailey Circus; Senator John McClellan, Democrat, Arkansas; Senator Harry Byrd, Independent, Virginia; Joseph Duffey, chairman of the National Endowment for the Humanities; Lesley Stahl, CBS correspondent; Senator Joseph Montoya, Democrat, New Mexico; U.N. Ambassador Charles Yost; Congressman Frank Annunzio, Democrat, Illinois; and Mary Hoyt, press secretary to Rosalynn Carter. (The Colonnade is often perceived as a Democratic stronghold, the Watergate a Republican one.)

Immediately after Nathan Landow sold the Colonnade to Stuart Bernstein and John Mason in 1974 for more than $15 million, plans were made to convert it to a condominium. Bernstein had previously converted the nearby Greenbriar (4301 Massachusetts Avenue, N.W.). The new owners received approval in July 1974 to convert, just weeks before the D.C. government placed a moratorium on condo conversions. Approximately half of the residents purchased their apartments. Although the developers offered the condos to the residents for only 5 percent down, with a 9 percent mortgage, half of the buyers paid cash.

Many of the tenants banded together to protect their interests, forming the Colonnade Residents Association (CRA) when the decision to convert was announced. At first the residents were given three months to decide whether to buy before sales were opened to the public (this was later extended another thirty days). At that time, the CRA negotiated several concessions from the developers: the association's attorney was allowed to inspect all ownership documents; the developers permitted tenants to advise on redecoration of the lobby and public areas, and to establish guidelines for the allocation of revenues and expenses between the developers and the condominium; and the developers agreed to have an independent engineering firm inspect the entire apartment

The handsome outdoor swimming pool at the Colonnade, one of the finest of any Washington apartment house, includes wide terraces with cabanas.

house and have any faulty plumbing, heating, air conditioning, wiring, or elevators repaired or replaced.

These negotiations between tenants and developers worked smoothly for several reasons. The president of the tenants association, Aaron Goldman, stated at the time that tenants should always follow three rules during a conversion to condominium ownership. First, a tenants association should be established as quickly as possible to "deal with the converters from a position of power." Second, tenants must demand adequate time to decide whether to buy their units. Finally, the tenants association should be up to date on negotiations with the developers at all times. Goldman added that the early formation of a tenants association also provided good training for the new owners' management of the condo, once it was established.

When the Colonnade began operation as a condo in 1976, the first board of directors, formed from owner-residents, drew up a set of rules for residents. Dogs, for instance, would be allowed in the apartments provided they weighed less than fifteen pounds. Dog owners were required to either carry their pets in the passenger elevators or use the freight elevator. The most controversial rule, however, involved the swimming pool. Known as the Great Yellow Towel Affair of 1976, the board-appointed pool committee voted that only yellow towels could be used at the pool in order to match the yellow awnings of the cabanas. Some residents who had yellow towels bought orange towels "just for the hell of it." After the nonconformist faction not only gained control of the pool committee but of the board as well, this rule was abolished.

129

FOXHALL

4200 Massachusetts Avenue, N.W.

ARCHITECT: Fischer and Elmore, 1970

ORIGINAL APARTMENTS: 126 (31 one-bedrooms; 77 two-bedrooms; 18 three-bedrooms)

STATUS: opened as co-op in 1974

The Foxhall, like Potomac Plaza in Foggy Bottom, developed very differently from its original plans. Neither enormous project was finished because of failure to obtain adequate financing. Had the Foxhall complex been completed according to the original 1970 design by architects Fischer and Elmore, its five hundred units would have made it the most important luxury apartment house in the city. The size of the apartments and the interior details would have been superior to the Watergate, although the view would not have been as dramatic.

The original 13-acre site was acquired by the Magazine Brothers Enterprise, headed by Samuel and Sheldon Magazine. Their projected $70 million project included three large ten-story curvilinear high-rises and fifteen rowhouses. Only 16 percent of the sloping wooded tract would have been used for construction, with many of the large trees on the former Glover estate retained. Landscaping was to include two swimming pools, ponds, and a stream. Automobile traffic was to enter through driveways on both Massachusetts and New Mexico avenues, N.W. The underground parking garage would have accommodated four hundred cars with two parking spaces for each townhouse, in addition to generous guest parking.

After more than a year of hearings, in which the project was vigorously opposed by the Spring Valley-

Wesley Heights Citizens Association, the D.C. Zoning Commission approved the Foxhall project in October 1970. Neighboring home owners had objected, fearing traffic congestion, parking problems, and a decline in the value of their homes. Approval was contingent on two changes to the Magazine brothers' plans—moving two of the three apartment houses away from property lines and providing at least one parking space per apartment. After considerable effort, the Magazine brothers obtained approval to build the enormous balconies wider than the standard 6 feet specified in the building code. Original plans were to construct Foxhall in three stages, one building at a time, Foxhall East, Foxhall West, and finally Foxhall North.

The site, just south of Ward Circle and American University and across from the Greenbriar and Berkshire apartment houses, was formerly the country estate of Charles C. Glover I, chairman of the board of the Riggs Bank. His house, known as Westover, was demolished in 1967 for the National Presbyterian Church, then located at Connecticut Avenue and N Street, N.W. When the church fathers decided to build on Nebraska Avenue, N.W., instead, they sold the Massachusetts Avenue tract to sportsman and developer Jerry Wolman. In 1968 Wolman planned an enclave of five embassies there, but—

Front facade of the Foxhall showing the main entrance.

failing approval from the zoning commission—he decided to build a luxury apartment house complex instead. Costing $30 million, it would have had 1,244 units in three high-rises, based on the Watergate complex, then under construction. Because of financial reverses, the property was taken over by the American National Bank of Maryland before Wolman could start any construction. The site was purchased from the bank by the Magazine brothers in early 1969 for more than $5 million. At the time it was still partially surrounded by Orchard Hill, the estate of Charles C. Glover II.

Construction of Foxhall East, as the first building was then called, was briefly delayed in October 1971, when 150 students from American University staged a demonstration and attempted to save the trees. After police arrived, the students left and work proceeded. Even

before construction of the apartment house was finished, the Magazine brothers began building Foxhall Square on New Mexico Avenue, N.W. The three-story, $8 million enclosed shopping mall and office building was located on 3 acres of adjacent land. The mansard-roofed structure, also designed by Fischer and Elmore, provides market facilities for the Foxhall residents as well as those of several newer apartment houses, such as Sutton Towers.

The Magazine brothers, Washington builders since 1946, had been stockholders and builders of the Watergate complex. They, like Wolman, based their plans for Foxhall on Watergate, but improved on its design. The Magazines had built more than two dozen apartment houses in the Washington area since the war, including the enormous twelve-hundred-unit Riverside Park in Alexandria. Because of material shortages, the first Foxhall building

UPPER LEVEL DUPLEX

KEY PLAN

Massachusetts Avenue, NW

LOWER LEVEL DUPLEX

Plan of several of the spacious duplex apartments of Foxhall.

was not completed until January 1974. Half of the 126 units had been sold by that time as cooperatives. The one-, two-, and three-bedroom units were originally priced from $60,000 to $120,000. An unusual feature is the connection of the living room, dining room, and bedrooms by sliding glass doors to the extra-wide balconies. The balconies completely encircle some of the large apartments.

The most unusual apartments at Foxhall are the twenty-two duplexes on the first and second floors. At Foxhall each duplex, entered through double doors from the public corridor, has at least 1,800 square feet and its own patio. In most, the lower level includes a living

Opposite: The luxurious duplex apartments at the Foxhall, on the first two floors, feature double doors, circular staircases, and private patios.

room, dining alcove, kitchen, powder room, and, in some, a library. Reached by an elegant staircase, the upper level has either two or three bedrooms, two large bathrooms, and abundant closet space.

Many of the apartments have exceptional features, such as master baths with marble floors—some with both bathtub and shower stall—and side-by-side refrigerators and freezers. All public corridors are exceptionally wide. Other amenities include a large indoor swimming pool that faces the rear lawn through a glass wall, a roofdeck, two levels of underground parking, storage areas, a security gate, twenty-four-hour secretarial service, six elevators, a tennis court, and a staff locker room.

In 1976, when the Magazine brothers could not obtain adequate financing to complete the project, they sold the unused land. In the late 1970s the Sutton Towers high-rise and its adjacent rowhouses and shopping mall,

Several apartments at the Foxhall have elegant circular foyers such as this.

Sutton Center, were built on most of the site. This complex has its own entrance from New Mexico Avenue. In 1980–81 the last unused land was occupied by yet another high-rise, 4100 Massachusetts Avenue, N.W., to the east of the Foxhall.

The name Foxhall was taken from nearby Foxhall Road, one of the most prestigious residential addresses in the city. In 1976, with construction of the other two apartment houses in the proposed complex halted, the co-op board of Foxhall East voted to change the name of the sole building to the Foxhall.

A modern bathroom in a Foxhall apartment.

130

SUMNER VILLAGE

4910 Sentinel Drive, Sumner, Maryland

ARCHITECT: Cohen, Haft, and Associates, Silver Spring, Maryland, 1971

ORIGINAL APARTMENTS: 395 (28 one-bedrooms; 293 two-bedrooms; 74 three-bedrooms)

STATUS: opened as condo in 1973–76

The most impressive feature of this 27-acre residential complex is its parklike setting. The sixteen mid-rise apartment houses, each four or five stories, occupy only one-third of the land. Built on a steep hill in Sumner, a small community adjacent to Bethesda, Maryland, the heavily wooded site is so quiet that it seems much farther removed than its actual location of half a mile from the District boundary and thirty minutes from the Mall in downtown Washington. The surrounding village of Sumner was developed at the turn of the century as an early suburb of Washington.

Each modernistic apartment building, of buff brick with massive windows, has garage parking on the ground floor. Twenty-four to twenty-eight apartments occupy each building, with several entrances in each. Many have covered balconies; others, on the top floor, have open terraces, usually shaded by canvas awnings. The apartments are mostly two- and three-bedroom units, varying from 1,360 square feet to 2,185 square feet, all on one level. Privacy is afforded by a building entrance for every six apartments. Parking, two spaces per apartment, is provided at the rear of the apartment buildings, which were built in clusters. Two entrances, front and rear, are available for each building. Many of the ground-floor units have sliding glass doors that open directly to the lawn.

Judy Miller, a resident at Sumner Village, walks her dog in this wooded setting.

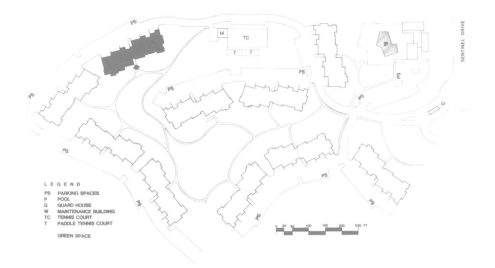

LEGEND

PS PARKING SPACES
P   POOL
G   GUARD HOUSE
M   MAINTENANCE BUILDING
TC TENNIS COURT
T   PADDLE TENNIS COURT

GREEN SPACE

Site plan of Sumner Village. The floor plan of the shaded building in the upper left appears on the following page.

Sumner Village has two tennis courts, typical of most large apartment house complexes built in Washington since 1965.

Sumner Village includes both a clubhouse and an adjacent outdoor pool.

Total parking includes 517 tandem (two spaces, end to end) garage spaces plus 348 open spaces. All apartment houses have elevators. A number of units have wood-burning fireplaces.

Even though the various buildings extend down a steep hill, they are connected by both walkways and driveways. A circular perimeter road, privately owned and maintained by the condo association, follows the topographic contours. On the western side of the complex, bermed landscaping offers protection from the adjacent shopping center.

Residents have many amenities. At the top of the steep hill is a twenty-four-hour security gatehouse, where all traffic must enter; a clubhouse with an outdoor swimming pool; terrace; two tennis courts; and paddle tennis courts. The developer, George G. Mulligan, originally advertised that Sumner Village was an agreeable alternative to life in "stark high-rise" apartment houses in the Washington area. He was right. One of several prominent residents here was Thomas P. (Tip) O'Neill, Democrat of Massachusetts, while he was Speaker of the House of Representatives during the 1980s.

Typical fourth-floor plan at Sumner Village.

131. GREENBRIAR

4301 Massachusetts Avenue, N.W.
ARCHITECT: Koenig and Moore, 1950
STATUS: opened as rental in 1951;
converted to condo in 1973

132. WOODNER

3636 16th Street, N.W.
ARCHITECT: Wallace F. Holladay, Sr., and Ian Woodner, 1950–51
STATUS: opened as rental in 1951–52

133. 3900 WATSON PLACE, N.W.

ARCHITECT: Harry Price, New York City;
Berla and Abel, associate architects, 1959

STATUS: opened as rental in 1960;
converted to co-op in 1963

134. RITTENHOUSE

6101 16th Street, N.W.

ARCHITECT: Berla and Abel, 1955

STATUS: opened as rental in 1956

135. CATHEDRAL

4101 Cathedral Avenue, N.W.

ARCHITECT: Corning, Elmore, and
Fischer, 1961

STATUS: opened as rental in 1963;
converted to co-op in 1977

136. COLUMBIA PLAZA *(right)*

2400 Virginia Avenue, N.W.

ARCHITECT: Keyes, Lethbridge, and Condon; DeMars and Reay, associate architects, San Francisco, 1960–65; Cosgrove and Associates, final office building and courtyard design, 1970

STATUS: opened as rental in 1967

137. TOWN CENTER WEST, now MARINA VIEW TOWERS

1100 6th Street, S.W.

ARCHITECT: I. M. Pei, New York City, ca. 1960

STATUS: opened as rental in 1962

138. TIBER ISLAND

468 M Street, S.W.

ARCHITECT: Keyes, Lethbridge, and Condon, 1961

STATUS: opened as rental in 1963; converted to condo in 1984

139. NEWPORT WEST

1415 Rhode Island Avenue, N.W.
ARCHITECT: Saunders and Pearson,
Alexandria, Virginia, 1966
STATUS: opened as rental in 1967

140. PROMENADE

5525 Pooks Hill Road, Bethesda, Maryland
ARCHITECT: Donald Hudson Drayer, 1972
STATUS: opened as rental in 1973; converted to condo in 1985

141. PLAZA, formerly the FOGGY BOTTOM

800 25th Street, N.W.
ARCHITECT: Edmund W. Dreyfuss and Associates, 1973
STATUS: opened as rental in 1974; converted to condo in 1975

6

POSTMODERNISM ARRIVES,

1974–1988

INTRODUCTION

NOTABLE ADDITIONS

Significant developments from 1974 to 1987 have affected the design, location, and type of apartment houses built in the Washington metropolitan area. Home rule came to the District of Columbia in 1974 with an elected mayor and city council. Coincidentally, this was also the year rent control was reestablished within the city, to compensate for the cancellation of national price and wage controls.

Although introduced as temporary at the time because of high inflation, rent control has been continuously extended ever since. It has drastically curtailed the construction of new rental apartment houses. Simultaneously, amenities in existing rental apartment houses have been adversely affected. Some landlords have simply closed their apartment houses; others have lessened services and other established amenities to make ends meet. Janitorial staffs have been cut in half and doormen are seldom seen, nor lobby switchboard operators, nor even resident managers. Many fine apartment houses have been converted from rentals to condominiums.

Cathedral Mansions is a good example. Of the three large buildings in this complex, the city's largest when it opened in 1923, only the south building remains rental, and it has declined as a luxury residence since services and staff were sharply curtailed. The center building is now mostly offices, while the north building has become a condo. Even though a city council provision of 1982 exempted new apartment houses from rent control, few buildings have been constructed since then. A 1985 attempt by the city council to modify the more stringent provisions of the rent control law was overturned by a small majority of voters in a general referendum late that year.

Although the first condominium had been established in the city in 1966—the rowhouses in the Tiber Island complex in Southwest Washington—this type of home ownership remained rare in Washington until the mid-1970s. With mounting inflation, caused in part by the rise in the price of Mideastern oil, many Washingtonians sought inner-city condominiums for economic security. The main advantage of a condominium over a cooperative lies in financing. Because in terms of ownership they are treated as real estate, instead of mere

Architect Wilfred V. Worland, after whom the Worland, which he designed, is named.

stock in a building, condo apartments can be much more easily financed than cooperatives.

Since 1970 a large number of older rental Washington apartment houses have been converted to condo status by developers. Some of those discussed here include the Woodward, the Wyoming, the Cairo, Windsor Lodge (now the Chancellery), 4701 Connecticut Avenue, N.W., the Marlyn, the General Scott, the Carlyn (now Gateway Georgetown), McLean Gardens, and the Towers. Even two-story single-family rental rowhouses have been converted to condo apartments, one to a floor. In 1987 it is estimated that among the District of Columbia's approximately 4,000 apartment buildings are 110 cooperatives, 400 condominiums, and 3,500 rentals. In addition, more than fifty older rental buildings were converted to offices or hotels. The number of rental apartment buildings thus slowly but steadily declines each year.

Almost all apartment houses built since 1974 have been condominiums, such as the Westbridge, Washington Harbour, the Griffin, the Worland, the Penn Mark, and the Flour Mill. Other new or recently renovated apartment houses planned as condos remain as rentals only because of the collapse of the real estate market in 1981—such as Meridian Mansions (now the Envoy), the Mondrian, and the Washington House.

SWIMMING POOLS

Apartment house swimming pools continued to gain popularity during the 1970s and 1980s. By 1987 more than three hundred Washington area apartment houses had swimming pools—90 percent of them outdoors. Outdoor pools are usually on the ground level in the suburbs; most rooftop pools are within the city where space is at a premium. The Colonnade, Van Ness Centre, Sumner Village, and the Towers have outdoor ground-level pools— all with spacious terraces and other amenities.

The most successful outdoor swimming pools are those that were planned and constructed when the apartment house involved originally opened. Those that were added later are often crowded onto some corner of the site, with lack of privacy and landscaping. Apartment pools appear in a great variety of shapes and sizes. One of the most unusual is the courtyard pool found at the Plaza, 801 North Howard Street in Alexandria. This 240-unit condominium, opened in 1982, contains an outdoor pool and clubhouse located in the center of a completely enclosed landscaped courtyard. The first rooftop pool at a Washington apartment house was built on the James near Thomas Circle in 1959. The most unusual is at the Irene in Chevy Chase, where the roof includes an Olympic-size swimming pool as well as a small diving pool on an upper level of the roof. This pool, and that of Van Ness Centre, are the largest, while Georgetown Park has the smallest.

Both outdoor and indoor apartment house swimming pools were rare in Washington until the 1960s. The earliest known indoor pool was in the basement of the Everett, a chic 1905 bachelor apartment house that has since been demolished. The oldest surviving one—although long since closed—is at Harvard Hall. Built in 1929 and closed since the 1950s, it survives as an empty, forgotten relic, sharing a small dark sub-basement room with a jungle of pipes and wires.

In the 1960s indoor pools became popular in Washington. The most successful ones have glass walls facing the outside—providing abundant natural light. Good examples are those at Harbour Square, the Promenade, and Cathedral West. At Cathedral West, the glass wall opens onto a terrace, providing a unique outdoor-indoor pool. By the late 1980s about thirty indoor swimming pools had appeared in Washington area apartment houses, still not many, because their year-round operation makes them very expensive to maintain.

SUBURBAN APARTMENT HOUSES

The marked growth of large suburban apartment house complexes—those with more than a thousand units in a number of high-rise buildings—was the major development of the 1970s and 1980s. The suburbs rather than the city itself claimed more than 90 percent of new apartment houses for obvious reasons: to avoid rent control in the city, to take advantage of cheaper land, to seek areas that seemed safer than the sometimes strife-torn inner city, and to attract clientele among the young singles living in the suburbs. Although such large Maryland

Architect Henry C. Holle of Holle and Lin is shown in the study of his apartment at Montebello. With Wayne Williams, Holle designed both Montebello and Porto Vecchio.

Architects David Jones (left) and Guy Martin (right) of Martin and Jones stand in front of the Madison Bank Building, a small mixed-use Postmodern building they designed in Georgetown.

Architect Arthur Cotton Moore designed two Postmodern apartment houses in Washington: Logan Park and, shown in the background, Washington Harbour.

apartment house complexes as Grosvenor Park and the Promenade—each with more than 20 acres, with several high-rises, pools, tennis courts, and spacious lawns—were unusual in the 1960s when they were built, their type became common in the 1970s and 1980s. Recent suburban examples include the Watergate at Landmark, the Rotonda, Montebello, and Somerset House.

Metro, the Washington metropolitan subway system, has had a marked impact on the development of apartment houses by reducing the commute between suburb and downtown to minutes. (The same phenomenon prevailed at the turn of the century with the extension of the streetcar on upper 14th Street, N.W., and along Columbia Road, N.W.) Much of the recent construction of suburban condo apartment houses has centered around Metro stations. Somerset House, near the Friendship Heights station in Chevy Chase, and the Belvedere and the Atrium, near the Rosslyn Metro station in Arlington, are typical examples. A number of the new condo apartment houses, such as Porto Vecchio in Alexandria, offer their own shuttle service to the closest subway station.

REVIVAL OF DOWNTOWN LIFE

From the 1920s through the 1960s, most American city planners felt that the various functions of city life should be segregated in the urban fabric. This philosophy was forced on many cities through zoning laws, separating house from office, shop from apartment. This then seemed especially appropriate to Washington, which is both city and national monument. Its weaknesses were revealed by the 1960s, when younger urban planners began to advocate diversity in downtown areas. Jane Jacobs, in *The Life and Death of Great American Cities* (1965), called for the integration of many functions within the same downtown sector. She believed apartment houses, shops, and offices should share, as in European cities, the same block. This arrangement would bring life back to the city at night. The revived concept of urban life was implemented in Washington in the 1960s by the Pennsylvania Avenue Development Corporation (PADC) and in 1974 by zoning changes in the West End, where many new office buildings had to include some residential units.

Architects Warren Cox (left) and George Hartman (right) of Hartman-Cox stand in front of their Georgetown office. They are responsible for the facade design of Market Square, a mixed-use complex scheduled to be built in 1988 opposite the National Archives.

The PADC further required the developers of selected sites on or near Pennsylvania Avenue downtown to do likewise.

Washington was certainly ripe for a revival of growth downtown by the mid–1970s. The riots were over; peace had returned. On a wave of affluence a new generation of higher-income professionals gravitated to the capital, both single and married couples who preferred city life and were willing to pay for it in terms of higher housing costs, restaurants, and stores. Everything changed. Washington transformed itself to receive them. Paradoxically, the enormous growth of the suburbs since Metro opened in 1976 was followed by a marked revival of downtown in the 1980s. Washington then entered a renaissance of its own.

The most important physical influence on the revival of downtown Washington was the master plan of the Pennsylvania Avenue Development Corporation for the revitalization of Pennsylvania Avenue between the Capitol and the White House. During the 1970s and especially the 1980s, the PADC planned and effected the construc-

tion of new hotels, office buildings, and mixed-use buildings on the north side of the avenue—causing a partial shift of business activity from K Street back to "the Avenue." The PADC encouraged the development of buildings with retail businesses on the ground level, office floors above, and apartments on the top floors.

The first such project, Market Square, an elegant Postmodern mixed-use building, is scheduled for construction opposite the National Archives in 1988–89. Other notable additions to the avenue include the magnificently enlarged Willard Hotel, the architecturally disappointing J. W. Marriott Hotel, the "restored" old Post Office Building and National Theater, the new Canadian Chancellery, the renovated Apex Building, the reerected Meade Monument, many elegant new office buildings including the Heurich Building, at 1201 Pennsylvania Avenue, N.W., and the facelifting of many decayed office buildings. Construction of the new Pershing Park and landscaping of both sides of this revived "national main street" also had resulted in renewed life for the inner city. Quite naturally, the appeal of downtown apartment living is thus increased.

MIXED-USE BUILDINGS

From the 1970s through the late 1980s, more than forty mixed-use buildings were constructed in the Washington area, often incorporating separate floors of offices, retail stores, and apartments. A change in the zoning law in 1979 allowed and even encouraged mixed-use buildings, especially to restore housing in areas of the city that had been almost exclusively commercial, such as the West End (the west end of downtown, adjacent to Georgetown).

These mixed-use buildings are of two basic types. The more successful appears to be that in which the residential area is actually separate from but adjacent to the commercial building. Good examples are the Washington Park Tower, the Penn Mark, and the Westbridge. Residents of these buildings seem to prefer, as ever, a structure that is somewhat domestic looking. Generally this is achieved by building two adjacent buildings, each with its own entrance. Often the residential building is red brick with Georgian detailing or some other traditional

Architect David M. Schwarz designed the Griffin and Penn Mark, both highly successful mixed-use buildings.

style, while the office-retail building is concrete and modern.

In the second major type of mixed-use structure, the various functions are horizontally layered, with two or three floors of apartments at the top of the building and the offices and stores below. Recent examples include 2501 M Street, N.W., the planned Market Square, the Madison Bank Building, and Georgetown Park. In an unusual third example, The Village of McLean Gardens, which occupies part of the site of the old World War II garden apartment complex of McLean Gardens, apartments are grouped in several ways. In the unusual arrangement there, apartments are included in the south tower, sharing half the space, vertically, with offices. A similar arrangement exists in the Price Tower by Frank Lloyd Wright in Bartlesville, Oklahoma, from the 1950s.

Pockets of zoning on major streets often permit mixed-use buildings. For instance, on Pennsylvania Avenue, S.E., on Capitol Hill; on Connecticut Avenue, north of the Taft Bridge to the Maryland boundary; and on Wisconsin Avenue, N.W., north of Calvert Street, sections of commercial development are permitted to serve marketing needs in predominantly residential neighborhoods. These areas, known as C2A in zoning designation, will probably attract more mixed-use buildings in the future. One of the best recent examples is the Penn Mark on Capitol Hill.

RETURN TO TRADITION

Most of the new Washington and suburban apartment buildings offer amenities not found in old apartment houses—outdoor swimming pools, indoor saunas, below-grade garage parking, and surrounding parkland and even tennis courts. Yet most apartment houses built since World War II lack the architectural charm of earlier buildings. The modern examples have little detailing—concrete floors that require wall-to-wall carpeting, little if any woodwork, 8-foot ceilings, and small, often tiny, rooms. The cost of labor and materials since 1970 has precluded wood floors except in the most expensive apartment units, such as Washington Harbour, although tenants sometimes add them.

Washingtonians have advanced considerably in recent years in their consciousness of the need for humanity in the streetscape. During the reign of Modernism, 1946–73, architects usually designed their International Style buildings with little or no regard for the scale, design, or even presence of adjacent landmark buildings. This represented the arrogance of the style itself, discarding the past. The International Style considered itself superior to all previous styles: clear the land and build anew was the theme, and for the *business* of architecture it seemed a neat idea. As a result, much of the area between the White House and Dupont Circle was razed in the post–World War II years and replaced by dozens of glass and concrete boxes.

The wide dissemination of early Postmodern styles by such nationally known architects as Michael Graves and Philip Johnson quickly reached developers, local architects, and the Washington public through architectural and design magazines. A new generation of developers and responsive architects adopted Postmodernism, knowing that in general the public was sick of Modern architecture. Washington, although an architecturally conservative city, welcomed the return of "traditional" styling. Beginning in the mid–1970s, architects reinter-

a

b

c

d

e

f

g

The design of elevator cabs has changed greatly over the past century. The early ones, including this example from the 1901 Farragut (a), which once stood on the northwest corner of 17th and Eye streets, and the existing example at the 1906 Wendell Mansions (b) were enclosed with iron grilles. Later, during the 1930s, a number of elevator doors were decorated with geometric Art Deco designs, as at the Kennedy-Warren (c), shown here. The streamlined version of Art Deco design lingered into the 1950s, as seen in this original elevator cab at the 1954 Potomac Plaza (d). Many installed after World War II, such as this Westinghouse model at 4000 Massachusetts Avenue (e), included handrails along the cab's walls. The Postmodern elevator cab at the Madison Bank Building (f) includes half columns, mimicking the columns at the building's entrances. The two passenger elevator cabs at the Atrium (g), completed in 1986, are glass-enclosed.

preted historical styles as best they could understand them, using a pidgin vocabulary of baroque, classical, Egyptian, and Romanesque—to name a few. And some new apartment houses actually were designed to complement their neighbors.

Another important change of the late 1970s was the attitude of the affluent toward apartment houses. Many elderly residents of large houses in such areas as Spring Valley, McLean, and Potomac elected to sell their property and move into large luxury apartments. This mode of life was popular during the first fifty years of Washington apartment house history, 1880–1930; it went out of fashion for two generations. In part because of recent racial conflicts, opulent apartments were scarce in the 1970s. Many, such as the Warder, had been razed. Others, such as the McCormick, with its 11,000-square-foot apartments, had been converted to offices. Still other large apartments, such as the eleven-room units in the Altamont, had been carved into smaller units.

Developers were unsure of demand at that time, especially with the recession and collapse of the real estate market in 1981 when interest rates were high. A number of developers changed their apartment house plans. Washington Harbour, for instance, had been designed in 1980 with 80 percent luxury apartments and 20 percent offices. In 1982, just before construction began, the space was redesigned, reversing the original plan. At that time offices were in short supply and luxury condo apartments were a glut on the market. By 1985, shortly before completion, the market had reversed itself: office buildings had been overbuilt and a marked scarcity of large luxury apartments had arisen. Most of the thirty-five units at Washington Harbour were sold before the building was completed in 1986. During the 1980s developers began to construct a number of luxury apartment buildings with large units in the Washington area—such as Washington Harbour, Porto Vecchio, and Somerset House. With renewed interest in fine apartment houses came a revival of exceptionally good design, fine detailing, and full service staffs, even chauffeurs.

For the past century the Washington apartment house has evolved with each generation to reflect changes in modes of living, technological and building advancements, and economic conditions. Never static, it is certain to see other major changes in the future. The apartment house is a fascinating building type for both its use and its rich variety—and Washington has one of the best collections, both old and new, to enjoy.

142

WORLAND

2828 Wisconsin Avenue, N.W., west side of Wisconsin Avenue between Fulton and Garfield streets

ARCHITECT: Wilfred Vollmer Worland, Bethesda, Maryland, 1975

ORIGINAL APARTMENTS: 41 (23 two-bedrooms; 18 three-bedrooms—all duplex units)

STATUS: opened as condo in 1977

Built at a time of national concern over energy conservation, the forty-one apartments in the Worland have individual heating and air conditioning units, and each resident is responsible for his own fuel and electricity consumption. Public areas, including the lobby, hallways, and garage, have no heat or air conditioning. All public corridors are lighted naturally by a large interior courtyard, a second unusual feature designed to save electricity during the day. With no resident manager or live-in janitor, residents take their own trash to the basement. Because of these economy features, the monthly maintenance fee is probably the lowest of any luxury apartment house in Washington. Units were first sold in 1977 for prices ranging from $105,000 (for 1,596 square feet) to $134,000 (for 1,848 square feet).

The basement garage, with its rear entrance, accommodates thirty-seven cars; four additional parking spaces are outside. Other public spaces in the six-story building include an unusual two-story lobby. Its massive Palladian window looks out onto a large open brick-laid courtyard. Much of the starkness of this enclosed space is relieved by brick arcades reminiscent of Thomas Jefferson's original design for the two ranges of student rooms and dining halls at the University of Virginia, as well as

Front facade of the Worland, the only Washington apartment house named for its architect.

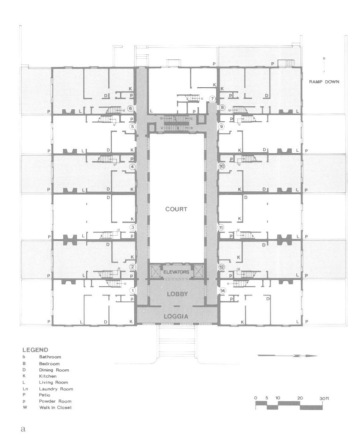

LEGEND
b   Bathroom
B   Bedroom
D   Dining Room
K   Kitchen
L   Living Room
Ln Laundry Room
P   Patio
p   Powder Room
W   Walk in Closet

a

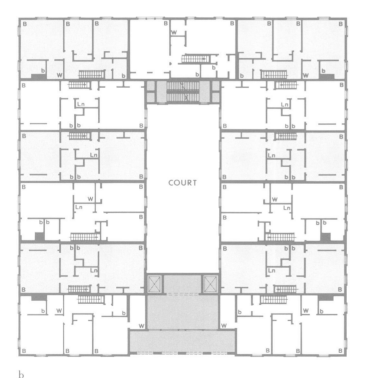

b

Plans for the lobby floor (a) and second floor (b), showing the two levels of the duplex apartments at the Worland.

The lobby of the Worland includes this impressive Palladian window, which overlooks the courtyard.

by planters and a series of iron window guards on the bedroom levels of the duplex apartments.

Laid in red brick, the front neo-Georgian facade is unusually severe. Interest is provided, however, by four tall entrance arches opening into a recessed porch. Other facade details include the rusticated first two floors, quoins, and a shallow cornice. The lobby contains a pair of elevators, one on each side. All of the first-floor apartments have handsome walled terraces that extend outward on each side of the building. They were designed to meet zoning requirements for side yards in this neighborhood.

The Worland was designed twice. Developer John Gerstenfeld assembled five adjoining lots and demolished several small 1920s houses; his original plan was to build modern brick rowhouses. After architect Wilfred V. Worland designed the rowhouses, Gerstenfeld abandoned this plan because the site was so small and asked his architect to redesign the project with duplex apartments around an open courtyard. The duplex apartments, like rowhouses, are consequently stacked on top of each other, three levels

The large enclosed courtyard of the Worland, looking east toward the lobby with Wisconsin Avenue beyond.

All of the Worland apartments are duplex units with the living room and dining room on the lower level open to one another.

The upper level of a duplex apartment at the Worland looking down the private staircase.

high. The Worland's apartments are basically the same—all duplex units, most with two rooms on the lower level (living room and dining room, plus kitchen and powder room) and either two large bedrooms or three smaller bedrooms on the upper level. Each apartment extends through to the courtyard, thus providing two exposures. An unusual feature is seen in the Worland's 8-inch outer walls—all load-bearing.

The developer named this apartment house for his architect, Wilfred V. Worland, in appreciation for designing the site twice. Worland, born in Jasper, Indiana, in 1907, graduated from the Carnegie Institute of Tech-

nology (now Carnegie-Mellon University) in Pittsburgh in 1931. Two years later he moved to Washington to practice architecture. He has specialized in Georgian Revival ever since, designing several hundred important houses over the past fifty years in Potomac, Westmoreland Hills, Leesburg, Fairfax County, and other Washington suburbs. Worland is one of the last practicing architects who personally knew most of Washington's prominent architects from the 1930s, such as Waddy Wood, Jules H. de Sibour, Horace Peaslee, Louis Justement, Leon Chatelain, Joseph Abel, and Jarrett White. The latter gave Worland his first job in Washington as a draftsman.

143

GEORGETOWN PARK

1080 Wisconsin Avenue, N.W.; southwest corner of Wisconsin Avenue and M Street

ARCHITECT: Lockman Associates, principal architect; Chloethiel Woodard Smith, consultant, and other associate architects, 1977

ORIGINAL APARTMENTS: 93 (2 efficiencies; 60 one-bedrooms; 30 two-bedrooms; 1 three-bedroom)

STATUS: opened as condo in 1982

Without question, one of the most sophisticated and intricately designed mixed-use buildings in Washington is the Georgetown Park complex at Wisconsin Avenue and M Street, N.W. Most of this site belonged for many years to the D.C. Transit Company, the city's major bus and streetcar system, owned by O. Leroy Chalk. Shortly after Chalk replaced the last streetcar with buses in 1962, he sold his company to the city government. A shrewd businessman, however, Chalk managed to keep most of the company's real estate holdings, which included numerous properties where streetcars and buses were repaired and stored. During the next two decades, he realized a considerable profit from the sale of those holdings for commercial development.

The first effort to develop this strategic site was in 1976, when Chalk attempted to build a commercial complex. His design was disapproved by the Commission of Fine Arts, however, as unsympathetic with Georgetown's historic appearance. In 1977 Chalk sold his holdings at the southwest corner of Wisconsin Avenue and M Street, N.W., to the Western Development Corporation. Its principal investor and president is Herbert S. Miller, a native Washingtonian. He was familiar with this area of Georgetown and its potential for development: while a graduate student at George Washington University, he had written

his master's thesis in urban planning on how to develop the Georgetown waterfront. Until the mid–1970s, most of the area had remained a backwater of abandoned warehouses, power plants, and unsightly industrial structures. By the mid–1980s, however, it had become one of the centers of development in the city, with dozens of new rowhouses, apartment houses, and office buildings under construction. Creation of the $100 million Georgetown Park was a principal catalyst for development of other new buildings between M Street, N.W., and the Potomac River.

The Western Development Corporation, established in the 1970s, quickly left its imprint on the evolution of lower Georgetown. This firm initiated, designed, and constructed several dozen shopping centers, mostly in the suburbs: Great Falls, Falls Church, Reston, and Dale City in Virginia; and Greenbelt, Brandywine, Germantown, and Gaithersburg in Maryland. One of its most spectacular shopping centers was created through adaptive use of the Main Street Station in Richmond, Virginia, an imposing Victorian train station that had been abandoned and threatened with demolition. The firm also developed two large industrial/office parks in Dale City and Germantown and renovated some older office buildings in downtown Washington. Its largest single project is

The south facade of Georgetown Park facing the Chesapeake and Ohio Canal.

View of both garage and apartment house entrances of the Georgetown Park complex on Wisconsin Avenue.

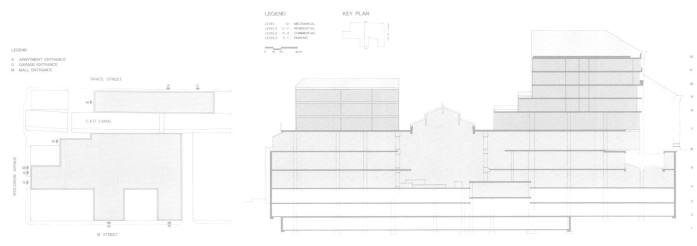

Site plan of Georgetown Park.

Longitudinal section of Georgetown Park showing the three levels—lower for the garage, central for the commercial space, and upper for apartments.

Washington Harbour on the Georgetown waterfront, a $175 million mixed-use complex completed in 1987, which includes office, retail, and luxury residential units.

BASIC DESIGN CONSIDERATIONS

A number of obstacles had to be overcome before the design and construction of Georgetown Park could begin. Several properties on this large tract could not be acquired, such as the historic firehouse at the northwest corner of Wisconsin Avenue and the Chesapeake and Ohio Canal, used as a store known as the Bowl and Board, and Clyde's, a popular bar and restaurant on M Street. The complex thus had to be designed around these structures.

Further, the design had to be approved by the Commission of Fine Arts, which carefully imposed restrictions to preserve the low Victorian streetscape. As a result, the facades and roof of the Victorian brick warehouse between Grace Street and the C and O Canal had to be retained. This first phase, Georgetown Park South, is now known as Canal House. The massive stone retaining wall on the north side of the canal, referred to by the developers as "the Great Wall of China," also had to be kept. All of the facades of Georgetown Park North, now Georgetown Park, had to be either retained or built to resemble Victorian commercial facades with elaborate brick cornices and appropriate window hoods. Most of the facades of Georgetown Park on both Wisconsin Avenue and M Street and all of Georgetown Park on the north side of the canal

The top floor of the apartment house lobby of Georgetown Park, fronting Wisconsin Avenue.

are new. Western Development was required to adhere to height limits of 40 feet on the street facades and 60 feet on the canal side. The final result demonstrates a sensitive solution to the problem of building a massive new building in the heart of an historic district. It is an instructive example for developers in other American cities.

Once building permits were issued, other construction problems surfaced. For phase 1 (Canal Square), the brick warehouse on the south side of the development site on Grace Street needed substantial underpinning to prevent it from collapsing. The warehouse walls had been supported for many years by a series of steel beams that extended across the canal every 30 feet to the massive north stone retaining wall to keep both structures from collapsing. The National Park Service had fortunately just drained the canal for repairs at the time Western Development began the underpinning process, thereby incidentally reducing construction and excavation problems.

The Victorian warehouse on the site had been used to store coal brought down to Georgetown from Cumberland, Maryland, the terminus of the canal 180 miles to the west. In the nineteenth century, coal was hoisted from canal barges to a bridge where a conveyor belt moved the coal into the top of the warehouse. A giant hopper then fed the coal into horse-drawn wagons below for delivery to Washington houses. The interior of this warehouse was completely open except for the large hopper.

TWO DESIGN PHASES

Once the warehouse was gutted, construction of the first phase of this project began. Additional windows and doors were cut into the Victorian walls to accommodate the lower two stories of commercial space (now in use by Conrans, Inc., a London and New York firm dealing in household furnishings) and the two and a half stories of condo apartments above. Part of the western end of the second commercial floor facing Grace Street is devoted to six one-bedroom flats; twenty-five two-bedroom duplex apartments are on the top two floors. The principal architect, Alan S. Lockman, cleverly reversed the duplex pattern—normally a living-dining room and kitchen on the lower level and the bedrooms above. Instead, he placed the living-dining room on the upper level to take advantage of the more desirable view, above the rooftops of the adjacent rowhouses to the south, of the Georgetown waterfront and Potomac River. The facades of this warehouse were kept flat after its original design by recessing the balconies of the duplex apartments on the Grace Street side. Originally conceived as Georgetown Park South, the name of the first phase was changed to Canal House

Rooftop courtyard of Georgetown Park showing the brick sidewalks and landscaping.

shortly before the apartments were sold as condos in 1980.

The design of the north section of Georgetown Park comprises three horizontal parts: three underground levels of parking for five hundred cars at the bottom; three levels of shopping, partly below grade in the center of the massive building; and 128 apartments on the top three floors. The arched garage entry is on Wisconsin Avenue. When a market study indicated that most shoppers disliked corkscrew parking ramps, diagonal ramps (which require more valuable space) were designed on all three levels. The main entrance to the apartment lobby is on Wisconsin Avenue under a shallow canopy marked *Georgetown Park Residences*. To the left of the garage also is an entrance to the shopping center, reached by a descending escalator.

From Wisconsin Avenue, one arrives at the shopping area on its lowest level. The ninety shops are located on three levels in a voluminous open space, designed in neo-Victorian detail. Its atrium is surrounded on all three levels by balconies, escalators, and an exposed glass elevator. A second entrance on M Street leads into the shopping center at its upper level. During the design process, considerable attention was paid to providing a smooth flow of pedestrian traffic on the three commercial levels. Part of this plan includes two bridges, which cross the canal, connecting the main shopping mall in the north

Shopping center at Georgetown Park with Victorian Revival detailing.

building (Georgetown Park) with the commercial space in the south building (Canal Square).

In addition to the main lobby entrance on Wisconsin Avenue, a second apartment entrance is on M Street, where an inconspicuous private elevator leads to the apartments above at the west end. Although the apartment complex in the north building is officially named Top of the Park, it is commonly known simply as Georgetown Park. Most of the apartment house consists of three floors, although two sections facing M Street, N.W., have five floors. The lower level of the apartment complex includes a network of brick walks that extend the length of the roof, forming a courtyard. These walks circle the glass-domed central roof of the shopping center atrium, which protrudes into the apartment house courtyard. In addition to the interesting landscaping of the roof courtyard, a small outdoor swimming pool and jacuzzi are on an upper terrace.

Few pedestrians on the street realize that most of Georgetown Park is below street level. This design was fortunately stipulated by the Commission of Fine Arts to protect the Georgetown streetscape.

144

2501 M STREET, N.W.

North side of M Street, N.W., at the intersection of 26th Street

ARCHITECT: Vlastimil Koubek, 1978

ORIGINAL APARTMENTS: 38 (20 one-bedroom flats; 18 two-bedroom duplexes)

STATUS: opened as condo in 1980

The eight-story 2501 is designed with 100,000 square feet of office space on the lower five floors and thirty-eight apartments on the top three floors. The sixth floor consists of twenty one-bedroom flats, while eighteen two-bedroom duplexes occupy the seventh and eighth floors.

A number of the two-bedrooms have private roofdecks. The step-down lobby on the south side of the building, facing M Street, provides entry to both the offices and the apartments. This mixed-use building is served by three elevators—one exclusively for the residents, a sec-

The top three floors of 2501 M Street, a mixed-use building, are condominium apartments.

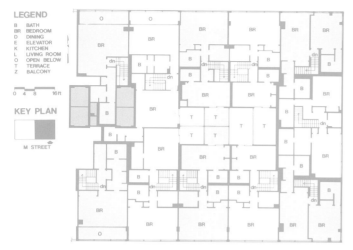

EIGHTH FLOOR (UPPER DUPLEX LEVEL)

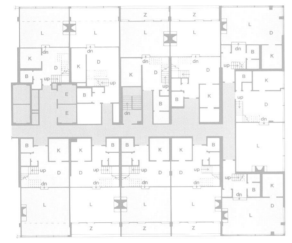

SEVENTH FLOOR (LOWER DUPLEX LEVEL)

SIXTH FLOOR (FIRST RESIDENTIAL LEVEL)

Floor plan of the right or east half of the residential section of 2501 M Street, showing the simplex apartments on the sixth floor and the duplex apartments on the seventh and eighth floors.

The typical duplex apartment at 2501 M Street has a step-down living room opening onto the dining room.

ond only for the commercial floors, and a third serving both. Only this third one is used in the evenings to conserve energy.

The most noteworthy features of the 90-foot-high facade include the recessed first floor, the protruding balcony on the second floor for office occupants, and the projecting top three floors, which help to define the residential area. All apartments have closed-circuit television to monitor visitors entering the lobby. The recessed balconies found on many of the apartments are less successful than those found on other apartment buildings because they are so narrow they can barely accommodate chairs. Although the building was designed to have thirty-eight residential units, plans were changed during construction to combine two duplex apartments in the rear for the owner, Melvin Lenkin of the Lenkin Company.

A garage on the two levels below the building provides parking for 150 cars, with 38 spaces reserved for the residents. Although the condo apartments were sold in 1980, the Lenkin Company continues to own both the land and the office space, which remains rental.

The architect, Vlastimil Koubek, is noted mainly for his office buildings in the K Street, N.W., area of the city, but he has also designed a number of apartment houses. Others include Normandie House, London House, and the Chatham in Arlington, and Horizon House in Baltimore.

145

WESTBRIDGE

2555 Pennsylvania Avenue, N.W.
ARCHITECT: Weihe, Black, Jeffries, and Strassman, 1978
ORIGINAL APARTMENTS: 157 (109 one-bedrooms; 48 two-bedrooms)
STATUS: opened as condo in 1979

Built by the Oliver T. Carr Company as a condominium in 1977, the Westbridge was designed as a mixed-use building: apartments occupy the southern half while the northern half has retail and office space. Because of its prominent location at the western end of Pennsylvania Avenue adjacent to Georgetown, it was not economically feasible to devote an entire structure on such expensive land to apartments.

The lobby entrance of the apartment house is located on Pennsylvania Avenue at the corner of 26th Street, N.W. The spacious, two-story lobby has a front desk and receptionist at the far end adjacent to a bank of three elevators; one is a freight elevator cleverly designed with a removable ceiling to accommodate large furniture, as well as doors on opposite sides for convenient trash removal by the custodian. Although common in hospitals, this door arrangement is unusual in apartment house elevator cabs. The apartment house was originally designed with 157 units. A recent combination of two apartments, to create a unit with three bedrooms and a den, has reduced the total to 156. Typical of luxury apartment house design in Washington in the 1970s and 1980s, the dining room is not treated as a separate room but opens onto the living room in all units. Before construction began, a study was conducted to determine what the

Located adjacent to Georgetown at Pennsylvania Avenue and 26th Street, the Westbridge remains one of the most successful mixed-use buildings in Washington.

market demanded at this location. The results, which pointed to large apartments for upper-income residents, dictated the design.

A number of apartments within the Westbridge offer

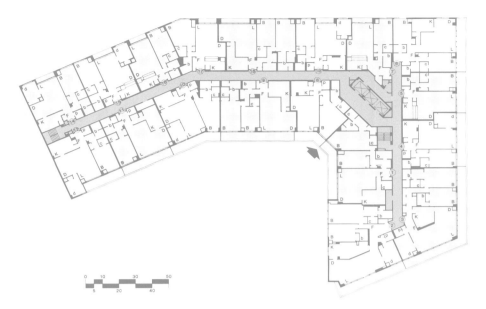

Typical floor plan of the Westbridge.

Typical apartment at the Westbridge.

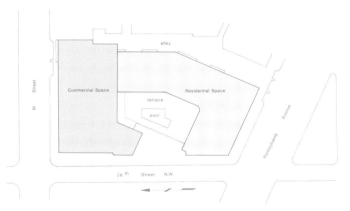

Site plan of the Westbridge.

floor, providing additional light and air for the apartments as well as space for the pool and adjacent terrace. (The pool space is leased from the adjacent Westbridge Office Building, which is still owned by Oliver T. Carr.) Although small, this outdoor swimming pool is surrounded by a spacious terrace for lounge chairs, a design feature often lacking at other apartment house swimming pools.

The brick-faced facades of the Westbridge include balconies for those apartments facing both Pennsylvania Avenue and 26th Street, N.W. The units on the front of the second floor have outdoor patios screened by a low, brick serpentine wall facing the outdoor pool. The six rear apartments on the ground floor that face the alley have larger patios enclosed by tall brick walls. Both patios and balconies are unusual for an intown apartment house that occupies such prime space.

unusual features. Those on the second floor front face an outdoor swimming pool, located on a terrace overlooking 26th Street. This section of the irregular L-shaped apartment house is set back from the street above the first

146

MADISON BANK BUILDING

2833 M Street, N.W.; northeast corner of M and 29th streets
ARCHITECT: Martin and Jones; Deupi and Associates, designers; 1980
ORIGINAL APARTMENTS: 5 (5 two-bedrooms)
STATUS: opened as rental in 1981

This survey of well-designed apartment houses includes not just the large buildings but occasionally the unnoticed very small ones as well. The Madison Bank Building has been included here because it is a good example of a small (five-unit) Postmodern building that fits successfully into its surroundings. This structure has been welcomed by the neighboring residents not only for its sensitive design but also because it replaced a gas station.

This structure was built as the Georgetown branch of the Madison National Bank, an institution founded in 1963 with headquarters at 1730 M Street, N.W. The architects, Martin and Jones, kept the red-brick building

Designed in the Postmodern mode, the Madison Bank Building is well integrated with its M Street neighbors.

A staircase descends to the interior of the bank on the basement floor of the Madison Bank Building.

small in scale, with a 50-foot height, to complement the adjacent Federal and Victorian rowhouses on 29th Street, N.W., and the 1920s classically inspired limestone-faced Biograph Theatre beside it on M Street.

The interior of this building is divided for three uses. The basement and first floor are occupied by the bank, the second floor is used for rental offices, and the third and fourth floors accommodate rental apartments. The M Street facade has two entrances adjacent to a large column; the bank door is to the left, while the second-floor offices are reached by two flights of steps to the right. Access to the apartments is through the 29th Street entrance with its private elevator.

The plan of the five apartments—two flats and three duplexes—is innovative because of the restricted space available for the architect to work with. Although each

Third Floor (First Residential Level)

a

Fourth Floor (Second Residential Level)

b

Plan of both the lower (a) and upper (b) levels of apartments (third and fourth stories) of the Madison Bank Building.

contains two bedrooms and two bathrooms, the units vary in size from 900 to 1,210 square feet. One flat is located on each of the third and fourth floors, while the three duplex apartments occupy both levels. The third-floor flat above the front entrance has a balcony with a sweeping view of M Street. The flat on the fourth floor extends along the 29th Street facade. All three duplexes were designed with living-dining rooms on the third floor and bedrooms above.

The apartment elevator stops only on three levels— basement (garage), first floor, and third floor. The flat on the fourth floor can be reached only by a private staircase extending from the third to the fourth floor. Stopping the elevator at the third floor gained a considerable amount of extra space, since the fourth-floor public corridor could be eliminated. Also, the elevator machinery could be placed on the fourth floor, thereby preventing the roof from being punctured and the clean lines of the gable defaced by a protruding penthouse. The elevator cab itself is unusual: its Postmodern design includes a pair of engaged columns simulating those at the front and side entrances.

The two duplex apartments facing the rear have direct access to a long terrace that runs the length of the building at the third-floor level. Other tenants can use it as well, since it is connected to the third-floor public corridor. Below the terrace, a ramp leads down two levels to a small garage providing parking for thirteen cars. These spaces are divided among the bank staff, office tenants, and apartment residents. At the fourth floor dramatic 12-foot-high interior spaces are formed by the oversize gabled windows.

A domestic appearance is reflected in the facade design, with massive expanses of multipaned glass, fanlights, gabled roof, dormers, and columns. Palladian elements are incorporated throughout in a Postmodern manner. Although the windows have no shutters, they are emphasized by flat brick surrounds of a lighter shade of red. Five rows of lighter brick are used above each flatheaded window to create the effect of a Federal lintel. The center of the front facade is articulated by a massive Palladian window with paired columns and a large fanlight, an indented third-floor balcony, and a central dormer window.

Third floor of the Madison Bank Building showing the study of an apartment that opens to the balcony over the M Street entrance.

The single large column on the front facade echoes the pilasters of the adjacent Biograph Theatre, built as an auto showroom in the 1920s. Even the classical entablature above this column corresponds in scale and height with the Biograph. The rear of the Madison's column is flat, also corresponding to the adjacent pilasters. The right front wall is separated from the mass behind, creating a major opening with the classical column and its entablature placed in the center. Likewise, the small scale of the single column at the 29th Street entrance relates to the porch columns and doorjambs of the historic rowhouses beyond.

The architects themselves said of the Madison Bank Building:

> The building responds to its historic context through its basic massing and use of a traditional wall and window fenestration. It seeks neither to mimic the historic buildings, nor to act as a bland backdrop for them, but to respond to the importance of its site, the complexity of its program, and the variety of scales of surrounding buildings.

Completed in 1981, this building was awarded a citation from the American Institute of Architects for "achievement of excellence in historic preservation and architectural design."

In addition to the Madison Bank Building and the Barclay House, Martin and Jones won the competition to redesign the East Capitol Street Car Barn on Capitol Hill in 1982. This project entailed adapting a landmark Victorian structure for 52 rowhouses and 144 new apartments. Their plan at 1752 N Street, N.W., involved designing a large downtown office building behind and connected to landmark Victorian rowhouses that were remodeled for office use. The architects' largest building to date is the $22 million Olmsted Foundation Building, a Postmodern high-rise office and retail center in Arlington, built in 1985–86.

147

WASHINGTON PARK TOWER

1099 22nd Street, N.W.; east side of 22nd Street, between K and L streets

ARCHITECT: Smith, Segreti, and Tepper, Arlington, Virginia, 1980

ORIGINAL APARTMENTS: 67 (17 one-bedrooms; 38 two-bedrooms; 12 three-bedrooms)

STATUS: opened as rental in 1982

When developer David E. Evans and his three partners first assembled this long narrow site, they planned to build a small, exclusive hotel. Although the south end of the site was zoned commercial, most of the area was still zoned residential, and an Advisory Neighborhood Commissioner blocked plans for a hotel, arguing that it was commercial and unwanted by the residents of the neighborhood.

Four years later, Evans decided on a mixed-use structure with a small eight-story office building on the south and an eleven-story apartment house, the Washington Park Tower, on the remaining two-thirds of the site. When construction began in 1980, the apartments were planned as luxury cooperatives. The building remained rental, however, since few units could be sold because of the high mortgage interest rates in early 1982 when the apartments were completed. Many potential purchasers also considered the original prices, which ranged from $170,000 to $550,000, to be excessive.

The office building section is clearly demarcated because it sets well back from the facade of the Washington Park Tower, which borders the sidewalk. The offices are completely separated from the apartments; there are no internal connections, and each building has its own entrance, lobby, and elevator. The only shared area is the three-level underground garage, which has space for sixty-seven cars; the residents use the first two levels, while the office tenants park on the lowest level. The garage has a common entrance on L Street. Those residents assigned parking spaces under the front of Washington Park Tower, facing 22nd Street, may rent additional space under the sidewalk for a nominal fee. These "vault" areas, owned by the city, provide space for small cars or storage chambers for residents. Few if any apartment houses have rented this unusual city-owned space before. But the developers felt that Washington Park Tower, situated on its narrow inner-city site, should take advantage of every usable square foot of space.

Within the step-down lobby is a curved ramp for the handicapped (required by a new building code for apartment houses in the late 1970s), as well as the reception desk. Because of its narrow shape, the building is only one apartment deep, and the resulting plan includes a total of sixty-seven apartments. On the first three floors are twenty-three flats, while the upper eight stories contain four levels of duplex units (forty-four duplexes).

Except on the upper levels of the duplexes (which extend through the building), a long corridor is at the rear of each floor, with spacious windows facing a rear courtyard. These corridors are thereby naturally lighted

Facade of the Washington Park Tower, a mixed-use building, with the apartment section to the left and the office section to the right.

Plan of a duplex apartment, including private roofdeck, on the upper two stories of the Washington Park Tower.

during daylight hours, a concept also employed at the Worland apartment house, designed slightly earlier. Public hallways with natural light are rare in Washington. Perhaps the best example is in the Worland, where the corridor walls are glazed on the courtyard side. (Many local pre–World War I apartment houses have skylights, however, to admit light to the top-floor corridors.) In addition to the natural lighting, the Washington Park Tower also features public elevators that skip floors, stopping only on the lower level of each duplex, thus allowing the second floor of these duplexes to extend through the building.

Local fire regulations require that staircases within the duplexes be within 10 feet of the door. When originally designed they were 14 feet from the apartment door, but were altered to comply with regulations just before construction was completed. The architect simply extended the last step of each staircase 4 feet, thus creating a long "landing" that is considered part of the staircase.

Arranged in eleven tiers, nine of the duplex apartments also have working fireplaces. Even though each tier has a different floor plan, all of the duplexes are large with 1,500 to 2,300 square feet of floor space. The flats, each with two or three rooms, are also unusually large, averaging 1,200 square feet. The apartments were designed in a wide range of thirty-four different floor plans. All of the upper-level duplexes have private penthouse-terraces reached by circular staircases.

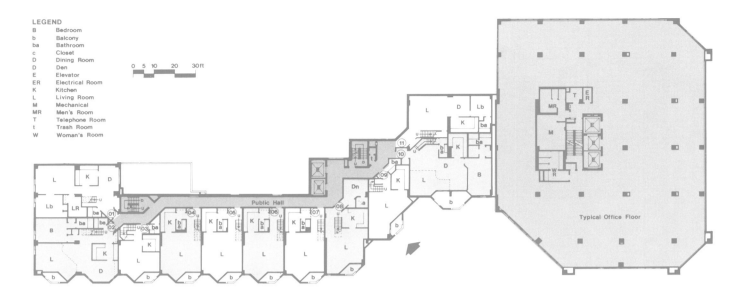

Floor plan of the Washington Park Tower duplex apartments.

A living room and overhanging balcony in a typical duplex apartment at the Washington Park Tower.

A circular staircase leads from a duplex apartment to its private roofdeck at the Washington Park Tower.

Also unusual at Washington Park Tower are the triangular bays that project 4 feet from the property line to the sidewalk. There are open two-story balconies in the duplex units, and glassed-in solaria for flats in the lower three levels. The duplex living room windows facing the tall exterior balconies are two stories high. Within, overlooking the living room, are interior balconies from which the bedrooms radiate to the rear courtyard. Each of the flats on the first floor has a private door to the outside. Because of the unusual triangular bays and penthouses and other innovative designs, the Washington Park Tower was particularly expensive to build.

Even though the building was placed back on the market as a condominium in the spring of 1986, the units did not sell because of their unusually high prices.

148

WASHINGTON HARBOUR

3020 K Street, N.W.; south side of K Street between 30th and 31st streets

ARCHITECT: Arthur Cotton Moore, 1980–82

ORIGINAL APARTMENTS: 35 (1 efficiency; 10 one-bedrooms; 21 two-bedrooms; 1 three-bedroom; 1 four-bedroom; 1 six-bedroom)

STATUS: opened as condo in 1986

One of the most striking of all Postmodern style buildings erected in Washington during the 1980s is Washington Harbour, a mixed-use complex occupying a site of slightly more than 6 acres at the foot of Georgetown. It is bordered by K Street and the Whitehurst Freeway to the north, 30th Street to the east, 31st Street to the west, and the Potomac River to the south. Washington Harbour received a great deal of public attention when it opened in 1986 because of the excessive use of various classically inspired details in the facade design.

Built of buff and brown brick and limestone, the complex was designed in two massive sections divided

Above: The river facade of Washington Harbour, a Postmodern mixed-use building whose apartments exceed those at the Watergate in luxury appointments. *Opposite:* Detail of the south, or riverfront, facade of Washington Harbour showing the range of large pylons that serve as lampposts and support the floodgates after they have been raised electronically.

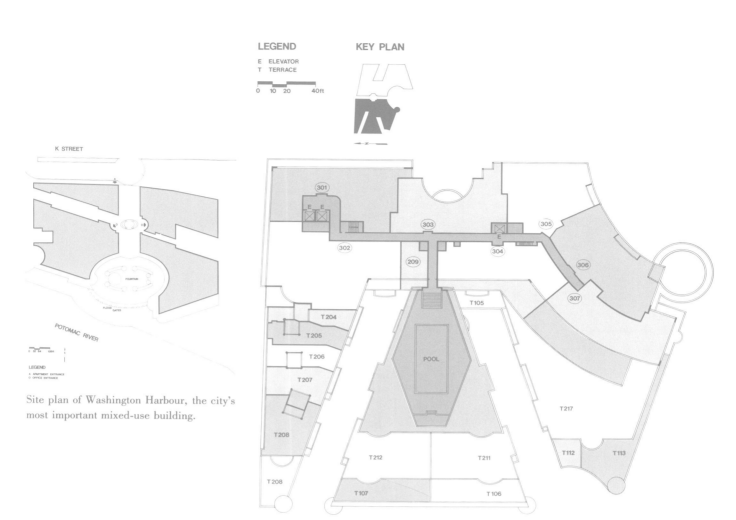

K STREET

POTOMAC RIVER

0 30 64   1200

LEGEND
A APARTMENT ENTRANCE
O OFFICE ENTRANCE

Site plan of Washington Harbour, the city's most important mixed-use building.

Plan of the apartment section of Washington Harbour.

in the center by the extension of Thomas Jefferson Street. The focal point is the south facade facing the Potomac River. On both the east and west buildings the south facades are semicircular, designed to frame the large fountain and pool with its playful Postmodern decorative tower just west of the axis of the fountain.

UNPRECEDENTED RESISTANCE

More problems faced the design and ultimate development of Washington Harbour than almost any other Washington apartment house. As early as 1974 Inland Steel purchased the site from the Potomac Land and Gravel Company, planning a large mixed-use building. Inland Steel commissioned Arthur Cotton Moore as the architect. He had already successfully worked for Inland Steel, redesigning the interior of the nearby historic Foundry building for the firm's adaptive reuse as a restaurant. Inland Steel's

proposed new large building, basically Victorian in feeling, was to have been part of the Foundry project, extending from the Foundry down to K Street.

Constant and unrelenting opposition to any new commercial development of the 19-acre Georgetown waterfront came from the Citizens Association of Georgetown as well as the Commission of Fine Arts. Both groups wanted the then-forlorn area that was covered with cement and gravel plants, incinerators, and parking lots to be converted into either a federal or city public park. Although Moore's initial concept was approved, Inland Steel declined to build. In 1978 the Chicago-based firm decided to abandon further involvement in real estate development, even though it had been successful in several Washington ventures, including conversion of the Cairo apartment house into a condominium as well as the adaptive use of the Foundry building.

Inland Steel sold the site to CSX Resources, Inc., the real estate division of the Chessie and Seaboard Coast-

The lobby of the apartment house wing at Washington Harbour.

line railroads. The next proposal for development came when the Georgetown firm Western Development Corporation formed a partnership with CSX Resources, Inc., and KanAm, Inc., the Atlanta-based investment branch of a German oil and gas company, to build on the site. They commissioned architect Elliott Gitlin to design a mixed-use building. The massive 1,500-foot-long triangular structure, dubbed a "beached whale," with no streets or sidewalks around it, was disapproved by the Commission of Fine Arts.

In 1980 Arthur Cotton Moore was commissioned once again—this time by Western Development—to design a third mixed-use building. His new design, markedly different from that of 1974, was not approved by the Commission of Fine Arts. Against the advice of the commission, however, the mayor approved this Washington Harbour plan. (Since neither the District of Columbia nor the federal government was willing to invest the millions of dollars necessary to buy the entire Georgetown waterfront for a public park, permission was given by the city to proceed with construction in 1982.) The design was altered in 1982 to substitute a large fountain for the boat basin originally planned for the circular area on the south side of the complex facing the Potomac River. It was felt that pollution from the river would become a problem if a boat basin were so close to the proposed building.

Western Development compromised in a number of ways to meet criticism of the project. The complex was reduced by one-third of its original size, occupying only half of the 6-acre site. In addition the height was reduced from 90 to 70 feet. Further changes set the complex back from the river to allow a wide public walkway next to the water.

Negotiations were also concluded for phase two, which involved construction of a hotel and office building on the land between 30th Street and Rock Creek. Western Development Corporation and its partners sold this site to a Texas development firm, Rosewood, which also employed Moore as its architect. The National Park Service allowed this phase of development after Rosewood agreed to reduce the height of the two structures to 60 feet. The new developer also agreed to build wide public walkways

around them, extensively landscape the area, and restore the deteriorated historic Chesapeake and Ohio Canal lock near the mouth of Rock Creek. In 1987 the city planned to donate 9 acres of blighted land to the west of Washington Harbour to the National Park Service for a public park.

One of the unresolved problems at that time was the Whitehurst Freeway, an elevated highway constructed over K Street in 1948 to relieve congestion on M Street and to connect automobile traffic from Key Bridge to K Street downtown. After extensive study, the city government decided in 1985 to repair the aging structure rather than tunnel car traffic under K Street because of the greatly increased cost. Recommendations to simply demolish the structure were also rejected. The noise created by the Whitehurst Freeway is unpleasant, and its unsightly bulk blocks views of the river from most of Georgetown.

UNIQUE DETAILS

Moore's original conception of a boat basin was subsequently changed to a circular fountain in order to avoid

LEGEND
B Bedroom
BR Breakfast Room
c Closet
D Dining Room
DC Dressing Closet
F Foyer
K Kitchen

L Living Room
Lb Library
LR Laundry Room
M Mechanical
SL Staff Lounge
SR Sitting Room
T Terrace

0 5 10 20 ft

A unit plan at Washington Harbour.

A number of apartments at Washington Harbour have private rooftop patios.

Detail of unusual chimneys on the apartment house section of Washington Harbour.

the possibility of both flooding and pollution. To protect the building when the Potomac River is at flood stage, Moore designed a row of submerged steel floodgates, which can be raised 17 feet between concrete pylons in an emergency. The lower garage also is designed to be filled with water to anchor the foundation and prevent the building from being torn loose in a major flood. During the final stage of construction of Washington Harbour, the developer had a chance to test the newly installed floodgates: when the Potomac rose 11 feet above its normal level in November 1985, the electronically operated floodgates were quickly raised, successfully protecting the complex.

Moore's 1980 design called for 80 percent luxury apartments. The following year, however, because of extremely high interest rates, the market for luxury apartments collapsed in Washington. At the same time, a critical shortage of office space became apparent in the city. Because of these developments, the design was reversed in 1982, reducing the apartments to 20 percent of the space. If the developers could have forecast market conditions in 1986, however, they would have retained the original concept!

The thirty-five apartments, ranging from one to six bedrooms, are now located only in the west building on the top three floors. The smallest efficiency is 880 square feet, while the largest unit of three bedrooms and three baths—as originally designed—consisted of 4,000 square

Washington Harbour residents' outdoor swimming pool is on the top level of the three stories of apartments.

feet. Many of the condominium apartments have large terraces of 2,000 square feet or larger, located in the triangular central section of the west building on the fifth, sixth, and seventh floors—known as PH (penthouse) 1, PH2, and PH3. Five of the apartments, termed townhouses, are duplexes with roof gardens. At the time of construction two adjacent apartments were sold together and combined by the owner into a six-bedroom 6,500-square-foot apartment. The original owner of one apartment had the architect design a private swimming pool on his spacious private roof terrace. The other condo owners share a common pool on a terrace on PH3.

All apartments in Washington Harbour are designed as luxury units with such features as marble foyers and elegant wood floors in the living room, dining room, and library. The original purchasers had a choice of floor plans and interior finishes such as flooring of mahogany parquet, wood block, or planks of teak, oak, or mahogany. (Purchasers' preconstruction choice of floor plans and finish materials began with the erection of the Watergate apartments and has since become more common in Washington luxury apartment houses.) Both walls and floors are mar-

ble in Washington Harbour's master bathrooms.

The original residents purchased an average of two parking spaces at $30,000 each on the two garage levels, which have a total of 550 parking spaces. The health club in the east building is available to both apartment residents and office tenants. All but three of the thirty-five apartments, ranging in price from $250,000 to $1.8 million, were sold by 1986, shortly before the building was opened. Most of the buyers were owners of large houses who decided to move into the heart of the city. The success in the sale of these apartments indicated a reverse in market conditions in just four years.

A unique feature of Washington Harbour is its enormous perimeter, the greatest of any building ever constructed in Washington. Although built as one structure, the complex appears to be several buildings because it is sliced by extensions of both Virginia Avenue and Thomas Jefferson Street (not to be confused with Jefferson Drive on the Mall or Jefferson Street near Dupont Circle). The twenty-two different facades provide an abundance of light and air and unusual vistas of the river for both the residents and office workers.

The public hall on the top floor of the apartment house section at Washington Harbour, showing a typical recessed apartment entrance with its double doors.

In addition to the condominium apartments on the top three floors of the west building, Washington Harbour has retail space on its ground floor and offices above the shops. Several public restaurants were planned for the lower floors of the east building, facing a wide terrace with an outdoor cafe. The largest was the Potomac Restaurant, which received considerable public notice when it opened in 1986 because of the flamboyance of its decoration and its owner. Because of many problems, the owner closed the Potomac and declared bankruptcy in late 1987. The small luxury hotel planned for the site east of Washington Harbour in 1986 was never built. The construction of Washington Harbour in the 1980s was the most important event marking the increased commercial, residential, and recreational use of the Georgetown waterfront. This long-neglected but vital space in the city's core at last began to be fully utilized.

149

PORTO VECCHIO

1250 South Washington Street, Alexandria, Virginia

ARCHITECT: Wayne Williams, Smith/Williams Group, Los Angeles and Alexandria, Virginia (facade and site plan);
Holle and Lin Associates (floor plan), 1982

ORIGINAL APARTMENTS: 170 (50 one-bedrooms; 80 two-bedrooms; 40 three-bedrooms)

STATUS: opened as condo in 1985

The most striking feature of the 170-unit Porto Vecchio is its richly detailed facade treatment. Resembling a castle with its own moat and drawbridge, this Postmodern apartment house has an eclectic arrangement of twenty-three varying tiers of balconies and a massive three-story mansard roof laid in black asphalt shingles. Located just south of Old Town Alexandria, Porto Vecchio is one of only a dozen local apartment houses built directly on the Potomac River. Most of the riverfront land is owned by the federal government and is reserved for parkland, military reservations, or airports.

The concept and design of Porto Vecchio differ markedly from the other luxury apartment houses built by Giuseppe Cecchi, president of International Developers, Inc. Most of his others built after 1970 in northern Virginia—such as the Watergate at Landmark, the Rotonda, and Montebello—are large complexes of high-rises occupying sites of 20 to 35 acres. Their facades are plain, while their major features are expansive sites with elaborate landscaping and parkland. Those three apartment complexes, each with more than a thousand apartments, were designed as small self-contained cities. At Porto Vecchio, however, which occupies a small site of slightly less than 5 acres, great attention was paid to the detail of the facade to establish its prestige and to create interest.

Model of Porto Vecchio, one of the few Washington area apartment houses built directly on the Potomac River.

The river facade of Porto Vecchio with its outdoor swimming pool and pergola.

Detail of the unusual balconies of Porto Vecchio, facing the George Washington Parkway on the south side of Old Town in Alexandria.

Porto Vecchio consists of two eight-story wings joined by a central lobby. This basic design was employed in several other Washington area apartment houses, including the Towers, the Promenade, the Belvedere, and Van Ness South. The first five stories of this tan-brick building are crowned by a massive three-story black mansard roof. Interest is added to the entire facade by the varying tiers of balconies. The largest are glassed-in rectangular units, nine bays wide, which are technically oriel windows since they begin at the second floor and terminate on the eighth or top floor. They house the libraries in the larger two-bedroom units. Other tiers contain as many as three varieties of balconies: rectangular glassed-in ensembles on the top floors, with glassed-in units below, and staggered, open-bowed balconies of two different configurations on the lower floors.

The two wings form an irregular U shape, creating a partially enclosed courtyard oriented toward the Potomac River. Pedestrians enter Porto Vecchio (Italian for "old port") via a canopy-covered ramp that connects the building to the front driveway. The two-story moat below serves as a service driveway that encircles the building. The square two-story lobby contains an anteroom on each side—the one on the right for the receptionist and the one on the left for the manager. A wide door, crowned by a Palladian-inspired shell-shaped cornice, leads from the lobby to the rear lounge, an octagonal room facing the formal garden and the river beyond. The adjacent

terrace is laid with hexagonal concrete pavers, which provide a rich pattern in contrast to the rather stark walls and windows of the building. The garden is framed in the center by a handsome U-shaped, classical projecting pergola that overlooks an outdoor circular pool. Outside stairs lead from the terrace of the swimming pool area down to a rear walkway. A wharf extends 100 feet into the river to a floating barge, which can be reserved for parties.

To stay within the 130-foot height limit established by the city of Alexandria and to fully utilize the constricted site, a two-story berm—or artificial mound of earth—was built as the foundation of the north and south wings. Height is measured from the top of this mound. The berm also provides a deep basement with two levels of garage space for 245 cars. Residents enter and leave the garage on the north (left) side of the building. The entrances are on two levels via a ramp for the upper garage and the service driveway for the lower garage. Parking spaces were originally sold for $10,000 each or $17,000 for tandem parking with two spaces end to end. The lower basement also has two service entrances. Additional parking for twenty cars for visitors is provided at the front of the building.

The lower garage entrance is 15 feet above the high-tide level of the Potomac River. The possibility of flooding is remote, however, because the river is much broader at this point than in Georgetown, five miles northward. During the flooding caused by a hurricane in November 1985, only the service drive on the river side was flooded. The building was designed to survive even a major flood, since water can flow into the lower basement to anchor the apartment house and prevent it from being torn from its foundation.

In addition to the outdoor swimming pool, residents have access to men's and women's exercise rooms on the B-1 level adjacent to the upper garage. Each facility includes a locker room, shower, and bathroom. They are joined in the center by a large room with a whirlpool and hot tub. This glass-walled room overlooks the outdoor swimming pool. Residents also have access to a tennis court on the south side of the property. Other amenities include a shuttle bus that runs from Porto Vecchio to the shopping area of Old Town Alexandria as well as to the King Street Metro station during morning and evening rush hours.

The plan of Porto Vecchio includes fifty different shapes and sizes of apartments in twenty-six tiers. Four

Lobby of Porto Vecchio with the reception desk on the right and the card room in the left background.

different styles of one-bedroom apartments are offered, for example. The largest unit, the only duplex apartment in the complex, contains three bedrooms, a den, and a maid's room. Located over the lobby, it has its own private elevator and stairs from the lobby as well as a large private outdoor terrace on the roof of the lounge. Originally sold in early 1985 for $500,000, this large apartment was resold by the first owner later that year for $600,000.

Interior details of the apartments include marble foyers with chair rails, teakwood parquet-style block floors, and cornices in the foyers and living-dining rooms. Bathrooms in most apartments have both a shower stall and a whirlpool bathtub and connect to a small dressing room. The ceilings are 8 feet high on the lower floors and 8½ feet on the upper three floors. Apartments on the upper floors also include working living room fireplaces. In most

Opposite: The card room.

Double doors on the right open into the foyer of this two-bedroom apartment at Porto Vecchio.

A number of apartments at Porto Vecchio have custom-designed features such as this Postmodern foyer, which opens onto the living room with its decorative fireplace mantel.

apartments a balcony opens from the living room; a number of the larger units have two, and some even three, balconies. Each wing of the building has two passenger elevators and one freight elevator; all descend to the two garage levels. Since the building is U shaped, the problem of long, boring public corridors was carefully avoided.

The site of Porto Vecchio was originally developed in 1948 as part of the grounds of Hunting Towers, which borders it to the north. When it opened in 1950, Hunting Towers—a large rental apartment house with three massive brick cross-shaped buildings—had an outdoor swimming pool and marina on the site of what is now Porto Vecchio. The marina became unusable because it rapidly began to fill with silt from Hunting Creek, which empties into the Potomac at this point. Dozens of piers from this 1950 marina are still in place along the shore in front of Porto Vecchio. When Hunting Towers was completed, its owners sold the south grounds to the Teamsters Union but continued to rent the swimming pool from them for its tenants. When rent on the pool was raised, the owners decided to build another pool on their remaining land.

At that time the Teamsters filled in the first swimming pool. In 1980 International Developers, Inc., purchased the site for Porto Vecchio and were surprised to discover, when they began excavation for the 510 wooden pilings that support the foundation of Porto Vecchio, the old swimming pool still in place.

Although the condominium apartments of Porto Vecchio were sold as early as November 1982, it was not until May 1983 that a temporary building was erected on the site to house the model units. Construction actually began in early 1984 and was completed in June 1985 when the first residents moved in. One of the original residents was Henry Holle, the architect of Porto Vecchio, who moved there from his former condo apartment at nearby Montebello, which he also designed.

Porto Vecchio is protected from encroachment on the south and west by Hunting Creek, which is preserved as a bird sanctuary, and by the river on its east. Although some find the facade design a bit bizarre, Porto Vecchio remains the finest apartment house in Alexandria for its views, interior detailing, and amenities.

150

PENN MARK

649 C Street, S.E. (residential entrance) and 650 Pennsylvania Avenue, S.E. (commercial entrance)

ARCHITECT: David M. Schwarz, 1983

ORIGINAL APARTMENTS: 35 (8 efficiencies; 21 one-bedrooms; 6 two-bedrooms)

STATUS: opened as condo in 1986

The commercial section of Penn Mark, a mixed-use building on Capitol Hill, incorporates part of the original Art Deco facade of the Penn Theatre.

Site plan of Penn Mark.

The courtyard of Penn Mark, looking from the commercial to the residential section, showing the spectacular freestanding screen that extends from the apartment wing.

Located on the block opposite the Eastern Market on Capitol Hill, Washington's best-preserved Victorian food market, the Penn Mark contains several unusual design features. Architect David Schwarz designed this mixed-use complex in three principal parts—the commercial building facing Pennsylvania Avenue, an open courtyard in the center of the complex on several levels, and the residential building facing C Street to the rear.

The complex was built around the front facade of the 1933 Art Deco Penn Theatre, which had remained vacant for a number of years before this mixed-use building was designed. Schwarz saved the original limestone-faced theater facade, including the streamlined marquee, curving canopy, and even the ticket booth. The lobby has become a concourse leading to the courtyard and apartment house beyond. The facade of the new commercial building that envelops the old theater front was designed with a handsome blue-glazed brick, defined with white-brick Art Deco beltcourses and vertical strips set in the center of the wings and central pavilion. Red tiles and balcony rails provide additional interest to this blue and white facade. New limestone-faced storefronts, set half a floor below street level, were provided on each side of the theater entrance for the stores. The commercial

building's mass is broken by balconied setbacks on each side of the entrance and by stylish parapets above the end wings. The elevator penthouse and cooling towers are cleverly hidden behind an Art Deco–inspired setback in the center of the four-story structure.

The four-story red-brick and gabled apartment house, designed to present a domestic appearance, faces C Street, S.E., across the street from the Eastern Market and late nineteenth-century rowhouses. The garage entrance is at the left side through an alley.

The multilevel interior courtyard that separates the two buildings serves the residents, office workers, and shoppers. Its principal feature is the massive freestanding white stucco-covered grid that screens the rear of the residential building. The awkward leftover wedge between the two buildings, as well as the difference in grade between the two streets, was a design problem that the architect skillfully solved by slicing the condominium building on the diagonal. The pie-shaped plaza is divided by stairs, terraces, and fountains to create one of the most interesting Postmodern courtyards in Washington. An additional amenity is the Eastern Market Metro stop half a block away at the corner of Pennsylvania Avenue and 7th Street, S.E.

The Georgian Revival residential section of Penn Mark faces
C Street.

LEGEND

B   BATH
BR   BEDROOM
C   CLOSET
D   DINING
E   ELEVATOR
K   KITCHEN
L   LAUNDRY
LR   LIVING ROOM
M   MECHANICAL
Z   BALCONY

0   4   8   16ft

KEY PLAN

C STREET, SE

Typical floor plan of Penn Mark.

151. FLOUR MILL

1015 33rd Street, N.W.
ARCHITECT: Peter Vercelli, 1976
STATUS: opened as condo in 1981

152. ROTONDA

8352 Greensboro Drive, McLean, Virginia
ARCHITECT: Wayne Williams, Los
Angeles, California, and Arlington,
Virginia, 1976
STATUS: opened as condo in 1978–80

153. LINDSAY

5025 Wisconsin Avenue, N.W.
ARCHITECT: Hellmuth, Obata, and
Kassabaum, Washington and St. Louis, 1979
STATUS: opened as rental in 1980

154. WESLIE

1401 North Oak Street, Arlington, Virginia
ARCHITECT: Helbing Lipp, Ltd., Vienna, Virginia, 1978
STATUS: opened as condo in 1980

155. BARCLAY HOUSE

2501 K Street, N.W.
ARCHITECT: Martin and Jones, 1980
STATUS: opened as rental in 1981;
converted to condo in 1985

156. LOGAN PARK

1245 13th Street, N.W.
ARCHITECT: Arthur Cotton Moore, 1980
STATUS: opened as rental in 1981

157. MONTEBELLO

5905 Mount Eagle Drive, Alexandria, Virginia

ARCHITECT: Wayne Williams, Smith/Williams Group, Los Angeles, California, and Arlington, Virginia (site plan); Holle and Lin (floor plan), 1980

STATUS: opened as condo in 1982–84

158. ATRIUM

1530 North Key Boulevard, Rosslyn, Virginia

ARCHITECT: Thomas G. Georgelas and Associates, McLean

STATUS: opened as condo in 1986

159. GRIFFIN

955 26th Street, N.W.

ARCHITECT: David M. Schwarz, 1984

STATUS: opened as condo in 1985

160. ASTORIA

2120 Lee Highway, Rosslyn, Virginia
ARCHITECT: CHK Associates, Silver Spring, Maryland, 1985–86
STATUS: opened as condo in 1987

161. SOMERSET HOUSE

5530 Wisconsin Avenue, Somerset, Maryland
ARCHITECT: CHK Associates, Silver Spring, Maryland, 1985
STATUS: opening as condo in 1988–90

162. MARKET SQUARE

701–801 Pennsylvania Avenue, N.W.
ARCHITECT: Hartman-Cox (facade), and CHK Associates (apartment floor plan), Silver Spring, Maryland, 1985–86
STATUS: opening as condo in 1989

APPENDIX 1: EUROPEAN AND AMERICAN ORIGINS

The arrival of the apartment house in the United States just over a century ago is a recent event compared with the long history and evolution of the building type in Europe. A brief survey of the origins of the apartment house in four European cities—Rome, Paris, London, and Edinburgh—helps place its American development in context. A comparison of apartment house development in Boston and New York further highlights important differences in Washington apartment house design.

PART I: EUROPEAN ORIGINS

Roman Insulae

Developed as early as the fourth century B.C., the apartment house soon became the most popular residence for citizens living in Rome and other large cities of the Roman Empire. At its height during the fourth century A.D., Rome had a population of from 800,000 to as many as 3 million people, according to various estimates. By economizing on the amount of land used, the apartment house solved the problem of housing the lower and middle classes near urban centers. Only the rich could afford a *domus*, or private detached house.

The Latin name for apartment house, *insula*, which literally means "island," designated a number of self-contained residences under one roof, set apart from other buildings. By the first century A.D. apartment houses had multiplied so quickly in Rome that building regulations were established requiring that *insulae* be set back at least 5 feet from the street and from adjacent buildings to provide better light and air circulation. Although initially intended only for working-class residents, the apartment house eventually became widely accepted. Apartment units ranged from two-room working-class tenements to elegant twelve-room apartments for the affluent.

Building regulations were further refined to ensure better design and construction. To resist fire *insulae* had to be built of brick, stone, or concrete; a height limit of 70 feet was also imposed. The laws were often evaded, however, and the cheaper apartment houses, most of which were owned by absentee landlords, commonly collapsed or were destroyed by fire.

Italian archaeologists discovered much about the development and history of apartment houses in Ostia, the port of ancient Rome, during excavations there in the 1930s. They made this accurate model of a high-quality Ostia apartment building typical of A.D. 100.

A view of the remains of the House of Diana, one of the best-preserved apartment buildings from the first century in Ostia, Italy. It was named for a mural depicting Diana, the goddess of the hunt and of the moon, still preserved on the inside walls.

By the first century A.D. the floor plan of the Roman apartment house had become fairly standardized. Typically two entrances opened from the street, often protected from the weather by a portico, projecting arcade, or massive cornice. The main entrance opened onto a passage that ran through the building to a large, open interior courtyard or *atrium*. The second entrance opened onto a staircase leading to the apartments above. All but the most exclusive apartment houses contained shops, or *tabernae*, on the ground floor and sometimes even around the *atrium*, because commercial space commanded more rent than residential. The average *insula* included a common kitchen on the ground floor, where individual families cooked their own food. There was no heat except for braziers, and water was not piped to the upper floors except in the most opulent buildings. Some apartment houses also contained communal latrines on the ground floor, but most residents used the public latrines and bathhouses located every two or three blocks.

Some of the best-preserved *insulae* can be seen today in the city of Ostia, the old port of Rome on the Tiber River. Indeed, much of our knowledge of the design of the Roman apartment house comes from extensive archaeological studies carried out by the Italian government in Ostia during the 1930s. The exterior walls of a number of these first apartment buildings, built in the first and second centuries A.D., still stand. They were faced with narrow Roman brick and had arches throughout for additional strength. The surviving floors of some of the ruins were built with long ranges of arched windows and doors. Many buildings included balconies as well as roofdecks.

The average apartment consisted of either one large room, called a *tablinum*, or a small living room with several very small bedrooms, known as *cubiculae*. A very large apartment, however, might have a dozen or more rooms, including spacious living and dining rooms with 20-foot ceilings and bedrooms with 10-feet ceilings. The interiors of these better-class *insulae* had public corridors, decorated with elaborate murals, that often opened onto intricately landscaped square inner courtyards. One of the most luxurious, the "House of Diana" in Ostia, contained large duplex apartments, each with its own bathroom and kitchen as well as bedrooms for slaves.

After the fall of the Roman Empire in the late fifth century A.D. and the drastic decline of major urban centers in Europe, the necessity for apartment houses such as those in Ostia and Rome vanished. The apartment house was not revived until the Renaissance, a thousand years later.

Renaissance Apartment Houses

At the end of the medieval period, a dramatic increase in trade, stability, wealth, and population led to a rebirth of urban centers in Europe. Since most of the major cities were surrounded by walls for defense, land values rose rapidly as urban populations grew, and the apartment house again became an attractive and economic solution. By 1550 Venice, which then had a population of 150,000 and was the largest city in Europe, had become a major apartment house center. A number of these Renaissance apartment houses still stand—such as the Procuratie Vecchie on the Piazza San Marco—and are among the oldest surviving examples. Vienna also boasts a fine collection of Renaissance residences; more than a dozen sixteenth-century apartment houses are preserved in the heart of the old city. In addition, at least six medieval apartment houses from the sixteenth and early seventeenth centuries survive in Edinburgh, the principal apartment house city in the British Isles.

Paris

Paris is the continental capital of European apartment house cities, with more than 95 percent of the population still living in multifamily dwellings today. By 1600 Paris, with a population of 250,000, overtook Venice as the largest city in Europe, and the high price of land forced almost all Parisian families to live in multifamily dwellings. Few of the city's Renaissance apartment houses still stand. Most were destroyed in the 1850s and 1860s when Emperor Napoleon III commissioned Baron Haussmann to cut broad, axial boulevards through the city's existing maze of narrow, medieval streets. These improvements resulted in grand public buildings, impressive squares and parks, an improved water and gas system, and, by the late nineteenth century, "grand boulevards" lined with imposing Beaux Arts apartment houses.

The design of this typical 1830 Paris apartment house at 8–10 rue de Louvois shows the ground floor used for shops; the second level, or "mezzanine," with small flats for the shopkeepers; and the attic, for servants' rooms.

By 1880 the typical Paris apartment house facade had changed again. Here at 21 rue de Marignan the shops and shopkeepers' flats are gone, the louvered blinds are inside, and two balconies decorate the facade.

Of the late eighteenth-century apartment houses that survive, most have been altered in some way. Several dozen are located along the rue Chabanais and adjacent streets, behind the Palais Royale on the Right Bank. These apartment houses are five stories high, with double doors opening from the street to an inner courtyard. A wide shopfront flanks each side of the main entrance on the ground floor. The second level (sometimes called the "mezzanine") has small, almost square windows, often set in simple heavy arches with plain iron bars within the window frame. Typically it contained small apartments for shopkeepers. The only decoration of the stone facade at this time was simple rustication or high-relief stone banding on the first two levels and wrought-iron guards on the full-length windows on the upper three floors. Exterior louvered blinds and window guards, which varied on each floor, added subtlety to an otherwise plain facade. Many of the roofs had gables and dormer windows; the attic space was traditionally used for servants' quarters.

By 1830, the facade of the Parisian apartment house had changed completely. Although shops still occupied the ground floor, shopkeepers no longer resided in the building and tenants enjoyed greater privacy. Windows on the top four levels became uniform in shape and decorated with outside shutters and simple neoclassical pediments. A plain neoclassical cornice appeared at the roof level.

Within fifty years the facade had evolved once again. The shops on the ground floor disappeared, and wide iron balconies decorated the third- and fifth-floor levels of the facade. The louvered blinds moved into the interior of the apartments.

The typical Paris apartment house courtyard of the eighteenth century, as shown here at 11 Quai Voltaire, is irregular with many additions and variations in roof height. At that time shops with shopkeepers' apartments were often located within the courtyard.

In the 1880s the courtyards of Parisian apartment houses also underwent a basic change in design. The main courtyard of a better building (the courtyard deluxe) was used for storing carriages, while a smaller rear courtyard housed the stables. The main courtyard now became more private and uniform in design; earlier courtyards, which often had public shops on the ground floor, had tended to be irregular because they were built in sections over many decades.

The advent of passenger elevators in the 1880s changed the living pattern inside apartment houses as well. Before the arrival of the elevator, all social classes lived in the same building. As no one wanted to climb stairs, those who could afford to lived on the lower floors. Typically merchants lived directly above their street-level shops, with upper-class residents on the third level, middle-class tenants on the fourth level, lower-income families on the fifth level, and servants and sometimes artists in the garret. The most desirable level was the third floor—not too far to climb, but far enough from the noise and smell of the street. The introduction of the elevator led to a more pronounced social division among classes, as the location and quality of a building became the principal measures of status.

The golden age of Parisian apartment houses coincided with the final flowering of the Beaux Arts style between 1890 and 1910. The facade became increasingly plastic, with massive projecting bays, huge stone brackets, exaggerated windows, and carved deco-

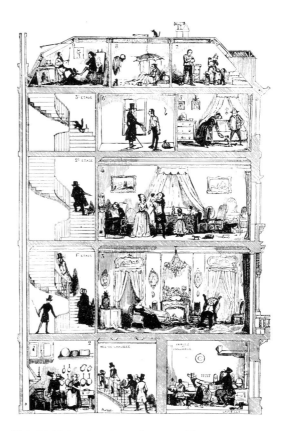

This 1845 drawing shows the typical living pattern in a Paris apartment house, with the concierge's apartment on the ground floor. Poor residents lived on the upper stories before 1880 (when the elevator was introduced), since climbing stairs was undesirable.

A typical upper-class drawing room in an 1850 Paris apartment house such as that at 39 rue de Turenne contains a gilded plaster ceiling medallion, cornice, and paneled walls, as well as a built-in mirror over the working fireplace, casement or "French" windows, and a handsome parquet floor.

During the 1890s the rigid exterior facade composition of the Paris apartment house disappeared as the Beaux Arts reached its climax with projecting bays, ornate window surrounds and balconies, massive brackets, exaggerated dormers, and a facade plasticity—as in this example at 1 rue de Messine.

The most romantic of all Paris apartment houses were built in the Art Nouveau style at the turn of the century. Here the author stands in front of 29 avenue Rapp to provide scale to the massive door and the ornate applied ornament that covers the facade.

ration everywhere. The height of the building increased from five to six stories, and interiors often boasted 14-foot ceilings. Elaborate wrought-iron ornamental grilles and railings appeared on windows, and the custom of two long balconies on the third and fifth levels gave way to one long iron balcony on the top floor. Because many American architects trained in Paris during the late nineteenth and early twentieth century, the influence of the Beaux Arts mode was directly felt in dozens of American cities.

Perhaps the most exuberant of all Parisian apartment houses were the Art Nouveau residences built at the turn of the century. This curvilinear style, featuring sinuous plantlike motifs on exterior and interior detailing, was a brief reaction against the formalism and symmetry of Beaux Arts design, which continued to dominate architectural design through the mid-1920s.

Edinburgh

Although the apartment house has never been popular in England, Wales, or Ireland, and was only introduced in those countries in the nineteenth century, it developed steadily in Scottish cities from as early as 1500, and above all in Edinburgh. The unique development of Edinburgh helps explain why apartment house design evolved differently here than on the continent.

The city of Edinburgh began in the thirteenth century when a market and trading center (or "burgh") was established adjacent to Holyrood Castle during the reign of Scottish King David I. It comprised only 130 acres extending along a narrow high ridge that was considered reasonably safe from attack by the English. The population within this small area grew from 2,000 in 1300 to 20,000 in 1635 and 31,000 in 1755, and the city was forced to

build vertically to supply adequate housing and workshop accommodation. Longstanding rules of the burghs of Scotland made it necessary for merchants and craftsmen to live and work within the burgh boundaries.

By 1600, the average apartment house in Edinburgh had six or seven stories, thought to be the tallest in Europe at that time. Several, built on the side of steep cliffs, had thirteen or fourteen stories with dual entrances—one on the lowest floor at the foot of the hill, the other halfway up at ground level on the hill's upper side. Since tall structures cut off sunlight to neighboring properties, in 1698 the Scottish parliament passed a law limiting apartment houses to five stories. The law did not, however, prevent builders from extending hillside apartment houses several stories down in the rear. In contrast to Paris, the lower units were considered least desirable. For the affluent, climbing stairs to the upper units was preferable to living with the stench from High Street and the narrow alleys between the buildings.

Scottish apartment house terminology differs markedly from American usage. The word "flat," which appeared as early as the fifteenth century in Scotland, originally meant the interior of a house. During the eighteenth century the term evolved to mean a single story inside an apartment building, and by the mid-nineteenth century it acquired its two current meanings: either an entire floor of a residential or commercial building or, more usually, an apartment within a building. The sixteenth-century term for an apartment house was a "land," but since the nineteenth century the most common term used has been "tenement." The word does not carry the derogatory connotation it has in the United States, and even the finest apartment houses in Scotland today are called "tenements." The term "apartment house" remains unknown, but an individual apartment has been called a "house" in Scotland for the past two hundred years.

Late medieval and Renaissance Scottish flats that were not built on hillsides typically had a single street entrance. One walked from the street through a passageway or "close" to the courtyard, which in turn led to a "turnpike," a steep spiral staircase enclosed in a circular brick tower, usually attached to the rear of the building. This curious medieval feature (which was also used in Paris, although none survives there today) disappeared in the mid-nineteenth century when straight stairs with landings became the common arrangement. The rear walled yard provided privies as well as laundry facilities. Lack of air and light, poor sanitation, the threat of fire, and the great height of the load-bearing walls (which often collapsed) presented architects with the same problems that had worried the Romans more than a thousand years earlier.

It was not until the late eighteenth century that living conditions improved—at least for wealthier residents. With the construction of the "New Town," an elegant "suburb" just outside the old city (which has now become the inner city of Edinburgh), conditions in the Scottish capital changed markedly. Built between 1767 and the 1830s, the Edinburgh New Town consists of more than fifty square blocks of Georgian architecture; elegant stone rowhouses extend the full length of each block, usually terminating in an apartment house at the corner. The rowhouses were built at the same time and in the same style as the apartment houses. The latter can be identified only by their sets of three doors. Both the rowhouses, called "terrace houses" throughout Britain, and the "tenements" are usually five stories high with spacious basements below street grade.

The Georgian apartment houses of Edinburgh differ in design from those found in any other European city. Two of the three outer doors provide separate entrances to spacious three-story flats, each occupying part of the basement, ground floor, and first floor. They are the largest flats in the building and are known as main door flats since they open directly to the street. The central door, called the "stair-door," opens to a staircase leading to the two duplex apartments on the third and fourth levels (the second and third floors in the European counting system). A typical Georgian tenement thus contains two triplex and two duplex units, with additional flats occupying the top or fourth floor of the five levels. A mews is usually found in the rear alley.

The Georgian apartment houses built in Edinburgh between 1767 and 1830 have several unique features. An ingenious device allows the stair-door, which is hung at an angle, to be opened by residents of the upper apartments by pulling a brass lever on the third- or fourth-floor landings. The lever is connected to a wire that

The neoclassical buildings in Edinburgh's "New Town," dating from 1767 to 1830, usually included rowhouses in the center of each block with apartment houses on the corners, as on Murray Place.

One of the best-preserved medieval apartment houses in Europe is the six-story Gladstone's Land in Edinburgh, built about 1550 and enlarged in 1620. It is now a museum of the National Trust of Scotland.

The rear of Gladstone's Land shows the typical passage through the building from the street into the courtyard, as well as the steep circular "turnpike" stair—always attached to the rear of the apartment house to save space within.

This main room in the front second-floor apartment at Gladstone's Land remains in original condition, as built in 1620.

The first apartment house in London, and the only freehold that is a cooperative in England today, is The Albany, established in 1802.

is channeled through the walls to the front stair-door latch. Many of the Georgian houses in the New Town also contain bed-recesses, or closets with beds in them, to conserve space.

Not only have most of the elegant Georgian blocks of Edinburgh survived intact but so have a number of the late medieval apartment buildings in the Old Town. One of the best-preserved Renaissance apartment buildings is Mylne's Court, a seven-story stone structure built in 1690 by Robert Mylne, a successful architect and one of a dynasty of Master Masons to the Crown. Threatened with demolition in 1966, Mylne's Court was rescued by the University of Edinburgh and has recently been converted to an undergraduate dormitory.

Another remarkably intact Renaissance structure is Gladstone's Land, a six-story apartment building built around 1550 and later purchased and enlarged in 1620 by Thomas Gladstone, a successful merchant. Owned since 1934 by the National Trust of Scotland, this building is now a museum. Its second-floor flat, possibly the world's oldest surviving purpose-built apartment—with its original beamed parlor ceiling, massive fireplace, bed-recess, and restored turnpike staircase—is open to the public. Continuing a five-hundred-year tradition, a number of flats are still rented as residences.

London

London developed differently from both continental cities and Edinburgh. These cities had been surrounded by walls for defense, and as populations grew new rings of walls were constructed farther out. Most of England, however, had not been invaded by land since 1066, except by the Scots on the northern boundary, and, by the time London's original Roman walls became too restrictive, they were no longer considered necessary. Instead each village on

the outskirts became the nucleus of a new town, and over a thousand-year period the city evolved into the collection of towns we know as greater London today. As London continued to expand outward, many English nobles turned their country estates into squares of rowhouses, after the pattern of Covent Garden, the first rowhouse square, which was developed by the Duke of Bedford in the 1630s. Rowhouses, often arranged around an open landscaped square, thus became the principal residential mode in London.

The first apartment house in London was The Albany, a former mansion off Piccadilly built between 1770 and 1774 by Lord Melbourne. When it was subdivided into apartments in 1802, a front courtyard was added for the carriages, stables, kitchen, and staff, and two long, four-story brick ranges of apartments were built in the rear. The sixty-nine apartments were sold as freehold to a number of wealthy residents as soon as the speculative project was completed. Similar to a condominium, The Albany is still in use today.

While the tremendous growth of London during the first half of the nineteenth century resulted in the construction of many "philanthropic trusts"—as the early English tenements were called—The Albany remained the only luxury apartment house in London for fifty years. It was not until the 1850s that other first-class apartment buildings, all rental, appeared. Called "mansion flats" or "mansion blocks," they had large units, a staff, and adjacent mews for the residents' carriages, horses, and servants. These early mansion flats were built on Victoria Street, which was then being cut through Westminster to clear slums and create a new upper-middle-class neighborhood. Most of the other apartment houses built in the 1860s and 1870s were also located on or near Victoria Street, creating the city's first apartment house corridor. One of the earliest surviving examples is Grosvenor Gardens, built

One of the most prominent Victorian apartment houses in London is Albert Hall Mansions, designed by Richard Norman Shaw in 1879.

American apartment house facade design was influenced by that of London during the 1880s. A typical upper-middle-class apartment house of that decade is Carlisle Mansions, on Carlisle Street near Victoria Street.

in 1865 at the end of a row of fashionable French-style rowhouses.

The first truly large luxury apartment house was Queen Anne Mansions, also built near Victoria Street, between Birdcage Walk and Petty France and overlooking St. James's Park. Begun in 1873 and completed in 1889, it incorporated hydraulic lifts and had fourteen stories—by far the tallest apartment house in England at the time. Destroyed in the 1970s to make room for commercial development, this enormous structure was criticized by Queen Victoria because it overlooked the grounds of Buckingham Palace. The controversy over Queen Anne Mansions resulted in the passage of a height law designed to prevent any further high-rises.

Perhaps the two most important of all surviving Victorian luxury apartment houses in London are the Albert Hall Mansions and Albert Court, located next to one another and across from the Albert Memorial in Kensington. Built in the Queen Anne style in the 1880s, both buildings have large apartments of from eight to twelve rooms and remain in excellent condition. Albert Hall Mansions, considered by many to be the most famous of all intact London apartment houses, was designed in 1879–80 by Richard Norman Shaw. Having no experience with this building type, Shaw traveled to Paris to study apartment house design. Important changes were incorporated, however, to appeal to traditional English taste. To ensure greater privacy, Shaw eliminated the customary open passages and central interior courtyards. He also designed the apartments as duplexes—with private staircases in each unit as in the English rowhouse, removing the bedrooms to another level for greater privacy.

Several other large Victorian apartment houses from the 1880s and 1890s—such as the elegant Harley House on Marylebone Road—are still in use today. A well-preserved and important group of smaller luxury dwellings is found on Carlisle Place and adjacent Morpeth Place. These groups of flat buildings—including Carlisle, Cardinal, and Morpeth Mansions—resemble five-story first-class rowhouses and were designed in the Queen Anne and Georgian Revival styles, with two five-room flats on each floor. Another impressive group of blocks of early luxury apartment houses, built at the turn of the century, is located miles away on the south side of the Thames on Prince of Wales Drive. Each of these sixteen "mansion flats," built in the Georgian Revival style, forms an impressive row extending for nearly one and a half miles.

Exterior architectural features of these late nineteenth-century buildings are unique in comparison with residences on the continent. In Vienna and Paris, facades were built of limestone in an ordered, classical style until the flamboyant Beaux Arts version appeared at the end of the century. Edinburgh's dozens of Georgian apartment buildings fit easily into the streetscape because they match the height and building material of the adjacent rowhouses. They maintain their elegance through their simplicity. Visual relief from the blocks upon blocks of granite architecture is achieved through the finely proportioned and detailed doorways, iron railings, and window guards. By contrast, most of London's nineteenth-century apartment houses were built of red brick in either the eclectic Queen Anne style, with a maze of balconies, bays, and gables, or in the Georgian Revival style.

For one generation the luxury apartment house enjoyed a brief vogue in London; by the outbreak of World War I, there were more than fifty thousand units in a thousand apartment houses. But with the exception of a building boom in the 1930s, few have been built since, and today a much smaller percentage of the London population lives in apartment houses in comparison with other metropolitan inhabitants. The rowhouse remains the basic type of residential housing both in London and throughout England.

PART II: AMERICAN ORIGINS

The American apartment house was first developed on a major scale in Boston, New York, and Chicago during the 1870s. In the following decade its popularity spread rapidly to other cities, including Washington, D.C. Since then its growth as a distinct building type has been phenomenal, with the majority of many metropolitan populations now residing in apartments. Like the population itself, a melting pot of diversity, nineteenth-century American apartment houses varied widely in size and the types of amenities offered—from two-story walk-ups with modest units to twelve-story luxury buildings with sixteen-room apartments attended by full staffs.

Three significant factors influenced the development of the American apartment house. Of foremost importance was the introduction of practical hydraulic passenger elevators in the 1870s. Other improvements in building technology in the late 1870s and 1880s—notably the widespread use of iron and later steel frame construction, as well as effective fireproofing materials—allowed progressively taller apartment houses to meet fire and safety codes. Finally, the dramatic growth of American cities in the increasingly industrialized post–Civil War period placed a strain on the space available for burgeoning populations. The apartment house, by economizing on the amount of land used, solved the problem of housing urban dwellers near city centers.

It is often erroneously thought that the Pontalba Buildings, constructed in New Orleans in 1849, represent the first apartment house in the United States. The Upper Pontalba Building and the Lower Pontalba Building, two handsome brick structures facing one another across Jackson Square, are each a block long, with two striking ranges of iron balconies decorating the facades. They were designed by James Gallier and modified by Henry Howard, both New Orleans architects, for Baroness Micaela Almonester de Pontalba as a rental investment.

The common roof of each of the Pontalba Buildings, however, actually covered sixteen self-contained rowhouses, not apartment units. Originally, each rowhouse had its own entrance on the street from which a passageway led back to a staircase and courtyard beyond. Stores, completely separated from the rowhouses above, took up the ground floor. The four-bay-wide houses occupied the second and third floors and attic. After Baroness Pontalba's death in 1874, the fashionable buildings fell into decay, and the rowhouses were divided into apartments, one to a floor. Restored during the 1930s, the Pontalba Buildings are in excellent condition and still in use, one as commercial and the other as residential property.

The American middle classes were slow to accept the apartment house because of its resemblances to the earlier, working-class multifamily dwelling, derisively referred to in this country as tenements. The tenement, cramped and primitive, offered no amenities and had poor ventilation and little light. It had been introduced in the 1830s to house factory workers in New England textile towns and the growing flood of immigrants in New York City. To Victorians, the tenement was an all-too-visible manifestation of poverty and social ills. According to an 1874 article in *Scribner's Monthly*, it was only after luxury units had been built for the rich that the middle classes began to accept apartment house living.

To distinguish the apartment house from the tenement, developers referred to it during the 1870s and 1880s as a "French flat" because Paris was then the leading apartment house city and influenced design elsewhere. The French flat—a far cry from the tenement indeed—had a main entrance from the street, a lobby, an elevator, and self-contained units with their own kitchens and bathrooms. In addition, a full staff served the residents—manager, desk clerk, janitors, and doorman. Facades resembled the eclectic exteriors of London—red brick based on Queen Anne, Romanesque Revival, and other Victorian styles then in vogue—rather than the tightly ordered classical designs in limestone that predominated in Paris.

By the early twentieth century, however, the floor plans of American apartment houses were modeled after their Parisian counterparts, with interior units carefully divided into three zones—public for entertaining (parlor, dining room, and library), private (bedrooms for family members), and service (kitchen, pantry, and maid's room). The Parisian fashion of having the master bedroom connect to the parlor so that the mistress of the household could conveniently entertain close friends in her boudoir was followed briefly in better New York apartment houses during the 1880s. In the early 1890s the term "French flat" for first-class apartment houses in the United States was replaced by the term "apartment house." By 1900 the once prestigious word "flat" was used only for lower-income multifamily dwellings.

Boston

The first authentic apartment house in the United States was the Hotel Pelham, constructed in 1857 at the southwest corner of Boylston and Tremont streets in Boston. The word "hotel" was used in the French sense of a private mansion. Designed for a Boston physician, Dr. John H. Dix, who also owned the building, and by a local architect, Alfred Stone, the Pelham was modeled on the latest Parisian-style apartment house. It was named for Dix's wife, Helen Pelham Curtis.

Built in a fashionable residential neighborhood adjacent to the Boston Common, the six-story Pelham included commercial space on the ground floor. It also had one of the first "French" or mansard roofs in the city. From newspaper descriptions it is clear the building had a public dining room on the ground floor and approximately eighteen apartments above. Designed for permanent rather than transient residents, this landmark building featured modern plumbing in the shared toilets and baths on each floor. Because the apartments contained no kitchens, the building would be termed an apartment-hotel today.

Top: The first true apartment house in the United States was the Hotel Pelham, shown in this Civil War photograph, built in Boston in 1857. *Bottom:* The Charlesgate was Boston's most elegant apartment house when it was opened by John Pickering Putnam, its developer and architect, in 1890.

The Pelham's lack of private kitchens, toilets, and bathing rooms was typical of contemporary first-class American hotels. While the public accepted these inconveniences when traveling, the arrangement was distinctly unpopular with permanent residents and was not repeated in later apartment houses. The Hotel Pelham established the Boston custom of calling most late nineteenth-century apartment houses "hotels," a peculiarity unique to this city.

Twelve years elapsed before architect Nathaniel J. Bradlee designed the second Boston apartment house, the Hotel St. Cloud, in then-fashionable Union Park in the South End. The depression of 1857 and the disruption of the Civil War accounted, in part, for the gap in apartment house construction in Boston between 1857 and 1869. The five-story marble-faced building, with its French classical and Italianate details, was more eclectic than the Hotel Pelham and incorporated several improvements, including an elevator—the first in an American apartment house—and a toilet, bathing room, and kitchen in each unit. Although the Hotel Pelham was demolished in 1916, the Hotel St. Cloud still stands on Tremont and Union streets. Though abandoned and dilapidated today, as one of the oldest surviving apartment houses in the country it is certainly worthy of restoration. Boston's surviving stock of more than two dozen nineteenth-century luxury apartment houses is exceeded only by those still standing in New York City.

The Boston apartment house differed in many ways from nineteenth-century luxury apartments in other American cities. Stores usually occupied the ground floor; kitchens in some apartments were located on the top floor to isolate cooking odors; and servants' rooms were often in the basement. Five rooms with kitchen and bath were an absolute minimum for upper-class Boston apartments, and many were much larger. The apartments in the Hotel Cluny, for example, all had seven bedrooms and five public rooms located on one floor—reception room, parlor, dining room, library, and smoking room. The ease of entertaining in such apartments was often superior to the better rowhouse of the same period.

Boston also developed the "triple-decker" in the 1870s. These three-story middle-class apartment houses, with one apartment per floor, resembled large houses from the outside. "Double triple-deckers" were also built—two standard "three-deckers" joined by a common center stairhall that gave access to two dwelling units on each floor. One of the oldest surviving double three-deckers was built in 1875 at 15 Upland Road in Cambridge. Especially popular near trolley lines in the Boston suburbs, double triple-deckers were inhabited by all social classes and varied greatly in quality. Though common throughout New England cities, the three-decker is rare in Philadelphia, Baltimore, or Washington.

One of Boston's most significant early apartment house architects was John Pickering Putnam (1847–1917). Born into a wealthy and socially prominent Boston family, Putnam graduated from Harvard and then studied architecture at the Ecole des Beaux Arts in Paris and at the Bauakademie in Berlin. In 1872, two months after he returned to Boston and opened his own architectural firm, a fire destroyed more than 750 buildings in the central section of the city, creating a massive demand for new construction. Putnam soon became a specialist in luxury apartment house design. His first building was the Hotel Cluny, built in 1876 on Boylston Street in Copley Square. Based on the Parisian model, it was one of the earliest American apartment houses with a clear separation of public, private, and service quarters.

The Charlesgate, Putnam's elegant Queen Anne style building located near the Charles River in Boston's Back Bay, had a facade more typical of a London than a Parisian apartment house. It was the most advanced and expensive apartment house design in Victorian Boston, and Putnam and his family resided there until his death. Built of brick with limestone trim, the facade was enlivened with turrets, oriel windows, bay windows, and a mansard roof. Designed in an L shape, the Charlesgate faced an expansive landscaped garden that occupied half of the large site, supplying abundant light and air to every unit. Putnam's advanced heating, ventilating, and sanitary systems resulted in the rental of all thirty apartments before the building was completed. In addition to the spacious lobby and adjacent public dining room, the Charlesgate's apartments featured elaborate carved woodwork, stained glass, and tile fireplaces. Because of its many amenities, it remained one of Boston's "best addresses" until 1920. Though subsequently converted to a dormitory for Boston University, most of its first-floor public rooms remain intact.

Putnam's third great apartment house, the Haddon Hall, caused a furor when it opened in 1894 at Commonwealth Avenue and Berkeley Street. Its ten stories created a jarring effect on the sedate and uniform cornice line of the adjacent upper-class Victorian rowhouses. As a result, a law limiting building height to 80 feet was passed in 1896 to prevent future intrusions on the residential streetscape.

The design and development of the Boston apartment house, especially the triple-decker, was influential in other New England cities, but had little, if any, impact on the development of Washington apartment houses. New York is another story.

New York

Even though New York architect Calvert Vaux called for the adoption of the apartment house as an urban building type as early as 1857, it was not until after the Civil War that the construction of apartment houses began in New York City. The overcrowded living conditions in Manhattan made the apartment house obviously attractive. Already in the 1850s ownership or even rental of private rowhouses for middle-class families had become prohibitive, and in that decade hundreds of older rowhouses were divided into multifamily units or apartments, one to a floor. This development temporarily solved the housing problem for the middle-income New Yorker, but conditions worsened after the Civil War because of the city's tremendous growth.

It was not until 1869 that the first apartment house in New York, architect Richard Morris Hunt's Stuyvesant Flats, opened at 142 East 18th Street.

The first apartment house erected in New York was Stuyvesant Flats, designed by Richard Morris Hunt in 1869. Hunt, the first American trained in architecture at the Ecole des Beaux Arts in Paris, became a leading American architect during the late nineteenth century and a founder and later president of the American Institute of Architects.

The Stuyvesant, located on East 18th Street, was an elegant and comfortable four-story structure. Designed for affluent younger couples, it contained a total of sixteen apartments, most with five rooms, with small studio units under the mansard roof. Every room opened directly to the outside for maximum fresh air. The plan of the building was similar to that of the typical New York rowhouse of the period, with long, narrow light courts in the rear. Its low scale fit nicely into the streetscape and, with two entrances, the structure did not draw attention to itself as an apartment house. An important early prototype that helped make the American apartment house respectable, the Stuyvesant was unfortunately demolished in 1957.

In the mid-1870s the French flat began to be popular with upper-income New Yorkers. Most apartment houses built during the decade were relatively small since they were typically situated on a rowhouse lot measuring 25 by 100 feet. As a result, the floor plan of each flat was arranged along a long hall, as in the separate floors of a rowhouse, to allow different functions on one floor. Only a few first-class New York apartment houses survive from the 1870s. One, built in 1878, is located at 129 East 17th Street. Designed by an architect personally familiar with Parisian flats, Napoleon E. LeBrun, this relatively unknown five-story red-brick and brownstone walk-up contained one unit per floor. The five-room apartments still possess the original woodburning fireplaces with marble mantels in each room, although both electricity and steam heat have been added. A second important survivor from this period is an 1878 apartment house by Bruce Price at 21 East 21st Street.

In the early 1880s New York developers began to build large apartment houses often occupying an entire block. Larger buildings allowed for bigger units with more convenient floor plans. One of the most prominent was the Central Park, erected in 1883 at Seventh Avenue and 59th Street. At the time it was the largest apartment house in the United States. Although it was also sometimes called the "Spanish Flats," it was best known as the "Navarro" after its builder, Juan de Navarro. This impressive residence, comprising eight ten-story towers joined by courtyards between, was one of the first fashionable apartment houses in New York City. The architects, Hubert, Pirsson and Company, were New York's first apartment house specialists.

The Navarro's floor plan, probably the most successful of any American apartment house at that time, was based on Parisian models. (Its massive brick facade, however, more nearly resembled the typically large and eclectic Queen Anne style apartment houses of London.) Apartment sizes varied, but many were large seven-room units—with the parlor, library, and dining room separated by wide arches holding double sliding doors that could be opened to form a great chamber for entertaining. The kitchen was often arranged next to the servant's bedroom and was shielded from the dining room by the pantry. The service rooms acted as a buffer between the public rooms near the entrance and the three principal private bedrooms in the rear. Although the Navarro was planned as one of the first cooperatives in the United States, it opened as a rental apartment house because the owner and builder declared bankruptcy shortly before it was completed.

More than any other city, New York had an impact on the treatment of Washington apartment house facades. A number of landmark New York buildings that inspired Washington architects remain in good condition. The massive Osborne at 205 West 57th Street, built in 1885, served as the model for the design of Washington's Cairo a few years later. Similarly, the early twentieth-century terra cotta–faced Alwyn Court at Seventh Avenue and 58th Street inspired the design of 2029 Connecticut Avenue, N.W., whereas New York's Henrick Hudson influenced the facade of Washington's Woodward. The facade treatment of 2101 Connecticut Avenue was based on the slightly earlier 1924 Shelton Club Hotel at Lexington Avenue and 49th Street in New York by architect Arthur Loomis Harmon. Art Deco apartment houses in Washington during the 1930s were also modeled mainly after New York examples. New York's Rockefeller apartments, for instance, are a direct ancestor of Washington's Majestic. Furthermore, New York architects designed more Washington apartment houses than architects from any other outside city, including the Champlain, the Connecticut (at Connecticut Avenue and M Street, N.W., now demolished),

The 1906 Alwyn Court at Seventh Avenue and 58th Street in New York, entirely clad in terra cotta, influenced the detailing on 2029 Connecticut Avenue in Washington.

3900 Watson Place, N.W., the Shoreham Hotel, and others. Indeed, Washington's first two apartment houses, the Portland Flats and the Fernando Wood Flats, were built by two New York developers in 1880.

Differences did exist between early New York and Washington apartment houses, however. One example is the completely enclosed courtyard plan, which was most successful in large apartment houses occupying an entire city block. Since apartment houses in the nation's capital were much smaller than those in New York, the large interior landscaped courtyard plan was adopted in only one Washington building, the 1922 Kew Gardens. Three excellent examples of early New York courtyard apartment houses are the Dakota (1880) by Henry Janeway Hardenbergh at Central Park West and 72nd Street, the Apthorp (1908) by Clinton and Russell at 2201 Broadway, and the Belnord (1908) by H. Hobart Weekes at 225 West 86th Street. The New York design had several advantages. Carriages could conveniently turn around in the courtyard and deliver passengers to the four corner entrances. The arrangement also meant that long, dark, and monotonous public interior hallways could be avoided. Larger apartments had windows on both the interior courtyard and the exterior streets, increasing the light and air circulation. Bedrooms faced the courtyard and were therefore quieter.

Of course during the late nineteenth century thousands of small flat buildings for lower-income and middle-income residents were also built in New York City. The true luxury examples—usually the most architecturally distinguished—have always constituted a very small percentage of all apartment houses built. During the decade of the 1880s apartment living became increasingly popular with upper-class New Yorkers, since these large apartments provided accommodations equal in size to the average Manhattan rowhouse for less expensive maintenance and service costs.

New York made another important contribution to American apartment house development when the architectural firm of Hubert, Pirsson and Company pioneered the cooperative apartment house. Influenced by Parisian models, the firm built several dozen cooperatives between 1880 and 1900. Apartment owners purchased stock in a private corporation, known as the Hubert Home Clubs, which owned the building. An owner's amount of stock and voting power was determined by three factors: the square footage of the unit, its location within the building, and its view. Many of these early co-ops, as designed and built by Philip G. Hubert, were duplex units that attempted to reproduce the ambiance of a private home. They were also expensive, costing as much as a substantial New York rowhouse in 1900.

One of the Hubert firm's most famous surviving co-ops (now rental), is the Chelsea, built at 222 West 23rd Street in 1883. A unique feature of this eleven-story red-brick building are the massive tiers of richly decorated iron balconies with French doors opening onto them. The central and two projecting pavilions at the

The grande dame of all nineteenth-century New York apartment houses is the Dakota, which retains almost all of its elegant exterior and interior 1884 detailing.

ends, as well as the dormer windows set into the slate-covered mansard roof, create a facade with movement and rich detail. A rental apartment-hotel since 1905, the Chelsea has been the home of many notable American authors, including Mark Twain, O. Henry, Eugene O'Neill, Thomas Wolfe, Arthur Miller, Tennessee Williams, and Andy Warhol.

Of course the most prominent of all surviving nineteenth-century American apartment houses is the justly famous Dakota. It was so named because at the time it was built in 1880, its location on Central Park on the upper West Side seemed as remote as the Dakota Territory. Designed for Singer sewing machine magnate Edward Clark, the seven-story Dakota, now a co-op, was constructed in the Châteauesque style at a cost of $1 million. It had forty-two large apartments and a number of small suites for guests. Dozens of servants' rooms were located in the two-story attic as well as in the spacious English basement. Steep gables, romantic dormer and oriel windows, high chimneys, niches, arches, balconies, and rich ironwork created a picturesque domestic ambience. The main feature was an enormous central courtyard with entrances at each of the interior corners. Carriages and pedestrians entered through two great, arched portals on opposite sides of the building.

During the 1880s New York developers also began to construct luxury "bachelor apartment houses" of two- or three-room suites with a bathroom but no kitchen. These early buildings were first designed as complexes for single men or single women. Usually a public restaurant was provided on the first floor.

Another New York innovation was the development of the "studio" apartment house, designed as a residence for affluent artists. Even though Richard Morris Hunt had designed a studio building on 10th Street in the late 1850s, the type did not become popular until the 1890s. The center of each duplex unit typically contained a large studio for painting, facing north, with a 20-foot ceiling. Often adjoining on the lower level were a dining room and library, while two or three bedrooms were on the second floor. The rooms on the upper level usually opened onto a balcony that looked down on the living room below. The studio soon became popular with others who found the economy of space and the ease of entertaining attractive.

Shortly before World War I, a number of luxurious studio apartment houses were built in New York. One of the finest, built as a co-op, is the Studio at 44 West 77th Street. Designed by Harde and Short in 1907, this fourteen-story building contained apartments with a two-story artist's studio and a duplex with foyer, living room, dining room, library, conservatory, and four bedrooms. The three-room public lobby is richly decorated in the Gothic style with groin-vaulting, paneled walls, and lead-paned windows.

During the 1910s and 1920s, the New York luxury apartment house reached its zenith in terms of facade and floor-plan design as well as quality construction. Usually built as cooperatives, these opulent residences often boasted units of twelve to sixteen rooms, covering an area of 8,000 to 10,000 square feet. Apartment house towers, ranging from twelve to twenty stories, generally contained one to three apartments per floor to maintain privacy. Two New York architects, J. E. R. Carpenter and Rosario Candella, stand out as leaders in refining the luxury apartment house. Their designs have never been equalled in either the quality of their interior detailing or the sophistication of their floor plans.

This brief history can only begin to suggest the rich variety of regional experiments with the luxury apartment house as a building type. Other cities might have been included, but the six treated here—Rome, Paris, Edinburgh, London, Boston, and New York—provide a broad background against which to measure the similarities and differences in Washington apartment house design.

APPENDIX 2: ARCHITECTS OF WASHINGTON APARTMENT HOUSES

All of the architects whose buildings are included in *Best Addresses* are listed below along with the apartment houses they designed. A number of firms changed names frequently. For example, Joseph Abel, one of the most prolific apartment house architects in Washington, practiced alone in the early thirties and has had several partners since then. His firm was known as Dillon and Abel in the late thirties and as Berla and Abel in the forties and fifties; today it is known as Abel and Weinstein. To find all of the apartment houses included in *Best Addresses* with which Joseph Abel was associated the reader should refer to each of these firm names. Founded in the fifties, the architectural firm of Cohen and Haft is today known as CHK Associates. Another firm, active between 1950 and 1970, had four names: Corning and Elmore; Corning, Elmore, and Fischer; Corning, Moore, Elmore, and Fischer; and finally Fischer and Elmore. The name of each firm is listed as it appears on the building permit and is not cross-indexed except as mentioned here.

Readers can easily refer to apartment houses by the building numbers that are used throughout the book—as part of the heading of all entries, on the two maps that form the endpapers, and in this list. The date given for each apartment house is the date of the building permit (just before construction began) rather than the date of completion. All architects are from Washington unless otherwise noted.

JOSEPH ABEL
79. 2101 Connecticut Avenue, N.W. (with George T. Santmyers); 81. Broadmoor; 86. Shoreham Hotel.

FREDERICK G. ATKINSON
46. Plymouth.

ALVIN L. AUBINOE, SR. (with HARRY L. EDWARDS)
103. Majestic; 117. Hightowers.

AVERILL, HALL, AND ADAMS
27. 1509 16th Street, N.W.; 52. Netherlands.

WALTER F. BALLINGER, Philadelphia
69. Methodist Building.

ALBERT H. BEERS
25. Dresden; 28. Northumberland; 51. Toronto.

ROBERT F. BERESFORD
65. Mayflower Hotel (with Warren and Wetmore, New York City).

BERLA AND ABEL
119. Towers; 133. 3900 Watson Place, N.W. (with Harry Price, New York City); 124. Van Ness Centre (with Van Fossen Schwab and Shanti Singh Sukthankar, Baltimore); 125. Irene; 134. Rittenhouse.

HARRY BLAKE (with EDGAR S. KENNEDY)
21. Westmoreland.

EDWARD L. BULLOCK, JR., Philadelphia
69. Methodist Building addition.

CHK ASSOCIATES, Silver Spring, Maryland
160. Astoria; 161. Somerset House (in Chevy Chase, Maryland); 162. Market Square (with Hartman-Cox).

APPLETON P. CLARK, JR.
29. 2852 Ontario Road, N.W.; 59. 1424 16th Street, N.W.; 62. Roosevelt Hotel; 67. Presidential.

ADOLPH CLUSS
1. Portland Flats.

COHEN, HAFT, AND ASSOCIATES, Silver Spring, Maryland
130. Sumner Village.

GEORGE S. COOPER
6. Analostan; 10. Balfour; 11. Hawarden; 26. Dumbarton Court.

JAMES E. COOPER
71. Cleveland Park; 84. Hampshire Gardens; 93. 1705 Lanier Place, N.W.

CORNING, ELMORE, AND FISCHER
135. Cathedral.

CORNING, MOORE, ELMORE, AND FISCHER (with LUIGI MORETTI, Rome, principal architect)
122. Watergate.

WILLIAM I. DEMING
14. Stoneleigh Court addition.

JULES H. DE SIBOUR, New York City and Washington, D.C.
19. Warder; 35. McCormick; 70. Anchorage; 91. Jefferson.

LEON E. DESSEZ
24. Chevy Chase.

CLEMENT A. DIDDEN, JR.
9. Portner Flats.

DILLON AND ABEL
102. 2929 Connecticut Avenue, N.W.; 104. Governor Shepherd; 115. 2407 15th Street, N.W.

DIXON AND WEPPNER
118. Potomac Plaza.

DONALD HUDSON DRAYER
123. Prospect House; 128. Colonnade; 140. Promenade.

EDMUND W. DREYFUSS AND ASSOCIATES
141. Plaza (formerly Foggy Bottom).

HARRY L. EDWARDS
72. Army and Navy; 103. Majestic (with Alvin L. Aubinoe, Sr.); 105. Gwenwood; 117. Hightowers (with Alvin L. Aubinoe, Sr.).

FISCHER AND ELMORE
129. Foxhall.

KENNETH FRANZHEIM, New York City (with ALLAN B. MILLS)
112. McLean Gardens.

THOMAS G. GEORGELAS AND ASSOCIATES, McLean, Virginia
158. Atrium.

EDWARD H. GLIDDEN, SR., Baltimore
23. Wendell Mansions.

GRAY AND PAGE
2. Richmond Flats.

NICHOLAS T. HALLER
7. Cambridge.

ISAIAH T. HATTON
39. Whitelaw.

HARDING AND UPMAN
30. Woodward.

WILLIAM HARRIS
99. Park Tower.

HARTMAN-COX
162. Market Square (with CHK Associates).

RALPH HEALY
54. Covington.

ARTHUR B. HEATON
13. Highlands; 34. Altamont; 42. Marlborough.

HELBING LIPP, LTD., Vienna, Virginia
154. Weslie.

HELLMUTH, OBATA, and KASSABAUM, St. Louis and Washington, D.C.
153. Lindsay.

JAMES G. HILL
12. Mendota; 14. Stoneleigh Court; 16. Ontario.

HILL AND KENDALL
16. Ontario addition.

WALLACE F. HOLLADAY, SR. (with IAN WOODNER)
132. Woodner.

HOLLE AND LIN (with WAYNE WILLIAMS)
149. Porto Vecchio; 157. Montebello.

HUNTER AND BELL
36. 2029 Connecticut Avenue, N.W.; 53. Stafford; 57. 1868 Columbia Road, N.W. (now the Norwood).

PHILIP M. JULLIEN
61. Chastleton.

LOUIS JUSTEMENT, JR.
75. 2120 Kalorama Road, N.W.; 82. Harvard Hall; 114. Falkland.

EDGAR S. KENNEDY (with HARRY BLAKE)
21. Westmoreland.

KEYES, LETHBRIDGE, AND CONDON
136. Columbia Plaza; 138. Tiber Island.

FRANCIS L. KOENIG
100. Colonial Village addition; 106. Marlyn (with Harvey H. Warwick, Sr.); 109. Carlyn (now Gateway Georgetown); 111. Dorchester House.

KOENIG AND MOORE
131. Greenbriar.

VLASTIMIL KOUBEK
144. 2501 M Street, N.W.

LOCKMAN ASSOCIATES
143. Georgetown Park (with numerous associate architects).

MACLANE AND CHEWNING
127. Cathedral West.

MARTIN AND JONES
146. Madison Bank Building; 155. Barclay House.

MIHRAN MESROBIAN
83. Wardman Tower; 89. Sedgwick Gardens; 96. Dupont Circle
(with Joseph J. Moebs and Claughton West, associate architects).

ALLAN B. MILLS (with KENNETH FRANZHEIM, New York City)
112. McLean Gardens.

ARTHUR COTTON MOORE
148. Washington Harbour; 156. Logan Park.

LUIGI MORETTI, Rome, Italy
122. Watergate (with Corning, Moore, Elmore, and Fischer, associate architects).

PARKS AND BAXTER
78. Tilden Gardens.

HORACE W. PEASLEE
77. Moorings.

I. M. PEI, New York City
137. Town Center

HARRY PRICE, New York City
133. 3900 Watson Place, N.W. (with Berla and Abel, associate
architects).

GEORGE N. RAY
95. 1700 Connecticut Avenue, N.W.

HILYARD R. ROBINSON
101. Langston Terrace.

EMERY ROTH AND SONS, New York City
126. Shoreham West.

LOUIS T. ROULEAU, SR.
85. Woodley Park Towers.

GEORGE T. SANTMYERS
76. 4701 Connecticut Avenue, N.W.; 79. 2101 Connecticut
Avenue, N.W. (with Joseph Abel); 98. 3901 Connecticut Avenue,
N.W.; 110. Delano.

SAUNDERS AND PIERSON, Alexandria, Virginia
139. Newport West.

A. M. SCHNEIDER
56. 2001 16th Street, N.W.

T. FRANKLIN SCHNEIDER
3. Cairo; 5. Story Flats; 20. Florence Court; 40. Albemarle; 41.
Iowa; 43. Farragut; 44. Sherman; 45. Cecil; 47. Rochambeau; 48.
Woodley; 50. Portsmouth.

ROBERT O. SCHOLZ
80. Alban Towers; 108. General Scott.

LEONARD SCHULTZE AND ASSOCIATES, New York City
113. Parkfairfax.

VAN FOSSEN SCHWAB AND SHANTI SINGH SUKTHANKAR,
Baltimore
124. Van Ness Centre (with Berla and Abel).

DAVID M. SCHWARZ
150. Penn Mark; 159. Griffin.

LOUIS E. SHOLTES
68. 2500 Massachusetts Avenue, N.W.

B. STANLEY SIMMONS
8. Mt. Vernon Flats addition; 22. Wyoming; 37. 1870 Wyoming
Avenue, N.W.; 92. Belvedere; 94. Embassy.

SMITH, SEGRETI, AND TEPPER, Arlington, Virginia
147. Washington Park Tower.

CHLOETHIEL WOODARD SMITH
121. Harbour Square.

CLINTON SMITH
49. Champlain.

ALEXANDER H. SONNEMANN
18. Cordova addition; 38. Meridian Mansions (now the Envoy); 64.
Kew Gardens; 88. Kennedy-Warren addition.

ROBERT STEAD
4. Maltby House.

STERN AND TOMLINSON
90. Argonne (now the Park Plaza).

DAVID L. STERN
116. 4801 Connecticut Avenue, N.W.

GEORGE W. STONE, SR.
15. Kenesaw.

GEORGE OAKLEY TOTTEN, JR.
66. Meridian Hill Studio.

MERRILL T. VAUGHN
31. Windsor Lodge; 32. St. Regis.

PETER VERCELLI
151. Flour Mill.

WARDMAN AND WAGGAMAN
63. Cathedral Mansions.

WARREN AND WETMORE, New York City
65. Mayflower Hotel (with Robert F. Beresford, associate architect).

HARVEY H. WARWICK, SR.
73. Chalfonte; 87. Westchester; 97. Hilltop Manor; 100. Colonial
Village (with Francis L. Koenig); 106. Marlyn (with Francis L.
Koenig).

EDWIN WEIHE AND ASSOCIATES
120. Army Distaff Hall.

WEIHE, BLACK, JEFFRIES, AND STRASSMAN
145. Westbridge.

HENRY T. E. WENDELL
2. Richmond Flats (1887 addition).

CLAUGHTON WEST
55. Biltmore; 96. Dupont Circle (with Mihran Mesrobian, principal architect, and Joseph J. Moebs).

FRANK R. WHITE
33. Avondale; 58. Somerset House; 60. Northbrook Courts.

WAYNE WILLIAMS, Los Angeles, California, and Arlington, Virginia
149. Porto Vecchio (with Holle and Lin); 152. Rotonda; 157. Montebello (with Holle and Lin).

WOOD, DONN, AND DEMING
17. Bachelor Flats; 18. Cordova.

IAN WOODNER (with WALLACE F. HOLLADAY, SR.)
132. Woodner.

WILFRED VOLLMER WORLAND
142. Worland.

FRANK LLOYD WRIGHT, Scottsdale, Arizona, and Spring Green, Wisconsin
107. Crystal Heights.

JOSEPH YOUNGER
74. 1661 Crescent Place, N.W.; 88. Kennedy-Warren.

APPENDIX 3: LOCATION OF APARTMENT HOUSES BY NEIGHBORHOOD

The 162 apartment houses featured in *Best Addresses* are listed below by neighborhood. A number of apartment houses located downtown are listed according to the closest circle or park. One apartment house corridor is also included—14th Street, N.W., north of Massachusetts Avenue. Demolished buildings are italicized; in the case of No. 107, Crystal Heights, the building was never built. Readers may also refer to the two endpaper maps of north-central Washington and of south-central Washington.

ALEXANDRIA, VIRGINIA
113. Parkfairfax; 149. Porto Vecchio; 157. Montebello.

ARLINGTON, VIRGINIA
100. Colonial Village; 123. Prospect House; 153. Weslie; 158. Atrium; 160. Astoria.

ADAMS-MORGAN
16. Ontario; 22. Wyoming; 29. 2852 Ontario Road, N.W.; 37. 1870 Wyoming Avenue, N.W.; 38. Meridian Mansions; 52. Netherlands; 53. Stafford; 54. Covington; 57. 1868 Columbia Road, N.W., now the Norwood; 73. Chalfonte; 74. 1661 Crescent Place, N.W.; 82. Harvard Hall; 90. Argonne, now the Park Plaza; 93. 1705 Lanier Place, N.W.; 99. Park Tower; 107. Crystal Heights; 111. Dorchester House.

BETHESDA, MARYLAND
130. Sumner Village; 140. Promenade.

CAPITOL HILL
4. *Maltby House*; 69. Methodist Building; 150. Penn Mark.

CATHEDRAL HEIGHTS
80. Alban Towers; 87. Westchester; 106. Marlyn; 112. McLean Gardens; 119. Towers; 127. Cathedral West; 128. Colonnade; 133. 3900 Watson Place, N.W.; 135. Cathedral; 142. Worland.

CHEVY CHASE, D.C.
24. Chevy Chase; 120. Army Distaff Hall

CHEVY CHASE, MARYLAND
125. Irene; 161. Somerset House.

CLEVELAND PARK
71. Cleveland Park; 78. Tilden Gardens; 81. Broadmoor; 89. Sedgwick Gardens; 98. 3901 Connecticut Avenue, N.W.

COLUMBIA HEIGHTS
66. Meridian Hill Studio; 115. 2407 15th Street, N.W.

DUPONT CIRCLE
3. Cairo; 6. Analostan; 10. Balfour; 18. Cordova, now the President Madison; 28. Northumberland; 33. Avondale; 35. McCormick; 40. Albemarle; 50. Portsmouth; 51. Toronto; 56. 2001 16th Street, N.W., now the Brittany; 58. Somerset House; 61. Chastleton; 62. Roosevelt Hotel; 70. Anchorage; 77. Moorings; 95. 1700 Connecticut Avenue, N.W.; 96. Dupont Circle; 117. Hightowers.

FARRAGUT SQUARE
14. *Stoneleigh Court*; 42. *Marlborough*; 43. *Farragut*; 65. Mayflower Hotel.

FEDERAL TRIANGLE
162. Market Square (construction planned for 1988).

FOGGY BOTTOM

104. *Governor Shepherd*; 118. Potomac Plaza; 122. Watergate; 136. Columbia Plaza; 141. Plaza; 155. Barclay House; 159. Griffin.

14TH STREET, N.W., CORRIDOR (north of Massachusetts Avenue)

9. *Portner Flats*; 11. Hawarden; 39. Whitelaw; 97. Hilltop Manor.

FRANKLIN PARK

5. *Story Flats*; 49. Champlain.

GEORGETOWN

26. Dumbarton Court; 64. Kew Gardens; 109. Carlyn; 143. Georgetown Park; 146. Madison Bank Building; 148. Washington Harbour; 151. Flour Mill.

KALORAMA

13. Highlands; 20. Florence Court, now California House and California Court; 21. Westmoreland; 23. Wendell Mansions; 25. Dresden; 31. Windsor Lodge, now the Chancellery; 32. St. Regis; 68. 2500 Massachusetts Avenue, N.W.; 72. Army and Navy; 75. 2120 Kalorama Road, N.W.

KALORAMA TRIANGLE

12. Mendota; 30. Woodward; 34. Altamont; 36. 2029 Connecticut Avenue, N.W.; 48. Woodley; 55. Biltmore; 79. 2101 Connecticut Avenue, N.W.

LAFAYETTE SQUARE

2. *Richmond Flats*; 17. Bachelor Flats; 47. *Rochambeau*; 67. Presidential.

LOGAN CIRCLE

41. Iowa; 46. Plymouth; 156. Logan Park.

McLEAN, VIRGINIA

152. Rotonda.

MOUNT PLEASANT

15. Kenesaw, now La Renaissance; 60. Northbrook Courts; 94. Embassy; 103. Majestic; 132. Woodner.

MOUNT VERNON SQUARE

7. Cambridge; 8. *Mount Vernon Flats*.

PETWORTH

84. Hampshire Gardens.

SCOTT CIRCLE

19. *Warder*; 27. 1509 16th Street, N.W.; 45. *Cecil*; 59. 1424 16th Street, N.W.; 91. Jefferson; 108. General Scott.

SILVER SPRING, MARYLAND

114. Falkland.

SHEPHERD PARK

134. Rittenhouse.

SOUTHWEST

121. Harbour Square; 137. Town Center (West), now Marina View Towers; 138. Tiber Island.

THOMAS CIRCLE

1. *Portland Flats*; 44. *Sherman*; 92. Belvedere; 139. Newport West.

TRINIDAD

101. Langston Terrace.

VAN NESS

76. 4701 Connecticut Avenue, N.W.; 116. 4801 Connecticut Avenue, N.W.; 124. Van Ness Centre.

WARD CIRCLE

129. Foxhall; 131. Greenbriar.

WASHINGTON CIRCLE

105. *Gwenwood*; 147. Washington Park Tower.

WEST END

144. 2501 M Street, N.W.; 145. Westbridge.

WOODLEY PARK

63. Cathedral Mansions; 83. Wardman Tower; 85. Woodley Park Towers; 86. Shoreham Hotel; 88. Kennedy-Warren; 102. 2929 Connecticut Avenue, N.W.; 110. Delano; 126. Shoreham West.

GLOSSARY

To assist the reader the following brief glossary of terms relating specifically to apartment buildings has been compiled. These definitions apply specifically to Washington usage; some of their meanings vary slightly among other American cities.

APARTMENT-HOTEL   A residential building with a combination of bedrooms with baths for transient occupants and small apartments (with kitchens) for permanent residents who benefit from the availability of hotel services.

ASSESSMENT   The levying of a special fee on the owners of either a co-op or a condominium apartment, usually for a particular project such as replacement of the roof, purchase of a new boiler, or installation of central air conditioning. Also known as a special assessment.

BACHELOR APARTMENT   A one- or two-room apartment with a bathroom but without a kitchen. Popular in the early twentieth century, they were often found in buildings solely comprising bachelor units.

CONDOMINIUM   An apartment owned outright as an individual piece of real estate with percentage interest in the common areas of the building and grounds.

COOLING CHAMBER   A vegetable storage cabinet located in the wall of an apartment, usually under the kitchen window, with perforated bricks in the outer wall to allow cold air to enter. Popular in Washington apartment houses between 1900 and 1925 before the widespread use of electric refrigerators.

COOPERATIVE   An apartment house organized as a corporation with shares of stock issued to owners according to apartment size,

location, and view. Shareholders do not own their units outright but enjoy the right of perpetual use. Also known as a co-op.

DUMBWAITER   A small rope-operated elevator located in a shaft adjoining either the kitchen or pantry of an apartment. Operated by the janitor from the basement, a bell system alerted residents of daily trash removal. Popular between 1880 and 1925.

DUPLEX   A two-story apartment.

EFFICIENCY   An apartment with one room, kitchen, and bath. Also known as a studio in New York.

ELEVATOR PENTHOUSE   A projecting structure on the roof of a multistory apartment building housing the elevator machinery.

FLAT   A term in common use in Washington between 1890 and 1920 meaning an apartment on one level in an inexpensive two- or three-story purpose-built walk-up apartment building.

FRENCH FLAT   The term in popular use in Washington during the 1880s for an apartment in a luxury apartment house with lobby, elevator, and full service. The term was superseded by apartment in the 1890s.

GALLEY KITCHEN   A long narrow kitchen, usually with all appliances and cabinets located on one wall. The most widespread type of apartment kitchen used by builders to conserve space.

GARDEN APARTMENT   Three or more buildings of no more than three stories with no elevator or lobby, usually arranged around a well-landscaped open space. Popular between the two World Wars.

LOFT   An open-plan apartment in converted light-industrial buildings. Popular in New York but rare in Washington, since old industrial buildings (in convenient locations) are in short supply.

Dumbwaiters were popular in many Washington apartment houses for trash removal before 1925. Four apartment houses still use them. In this apartment at the Stafford, 1789 Lanier Place, the pantry door is on the right while the dumbwaiter is open on the left.

The janitor at the St. Regis signals the resident of each apartment with a bell, then sends the rope-operated dumbwaiter up on schedule from the basement for trash removal.

In Dumbarton Court and a number of other small pre–World War I apartment buildings without lobbies or receptionists, vestibules were used for brass mailboxes and speaking tubes through which visitors requested admittance.

LOW-YIELD CO-OP   A cooperative apartment building that limits the profit an owner can realize when the apartment is sold. Any increase in the price of a unit is usually determined by the original cost plus an adjustment for yearly inflation. Designed to preserve modestly priced housing.

MAISONETTE   An apartment, usually a duplex, with a private entrance to the street.

MIXED-USE BUILDING   A single building combining office and residential functions, and often retail use as well. The most common arrangement in Washington is horizontal, with retail space on the street floor, apartments on the upper floors, and offices in between. Less common is the vertical division of the building for commercial and residential use.

MURPHY BED   A folding bed that swings out of a closet or dressing room into the single room of an efficiency apartment. Popular in Washington between the two World Wars.

PENTHOUSE   Any freestanding structure built on the roof of an apartment house. It is usually nonresidential, such as an elevator penthouse or boiler-room penthouse. Many realtors (incorrectly) use the term for a luxury apartment, usually with a terrace, located on the top floor of an apartment house. A more accurate description would be simply a top-floor apartment.

PULLMAN KITCHEN   A small compact kitchen that opens directly onto an efficiency apartment. The refrigerator is located below the counter and in some cases a folding screen is used to conceal the kitchenette.

SIMPLEX   A one-level apartment.

SPEAKING TUBES   An early communication system connecting vestibule with individual apartments; popular between 1890 and 1915 in small apartment buildings.

STUDIO   The original meaning, in use between 1880 and 1930, was a luxury duplex apartment for painters, with a large north window or a skylight and often designed with a two-story-high living room with bedrooms on the second level. Since World War II, the term has evolved to mean a one-room apartment, with kitchen and bath, in New York—or an efficiency in Washington usage.

SUMMER PAVILION   A roofed open-air structure on an apartment house roofdeck where residents can read, converse, or catch the breeze during the summer months. Popular between 1900 and 1930.

TIER   The vertical arrangement of identical apartments in a multistory apartment house.

TRIPLEX   A three-level apartment.

BIBLIOGRAPHICAL NOTES

My research on the social and architectural history of Washington apartment houses focused on seven major sources—building and raze permits, newspaper articles, floor and site plans, photographs, architectural periodicals, interviews, and the most important—the buildings themselves.

Building permits are in many ways the most important single source since they list the architect, owner, builder, cost, date, and often the original number of units. Those issued between 1877 and 1950 are housed in the National Archives; post-1950 permits are kept in the D.C. Archives. Raze permits, dating from 1907 (when they were first issued) to 1950, are also located in the National Archives, with more recent ones in the D.C. Archives.

The majority of newspaper articles cited are from the [Washington] *Evening Star*, the city's leading periodical from 1880 through the mid-1950s. The index to the *Evening Star*, covering the period 1904–75, was frequently consulted in the Washingtoniana Collection of the Martin Luther King, Jr., Public Library. Of particular interest was the Saturday real estate section of the *Evening Star* between 1880 and 1980—each was surveyed on microfilm in order to assemble over two thousand articles on the development of the Washington apartment house over the past century.

Floor plans were also a revealing source of information. A few were published in architectural journals soon after the building was completed, including the Portland Flats, the Ontario, the Northumberland, the Dresden, and the McCormick. Others appeared in brochures prepared by the developer at the time the building opened for rent, such as the Highlands, the Connecticut, the Altamont, and Tilden Gardens. Still others were located by apartment house board members, building managers, or janitors—often

hidden away in basement storage bins and in poor condition. It is surprising how many apartment houses, both old and new, are missing all floor plans. In many cases typical floor and site plans could be secured from the architectural firm that designed the building, including Abel and Weinstein, Lockman Associates, CHK Associates, Martin and Jones, and many others. Architecture students from the University of Maryland were employed over a period of seven years to redraw these plans, ink on mylar, for publication. They also prepared measured drawings for two dozen apartment houses in which the original plans were lost.

Photographs of the Ontario, dating from 1904, were the earliest interior views found of private units within a Washington apartment house. Early exterior photographs provided clues to important facade changes. For instance, the portico of the Albemarle was moved from T to 17th streets soon after the building opened in 1901 and the entrance to the Wyoming was changed from the west to the central wing when additions were made to the building shortly before World War I. Old photographs of apartment houses, however, are rare in comparison to those of old houses. In order to properly document the exteriors and interiors of apartment houses two private photographers accompanied the author on visits to over two hundred apartment houses. The five thousand photographs taken include views of over six hundred privately occupied apartments and form an important documentary on the history of decoration and interior design, as well as the life style of apartment house residents in the 1980s. The collection also includes 1,200 interior and exterior photographs of over 100 historic European apartment houses—in Vienna, Paris, London, Edinburgh, and Glasgow, which I took during a research trip in the summer of 1985. Fifty historic photographs of early apartment houses in

Boston, New York, and Chicago were also assembled. The entire collection of 6,250 photographic negatives, known as the Goode-Phillips Collection, has been deposited in the Photographic Archives of the National Gallery of Art and is open to the public for scholarly use.

Another valuable source were the four hundred articles on apartment houses published in American architectural journals between 1875 and 1980. These were located and xeroxed in the library of the American Institute of Architects. Filed chronologically they form an important reference source on the development of the apartment house in other American cities. These articles, other papers collected by the author, and many of the photographic prints form the Goode Apartment House Collection at the Columbia Historical Society and are also available for research.

Interviews with over two hundred architects, developers, builders, owners, residents, and managers provided crucial information on the development of Washington apartment houses. Although these are not cited in the bibliography for lack of space, several important letters from long-time residents have been quoted in the text. Other accounts were found in the published letters or autobiographies of leading Washington figures, such as Harry Truman and Frances Parkinson Keyes. These sources are particularly important since little has been published on the social history of the Washington apartment house. Biographical data was also collected on the major architects of Washington apartment houses and on noteworthy developers such as Harry Wardman, Gustave Ring, and Morris Cafritz.

The bibliography is organized by chapter, each section listing general reference information as well as the type of sources consulted on each building. Citations within subheadings are organized alphabetically by author's last name or by title, with material quoted in the text designated in parentheses. Building and raze permits are listed chronologically, as are multiple entries when no author or title is given. Newspaper section and page numbers are also given when known (in some cases only a clipping was consulted).

To conserve space the following abbreviations have been devised for frequently cited manuscripts, books, and periodicals.

AA—*American Architect*

AABN—*American Architect and Building News*

Abel-Severud—Joseph H. Abel and Fred N. Severud, *Apartment Houses* (New York: Reinhold, 1947).

ABJ—[Baltimore] *Architects and Builders Journal*

AF—*Architectural Forum*

AG—*Alexandria Gazette*

AH—*Apartment House Magazine*

AJ—*Alexandria Journal*

Alley—Paul Alley, "The Development of the Washington, D.C. Apartment House, 1900–1905," M.A. thesis, University of Virginia, School of Architectural History, 1979, pp. 1–130.

AR—*Architectural Record*

AM—*Architecture* (magazine)

BM—*Brickbuilder Magazine*

Blouir—Clark Hollis Blouir, "An Urban Building Block—Mixed-use Buildings, Commercial/Residential Development, Washington, D.C.: A Case Study," M.A. thesis, Virginia Polytechnic Institute and State University, School of Architecture, 1987, pp. 1–76.

BP—District of Columbia building permit

ES—[Washington] *Evening Star*

FHA—*FHA Insured Mortgage Portfolio*

Goode—James M. Goode, *Capital Losses: A Cultural History of Washington's Destroyed Buildings* (Washington, D.C.: Smithsonian Institution Press, 1979).

Green—Constance McLaughlin Green, *Washington, Capital City, 1879–1950* (Princeton, N.J.: Princeton Univ. Press, 1963).

GPO—Government Printing Office

Gutheim—Frederick Gutheim, *Worthy of the Nation: The History of Planning for the National Capital* (Washington, D.C.: Smithsonian Institution Press, 1977).

Hickman—Caroline Mesrobian Hickman, "Mihran Mesrobian, Washington Architect," *Building News*, vol. 2, no. 3 (June 1983), 1–4.

HP—*Historic Preservation*

JG—[Washington] *Journal and Guide*

McAndrew—John McAndrew, editor, *Guide to Modern Architecture, Northeast States* (New York: Museum of Modern Art, 1940).

MMS—Montgomery Meigs Scrapbooks, Engineering Division, National Museum of American History, Smithsonian Institution.

NR—National Register of Historic Places Inventory–Nomination, National Park Service, U.S. Department of the Interior.

NYT—*New York Times*

Perks—Sydney Perks, *Residential Flats of All Classes* (London: B. T. Batsford, 1905).

Placzek—Adolf F. Placzek, editor, *Macmillan Encyclopedia of Architects*, vols. 1–4 (New York: The Free Press, 1982).

PP—*Pencil Points*

PR—*Progressive Architect*

Proctor—John C. Proctor, editor, *Washington, Past and Present, a History*, vols. 1–4 (New York: Lewis Historical Publishing Company, 1930).

REG—"Real Estate Gossip" column, [Washington] *Evening Star*.

RM—*Regardie's, The Magazine of Washington Business & Real Estate*

RP—District of Columbia raze permit

Sexton—R. W. Sexton, *American Apartment Houses, Hotels, and Apartment Hotels of Today* (New York: Architectural Book Co., 1929).

Slauson—Allan B. Slauson, *A History of the City of Washington, Its Men and Institutions* (Washington, D.C: Washington Post Co., 1903).

TL—[Washington] *Trans-Lux*

WAA—*Washington Afro-American*

WB—[Washington] *Bee*

WDN—*Washington Daily News*

WH—*Washington Herald*

WHT—*Washington Herald Tribune*

Wirz-Striner—Hans Wirz and Richard Striner, *Washington Deco: Art Deco in the Nation's Capital* (Washington, D.C.: Smithsonian Institution Press, 1984).

Withey—Henry F. Withey and Elsie Rathburn Withey, *Biographical Dictionary of American Architects (Deceased)* (Los Angeles: Hennessey & Ingalls, 1970).

WM—*Washingtonian* (magazine)

WN—[Washington] *Westchester News*

WP—*Washington Post*

WS—*Washington Star*

WT—*Washington Times* (First published, 1895–1939; revived under the same name by New World Communications, Inc., in 1982.)

WTH—*Washington Times Herald*

CHAPTER 1

INTRODUCTION

Manuscripts Clark Hollis Blouir, "Moving Up: the Emergence of the Luxury Apartment House in Our Nation's Capital, 1880–1900," research paper, Virginia Polytechnic Institute and State University, 1983, pp. 1–28. Books Grace Dunlap Ecker, *A Portrait of Old Georgetown* (Richmond, Va.: Garrett and Massie, 1933); Goode; Green. Pamphlets *North Columbia Heights, the New Addition to the Great Northwest* (Washington, D.C.: n.p., ca. 1900), pp. 1–14. Periodicals "Apt. Bldg. in Georgetown Altered," ES, 14 Feb. 1953, p. B7; Christopher Gray, "The 'Revolution' of 1881 Is Now in Its 2d Century," NYT, 28 Oct. 1984, sect. 12, p. 61.

1. PORTLAND FLATS.

Manuscripts BP 1596, 16 June 1880, lots 9–10, sq. 215; BP 812, 3 Feb. 1883. Books Goode, pp. 183–85; Proctor, vol. 1, p. 151, and vol. 2, p. 516. Periodicals Robert L. Buchanan, "Iron Works Turns 75," ES, 2 May 1973; "The First French Flat," unidentified Washington newspaper clipping, 22 Apr. 1880, in MMS, vol. 1, p. 89; F. W. Fitzpatrick, "The Brick Architecture of Washington, D.C.," BM, vol. 8, 1899, pp. 54–57; "The French Flat Building," unidentified Washington newspaper clipping, 1880, in MMS, vol. 1, p. 89; "Gichner Leases Drury Plant for War Work," WDN, 12 Apr. 1944, p. 31; Hugh Humphrey, "District Iron Works Approaching Status of Heavy Industry," ES, 25 Mar. 1953; "The Improvement Boom," unidentified Washington newspaper clipping, 1880, in MMS, vol. 1, p. 89; William A. Miller, "Gichner Plant First Unit of New Industrial Center," ES, 15 Oct. 1956, p. A18; Edwin D. Neff, " 'Iron Man' Hale and Hearty at 80," WTH, 23 Nov. 1950; "The Portland," AABN, vol. 14, Jan.–June 1884, pp. 433–34; "Portland Hotel Sold for $600,000," ES, 5 May 1928, p. 17; "Portland Hotel Sold to Woman," ES, 3 May 1928, p. 7; Wolf Von Eckardt, "City's First Apt. House To Be Razed," WP, 13 Mar. 1962; "Wardman Buys Portland Here," ES, 5 Oct. 1923, p. 2.

2. RICHMOND FLATS.

Manuscripts BP 917, 1 Mar. 1883, lots 23–24, sq. 165; BP 75, 11 July 1887; RP 3121, 28 Sept. 1922. Books Goode, p. 182; *Red Book Society, The Catholic Red Book of Washington and Environs* (Baltimore: Kohn and Pollock, 1908). Periodicals "City and District," ES, 19 May 1883, p. 2; "For Rent—Flats," ES, 1 Nov. 1883; "Progress in Bldg.," ES, 8 Sept. 1883, p. 1; REG, 1 June 1901, p. 17.

3. CAIRO.

Manuscripts BP 1121, 19 Feb. 1894, lot 800, sq. 179; Elizabeth Bloom Applebaum, "The Early Tall Buildings of Washington, D.C., 1880–1900," M.A. thesis, George Washington University, American Civilization Dept., May 1983, p. 1–115. Books and pamphlets *The Cairo, Washington, D.C.* (St. Louis: I. Haas and Co., 1894), pp. 1–10; *Limitations on Building Heights in the District of Columbia, 1791–1975,* 94th Congress, 2nd Session, 1976, H. Doc.-Committee on the District of Columbia (first quote, p. 15); Russell Lynes, *The Art Makers of Nineteenth Century America* (New York: Atheneum, 1970). Periodicals "The Cairo," in *The Inventive Age and Industrial Review* (Washington, D.C.: n.p., Dec. 1894); "Cairo Hotel Leased by James T. Howard," ES, 1 Jan. 1938; Patricia Camp, "Cairo Condo Conversion Under Way," WP, 4 Aug. 1979, p. E2; "11 Pieces of D.C. Realty Sold in $3 Million Deal," ES, 4 May 1955; Lawrence Feinberg, "Jaded Cairo to Get a Facelift," WP, 8 Aug. 1972; Harvey Kabaker, "A Lease on Life," ES, 17 May 1973; "Nearing Completion," WP, 1 Feb. 1975; "A New Life at 85 for the Cairo," WP, 10 Aug. 1979; REG, 9 Apr. 1904, pt. 2, p. 14; "Renovation," WP, 5 Mar. 1974; "Renting Begins at the Cairo," WS, 26 Mar. 1976; "Representative Gregg Is Defendant in Suit," ES, 18 Oct. 1918, p. 28; Aaron Ruvinsky, "Cairo Gets New Life as Apt. House," WP, 23 Jan. 1976; Montgomery Schuyler, "Architectural Aberrations: no. XIII—The Cairo," AR, vol. 4, no. 4, 1894–5, pp. 473–76 (second quote); "$3 Million Property Sale Told," WP, 4 May 1955; Wolf Von Eckardt, " 'Schneider's Folly' to Live Again," WP, 30 Aug. 1972; John B. Willmann, "Cairo Sale, Shift to Condos Planned," WP, 22 Feb. 1979.

4. MALTBY HOUSE.

Manuscripts BP 891, 8 Oct. 1887, lot 1, sq. 633. Books and pamphlet *Enlarging the Capitol Grounds,* 58th Congress, 2nd Session, 1943, S. Doc. 201; Harrison W. Fox, Jr., and Susan Webb Hammond, *Congressional Staffs, the Invisible Force in American Lawmaking* (New York: The Free Press, 1975); *Safety of the Maltby Building,* 81st Congress, 2nd Session, 1904, S. Doc. 201; *Space Requirements of the U.S. Senate,* 81st Congress, 2nd Session, 1950, S. Doc. 137. Periodicals "Additions to Capitol," WP, 4 Apr.

1905; "In the Senate—To Purchase the Maltby House,"
[Wilmington, Dela.] *Every Evening*, 26 Sept. 1890, p. 3; "Landmark to Make Way for Union Station Plaza," ES, 24 Jan. 1914, pt.
2, p. 2.

5. STORY FLATS.
Manuscripts BP 220, 3 July 1889, lot 830 (34 and 35), sq. 288.
Books *Selections from the Work of F. T. Schneider, Architect, Washington, D.C., 1894* (St. Louis: National Chemigraph Company,
1894). Periodicals REG, 10 Aug. 1889, p. 11.

6. ANALOSTAN.
Manuscripts BP 2002, 11 Apr. 1893, lot 803, sq. 155. Periodicals
"The Analostan, Before and After," WS, 19 Aug. 1977; "Financing
Set," WP, 14 Dec. 1973; "Old Apt. House Sold," ES, 15 Dec.
1917, pt. 2, p. 2.

7. CAMBRIDGE.
Manuscripts BP 1764, 1 June 1894, lot 40, sq. 485.

8. MT. VERNON FLATS.
Manuscripts RP 301924, 19 Dec. 1947, lot 32, sq. 373; RP
301994, 26 Dec 1947. Periodicals "Landmark Sold for Hotel," ES,
8 Sept. 1945, p. B2; "Owner Plans Empire-Building Restoration,"
WP, 23 Mar. 1950; REG, 6 May 1893; REG, 29 Mar. 1902;
REG, 21 Feb. 1903, pt. 2, p. 17.

CHAPTER 2

INTRODUCTION
Bachelor apartment houses.
Periodicals "Apt. Houses," ARBN, vol. 31, Jan.–Mar., 1891, pp.
37–39; REG, 25 Feb. 1905, pt. 2, p. 16; "Suggests an Ideal
Home for the Bachelor Woman," ES, 16 Nov. 1915, pt. 2, p. 2.

Children refused in apartment houses.
Periodicals REG, 21 Oct. 1905, pt. 3, p. 1.

Growth of apartment houses.
Periodicals "Flocking to Live in Flats," ES, Sept. 1897 (first
quote); REG, 13 Dec. 1902, pt. 2, p. 29; REG, 28 Mar. 1903, pt.
2, p. 32; REG, 4 Apr. 1903, pt. 2, p. 32; REG, 30 May 1903, pt.
2, p. 17; REG, 4 July 1903, pt. 2, p. 28; REG, 25 July 1903, pt.
2, p. 17; REG, 6 Feb. 1904, pt. 2, p. 1; REG, 26 Mar. 1904, pt.
2, p. 16; REG, 25 June 1904, pt. 2, p. 6; REG, 31 Dec. 1904,
pt. 2, p.1; REG, 3 June 1905, pt. 2, p. 6; REG, 2 Sept. 1905, pt.
2, p. 7; REG, 14 Oct. 1905, pt. 2, p. 6 (second quote); REG, 19
Sept. 1908, pt. 2, p. 17.

Height of buildings.
Periodicals "Height of Bldgs.," ES, 21 Mar. 1903, pt. 2, p. 7;
REG, 21 Mar. 1903, pt. 1, p. 7.

Two-story flat buildings.
Periodicals "New Bldgs. Going Up," ES, 9 Apr. 1904, pt. 2, p.
14; REG, 26 Mar. 1904, pt. 2, p. 16; REG, 16 Apr. 1904, pt. 2,

The marble balustrade in the lobby of the
1901 Balfour.

p. 9; REG, 23 Apr. 1904, pt. 2, p. 9; "Two-Story Apts.," ES, 12
Dec. 1903, pt. 2, p. 1.

9. PORTNER FLATS.
Manuscripts BP 1596, 16 June 1980, lot 9–10, sq. 215; BP 812,
3 Feb. 1883. Books Goode, pp. 183–85; Slauson, p. 435. Periodi-
cals "Dunbar House," WAA, 24 Jan. 1948; "Dunbar House
License Protest Weighed," ES, 18 Aug. 1948; "New License Is
Denied to Dunbar Hotel," WP, 28 Apr. 1951; John Stevens,
"Tribute to Dunbar at Library Opening Stirs Old Memories," WP,
4 Oct. 1979; "Two New Apt. Bldgs. Planned for 15th Street NW,"
WP, 15 Apr. 1978; "Virginia Apts.," WT, 14 May 1928.

10. BALFOUR.
Manuscripts BP 1328, 27 Mar. 1900, lot 1, sq. 175; Alley. Peri-
odicals "Apt. House Sold," ES, 14 Apr. 1917, pt. 2, p. 2;
"Balfour Apts. Will Become Hotel," ES, 6 Oct. 1934; "Large
Properties Traded," ES, 27 May 1909, pt. 2, p. 9.

11. HAWARDEN.
Manuscripts BP, 2 July 1901, lot 109, sq. 207. Books *Interna-
tional Who's Who, 1980–81, 44th Edition* (London: Europa
Publications, Ltd., 1980); Michael Joseph and George Rainbird,
The Shell Guide to Wales (London: George Rainbird, Ltd., 1969);
John Morley, *The Life of William Ewart Gladstone* (London:
Macmillan and Co., 1903). Periodicals Bernhart Mingia, "Six
Elderly Tenants Fight to Keep Apts.," WP, 7 Aug. 1986, p. DC1;
"Sale Is Reported of Two Apts.," ES, 1 Sept. 1917, sect. 2, p. 2.

12. MENDOTA.
Manuscripts BP 1307, 1 Apr. 1901, lot 148, sq. 2537; Alley;
Mark Andrich, "The Mendota Apts.," 1984, pp. 1–10. Periodicals
"The Mendota," ABJ, Jan. 1902, p. 31; Kirk Scharfenberg, "Apts.
Fined; Denied Negro Lease," WP, 18 Nov. 1972.

13. HIGHLANDS.
Manuscripts BP 1308, 13 Mar. 1902, lot 155, sq. 1530; Alley;
Arthur B. Heaton Architectural Drawings Collection, Prints and
Photographs Div., Library of Congress. Pamphlets *Catalogue,
Annual Exhibit of the Washington Architectural Club, 1904,*

Corcoran Gallery (Washington, D.C.: 1904); *The Highlands: An Exclusive Hotel Apartment House* (Washington, D.C.: Weaver Bro., 1904). Periodicals "Apt. Hotel Conversion Sparks Growing Controversy," WP, 13 Aug. 1977; "Apts. Due for Remodeling," ES, 8 Oct. 1955; "Apts. Sold," ES, 1 Feb. 1958; "Change in Ownership," ES, 27 Jan. 1906, pt. 1, p. 1; "Connecticut Ave. Apts. Sold," WP, 18 Jan. 1964; "Easier Money Market," ES, 10 Oct. 1903, pt. 2, p. 32; Neil Henry, "Connecticut Ave. Bldg. to Become Apt. Hotel," WP, 1 Aug. 1977; "Highlands and Westmoreland Sold," ES, 22 May 1924, p. 4; "Highlands Purchased," ES, 23 July 1960; "$1 Million Transforms the Highlands," WP, 17 June 1956; "Wallace Takes Leave of Spacious Apt.," ES, 3 Mar. 1921, p. 13; "Wardman Realty Deals Recalled," ES, 13 Apr. 1934; "A Washington Type of the High Class Apt. House," *The American Spectator*, 11 Aug. 1906, pp. 15–16.

14. STONELEIGH COURT.
Manuscripts BP 458, 5 Sept. 1902, lot 35, sq. 164; Alley; letters, Mrs. Alice Stephan Joyce, McLean, Va., to the author, 18 Sept. 1982 (quote) and 2 Apr. 1983; letter, Rear Admiral Edward S. Stephan, Ft. Pierce, Florida, to the author, 16 Feb. 1982. Periodicals "Announce Sale of Stoneleigh Court Bldg.," WTH, 24 Jan. 1953; "Apts. Rented," ES, 22 Sept. 1934; "Appointed Receivers," ES, 31 Mar. 1927, p. 52; "Business Replaces Fashionable Homes," ES, 12 Aug. 1916, pt. 2, p. 2; "Famous Connecticut Ave. Residential Bldgs. Sold," ES, 27 Feb. 1926, p. R15; "Huge Apt. Bldg. Sold," ES, 26 Feb. 1926, p. 21; "Landmark Sold for $3 Million," ES, 25 Sept. 1957; "Metropolitan Life Buys Stoneleigh Court," ES, 22 Feb. 1933; Thomas Plate, "Stoneleigh Court Being Torn Down," WP, 25 Aug. 1965; REG, 24 May 1902, pt. 2, p. 17; REG, 17 Oct. 1903, pt. 2, p. 32; REG, 30 Jan. 1904, pt. 2, p. 1; "Stoneleigh Court Apts. Undergo a Complete Remodeling," WH, 16 Sept. 1934; "Stoneleigh Court Apts., Washington, D.C.," AA, 22 Dec. 1909; "Stoneleigh Court Apts. Sold for $2 Million," WP, 25 Jan. 1953; "Stoneleigh Court Improvement Due," WP, 24 Dec. 1933; "Stoneleigh Court, or Look Before You Leap," AABN, Apr.-June, 1903, p. 24; "Stoneleigh Court to Be Renovated," WP, 28 Sept. 1957; "Stoneleigh Court Renovated with Up-to-Minute Equipment," ES, 15 Sept. 1934; "Stoneleigh Court Sold at Auction," WP, 22 Feb. 1933; "Stoneleigh Court Sold, Management Will Be Unchanged," WP, 17 Apr. 1941; "Stoneleigh Court Sold for $2 Million," ES, 24 Jan. 1953; "Stoneleigh Court Work Will Begin," ES, 13 Jan. 1934; "$3 Million Buys Stoneleigh Court," WP, 24 Sept. 1957; "$200,000 Spent in Remodeling Stoneleigh," WP, 19 May 1935; "Venetian Blind in Stoneleigh Court Rooms," WP, 16 Sept. 1934; "Wardman Buys Apt. House," ES, 7 Apr. 1927, p. 24; "Wardman Sells Stoneleigh Court," ES, 3 Sept. 1927, p. 14; John B. Willmann, "Stoneleigh Court Sold for $4.5 Million," WP, 19 Dec. 1962.

15. KENESAW.
Manuscripts BP 2025, 16 Mar. 1905, lot 175, sq. 2594; Alley; Karen J. Schiffres, "A History of the Kenesaw Apt. House," Dec.

1983, pp. 1–33; George W. Stone, Jr., "Roots and Future, the Kenesaw Apt. House," Mar. 1984, pp. 1–24 (quote). Pamphlets *Catalogue, Annual Exhibit of the Washington Architectural Club, 1904, Corcoran Gallery* (Washington, D.C.: 1904). Periodicals Anne Chase, "The Battle of the Kenesaw Apts.: Round 2," WP, 13 Oct. 1983; Christopher Dickey, "Kenesaw Bldg. Purchase by Tenants Delayed by Trial," WP, 23 Aug. 1978, p. B12; Dickey, "90 Tenants pay $25,000 on Bldg.," WP, 14 Nov. 1978; Dickey, "Tenants Lose a Court Fight to Buy Kenesaw," WP, 31 Aug. 1978; Dickey, "Tenants' Victory," WP, 16 Dec. 1978; Dickey "This Must Be a Dream Come True," WP, 9 June 1978; Allan Frank, "Court Stops Antioch Sale of Bldg.," WS, 23 Aug. 1978; Roger S. Glass, "Tenant Group Purchases Kenesaw Apts.," WAA, 3 June 1978; "Kenesaw Apts., Washington, D.C.," AA, 22 Dec. 1909; Charles A. Krause, "Legation Legal Fight is Settled," WP, 3 July 1975; "150 Tenants Are Routed by Apt. Fire," ES, 13 Apr. 1962; REG, 14 Mar. 1903, pt. 1, p. 11; REG, 28 May 1904, pt. 2, p. 14; REG, 18 Mar. 1905, pt. 2, p. 1; Walterene Swanston, "Kenesaw Apts. Sold to Private Developer," WP, 3 Nov. 1977; Swanston, "Kenesaw Tenants' Co-op Hopes to Purchase Bldg.," WP, 2 Mar. 1978.

16. ONTARIO.
Manuscripts BP 1211, 2 Feb. 1903, lot 200, sq. 2586; BP 1808, 21 Mar. 1905. Books Penelope Engel, Katherine Frederic, and the Ontario History Committee, *The Ontario* (Washington, D.C.: The Ontario, 1983). Periodicals "Apt. Agrees to Racial Pact," WP, 12 Apr. 1969; "Apt. House Overlooking Zoo," WT, 18 Feb. 1906; Kitty Chism, "The Grand Old Ontario," WP, 25 May 1983, p. DC7; Art Harris, "The Ontario," WP, 8 July 1979; Thomas W. Lippman, "Cooperative Sued to Halt Race Policy," WP, 18 Jan.

The vestibule of the Cordova includes two ranges of brass mailboxes as well as an unusual vaulted and coffered ceiling.

Top: This unusual dining room cabinet at the Westmoreland was designed to camouflage two projecting supporting steel beams. *Bottom:* Detail of the classical cornice at the Westmoreland, rarely noticed by sidewalk pedestrians six floors below.

1969, p. E1; "The Ontario," AA, 22 Dec. 1909; "Ontario Apt. Company," ES, 22 Nov. 1902, pt. 2, p. 25; Alice L. Powers, "Gracious Living at the Ontario," WP, 10 Nov. 1983; REG, 8 Mar. 1902, pt. 2, p. 17; REG, 15 Nov. 1902, pt. 2, p. 24; REG, 22 Nov. 1902, pt. 2, p. 25.

17. BACHELOR FLATS.
Manuscripts Alley; Edward W. Donn, Jr., "Architectural Reminiscences," Nov. 1948, pp. 1–25 (AIA Library); Reed M. Fawell, III, "Bachelor Apt. House," NR, 15 Apr. 1977, pp. 1–10. Pamphlets *The Bachelor* (Washington, D.C.: Geo. E. Howard Press, 1905); *Catalogue, Annual Exhibit of the Washington Architectural Club, 1904, Corcoran Gallery* (Washington, D.C.: 1904); Emily Hotaling Eig and Gray Bryan III, *Waddy Wood in Kalorama: A Walking Tour* (Washington, D.C.: Preservation Press, 1975). Periodicals

"Apt. Acquired by Evans Estate," ES, 6 Mar. 1915, pt. 2, p. 2; "Bachelor Apt. House Sold," ES, 4 Feb. 1922, pt. 3, p. 1; "The Benedick" (advertisement), ES, 30 Dec. 1905, pt. 2, p. 4; Sarah Booth Conroy, "Stamped with Waddy Wood Architectural Personality," WP, 6 July 1975, p. F1; "Home for Bachelors," ES, 13 Mar. 1915, pt. 2, p. 2; REG, 25 Feb. 1905, pt. 2, p. 16; Leila Mecklin, "The Work of Wood, Donn & Deming, Washington, D.C.," AR, Apr. 1906, pp. 245–58.

18. CORDOVA.
Manuscripts BP 2656, 6 June 1905, lot 35, sq. 109; BP 4903, 27 May 1915; BP 2707, 4 Dec. 1916, lot 48, sq. 109. Pamphlets Emily Hotaling Eig and Gray Bryan III, *Waddy Wood in Kalorama: A Walking Tour* (Washington, D.C.: Preservation Press, 1975). Periodicals "Cordova," AA, 22 Dec. 1909; "Cordova Annex Sold," ES, 22 Apr. 1916, pt. 2, p. 3; "The Cordova Apts.," AA, 22 Dec. 1909; Paul M. Herron, "President Madison Would Sleep Here," WP, 15 May 1953; Leila Mecklin, "The Work of Wood, Donn & Deming, Washington, D.C.," AR, Apr. 1906, pp. 245–58; "Northwest Apts. Sold," WP, 20 July 1952; "Out-of-Town Investor Buys Cordova Apts.," ES, 27 May 1916, pt. 2, p. 3; REG, 13 Jan. 1906, pt. 1, p. 8; REG, 22 Apr. 1916, pt. 2, p. 3; "Rehabilitation Committee for D.C. Housing Planned," WDN, 14 Mar. 1953.

19. WARDER.
Manuscripts BP 377, 8 Aug. 1905, lot 17–18, sq. 197; Alley; Elizabeth B. Applebaum, "The Early Tall Buildings of Washington, D.C.: 1880–1900," M.A. thesis, George Washington University, Dept. of American Civilization, 1983. Periodicals Wallace R. Brode, "ACS Addresses—From Pre-P.O. Box to the Present," *Chemical and Engineering News* (Oct. 1960), pp. 114–20 and 130; "Old Plush Apt. To Be Razed for Office," ES, 28 July 1957; REG, 16 Mar. 1901, pt. 2, p. 17; REG, 3 June 1905, pt. 2, p. 6; REG, 22 July 1905, pt. 2, p. 1.

20. FLORENCE COURT.
Manuscripts BP 1796, 20 Mar. 1905, lots 297 and 844, sq. 2528. Periodicals "Apt. Bldg. Sold," ES, 3 June 1961; "Bernstein Undaunted by Conversion Ban," WP, 8 Nov. 1974; "Condominiums Selling Fast in City Despite High Prices," ES, 18 Aug. 1978; John B. Willmann, "California House Owner Keeps Rentals with Condos," WP, 19 Aug. 1978, p. D8.

21. WESTMORELAND.
Manuscripts BP 2466, 15 May 1905, lot 179, sq. 2530; Alley; letter, Mrs. Stephen M. Conger, Lovettsville, Virginia, to the author, 13 Jan. 1986, pp. 1–6 (quote); Robert W. Kilpatrick, "Notes on the History of the Westmoreland," 9 Oct. 1984, pp. 1–28; letters, Robert W. Kilpatrick, Washington, to the author, 28 June 1980 and 1 July 1980. Periodicals "Apt. Rezoning Bid Denied," WP, 12 July 1955; "Apts. Bought by Syndicate Here," ES, 15 Feb. 1930, p. B1; Lysbeth Bledsoe, "They Prefer Posies to Progress," WDN, 10 June 1961; "15 Westmoreland Tenants Face

Detail of the elaborate marble and plaster lobby in the Wyoming.

Eviction Next Week," ES, 29 Jan. 1949; Richard J. Maloy, "Blocked View Creates Bitter Apt. Row," WP, 21 June 1955; "Ouster of Westmoreland Tenants by Co-op Upheld," ES, 20 May 1949; REG, 15 July 1905, pt. 2, p. 7; "Two Apts. Sold," ES, 22 May 1924, p. 4.

22. WYOMING.
Manuscripts BP 1672, 3 Mar. 1905, lot 26, sq. 2535; BP 3303, 9 Mar. 1909; BP 3632, 20 Feb. 1911; Alley; letter, John L. Barr, Jr., Washington, to the author, 27 Feb. 1980; letter, Robert W. Kilpatrick, Washington, to the author, 26 Feb. 1980; letter, Benjamin S. Simmons, Jr., Sarasota, Florida, to Emily Eig, Washington, 22 Feb. 1980; letter, William L. Simmons, Deltona, Florida, to Emily Eig, Washington, Jan. 1980; *Wyoming Apts.*, D.C. Landmark Application and Staff Report, Joint Committee on Landmarks of the National Capital, case 80–81, 10 July 1980. Books and pamphlets Dorothy Brandon, *Mamie Doud Eisenhower: A Portrait of a First Lady* (New York: Charles Scribner's Sons, 1954); Kenneth S. Davis, *Soldier of Democracy: A Biography of Dwight Eisenhower* (Garden City, N.Y.: Doubleday, Doran and Co., 1945) (quote, p. 221); *The Wyoming* (Washington, D.C.: Swartzell, Rhemm and Hensey Co., 1906); *The Wyoming* (Washington, D.C.: Wyoming Associates, 1983). Periodicals "Addition Planned to the Wyoming," ES, 10 June 1922, p. 14; Hank Burchard, "Presidents in Residence," WP, *Weekend* mag., 7 Mar. 1986, pp. 4–5 and 7; "John L. Barr, 82, Builder in District," WP, 27 Nov. 1969; "B.S. Simmons Dies after Operation," ES, 9 Sept. 1931; "B.S. Simmons Dies, Eminent Architect," WP, 9 Sept. 1931; "His Work Excellent," ES, 10 Dec. 1902; Betty James, "Residents Oppose Hilton Expansion on Columbia Road," WS, 5 Aug. 1979; Mary Ann Kuhn, "'Nuts!' Is Again the Reply to Surrender," ES, 28 Apr. 1974, p. B1; Ann Mariano, "'Wyoming' Connected to Condo,"

WP, 5 Feb. 1983; Joe Pichirallo, "Gas Leak Fuels Blast at Elegant Old Apts.," WP, 24 Mar. 1983; "Real Estate Dealer Adjudged Bankrupt," ES, 28 Nov. 1928, p. 17; REG, 11 Feb. 1905, pt. 2, p. 16; Wolf Von Eckardt, "Ungrand Hotel," WP, 2 Feb. 1980.

23. WENDELL MANSIONS.
Manuscripts BP 1759, 2 Jan. 1906, lot 14, sq. 2517; Deborah Anne Fulton, "Classical Imagery in Baltimore 1900–1925: The 1909 City Plan of Carrere, Brunner and Olmsted, Jr., and the Apt. Houses of Edward Hughes Glidden (1873–1924)," May 1985, pp. 1–88 (author's files). Books and pamphlets Edward Hughes Glidden, Jr., *Architecture: Selections from the Work of Edward Hughes Glidden, Jr., Baltimore* (Baltimore: Barton-Cotton, Inc., ca. 1925); Withey, p. 237. Periodicals "Edward H. Glidden," *Journal of the American Institute of Architects*, vol. 13, 1925, p. 39.

24. CHEVY CHASE.
Manuscripts BP 4730, 2 June 1909, lot 1, sq. 1863; Snowden Ashford, "Leon Emile Dessez, 1858–1918," ca. 1930, pp. 1–5 (author's files); Kevin J. Parker, "Leon Emile Dessez, Washington Architect: 1858–1918," 1979, pp. 1–25 (CHS). Books and pamphlets John Jay Daly, *Landmark in Chevy Chase: Story of the Most Blessed Sacrament, 1911–1961* (Washington, D.C.: Arrow Printing Service, 1961); *Origins, No. 1* (Washington, D.C.: Woodrow Wilson High School, 1974). Periodicals "Apt. House Sells for $95,000," ES, 21 Nov. 1921, pt. 2, p. 2; Edith Claude Jarvis, "Chevy Chase Looks Back," *Maryland*, summer 1970, pp. 28 and 30.

25. DRESDEN.
Manuscripts BP 3184, 20 Feb. 1909, lot 187, sq. 2277; George S. Carnett, "The Northumberland," NR, 5 Jan. 1979, pp. 1–10; letter, Helen J. Sioussat, Washington, to the author, 28 Jan. 1980. Periodicals "Apt. House Sold," ES, 25 July 1910, p. 2; "To Build Sixty-Nine Homes," ES, 20 Oct. 1909, sect. 1, p. 2; "Dowager Units Go Condo," WDN, 18 Jan. 1974, p. E10; Maureen Dowd, "Julia Cantacuzene, 99, Dies; U.S. Grant's Granddaughter," WS, 7 Oct. 1975, p. B5; "Dresden Apt.: Week's Largest Deal," ES, 28 Oct. 1916, pt. 2, p. 2; "The Present Situation in Washington," AH, Feb. 1911, pp. 22–26.

26. DUMBARTON COURT.
Manuscripts BP 1282, 14 Oct. 1909, lot 819, sq. 1282; letter, Mrs. Katharine Brown Ivison, Chevy Chase, Maryland, to Mrs. T. C. Alford, research assistant, Washington, 8 Oct. 1980 (quote). Books *Illustrated Washington: Our Capital* (New York: American Publishing and Engraving Co., 1890); "George S. Cooper," in Slauson, pp. 307–8. Periodicals "Decatur Apt. Reported to be Sold," ES, 26 Feb. 1916, pt. 2, p. 2; "G.S. Cooper, Retired Architect, Is Dead," ES, 13 Mar. 1929; "In the Midst of Lawns," ES, 9 Oct. 1909, p. 8; REG, 22 Mar. 1902, pt. 2, p. 17; REG, 25 Mar. 1905, pt. 2, p. 9.

27. 1509 16TH STREET, N.W.
Manuscripts BP 3364, 17 Mar. 1909, lot 98, sq. 194. Pamphlets

1509 Sixteenth Street, Northwest (Washington, D.C.: J.N.C. Enterprises, Inc. and Success Trust Corp., 1982). Periodicals "1509 16th St., N.W.," AA, 29 Nov. 1911; "16th Street Apt.," ES, 23 May 1909, pt. 1, p. 13.

28. NORTHUMBERLAND.
Manuscripts BP 4144, 4 May 1909, lot 60, sq. 189; George S. Carnett, "The History of the Northumberland Apt. Bldg.," Jan. 1978, pp. 1–16; letter, J. A. Moore, Edenton, N.C., to Edmund J. Flynn, Washington, 11 July 1944; "The Northumberland Apts.," NR, 5 Jan. 1979. Books *The New Washington* (Washington, D.C.: Chamber of Commerce, 1913), p. 24. Periodicals Russell T. Adams, "The Northumberland," *Condo News*, 24 Sept. 1982, vol. 1, no. 2, p. 4; "Apt. Bldg. Exchanged for Hotel," ES, 23 June 1917; "Buys the Northumberland," ES, 17 Mar. 1914, pt. 1, p. 2; Dennis Collins, "Northumberland: Economy and History," WP, 15 Feb. 1976, p. H25; Blair Gately, "The Push to Renew at 16th and U," WP, 12 Apr. 1986, p. F10; Ron Harris, "Beaux Arts Style Concrete 'Marble' Again Available," WP, 30 Oct. 1982; William Hogan, "The First Tycoon," RM, May–June 1981, pp. 60–65; "Kehoe Acquires Store," ES, 25 Sept. 1915, pt. 2, p. 2; "Lifelong Resident of District, 87," WP, 9 Apr. 1981; "May Build Apt.," ES, 20 Feb. 1915, pt. 2, p. 2; "The Northumberland" (advertisement), ES, 19 Jan. 1921, pt. 2, p. 2; Tom Precious, "Hope Kindled at 14th and U," WP, 12 Apr. 1986, p. F1; "The Present Situation in Washington," AH, Feb. 1911, pp. 22–26; "Realty Deal Involves Hotel and Apt.," ES, 18 Sept. 1915, pt. 2, p. 2; "Sale Involves $750,000," ES, 22 Aug. 1913, p. 5; "Sold to Co-operative Owners," ES, 16 Oct. 1920, pt. 2, p. 2; Walter Taylor, "Kissinger Circle in Rights Case," ES, 28 Sept. 1972.

29. 2852 ONTARIO ROAD, N.W.
Manuscripts BP 4037, 27 Apr. 1909, lot 829, sq. 2583. Periodicals Earl Byrd, "How the Jubilee Community Built a New Environment Here," ES, 9 Oct. 1977; "On Co-operative Plan," ES, 16 Aug. 1909, p. 22 (quote).

30. WOODWARD.
Manuscripts BP 5099, 29 June 1909, lot 811, sq. 2541; letter, David P. Bindeman, Washington, to Constance Minkin, Arlington, Va., research assistant, 6 July 1982. Books and pamphlets *Apartment Houses of the Metropolis* (New York: G. C. Hesselgren Pub. Co., 1908), pp. 11–15; Withey, p. 613; *The Woodward Apartments* (Washington, D.C.: F. H. Smith Co., 1910), pp. 1–11; *The Woodward Apartments* (Washington, D.C.: Landmark Realty, 1971), pp. 1–4. Periodicals "Architectural Criticism," AM, 15 Mar. 1910, vol. 21, no. 3, p. 33 and plate 28; "New Apt. House," ES, 30 June 1909, p. 22; "New York Architectural Terra Cotta Company" (advertisement), AM, Index for 1912, p. 17; "Numbers Work for Rehabilitated Apts.," *NAHB Journal–Scope* (National Association of Home Builders), vol. 4, no. 14, 7 Apr. 1975, pp. 19–20; "Ornate Face," WP, 6 June 1970; "Renovating Older Units for Profit," *Realtor*, vol. 39, no. 2, Feb. 1971, pp. 15 and 48; "Sale of Apt. House," ES, 19 Nov. 1909, p. 2; John B. Williams, "It's

Happening in Real Estate," WP, 13 Dec. 1969; "Woodward Apts.," AA, vol. C, no. 1875, 29 Nov. 1911; "Woodward Apts. Renovated," ES, 17 July 1980.

31. WINDSOR LODGE.
Manuscripts BP 4586, 21 Feb. 1910, lot 815, sq. 2527; BP 3687 1/2, 23 Feb. 1911, lot 814, sq. 2527; letter, Leo Simmons to Sen. William E. Borah, Washington, Sept. 1920, Borah Papers, MSS Division, Library of Congress (quote); "William Edgar Borah Apt., No. 21, Windsor Lodge," NR, Jan. 1976, pp. 1–12.

32. ST. REGIS.
Manuscripts BP 4701, 8 Apr. 1912, lot 236, sq. 2528.

33. AVONDALE.
Manuscripts BP 5080, 23 Apr. 1913, lot 107, sq. 157. Periodicals "Avondale Apt. Figures in Exchange," ES, 16 Mar. 1914, p. 8; "Avondale Apts." (advertisement), ES, 24 July 1920, pt. 2, p. 2; "Avondale Apts." (advertisement), ES, 9 Oct. 1920, pt. 2, p. 6; Kenneth Bredemeier, "D.C. Zoning Panel Approves Brookings Institution Plan," WP, 9 Apr. 1985, p. B1; "Houses for Sale," ES, 16 Oct. 1920, pt. 2, p. 6; Robert H. Melton, "Brookings' Plan for P Street Site Stirs Opposition," WP, 1 Dec. 1982; Eric Pianin, "Way Cleared for Dupont Circle ANC Recall Vote," WP, 4 Aug. 1983; Tom Vesey, "Panel Approves Proposal For Brookings Complex, But Orders Modifications," WP, 18 Oct. 1983; "Zoning Commission Acts on Brookings; Citizen Groups Hail Decision," [Washington] *InTowner*, Nov. 1983, p. 1.

34. ALTAMONT.
Manuscripts BP 1325, 18 Sept. 1915, lot 2, sq. 2538; Kathleen Wood, "Arthur B. Heaton," pp. 1–13, Dec. 1985. Pamphlets

The small staircase in the lobby of the Windsor Lodge features an elegant balustrade and a stained-glass window.

The revolving door in the lobby of 2029 Connecticut Avenue, once common in first-class Washington apartment houses before World War I, is one of only two surviving examples.

The mail chute and letter box in the lobby of 2029 Connecticut Avenue.

George Truesdell, *The Altamont* (Washington, D.C.: Byron S. Adams, 1916), pp. 1–18. Periodicals "The Altamont" (advertisement), ES, 14 Apr. 1917, ES, pt. 2, p. 2; "Apt. House Sold in Big Deal," ES, 25 Oct. 1919, pt. 2, p. 2; "Arthur B. Heaton Dies; Designed Bldgs. in Capital 53 Years," ES, 7 Dec. 1951; "Arthur Berthrong Heaton," *Cosmos Club Bulletin*, vol. 6, no. 7, May 1953; "An Attractive Design for Apt. House," ES, 7 May 1915, p. 5; Sarah Booth Conroy, "The Affordable Dream Apt.," WP, 10 Aug. 1980, p. E1; "D.C. Suit Challenges New Rent Law and Cooperative Curbs," ES, 22 June 1949; "Heaton Is Honored by Architects Institute," ES, 28 June 1942, p. A10; "Houses of Arthur B. Heaton," AABN, 22 Nov. 1911; "How Truesdell Apt. Will Look When Completed," ES, 18 Mar. 1916, pt. 2, p. 2; Robert J. Lewis, "Altamont Units Put on Sale as 'Cooperatives,' " ES, 7 Jan. 1949; REG, 23 Mar. 1901, p. 17.

35. McCORMICK.

Manuscripts BP 1987, 25 Oct. 1915, lot 800, sq. 157; Janet L. Davis, "J. H. de Sibour: Five Bldgs. on Massachusetts Avenue, Washington, D.C.," M.A. thesis, University of Virginia, School of Architectural History, 1980, pp. 1–78. Books and pamphlets Charles H. Atherton, Donald B. Myer, Jeffrey R. Carson, Lynda L. Smith, and J. L. Sibley Jennings, Jr., Commission of Fine Arts, *Massachusetts Avenue Architecture, Vol. I: Northwest Washington, District of Columbia* (Washington, D.C.: GPO, 1973); David Alan Brown, *Raphael and America* (Washington, D.C.: National Gallery of Art, 1983); David N. Yerkes and Associates—Nicholas A. Pappas, Partner in Charge, *Survey and Program, The New Headquarters of the National Trust for Historic Preservation* (Washington,

D.C., 1977), pp. 1–84; S. N. Behrman, *Duveen* (New York: Random House, 1951). Periodicals "AIA Makes Temporary Bed in a Smashing Old Mansion," WP, 13 Feb. 1971; Gale Shipman Alder, "1785: Architect and Imagemaker Jules Henri de Sibour," HP, July–Aug. 1979, pp. 12–14; "Apt. House at 1785 Massachusetts Avenue, Washington, D.C.," AR, Jan.–June, 1979, pp. 2–7; "Building Sold," ES, 20 May 1950; Sarah Booth Conroy, "AIA Honors the Rebuilders of History," WP, 21 Sept. 1980, p. E1; "Funeral Rites Today for Jules de Sibour," WP, 5 Nov. 1938; Evelyn Peyton Gordon, " 'Mellon Apt.' Apparently Vacated on White House Order," WDN, 28 Feb. 1941; Judith Helm Robinson, "1785: Where the National Gallery Began," HP, July–Aug., 1979, pp. 8–11; "Jules Henri de Sibour, Famous Architect, Succumbs to Illness," ES, 4 Nov. 1938; "Sale of a Residence," ES, 10 Sept. 1906, p. 16; "Soon to Begin Construction of McCormick Apt.," ES, 25 Sept. 1915, pt. 2, p. 2; "Start $1,600,000 Apt. Hotel at 15th and L Streets," ES, 9 July 1921, pt. 2, p. 1; "Trust to Restore Mellon Apts.," ES, 21 Jan. 1977; Anne Woodward, "1785: a Landmark for the National Trust," HP, July–Aug., 1979, pp. 2–7.

36. 2029 CONNECTICUT AVENUE, N.W.

Manuscripts BP 38, 24 June 1915, lot 272, sq. 2536; "Alwyn Court Apts., 180 West 58th Street, N.Y., N.Y.," NR, 26 Dec. 1979; letter, Walter Angst, Silver Spring, Maryland, to the author, 12 July 1981. Books and pamphlets Desmond Seward, *Prince of the Renaissance: The Life of Francois I* (London: Constable, 1973); Bates Warren, *2029 Connecticut Avenue: A Residence for Particular People* (Washington, D.C.: 1916), pp. 1–14. Periodicals "Alwyn

Court," AM, Feb. 1910, plates xvi and xvii; Hank Burchard, "Presidents in Residence," WP, *Weekend* mag., 7 Mar. 1986, pp. 4–5 and 7; "Justice Stone's Mansion is Sold," ES, 23 Feb. 1950, p. B1; John Mintz and Joe Brown, "McGovern's NW Condo Gutted, Son Slightly Hurt," WP, 17 May 1983; "Modern Solutions of Modern Problems" (advertisement), PP, vol. 2, no. 1, 1921, p. 45; "New Apt. at Connecticut and Wyoming Avenues to Be Ready Sept. 1," ES, 20 May 1916, pt. 2, p. 4; "Plans Big Apt.," ES, 2 Jan. 1915, p. 4; "Remarkable Conversion, Both Inside and Out," ES, 9 Sept. 1977.

37. 1870 WYOMING AVENUE, N.W.
Manuscripts BP 4127, 30 Mar. 1916, lot 14, sq. 2554. Periodicals "Apt. for John L. Barr," ES, 11 Mar. 1916, pt. 2, p. 2; "Plans for Apts.," ES, 4 Mar. 1916, pt. 2, p. 1.

38. MERIDIAN MANSIONS.
Manuscripts BP 388, 21 July 1916, lot 99, sq. 2571; Helen Dillon, "Meridian Hill Park," NR, 25 Oct. 1974, pp. 1–8; Lucinda P. Janke, "History of 2400 Sixteenth Street, N.W.," 1979, pp. 1–3. Books and pamphlets *The Envoy, 1918–1981* (Washington, D.C.: David Clark and Associates, 1981), pp. 1–12; Frances Parkinson Keyes, *All Flags Flying* (New York: McGraw-Hill, 1972), pp. 145–49 (quote); Sue A. Kohler and Jeffrey R. Carson, Commission of Fine Arts, *Sixteenth Street Architecture* (Washington, D.C.: GPO, 1978), vol. 1. Periodicals "Acquires Apt. Site on Sixteenth Street," ES, 15 May 1915, pt. 2, p. 2; Norman Beebe, "Going Once . . . Gone for $250,000," WDN, 14 Mar. 1967; Bill Black, "Preservation Tax Aid Saves Some Condos," WP, 23 Apr. 1983; LaBarbara Bowman, "Empty Apts.," WP, 1 June 1977; Jeff Burbank, "Venerable 'Envoy' Is Home at Last," WP, 28 Mar. 1985; "Envoy Getting Specialty Shops," WDN, 23 Apr. 1965; "Envoy Towers," WDN, 24 July 1964; "Envoy Towers Adds Spark to 16th St.," WP, 21 Aug. 1965; "$4.6 Million Mortgage Foreclosed, Envoy Towers to Be Auctioned," WP, 3 Mar. 1967; "Hotel Penthouse Dispute Carried to Congress," ES, 11 Nov. 1945; "Hotel 2400 Penthouse Occupancy Disapproved," ES, 13 June 1951, p. A3; "Hotel 2400 Sold for $1,500,000," 3 June 1945, p. B10; "House for Rent," WP, 12 Dec. 1945; Robert G. Kaiser, "Building Leased for Riot Homeless," WP, 30 Apr. 1968; "Large Orders Set for Carpets for Apts.," WP, 4 Oct. 1966; "Lofty Penthouse Rental Opposed by Commissioners," WP, 13 June 1951; "Meridian Mansions on Sale at Auction," ES, 7 Oct. 1924, p. 1; "Million-Dollar Hotel for Sixteenth Street," ES, 20 July 1916, p. 22; "Old Hotel Finds No Takers," WP, 14 Mar. 1967; Drew Pearson, "FHA Takes 2d Look at Powell Loan," WP, 14 Sept. 1962; Paul A. Schuette, "Neighbors Oppose Rep. Powell's Plan for Hotel 2400," WP, 20 Sept. 1962; "Shops to Ring Apt. Lobby," WP, 2 Jan. 1965; "Sixteenth Street Apt. Modernized," ES, 3 Oct. 1936; "16th Street Apt. Rent Returns Low by Comparison," ES, 9 Oct. 1929, p. 2; "Truman Signs Bill Allowing Hotel 2400 to Use Penthouse," ES, 16 May 1952; "Work on New Seven-Story Apt. Bldg. Begun," ES, 22 July 1916, pt. 2, p. 2.

39. WHITELAW.
Manuscripts BP 556, 5 July 1918, lot 10, sq. 275; BP 6879, 3 Dec. 1920, lots 9, 10, 11, sq. 275; Harrison M. Ethridge, "Architects of the Secret City: The Black Architects of Washington, D.C., 1902–1979," Ph.D. dissertation, Catholic University, Dept. of History, Washington, 1979, pp. 1–154; letter, Betty Bird, Washington, to the author, 2 Nov. 1983; "Whitelaw Apt. Hotel," NR, no. HABS-DC-363, 1979, pp. 1–10; "Whitelaw Apt. Hotel," Application for Historic Preservation Certification, D.C. Historic Preservation Office. Books William Henry Jones, *The Housing of Negroes in Washington, D.C.* (Washington, D.C.: Howard University Press, 1929) (quote); Jones, *Recreation and Amusement among Negroes in Washington, D.C.* (Washington, D.C.: Howard University Press, 1927). Pamphlets *The Whitelaw Apartment House Company* (Washington, D.C.: n.p., 1918), pp. 1–2. Periodicals "Building to Cost $125,000," ES, 6 Aug. 1918, p. 7; Dorothy Gilliam, "Landmark," WP, 12 Sept. 1983; "Hotel for Colored People Completed," ES, 22 Nov. 1919, pt. 2, p. 2; "Let Us Help Him over the Top," WB, 5 Oct. 1918; "The New Industrial Savings Bank Building," WB, 30 June 1917; "2 Firefighters Hurt in Blaze in Boarded Up Hotel in N.W.," WP, 12 Dec. 1981, p. B5; "What the Educated Colored People of Washington Have Done," WB, 13 Dec. 1919; "Whitelaw Hotel," WB, 29 Nov. 1919; "Whitelaw Hotel," WB, 13 Dec. 1919; "The Whitelaw Hotel" (advertisement), WB, 17 Jan. 1920.

40. ALBEMARLE.
Manuscripts BP 987, 31 Dec. 1900, lot 20, sq. 152; Alley. Periodicals REG, 12 Jan. 1901, p. 17.

41. IOWA.
Manuscripts BP 1124, 24 Jan. 1900, lot 25, sq. 280. Periodicals Sarah Booth Conroy, "The Rescued and the Rescuers," WP, 15 Nov. 1981, p. E1; "Iowa Apts. Sold," ES, 17 Mar. 1951; "Iowa Restoration Under Way," WS, 6 Oct. 1978, p. F1; Beverly A. Reece, "A Beaux Arts Rehabilitation," WP, 10 June 1968; John B. Williams, "Iowa Building, 77, Taking in New Life," WP, 9 Dec. 1978, p. E1.

42. MARLBOROUGH.
Manuscripts BP 1963, 17 June 1901, lot 52, sq. 126; Alley. Pamphlets *Catalogue, Annual Exhibit of the Washington Architectural Club, Held at the Corcoran Gallery of Art, MCMIII* (Washington, D.C.: 1903).

43. FARRAGUT.
Manuscripts BP 1931, 12 June 1901, lot 51, sq. 126. Periodicals "Farragut Apts. To Be Remodeled," ES, 1 July 1922, p. 14.

44. SHERMAN.
Manuscripts BP 1338, 28 May 1901, lot 80, sq. 214. Periodicals William A. Miller, "Rebuilding Properties at 15th and L Pushed," ES, 28 Oct. 1958.

45. CECIL.
Manuscripts BP 1241, 28 Jan. 1903, lot 31 (800), sq. 198.

Many of Washington's first-class pre–World War I apartment houses, such as the Cecil, have been demolished for commercial development.

Oriel window at the Portsmouth.

Adamesque style lobby of the Somerset House on 16th Street.

46. PLYMOUTH.
Manuscripts BP 1870, 8 June 1903, lot 45, sq. 314; "The Plymouth," NR, 11 May 1983, pp. 1–15. Periodicals Courtland Milloy, "Heroin: 'Murder One' for Sale," WP, 10 Aug. 1981.

47. ROCHAMBEAU.
Manuscripts BP 2034, 19 June 1903, lot 38, sq. 186; RP B88628, 27 June 1962; Alley.

48. WOODLEY.
Manuscripts BP 1411, 12 Feb. 1903, lot 161, sq. 2550; Alley.

49. CHAMPLAIN.
Manuscripts BP 2552, 25 May 1905, lot 14, sq. 218.

50. PORTSMOUTH.
Manuscripts BP 1550, 6 Feb. 1905, lot 38, sq. 154. Periodicals "Dupont Condo," WP, 25 Apr. 1981; "New Hampshire Avenue Apt. House," ES, 9 Apr. 1904, pt. 2, p. 14; "Seven Stories High," ES, 7 Jan. 1905, pt. 2, p. 1.

51. TORONTO.
Manuscripts BP 3123, 13 Apr. 1908, lot 99, sq. 96. Periodicals "Apt. Suit Filed by Woman," ES, 11 Sept. 1927, p. 4; "Near Dupont Circle," ES, 13 Mar. 1908, p. 2; "Owner Asks Injunction," ES, 28 June 1929, p. 17; "Starts to Rebuild," ES, 20 June 1908, p. 5; "Tenant Stock Sale Stopped by Court," ES, 13 July 1929, p. 13; "Toronto Apts. Sold," ES, 4 Sept. 1920, pt. 2, p. 1; "Toronto Changes Hands," ES, 24 Apr. 1915, pt. 2, p. 2.

52. NETHERLANDS.
Manuscripts BP 4268, 11 May 1909, lot 61, sq. 2551. Periodicals Thomas W. Lippman, "District Suit Charges Apt. Bias," WP, 18 Sept. 1969, p. A28.

53. STAFFORD.
Manuscripts BP 2173, 31 Oct. 1910, lot 382, sq. 2583. Periodicals "Tenants Purchase Apts.," ES, 5 Mar. 1932.

54. COVINGTON.
Manuscripts BP 5–64, 29 May 1911, lot 806, sq. 2551; Bill Black, "Covington Apt. Bldg.," Apr. 1981, pp. 1–4. Periodicals Bill Black, "Low-Yield Co-ops Restore Shelter's Priority," WS, 10 Apr. 1981, p. D1; Black, "Perspectives: Digging into Your House's History," WP, 6 July 1982, p. B5; Black, "Report of the General Meeting," [Washington] Communicator, 14 Oct. 1980; Black, "$3,000 Efficiencies in Adams Morgan Prove Hard to Sell," WS, 3 Oct. 1980.

55. BILTMORE.
Manuscripts BP 4834, 11 Apr. 1913, lot 273, sq. 2545. Periodicals "Attractive Apt. Nearing Completion," ES, 5 July 1913, pt. 2, p. 3; "Court Ruling Defines Rights of Tradesmen," ES, 29 Dec. 1913, p. 12; "Reported to Have Been Sold," ES, 28 Aug. 1915, pt. 2, p. 2.

56. 2001 16TH STREET, N.W.
Manuscripts BP 3952, 22 Mar. 1916, lot 4, sq. 188.

57. 1868 COLUMBIA ROAD, N.W.
Manuscripts BP 3485, 17 Feb. 1916, lot 812 (61), sq. 2552.

58. SOMERSET HOUSE.
Manuscripts BP 2587, 24 Nov. 1916, lot 103, sq. 191. Books Biographical Directory of the American Congress, 1774–1971 (Washington, D.C.: GPO, 1971). Periodicals "Newest Apt. Is Somerset House," ES, 11 Aug. 1917, pt. 2, p. 2; "$1,000,000 Realty Exchanges Made Here," ES, 17 Nov. 1917, pt. 2, p. 2; "Somerset Apts. Sold," WP, 15 Apr. 1916.

59. 1424 16TH STREET, N.W.
Manuscripts BP 3689, 23 Feb. 1917, lots 100–112, sq. 181. Periodicals "Apts. for Rent—1424 Sixteenth Street" (advertisement), ES, 24 June 1922, p. 15.

60. NORTHBROOK COURTS.
Manuscripts BP 2965, 3 Jan. 1917, lot 752, sq. 2622; BP 3352, 30 Jan. 1917, lot 751, sq. 2622. Periodicals "Big Apts. for Upper 16th Street," ES, p. 5; "Northbrook Court," ES, 8 June 1979; "Northbrook Court II" (advertisement), WP, 11 July 1981, p. E22; "Northbrook Courts Bought for $725,000," ES, 29 Jan. 1920, pt. 1, p. 7; "Northbrook Courts Nearing Completion," ES, 11 Aug. 1917, pt. 2, p. 2.

CHAPTER 3

INTRODUCTION.

Congressional apartment house.
Periodicals "Apt. House City Is Planned," ES, 9 Nov. 1929, p. 17; "Apt. House for Congressmen," ES, 22 Jan. 1922, pt. 2, p. 2; "Congressman Norton against Congress Apt. Hotel," ES, 10 Dec. 1936, p. B1; "Erection of Apts. Here for Congress Members Asked," ES, 24 June 1935; "Sabath Charges 'Gouge' on Rent for Legislators," ES, 8 Jan. 1945, p. B1; "$6,000,000 Housing Project for Congressmen Proposed," ES, 16 Jan. 1937.

Connecticut Avenue apartment house corridor.
Manuscripts Mark Andrich, "Washington Apt. Houses on Connecticut Avenue, 1920–1940," George Washington University,

Even though the lobby and many of the original interior features of the Woodley were gutted in an insensitive renovation in the 1970s, the balustrade of the main staircase remains intact.

research paper, 1985, pp. 1–11. Periodicals Caryle Murphy, "Along the Road to a Good Life," WP, 24 Oct. 1983, p. D3; Don S. Warren, "Cites Transformation of Connecticut Avenue," ES, 21 Sept. 1929, p. 13.

Co-op apartment houses.
Periodicals "Apt.. Home Division Created," ES, 19 Feb. 1927, p. 22; "Apt. Houses Sold on Co-operative Plan," ES, 21 Jan. 1922, pt. 1, p. 13; "Apt. Sales Rules Are Given," ES, 20 Aug. 1927, p. 17 (quote); "Cafritz Enters New Field," WT, 21 July 1926; Robert J. Cottrell, "Bldg. Here Leaps Ahead: $1,000,000 Past 1925 Mark," ES, 30 Oct. 1926, p. 17; "Five Rooms at $35 a Month Seen as Possibility Here," ES, 9 Oct. 1926, p. 13; Edmund J. Flynn, "Apt. Ownership by Tenants Grows," WT, 7 Nov. 1925; Flynn, "Co-operative Apt. Less Expense Than House," WH, 8 Nov. 1925; Flynn, "Co-operative Apt. Plan Declared Sound in Principle," ES, 18 Sept. 1926, p. 17; Flynn, "Co-operative Apt. Plan Is Successful in Washington," ES, 11 Sept. 1926; Flynn, "Expert Limns Development of Co-operative Apt.," WH, 9 Jan. 1927; Flynn, "Says Co-operative Apts. Pay," ES, 25 Sept. 1926, p. 25; Hulst Glenn, Jr., "Plan in Vogue for Six Years," WH, 26 July 1925; "Group Ownership of Apts.," AA, vol. 118, July–Dec. 1920, p. 378–79; "Joint Apts. Cost Much Money," ES, 24 Aug. 1929, p. 19; "New Apts. Find Ready Sale to Tenants," ES, 5 Sept. 1925, p. 16; "Own Your Own Home," ES, 6 Nov. 1920, pt. 2, p. 5; "Parkwood Sold," ES, 28 Aug. 1920, pt. 2, p. 1; "Traces Co-operative Apt. Growth," ES, 12 Feb. 1927, p. 18; "Two District Apts. To Be Co-operatively Owned," ES, 31 July 1920, p. 1; R. Bates Warren, "Apt. Home Owning Idea Is Old," ES, 30 Oct. 1926, p. 23; Warren, "Says Co-operative Apts. Save," ES, 2 Oct. 1926, p. 23; "Wardman Co. Reports Big Apt. Demand," 6 Sept. 1925; Louis L. Young, "Great Opportunity Is Seen for Co-operative Apt.," ES, 3 July 1926, p. 14.

Co-operative Apartment House Bureau.
Periodicals "Adopt Standards For Co-operatives," ES, 22 Dec. 1928, p. 16; "Apt. Expert Board Is Planned," ES, 28 Apr. 1928, p. 17; "Apt. Home Division Created," ES, 19 Feb. 1927, p. 22; "Apt. House Tour To Be Made," ES, 13 Oct. 1928, p. 20; "Apt. Sales Rules Are Given," ES, 20 Aug. 1927, p. 17; "Bungalow Sites on Apt. Tops Held as Typical of 'Castles in Air'," ES, 26 Dec. 1928, p. 13; "Bureau Provides Apt. Check," ES, 4 Dec. 1928, p. 5; "District Realtors in Leading Roles," ES, 27 Aug. 1927, p. 17; "Division Will Discuss Apt. Economics," ES, 12 Nov. 1927, p. 19; "50 Co-operative Apt. Experts to Convene Monday," ES, 1 Dec. 1928, p. 17; "Local Apts. Studied by Group," ES, 3 Dec. 1928, p. 28; "Move to Protect Investors in Co-operative Ownership," ES, 31 Mar. 1928, p. 17; "National Real Estate Body Sets Up Bureau to Make Technical Study of Group Projects," ES, 8 Dec. 1928, p. 15; "New Safeguard Is Placed on Co-operative Buying," ES, 17 Aug. 1929, p. 15; "Protection Offered Buyer of Co-operative Apt.," ES, 8 Dec. 1928, p. 15;

"Realtors of U.S. Plan Bureau to Study Apt. Sales," ES, 26 Nov. 1927, p. 17; R. Bates Warren, "Co-operative Men Meet in New York," ES, 11 Dec. 1926, p. 15; Warren, "Says Co-operative Apts. Save," ES, 2 Oct. 1926, p. 17.

Developers of apartment houses.
Manuscripts Adam Scher, "Harry Wardman and the Washington Construction Boom, 1925–1928," George Washington University, research paper, 1982, pp. 1–15 (author's files). Periodicals "Cafritz Enters New Field," WT, 21 July 1926; "Leaders in Apt. House Construction Industry," ES, 30 Aug. 1930; J. Y. Smith, "Gustave Ring, Noted Builder In Area, Dies," WP, 5 May 1983; "Wardman Co. Reports Big Apt. Demand," ES, 6 Sept. 1925.

Garden apartments.
Periodicals "Construction of First Unit of Petworth Gardens Begun," ES, 8 Oct. 1921, pt. 2, p. 1; "Giant Apt. Community Started Here," WDN, 11 May 1929.

Growth of apartment houses.
Periodicals "Apt. to Cost $5,000,000 Going Up Soon in N.W.," ES, 28 Sept. 1926, p. 1; "Apt. Dwelling Trend Continues in Full Swing," ES, 1 June 1929, p. 13; "Apts. Represent Gigantic Industry Here," ES, 30 Aug. 1930; "Apt. Sites Playing More Important Role," ES, 30 Aug. 1930; "Apt. Value Formulae Drawn," ES, 6 Sept. 1930; "Apts. Lead in Bldg. Work," ES, 10 Mar. 1928, p. 17; "Building Here Leaps Ahead, $1,000,000 Past 1925 Mark," ES, 30 Oct. 1926, p. 17; "Building Records Smashed by $15,000,000 during Year," ES, 2 Jan. 1926, p. 17; "Capital Advances in Architecture," ES, 30 Aug. 1930, p. C4; Harden Colfax, "Building Figures Show 'Cliff-dwelling' Tendency," ES, 20 Oct. 1929, pt. 2, p. 2; "Construction Volume in 1925 Surpasses All Precedents," ES, 16 Jan. 1925, p. 17; "Projected Club and Apt. Bldg.," ES, 31 Mar. 1928, p. 21; "Ratio of Apts. to Single Family Houses Shows Increase in Washington," ES, 22 Apr. 1927, p. 6; "Richards Reveals Apt. Data," ES, 13 Sept. 1930; "Tenants Benefit from Apt. Bldg. in D.C.," ES, 6 Sept. 1930; "Trend to Apt. Homes in District Growing Rapidly," ES, 4 June 1927, p. 16; Don S. Warren, "Apt. House Bldg. in District Shows Big Gain," ES, 24 Nov. 1928, p. 17; Warren, "Private Bldg. Work in D. C. Gains 27 Percent Over 1927," ES, 29 Dec. 1928, p. 15; "Washington Is Apt. City," ES, 14 Dec. 1929, p. 15.

Inflation.
Periodicals Willis Polk, "The Present Cost of Bldg.," AM, vol. 39, 1919, p. 28; Polk, "Pre-War Prices and Pre-War Wage Scales Are Out of the Question," AM, vol. 39, 1919, p. 304.

Moving day.
Periodicals "Apt. Dwellers in Annual Move Are Finding Slight Reductions in Rentals," ES, 11 Oct. 1927, p. 17; "Baltimore Wants Moving Curb Made," ES, 14 Sept. 1929, p. 28; "Moving Day Brings Shuffle Of Residents," ES, 1 Oct. 1940, p. B1; "Moving Day in Washington," ES, 30 Sept. 1936, p. 1; "Moving Vans Are Kept Busy in Washington," ES, 30 Sept. 1919, p. 21; "Moving Vans Fly Streets as Hundreds Change Homes," ES, 2 Oct. 1928, p. 17; "Realtors Take Steps to End Tenant's Annual Moving Day," ES, 24 Aug. 1929, p. R17; "Record Moving Day Keeps Transfer Men Busy," ES, 1 Oct. 1937; "Tenant Migration Is Started Today," ES, 30 Sept. 1932; "Vacancies Scarce, Moving Day Quiet," ES, 1 Oct. 1935.

Names of apartment houses.
Books Richard Kenin, *Return to Albion, Americans in England, 1760–1940* (New York: Holt, Rinehart, and Winston, 1979). Periodicals "Does the Name Influence Apts.' Popularity?," ES, 2 May 1914; James Waldo Fawcett, "Washington Apts. Bear Names That Reflect Romance," ES, 6 Apr. 1935.

Opposition to apartment houses.
Periodicals "Acquires Wardman Holding to Block Apt. House," ES, 9 Jan. 1915, p. 4; "Apts. Barred on Woodley Place," ES, 20 June 1924, p. 10; "Apt. House Exclusion Asked," ES, 19 June 1924, p. 2; "Apt. Zone Ruling Announced," ES, 21 Apr. 1925, p. 2; "Bill to Limit Height of Apt. House," ES, 5 Sept. 1919, p. 27; "Citizens Protest Apt. Site," ES, 6 Oct. 1931; "Citizens Renew Fight for Zoning," ES, 19 Apr. 1925, p. 23; "Curb on Apt. Bldgs. Favored in Residential Area," ES, 17 Mar. 1928, p. 20; " 'Esthetic Zoning' Asked by Citizens," ES, 16 Apr. 1925, p. 2; "Forbid Apts. in Large City Area," ES, 24 June 1924, p. 1; "Irving Street Owners Want Apt. Curb," ES, 31 Jan. 1927, p. 5; "Land Owner Seeks Zoning Injunction," ES, 13 May 1926, p. 50; "New Apts. Barred in 7 Areas," ES, 31 Oct. 1923, p. 2; "Suburban Citizens Oppose Apts.," ES, 27 Sept. 1923, p. 10; "Withdraws Senate Bill Fixing Building Height," ES, 16 Sept. 1919, p. 1; "Zoning Proposal Argued at Hearing," ES, 26 Oct. 1923, p. 12.

Parkway co-op collapse.
Periodicals "Apt. Probe Starts Tomorrow," ES, 17 Jan. 1929, p. 17; "D.C. Protection Held Minimum," ES, 19 Jan. 1929, p. 2; "18 Face Eviction From Apt.," ES, 3 Nov. 1928, p. 2; "Gilbert Pushes Parkway Probe," ES, 22 Jan. 1929; "Grand Jury to Get Apt. Deal," ES, 10 Apr. 1929, p. 17; "New Co-operative Apt. in N.W.," ES, 12 Nov. 1927, p. 18; "New Effort Made to Oust Tenants," ES, 21 Dec. 1928; "Parkway Apts. Summonses Are Issued," ES, 23 Jan. 1929, p. 4; "Parkway Failure Hit by Committee," ES, 26 Jan. 1929, p. 2; "Parkway Ouster Upheld by Aukam," 5 Jan. 1929; "Parkway Tenants Lose Court Fight," ES, 30 Jan. 1929, p. 17; "Parkway Tenants Quit Apts.," ES, 4 Feb. 1929, p. 17; "Price On Parkway Called Too High," ES, 24 Jan. 1929, p. 2; "Suit under Arrest By Illinois Police on Theft Charges," ES, 28 Feb. 1929, p. 17.

Suburban growth.
Books Gutheim. Periodicals Leonard Cox, "Suburban Home Demand Grows," ES, 30 Nov. 1929, p. 17.

Technological improvements.
Periodicals "Apts. Near Ultra-Modern Era," ES, 19 Oct. 1929, p.

17; "Modern Kitchen Is Held Big Aid to Housewives," ES, 17 Dec. 1927, p. 17; "Two Baths in Home Increase Sales Value," ES, 22 Oct. 1927, p. 18.

Zoning.

Manuscripts Mark Andrich, "The Impact of Zoning on Apt. House Development, Washington, D.C., 1920–1985," George Washington University, research paper, Feb. 1985, pp. 1–28. Books and pamphlets Steven J. Diner, *The Regulation of Housing in the District of Columbia, Studies in D.C. History and Public Policy, Paper No. 5* (Washington, D.C.: Univ. of D.C., 1983); Gutheim; S. G. Lindholm, *Experiences with Zoning in Washington, D.C., 1920–1934* (Washington, D.C.: D.C. Zoning Commission, 1935). Periodicals "Acquires Wardman Holding to Block Apt. Plans," ES, 9 Jan. 1915, p. 4; "Apt. Zone Ruling Announced," ES, 21 Apr. 1925, p. 2; "Apts. Barred on Woodley Road," ES, 20 June 1924, p. 10; "Bill to Limit Height of Apt. Argued," ES, 22 Sept. 1919, p. 14; "Bill to Limit Height of Apt. House," ES, 5 Sept. 1919, p. 27; David Braaten, "Churchmen See Crisis as Apts. Grow," ES, 10 Nov. 1965; "Citizens Renew Fight for Zoning," ES, 19 Apr. 1925, p. 23; "Curb on Apt. Bldgs. Favored in Residential Area," ES, 17 Mar. 1928, p. 20; Paul Delaney, "75 in NW Area Urge Denial of High-Rise Rezoning Bid," ES, 28 Mar. 1968; " 'Esthetic Zoning' Asked by Citizens," ES, 16 Apr. 1925, p. 2; "Forbid Apts. in Large City Area," ES, 24 June 1924, p. 1; "New Apts. Barred in 7 Areas," ES, 31 Oct. 1923, p. 2; "New Regulations for City Zoning Put Into Effect," ES, 30 Aug. 1920; Miriam Ottenberg, "Chevy Chase Center Is in the Middle of Real Estate Fight over Future of Upper Connecticut Ave.," ES, 30 Apr. 1952, p. B1; "Protests Height Limit for 16th St. Bldg.," ES, 6 Nov. 1919, p. 2; "Regulating Apt. Bldgs.," ES, 6 May 1905, pt. 2, p. 2; "Rezoning for Apt. Protested at Hearing," ES, 21 June 1955, p. A10; "Two Zoning Decisions Aid Apt. Growth," ES, 30 Aug. 1930, p. C1; Don S. Warren, "Concessions in Apts. Up for D.C. Hearing Mar. 27," ES, 16 Mar. 1929, p. 15; "Withdraws Senate Bill Fixing Bldg. Height," ES, 16 Sept. 1919, p. 1; "Would Limit Height of Apt. House," ES, 23 Oct. 1919, p. 9; "Zoners Reject Apt. Bid in NW," ES, 12 July 1955.

61. CHASTLETON.

Manuscripts BP 4930, 30 June 1919, lots 63–72, sq. 192; BP 2631, 23 Oct. 1919, lot 104, sq. 192; letter, James Durham, Norman Bernstein Management, Inc., Washington, to the author, 24 Aug. 1982; press release, IGC, Inc., St. Charles, Maryland, "Interstate General Corporation Raises $19 Million to Rehabilitate Historic Chastleton Apts. in D.C.," 2 Aug. 1985, pp. 1–7. Pamphlets *The Chastleton* (Washington, D.C.: F. H. Smith Co., 1919), pp. 1–8. Periodicals "Apt. Is Sold; Will Become Hotel," ES, 5 Mar. 1925, p. 12; Beth Bropsky, "Tenants Dismayed by Plan to Convert the Chastleton," WS, 5 Mar. 1979; "The Chastleton," ES, 5 Jan. 1958; "Chastleton Annex Building Starts," ES, 1 Nov. 1919, pt. 2, p. 2; "Chastleton Apts. Completed," ES, 28 Aug. 1920, pt. 2, p. 2; "Chastleton Apts. Renovated," ES, 11 Feb. 1966; "Chastleton Auctioned, Brings Only $2,453,750," ES, 26 Sept. 1922, p. 30; "Chastleton Corporation Sold," WP, 12 Mar. 1960; "Chastleton Deal Fair, Lake Avers," ES, 6 Sept. 1922, p. 1; "Chastleton Given New Look, Life," WP, 20 Feb. 1966; "Chastleton Rent Boost Asked; 3 Apts. Are Granted Increases," ES, 29 July 1943; "Chastleton Residents Told Navy Won't Take Home," ES, 20 Nov. 1943; Kitty Chism, "Chastleton Apts. Win Approval to Relocate Tenants," WP, 20 Oct. 1983; "Columbia Realty Trust Buys the Chastleton," WP, 16 Oct. 1964; "Elderly Bldgs. Find a Champion," ES, 11 Dec. 1964; "474-Room Apt.," ES, 14 June 1919, pt. 2, p. 1; "Judge Issues Rule in Big Apt. Receivership Suit," ES, 15 Dec. 1925, p. 11; "Knox Cites Housing Needs in Abandoning Chastleton," ES, 5 Dec. 1943; "Modern Apt. Arrangement," ES, 13 Mar. 1920; "Mr. and Mrs. A. I. duPont Buy the Chastleton," ES, 24 Feb. 1922, pt. 2, p. 1; "Mrs. duPont Loses Chastleton Suit," ES, 12 Sept. 1922, p. 2; "New Apt. to Offer Relief," ES, 13 Mar. 1920, pt. 2, p. 3; "New Battle Brews Over Chastleton Conversion Plan," WP, 20 July 1983; "Philip Jullien, 88, Retired Architect," WP, 19 Sept. 1963; "Philip M. Jullien Dies; Architect and Teacher," ES, 19 Sept. 1963; "Postwar Plans Will Force 800 from Chastleton," TH, 10 Jan. 1946; "16th Street Apt. Rent Returns Low by Comparison," ES, 9 Oct. 1929, p. 2; "Sixteenth Street Mansions Auctioned," ES, 10 Nov. 1925, p. 2; "16th Street Mansions Sold for $2,500,000," ES, 6 Feb. 1925, p. 2; "Sues for $25,600 Fee," ES, 16 Oct. 1925, p. 39; "$3,500,000 Realty Deal Announced," ES, 27 Apr. 1921, p. 1; "Time Runs Out for Old-Fashioned Pharmacy," WP, 3 Nov. 1983; Jacqueline Trescott, "The Once and Present Chastleton: It's a Bustling Crossroads of City Faces," WP, 3 May 1977; "2 Apts. Sold; Bring $4,850,000," ES, 12 Sept. 1924, p. 1; "Wardman Interests Extending Hotel Activities," [Washington] *Wardman Park Vista* mag., vol. 4, no. 34, 30 May 1926, pp. 3 and 15; Ardrienne Washington, "Court Allows Chastleton Owner to Convert Building to Hotel," WS, 23 July 1980; "Would Set Aside Chastleton Sale," ES, 1 Sept. 1922, p. 1.

62. ROOSEVELT HOTEL.

Manuscripts BP 819, 29 July 1919, lot 71, sq. 188; letter, Charles H. Hillegeist, Washington, to Alfred T. Jenkins, New York, 25 Feb. 1941 (author's file). Periodicals Sandra Evans, "D.C. Seeks the Roosevelt," WP, 24 Oct. 1985; Evans, "Roosevelt Tenants to Bid," WP, 3 Apr. 1986, p. C3; "Hadleigh Apts. Nearing Completion," ES, 3 Apr. 1920, pt. 2, p. 3; "Hotel Apt. to Cost $1,600,000," ES, 3 Aug. 1918, p. 3; "New Apt. Hotel Will Cost 2 Million," ES, 8 Aug. 1919, p. 2; "New Apts. to Offer Relief," ES, 13 Mar. 1920, pt. 2, p. 3; "Protests Height Limit for 16th Street Bldg.," ES, 6 Nov. 1919, p. 2; "Receiver Appointed for Roosevelt Hotel," ES, 24 Oct. 1929, p. 48; "Receiver to Take Roosevelt Hotel," ES, 22 Oct. 1929, p. 17; "Roosevelt Hotel Faces Move to Force Repairs," ES, 2 Oct. 1952, p. A25; "Roosevelt Hotel Fined $250, But Will Stay Open," ES, 7 Oct. 1952, p. B1; "Roosevelt Hotel Sold by Wardman," ES, 5 Feb. 1928, p. 24; "Roosevelt

Hotel Sold to Wardman," ES, 22 Sept. 1926, p. 1; "Roosevelt Refinance Accounting Is Asked," ES, 28 Dec. 1928, p. 2; "Tenants Set to Purchase Roosevelt," [Washington] *InTowner*, May 1986, p. 1; "Would Limit Height of Apt. House," ES, 23 Oct. 1919, p. 9.

63. CATHEDRAL MANSIONS.
Manuscripts BP 8595, 17 May 1922, lot 1, sq. 2106; BP 2500, 9 Sept. 1922, lot 2, sq. 2106; BP 9025, 12 Apr. 1923, lot 3, sq. 2106. Pamphlets *Cathedral Mansions* (Washington, D.C.: Wardman Construction Co., 1924), pp. 1–15. Periodicals "Better Not Mess with Smokey Bear," WP, 12 Sept. 1974; "Cathedral Mansions and Chastleton Sold in 7-Apt. Deal," ES, 6 Jan. 1946; "Cathedral Mansions to Cover Eight Acres in Three Sections," ES, 27 May 1922, p. 14; "Cathedral Mansions Shop Ban Is Lifted," ES, 20 June 1925, p. 5; "Cathedral Park," WSN, 11 Oct. 1974; "Center Bldg. of Cathedral Mansions To Be Erected on Connecticut Ave.," ES, 13 Jan. 1923, p. 14; "Elderly Bldgs. Find a Champion," ES, 11 Dec. 1964; "$5,000,000 Realty Deal," ES, 13 June 1924, p. 5; Thomas W. Lippman, "Evictions from Apts. Protested," WP, 28 Mar. 1974; "Security Board Is Seeking Power," ES, 29 June 1936; John C. White, "Hopeless Housing Dilemma," WSN, 28 Mar. 1974; John B. Willmann, "Four Brothers Pull Together," ES, 1 Jan. 1964, p. D1.

64. KEW GARDENS.
Manuscripts Letter, Mrs. Mildred Trimble, Washington, to Jack G. Leo, Roevmar Realty Corp., Washington, 5 Apr. 1946 (author's files). Periodicals "Kew Gardens" (advertisement), ES, 28 June 1930; "Kew Gardens Awarded 7 Pct. Rent Increase," ES, 18 Nov. 1947; "Kew Gardens Rent Hike Plea Is Continued," ES, 17 July 1947; "$900,000 Building Sold," ES, 3 June 1925, p. 4; "Sonnemann, Architect, Dies Here at 84," WP, 27 Apr. 1956; "Work on Kew Gardens Is Nearing Completion," ES, 24 Mar. 1923, p. 17.

65. MAYFLOWER HOTEL.
Manuscripts BP 8596, 5 June 1922, lots 88 and 91, sq. 162; James C. Massey and Shirley Maxwell, "Mayflower Hotel," NR, Aug. 1983. Pamphlets *A Brochure Concerning Semi-Housekeeping Apartments in The Mayflower* (Washington, D.C.: Mayflower Hotel, 1926), pp. 1–22 (quote). Periodicals Betts Abel, "Federal Tax Credit Fuels Fix-Up Drive," WP, 17 Jan. 1985, p. DC-1; David Beacom, "Home Is Where the Hotel Is," WP, *Washington Home* mag., pp. 16–19; "December in The Mayflower," *The Mayflower's Log*, vol. 3, no. 10, Dec. 1927; "Large New Hotel," ES, 30 Jan. 1910, sect. 1, p. 12; "A Massive Design," ES, 22 Feb. 1910, p. 8; "Millions To Be Spent on Two New Buildings," ES, 26 Feb. 1910, sect. 2, p. 2; "R. F. Beresford, Was Architect for Notable Buildings," ES, 21 Dec. 1966; "$6,200,000 Hotel to Rise at Once," ES, 18 Apr. 1922, pt. 1, p. 1.

66. MERIDIAN HILL STUDIO.
Manuscripts BP 8460, 2 May 1922, lots 817–21, sq. 2666. Periodicals "Concrete Sides Lifted in Place," ES, 6 Jan. 1923, p. 16;

Sarah Booth Conroy, "How Washingtonians Live in Harmony and Scale with the Grand Dames of Music," WP, *Washington Home* mag., 26 Aug. 1982; Conroy, "The Roomy Cube Solution," WP, 31 Jan. 1982; Andy Leon Harney, "The Fire This Time," WP, *Washington Post* mag., 7 Dec. 1980, p. 62; "The House in Washington, D.C., of George Oakley Totten, Architect," AA, 6 July 1921, pp. 1–7; "Noted Landmark Now on New Site," ES, 21 Nov. 1925, p. 19; "Resume Building on 'Embassy Row'," ES, 9 Apr. 1927, p. 30; "Studio Is Latest Apt. Idea," ES, 23 June 1923, p. 20.

67. PRESIDENTIAL.
Manuscripts BP 384, 11 July 1922, lot 830, sq. 184. Books Proctor; Slauson. Pamphlets *Certificate of Incorporation and By-Laws* (Washington, D.C.: Presidential Owners, Inc., 1959); *Presidential Apartments, Cooperative Home Ownership* (Washington, D.C.: Edmund J. Flynn Co., 1959). Periodicals "Appleton Clark, Jr., Architect in District More Than 50 Years," ES, 26 Mar. 1955; "Appleton Clark, 89, Dean of Architects," WP, 27 Mar. 1955; Herbert W. Congdon, "A Shot at Two Targets," AA, 24 May 1916, pp. 333–39; "House of J. Philip Herrmann, Esq., Washington, D.C.," AA, 2 Aug. 1911; "Residence of Mrs. James M. Green, Washington, D.C.," AABN, 14 July 1906; "Eight-Story Apt. under Construction," ES, 30 Apr. 1922, pt. 1, p. 15; "Flynn Plans Cooperatives on 16th Street," WP, 11 Sept. 1959; "Presidential Apts." (advertisement), ES, 5 May 1923, p. 13; "16th Street Apt. Rent Returns Low by Comparison," ES, 9 Oct. 1929, p. 2.

68. 2500 MASSACHUSETTS AVENUE, N.W.
Manuscripts BP 1836, 21 Aug. 1922, lots 4 and 801, sq. 2500. Pamphlets *#2500 Massachusetts Avenue, N.W., Washington, D.C.* (Washington, D.C.: 1927). Periodicals "Diplomatic Apts. Planned," ES, 29 July 1922; Robert J. Lewis, "2500 Massachusetts, Bought by Mrs. Clark, Will Become Co-op," ES, 9 Sept. 1948.

69. METHODIST BUILDING.
Manuscripts BP 5963, 2 Jan. 1923, lots 4–5, 6–8, 802, 809, sq. 726; BP 144, 548, 8 July 1931; Minutes of the Commission of Fine Arts, 13 Dec. 1930 and 1 July 1931. Periodicals "Building Design Studied," ES, 18 Feb. 1928, p. 16; "Church Property Contest Looming," ES, 10 Dec. 1930; "M.E. Property Near Capitol to Be Bought by U.S.," ES, 25 Apr. 1931; "Methodist Bldg. Addition Studied," ES, 3 Apr. 1930; "Methodists File Bldg. Plans," ES, 5 June 1923; "Methodists Plan Apt. House," ES, 24 Apr. 1931; "The Story of the Methodist Building in Washington, D.C.," *The Voice of the Board of Temperance, Prohibition, and Public Morals of the Methodist Episcopal Church*, Mar. 1925, p. 1; "Why a Building Is Needed," *The Voice of the Board of Temperance, Prohibition, and Public Morals of the Methodist Episcopal Church*, Sept. 1920, pp. 1–4.

70. ANCHORAGE.
Manuscripts BP 9164, 1 May 1924, lots 1 and 2, sq. 112; letter,

Stained glass skylight in a public hall at the Methodist Building.

Frederica Sterling Bacher, Gordonsville, Va., to the author, 27 June 1982; letter, Clifford J. Hynning, Arlington, Va., to the author, 3 June 1982. Books Slauson. Periodicals "Anchorage to Become Offices," ES, 9 Nov. 1963; "Anchorage Remodeled," ES, 19 Mar. 1965; Fred Barnes, " 'Anchorage' Suing Miles," ES, 30 Jan. 1972; "Complete Bachelor Apt. Planned," ES, 4 Oct. 1924, p. 14; Betty Nowell, "Shop Venture Developed As Social Center," WH, 6 May 1934; Daniel Poole, "One Million Dollars Invested by Accident," ES, 1 June 1983; "Three Apts. Sold to Investor," WP, 29 Sept. 1962; Gayle Young, "Mansion on Mass. Avenue Is Headed for the Auction Block," WP, 22 Oct. 1983.

71. CLEVELAND PARK.
Manuscripts BP 8799, 22 Mar. 1924, lots 63–68, sq. 2067. Periodicals "Co-operative" (advertisement), ES, 14 Aug. 1924; "$400,000 in Sales Listed by Flynn on Cooperative Plan," WP, 22 Nov. 1924.

72. ARMY AND NAVY.
Manuscripts BP 10750, 25 May 1925, lots 19–21, sq. 2500; Major General Charles G. Hall, "The Story of '2540'," 1981, pp. 1–9 (author's files); letters, Monroe Warren, Sr., Sauveterre de Bearn, France, to the author, 19 Oct. 1982 and 5 Jan. 1983. Periodicals "50-Apt. House Is Now Ready for Use," ES, 12 Feb. 1927, p. 21; "Hotel Changes Name to Avoid Confusion," ES, 26 May 1934; "Huge Apt. Bldgs. Planned," ES, 19 Nov. 1927, p. 7; "Irene Sheridan Dead; Daughter of General," WP, 8 Dec. 1964; "Miss Sheridan, Daughter of Civil War General," ES, 7 Dec. 1964; "New Apt. Will Start Soon," ES, 26 Nov. 1927, p. 19; "Some Apts. Owned by Tenants," WH, 26 July 1925.

73. CHALFONTE.
Manuscripts BP 11172, 5 June 1925, lot 27 (801), sq. 2590; letter, Harvey H. Warwick, Jr., St. Petersburg, Fla., to the author, 15 Feb. 1982. Periodicals "Apt. Bldg. Sold," ES, 27 Jan. 1962, p. B3; "Apt. Planned to Cost $1,800,000," ES, 21 Feb. 1925, p. 19; "Citizens Lose Plea to Halt Bldg.," ES, 14 May 1923; "Citizens Oppose More Apts.," ES, 20 Nov. 1924; "Height Limit Raised for New Apt.," ES, 11 May 1923; "New Apt. House Planned for Mount Pleasant," ES, 21 Feb. 1925; "$1,500,000 Reported Paid for Chalfonte," ES, 1 Mar. 1930, p. B1; "300 Tenants Receive Eviction Notices in Rent Raise Move," ES, 28 July 1953; "2 Apts. Sold at Public Auction," WP, 15 Apr. 1932.

74. 1661 CRESCENT PLACE, N.W.
Manuscripts BP 4133, 5 Nov. 1925, lot 942, sq. 2571; Mary Adams Catanzaro, "The People of 1661," 1981, pp. 1–47 (quote); letter, Monroe Warren, Sr., Sauveterre de Bearn, France, to the author, 5 Jan. 1983. Books and pamphlets Sexton; *1661 Crescent Place, N.W.* (Washington, D.C.: M. and R. Bates Warren, 1926), pp. 1–34. Periodicals "50-Apt. House Is Now Ready for Use," ES, 12 Feb. 1927, p. 21; "Senator Walsh Buys an Apt. House," ES, 19 Nov. 1927, p. 17.

75. 2120 KALORAMA ROAD, N.W.
Manuscripts BP 4276, 9 Nov. 1925, lot 49, sq. 2527. Pamphlets *Justement and Callmer, Architects* (Washington, D.C.: n.p., 1964), pp. 1–25. Periodicals "Louis Justement Dies, Washington Architect," ES, 28 July 1968; "Sibley Hospital Architect Dies," WP, 28 July 1968.

76. 4701 CONNECTICUT AVENUE, N.W.
Manuscripts BP 7884 and 7911, 4 Apr. 1927, lots 1–2, sq. 2037. Books Robert H. Ferrell, ed., *Dear Bess: The Letters from Harry to Bess Truman, 1910–1959* (New York: Norton, 1983). Periodicals Hank Burchard, "Presidents in Residence," WP, *Weekend* mag., 7 Mar. 1986, p. 4–5 and 7; "New Apt. Bldg. for Northwest Section," ES, 10 Sept. 1927, p. 14; Aaron Ruvinsky, "Converting Rentals to Rentals," WSN, 5 Apr. 1974; John Sherman, "Last of All Farewells," WSN, 29 Aug. 1973.

77. MOORINGS.
Manuscripts BP 8488, 21 Apr. 1927, lot 54, sq. 111. Periodicals "A 'Nautical' Apt. Bldg.," AR, Mar. 1928, pp. 223–25; "New Type Apt. House," ES, 25 June 1927, p. 15.

78. TILDEN GARDENS.
Manuscripts BP 8027, 7 Apr. 1927, lot 3, sq. 2059; BP 2989, 7 Oct. 1927, lot 4, sq. 2059; BP 5347, 9 Jan. 1928, lot 5, sq. 2059; BP 7290, 4 Apr. 1928, lot 2, sq. 2059; BP 1212707, 19 Mar. 1929, lot 6, sq. 2059; BP 130348, 20 Jan. 1930, lot 7, sq. 2059; Helen M. Dyer, "Reminiscences of Dr. Helen M. Dyer at 50th Anniversary Garden Party of Tilden Gardens, Inc.," 1979, pp. 1–9 (author's files); letters, Monroe Warren, Sr., Sauveterre de Bearn, France, to the author, 19 Oct. 1982 and 5 Jan. 1983. Books and pamphlets *Certificate of Incorporation and By-Laws of Tilden Gardens, Inc.* (Washington, D.C.: M. and R. Bates Warren, 1928), pp. 1–9; Sexton; *Tentative Plans of Development of Tilden Gardens* (Washington, D.C.: National Publishing Co., 1928), pp. 1–8; *Tilden Gardens: The Distinctive Cooperative Apartment Home Development of M. and R. B. Warren* (Washington, D.C.: M. and R. Bates Warren, 1929), pp. 1–14; Judith and Milton Viorst, *The Underground Washington, D.C.*, Gourmet (New York: Simon and Schuster, 1970) (quote). Periodicals Russell T. Adams, "Tilden

An original kitchen in the 1929 Tilden Gardens.

Gardens," [Washington] *Condo News,* 22 Oct. 1982, p. 2; "Apt. Project to Cost $3,000,000," ES, 13 Aug. 1927; "Apt. Unit Permit Is Issued," ES, 1 Feb. 1930, p. B1; Hank Burchard, "Presidents in Residence," WP, *Weekend* mag., 7 Mar. 1986, pp. 4–5, 7; "18 Apt. Homes Sold in Tilden Gardens," ES, 13 Sept. 1930; "Exhibit Apt. Home Is Opened to Public Inspection," ES, 8 Mar. 1930, p. B3; "Exquisite Planning in Tilden Gardens," WP, 11 Aug. 1929; "Fifth Tilden Gardens Unit to Contain Club Features," ES, 2 Mar. 1929; "Final Bldg. in Tilden Gardens Is Begun," ES, 15 Feb. 1930, p. B1; "First Unit of Big Apt. Built," ES, 1 Oct. 1927; "Bldg. Operation O.K.'d Second Week of Year," ES, 14 Jan. 1928; David Holmberg, "Eastman Spurred Bias Suit," ES, 25 Sept. 1969; "Justice Dept. Sues Firm after City Circle Complains," WAA, 14 June 1969; "Last Unit of Tilden Gardens Completed," ES, 2 Aug. 1930; "New Apts. on Connecticut Avenue," WP, 14 Aug. 1927; "New Cooperative Apt. Cost Estimated at $400,000," ES, 7 Apr. 1928; "New Trend Seen in Rear Grounds," ES, 14 Sept. 1929, p. 14; Hugh Shaber, "Rehab Set at 19th and Q Sts.; Washington School to Relocate," *The InTowner,* Feb. 1988, p. 1; "Tilden Gardens Unit Advances," ES, 1 Sept. 1928, p. 15; "Tilden Gardens Unit To Be Built," ES, 17 Dec. 1927, p. 18; "Towne Purchases Tilden Apt.," ES, 28 Sept. 1929, p. 18; Alton L. Wells, "Promoting a Cooperative Apt.," AF, Apr. 1932, pp. 401–6; John B. Willmann, "Tilden Gardens: 50 Stately Years, But Almost Ageless," WP, 22 Sept. 1979, p. E1; Sanford J. Ungar, "NW Co-op Ordered to Halt Alleged Bias," WP, 8 Dec. 1970.

79. 2101 CONNECTICUT AVENUE, N.W.
Manuscripts BP 3831, 3 Nov. 1927, lots 77–78, 93–94, 805–8, sq. 2537. Pamphlets *2101 Connecticut Avenue: Plan of Cooperative Organization* (Chevy Chase, Maryland: B. F. Saul Co., 1975), pp. 1–82; *Washington Architecture Club Catalogue, 1906* (Washington, D.C.: n.p., 1906). Periodicals "Atlantic Terra Cotta Company" (advertisement), PP, Jan. 1923, p. 1; "Atlantic Terra Cotta in a Zoning Law Building" (advertisement), PP, May 1924, p. 1; Sarah Booth Conroy, "High Life," WP, 5 Aug. 1982; "The Farmers Loan and Trust Company Bldg.," AM, Jan.–June 1926, pp. 199–200;

Joanna Shaw-Eagle, "The Collectors: Treasures from the East: The Washington D.C. Apt. of John W. Gruber," AD, June 1984, pp. 128–35; John B. Willmann, " '2101' Sold . . . Prestige Address," WP, 6 Apr. 1974, p. E1.

80. ALBAN TOWERS.
Manuscripts BP 6054, 11 Feb. 1928, lot 12, sq. 1929; BP 127222, 13 Sept. 1929, lot 802, sq. 1929. Pamphlets *Alban Towers, 3700 Massachusetts Avenue, N.W.* (Washington, D.C.: 1929), pp. 1–4. Periodicals "ABC Liquor License Granted Alban Towers Despite Protest by Cathedral," ES, 30 June 1952; "Addition Planned for Alban Towers," ES, 21 Sept. 1929, p. 15; "Alban Towers" (advertisement), WP, 16 Oct. 1932, p. R7; "Alban Towers Add 84 Apt. Units," ES, 8 Feb. 1930, p. B1; "Alban Towers Purchased for $2,000,000," WP, 21 Mar. 1948; "Large Apt. House To Be Erected Here," ES, 18 Feb. 1928, p. 19.

81. BROADMOOR.
Manuscripts BP 118777, 7 Nov. 1928, lots 56/53, 2223–24, sq. 2226. Pamphlets Edmund J. Flynn, Jr., *Own Your Own Apartment Home in the Broadmoor* (Washington, D.C.: 1948); Kevin and Sue Murray, Stephen Kent, and members of the Broadmoor History Committee, *The Broadmoor of Cleveland Park, Since 1929* (Washington, D.C.: Broadmoor, 1984). Periodicals Dorothea Andrews, "Broadmoor Tenant Anger Seethes," WP, 26 Aug. 1948; "Apt. House to Cost $2,750,000," WP, 9 Sept. 1928; "Apts. Can Be Had," WDN, 25 Aug. 1948; "Broadmoor Co-op Taken to Court," WP, 23 Sept. 1948; Hank Burchard, "Presidents in Residence," WP, *Weekend* mag., 7 Mar. 1986, pp. 4–5, 7; "Cooperative Flat Purchase Goes to Court," WP, 26 Oct. 1948; "40 Purchase Broadmoor Cooperative Apts.," WP, 25 Aug. 1948; Robert J. Lewis, "Angry Tenants Protest Plan to Sell Broadmoor," ES, 25 Aug. 1948; Lewis, "More Than 500 D.C. Apt. Units Converted in Year for Sale as 'Co-ops,' " WP, 22 Jan. 1949; Lewis, "197-Unit Broadmoor Apts. for Sale on Co-operative Plan," ES, 24 Aug. 1948; "Mammoth Apt. House to Rise on Five-Acre Site," ES, 8 Sept. 1928, p. 14; "$951,000 Notes Out on the Broadmoor," ES, 24 Apr. 1931; "Plan New Apt. on Five-acre Plot," ES, 6 Sept. 1928, p. 29; "Sues for Commission," ES, 18 July 1929; "39 at Broadmoor Are Out on Strike as Parleys Fail," ES, 10 Oct. 1938.

82. HARVARD HALL.
Manuscripts BP 119742, 18 Dec. 1928, lots 266, 267, 805, 830, 840, sq. 2589. Books *Biographical Directory of the American Congress, 1774–1961* (Washington, D.C.: GPO, 1961). Periodicals "Apt. Costing $1,100,000 Now Being Erected," ES, 5 Jan. 1929, p. 17; "Apt. Deadline Set," ES, 14 Feb. 1940, p. A7; "Author Besieges Apt. She Sublet to Zionchecks," ES, 29 May 1936; "Harvard Apt. Figures in Exchange," ES, 16 Oct. 1948; $1,100,000 Apt. House Planned on Harvard Street," ES, 22 Dec. 1928, p. 15; "Two Apts. Sold at Auction," ES, 15 Apr. 1932; "Zioncheck Is Dispossessed as Landlady Views 'Losses'," ES, 21 May 1936 (first quote); "Zioncheck Evicts Mrs. Young, Who Goes

to Hospital," ES, 30 May 1936 (second quote); "Zioncheck Sought for Commitment to Hospital Here," ES, 29 June 1936.

83. WARDMAN TOWER.
Manuscripts BP 8312, 9 May 1928, lots 25, 802–3, 817, sq. 2132; Caroline Isabelle Mesrobian, "A Selection of the Architectural Oeuvre of Mirhan Mesrobian," M.A. thesis, Tulane University, Art History Dept., 1978, pp. 1–99; "Wardman Park Annex (Wardman Tower and Arcade)," NR, 3 Aug. 1978, pp. 1–18. Pamphlets Nord Schwiebert, Wardman Park Hotel, 1918–1953; Sheraton-Park Hotel, 1953–1980 (Washington, D.C.: n.p., 1980), pp. 1–7. Periodicals Carl Bernstein, "The Washington Wardman Built," WP, 16 Feb. 1969, Potomac mag., pp. 25–32; "Contemplates the Erection of Ten Large Apts.," ES, 8 Apr. 1916; Ruth Dean, "Madame Ambassador on the Move," ES, 20 Aug. 1967, p. E2; Hickman; "Hotel to Celebrate," ES, 17 Nov. 1928, p. 17; "Mamie Eisenhower's Life Comes Full Circle," WS, 5 Nov. 1978; "Mammoth Hotel Opens This Evening," ES, 23 Nov. 1918, p. 4; "1,136 Rooms in Hotel," WP, 24 Nov. 1918; "Plans $5,000,000 Apt. House," ES, 6 Apr. 1916, p. 1; "Mirhan Mesrobian, 86, Award-Winning Architect," WSN, 25 Sept. 1975; "Two Apts. Will be Erected," ES, 28 May 1929, p. 4; "Work to Start Soon on Woodley Courts," ES, 30 Dec. 1916, p. 3; "Wardman Park Annex Planned," ES, 10 Apr. 1928, p. 20; "Wardman Park and Carlton Control Bought for $2 Million," ES, 25 May 1953; "Will Raze $100,000 Home to Build Big Apts.," ES, 22 Apr. 1916, pt. 2, p. 2.

84. HAMPSHIRE GARDENS.
Manuscripts BP 123508, 10 May 1929, lot 1, sq. 3324; BP 123507, 10 May 1929, lot 2, sq. 3324; BP 123510, 10 May 1929, lot 3, sq. 3324; BP 125744, 24 July 1929, lot 6, sq. 3324; BP 125742, 25 July 1929, lot 4, sq. 3324; BP 125743, 25 July 1929, lot 7, sq. 3324; BP 126386, 16 Aug. 1929, lot 9, sq. 3324; BP 126387, 16 Aug. 1929, lot 8, sq. 3324; BP 125839, 29 July 1929, lot 5, sq. 3324. Periodicals "Apt. House Group Certified," ES, 12 Oct. 1929, p. 17; "Apt. Plans Win Jury Approval," ES, 14 Sept. 1929, p. 17; "Co-Operative Dwelling Plan Has Several New Features," ES, 31 Aug. 1929, p. 13; James P. Fremgen, " 'Flynn's Folly' Endures after 53 Years," WP, 5 June 1982; "Giant Apt. Community Started Here," WDN, 11 May 1929; "Hampshire Gardens" (advertisement), ES, 14 Sept. 1929, p. R19; "Hampshire Gardens" (advertisement), ES, 28 June 1930; "Hampshire Gardens Co-operative Apt. Development," ES, 11 May 1929; "Huge Housing Project," WT, 11 May 1929; Malcolm Lamborne, Jr., "Apt. Co-op Built in 'Wilds' Still Going Strong after 19 Years," ES, 26 June 1948; "National Board Approves D.C. Project," WT, 12 Oct. 1929; "Plan Project for Housing 7,500," WN, 11 May 1929; "Skyviews of Washington—No. 38," WP, 8 Dec. 1931.

85. WOODLEY PARK TOWERS.
Manuscripts BP 121086, 25 Feb. 1929, lots 55–56 and 811, sq. 2106. Periodicals "Apt. House Changes Owners," ES, 5 Oct. 1929, p. 13; Hank Burchard, "Presidents in Residence," WP, Weekend mag., 7 Mar. 1986, pp. 4–5, 7; "D.C. Permits Reach Highest Weekly Total This Year," 2 Mar. 1929, p. 18; "Large Apt. Bldg. Sold," ES, 29 June 1929, p. 19; "Lobby," WP, 15 Sept. 1973; "New Apt. House Is Planned," ES, 6 Oct. 1928, p. 19; "New Apt. House for Kalorama Heights," ES, 16 Mar. 1929, p. 16; "New Apts. Swell District's Bldg. Activity," ES, 12 Dec. 1936; "New $700,000 Apt. at 1845 Columbia Road," ES, 22 June 1929, p. 19; "$300,000 Apt. Bldg. Is Planned," ES, 1 June 1929, p. 14; "Views from Woodley Park Towers," WH, 27 Apr. 1930.

86. SHOREHAM HOTEL.
Manuscripts BP 129956, 8 Jan. 1930, lot 6, sq. 2138; BP 182200, 8 July 1935, lots 5–6, sq. 2138. Books Goode; Josiah F. Goodhue, History of the Town of Shoreham, Vermont (Shoreham, Vt.: Trustees of the Platt Memorial Library, 1975); Esther M. Swift, Vermont Place-Names (Brattleboro, Vt.: Greene Press, 1977). Periodicals "Apt. Is Sold," ES, 2 Dec. 1934; "Apt. Hotel To Be Constructed on Calvert Street," ES, 30 Dec. 1929, p. 17; Betty Beale, "When This Bash Is Held, Barnee Breeskin'll Be Back Where He Belongs," WS, 9 Sept. 1979, p. D3; "Bernard R. Bralove Dies, Ex-Owner of Shoreham," WP, 19 Jan. 1981, p. C4; "Building Planned on Shoreham Site," ES, 15 Sept. 1928, p. 2; "First Shoreham Unit Completed," ES, 5 Oct. 1930, p. B1; "$5,000,000 Hotel To Be Built Here," ES, 10 Dec. 1927, p. 2; Benjamin Forgey, "Checking Out Washington's Inn Crowd," WP, 27 Mar. 1982, p. C1; Mary Law Harris, "Shoreham Suite Features Chromium Furniture and Vari-Colored Walls," WP, 16 Aug. 1933; "Harry Bralove Dies, Built Shoreham Hotel," ES, 21 Mar. 1961; "Harry Bralove, Hotel Operator," WP, 21 Mar. 1961, p. B4; "Man Who Loaned Shoreham Funds Kept Anonymous," ES, 16 Apr. 1935; "Name of Historic Shoreham Hostelry To Be Perpetuated in Project, Furnishing Suites and Recreational Facilities," ES, 25 Jan. 1930; "New Shoreham Hotel Opens Tomorrow," WH, 30 Oct. 1930, p. 1; " 'Permanent' Shoreham Guests Evicted to Admit Transients," WP, 6 Oct. 1950; "Report on the Accident to the Shoreham Apt.-House," AABN, 12 Dec. 1891, pp. 167–68; "Rheem Co. Trustees to Take $140,000 Bid to Firm's Creditors," ES, 18 July 1939, p. B1; "Shoreham Asks Its Permanent Guests to Leave," WN, 6 Oct. 1950, p. B1; "Shoreham Asks Zoning Change for Addition," WP, 22 Nov. 1945; "Shoreham Bldg. Sold to Oil Magnate," WS, 22 Mar. 1930, p. A1; "Shoreham History Anecdotes," [Washington] Shoreham Americana News, 1983, pp. 1–3; "Shoreham Hotel Receiver Is Asked by Furniture Firm," ES, 29 Jan. 1931, p. 1; "Shoreham Hotel Receivers Named," ES, 30 Jan. 1931; "Shoreham Hotel to Be Torn Down," ES, 22 Jan. 1927, p. 2; "Shoreham Hotel to Open Thursday," WP, 26 Oct. 1930; "Shoreham Hotel to Raise Chicks in Old Riding Hall," WTH, 3 Aug. 1943; "The Shoreham Motor Inn," WP, 5 July 1959, pp. K1–12; "Shoreham Moves to Build Addition," ES, 12 May 1935, p. D10; "Shoreham to Open," ES, 21 Oct. 1930; "Shoreham to Replace Pool with Dining Room," ES, 27 Mar. 1946; Edward C.

Stone, "Shoreham Is Paying Holders of Second Trust in Full," ES, 6 May 1941; "Two Apts. Will Be Erected," ES, 28 May 1929; "Ultra-Modern Apt. Hotel Soon to Rise," ES, 25 Jan. 1930, p. B1; "Washington Landmark Is Soon to Disappear," NYT, 30 Sept. 1928.

87. WESTCHESTER.
Manuscripts BP 130047, 6 Mar. 1930, lot 31/39, sq. 1805; BP 131963, 11 Apr. 1930, lot 31/80, sq. 1805; Rosamond Lewis, "Notes on Westchester History," 1978, pp. 1–5 (author's files); "The Westchester Tenants Protective Committee: An Analysis of the Westchester Occupant-Ownership Plan," 1950, pp. 1–8 (author's files). Pamphlets *The Westchester Occupant-Ownership Plan* (Washington, D.C.: Randall H. Hagner & Co., 1950), pp. 1–16. Periodicals "Apt. for Cathedral Ave. Is Largest Yet," WH, 9 Feb. 1930; "Apt. House Bldg. in District Shows Big Gains," ES, 24 Nov. 1928, p. 17; "Apt. House Permit Granted," ES, 12 Apr. 1930, p. B2; "Business Romance Hidden in Bldg.," ES, 30 Aug. 1930; "Capital Improvements Program," WN, Nov. 1976, p. 3; "Company Planning Beautiful Garden," WP, 21 Sept. 1930; "Court Ban Asked on Apt.," ES, 23 Apr. 1958, p. A33; "Decision on Rent Increase Petition Slated for July," WTH, 22 June 1947; Morrey Dunie, "Tenants Protest Plan to Turn Plush Westchester into Co-op," WTH, 8 June 1950; "Early Start Planned on Apt. Project," ES, 18 Jan. 1930; "First Units of Huge Westchester Apt. Development Now Underway," ES, 8 Feb. 1930, p. B1; S. L. Fishbein, "400 Tenants of Westchester Battle Cooperative Project," WP, 6 June 1950; "From the President's Desk," WN, Apr. 1977, pp. 1 and 4; "Gates from England at Westchester," ES, 21 June 1952; "Gen. Clarke Receives Westchester Post," ES, 1 Jan. 1955; "Glover Parkway Apt. Will Cost $4,000,000," ES, 7 Dec. 1930; "Ground Sold by Realest," WN, June 1962, p. 1; "Harvey Warwick, Architect for Colonial Village," ES, 13 July 1972; Alexander Henderson, "Westchester Corp. Elects Officers," WP, 24 Feb. 1957; "Huge Westchester Bldg. Rated City's Largest of Its Kind," ES, 12 Sept. 1931; "Imposing Gate Due to Battle of Britain," WP, 16 June 1952; David Jacobson, "A New Life for the Westchester," WS, 24 Sept. 1978, *Home-Life* mag., pp. 8 and 29; "Land Owned by Realest May Be Sold," WN, Aug. 1962, pp. 1 and 3; "Landmark Replaced," WT, 5 Jan. 1935; "Large Apt. House Is Sold," ES, 2 June 1937; "Large Apt. Sold to Syndicate," ES, 2 June 1937; Robert J. Lewis, "19-Year-Old Westchester May Keep Rank As Biggest Elevator Apt.," ES, 1 Apr. 1950, p. B1; Lewis, "Site Deal Seen at Westchester," ES, 14 Oct. 1956; Lewis, "Tenants' 'Analysis' of the Hagner Plan for Westchester Co-op Sale Due Soon," ES, 10 June 1950; Lewis, "Westchester Apt. Sales to Tenants to Open Tomorrow," ES, 6 Oct. 1953; Lewis, "Westchester Sale to Tenants May Be Sought Again," ES, 1 Sept. 1956; Wilma Martin, "Westchester Club Holds Apt. Tour," WN, Mar. 1979, pp. 1 and 4; "Member-Owners Patronizing Shops," WN, June 1941, p. 4; "New Unit Started for Westchester," WP, 7 Dec. 1930; "New Westchester Apts. Open," WP, 9 Sept. 1930; "Queen Held Interest in Apt. Here," WDN, 29 Nov. 1962; "Resumes Bldg. of Big Apt.," ES, 16 Apr. 1931; "Security Officers Efficient in Many Jobs," WN, Oct. 1962, p. 4; "Standing and Other Committees Appointed and Approved By President," WN, May 1970, p. 3; "Tenants' Committee Wins Better Terms In Apt. Sale," ES, 30 Oct. 1953; "$3,000,000 Building for Westchester Development," ES, 25 Apr. 1931; Franklyn Waltman, "Private Housing Projects in Capital Set Example for United States," WP, 28 Nov. 1937; "Westchester Apts. Sold; Price Believed Over 5 Million," WTH, 28 Feb. 1947; "Westchester Club Activities Flourishing," WN, May 1981, p. 2; "Westchester Establishes Co-op Firm," WP, 1 Dec. 1953; "Westchester Prices 'Reasonable', Asserts Hagner Firm Head," ES, 17 June 1950; "Westchester Tenants' Analysis Holds Co-op Sale Disadvantageous," ES, 16 June 1950; "Westchester Tenants Hear About Repairs," WP, 11 Nov. 1953; "Westchester Tenants Meet on Lawn to Fight Co-op Move," WP, 21 Oct. 1953; "Westchester Tenants Rally to Halt Sale as Co-op Apt.," ES, 8 June 1950, p. A5; "Westchester Tenants Told of Concessions," WP, 30 Oct. 1953; "Westchester Tenants Vote Against Co-op," ES, 22 June 1950, p. A5; "Westchester Unit Now in Operation," WP, 15 Nov. 1931; John B. Willmann, "Cooperative Life Continues Serene at Westchester," WP, 1 Aug. 1964, p. E1; Estelle Wood, "Westchester Co-operative New to City," WTH, 16 Oct. 1953.

88. KENNEDY-WARREN.
Manuscripts BP 140167, 28 Feb. 1931, lot 55/214, sq. 2214; "B. Francis Saul," biographical sketch, ca. 1935, pp. 1–7 (files of B. F. Saul Co., Chevy Chase, Maryland); letters, Monroe Warren, Sr., Sauveterre de Bearn, France, to the author, 19 Oct. 1982 and 5 Jan. 1983. Books and pamphlets *The Kennedy-Warren* (Washington, D.C.: Kennedy-Warren, Inc., 1931), pp. 1–8; *The Kennedy-Warren* (Washington, D.C.: B. F. Saul Co., ca. 1935), pp. 1–4; Wirz-Striner. Periodicals "Art Stone Is Used in Hotel Entrance," WP, 13 Sept. 1931; "Bankrupt Petition Filed by Warrens," ES, 30 Apr. 1933; "Bird's-eye View of the Kennedy-Warren," WP, 13 Sept. 1931; Hank Burchard, "Presidents in Residence," WP, *Weekend* mag., 7 Mar. 1986, pp. 4–5 and 7; "Dining Room Will Open October 15," WP, 11 Oct. 1931; "H. P. Amos, Master Painter 50 Years," WP, 13 Sept. 1931; "Huge Apt. Hotel Project to Start Soon," ES, 11 Oct. 1930; Bill Ivory, "Sophisticated Lady of Connecticut Ave.: The Kennedy-Warren," TL, vol. 1, no. 3, July 1983, pp. 1–2; "The Kennedy-Warren" (advertisement), WP, 25 Sept. 1932; "Kennedy-Warren Receiver Is Named," WP, 20 Apr. 1932; "Kennedy-Warren To Be Enlarged," ES, 12 May 1935; "Large Apt. Nears Completion," ES, 20 June 1931; "A Man in the News Lives Here . . . ," WP, 21 Oct. 1961; "Permit Is Asked for Large Hotel," ES, 10 Oct. 1930; Alice L. Powers, "Blending Classic Elements and Stylish Elegance," WP, 26 May 1983, *Washington Home* mag., pp. 18–21; Anne Simpson,

One of the many outstanding features of the Kennedy-Warren is the elaborate aluminum detailing, as shown in the balustrade of the main staircase.

"Kennedy-Warren: Bastion of Gentility," WP, 6 Mar. 1986, p. DC1; "Suit for Discovery of Assets Is Filed," ES, 15 Aug. 1932; "Tiles and Marble Supplied in Capital," WP, 13 Sept. 1931.

89. SEDGWICK GARDENS.
Manuscripts BP 146687, 18 Sept. 1931, lot 31, sq. 2060; Judy Catlin, "Looking Back at Sedgwick Gardens," 1982, pp. 1–3 (quote). Pamphlets Sedgwick Gardens Apartments (Washington, D.C.: Legum and Gerber Realty Co., ca. 1955), pp. 1–4. Periodicals "Bldgs. Razed for New Project," ES, 12 Oct. 1929, p. 20; Hank Burchard, "Presidents in Residence," WP, Weekend mag., 7 Mar. 1986, pp. 4–5; Judith Catlin, "Coming of Age in Cleveland Park," WP, 27 Sept. 1984; "$500,000 Apt. Heads City Building Permit List," ES, 15 Aug. 1931, p. B1; Bill Ivory, "Sedgwick Gardens," TL, vol. 2, no. 1, Mar. 1984, pp. 1–2; "Sedgwick Gardens Sold," WP, 8 Mar. 1958; "Northwest Apt. Bldg. Sold," ES, 15 Mar. 1958.

90. ARGONNE.
Manuscripts BP 570, 1 June 1922, lot 476, sq. 2589. Periodicals "Apt. House to Cost $2,000,000," ES, 27 May 1922, p. 14; "Apt. House Sold for $2,000,000," ES, 17 Nov. 1923, p. 17; "Argonne Apt. Will Open Tomorrow," ES, 31 Mar. 1923; "Columbia Road Apts. Sold for $2 Million," WP, 13 Jan. 1962; John Maffre, "Moving Van a Regular at Argonne," WP, 1 Apr. 1962; "Mensh Corp. Offers Arena Season Tickets," ES, 29 Apr. 1966; "New Park Plaza Has Unusual Features," ES, 3 July 1964; "Park Plaza Apt. Renovated," ES, 20 Aug. 1965, p. D10; "Park Plaza Nearly Ready," WP, 1 Feb. 1964; "Park Plaza Retains the Past," ES, 1 May 1964; "Rental Reception," WP, 28 Aug. 1965, p. D18; "Settlement Held for Park Plaza," ES, 28 Feb. 1969.

91. JEFFERSON.
Manuscripts BP 3146, 27 Sept. 1922, lots 19, 61–64, 815, sq. 182. Periodicals Barbara Gamarekian, "At Home Near the White House," NYT, 15 Mar. 1981, p. 54; Evelyn Hayes, "She Makes a Pretty Home for Her Guests," WP, 3 June 1955; "Jefferson Change," WP, 5 June 1963; "Jefferson Hotel on 16th St. Sold to Realty Trust for $1 Million," WP, 3 Mar. 1963; "Jefferson Hotel Sold to Trust," ES, 2 Mar. 1963; "Jefferson Sold for $250,500, to J. McD. Shea," WP, 4 Nov. 1934; Elizabeth Mehren, "Catering to the Californians," WP, 19 Apr. 1981, p. G1; Mehren, "The Jefferson—Anything But Humble and Almost Like Home," Los Angeles Times, 12 Apr. 1981, part 4, p. 1; "Nature Institution Enlarges Home," ES, 9 Apr. 1927, p. 23; "New Receiver Named for Apt. House," ES, 15 May 1930, p. B1; "$900,000 Apt. for 16th and M Sts.," ES, 16 June 1922, p. 3; David Schoenbrun, "There's a Small Hotel," Town & Country, July 1962, pp. 16, 23, and 94; "16th Street Apt. Rent Returns Low by Comparison," ES, 9 Oct. 1929, p. 2.

92. BELVEDERE.
Manuscripts BP 5423, 22 Dec. 1923, lots 4–16, sq. 246; letter, James Durham, Norman Bernstein Management, Inc., Washington, to the author, 24 Aug. 1982. Periodicals "Apt. Auction Brings Half-Million," ES, 3 Dec. 1930; "Woman Asks Injunction to Prevent Eviction," ES, 28 June 1928.

93. 1705 LANIER PLACE, N.W.
Manuscripts BP 4528, 21 Nov. 1923, lot 800, sq. 2582. Periodicals "Apts. on Cooperative Plan Sold," WH, 6 Apr. 1924; "Cooperative," ES, 14 Aug. 1924; "New Apt. House Sold," ES, 4 June 1927, p. 19.

94. EMBASSY.
Periodicals "Embassy Apts. Being Erected," ES, 13 Sept. 1924, p. 11; "Embassy Apts. Sale Brings $400,000," ES, 30 Aug. 1933; "Trade Deal Here Involves Acreage," ES, 23 May 1931.

The ceiling of the Embassy, with its detailed decorative Gothic Revival ribbed vaulting and bosses.

95. 1700 CONNECTICUT AVENUE, N.W.
Manuscripts BP 9754, 30 Apr. 1925, lot 800 (58), sq. 92. Periodicals "Schwartz Drug Facelift," *The InTowner*, Mar. 1988, p. 1.

96. DUPONT CIRCLE.
Manuscripts BP 139153, 22 June 1926; BP 139253, 30 Jan. 1931, lot 13, sq. 138. Periodicals "Bradley Mansion Site Sought for Apt.," ES, 6 Aug. 1925, p. 13; "The Dupont Circle," WP, 16 Oct. 1932; p. R7; "Dupont Circle Bldg. Denied Offices Permit; 175 Facing Ouster," ES, 17 May 1950, p. A14; "Dupont Circle to Have Big Hotel," WDN, 14 Mar. 1930; Hickman; "Ouster Stirs 'Meeting' at Dupont Apts.," WTH, 7 July 1941; Arthur H. Purcell, "The Offices with a Soul," WP, 30 Mar. 1986, p. K1; "10-Story Building for Dupont Circle," ES, 20 May 1926, p. 5; "12-Story Hotel Plans Completed," ES, 17 Jan. 1931.

97. HILLTOP MANOR.
Manuscripts BP 8148, 2 Apr. 1926, lot 43, sq. 2688. Pamphlets Edmund J. Flynn, *Hilltop Manor: A 100% Co-operative Apartment Building* (Washington, D.C.: Cafritz Co., 1927). Periodicals "Big Apt. Bldg. for 14th and Oak," ES, 10 Apr. 1926, p. 19; "Cafritz Resources Brought to Front for Hilltop Manor," ES, 17 Oct. 1926, p. 2; "Cavalier Trustee Removal Sought," ES, 8 May 1930, p. B1; Anne Chase, "Cavalier to Reopen After Major Facelift," WP, 16 Feb. 1984, p. DC12; Edmund J. Flynn, "Inspection Urged for Many Features of Hilltop Manor," ES, 17 Oct. 1926, p. 2; "14th St. Landmark Sold," WP, 12 May 1964; Margaret Green, "Cavalier Rent Suit is Decided," SN, 2 Mar. 1973; "Here Is the Whole Proposition," WP, 17 Oct. 1926, p. 3; "Hilltop Manor, Largest of Cooperative Apts., Has Many Unusual Features," WP, 17 Oct. 1926, p. R1; David Holmberg, "Tenants with Children Fight Eviction Notice," SN, 11 Jan. 1973; "Landmark Work Beautifies Tract at Hilltop Manor," ES, 17 Oct. 1926, p. 6; "Many Apt. Homes Bought in Hilltop Manor," ES, 17 Oct. 1926, p. 2; "Service To Be Motto of Hilltop Management," ES, 17 Oct. 1926, p. 2; "Tenants Gird," SN, 12 Jan. 1973; "Top City Officials," WAA, 10 Mar. 1984.

98. 3901 CONNECTICUT AVENUE, N.W.
Manuscripts BP 2985, 7 Oct. 1927, lot 2, sq. 2234. Periodicals "New Apt. Started in N.W.," ES, 15 Oct. 1927, p. 18.

99. PARK TOWER.
Manuscripts BP 117740, 2 Oct. 1928, lot 101, sq. 2571. Books Sexton. Periodicals "Apt. Being Erected on Sixteenth Street," ES, 15 Sept. 1928, p. 20; LaBarbara Bowman, "Tenant Clings to Her Home in Empty Bldg.," WP, 18 Apr. 1981, p. B1; "Five Story Apt. House Planned on Sixteenth Street," ES, 25 Aug. 1928, p. 13; "Landlord Wins Two-and-a-Half-Year 'War' with His Tenants," WP, 28 Feb. 1981, p. C1; "Large Apts. Change Ownership," ES, 5 Oct. 1929, p. 15; "Woodney Buys Park Towers," ES, 8 July 1961.

CHAPTER 4

INTRODUCTION.

Apartment shortage, 1935–45.
Periodicals "Apt. Project Patterned Along Lines of Tomato Can," ES, 5 Sept. 1944; "Apt. Scarcity Gives Rise to Fear of Rent 'Black Market,' " ES, 6 Sept. 1942; "Bldg. Owners Seek Action on Shortage of Elevator Boys," ES, 12 June 1942; "Capital Apt. Managers Asked to Aid Salvage Drive," ES, 8 Aug. 1942; "District Tops Entire Nation in Bldg.," ES, 23 May 1942; "8 Apt. Houses Win Raid Security Awards," ES, 22 Sept. 1944; John F. Gerrity, "Housing Shortage Relief Seen as Foreign Agencies Move Out," WP, 16 Nov. 1945; Harriet Griffiths, "Thousands on Waiting Lists for Higher Priced Apts.," ES, 27 Aug. 1944; James Y. Newton, "Construction in D.C. Best Since 1928," ES, 6 Jan. 1940, p. B1; Newton, "D.C. Bldg. Activities Show Boom-Like Gains," ES, 28 Dec. 1935; Newton, "1,934 D.C. Apts. Occupied as Offices Survey Discloses," ES, 29 Oct. 1941; Newton, "Permits Reveal Bldg. 'Boom' Underway Here," ES, 11 May 1935 (quote); Newton, "Private Bldg. in D.C. Breaks Records in '41," ES, 10 Jan. 1942; "Record Bldg. Cited by Realtor," ES, 23 May 1936; "Rents in District Average $52.68, Nation's Highest," ES, 8 June 1942; "Soaring City Rents Feared by Meyer," ES, 23 Nov. 1934; "Suitland Slated to Get 682-Unit Housing Project," ES, 28 Mar. 1942.

Government takeover of apartments.
Periodicals "Biddle Rules Dupont Lease to U.S. Valid," WP, 28 Aug. 1941; "British Air Office To Be Moved Here from New York," ES, 22 Oct. 1940; "British Lease Another Apt. House," ES, 18 Mar. 1941; "British Office to Take Over John Marshall Apt.," ES, 2 Aug. 1941; "Dupont Circle Residents Plan Court Action," WP, 23 Aug. 1941; "Dupont Circle Tenant Ousted by Noise After 6-Year Fight," WP, 31 Mar. 1948; "Government Leases Apt. Bldg.," ES, 25 Aug. 1917; "Government Vacates 117-Unit Apt.," ES, 9 May 1946; Robert J. Lewis, "More Sue Dupont Hotel Over Leases," WP, 29 Aug. 1941; "Navy Explains Apt. Seizure Here," 9 Jan. 1943; "Navy Files Court Action to Take New Bldg.," ES, 5 Jan. 1943; "118 Tenants Evicted to Permit Alterations for War Workers," ES, 20 Apr. 1944; "350 More D.C. Tenants 'Evicted' to House British," WTH, 2 Aug. 1941; "U.S. Pays $550,000 for Apts.," ES, 17 Oct. 1935; "U.S. to Take Potomac Park Apts.," WP, 3 Aug. 1935; "USSR Gives Up 16th Street Apts.," ES, 17 May 1947.

Murphy beds.
Pamphlets *Murphy's Blue Print Manual* (New York: Murphy Door Bed Co., 1925). Periodicals "New Apt. House Plan Has Developed Good Results," AA, vol. 18, July–Dec. 1920, p. 379.

Rent control.
Pamphlets Steven J. Diner, *The Regulation of Housing in the District of Columbia, Studies in D.C. History and Public Policy No. 5* (Washington, D.C.: Univ. of D.C., 1983). Periodicals James E.

Chinn, "Rent Control Bill Effective Only for Emergency," ES, 16 July 1961; "Commissioners Urged by Realtors to Seek End of Rent Control," ES, 30 Jan. 1948; James Free, "Henderson Asks Rent Control for District," ES, 11 July 1941; "Kenesaw Rent Boost Granted," WTH, 15 Nov. 1947; "Rent Cut in 75 Percent of Cases Handled, Cogswell Testifies," ES, 6 Apr. 1942; Samuel Shaffer, "Cogswell Appointed Rent Czar," WTH, 18 Dec. 1941.

Popularity of garden apartments.
Periodicals "Construction of First Unit of Petworth Gardens Begun," ES, 8 Oct. 1921.

100. COLONIAL VILLAGE.
Manuscripts "Colonial Village," NR, 1979, pp. 1–47; Colonial Village Preservation Committee, "Colonial Village: The Cultural and Architectural Heritage," 1978, pp. 1–50. Books *Historic Arlington* (Arlington, Va.: Arlington County Bicentennial Commission, 1976); Eleanor Lee Templeman, *Arlington Heritage* (Arlington, Va., 1959). Periodicals "Air Conditioning For Homes," AF, Aug. 1935, pp. 136–39; "Arrange for $1,800,000 Extension to Colonial Village," ES, 2 Nov. 1935; "Big F.H.A. Project to Begin Tuesday," ES, 21 Apr. 1935; William D. Blair, "Solving an Estate Investment Problem," IMP, Nov. 1937, pp. 8–10; Sandra G. Goodman, "Colonial Village in Arlington Is Sold," WP, 15 Oct. 1977; Miles L. Colean, "An Early FHA Experiment," *Mortgage Banker*, May 1978, pp. 86 and 88; "Colonial Village Addition Planned," ES, 18 Aug. 1935; "Colonial Village Being Occupied," ES, 31 Aug. 1935; "Colonial Village Builds More Homes," ES, 27 July 1935; "Complex Under Way," WP, 14 Nov. 1981, p. E10; Alison Cumming, "Colonial Village Tenants Dislike Mobil's Plans," *Arlington Journal*, 13 Oct. 1978; "The Development of Colonial Village," WP, 20 Mar. 1984; Guy T.O. Hollyday, "America Builds for Her Renter Millions," IMP, May 1939, pp. 5–7; "Housing," *Fortune*, May 1938, p. 94; "Large-Scale Housing," AF, Feb. 1938, pp. 110–24; "Low-Cost Apt. Project at Clarendon Approved by FHA," WDN, 25 Feb. 1935; "Low-Cost Suburban Apt. Bldgs.," AR, Sept. 1939, pp. 88–114; Seward H. Mott, "Land Planning in the FHA: 1934–44," FHA, second qtr., 1944, pp. 12–14; Mott, "Projects Actively Under Way," FHA, Sept. 1938; Sue Mullin, "Tenants Battling Oil Giant to Keep Their Homes in Colonial Village," WS, 25 Oct. 1978; "A New Policy for Housing," AF, Aug. 1936; "New Apt. Project in Clifton May Cost $3,000,000," *Cincinnati Times-Star*, 7 Mar. 1937; "Progress in Large-Scale Housing," IMP, May 1937, pp. 10 and 23; Gustave Ring, "Large-Scale Housing as a Business," FHA, June 1937, pp. 5–7; Ring, "Modern Trends in Garden Apts.," *Urban Land*, May 1948, pp. 1 and 3–4; Ring, "Pointers on Garden Apt. Operation," *Urban Land*, July-Aug. 1948, pp. 2–5; "Shop Center Opened in Arlington County," ES, 2 Apr. 1936; "Starts $1,500,000 Apt. Project," [Baltimore] *Sun*, 18 Mar. 1938; "Store Property Sales Reported," ES, 11 July 1936; "Waiting List," ES, 11 Sept. 1935; Franklyn Waltman, "Private Housing Projects in Capital Set Example for U.S.," WP, 28 Nov. 1937; "Washington Housing," AF, Jan. 1944,

pp. 53–64; J.Y. Smith, "Gustave Ring, Noted Builder in Area, Dies," WP, 5 May 1983.

101. LANGSTON TERRACE.
Manuscripts "Hilyard R. Robinson," vertical file, Howard University Library, Washington; Record Group 192, U.S. Housing Administration, WPA, National Archives. Books John McAndrew, ed., *Guide to Modern Architecture, Northeast States* (New York: Museum of Modern Art, 1940), p. 26. Periodicals "Absence of Child Delinquency Noted in U.S.H.A. Survey," ES, 14 Jan. 1940; "Colored Tenants Rush to Langston," ES, 7 Mar. 1938; "First Low-Cost Housing Project for D.C.," WT, 17 Dec. 1935; "Frieze Shows Progress of Race," ES, 11 Oct. 1936; "H.R. Robinson Named to Planning Group; Wurster Is Chairman," ES, 30 June 1949, p. A6; "Langston Rents under $8 Weekly," ES, 1 Mar. 1938; "Langston's Tenants," ES, 27 Mar. 1940; "Langston Terrace," WP, 24 July 1936; "Langston, U.S. Housing Project, Is Year Old Tomorrow," ES, 4 May 1939; Glen B. Leiner, "The Langston Terrace Dwellings," TL, vol. 2, no. 3, Aug. 1984, p. 1 and p. 9; Agnes E. Meyer, "Negro Housing," WP, 6 Feb. 1944; "Mrs. Roosevelt to Address D.C. Project Group," JG, 11 Apr. 1936; Art Peters, "Langston Awards Made for High Maintenance," *Pittsburgh Courier*, 11 June 1949; "Program Marks 10th Year of Langston Homes Project," WAA, 19 June 1948; "PWA Head Awards Contract for Colored Housing Project," WP, 11 Nov. 1936; Rick Roberts, "Langston Terrace Memorial to Virginia Pioneer," *Pittsburgh Courier*, 8 July 1950; Joe Shepherd, "Washingtonians You Should Know," WAA, 8 June 1940; Nelson M. Shephard, "Thousands To Be Turned Away in Langston Rent Scramble," ES, 23 June 1938; "Survey of the Month," *In Opportunity* mag., Sept. 1941, p. 179; Wolf Von Eckardt, "Blueprints of an Unheralded Past," WP, 13 Dec. 1980; Von Eckardt, "House Keeping," WP, 9 May 1981; "Where Shall We Live?," WDN, 2 Oct. 1937, p. 4; "Washington Housing Project to Rent for $5.58 a Room," JG, 18 July 1936.

102. 2929 CONNECTICUT AVENUE, N.W.
Manuscripts BP 196436, 18 Sept. 1936, lot 6, sq. 2210. Books Wirz-Striner. Periodicals "Large Apt. Planned," ES, 26 Sept. 1936; "Dunbar Rosenthal, 91," WP, 2 Feb. 1982.

103. MAJESTIC.
Manuscripts BP 202089, 4 May 1937, lots 9–10, sq. 2608. Books Wirz-Striner. Periodicals "Alvin Aubinoe, Builder, Architect, Dies at 71," WP, 21 June 1974; "Bldg. Planned as Embassy Home," ES, 26 May 1928; "D.C. Architectural Firm Designs Apt.," ES, 29 Sept. 1951; "Harry Edwards, Architect, Dead," WP, 17 Jan. 1958; Richard Slusser, "Alvin L. Aubinoe Dies, Area Builder, Architect," WDN, 21 June 1974.

104. GOVERNOR SHEPHERD.
Manuscripts BP 216080, 30 Aug. 1938, lots 802 to 806, sq. 81; Richard Striner, "The Governor Shepherd," 1984, pp. 1–8 (author's files). Books Abel-Severud; McAndrew; Wirz-Striner.

The entrance to the Gwenwood, recently demolished, was one of several Art Deco apartment house examples built by Morris Cafritz with circular windows set within a pair of front doors.

Periodicals Bill Allegar, "D.C. Historic Preservation Board Weighs Fate of Apt. Bldg.," WT, 8 May 1985, p. B7; "Berla Firm Works on US-Danish Bldg. Plan," *Washington Building Congress Bulletin*, Oct. 1951, pp. 4 and 7; "Governor Shepherd Apts., Washington, D.C.," AF, May 1941, pp. 322–23; "In Danger: The Governor Shepherd Apts. and the Star Parking Complex," TL, vol. 1, no. 1, Nov. 1982, pp. 4–5; "New Apt. Under Construction," ES, 8 Oct. 1938; "A Portfolio of Work by Berla & Abel," AF, Aug. 1946, pp. 81–96; "Prince George Apts., Hyattsville, Maryland," AR, pp. 76–77; Anneke Reems, "Modern Architecture Comes of Age," *Magazine of Art*, vol. 37, no. 3, Mar. 1944, pp. 89–93.

105. GWENWOOD.
Manuscripts BP 219284, 30 Dec. 1938, lots 19–21, sq. 85. Books and pamphlets *Murphy's Blue Print Manual* (New York: Murphy Door Bed Co., 1925); Wirz-Striner. Periodicals "Apt. Bldgs. to Cost $1,000,000," ES, 11 Nov. 1922, p. 17; "Big Apt. Planned," ES, 31 July 1925, p. 5; "Cafritz Co. Plans Large Apt.," ES, 13 Dec. 1930; "Couple Trapped in Folding Bed Sue House Owner," ES, 20 Apr. 1928, p. 17; "Disappearing Beds Not New for Apts.," ES, 24 July 1920, sec. 2, p. 4; "Folding Beds," ES, 28 Mar. 1914, pt. 2, p. 2; "Group Inspects New Capital Apt.," ES, 12 Dec. 1936; "Harry Edwards, Architect, Dead," WP, 17 Jan. 1938; "Holmes Roll-Out Bed" (advertisement), PP, Mar. 1926, p. 43; "Leaders in Apt. House Construction Industry," ES, 30 Aug. 1930; "New Ambassador Will Open Today," ES, 22 Sept. 1929, p. 21; Robert Park, "The Streets Were Paved with Gold," WM, Apr. 1984, pp. 114–17; Richard Slusser, "Alvin L. Aubinoe Dies, Area Builder, Architect," WS, 21 June 1974.

106. MARLYN.
Manuscripts BP 207398, 12 Oct. 1938, lot 822, sq. 1815; letter, Francis L. Koenig, McLean, Va., to the author, 15 May 1982, pp. 1–6 (quote). Periodicals "Carrier Air Conditioning" (advertisement), *Time*, 11 Apr. 1938, p. 57; "The Marlyn," AF, Oct. 1938; "The Marlyn," WS, 18 July 1975; "Marlyn Apts. Sold for $1,185,000," WP, 1 June 1956; "Tenants Stand Firm with Pets, Appealing Eviction Action," ES, 21 Oct. 1942 (quote).

107. CRYSTAL HEIGHTS.
Books Arthur Drexler, *The Drawings of Frank Lloyd Wright* (New York: Horizon Press, 1962); Goode; Placzek; Bruce Brooks Pfeiffer, *Treasures of Taliesin; Seventy-six Unbuilt Designs of Frank Lloyd Wright* (Carbondale, Ill.: Southern Illinois University Press, 1985). Periodicals Al Chase, "A 'Radio City' in Washington," *Chicago Tribune*, 21 Apr. 1940; "Crystal City," WP, 25 Sept. 1940; "Crystal City Faces Another Hurdle in 130-Foot Limit," ES, 1 Dec. 1940, p. B1; "'Crystal City' May Require Special Act of Congress," ES, 9 Oct. 1940, p. B1; "Crystal City Plan Rejected by Zone Unit," WTH, 17 Jan. 1941; "Crystal City Project Zoning Decision Expected Thursday," ES, 27 Dec. 1940, p. B1; "'Crystal City' to Rise on Temple Heights," ES, 24 Sept. 1940; "Decision on 110-Foot Over-All Height of Bldgs. Deferred," ES, 5 Dec. 1940, p. B1; "Definite Plan Is Adopted for New Masonic Temple," ES, 21 May 1927, p. 24; "Developer Hopes to Create a Temple Heights 'Radio City,' " ES, 11 Dec. 1940; "$15,000,000 'Crystal Palace' to Rise on Connecticut Avenue," WTH, 25 Sept. 1940; Gerald G. Gross, "Architect Visions $15,000,000 City of Future on Temple Heights," WP, 25 Sept. 1940; Frederick Gutheim, "Critic Urges Another Look at Design for Hilton," WP, 10 Sept. 1961, p. E2; Elizabeth Mooney, "Fallingwater," WP, 12 July 1981, p. E1; "Nary One Window in 'Crystal City'," WDN, 25 Sept. 1940 (first quote); "New York Syndicate Buys Temple Heights to Build Apts.," ES, 8 Jan. 1945, p. B1; "Nolen Offers Plan to 'Save' Crystal City," WP, 27 Dec. 1940; Bruce Brooks Pfeiffer, "Oh, What We Missed," *Washington Post* mag., 5 Jan. 1986, pp. 16–19; "Side View of Project White Is to Dim the Glory of Versailles," WTH, 24 Sept. 1940; "Temple Heights Plans Call for $2,500,000 Bldg. Project," ES, 22 Jan. 1945; "Trade Group Assured on Crystal City Plans," ES, 9 Oct. 1940, p. B1; "Wright Designs 'Crystal City' for Temple Heights," ES, 24 Sept. 1940, B1 (second quote); "Wright's Lance Hurled at D.C.," ES, 26 Oct. 1938 (third quote).

108. GENERAL SCOTT.
Manuscripts BP 239352, 16 Dec. 1940, lots 806–7, sq. 195. Pamphlets *The General Scott* (Washington, D.C.: Herbert Harvey Realty, 1941), pp. 1–3; *The General Scott* (Washington, D.C.: Hoskinson and Davis Realty, 1982), pp. 1–9. Periodicals Bill Black, "Taking Risks Paid Off for Tenants of the General Scott Apts.," WP, 6 Nov. 1982, p. E21 (quote); "Blasts of Rays to Germ-Proof New 16th Street Apts.," WTH, 24 July 1941; "Rent Boost Weighed after Protests by 30 General Scott Tenants," ES, 16 Nov. 1948.

109. CARLYN.
Manuscripts BP 244299, 4 June 1941, lot 846 (21), sq. E–1264. Periodicals "New Apt. Under Construction," ES, 14 June 1941; Lynn Rosellini, "Power in the Aisles of a Capital Market," NYT, 8 July 1981.

110. DELANO.
Manuscripts BP 243555, 14 May 1941, lot 825, sq. 2132. Books

Wirz-Striner. Pamphlets *The Delano Apartments* (Washington, D.C.: Brown Bros. Corp., 1941).

111. DORCHESTER HOUSE.
Manuscripts BP 240243, 14 Jan. 1941, lot 808, sq. 2572. Books and pamphlets *Dorchester House* (Washington, D.C.: Randall H. Hagner and Company, 1941), pp. 1–6; Lynne McTaggart, *Kathleen Kennedy, Her Life and Times* (New York: Dial Press, 1983); Herbert S. Parmet, *Jack, The Struggles of John F. Kennedy* (New York: Dial Press, 1980). Periodicals Kenneth Bredemeir, "Laws Attacked for Scaring Off Investment," WP, 11 July 1984; Hank Burchard, "Presidents in Residence," WP, *Weekend* mag., 7 Mar. 1986, pp. 4–5; "Dog Owners Unite to Keep Pets," WTH, 29 Mar. 1945; "Dorchester House Gets Hot Water and Heat During Strike," ES, 23 Jan. 1954; "Dorchester House Tenants Unite to Protect Leases and Leashes," ES, 29 Mar. 1945; "Dorchester House Told to Refund Excess Rent," WP, 27 May 1984; Linda Ellis, "Rent Refunds Due to Tenants of Bldg. in Northwest," WS, 25 July 1980; "Huge Apt. Planned," ES, 21 Dec. 1940; "No One Laughed When She Sat Down and Played Mozart," ES, 20 Oct. 1953; Drew Pearson, "Washington Merry-Go-Round," WP, 26 Sept. 1942; Eugene Robinson, "D.C. Firm Told to Pay Tenants Over $1 Million," WP, 19 Aug. 1981; "Running Sore," WP, 22 Nov. 1954; Jacqueline Trescott, "Tenacious Tenants' Triumph," WP, 25 May 1981.

112. McLEAN GARDENS.
Manuscripts Letter, Alan B. Mills, Jr., Ponte Vedra Beach, Fla., to the author, 12 May 1983. Books *Guide to the National Archives of the United States* (Washington, D.C.: GPO, 1974); Charles Zaid,

Detail of the original 1941 carpet still in use in the public corridors of the Delano.

compiler, *Preliminary Inventory of the Records of the Reconstruction Finance Corporation, 1932–1964* (Washington, D.C.: GPO, 1973). Periodicals Andrew Alexander, "Tragedy on Wisconsin Ave.," RM, Aug.-Sept. 1982, pp. 75–81; LaBarbara Bowman, "Big New Complex Approved for McLean Gardens," WP, 10 Aug. 1982; Patricia Camp, "McLean Gardens Tenants Plan Own Development," WP, 1 Dec. 1978; Camp, "McLean Gardens Tenants Sign Pact to Bury Project," WP, 6 Dec. 1978; Camp, "Obstacle Looms for McLean Gardens," WP, 25 May 1978, p. C12; Camp, "Tenants Complain Purchase of McLean Gardens," WP, 29 Sept. 1979; H. Bradford Fish, "McLean Gardens Groups Oppose High-Rise Plans," WP, 8 May 1982; Barbara J. Graham, "New Developer Unveils Plan for McLean Gardens Complex," WP, 20 Aug. 1983, p. F1; Donald Hirzel, "McLean Gardens Tenants Win Reprieve from Mass Eviction," WS, 11 Aug. 1978; George Kennedy, "Friendship, Dating to 1695, Houses 4,000 in Modern Apts.," ES, 12 Mar. 1951, p. B1 (quote); Michael Kierman, "Council to Air McLean Gardens Rent Increases," WSN, 17 Jan. 1974; "Letters to the Editor: The McLean Gardens Dispute," WP, 26 June 1978; Thomas W. Lippman, "Rent-Rise Scare Hits Project," WP, 23 Jan. 1975; Margaret Mason, "Grand Tradition Preserved," WP, 13 July 1980, p. D1; "McLean Gardens To Be Converted to Condominiums," WS, 24 May 1978; Howard Means, "The Battle of McLean Gardens," WM, Nov. 1979, pp. 112–31; Peter Perl, "Uncertainty at McLean Gardens," WP, 19 May 1982, p. C1; Karen Riley, "Condo Push Comes to Shove," WP, 30 May 1981, p. E1; Duncan Spencer and Donia Mills, "Tenants Hail Agreement on N.W. Complex," WS, 3 June 1979; Sandra Evans Teeley, "McLean Gardens Taking Up Where Tenants Left Off," WP, 3 Oct. 1981, p. E1; "Tenants Announce Development Plan," WP, 2 Dec. 1978, p. B12.

113. PARKFAIRFAX.
Manuscripts Letter, Richard M. Nixon, New York, to Robert Cullinane, research assistant, Washington, 20 Dec. 1985 (quote); letter, Gerald R. Ford, Rancho Mirage, Calif., to Robert Cullinane, research assistant, Washington, 12 Dec. 1985. Periodicals Gloria Borger, "Parkfairfax Takes a Shaky Step into Our Modern Times," WS, 13 Mar. 1977; Hank Burchard, "Presidents in Residence," WP, *Weekend* mag., 7 Mar. 1986, pp. 4–5; Patricia Camp, "Parkfairfax Sold, Will Become Condominiums," WP, 12 Feb. 1977; Abby Chapple, "Inside Living," WS, 6 Aug. 1978; "Citizen-Developer Conflicts Easing," AP, 17 May 1978; "Conversion Finds Key to Keeping Its Tenants," WS, 4 Aug. 1978; Richard Corrigan, "Parkfairfax," WP, *Potomac* mag., 22 Sept. 1968, pp. 18–19; Lynn Darling, "The All-Night Town House Vigil," WP, 23 Nov. 1977; Barbara Halliday, "278 Former Parkfairfax Tenants Go Condo," AJ, 21 June 1978; Sandra Hemingway, "Condo Transition to Oust Tenants," AJ, 1 Feb. 1978; Hemingway, "Parkfairfax to Roll Back Rent Increases," AJ, 25 Nov. 1977; Shirley Johnson, "Parkfairfax to Roll Back Rent Increases," AG, 18 Apr. 1975; D.L. Kennedy, "West Plays Catch-Up with Time," AP, 28 Apr.

1977; Cynthia Keyworth, "Parkfairfax: 'Revitalized' into 'Immodesty,' " WP, 5 Mar. 1977; Stephanie Mansfield, "Housing Bias," WP, 16 July 1978; Jane Mayer, "Ford's Old Apt. Listed at $75,000," WS, 19 June 1980; Sharon Obermiller, "Parkfairfax Potpourri," AP, 12 Dec. 1979; "Parkfairfax Evictions Canceled," AP, 15 Feb. 1978; "Parkfairfax Sells Out 2nd Village," AP, 19 July 1978; "Parkfairfax Tenant Defends Condo Development Firm," AG, 26 Apr. 1978; "Residents Line Up for Parkfairfax Units," AP, June 1978; "Tenants Buy Most Parkfairfax Units," AG, 19 July 1978; Lexie Verdon, "Staying Put: Apt. Renovations Irritate Some Parkfairfax Residents," AJ, Jan. 1978; "Waiters," AP, 13 Dec. 1979; John B. Willmann, "Condo Managers: New Breed," WP, 15 July 1978; Willmann, "Parkfairfax Conversion Continues," WP, 18 Feb. 1978.

114. FALKLAND.
Manuscripts "Falkland Apts.," Maryland Historical Trust Inventory Form for State Historic Sites Survey, 1981, pp. 1–31; letter, David E. Betts, and Henry H. Glassie, Washington, to Historic Preservation Commission of Montgomery County, Rockville, Maryland, 20 May 1981, pp. 1–3; letter, Nicholas A. Pappas, Washington, to Henry H. Glassie, Washington, 8 May 1981; Andrea Rebeck, "Evaluation of Falkland Apts. for National Register Nomination," Jan. 1984, pp. 1–11; statements of Anne H. Helwig, Perry Gerard Fisher, and Nicholas Pappas, Montgomery County Historic Preservation Commission, Rockville, Maryland, 5 Feb. 1981, pp. 1–14; Mark Walston, "Falkland Apts. in Relation to the Pre-World War II Suburban Apt. Movement in Montgomery County," 1981, pp. 1–72. Periodicals Jack Allen, "New Apts. Are Planned on Sixteenth Street," ES, 10 Jan. 1937; Miles L. Colean, "Multiple Housing Under FHA," AR, Sept. 1938; John Hanrahan, "$100 Million Project Planned," ES, 2 July 1968; Robert J. Lewis, "Planning Panel Opposes Huge Falkland Complex," ES, 2 Apr. 1970; "Locations for Large-scale Housing," FHA, Mar. 1937, pp. 15–17 and 24–26; Virginia Mansfield, "Tenants Seek to Purchase Falkland Apts.," WP, 11 Sept. 1980, p. MD3; Mansfield, "Historic Group Delays Decision on Falkland," WP, 13 Nov. 1980; "Maryland Large-scale Housing Project Insured," FHA, Feb. 1937, p. 20; "Planning Is Related to Sound Land Use and Financing," AR, Mar. 1941; "Rental Projects of F.H.A. Praised," ES, 20 Nov. 1937; "Suburban Apt. Bldgs.," AR, Sept. 1939, pp. 89–100; Wendy Swallow, "Older Garden Projects Face Pressure," WP, 10 Mar. 1984, p. F1; "A Tribute to Louis Justement," *Washington Building Congress*, Sept. 1968, pp. 12–13; Wolf Von Eckardt, "Falkland Plans: Potential Disaster," WP, 13 Nov. 1971; Mark Walston, "Montgomery County's First Garden Apts.," *Montgomery County Story*, vol. 27, no. 1, Feb. 1984; Franklyn Waltman, "Private Housing Projects in Capital Set Example for United States," WP, 28 Nov. 1937.

115. 2407 15TH STREET, N.W.
Manuscripts BP 199232, 3 Feb. 1937, lot 848–50, sq. 2662. Books John McAndrew, editor, *Guide to Modern Architecture,*

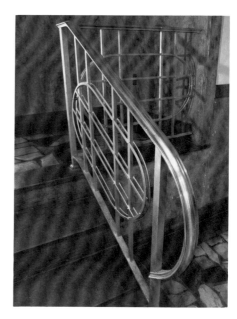

Detail of the Art Deco balustrade in the lobby of the Normandie, near Walter Reed Hospital.

Northeast States (New York: Museum of Modern Art, 1940).

116. 4801 CONNECTICUT AVENUE, N.W.
Manuscripts BP 217990, 3 Nov. 1938, lots 3, 803–4, sq. 2035; Alvin L. Aubinoe, Sr., "Biography of Alvin L. Aubinoe, Sr.," 1965, pp. 1–3. Books Wirz-Striner. Pamphlets *4801 Connecticut Avenue, N.W.* (Washington, D.C.: Real Estate Mortgage and Guaranty Corp., 1940), pp. 1–4. Periodicals "Alvin L. Aubinoe, Builder, Architect, Dies at 71," WP, 21 June 1974, p. B12; "Big Apt. Bldg. Sold to Group of Investors Here," ES, 15 July 1950, p. B3.

117. HIGHTOWERS.
Manuscripts BP 215355, 4 Aug. 1938, lot 801, sq. 180. Books Wirz–Striner.

CHAPTER 5

INTRODUCTION.
Building boom, 1955–69.
Periodicals Conrad P. Harness, "Vast Rental Program to Cover Washington with New Apts.," WP, 10 Apr. 1949; Robert J. Lewis, "Congress Fails to Push Apt. Production," ES, 15 Mar. 1958, p. B1; Sylvia Porter, "Your Money's Worth," ES, 3 Sept. 1959; "Survey Shows Low Apt. Vacancy Rate," ES, 19 May 1956, p. B1; "3.5 Pct. Vacancies Noted in Area Big Apts.," ES, 5 Nov. 1955.

Cooperative conversions.
Periodicals "Cooperative Protection," WP, 22 Oct. 1948; "District Heads to Ask Rent Control Till '50, Restriction on Co-ops," ES, 10 Nov. 1948; "House Groups Weigh Rent Control Curb in Co-op Apts.," ES, 1 Mar. 1949.

Government takeover of apartments in Korean War.
Periodicals "Defense Agencies to Take Over Apt. Houses as Offices," ES, 20 Feb. 1951; "GSA Drops Move to Lease Apts.,"

ES, 10 Apr. 1951; "Marshall Fights Plan to Give Up Offices in New Apts.," ES, 28 Apr. 1951; Crosby S. Noyes, "Bates Questions U.S. Agencies Apt. Use," ES, 5 Mar. 1951; Noyes, "House Group Frowns on Apts.' Use for Defense Offices," ES, 7 Mar. 1951; "Pentagon Plan to Lease Offices Is Probed," ES, 16 Mar. 1951; "Truman Vetoes Curb on Executive Realty Deals; Hits Congress," ES, 16 May 1951.

Modernism.

Books John Ely Burchard and Albert Bush-Brown, *The Architecture of America: A Social and Cultural History* (Boston: Little, Brown, 1961); William J.R. Curtis, *Modern Architecture since 1900* (Englewood Cliffs, N.J.: Prentice-Hall, 1983); Kenneth Frampton, *Modern Architecture: A Critical History* (London: Thames and Hudson Ltd., 1985); Green; Talbot Hamlin, ed., *Forms and Functions of Twentieth-Century Architecture* (New York: Columbia Univ. Press, 1952), 4 vols.; Henry-Russell Hitchcock and Arthur Drexler, ed., *Built in USA: Post-War Architecture* (New York: Museum of Modern Art, 1954); Henry-Russell Hitchcock and Philip Johnson, *The International Style* (New York: W.W. Norton & Co., 1966); Spiro Kostof, *A History of Architecture: Settings and Rituals* (New York: Oxford Univ. Press, 1985); Vincent Scully, *American Architecture and Urbanism* (New York: Praeger, 1969); Robert A. M. Stern, *New Directions in American Architecture* (New York: Geo. Braziller, 1969); Wolf Von Eckardt, ed., *Mid-Century Architecture in America* (Baltimore: Johns Hopkins Univ. Press, 1961); Marcus Whiffen, *American Architecture since 1780: A Guide to the Styles* (Cambridge, Mass.: MIT Press, 1969). Periodicals Roger K. Lewis, " 'Modernist' Bldgs. Spoiled Architects' Fun," WP, 2 Feb. 1985; Lewis, "New Materials Foretold Architectural Changes," WP, 19 Jan. 1985, p. F8; Lewis, "What Makes for a Modern Bldg.?," WP, 9 Feb. 1985, p. F2.

Rent control.

Periodicals "Applications To Raise Rents Triple in Year," ES, 27 Aug. 1948; LaBarbara Bowman, "Council Gives Preliminary Nod to New District Rent Control Bill," WP, 15 Nov. 1980, p. B1; Kenneth Bredemeier, "Lines Drawn in D.C. Rent Control Battle," WP, 17 Mar. 1985; "Each Side Has Supporters in Crowd of 200 at District Rent Control Hearing," WP, 21 May 1947; Lance Gay, "Rent Control: Economic Scourge or Inflation Shield?," WS, 16 Jan. 1977; Marcia Slocum Greene, "Divided Council to Take Up Rent Control," WP, 28 Feb. 1985; Greene, "FTC Report Says Rent Control Harmful to D.C. Economy," WP, 15 Mar. 1985, p. A15; Gilbert Hahn, Jr., "Who Pays—Landlord or Tenant?," *Journal of the Bar Association of D.C.*, Dec. 1948, pp. 495–507; Michael Kiernan, "Rents Frozen in District," WS, 27 Apr. 1974; "Prompt Ruling Sought by Lusk on Proposed Rent Boost Formula," ES, 26 Nov. 1947; Lew Sichelman, "Citing D.C. Rent Curbs, Investors Want Out," WS, 12 Nov. 1977; "Truman Signs Bill Extending D.C. Rent Control," ES, 13 July 1949.

Southwest urban renewal.

Manuscripts Mary Alice Riley, "An Ecological Study of South West Washington," M.A. thesis, Catholic University, Philosophy Dept., 1929, pp. 1–42; letter, John R. Searles, Jr., Ponte Vedra Beach, Fla., to the author, 15 July 1983, pp. 1–9 (quote). Books Green; Chalmers M. Roberts, *The Washington Post: The First 100 Years* (Boston: Houghton Mifflin, 1977); Robert A. M. Stern, *New Directions in American Architecture* (New York: George Braziller, 1969). Periodicals Al Alibrando, "Apt. Stores Favored in S.W.," ES, 4 Nov. 1958; "Apt. Dedicated As Renewal Milestone," ES, 9 Oct. 1959; "Architects Call Southwest Plan 'Unimaginative,' " ES, 21 Nov. 1952, p. A23; "Architects Dream," *Georgetowner*, 26 Mar. 1959; George Beveridge, "Builders to Get Bid to Invest in Redevelopment," ES, 14 Nov. 1952, p. A21; Beveridge, "2 Years Allotted to Find Homes for S.W. Slum Dwellers," ES, 19 Nov. 1952, p. A25; Paul Delaney, "Big Apts. Sought in City Renewal Areas," ES, 16 July 1968; "18 Designs Submitted for RLA Project," ES, 27 Feb. 1962; Jack Eisen, "Many Eager to Move into Southwest," WP, 5 Oct. 1958; Eisen, "Searles Leaves Big Job to Fill," WP, 20 Aug. 1961; " 520 S.W. Public Housing Units Planned," ES, 20 Nov. 1952, p. A25; "Grant and Mrs. Smith Disagree on Majority of S.W. Plan," ES, 3 Dec. 1952, p. A29; "Grant Urges Action on Redevelopment," ES, 11 Dec. 1945, p. B1; "Ground Broken for Apts.," ES, 31 Oct. 1960; Luther P. Jackson, "Affiliate of D.C. Transit Wins Contest for Design of Housing Development," WP, 27 Mar. 1962; Jane Jacobs, "Washington," AF, Jan. 1956, pp. 93–115; George Kennedy, "Historic S.W., Once an 'Island', Looks Forward to a Promising Future," ES, 29 Jan. 1951, p. B1; "Last Project Rising in Southwest Renewal," ES, 3 Apr. 1970; "New Luxury High-Rise to Start in S.W.," 7 Apr. 1966, p. E5; "New $6 Million Unit Opens in SW," WDN, 29 Jan. 1965; William A. Millen, "Area B Construction to Start Wednesday," ES, 6 Apr. 1958; Sibyl Moholy-Nagy, "Washington—A Critic of 'The Plan for the Year 2000'," AF, Dec. 1961, pp. 126–31; "Private Builder Displays 10 Remodeled Slum Area Homes," ES, 27 Nov. 1952, p. A29; "Program Drawn," ES, 12 Nov. 1952, p. A1; "Residents Ask Explanation of S.W. Plan," ES, 13 Nov. 1952, p. A3; "See Capitol Park As Reply to Reds," *Pittsburgh Courier*, 25 July 1955; "Southwest Is Center of Primary Planning for Redevelopment," ES, 17 Jan. 1951, p. A8; "S.W. Waterfront Urged by Donohue As Apt. Area," ES, 23 Nov. 1952, p. A14; "S.W. Plan," ES, 18 May 1952, p. C3; John W. Thompson, Jr., "Key to the Redevelopment Project," ES, 28 Sept. 1952, p. A29; John B. Willmann, "A Walk in S.W. Will Refresh Tired Eyes," WP, 16 Feb. 1963, p. D1; Sam Zagoria, "$500 Million Plan to Transform S.W. Told," WP, 17 Feb. 1954, p. 19.

118. POTOMAC PLAZA.

Manuscripts BP B-9324, 27 Mar. 1956, lot 826, sq. 31. Pamphlets *Cooperative Apartment Homes in Potomac Plaza Center* (Washington, D.C.: Edmund J. Flynn Co., 1956), pp. 1–6; *Potomac*

Plaza Medical Building, Inc.: A New Co-operative Medical Building (Washington, D.C.: Edmund J. Flynn Co., 1954). Periodicals Robert C. Albrook, "There's a Fire Going in Foggy Bottom," WP, 30 Oct. 1955; Wes Barthelmes, "Co-op Offices for Foggy Bottom," WP, 16 May 1954; George Beveridge, "Big Foggy Bottom Development Expected to Start by Fall," ES, 13 May 1954, p. A1; Beveridge, "First Permit Sought for Potomac Plaza," ES, 29 Oct. 1955, p. B1; Beveridge, "Plans for Two Big Bldgs. in Foggy Bottom Revealed," ES, 12 May 1954, p. A1; "Bldg. Plans for Property on Potomac Told," ES, 8 Mar. 1954, p. B2; "Center Planned on Capital Acres," NYT, 15 June 1955; "Developers Sign Contract for Foggy Bottom Project," ES, 14 June 1955; Jack Eisen, "Searles Leaves Big Job to Fill," WP, 20 Aug. 1961; "Face-Lifting for Foggy Bottom," WP, 8 Dec. 1954; "Foggy Bottom Association Backs Renewal Project," WP, 17 Nov. 1955; "Foggy Bottom Project Now at Go-Ahead Stage," ES, 15 June 1955, p. A10; "Foggy Bottom Redevelopers Spot 20 Doctor Prospects," WDN, 13 May 1954; "Foggy Bottom Site Bought for $1 Million," WP, 6 Dec. 1955; Harry Gabbett, "Foggy Bottom Jarred to Heels," WP, 16 Apr. 1956; Paul Herron, "N.Y. Firm to Build DeLuxe Center in Foggy Bottom Area," WP, 15 June 1955, p. 17; Herron, "Zoning Ruling Seen Key to Foggy Bottom Project," WP, 10 Mar. 1954; "Last Plaza Plan Hurdle Cleared," WP, 28 Oct. 1955, p. 33; Robert J. Lewis, "Business-and-Housing Project Planned on Foggy Bottom Site," ES, 7 Oct. 1952, p. A1; Hector McLean, "Foggy Bottom Project Drops Potomac Plaza," ES, 27 Dec. 1955, p. A1; William A. Millen, "Potomac Plaza Project Calls For Job Bids," ES, 28 Dec. 1955; "NCPC Opposes $75 Million Development for Foggy Bottom at D.C. Zoning Hearing," WP, 9 Mar. 1954; "New Look for Foggy Bottom," ES, 12 May 1954; Don Olesen, "Foggy Bottom Plan Rezoning Approved," WP, 12 Mar. 1954; "On the Way Out," ES, 26 May 1954; "$100 Million Bldg. Deal Is Clinched," WDN, 14 June 1955; "Papers Signed for Big Project in Foggy Bottom," ES, 14 June 1955; "Planners End Fight, Agree on Bridge Sites," WP, 29 July 1954, p. 17; " 'Potomac Plaza Center' Planned for Foggy Bottom," ES, 30 Nov. 1956; "Potomac Plaza Granted Bldg. Code Exception," ES, 27 Oct. 1955; "Progress on the Construction Front," WP, 17 Nov. 1956; "Rebuilding Foggy Bottom," WP, 11 Mar. 1954, p. 14; "Transforming Foggy Bottom," WP, 29 Dec. 1955.

119. TOWERS.
Manuscripts BP B-37152, 1 July 1958, lots 800–801, sq. 1601. Pamphlets *The Towers* (Washington, D.C.: Gelman Co., 1954), pp. 1–9; *The Towers Condominium Public Offering Statement* (Washington, D.C.: 1979), pp. 1–21. Periodicals Frances Albrecht, "Two Million Dollar Dream," WP, 8 Dec. 1963; "Lobby Elegance at the Towers," WP, 4 June 1960; "New Luxury 'Towers' Adjoins Glover Park," WP, 26 July 1958; "One Apt. House Yields $8200 in Loot," WP, 12 July 1960; Daniel Poole, "Luxury Is His Trademark," ES, 29 Oct. 1965; "Snap-Shots," WP, 11 Feb. 1968; "3 Give Up Towers Luxury Rather Than Their Dogs," WP, 1 Aug. 1961, p. A3; "Towers," ES, 18 June 1960; "The Towers Now

City's Highest-Taxed Property," WP, 5 July 1961; "Towers West," ES, 1 Aug. 1959; "Tradition Redefined," AD, Apr. 1982, pp. 114–21; John B. Willmann, "Sale, Conversion Set for Towers," WP, 7 Nov. 1978.

120. ARMY DISTAFF HALL.
Books and pamphlets *The Challenge—Funding the Future* (Washington, D.C.: The Army Distaff Foundation, 1982), pp. 1–22; Col. Rosemary T. McCarthy, *Army Distaff Hall* (Washington, D.C.: Army Distaff Hall, 1982), pp. 1–24; *Questions and Answers* (Washington, D.C.: Army Distaff Foundation, 1982), pp. 1–20 (quote); *Twenty Years, 1962–1982* (Washington, D.C.: The Army Distaff Foundation, 1982), pp. 1–8. Periodicals Sally Danforth, "The Service Set," [Columbia, S.C.] *State*, 19 Feb. 1960; Ruth Dean, "Mrs. Johnson Opens Army Distaff Hall," ES, 18 Jan. 1962; Elizabeth Ford, "First Lady Shovels Symbolic Dirt," WP, 14 Dec. 1960; Mike Sager, "The Widows of War," *Regardie's*, Mar. 1985, pp. 75–81; "William Montgomery, Acacia Chief, Dies at 85," ES, 5 Sept. 1955; Amelia Young, "Widows of Officers Get Dream Haven," ES, 19 Aug. 1959.

121. HARBOUR SQUARE.
Manuscripts D.C. Certificate of Occupancy, B57949, 2 Sept. 1966. Pamphlets *The Brook House* (Brookline, Mass.: Leatherbee and Co., ca. 1966), pp. 1–17; *Harbour Square* (Washington, D.C.: Chloethiel Woodard Smith and Associates, 1966), pp. 1–44; *A Washington Channel Bridge* (Washington, D.C.: Chloethiel Woodard Smith and Associates, 1966), pp. 1–44. Periodicals Arthur H. Keyes, Jr., "An Architect Talks about the Space between Bldgs.," AR, Sept. 1963, pp. 194–204; Scottie Lanahan, "Be It Never Humble—This Is Home," WP, 21 Nov. 1966; Robert J. Lewis, "Harbour Square Project Sponsor Shifts Name," ES, 17 Dec. 1963; Lewis, "Park Trees a Lively Issue," ES, 22 Jan. 1968; Lewis, "RLA to Check Shifts in Harbour Square Stock," ES, 1 Nov. 1963; Lewis, "Stock Transfer Bypassing RLA Upheld," WP, 2 Nov. 1963; Dorothy McCardle, "HHH Neighbors Borrow White House Red Carpet," WP, 6 July 1968; "Park Protested," WP, 23 Jan. 1968; Daniel Poole, "Everything's Unusual at Harbour Square," ES, 5 June 1963; J.V. Reistrup, "Cooperatives: 'Best of Both Worlds,' " WP, 24 Aug. 1963; "Two Bldgs. Get Age Honors in D.C.," ES, 1 Mar. 1926, p. 37; "View from the Roof," WP, 26 Nov. 1966, p. C6; Jean M. White, "Modern Renewers Won't Kill the Past," WP, 1 Feb. 1962; "Work Under Way at Harbour Square in S.W.," WP, 23 Nov. 1963.

122. WATERGATE.
Manuscripts BP B-123591, 20 Mar. 1964, lots 800–804, 807, 813–814, sqs. 2–3,7–9, 18; BP B-140238 and B-140241, 9 Mar. 1966. Pamphlets *Dedication, Watergate East* (Washington, D.C.: Riverview Realty Corp., 1965), pp. 1–16; Suzanne Berry Sherwood, *Foggy Bottom 1800–1975: A Study in the Uses of an Urban Neighborhood, Washington Studies No. 7* (Washington, D.C.: George Washington University, ca. 1975). Periodicals "Anti-Planning," WP, 22 Apr. 1962; Grace Bassett, "Apt. at Watergate

Draws 6,500 Protests," ES, 17 Dec. 1962; Carl Bernstein, "'Blackmail' Charged at Watergate," WP, 31 Oct. 1968; Michael Bernstein, "Arts Commission O.K.'s Watergate," WDN, 15 Nov. 1967; "Bill to Block Watergate Introduced," WDN, 11 Oct. 1967; Philip D. Carter, "Watergate: Potomac Titanic," WP, 3 May 1970; Maxine Cheshire, "Magnificent Penthouse," WP, 17 Jan. 1969; "City Backs Watergate Plan," WP, 17 Feb. 1968; Willard Clapton, "New Design Approved for Watergate Project," WP, 8 Nov. 1968; B.D. Colen, "Watergate Residents Happy," WP, 21 Feb. 1970; "Commercial Zoning Denied Watergate," WP, 8 Aug. 1968; "Computers Help Lay Out Plan at Watergate," WP, 14 Nov. 1964; Sarah Booth Conroy, "Prices Start as Low as $74,200," WP, 4 Mar. 1967; "Development of Watergate Towne Gets Go-Ahead on Ground Breaking," WP, 25 Jan. 1964; Ymelda Dixon, "Mitchells Sell Duplex," WDN, 5 Aug. 1972; Paul G. Edwards, "8-Acre High Rise Site Eyed," WP, 22 July 1970; Jack Eisen, "Architect Plans 'Touch of Rome'," WP, 6 Aug. 1963; "First Residents," ES, 24 Jan. 1969; "A Flag at Watergate," ES, 29 May 1979; Lee Flor, "Architect Says Curves Will Give Watergate a 'Living Shape'," ES, 7 Aug. 1963; "Foggy Bottom Project Gets Bldg. Loan," ES, 14 Dec. 1962; "4th Unit Rising at Watergate," ES, 27 Oct. 1967; Vera Glaser and Malvina Stephenson, "Watergate Residents Register Complaints," ES, 4 Jan. 1970; Martha M. Hamilton, "Watergate Is Most Valuable Commercial Property in City," WP, 14 May 1973; Helen Henry, "View of Potomac from Every Room," [Baltimore] Sun, 24 Jan. 1974; "High-Rise Watergate Towne Given Final D.C. Approval," WP, 14 July 1962; "High Tide at the Watergate," WP, 4 Apr. 1971; Jim Hoagland, "Alternatives Offered in Watergate Rift," WP, 8 Nov. 1967; Nancy Holmes, "At Home," Town & Country, June 1980, pp. 151–60; Roberts Hornig, "Suit to Block Watergate Hinted," ES, 15 Nov. 1967; Phillip M. Kadis, "Chi-chi Reaches Out," ES, 15 Aug. 1971; Robert J. Lewis, "Arts Center to Sue on Watergate Rule," ES, 1 Dec. 1967; Lewis, "Clark Defends Zoning of Watergate Towne," ES, 20 July 1962; Lewis, "$50 Million Project Set for Foggy Bottom," ES, 22 Oct. 1961; Lewis, "Zoning Adjusters Defer Decision in Watergate-Kennedy Rift," ES, 19 Oct. 1967; Myra MacPherson, "Foggy Bottom Takes Place among Addresses of Status," NYT, 25 June 1966; Jim Mann, "Watergate Residents Sue for $1.5 Million," WP, 3 Mar. 1972; Stephanie Mansfield, "Watergate," WP, 28 May 1981, p. D1; Dan Morgan, "Watergate Towne Gets Warning Over Height," WP, 17 June 1965; "New Watergate Concept Interests Zone Board," ES, 5 Aug. 1962; Charles D. Pierce, "Watergate Towne Hit As Overpowering Mass," ES, 19 Apr. 1963; Daniel Poole, "Watergate Is Unusual," ES, 10 Apr. 1964; Poole, "How Watergate Sells Views," ES, 22 Jan. 1965; Poole, "A 'Town' in the City," ES, 17 Dec. 1965; "Progress," WP, 25 Feb. 1966; Timothy S. Robinson, "Watergate Undressed," WP, 23 July 1970; "Sale Boom," WP, 30 Sept. 1978; "Sen. Morse Backs Watergate Plans," WP, 19 Oct. 1967; Isabelle Shelton, "Open Space for the Center," ES, 26 Sept. 1967; "Stock Value Guarantee Planned by Watergate," WP, 4 Aug. 1970; "The

Vatican Seen Selling Share in Watergate," WP, 19 June 1969; "The Vatican as World's Largest Property Owner," ES, 11 Apr. 1965, p. E2; Wolf Von Eckardt, "A Palace," WP, 23 Oct. 1965; "Warm Neutral Design," WP, 4 Oct. 1970; "Watergate," WP, 22 May 1971; "Watergate," WP, 24 July 1971, p. D20; "Watergate Apt. Hotel Opens," WP, 1 Apr. 1967; "Watergate Apt. Model Opens," WP, 19 June 1965, p. E12; "Watergate Complex Nears Completion," ES, 20 Aug. 1970; "Watergate Construction," WP, 25 Apr. 1970, p. D4; "Watergate Defers to Center; 5th Bldg. Set for Offices," WP, 28 Apr. 1968; "Watergate Developers Settle Defect Dispute for $600,000," WP, 16 July 1977; "Watergate East Gets First Tenants," WP, 24 Oct. 1965; "Watergate East Ready to Open," ES, 22 Oct. 1965; "Watergate Features Security Aids," ES, 25 June 1965; "Watergate Operating as 'Co-op'," WP, 9 Apr. 1966; "Watergate Plan Clears Final Zoning Hurdle," WP, 4 May 1963; "Watergate Plans Reaffirmed," WP, 16 Nov. 1967; "Watergate Project Enters Second Phase," WP, 5 Feb. 1965; "Watergate Ruling Due Soon," WP, 25 Nov. 1967; "Watergate Sales Boss Stroked for Boston U.," WP, 30 May 1964; "Watergate Style," ES, 27 Oct. 1963; "Watergate Towne Hits New Snag," WDN, 24 Sept. 1963; "Watergate Units To Be Sold Early," WP, 27 July 1963; "Watergate West Is Begun," ES, 30 June 1967; "Watergate, Where Republicans Gather," WP, 25 Feb. 1969; "Watergate Wins Battle, Looks to War," WDN, 25 Nov. 1967; "Watergate Wrinkle," WP, 5 Aug. 1970; Jean M. White, "More Woes Plague Watergate Project," WP, 18 Oct. 1963; Kim Willenson, "Watergate Towne Gets Financing, Awaits Permit," WP, 22 Oct. 1961; Willenson, "Watergate Sales Total $19 Million," WP, 11 Jan. 1967.

123. PROSPECT HOUSE.
Periodicals Mary Parrish, "Potomac Prospect," WM, Mar. 1966, p. 51; "Picture Window to the Nation," United States Gypsum Company Magazine, Feb. 1966, pp. 10–12; Mary M. Sullivan, "Faulty Title Claim Unsettles Prospect House," WP, 10 Sept. 1983.

124. VAN NESS CENTRE.
Manuscripts BP B-149274, 11 Oct. 1966, lot 6, sq. 2049. Periodicals "Capital Comment," WM, Nov. 1966; Jerry Knight, "District Moving to Block Van Ness Conversions," WP, 27 Feb. 1980, p. R2; Knight, "Last Van Ness Bldgs. Set for Conversion," WP, 26 Feb. 1980; Jura Koncius, "Sleek and Streamlined," WP, 19 Aug. 1982, WHM; "Lending Library at Van Ness East," WP, 18 June 1966; "March Occupancy," WP, 27 Apr. 1979; Kathleen Mirin, "Van Ness North Tenants Vote Yes on Co-op Offer," WS, 8 Aug. 1979; "New Uptown Center," ES, 19 Feb. 1967; Susan Schmidt, "Van Ness Centre Mall Closes Doors Despite Nearby Metro Station," WP, 6 Oct. 1983, p. DC1; "Van Ness East," WP, 26 Mar. 1966; "Van Ness East Opens Library," ES, 25 June 1966; "Van Ness to House 5000 Soon," WP, 20 June 1966; "Van Ness Readies 2nd Apt.," WP, 21 Aug. 1966; "Van Ness South Apts. Open," ES, 5 June 1970; John B. Willmann, "A $35 Million Project," WP, 27 Mar. 1965, p. E1; Willmann, "Van Ness North

Goes Co-op," WP, 27 Apr. 1979; Gayle Young, "Van Ness South's Tenants Turn Down Condo Proposal," WP, 29 Jan. 1983, p. F4.

125. IRENE.

Periodicals "Irene," WP, 8 Jan. 1966; "Irene Embraces Sports," WP, 19 Feb. 1966; Carol Krucoff, "Irene Pollin, Lost and Found," WP, 2 Oct. 1983, p. M1; Stephanie Mansfield, "The Irene: Tales From the Grand Dame of Apts.," WP, 18 Nov. 1979, p. B1; "The Rush to Apts.," *U.S. News & World Report*, 8 Dec. 1969, pp. 46–48.

126. SHOREHAM WEST.

Pamphlets *The Shoreham West* (Washington, D.C.: Bralove Co., 1965), pp. 1–17. Periodicals Maxine Cheshire, "A Palatial Abode for a Princess," WP, 9 Jan. 1975; "Shoreham West," ES, 4 Mar. 1966; "Shoreham West Progressing," ES, 25 June 1965.

127. CATHEDRAL WEST.

Periodicals "Allan MacLane, Architect, Veteran of World War II," ES, 17 Mar. 1968; "Atrium Apt.: A Touch of Luxury," WP, 19 June 1965; "Cathedral West Has Unusual Atrium Units," ES, 20 Jan. 1967; "Cathedral West Pool," WP, 21 May 1967; "High Rise Hill," WP, 19 Feb. 1967.

128. COLONNADE.

Manuscripts BP B-125943, 15 Mar. 1965. Periodicals Maryon Allen, "Collections of Mrs. John McClellan," *Southern Accents*, winter 1978, pp. 44–48; Samuel Allis, "The Colonnade," WP, 22 Oct. 1979, p. C1; "Bernstein Undaunted by Conversion Ban," ES, 8 Nov. 1974; Maxine Cheshire, "VIP," WP, 18 Sept. 1979; Richard L. Coe, "Irvin Feld's Eye for Talent," WP, 10 Sept. 1984; "Colonnade," WSN, 18 Apr. 1975; "Colonnade Goes Condo," ES, 16 Aug. 1974; Michael Kiernan, "Apt. Gets Condominium OK in Record Time," ES, 10 Aug. 1974; "Landow Sells Half Interest at Colonnade," ES, 15 Dec. 1967; Aaron Ruvinsky, "Conversion: A Case Study," ES, 17 Jan. 1975; "Sold," WP, 16 Dec. 1967, p. E2; John B. Willmann, "Apt. Designed for High Living," WP, 24 Oct. 1964; Willmann, "Young Builders on the Move," WP, 21 Oct. 1962.

129. FOXHALL.

Periodicals Michael Anders, "AU Students Fail to Save Tree Grove," ES, 12 Oct. 1971; "Architect's Model," *Potomac Current*, 26 Mar. 1970; William Basham, "$25 Million Plan Offered for N.W. Site," ES, 15 Mar. 1970; James Birchfield, "Luxury Is Appreciated," ES, 3 Dec. 1971; Willard Clopton, "New Design Approved For Watergate Project," WP, 8 Nov. 1968; "Foxhall, D.C. Condo, Ready for Occupancy," WSN, 8 Feb. 1974; "Foxhall Square Construction," ES, 1 Sept. 1972, p. B2; "Glover Estate Area Developed," WP, 13 Nov. 1981; Roberta Hornig, "Wolman Files Mass. Avenue High-Rise Bid," ES, 24 Mar. 1966; Aaron Ruvinsky, "A Condoful of Antiques," WSN, 2 July 1976; Christopher Wright, "Watergate Builder Plans New Luxury Complex," ES, 25 July 1969.

130. SUMNER VILLAGE.

Pamphlets *Sumner Village*, Urban Land Institute Project Reference File, vol. 5, no. 8 (Washington, D.C.: Urban Land Institute, Apr.–June 1975), pp. 1–4; *Sumner Village, Sumner, Maryland* (Washington, D.C.: Edmund J. Flynn Co., 1971), pp. 1–8.

CHAPTER 6

INTRODUCTION

Condominiums.

Periodicals Bill Black, "Condo Battle Heating Up," WP, 23 Apr. 1983; Jacqueline Bolder, "Costs Turn Off Apt. Giants," WS, 17 May 1974; Albert B. Crenshaw, "Condos Here Total More Than 100,000," WP, 29 Jan. 1983; "D.C. Condominium Conversions Multiply and Spread," WS, 12 July 1978; Michael D. Davis, "District Suspends Condo Conversion for 90-Day Period," WS, 23 May 1979; Davis, "Permanent Law Is Proposed to Slow Condo Conversions," WS, 14 Nov. 1979; Laura Murray, "Condo Ruling Generates Confusion," WS, 21 Oct. 1979; Linda Wheeler, "A Wide-Open Project," WP, 12 June 1986, p. DC1; John B. Willmann, "Condominium Plan Adopted Slowly Here," WP, 6 Apr. 1968.

Cooperatives.

Periodicals Christopher Gray, "The 'Revolution' of 1881 Is Now in Its 2d Century," NYT, 28 Oct. 1984, sect. 12, p. 61; "The Jargon of Co-ops and Condominiums," NYT, 28 Oct. 1984, sect. 20, p. 79; Matthew L. Wald, "Co-ops and Condominiums," NYT, 28 Oct. 1984, sect. 12, p. 1.

Growth of Washington apartment houses.

Periodicals "Area Apt. Market Tightest in the Nation," WS, 14 July 1974; Nancy Ferris, "D.C. Looks to More Apts. to Enliven Downtown," WS, 20 Aug. 1978; "Is High Density Necessarily Bad?," WS, 13 Sept. 1975.

Mixed-use buildings.

Manuscripts Blouir. Periodicals Corrie M. Anders, "D.C. 'West End' Rezoned for Residences and Offices," WSN, 13 Dec. 1974; David and Tirmazi Baumann, "West End Politics: Battle Over Redevelopment Has Not Ended," WP, 13 May 1978, p. E1; Paul Bedard and Sue Silver, "An Enclave for the Affluent: Old West End Community Reluctantly Gives Way to Change," WP, 27 May 1978, p. D1; Randy Sue Coburn, "Sharing the Castle," WP, 1 May 1983, WP mag., p. 14; Andy Leon Harvey, "Upstairs from the Office," WP, 1 May 1983, WP mag., p. 14; J. R. Hewitt, "Mixed-use Projects Boom," WT, 11 Apr. 1986, p. H1; Beverly and Marcia Murphy, "Filling the Hole in the Doughnut That Is the West End," WP, 6 May 1978, p. E1; Tom Precious, "West End Undergoes Bldg. Boom," WP, 21 June 1986, p. E1.

Looking from the roof of the Woodner down to its unique "floating terrace," used in the 1950s for cocktail parties and fashion shows.

Rent control.
Periodicals Nancy Ferris, "A Tale of 2 Bldgs. Exposes District's Housing Crisis," WS, 6 Aug. 1978; Marcia Slacum Greene, "FTC Report Says Rent Control Harmful to D.C. Economy," WP, 15 Mar. 1985, p. A15; Michael Kierman, "Monthly Leases, Higher Rents Seen," WS, 18 Jan. 1974; "Voting on Rent Control" (editorial), WP, 16 Apr. 1985, p. A18.

131. GREENBRIAR.
Manuscripts BP A13804, 18 Oct. 1950, lot 3, sq. 1717. Periodicals "Bernstein Undaunted by Conversion Ban," WS, 8 Nov. 1974; "Children's Museum Ordered to Vacate by End of Month," ES, 16 May 1945, p. A2; "Eig Buys Villa Rosa," ES, 9 Mar. 1944, p. A4; "Greenbriar Apts. Sold for $3.5 Million," WP, 10 Mar. 1962; "Greenbriar Luxury Apt.," WDN, 29 Dec. 1951; "Luxury Apts.," ES, 13 Oct. 1951, p. B3; Nelson M. Shepard, "Modern Design of Greenbriar Lobby Combines Quality and Conservatism," ES, 17 Nov. 1951, p. B1; "2 Apts. Planned on Villa Rosa Site," ES, 14 Oct. 1944, p. B3.

132. WOODNER.
Manuscripts BP A1020, 7 Oct. 1949, lots 824–27, sq. 2624; BP A18240, 28 May 1951. Pamphlets *Biennial Awards for Architecture* (Washington, D.C.: Washington Board of Trade, 1953); *Ian Woodner, Recent Paintings* (New York: Weintraub Gallery, 1969); *The Woodner* (Washington, D.C.: Jonathan Woodner Co., 1951). Periodicals "Air Conditioning at the Woodner," *Pepconian*, June 1953; "Appeal Upholds Woodner Hotel Status," WP, 1 May 1959; "Berkshire and Woodner Apply for Shopping Center Rezoning," WP, 18 Nov. 1954; Milton Berliner, " 'Fantastic' Reading in Woodner's Books," WDN, 7 Oct. 1954; Rosalind Browne, "Everyone Loves Flowers," *Woman's Day*, Apr. 1965, pp. 45–49; "Capehart Digs into Woodner Finances," WDN, 5 Aug. 1954; Gene Glasgow, "The Woodner Welcomes Its First Tenants," WTH, 14 Oct. 1951; "Government Sues to Bar Transients at Woodner," ES, 12 July 1955; Paul M. Herron, "The Luxurious Woodner Doffs Its Wraps Today," WP, 21 Oct. 1951; Albon B. Hailey, "FHA Basis for Woodner Loan Related," WP, 2 July 1954; "Imaginative Example of Architecture," *Diplomat*, Mar. 1957; Bob Levey, "Girding to Beat the Plan," WP, 13 Nov. 1980, p. DC1; Jo Ann Lewis, "The Master Collector," WP, 8 Jan. 1984; Robert J. Lewis, "Number of Rental Units," ES, 9 Apr. 1949; Lewis, "Single D.C. Bldg. Will Have 1,135 Units," ES, 4 Feb. 1950, p. B1; Richard J. Maloy, "Berkshire, Woodner Stores Sanctioned," WP, 23 Nov. 1954; "150 Workers Vote Strike at Woodner," WP, 30 Sept. 1959; "1,139 Apts. in Single Bldg.," ES, 30 May 1953; "Two Seized in Raid at Fashionable Hotel Face Lottery Charges," ES, 26 June 1953; "U.S. Sues Woodners Over Housing Funds," WP, 19 Oct. 1954; "Woodner Is Called Next," WDN, 4 Aug. 1954; "Woodner's Status Now Ifs and Buts," WP, 13 July 1955; "Woodner Collection in Display," LAT, 19 Dec. 1971; "Woodner Loan Was Made on 2-Project Basis, Suspended FHA Aide Tells Probers," WP, 2 July 1954; "Woodner Loses Hotel Appeal," WP, 13 Oct. 1959; "Woodner Operation As Hotel Extended," WP, 22 Nov. 1959; "Woodner Pool," WP, 16 Apr. 1966; "Woodner Wins Hotel Respite," ES, 3 Feb. 1960; "Zoners Okay Plans to Set Up Stores in Berkshire, Woodner," ES, 23 Nov. 1954.

133. 3900 WATSON PLACE, N.W.
Manuscripts Vearl Phillips, "3900 Watson Place, N.W., Inc.," 1975, pp. 1–2 (author's files). Periodicals "Apt. Project Nears Completion," ES, 4 June 1960; "Dog Sitter?," WDN, 25 Jan. 1963.

Columbia Plaza includes a complex of large apartment buildings, including this example facing the Kennedy Center with its striking arrangement of balconies and patios.

134. RITTENHOUSE.
Manuscripts BP 11079, 7 May 1956, lots 88/293, 295, 297 (801), sq. 2727. Periodicals "Construction Begun on New Apt.," ES, 12 May 1956; "Rittenhouse Sold," WP, 8 Dec. 1973; "Rittenhouse Sold," WS, 14 Dec. 1973.

135. CATHEDRAL.
Pamphlets The Cathedral Cooperative (Washington, D.C.: Lewis and Silverman Realtors, ca. 1977), pp. 1–4. Periodicals "4101 Cathedral Avenue," ES, 24 June 1977.

136. COLUMBIA PLAZA.
Manuscripts BP B-124277, 26 Jan. 1965, lot 84, sq. 33; letter, Dean Rusk, Secretary of State, Washington, to Lawson B. Knoll, Jr., General Services Administration, Washington, 19 July 1966, in RG 328 (NCPC), National Archives; letter, James F. Salkeld, Columbia Plaza Corp., Washington, to Thomas Appleby, D.C. Redevelopment Land Agency, Washington, 16 Jan. 1968, pp. 1–4, in RG 328 (NCPC), National Archives. Pamphlets Columbia Plaza (Washington, D.C.: Columbia Plaza Corp., ca. 1966), pp. 1–6; Suzanne Berry Sherwood, Foggy Bottom 1800–1975: A Study in the Uses of an Urban Neighborhood—Washington Studies No. 7 (Washington, D.C.: George Washington University, ca. 1975). Periodicals Patricia Camp, "Sale of Columbia Plaza to Canadians Approved," WP, 15 Jan. 1980; Camp, "Tenants Dealt Blow by Ruling," WP, 19 Jan. 1980; "Columbia Plaza," WP, 3 Sept. 1967; "Columbia Plaza Conversion Moves Ahead," WP, 2 Aug. 1980; "Columbia Plaza Co-op Plan Proposed," WP, 4 Oct. 1980, p. E25; Jack Eisen, "Columbia Plaza Project Hits Snag on Legal, Zoning Technicalities," WP, 3 Mar. 1961; Arthur H. Keyes, Jr., "An Architect Talks about the Spaces between Bldgs.," AR, Sept. 1963, pp. 194–204; "Looking Up," WP, 22 Feb. 1969; "Planners OK Foggy Bottom Plaza Design," ES, 3 Mar. 1961; "Sold," WP, 12 Feb. 1972; Wolf Von Eckardt, "Space Age Affecting Apt. Planning," WP, 13 Oct. 1963, p. G8.

137. TOWN CENTER (WEST).
Pamphlets Town Center Plaza (New York: Cole, Fischer and Rogow, 1961).

138. TIBER ISLAND.
Pamphlets Tiber Island (Washington, D.C.: 1971), pp. 1–6. Periodicals "Amateur Symphony Plays with Relish," WP, 2 June 1967; "Apts. Rising as Southwest Area Grows," ES, 8 Aug. 1965; Betsy Blair, "Busy Round of Activities at Tiber Island," WDN, 22 Apr. 1966; "Council Asks D.C. to Ensure against S.W. Housing Bias," WP, 21 Sept. 1966, p. B7; Gilbert Gimble, "$9.6 Million Housing Okayed for S.W.," ES, 7 Sept. 1961; "Gold Keys Given to Tenants at Tiber," WP, 6 Feb. 1965; Harvey Kabaker, "Tiber Tenant Pact Limits Rent Boost," ES, 8 Oct. 1970; Arthur H. Keyes, Jr., "An Architect Talks about the Spaces between Bldgs.," AR, Sept. 1963, pp. 194–204; Sidney Lippman, "Tiber Island Tenants Revolt," WDN, 31 Jan. 1969; Wendell Margrave, "D.C. Civic Symphony Gaining in Artistry," ES, 2 June 1967; Daniel Poole,

"Extras for the Home Owner," ES, 23 July 1965; William Raspberry, "Luxury Apt. Tenants Take on Landlord," WP, 3 Feb. 1969; Kirk Scharfenberg, "Tiber Island Tenants Lose Rental Plea," WP, 25 Aug. 1971; "Searles Wants Open Policy at Tiber Island," ES, 1 Oct. 1961; "Swedish Group Views Tiber Island," WP, 30 May 1964; "Tiber Island Units Feature New Phones," ES, 2 Apr. 1965; Wolf Von Eckardt, "Space Age Affecting Apt. Planning," WP, 13 Oct. 1963, p. 68; Martin Well, "High-Rise Tenant Trial Over Rent Rise Opens," WP, 24 June 1969; Woody West, "S.W. Tenants Win 2 Suits Against Owner," ES, 29 Sept. 1969; John B. Willmann, "New Plan of Owning Used Here," WP, 22 May 1965; Willmann, "Tiber Island Adds Newest Chapter to Southwest Saga," WP, 13 June 1964.

139. NEWPORT WEST.
Manuscripts BP B-141185, 4 Aug. 1966, sq. 210, lot 126. Periodicals Thomas F. Diamond, "Residents Again Battle N Street High-Rise Plan," ES, 9 Feb. 1966.

140. PROMENADE.
Pamphlets The Promenade (Washington, D.C.: Rosebeth Realty Corp., 1983); The Promenade, Property Report, Nov. 30, 1984 (Bethesda, Md.: Promenade Mutual Housing Corp., 1984). Periodicals Ann Mariano, "Things Looking Up at the Promenade," WP, 10 Mar. 1984; "The Promenade," WP, 14 Jan. 1984, p. F9.

141. PLAZA, formerly FOGGY BOTTOM.
Periodicals Judith Martin, "Residence Loaded with Elan," WP, 3 Nov. 1974, p. E1; Lorenze Middleton, "Condo Couple's Loneliness to End," WS, 19 Sept. 1975.

142. WORLAND.
Pamphlets The Worland Town Apartments (Washington, D.C.: SJG Properties, 1977). Periodicals "22 Worland Units Sold," ES, 29 Oct. 1977; "The Worland," ES, 3 June 1977.

143. GEORGETOWN PARK.
Manuscripts BP B-263795, 19 Sept. 1978, lot 64, sq. 1200. Pamphlets W. P. Dinsmoor and Nancy H. Noyes, Handbook on Storefront Design, Georgetown Park (Washington, D.C.: Georgetown Park Associates, 1978), pp. 1–56; One of a Kind: Top of the Park (Washington, D.C.: Western Development Corp., 1978). Periodicals Benjamin Forgey, "The New City in Town," WP, 24 Oct. 1981, p. B1; Paul Goldberger, "New Project: A Victorian Stage Set," NYT, 19 Oct. 1981; "Historic Preservation Integrates an Urban Mixed-use Complex," National Mall Monitor, Sept.–Oct. 1981.

144. 2501 M STREET, N.W.
Manuscripts BP B-265934, 7 Dec. 1978, lot 44, sq. 13.

145. WESTBRIDGE.
Manuscripts BP B-260033, lot 70, sq. 14, 10 May 1978. Pamphlets The Westbridge (Washington, D.C.: Oliver T. Carr Co., 1979).

146. MADISON BANK BUILDING.

Manuscripts BP B-280196, 23 Sept. 1980, lot 196, sq. 1212.
Pamphlets *James Madison Limited Annual Report 1981* (Washington, D.C.: Madison National Bank, 1981), pp. 1–27.
Periodicals "D.C. Architecture Turning to Post-Modernism," *Washington Business Journal*, 28 Mar. 1983; Benjamin Forgey, "Blending the Old and New," WP, 30 Jan. 1982, p. C1; "News Report," PA, 30 Jan. 1982, p. 27; "Philip Johnson, America's Foremost Architect Reviews Washington Architecture," WM, Sept. 1985; "Post Modern What?," *Builder*, Nov. 1983; "Post Modernism: Definition and Debate, " *AIA Journal*, May 1983; "Saving City Hearts," WP, 24 Jan. 1981.

147. WASHINGTON PARK TOWER.

Manuscripts D.C. Certificate of Occupancy, B-130046, 25 June 1982. Pamphlets *Washington Park at Washington Circle* (Washington, D.C.: Evans Co., 1980), pp. 1–9. Periodicals John B. Willmann, "Washington Park Bldg. Begins," WP, 2 Mar. 1982.

148. WASHINGTON HARBOUR.

Manuscripts BP B-288003, 18 Nov. 1981, lots 101, 800, 808, 811–12, sq. 1173; BP B-288660, 13 Jan. 1982; BP B-294170, 27 Dec. 1982; BP B-297169, Aug. 1983; BP B-298176, 29 Sept. 1983; BP B-300855, 13 Apr. 1984; BP B-303118, Oct. 1983.
Periodicals Karlyn Barker and John Ward Anderson, "Destructive Floods Hit D.C., Richmond," WP, 8 Nov. 1985, p. A1; Kenneth Bredemeier, "Approval Near for Complex on Waterfront," WP, 21 Aug. 1984, p. B1; Bredemeier, "Georgetown Waterfront Plans Unveiled," WP, 18 Oct. 1984, p. C1; Bredemeier, "War on Georgetown Is Unending Saga," WP, 12 Dec. 1984, p. B1; Sharon Denny, "Life at the Top," *Luxury Homes of Washington*, spring 1984, pp. 32–40; Lawrence Feinberg, "Court Clears Way for Hotel at Waterfront," WP, 9 Nov. 1985, p. D1; John H. Holdridge, " 'Whatchamacallit' on the Potomac," WP, 3 May 1986, p. A22; Jerry Knight, "Mega-Luxury Rises on Banks of Georgetown," WP, 28 Nov. 1983; Roger K. Lewis, "Washington's Ambivalent Relationship with Water," WP, 30 Mar. 1985, p. F4; Stephen J. Lynton, "Whitehurst Plan Announced," WP, 18 Oct. 1984, p. C5; Arthur Cotton Moore, "In Defense of the 'Whatchamacallit' (Cont'd.)," WP, 10 May 1986, p. A22; Wendy Swallow, "Washington Harbour Opens Doors," WP, 14 June 1986, p. E1; Sandra Evans Teeley, "Proposed Hotel Draws Protests in Georgetown," WP, 17 Jan. 1984; Alison Thresher, "City Set to Lease Land on River in Georgetown at Below-Market Rate," WP, 9 Mar. 1985, p. F1; Linda Wheeler, "Georgetown Readies with Floodgates and Car Rental Bargains," WP, 7 Nov. 1985, p. A40; John B. Willmann, "Georgetown Waterfront Project Started," LAT, 3 June 1984.

149. PORTO VECCHIO.

Pamphlets *Porto Vecchio* (Washington, D.C.: IDI, 1983).

150. PENN MARK.

Pamphlets *The Penn Mark* (Washington, D.C.: Carley Capital Group, 1985). Periodicals Benjamin Forgey, "The Color's Right at

Sculptor John L. Dreyfuss, left, and his assistant, Robert Bryant, display the bronze sculpture they designed for the entrance to the Griffin apartment house at K and 26th streets.

Penn Theater Site," WP, 1 Oct. 1983; Forgey, "Firm Foundations," WP, 20 Sept. 1986; Forgey, "The Penn Is Mightier," WP, 14 June 1985, p. D1; Margaret Gaskie, "Neo-eclecticism on the Potomac," AR, July 1984, pp. 86–107; "In Progress," PA, Sept. 1982, p. 82.

151. FLOUR MILL.

Periodicals "The Flour Mill," *Urban Land Institute Project Reference File*, vol. 12, no. 2, Jan.–Mar. 1982, pp. 1–4.

152. ROTONDA.

Pamphlets *The Rotonda* (Arlington, Va.: IDI, 1976), pp. 1–20.
Periodicals "High-Rise Hit in Suburban Washington," *Building Design and Construction*, Mar. 1978, p. 62; Bartlett Naylor, "Cecchi: The Man and His Empire," *Montgomery Journal*, 6 Jan. 1984, p. C1; "Price Mix," *Multi-Housing News*, Feb. 1979, p. 17; "The Rotonda," WP, 6 Nov. 1976, p. E16; "The Rotonda," *Builder*, 3 July 1978, p. 40; "The Rotonda," *Urban Land Institute Project Reference File*, July–Dec. 1980, pp. 1–4; Lew Sichelman, "Rotonda Plan Based on Roman Palace Grounds," WS, 8 Oct. 1976, p. C1; John B. Willmann, "Condomania in N. Virginia: From Glut to Glee," WP, 19 May 1979.

153. LINDSAY.

Pamphlets *The Amalgamated Transit Union Building* (Washington, D.C.: Urban Land Institute, ca. 1983).

154. WESLIE.

Pamphlets *The Weslie* (Washington, D.C.: Weissberg Development Corp., 1980).

155. BARCLAY HOUSE.

Manuscripts BP B–281798, 18 Dec. 1980, lots 20–22, 812–817, sq. 15. Periodicals Sarah Booth Conroy, "Harmony's Winning Way," WP, 21 Aug. 1982; Nadine Huff, " 'Time-Share' Project Bankrupt," WP, 19 June 1982, p. F1; Tim Miller, "West End Objects to Sharing," WP, 19 Sept. 1981, p. E1.

156. LOGAN PARK.

Manuscripts BP B–277733, 6 June 1980, lot 48, sq. 281.

157. MONTEBELLO.
Pamphlets *Montebello* (Washington, D.C.: IDI, 1982).

158 ATRIUM.
Pamphlets *The Atrium* (Washington, D.C.: Knightsbridge Development Co., 1985). Periodicals Tom Precious, "Judge Clears Way for Atrium Sale," WP, 28 Mar. 1987.

159. GRIFFIN.
Manuscripts BP B-301088, 1 May 1984, lot 104, sq. 16.
Pamphlets *The Griffin* (Washington, D.C.: Lenkin Co., 1985), pp. 1–6. Periodicals Carlton Knight III, "The Architect's Neighborly Approach," WP, 1 Feb. 1986, p. C1.

160. ASTORIA.
Pamphlets *Astoria, Rosslyn* (Washington, D.C.: Colonial Guardian Limited Partnership, 1985).

161. SOMERSET HOUSE.
Pamphlets *Somerset House* (Chevy Chase, Md.: Somerset House, Inc., 1986).

162. MARKET SQUARE.
Periodicals Kenneth Bredemeier, "Avenue Contract Awarded," WP, 16 Nov. 1984, p. A1; Bredemeier, "Developer Designated for Portal Site at 14th Street Bridge," WP, 13 Sept. 1985, p. A1; Benjamin Forgey, "Design on the Avenue," WP, 29 Sept. 1984, p. C1; John Mintz, "Agency Balks at Condemning Bldg. for Market Square," WP, 17 Apr. 1986, p. D1; "Showdown at Federal Triangle," WP, 18 Mar. 1986, p. C1.

APPENDIX I

Roman apartment houses.
Books Axel Boethius and J. B. Ward-Perkins, *Etruscan and Roman Architecture* (Harmondsworth, England: Penguin Books, 1970); A. G. McKay, *Houses, Villas and Palaces in the Roman World* (Ithaca: Cornell Univ. Press, 1975); Russell Meiggs, *Roman Ostia* (Oxford: Clarendon Press, 1960); Ernest Nash, *Roman Towns* (New York: J. J. Augustin Publisher, 1944); James E. Packer, *The Insulae of Imperial Rome: Memoirs of the American Academy in Rome* (Rome: American Academy, 1971), vol. 31; Perks; G. T. Rivoiva, *Roman Architecture* (Oxford: Clarendon Press, 1925); Peter Wyman, *Ostia* (London: Ginn and Co., Ltd., 1973).

European apartment houses.
Books Paul Bernard and Chemetov Marrey, *Architecture à Paris, 1848–1914* (Paris: Dunod, 1984); Norma Evenson, *Paris: A Century of Change, 1878–1978* (New Haven: Yale Univ. Press, 1979); Mark Girouard, *Cities and People* (New Haven: Yale Univ. Press, 1985); François Loyer, *Paris XIXᴱ Siecle, L'Inmeuble et la Rue* (Paris: Fernand Hazan, 1987); Perks; Anthony Sutcliffe, *The Autumn of Central Paris: The Defeat of Town Planning, 1850–1970* (London: Edward Arnold, 1970). Periodicals Hubert, Pirsson,

and Hoddick, "New York Flats and French Flats," AR, vol. 2, no. 1, July–Sept. 1892, pp. 55–64; Maurice Saglio, "City Apt. Houses in Paris," AR, vol. 5, no. 4, Apr.–June 1896, pp. 347–61; Jean Schopfer, "City Apts. in Paris," *Architectural Review*, Jan. 1904, pp. 91–99.

British apartment houses—Edinburgh and London.
Manuscripts Peter Robinson, "Life on a Stair: Five Centuries of Flats," Edinburgh, 28 Oct. 1981, pp. 1–12; Robinson, "Tenements: A Scottish Urban Tradition," Scottish Vernacular Bldgs. Working Group Conference, Univ. of Dundee, Hawkskill, Scotland, 22 Mar. 1980, pp. 1–20; Anne Turner Simpson and Sylvia Stevenson, "Town Houses and Structures in Medieval Scotland: A Seminar," Dept. of Archeology, Univ. of Glasgow, 1980, pp. 1–31. Books Philip Boardman, *The Worlds of Patrick Geddes* (London: Routledge and Kegan Paul, Ltd., 1978); Harry Furniss, *Paradise in Piccadilly* (London: John Lane, 1925); Mark Girouard, *Cities and People* (New Haven: Yale Univ. Press, 1985); Edward Jones and Christopher Woodward, *A Guide to the Architecture of London* (New York: Van Nostrand, 1983); Christopher Hartley, *Gladstone's Land* (Edinburgh: National Trust of Scotland, 1983); Collin McWilliam, *Edinburgh New Town* (Edinburgh: Edinburgh New Town Conservation Committee, 1984); Perks; Roy M. Pinkerton and William J. Wincham, *Mylne's Court* (Edinburgh: Edinburgh Univ. Press, 1982); Steen E. Rasmussen, *Towns and Buildings* (Liverpool: Edinburgh Univ. Press, 1951); Royal Commission on Ancient Monuments, Scotland, *The City of Edinburgh* (Edinburgh: HMSO, 1951); Andrew Saint, *Richard Norman Shaw* (New Haven: Yale Univ. Press, 1976); Ann Saunders, *The Art and Architecture of London* (Oxford, England: Phaidon, 1984); Anthony Sutcliffe, ed., *Multi-Storey Living: The British Working Class Tradition* (London: Croomhelm, 1974); Frank Worsdall, *The Tenement: A Way of Life* (Edinburgh: Chambers, 1979); A. J. Youngson, *The Making of Classical Edinburgh, 1750–1840* (Edinburgh: Edinburgh Univ. Press, 1975). Periodicals Chris Hammett, "London's Many Mansions," [London] *Estates Gazette*, 4 May 1985, pp. 462–64; Peter Robinson, "Tenements: A Pre-Industrial Urban Tradition," *Review of Scottish Culture*, 1985, pp. 52–64.

Types of American apartment houses.
Books Talbot Hamlin, ed., *Forms and Functions of Twentieth-Century Architecture* (New York: Columbia Univ. Press, 1952), 4 vols.; Teunis J. Van Der Bent, *The Planning of Apartment Houses, Tenements and Country Houses* (New York: Brentano's, 1917).

Boston apartment houses.
Manuscripts Deborah A. Fulton, "John Pickering Putnam, Visionary in Boston, Part I: A Systematic Approach to Apt. House Design," essay presented at the annual meeting of the Society of Architectural Historians, Minneapolis, Apr. 1984, pp. 1–12; Rebecca Zurier, "John Pickering Putnam, Visionary in Boston, Part II: The Charlesgate as Housing in a Nationalist Utopia," essay presented at the annual meeting of the Society of Architectural

Historians, Minneapolis, Apr., 1984, pp. 1–15. Books Bainbridge Bunting, *Houses of Boston's Back Bay* (Cambridge, Mass.: Belknap Press of Harvard Univ., 1967); Cambridge Historical Commission, *Survey of Architectural History in Cambridge, Report Three: Cambridgeport* (Cambridge, Mass.: MIT Press, 1971); Jane Holtz Kay, *Lost Boston* (Boston: Houghton Mifflin Co., 1980); Arthur J. Krim, Cambridge Historical Commission, *Survey of Architectural History in Cambridge, Report Five: Northwest Cambridge* (Cambridge, Mass.: MIT Press, 1977); Douglas Shand Tucci, *Built in Boston* (Boston: New York Graphic Society, 1978). Periodicals Jean A. Follett, "The Hotel Pelham: A New Bldg. Type for America," *American Art Journal*, vol. 15, no. 4, autumn 1983, pp. 58–73.

New York apartment houses.
Manuscripts Elizabeth Cromley, "The Development of the New York Apt. House, 1869–1902," Ph.D. dissertation, City University of New York, 1982; Donald F. Wrobleski, "The Development of the High Rise Apt. Bldg., As Seen in the New York Work of J.E.R. Carpenter, 1911–1926," essay presented at the Society of Architectural Historians annual meeting, Minneapolis, Apr., 1984, pp. 1–6. Books Andrew Alpern, *Apartments for the Affluent* (New York: McGraw-Hill Book Co., 1975); Paul R. Baker, *Richard Morris Hunt* (Cambridge, Mass.: MIT Press, 1980); M. Christine Boyer, *Manhattan Manners* (New York: Rizzoli, 1985); James Ford, *Slums and Housing* (Cambridge, Mass.: Harvard Univ. Press, 1936); John Hancock, "The Apt. House in Urban America," in *Buildings and Society*, edited by Anthony D. King (London: Routledge and Kegan Paul, 1979), pp. 151–89; Thomas E. Norton and Jerry E. Patterson, *Living It Up* (New York: Atheneum, 1984); Donald Martin Reynolds, *The Architecture of New York City* (New York: MacMillan, 1984); Nathan Silver, *Lost New York* (New York: American Legacy Press, 1967); Edward K. Spann, *The New Metropolis: New York City, 1840–1857* (New York: Columbia Univ. Press, 1981); Robert A. M. Stern, Gregory Gilmartin, and John Montague Massengale, *New York 1900* (New York: Rizzoli, 1983); Robert A. M. Stern, Gregory Gilmartin, and Thomas Mellins, *New York 1930* (New York: Rizzoli, 1987); Teunis J. Van Der Bent, *The Planning of Apartment Houses, Tenements and Country Houses* (New York: Brentano's, 1917). Periodicals Amy Kallman Epstein, "Multifamily Dwellings and the Search for Respectability: Origins of the New York Apt. House," *Urbanism Past and Present*, summer 1980, vol. 5, issue 2, no. 10, pp. 29–39; Hubert, Pirsson, and Hoddick, "New York Flats and French Flats," AR, July–Sept. 1892, pp. 55–64; Calvert Vaux, "Parisian Bldgs. for City Residents," *Harper's Weekly*, 19 Dec. 1957, pp. 809–10.

CREDITS FOR PHOTOGRAPHY AND DRAWINGS

Within sections, illustrations are listed according to the page on which they appear in the text; page position is indicated by the following abbreviations: T, top; M, middle; B, bottom; L, left; R, right. To conserve space abbreviations are also used for frequently cited sources: CHS = Columbia Historical Society; DCPL = District of Columbia Public Library; LC = Library of Congress; NA = National Archives; NGS = National Geographic Society; NTHP = National Trust for Historic Preservation; TH = photograph by Theodore Horydczak.

PHOTOGRAPHS BY JAMES STAFFORD PHILLIPS

© *James Stafford Phillips*

iii, xxi, 15, 39B, 42, 44T, 46, 60R, 61, 62R, 63T, 64, 65, 66, 70, 75, 76R, 78, 79B, 80, 81, 83, 87, 89, 90, 91L, 92, 94, 96T, 98, 100, 101R, 104R, 106, 107, 108, 110, 111T, 113T, 114, 116, 119, 121, 123T, 124, 129, 131, 132, 133, 137T, 140, 141, 143, 145T, 145BL, 146, 147, 148, 149, 150T, 162L, 162R, 165R, 166L, 167TL, 167BL, 168TR, 168BR, 169B, 182a, 182c, 193T, 194, 195, 205, 206L, 206R, 215, 216, 217, 218, 219T, 220, 221, 222, 223, 225, 233, 234TR, 235, 236T, 238, 240T, 243TL, 243BL, 245L, 245R, 246, 247, 248R, 249, 250T, 250B, 251B, 262, 263, 265T, 267L, 268, 269T, 269B, 271BL, 271R, 272B, 273R, 274, 276, 277, 278, 279, 280, 282, 283, 284, 285T, 290, 292T, 293, 294T, 296L, 296R, 302T, 303, 304, 305, 306L, 306R, 307, 310, 311, 312, 313, 318B, 319TL, 319TR, 319B, 321B, 321T, 340, 344, 347, 350, 351, 353, 355, 357, 358, 364, 365, 367, 368, 371, 373T, 373BL, 373BR, 380TR, 381, 394T, 395L, 398, 400b, 404g, 404h, 413, 416, 418, 419, 420T, 421T, 421B, 426, 427, 428L, 429, 430, 431TL, 431TR, 431BR, 434T, 437, 438, 439, 457B, 459T, 460TL, 460TR, 461, 463, 468, 470T, 470B, 471, 474B, 475B, 475M, 477TL, 485b, 485c, 485d, 487, 493BR, 494, 495, 549M, 553, 554, 555T, 555B, 557, 558L, 558R, 560R, 561, 572, 579T, 579B, 602

PHOTOGRAPHS BY JAMES F. TETRO

© *James F. Tetro*

x, 6, 20B, 21L, 37, 38, 45R, 56, 63B, 77, 84, 85, 96B, 104L, 125, 127, 128, 134, 135, 136, 144T, 164R, 166TR, 166BR, 167R, 168L, 169T, 182b, 197, 199, 200, 201, 202L, 204, 207T, 213, 224R, 226, 227T, 229, 231TL, 231LM, 231BL, 232B, 254TL, 254TR, 255, 257, 258, 260, 264L, 264R, 266, 271TL, 291B, 295, 301BL, 316, 320TL, 320TR, 320B, 330, 333T, 334, 335, 341, 342B, 370, 376T, 377B, 377T, 378, 380TL, 383T, 389T, 391, 392, 399B, 404a, 404b, 404c, 404i, 404m, 405d, 405e, 405f, 405j, 405k, 405l, 423, 425, 442, 443T, 444, 445T, 445B, 446, 449, 451, 453, 454, 455, 457T, 458, 462, 465, 467, 472B, 473T, 474T, 475T, 476TR, 476L, 476BR, 477TR, 477BL, 481, 482L, 482R, 483, 484, 485e, 485f, 485g, 488R, 489, 490L, 490R, 492B, 492T, 496, 497R, 498, 499L, 501, 503, 505L, 506B, 507, 508, 509, 511, 512B, 513, 514, 515, 517L, 517R, 518, 519, 520L, 520R, 521, 522R, 523T, 524T, 524B, 525TR, 525BR, 526T, 526BL, 526BR, 549L, 549R, 556, 560M, 565, 569B, 573, 574

ADDITIONAL PHOTOGRAPHIC CREDITS

5 Goode Collection, CHS; 8 Goode Collection, CHS; 9 Gichner Iron Works; 12 Leet Bros. photograph, Wright Collection, George Washington University; 14 Frances Benjamin Johnston photograph, LC; 16 LC; 17 Florence Schneider Christensen; 18T DCPL; 19 Florence Schneider Christensen; 20R CHS; 21R DCPL; 27 George W. Stone, Jr.; 28 Mrs. Catherine S. Roper; 30 Arthur Heaton Nash; 31 Janet Davis; 35L Goode Collection, LC; 49T Heaton Collection, LC; 62L Quentin Cabell Smith; 73L Thomas F. Scott photograph, American Chemical Society; 111B Northumberland Apartments, Inc.; 120T NA; 130T CHS; 139T Paul Mellon; 139B NTHP; 152T Clifton Adams photograph, NGS; 152B TH, LC; 154 TH, LC; 155B TH, LC; 155T TH, LC; 157 TH, LC; 158 Scurlock Studio photograph, Scurlock Studio; 159T Goode Collection, LC; 161 Scurlock Studio photograph, Scurlock Studio; 163BR LC; 165TL Underwood and Underwood photograph, LC; 174L CHS; 174R Helen White; 177 Mrs. Detlow Marthinson; 179L, Mitchell photograph, Mrs. Nancy H. Cooke; 180L Harvey H. Warwick, Jr.; 180R James P. Rouleau; 182d TH, LC; 188 Florence Schneider Christensen; 192 Del Ankers photograph, Norman Bernstein Management Co.; 202R Goode Collection, CHS; 209TL TH, LC; 209TR TH, LC; 211 Underwood and Underwood photograph, Mayflower Hotel; 228 United Methodist Church; 232T C. Thomas Clagett, Jr.; 234TL Edmund J. Flynn Co.; 242 Mark A. Bloomfield; 244 Frances Benjamin Johnston photograph, LC; 251T ACME Newspictures, UPI photograph, Truman Library, NA; 256 Buckingham Studios photograph, Tilden Gardens, Inc.; 272T TH, LC; 287 Ankers Capital photograph, Sheraton-Washington Hotel; 288 Ankers Capital photograph, Sheraton-Washington Hotel; 298 TH, LC; 300 Gustave Ring; 301T Gustave Ring; 308TR TH, LC; 308TL B. F. Saul Co.; 309T TH, LC; 309B, Joseph Younger, delineator, B. F. Saul Co.; 314 TH, LC; 315T TH, LC; 315B TH, LC; 318T Mrs. David Stern; 325 Harris & Ewing photograph, Francis L. Koenig; 326 Joseph Abel; 328 Harris & Ewing photograph, Alvin A. Aubinoe, Jr.; 329 Glen B. Leiner; 332 Van Durand photograph, Gustave Ring; 338L TH, LC; 338R Matthew Brady photograph, LC; 343 TH, LC; 345T TH, LC; 348 TH, LC; 354 TH, LC; 361 © Frank Lloyd Wright Memorial Foundation, 1942, 1970; 362 Harris & Ewing photograph, Roy Thurman; 375 V. E. Ruckett, delineator, Delano, Inc.; 383B Goode Collection, CHS; 384 Goode Collection, CHS; 386 McLean Gardens, Inc.; 394B TH, LC; 395R TH, LC; 399T George de Vincent photograph, Jack Cohen; 400T Studio Moretti, Rome, Italy; 402 Davis Studio photograph, Milton Fischer; 403L Mrs. J. Allan MacLane; 403R Adams Studio photograph, Mrs. Donald Hudson Drayer; 414T Pietro Belluschi; 424 Carl Schneider photograph, U.S. Army, NA; 433T J. Alexander photograph, Milton Fischer; 436 J. Alexander photograph, Milton Fischer; 480 Glogau Studio photograph, Wilfrid V. Worland; 500 Harlan Hambright and Associates photograph, Martin and Jones; 516 Mattox Studio photograph, International

Developers, Inc.; 524M International Developers, Inc.; 525L Harlan Hambright photograph, Martin and Jones; 525TL CHK Associates; 527TR CHK Associates; 527BR Hartman-Cox; 528 Art Resources of New York; 529 Art Resources of New York; 530TR author's photograph; 530TL author's photograph; 530BR author's photograph; 531T U.S. Embassy, Paris; 531BL author's photograph; 531BR author's photograph; 532 Mark Andrich photograph; 533TL author's photograph; 533BL author's photograph; 533BR author's photograph; 534L author's photograph; 534R author's photograph; 535L author's photograph; 535R author's photograph; 537T Boston Public Library; 537B Massachusetts Historical Society; 538 Charles von Urban photograph, Museum of the City of New York; 539 Wurts photograph, Museum of the City of New York; 540 Museum of the City of New York; 560L Gichner Iron Works; 566 Monroe Warren, Jr.; 569T TH, LC; 581 Mary Noble Ours photograph, John L. Dreyfuss

CREDITS FOR FLOOR AND SITE PLANS

9 Michael Kopp; 18L Thomas Ahmann and Beyhan Cagri; 39T Thomas Ahmann; 41B Thomas Ahmann; 45L Thomas Ahmann; 49B Michael Kopp; 52 Bruce Tobin and James Walsh; 57 Thomas Ahmann; 60L Timothy Newton; 67 Thomas Ahmann; 71 Michael Kopp; 73R James Walsh; 76L James Gerrity; 79T Michael Kopp; 86 Charles R. Lehner IV; 91R Mark Farber; 93 Beyhan Cagri; 97 Thomas Ahmann; 101L Thomas Ahmann; 105 Thomas Ahmann; 109 Michael Kopp; 113B Thomas Ahmann; 117 Thomas Ahmann; 120B Thomas Ahmann and Matthew Ford; 123B Thomas Ahmann and Mark Farber; 126 Leonard M. Kliwinski and Julie D. Perkins; 130B Michael Kopp; 137B Thomas Ahmann; 145BR Beyhan Cagri; 150B Michael Kopp; 153 Thomas Ahmann; 159B Thomas Ahmann and James Walsh; 193B Michael Kopp; 198 Mark Brenneman; 203T Thomas Ahmann; 203B Mark Brenneman and Beyhan Cagri; 207B James Gerrity; 209B Thomas Ahmann; 210 Thomas Ahmann; 214 Julie D. Perkins; 219B Michael Kopp; 224L Thomas Ahmann; 227B James Walsh; 231R Clark Hollis Blouir; 234ML Thomas Ahmann; 234BL Thomas Ahmann; 236B Thomas Ahmann; 240B Thomas Ahmann; 241 Thomas Ahmann; 243R Thomas Ahmann; 248L Thomas Ahmann; 252 Thomas Ahmann; 254B Michael Kopp; 259T Beyhan Cagri; 259B Beyhan Cagri; 265B Thomas Ahmann; 267R Beyhan Cagri; 273TL Hsueh-Mei Soong; 273BL Thomas Ahmann; 275 Clark Hollis Blouir; 281 Mark Brenneman and Beyhan Cagri; 285B Timothy Newton; 291T Thomas Ahmann; 292B Thomas Ahmann; 294B Mark Brenneman; 294M Mark Brenneman; 299 Thomas Ahmann; 301BR Dean Brenneman and Beyhan Cagri; 302B Dean Brenneman and Beyhan Cagri; 308BR Michael Kopp; 317 Thomas Ahmann and James Walsh; 333B Ming Hui Bon Hoa; 339 Thomas Ahmann; 342T Charles R. Lehner IV; 345B Bruce Tobin and Thomas Wilkinson; 352 Mark Farber and Bruce Tobin;

356 John Porter; 366 Thomas Ahmann; 372 Beyhan Cagri; 376B Charles R. Lehner IV; 380B Mark Brenneman; 389B Matthew Ford; 401 Thomas Ahmann and James Wang; 407 Mame Cohalan; 414B Dean and Mark Brenneman; 420B Thomas Ahmann; 424T Timothy Newton; 428TR Thomas Ahmann; 428BR Thomas Ahmann and James Walsh; 433B Clark Hollis Blouir; 434B Clark Hollis Blouir; 443B Charles R. Lehner IV; 447 Clark Hollis Blouir; 448 Robert L. Froman, Jr.; 452B Richard Lishner; 452T Richard Lishner; 456 Matthew Ford; 459B Julie D. Perkins; 460B Leonard M. Kliwinski; 464T James Gerrity; 464B James Gerrity; 469 Robert L. Froman, Jr.; 472T Julie D. Perkins; 473B Leonard M. Kliwinski; 488L Thomas Ahmann and Randy Davis; 493L Clark Hollis Blouir; 493TR Clark Hollis Blouir; 497L Clark Hollis Blouir; 499TR Mark Brenneman; 499BR Mark Brenneman and Beyhan Cagri; 502 Mark Brenneman and Beyhan Cagri; 505R Thomas Ahmann and Mark Farber; 506T Thomas Ahmann and Mark Farber; 510L Clark Hollis Blouir; 510R Clark Hollis Blouir; 512T Matthew Ford; 522L Clark Hollis Blouir; 523B Clark Hollis Blouir; 571L Clark Hollis Blouir

INDEX

The 162 apartment houses featured in *Best Addresses* appear in CAPITAL letters. Readers should also refer to the lists of architects and their buildings in Appendix 2 and of apartment houses by neighborhood in Appendix 3. Apartment houses not known by a name are alphabetized under the first digit of the street address; for example, 1870 Wyoming Avenue, N.W., is listed under ONE and 2120 Kalorama Road, N.W., under TWO. In some cases photographic material is indexed even though no mention of a specific term is made in the caption. Photographs appear in italics with page position indicated by the following abbreviations: T, top; M, middle; B, bottom; L, left; and R, right.

Reynolds Metals Development Corporation, 409–10
Richardson, Henry Hobson, 20, 216
RICHMOND FLATS, 5, 11–13
Ring, Gustave, *179B*, 300, 302–4, 332–34, 342, 354, 370, 372
RITTENHOUSE, *475MR*
River Park, 409–10
Riverside Realty Corporation, 439
Robinson, Hilyard R., *329*, 339
ROCHAMBEAU, xx, *165TL*
Roman apartment houses. *See* Appendix 1
Romanesque Revival, 4, 7, 14, 16, 20–21
roofdecks: private, 266–67, *269B*, 306, 372, *421B*, 428–29, *431TL*, 436, 496, 505, *507*, *512B*, 514, 519; public, 19, 66, 68, 71, 81, 97, 115, 131, 156, 196, 254, 266, 342, *349*, 429, *453*, 456, 495, 499, 502; pavilions, *60R*, *114*, 115, *129*, 131, *152T*, 156, *264TL*, 268–69
roofs: atriums, *460TR*, 461; chimneys, 136, 213, 256, *378*, 500, *513*; complex designs of, 452–54; mansard, 49, 126
ROOSEVELT HOTEL, 187, 196–99
Roosevelt, Mrs. Franklin D., 160
Rorke, Edwyn, 286
Rosenthal, Dunbar, 342
Rosewood, 511
ROTONDA, *524M*
Rouleau, Louis T., *180R*, 296
Rust, Harry L., 80

S

safes. *See* security systems
ST. REGIS, 122–24, *549M*
Santmyers, George F., *179TL*, 378, 421
Satterlee, Nicholas, *326*, 402
Saul Company. *See* B. F. Saul Company
Saunders and Pearson, 421
Schneider, T. Franklin, 5, 14, 16, *188*
Scholz, Robert O., 270, 364
Schuyler, Montgomery, 17
Schwarz, David, *484*
sculpture, *17*, *35B*, *264L*, 268–69, 270–71, 307–8, 314, *315T*, *338*, 354, 387, *419*, *581*. *See also* carvings
Searles, John R., Jr., 406–8
security systems, unusual: 440, 497; burglar alarms, 451–52; gatehouses, *404l*, 429, 469, 473; safes, 32, 68, 104, 108, 115, 138, *277*, 456; speaking tubes, 7, 32, 99, 248, 549; telephone intercom systems, *421T*; television monitors, 440, 452, 497
SEDGWICK GARDENS, *182d*, 314–17
servant rooms, 51, 53, 72, 91, 104, 115, 130, 138, 151, 222, 248, 264, 270, 294–95, 310, 519
Shannon and Lucks, 410, 429
Shapiro, J. B., 290
Shelton Club Hotel (New York), 269
Sheraton-Washington Hotel, 286, 289

SHERMAN, xx, *163B*
Shingle Style, 7, *21L*
Shipstead-Luce Act, 228
shopping: arcades, *405k*; centers, early, 335; malls, 436, 439–40, 446, 494–95
SHOREHAM HOTEL, 297–99, 455–56
SHOREHAM WEST, 455–57
Siegel, Meyer, 372, 374, 378
Silverman, Robert I., 446
Simmons, B. Stanley, *28*, 83, 86
Simmons, Leo, 118, 120–21
site plans: controversies over, 435, 440; innovative, 55, *57B*, *60L*, 63, 183, *207B*, *259T*, 260–61, 290–91, *301TL*, *301BR*, 334, 366, 388–90, *459B*, 493–95. *See also* apartment house shapes
16th Street, N.W., development of, 38, 55, 108–9, 151, 215, 218. *See also* Henderson, Mrs. John B.
Sixteenth Street Mansions. *See* Chastleton
sleeping porches, 7, 99, 185, 206, 239–40, 237, 244, 248, 249, *250B*, *282*
Smith, Chloethiel Woodard, *398*, 402, 406, 408–11, 429–30
Smithsonian Institution, 436
social activities, organized, 306, 338, 384, 392, 424–25. *See also* amenities
Societa Generale Immobiliare, 432, 435
Society of Architectural Historians, xiii
solaria, 185, *206R*, 222, *238*, 350, 364, 366, *368*, 452, 507
SOMERSET HOUSE (D.C.), 33, 161, *168BR*, 238, *560TR*
SOMERSET HOUSE (Md.), 238, *527TR*
Sonnemann, Alexander H., 157
Southeast Construction Company, 446
Southwest Washington, 406–12, 415, 429–30
Spanish Colonial style, 31, 69, 92, 99, *100T*, 114
Spectre, Jay, 421
split-level apartments. *See* floor plans
STAFFORD, *167TL*, 549
staircases, unusual: private, 217, *245BL*, 392, *431TL*, 444, 468–69, *490R*, 502, 505, *507*; public, *61*, 66, *70*, 71, 106–9, *116*, *202L*, *206T*, 215, 312, *501*, 553, 556, *557BR*, *561BL*, *569TL*. *See also* balustrades
Stein, Clarence S., 333
Stern, David L., *179B*, 180
Stinson and Capelli, 386
Stone, George W., Jr., 58
Stone, George W., Sr., 27, 57
STONELEIGH COURT, 50–54
storage rooms, innovative, 32, 131
STORY FLATS, 7, *20R*
streetcars, xix, 25, 27–28, 32, 34
Stuyvesant Flats (New York), *538*
subletting, 281–83
suburban apartment houses, 181, 324, 481–82
subway. *See* Metro stations

WASHINGTON PARK TOWER, *404i*, 504–7

Washington Post, 49, 80, 160

Washington, President George, xix, 390

WATERGATE, 415, 432–41, 467

Weese, Harry, 408

Weinstein, Jessie, *326*

WENDELL MANSIONS, *iii*, 29–30, 89–91, *485b*

WESLIE, *445B*, *525T*

WESTBRIDGE, 498–99

WESTCHESTER, *182c*, 300–306, *404h*

Western Development Corporation, 491, 493, 511

WESTMORELAND, 77–82, *555T*, *555B*

Westover. *See* Balfour

Wheat Row, 429

White, Frank Russell, *174R*

Whitehurst Freeway, 512

White, Jarrett C., 53

WHITELAW, 158–61

Williams, Mrs. John B., 230, 232, 253

Williams, Paul, *329*

Wilson, Mrs. Woodrow, 122–23

WINDSOR LODGE, 118–21, 556, 557

windows: casement, 184–85, 237; fanlight, 38, 107, *108T*, 112, 226, 287, 500, *519;* oriel, *20R*, *20B*, *38*, 43, 48, 55, *64*, 66, *92*, 93, *162R*, *163L*, *166TL*, *166BL*, *167BL*, *218*, *560TM;* Palladian, 38, 487, *488TR*, *500;* skylight, 8–9, 118, 217, *315T*, *342B*, *378*, *495*, 505, *565TL;* stained glass, 76, 106–7, 118, 159, 309, 556, *557BR*, *565TL;* transom, 40, *45B*, *62R;*

unusual, 95, *96B*, 103–4, 106–7, 135–36, *199T*, *226*. *See also* facade treatments

Wolman, Jerry, 466–67

Wood, Waddy B., 67

WOODLEY, *165BL*, *561BL*

WOODLEY PARK TOWER, 293–96

WOODNER, *474B*, *579TL*

WOODWARD, 33, 114–17

Woodward, Samuel W., 114–15, 263

WORLAND, 487–90

Worland, Wilfred V., *480*, 490

World Health Organization, 347, 350

World War I, effect on apartment houses, 33, 153, 226, 327

World War II, effect on apartment houses, xix, 195, 197–98, 206, 277, *279*, 299, 317, 326–28, 339, 359, 374, 382–84, 387, 400

Wright, Frank Lloyd, 360–63

Wright, Henry, 333

WYOMING, 33, 83–88, *556TL*

Y

Yerkes, Pappas, and Parker, 142

Z

Zeckendorf, William, Jr., 299, 408–9

Zioncheck, Congressman Marion A., 281–83

zoning, 51, 173, 185–88, 202, 218, 226, 260, 294, 346, 384, 386, 408, 419, 422, 433, 435, 482–84

Zupnik, Stanley, 446

BEST ADDRESSES was produced by the
Smithsonian Institution Press, Washington, D.C.

Set in Bodoni Book by World Composition Services, Inc., Sterling, Virginia.

Printed by Princeton University Press, Princeton, New Jersey,
on eighty-pound Warren's Lustro Offset Enamel Dull.

Photography and plans used in *Best Addresses* were made possible through generous grants from:

THE ALVORD FOUNDATION, Washington, D.C.
THE KIPLINGER FOUNDATION, Washington, D.C.
THE B. F. SAUL COMPANY, Washington, D.C.

Publication of *Best Addresses* was made possible through generous grants from:

THE GWENDOLYN AND MORRIS CAFRITZ FOUNDATION, Washington, D.C.
MARK G. GRIFFIN, Washington, D.C.